I0638399

INDIANS OF NORTH AMERICA

INDIANS OF NORTH AMERICA

INDIANS

OF

NORTH AMERICA

Harold E. Driver

UNIVERSITY OF CHICAGO PRESS

Library of Congress Catalog Number: 61-6504

THE UNIVERSITY OF CHICAGO PRESS, CHICAGO 37
The University of Toronto Press, Toronto 5, Canada

© *1961 by The University of Chicago. Published 1961. Composed
and printed by* THE UNIVERSITY OF CHICAGO PRESS, *Chicago
Illinois, U.S.A.*

PREFACE

THE AIM of this book is to offer a comprehensive comparative description and interpretation of native American cultures from the Arctic to Panama. It is designed for use as a text in anthropology courses, as a general introduction for anyone interested in Indians, and as a work of reference for scholars in other fields of thought. The customary line of division between Anglo and Latin America has been ignored except in the last chapter, where the two areas are contrasted with respect to Indian and White relations. To describe Indians north of Mexico without reference to Mexico and Central America is almost as inadequate as a botanical description of the branches and leaves of a tree without mention of the trunk and roots. Although the Indians north of Mexico were politically independent of those south of the border and produced a large number of innovations on their own, many fundamentals, such as domesticated plants, were first discovered and developed south of the border and later spread north to the Indians in what is now the United States. Any satisfactory discussion of Indian cultures in the United States must acknowledge the debt that they owe to the more advanced peoples to the south.

The variation in language and way of life of the Indians of North America was much greater than that in Europe at the time America was discovered by Europeans. There were literally thousands of Indian societies, each with its separate territory, language, or culture. In a broad work of this kind it is impossible even to mention each of these distinct ethnic units, but by grouping them into culture areas, one can study the essentials of their ways of life without getting lost in a plethora of detail. The pedagogical value of the culture area concept is sufficient to justify its use without getting involved in the technical task of objectively proving that such areal units are a reality.

The fundamental organization of the material, as shown by the chapter headings in the Table of Contents, is by subject, but within each chapter the subdivisions often refer to culture areas. The organization is, therefore, a combination of subject and areal classification. The culture areas most frequently mentioned are the Arctic, Northwest Coast, Plains, East, Oasis, and Meso-America. For many subjects it seemed advisable to ignore some of the culture areas in order to leave space for fuller and more meaningful descriptions and interpretations of the others. For teachers who prefer to proceed by area instead of by subject, the indexing of each culture area provides easy access to all information on it.

Although the principal purpose of this volume is to describe the salient features of Indian cultures at the high points of their histories, theory is not entirely lacking. Diffusion as a process of culture change has been given considerable attention because it has been unduly neglected for at least a decade; and significant correlations have been pointed out in the conclusions of many chapters, especially those in the last half of the book. If a few chapters, such as the one on kinship, seem a bit technical, it should be kept in mind that Indian cultures were by no means as simple as is generally believed and that some discussion of their more technical aspects is a necessary part of an authentic portrayal of them.

The time level varies from the sixteenth century for the Aztecs and their neighbors in Mexico to the nineteenth for the Indians of about half of the United States and most of Canada. Some peoples became extinct, at least as independent cultures and languages, before others were discovered, making it impossible to limit the time span of a work of continental scope even to a single century. To have salted in the proper century or decade to which each section or paragraph referred would have turned the book into a technical monograph unsuitable as an introduction to its subject. Someday, a competent ethnohistorian will write such a monograph, but so far every major synthesis on the Indians of North America has telescoped the time scale in favor of geographical differentiation and the culture area concept. I have attempted to describe Indian cultures as they were before serious disturbance by Whites, but, because no written records of any consequence were left by Indians before White contact, reliance almost exclusively on the writings of Europeans makes it impossible to rule out European influence altogether.

Twelve of the chapters, iii to x and xiii to xvi, cover subjects which appeared in a previous publication which William C. Massey and I co-authored: *Comparative Studies of North American Indians*, "Transactions of the American Philosophical Society," Volume XLVII, Part II, 1957. However, this material has been cut to less than half of its original length and most of it has been reorganized, updated, or rewritten. The remaining fourteen chapters are wholly new. Thus the subject coverage of the present book is over twice as extensive as that of the earlier *Comparative Studies*.

I am deeply indebted to William C. Massey of the University of Florida and L. P. Eisenhart of the American Philosophical Society for generously giving permission to reproduce part of the text, maps, and illustration from the *Comparative Studies of North American Indians*. I am also grateful for the indispensable help of my wife, Wilhelmine, who not only wrote the chapter on music but read and edited every draft of the manuscript as well as the printer's proofs. I also wish to acknowledge the friendship and encouragement of Stith Thompson of Indiana University, whose monumental achievements in comparative folklore have long served as inspiration for my more modest accomplishments in comparative ethnology. I am also indebted to Carl Voegelin of the same university for his many original insights into Indian language and culture and his unfailing optimism about the book. To Erminie Wheeler-Voegelin, also of Indiana University, I am grateful for many enlightening discussions of Indian ethnology and ethnohistory. I owe a further debt to two more colleagues at the same university: to George Herzog, whose publications and careful editing were indispensable to the chapter on music, and to Georg Neumann for lending photographs to serve as models for some of the clothing drawings and for much information over the years about the biological characteristics of Indians. I also wish to thank Deans John W. Ashton, Ralph E. Cleland, Shirley H. Engle, and Oscar O. Winther of the Indiana University Graduate School for grants in aid for the research that went into the book.

An acknowledgment is also due the Human Relations Area Files, from which some of the data for the book were drawn, and to the officers and directors of that organization, especially G. Peter Murdock and Clellan S. Ford, for stimulating discussion of the cross-cultural approach. To Harold and Kate Nachtrieb of Berkeley, California, my wife and I extend our appreciation for the hospitality of their home for the two summers when most of the writing was done.

I am also grateful to the following persons, mostly students and employees of Indiana University, for their loyal help in the actual production of the manuscript: Marilyn Lerch and Ester Maring for typing; Hilda Delgado, Wellawatte Ananda, Charles Pyne, and Rose Jaquith for indexing; Mickey Love for map drafting; and Robert Judah for the drawings in the chapter on clothing.

Acknowledgments to authors, publishers, universities, and museums for permission to reproduce photographs of art objects are included in the captions of the photos in the chapter on art and need not be repeated here, except to say that the positive responses of everyone we asked for illustrations were most gratifying.

CONTENTS

Contents

Contents

Illustrations

FIGURES

PLATES

(Following page 204)

MAPS

(Following page 612)

1: THE ORIGIN OF THE INDIANS

THE CLEAREST evidence bearing on the origin of the American Indians is zoological in nature. All scientists agree that man was not a separate act of creation but evolved from simpler forms of animal life. Man's nearest animal relatives, the anthropoid apes, are all found in the Old World today: the chimpanzee and gorilla in Africa, the orang and gibbon in southeast Asia and the neighboring continental islands. Man's next nearest animal relatives, the catarrhine monkeys, are likewise all confined to the Old World. The platyrrhine monkeys of the New World (South and Central America) share classification with man in the order of primates, but they are more distant than the Old World monkeys and apes and could not possibly have been the direct ancestors of the Indians. More important, there is a total absence in the New World of missing links and other intermediate fossil forms in man's family tree. In the Old World on the other hand, some hundreds of skeletons, of individuals intermediate in physical type between men and apes have been discovered by the spades of archeologists and paleontologists. The only conclusion to draw from this evidence is that man evolved from brute ancestry in the Old World and migrated to the New World only after he had become modern physically and a member of the single species of modern man called *Homo sapiens*, wise man.

Discoveries of early man in North America are fairly common back to about 11,000 years ago. But since man has existed as *Homo sapiens* for about 50,000 years, his inhabitance of the New World is short. The relatively late arrival of man in the New World is illustrated by Map 1, which is derived principally from Wormington, *Ancient Man in North America*, 1957. It locates the principal Paleo-Indian archeological sites and gives the date in centuries ago

1

of the earliest evidence of man at each site. For example, the number 43 in Alaska means that the evidence of man's presence in that locality dates from 43 centuries or 4,300 years ago. To convert this to Christian chronology, the present date, 1960, must be subtracted, leaving 2340 B.C. When two or more different dates were obtained for the same deposit, the dates were averaged. In some cases, however, only the earliest and latest dates for a deposit were given, and these have been joined by a hyphen. For example, in the Valley of Mexico, certain deposits are generally accepted as 110 centuries old, but, although the evidence is controversial, they may possibly extend back as far as 160 centuries. However, more than one scientific dissenter believes man first occupied the New World as far back as about forty thousand years ago (Carter, 1957; Crook and Harris, 1958). Although most archeologists, geologists, and paleontologists do not accept such an early date at the present time, a few new discoveries may change the picture and establish it beyond all reasonable doubt. But such discoveries would not change the fundamentals of our present knowledge, that man evolved from brute ancestry to *Homo sapiens* in the Old World and migrated to the New World only after he was a fully modern man.

Scientists who dig in the earth employ a number of intricate methods for dating the objects they uncover, but radiocarbon dating, which is based on measurement of radiation, is the latest and most useful. Ordinary carbon has an atomic weight of 12, but radioactive carbon has an atomic weight of 14. Radiocarbon is present in very small quantities in every living thing, plant or animal. In living wood, for example, only one out of every trillion carbon atoms is radioactive. This is enough, however, for the physicist to measure the radioactivity of a piece of wood.

Radiocarbon is produced by cosmic rays which bombard the upper atmosphere of the earth, producing fast-moving neutrons. These neutrons combine with nitrogen atoms to produce hydrogen and carbon-14. All vegetation absorbs carbon dioxide containing carbon-14 from the air and animals obtain the radioactive carbon by eating the plants or other animals which are plant eaters. When a plant or animal dies, its supply of carbon-14 is not renewed but gradually becomes less and less. At any time after death the amount of carbon-14 left in a portion of the remains of plants and animals may be measured by the amount of radiation still emanating from it. It has been found that when an organism has been dead for 5,568 years, its rate of radiation is half that of a living organism, and the amount of carbon-14 remaining is, therefore, half the original amount. After 11,136 years the rate of radiation is one-fourth of the original amount, and after 16,704 years only one-eighth.

The most commonly used organic material for determining the age of Indian remains is wood, most often in the form of charcoal, from the fire hearths of the Indians. By measuring the amount of radiation from the carbon-14 atoms in ancient pieces of wood or charcoal, it is possible to date them within a few centuries of their true ages and at the same time to date the stone spear points, human bones, and any other material associated with the wood in the same deposit. Shell, horn, and bone may also be dated by the same method. In spite of certain sources of error, which are gradually becoming recognized, the radiocarbon method is the most accurate so far devised by science for dating within the period from about 50,000 to 2,000 years ago and has yielded most of the dates shown on Map 1.

The physical type of the Paleo-Indian shows some differences from that of contemporary Indians, who are classed as Asiatics (Mongoloids) by all anthropologists today. On the whole the earliest Indians had longer and narrower skulls, with heavier jaws and teeth. Muscle attachments on the bones of the limbs as well as on the skull were heavier, indicating a more heavily muscled individual. The longitudinal crests of some of these early skulls tend to form a sort of ridge, with the skull bones sloping away somewhat like the two-pitched roof of a house from the ridge pole. This is a primitive characteristic found in pre-*sapiens* species of fossil men. However, all bones of Paleo-Indians so far discovered are unquestionably *Homo sapiens*, and some individuals fail to exhibit any of the primitive features and could even pass for contemporary Indians. On the whole, however, the Paleo-Indian is less Mongoloid than contemporary Indians, although the latter show variation in this respect. It therefore appears that the first immigrants to America from northeast Asia date from a time when the European (Caucasoid) and Asiatic (Mongoloid) races were less differentiated

3

than at the present time. The Paleo-Indian belongs to a more generalized type of Caucasoid-Mongoloid race with a slight bias in favor of the Mongoloid. As time went by and the Mongoloid race became more and more dominant in northeast Asia, successive waves of immigrants became more and more Mongoloid.

We have already suggested that the first Indians to enter the Americas came by way of northeast Asia and Alaska. Although we are certain that there was some contact between South Pacific islands and South America before A.D. 1492, this came much too late to account for the principal peopling of the New World. Boats or rafts capable of negotiating thousands of miles of open ocean did not exist 10,000 or more years ago, and knowledge of navigation was too scant for man to venture far from land. Whether the first men to negotiate the Bering Strait paddled across in hide boats, walked across on the ice, or walked over on a land bridge is not known. One thing, however, seems obvious. These first immigrants had no knowledge of the lands that lay beyond and would have had no incentive to travel a long distance to reach some objective ahead. The word infiltration is probably much more appropriate than migration for their first contact with the New World in Alaska. There is no reason to believe that any of these early arrivals traveled farther in any one day than was necessary to hunt the game they fed on.

At Bering Strait, Asia and North America are separated today by fifty-six miles of water broken by three islands. The widest expanse of open sea is only twenty-five miles and land may be seen across this gap on clear days and even on moderately cloudy days. The modern Eskimo have often negotiated these straits in their hide-covered boats propelled by paddles. Therefore any earlier group of people with hide boats of similar types could have made the crossing. We are not sure, however, that the earliest people to enter North America possessed hide boats or any other boats as seaworthy as those of the Eskimo. If the date of 11,000 years ago for man's first appearance in the Valley of Mexico is correct, the crossing at Bering Strait of the ancestors of these people must have taken place at least several thousand years earlier. Just as the early hunters and fishers around the strait would have had no incentive to travel rapidly across the strait and eastward across the Arctic, those peoples who went south knew nothing in advance about climate and hunting opportunities in that direction. They too probably never traveled farther in one day than their hunting, fishing, or gathering activities required. In spite of the absence of early archeological dates in Alaska, it seems clear from the earliest dates farther south that man must have first entered Alaska at least fifteen or twenty thousand years ago. At this early time we can surmise that boats were less skilfully made and less seaworthy than those of the modern Eskimo.

It seems more probable that the first infiltrators to reach Alaska walked all the way on a land bridge. The zoological and geological evidence for land bridges from Siberia to Alaska at several times during the Pleistocene (Ice Age) is overwhelming. The native animals in northern Asia and North America are so much alike that zoologists combine the two areas to form a single major life zone. The geologists estimate that during the maximum period of each major glaciation the ice cap was a mile high over vast areas of land and as much as 9,000 feet high in some localities. The enormous amount of water tied up in the ice caps came from the ocean in the form of fog and clouds and later fell in the form of snow. Because of the intense cold in the glaciated regions, the melting of ice and runoff of water in the summer was less than the deposit by precipitation in the winter. The result was a lowering of ocean level by as much as several hundred feet. Because the ocean bottom near Bering Strait is only 120 feet deep, it seems likely that land bridges as much as 100 miles wide may have existed for thousands of years at a time in this region.

A perplexing aspect of this theory is how man was able to migrate east or south from Alaska with ice packed a mile high or more on the landscape. Geologists answer this by explaining that the whole of northern North America was never covered by ice at one time. The ice cap of the last major glaciation, the Wisconsin, seems to have centered in the region of what is now Hudson Bay. Alaska and western Canada had less ice, and there were ice-free corridors of hundreds of miles in extent in these western areas. Although our knowledge today does not satisfy every query raised, it seems clear from the archeological evidence that man was living in

North America during the fourth major glaciation, at least at the time of the last phase of it called Mankato.

The life of these Paleo-Indians can be reconstructed in part from the material objects the archeologists have recovered from their campsites. Objects of stone are the most numerous because stone is preserved almost indefinitely in the soil in spite of changes in climate, moisture content of the soil, and soil chemistry. Stone tools and weapon parts made by chipping are more frequent than those made by grinding or abrading. The most frequent chipped stone objects are spear or dart points, suggesting that hunting was the dominant subsistence activity. The next most common items, scrapers and knives, were used in skinning, butchering, and dressing hides, again suggesting the dominance of hunting.

Other objects of stone, listed roughly in order of frequency are: grinding stones, hammerstones, mortars, pestles, abrading stones, grooved stone balls, and shaft smoothers. The grinding stones were used to grind wild seeds for food and the mortars and pestles to grind other food products. The grooved stone balls may have been tied together to make a weapon called the *bolas*, which was thrown at the legs of fleeing animals to trip them and facilitate capture. The shaft smoothers were stones of abrasive quality with a single groove on one face. Shafts of spears, and later arrows, were pulled back and forth in these grooves to smooth their surfaces and improve accuracy of flight. Grinding stones were more common than objects of chipped stone in the earliest level of the Cochise culture in southeastern Arizona, dated by radiocarbon at 7,756 years ago. Wild seeds, therefore, seem to have predominated in the diet in this locality as long ago as about 5800 B.C. By this early date the Paleo-Indian had already adapted his culture to changing geographic environment. As he moved south to drier areas where game was scarce and wild plants relatively abundant, he was forced to rely less on hunting.

Objects of other materials found by archeologists at Paleo-Indian sites, in a rough order of frequency are: basketry, bone awls, spear-throwers, cordage, paint pigments, shell objects, sandals, matting, copper tools, netting, harpoon heads, bone needles, shaft-straighteners, bone whistles, and bags. Objects made of plant materials, such as baskets, cord, sandals, matting, netting, and bags, have been found more often in the dry areas of the western United States and Mexico than in other regions. This areal localization is due in part to the fact that plant materials are better preserved in arid climates. Vegetal products were widely used in the south-eastern United States and in the tropics by Indians in the historic period but are not well preserved in archeological sites in these regions because of the moisture in the soil.

There is a tendency among some archeologists to divide Paleo-Indian cultures into an eastern and a western tradition, with the boundary about at the Rocky Mountains. The eastern people concentrated on big game hunting, as the abundant spear points found in their camp sites prove. The western people, on the other hand, relied more on wild plant foods, and left behind choppers, keeled scrapers, and grinding stones, as well as a more limited number of spear points. The hunting area of Map 3, which is based on conditions of the eighteenth and nineteenth centuries, probably matches rather closely the big game hunting area of the Paleo-Indian. The remaining area to the south would be assigned to those peoples who lived primarily on wild plant foods, because farming was unknown to the Paleo-Indian. A third major Paleo-Indian division may be distinguished in Alaska and northern Canada. Its beginning in time is later than the other two and its affiliations are with the Eskimo who later occupied the Arctic shoreline.

Ten years ago, before radiocarbon dates were much known, association of extinct animal bones with spear points and other objects of human manufacture, and occasionally with human bones, was important evidence bearing on man's antiquity in the New World. Most of these animals have been classed as different species from modern types but frequently fall within the same genus. Listed in approximate order of frequency in the archeological record, these are: bison, mammoth, horse, camel, mastodon, dire wolf, coyote, tapir, ground sloth, marmot, antelope, caribou, jaguar, musk ox, and llama. The mammoth, horse, camel, mastodon, ground sloth, and llama became totally extinct in North America long before A.D. 1492 without leaving any close modern relatives. The others became altered enough to be classed as new species in most cases, and the new species survive to this day. A few spear points have been found embedded in the bones of some of these

7

animals, proving beyond the shadow of a doubt that they were hunted by early man. Some anthropologists believe that man killed some of these animals in sufficient numbers to have contributed substantially to their extinction. None of them were domesticated by the Paleo-Indians.

A chapter on the origin of the Indians would be incomplete without some mention of the fabulous tales of origin that speculators have conjured up or lifted from literature. Among the most fantastic is the idea that the continent of Atlantis provided a partial land bridge to the New World from Europe or Africa. No reputable scientist today believes such a continent ever existed; so until we find some concrete evidence that it did, it has not been lost and remains pure fantasy, first recorded by the Ancient Greeks.

Another lost continent, Mu, in the Pacific Ocean, has been suggested to serve as a stepping stone to the New World from the Orient. But the Pacific is both wider and deeper, on the average, than the Atlantic and even less likely to have contained a continent.

A more tenable theory involving continents in places where oceans exist today is that of continental drift. This theory holds that North and South America were once joined to Europe and Africa and formed a solid land mass. Then, as the earth's crust cooled and shrunk, a cleavage appeared and the two portions gradually drifted apart. Although this theory may explain certain facts of geology, geography, and pre-human biology, it cannot account for man's presence in the New World because the separation, if it actually occurred, took place hundreds of millions of years before any form of man had evolved anywhere on the face of the earth.

Contact across the Atlantic by boat has also been suggested and serves to explain a few otherwise puzzling parallels shared by peoples of Africa and South America. However, the most enthusiastic proponents of this theory are only trying to show that it might have happened before A.D. 1492. They do not claim that it was done 11,000 or more years ago; knowledge of boats, navigation, and survival at sea were not sufficiently developed to make this feat possible at such an early date.

A more plausible, but still not acceptable, idea is that the first immigrants came to North America from Asia by way of the Aleutian Islands. A land bridge that far south from Bering Strait is out of the question fifteen to twenty thousand years ago, because of ocean depths of ten to twenty thousand feet; these hardy adventurers would have had to come by boat. Because some islands in the chain are too far apart to be visible from the nearest neighboring island even on a clear day, and because the climate is foggy and windy much of the time, the currents treacherous, and the shorelines rocky, it seems very unlikely that the earliest Paleo-Indians crossed by this route. There is some evidence to suggest contact by this route at a much later date, but there is no evidence that the first people to reach the New World came by way of the Aleutians. Another more fantastic notion is that Indians reached southernmost South America from Antarctica, and ultimately from Australia. This theory was put forward almost half a century ago to explain certain parallels in language in Tierra del Fuego and Australia but has had no acceptance by scientists.

Finally, religious groups have suggested that the Indians are the descendants of the Ten Lost Tribes of Israel who are thought to have wandered from that country all the way to the Americas. There is not a shred of evidence to suggest that any wanderers from Israel ever reached America in Old Testament times, but even if they had, it would have been much too late to account for the peopling of the New World.

There is no doubt that the first people to enter the New World fifteen or twenty thousand years ago lived primarily by hunting and secondarily by fishing. Edible wild plants were scarce in the Arctic and could not have furnished more than a small fraction of the diet. Farming was out of the question in such a cold climate and may not have been practiced anywhere in the world at this time. As the Paleo-Indian slowly drifted southward, he eventually penetrated the more arid geographical environments of the western United States and Mexico, where wild plant foods were more plentiful than game and fish were scarce. The first major change in his subsistence pattern occurred some eleven thousand years ago, when wild plant foods became important in his diet. The second major change in the Indian's way of life took place when he first domesticated plants, settled down as a farmer, and developed a still more reliable food supply. This took place about two thousand years later.

Experts on plant domestication believe in at least two separate origins of farming in the New World, one for root crops in the tropics of South America and around the Caribbean, another in the temperate upland region of Mexico or Guatemala for seed crops. Some authorities believe that plants were independently domesticated more than twice in the Americas. The oldest suggestion of farming comes from the lowest level in the Ocampo Caves in southwest Tamaulipas, Mexico. Here remains of gourds (*Lagenaria siceraria*), squash (*Cucurbita pepo* and *foetidissima*) Jack beans (*Canavalia ensiformis*, probably wild) have been found and dated from about 7000–5500 B.C. by the radiocarbon method. Although this date seems too early, material from the same culture in a nearby cave was dated at 6582 B.C., and radiocarbon dates from higher levels in the caves were consistent with the stratigraphy as well as with cross dates from other sites. Furthermore, there was nothing encountered in the excavation to contaminate the vegetable materials and later the radiocarbon content. The date of 7000–5500 B.C. must, therefore, be accepted until proven incorrect by a sufficient number of new discoveries and new dates. The dates quoted above are given by Crane and Griffin (1958:1103) and by Whitaker, Cutler, and MacNeish (1957). These authors say that one species of squash and possibly the beans are wild. Granting that this is correct, it seems unlikely that all four species were wild. It seems improbable that the wild ancestors of four plants would happen to be growing in one small area, say within a day's walk of the Ocampo Caves. Therefore it seems probable that the gourd and *pepo* squash were domesticated at the date given above. There is certainly no question about plant domestication in the next higher level about 2300–4000 B.C., where fragments of these and other plants show a sharp increase in frequency.

So far the earliest dates for corn (maize) are about 4000 B.C. at Bat Cave, New Mexico, and 5000 B.C. in southern Puebla, Mexico. The same type of corn has more recently been found in Romero's Cave, southwest Tamaulipas, and the date there is 2772 B.C. (Crane and Griffin, 1958).

From such early agricultural beginnings, more and more food

was produced by farming until it changed the way of life of the Indians. As hunters and gatherers, the Indians roamed about in small family groups or bands or lived in tiny seasonal villages. By the second millenium B.C., there were permanent villages in Meso-America (southern Mexico and Guatemala, Map 2). Such a sedentary settlement pattern was not achieved by Indians in the southwestern and southeastern United States until after the beginning of the Christian era. The villages in Meso-America grew into towns, cities, and ultimately the city-states of the Mayas, Aztecs, and their neighbors. Although the evidence on domesticated plants alone proves some contact before A.D. 1492 across the Pacific Ocean, most of the culture of the American Indians was independent in origin and development from that of the Old World.

REFERENCES

CALDWELL, 1958; CARTER, 1957; CRANE AND GRIFFIN, 1958; CROOK AND HARRIS, 1958; LIBBY, 1955; MACNEISH, 1960; SAUER, 1952; SELLARDS, 1952; WHITAKER, CUTLER, AND MACNEISH, 1957; WORMINGTON, 1957.

2: CULTURE AREAS

THE WORD "culture," as used by anthropologists and other social scientists, refers to the entire way of life of a people, not just the visual arts, music, dancing, drama, and literature. The chapter headings in this volume, with the partial exception of that on the origin of the Indians, all refer to culture, each to a different aspect of it. A culture area is a geographical area occupied by a number of peoples whose cultures show a significant degree of similarity with each other and at the same time a significant degree of dissimilarity with the cultures of the peoples of other such areas. In theory the delimitation of culture areas must be based on a representative sample of all aspects of the cultures of all the peoples being thus classified. The determination of significant degrees of similarity and dissimilarity is ultimately a statistical problem, but working approximations may be arrived at by other means, partly intuitive, by scholars familiar with a region.

The culture area, in its current stage of development, is a convenient way of describing the ways of life of hundreds of peoples covering a whole continent or a larger part of the earth's surface. Few readers are familiar with even a hundred names of Indian tribes, and the many names on the map at the end of this volume are much too numerous to be repeatedly mentioned in a book of this kind. Therefore, the entire North American continent, from the Arctic to Panama, has been divided into seventeen culture areas, which are relatively easy to remember (Map 2). With this simple scheme it is possible to give the approximate geographical distribution of some detail of Indian life, such as the custom of scalping, in a few words. As is evident from the many maps to follow, most details of culture do not fit the areas exactly. Nevertheless, the areas provide a convenient framework for introducing some degree

12

of order in the plethora of detail available about North American Indians.

In some respects the culture areas of the anthropologist are like the geographical regions of the geographer, and the dominance of geographical terms in the culture area labels is designed to help the reader remember where the areas are located. The boundaries of such areas on maps unavoidably give a false impression by over-emphasizing the sharpness of the break. Most boundaries are actually the approximate lines where the two neighboring types of phenomena are present in equal amounts. In one direction the first features become progressively more dominant, while in the opposite direction the second features become more and more noticeable.

For example, if you drive from New York to San Francisco you encounter a number of geographical zones. You start on a coastal plain, originally covered with broad-leaved trees, and as you proceed west you gain in altitude until you have reached the modest ranges of the Appalachians in Pennsylvania. Here trees of the pine family appear along with the broadleaves. After leaving the mountains around Pittsburgh, you travel through the slightly rolling Ohio country which gradually becomes flatter and flatter in Indiana and Illinois. If the natural vegetation had been undisturbed by the White man, you would notice at about the Indiana-Illinois line a balance between equal amounts of the forest, through which you have traveled so far, and a treeless prairie. As you proceed west in Illinois the forest cover gradually gives way to the tall grass of the prairie which dominates the landscape until you arrive in Nebraska. There at about the 100th meridian the grass becomes shorter and the trees still fewer. The first really abrupt change comes when you strike the magnificent peaks of the Rockies, which rise 9,000 feet above the mile-high plains at Denver. You suddenly find yourself in a wonderland of snow-capped peaks coniferous trees, and cascading mountain streams. But before you are out of Colorado, the land becomes drier and sagebrush makes its appearance, anticipating the deserts of the Great Basin. The Great Basin is so labeled because the streams there do not reach the ocean but flow inward to lakes, such as Great Salt Lake, or lose themselves in desert sands. After about a day's drive on the desert, you suddenly reach the eastern slopes of the Sierra Nevada which rise abruptly from the

13

desert floor. Again you see the snow-capped peaks and coniferous forest which gives way in California to valley grasslands and low coastal mountains.

If you could have traveled the same route in 1600, before Indian cultures had been disturbed by the Whites, you would have noticed similar changes in their way of life. You might travel for hundreds of miles with no appreciable change in Indian housing, clothing, and customs, and then suddenly you would notice abrupt changes within a few miles. In most cases, however, the change would be gradual. The permanent houses of the eastern United States would become salted with portable tipis in the prairie area before they were abandoned entirely in favor of the tipi out on the open plains. Nevertheless, it is convenient to draw a boundary at the line where the frequency of portable tipis matches that of stationary houses. The boundaries of culture areas, therefore, are generally the lines at which the two ways of life are in balance, and only occasionally represent an abrupt change. A brief description of the culture areas follows.

Arctic.—The home of the Eskimo in Alaska, Canada, and Greenland, this area is divided into a western portion, which includes the Aleut on the Aleutian Islands as well as the Eskimo of Alaska, and a combination central and eastern division, which embraces all the Eskimo from the Mackenzie River delta east to Greenland. The Alaskan Eskimo and Aleuts have been much influenced by both the cultures of Siberia on the west and of the Northwest Coast on the southeast. The Central and Eastern Eskimo retain more of the early and distinctive features of their way of life because they lived in greater isolation, with less contact with Indians to the south. The Eskimo in every locality but one or two had access to the sea and lived most of the year on the shoreline where they could obtain sea mammals.

Sub-Arctic.—This area lies directly south of the Arctic, as the name implies, in a belt of coniferous forest broken here and there by treeless tundra. It includes interior Alaska and most of interior Canada and was the home of the snowshoe and toboggan Indians who spoke languages of the Athapaskan and Algonquian families. For convenience this huge area has been split into three subdivisions: the Yukon Sub-Arctic in Alaska and Yukon Territory, Canada, drained by the Yukon River system; the Mackenzie Sub-Arctic in Northwest Territories and the northern parts of British Columbia, Alberta, Saskatchewan, and Manitoba, drained by the Mackenzie River; and the Eastern Sub-Arctic in Ontario, Quebec, and adjacent parts of Manitoba, and Coast of Labrador. Indians speaking languages of the Athapaskan family occupied the Yukon and Mackenzie regions, while people speaking Algonquian languages lived in the eastern part. The caribou and the moose were the principal sources of food over most of the Sub-Arctic, and the many streams, lakes, and swamps made travel in the birch bark canoe almost universal.

Northwest Coast.—This area includes the coastline from the panhandle in southeastern Alaska through British Columbia, Washington, and Oregon, to the northwestern corner of California. These Indians subsisted principally on fish, lived in plank houses, and enjoyed a considerable surplus of the necessities of life. Those in Alaska and British Columbia are famous for their totem poles which may be seen in many large museums there and in the United States. The culture of this area competes with that of the Arctic as the most distinctive or the most foreign of aboriginal North America. This is due partly to the geographical environment but also to its history, which shows much evidence of contact with Asia. The great emphasis on the acquisition of material goods, their display on public occasions, and the emergence of social classes and hereditary slavery set it off sharply from other non-farming culture areas of the continent.

Plateau.—This region is named after the Columbian plateaus drained by the Columbia River system. It includes parts of British Columbia, Alberta, Washington, Idaho, Oregon, and Montana. It embraces most of Fraser River drainage as well as that of the Columbia. It is a difficult area to characterize because its culture exhibits influences from both the Northwest Coast and the Plains, and the semidesert environment of the southern portion gives it something in common with the Great Basin as well. In the central part of the Plateau we find democratic peoples entirely free of the emphasis on rank of the Northwest Coast; they are also peaceful peoples largely lacking the war-drive of the Plains Indians. Fish was the staple food over most of this region as one might suspect

15

from the large numbers of salmon taken in its streams in modern times.

Plains.—This area stretches from central Alberta all the way south to the Mexican border. It is bounded on the west by the Rocky Mountains and on the east by the Missouri River. It includes parts of Alberta, Saskatchewan, Montana, Wyoming, Colorado, the Dakotas, Nebraska, Kansas, Oklahoma, and Texas. The Plains Indians are the ones best known to most people in the United States today. They ate the meat of the buffalo, rode horses after A.D. 1600, lived in conical tipis, and did not farm. After acquiring the horse, they became the most nomadic of all Indians and fought the White man bravely to defend their lands until as late as the 1870's. This was the home of the Blackfoot, Crow, Sioux (Dakota), Cheyenne, and Comanche Indians, among others.

Prairies.—This region matches pretty closely our modern term Middle West. It includes all of Wisconsin, Michigan, Illinois, Iowa, and Missouri, and parts of the Dakotas, Minnesota, Nebraska, Kansas, Oklahoma, Texas, Arkansas, Tennessee, Kentucky, and Indiana. These Indians were much like those of the Plains except that they farmed and lived in permanent villages near their farms part of the year. Most of them also hunted the buffalo, as well as other animals. Such familiar peoples as the Pawnee, Omaha, Iowa, Osage, and Illinois lived in this area.

East.—This area extends from a little beyond the St. Lawrence River in Canada to the Gulf of Mexico and from the eastern boundary of the Prairies area to the Atlantic. It includes all of New York and the Middle Atlantic states, southern New England, and most of the southern states as far west as Louisiana. The Iroquois of New York State belong in this region as do the Five Civilized Tribes of the South. These peoples were more sedentary than those of the Prairies, subsisted to a greater extent on farm crops, and were organized into the largest political units north of Mexico. The European colonists settling in the United States contacted these Indians and learned from them to raise corn, beans, and pumpkins, as well as tobacco.

California.—This culture area includes about two-thirds of the modern state of that name. Although the area is small, it is famous for its great diversity of physical type, speech, and culture. In spite

16

of the absence of farming, population was fairly dense but the political unit, called the tribelet, numbered only a few hundred. These Indians suffered a decline after the Spanish arrived in 1770 and the Gold Rush of 1849 put an end to their independence. The names of these peoples, such as Maidu, Miwok, Pomo, and Yokuts are not familiar to most people today.

Great Basin.—This area includes all of Nevada and Utah and parts of California, Oregon, Idaho, Wyoming, and Colorado. It is one of the driest regions in the United States and was inhabited by Shoshonis, Paiutes, and Utes. These peoples obtained a meager living from wild species of plants and animals available in their deserts and mountains. They lived in small family groups or bands until they got horses from the Spanish or from other Indians. Along with the horses came other influences from the Plains area and those living east of Great Salt Lake adopted the buffalo-hide tipis, Plains dress, and Plains customs after that time.

Baja California.—This small area is left separate because it doesn't fit very well with any of the neighboring areas. Most of it is desert, but in the south rainfall is heavier. From the number of village names left by the Spanish Padres, population appears to have been greater in the more favorable southern environment. Although none of these Indians farmed, their diet was superior to that of the Great Basin peoples because of sea foods. Few localities are more than fifty miles from the sea, and settlements were more numerous on the shore than inland. They were missionized by the Spanish before the California Indians and died of malnutrition and European diseases in such numbers that few survive today. Little is known about them.

Oasis.—This area includes most of Arizona, New Mexico, all of the Mexican states of Sonora and Sinaloa, and the western parts of Chihuahua and Durango. Because much of the land is desert, settlements tended to be located in oasis-like spots near streams. All of these Indians farmed, although some much more than others. Many of them lived in villages or towns, hence the name Pueblo for the village-dwellers of northern New Mexico and Arizona, such as Hopi and Zuñi. The Navaho and Apache also belong in this area, as do less known tribes such as the Mohave and Yuma. Of the Mexican tribes, the Yaqui are known to many people in the United

17

States today, and the Tarahumara may be familiar to those who have toured Mexico. On the whole the Indians in New Mexico and Arizona have been less disturbed by our own westward expansion than those in any other part of the United States, and they still retain many of their Indian attitudes and customs which make them interesting to tourists. The Navaho are now the largest tribe in the United States, with a population of about 80,000 in 1960.

Northeast Mexico.—This is a desert region formerly inhabited by the wild Chichimecs, who harassed the Spanish during the entire colonial period. They lived exclusively on wild plants and animals and were experts with the bow and arrow. They were extremely warlike and cost the Spanish many times as much in blood, sweat, tears, and money as did the successful campaign of Cortez against Montezuma and the Aztecs. On many occasions the Chichimecs fought to the last man to defend themselves against the Spaniards and, when captured, often escaped or committed suicide rather than acquiesce in a life of farming and peace. Today the few survivors of the Chichimecs live on little farms of their own or work as laborers on the farms and ranches of the Mexicans, but the oldest ones, who still speak no Spanish, remember the wild tales of the good old days when they raided the Spanish wagon trains to and from the silver mines at Zacatecas.

Meso-America.—In recent years this term has been applied to that part of Mexico lying south of about the twenty-first parallel, plus Guatemala and British Honduras. This is the land of the famous Mayas and Aztecs, who have been compared to the Greeks and Romans. The Mayas were the intellectuals who invented a place number system to record important dates on monuments and devised a remarkably accurate calendar, parts of which still survive today in the area. The Aztecs were the conquerors and politicians who dominated most of the peoples in southern Mexico when Cortez first set foot on Mexican soil. They compelled all the peoples they conquered to pay them tribute at regular intervals, and it is from similar tribute lists compiled by the early sixteenth-century Spaniards that much of our best data on population, settlement patterns, and political organization are obtained. The population of Meso-America in 1520 was greater than that of all the other culture areas combined, according to the best estimates. This

18

was made possible by intensive farming with large irrigation systems and well-organized totalitarian governments to regiment all available labor. Although we may not approve of this kind of government today, the peoples of this area achieved a much more complex and sophisticated civilization than that of any other area. The Aztecs and Mayas stemmed from humble Indian ancestors and, with the help of their Indian neighbors, developed their remarkable culture with practically no assistance from Europe and Asia.

Circum-Caribbean.—This area includes most of Central America, the northern shore of South America, and all the islands of the West Indies. Spanish colonization in the West Indies was more speedy and devastating than in any area of equal size on the mainland, with the result that the native inhabitants disappeared rapidly, to be replaced by Negro slaves from Africa. Indians on the mainland fared better and still retain some of their native way of life. The culture of this area was second only to that of Meso-America in general level of achievement. The people lived mainly by farming and were organized into tribes and kingdoms with populations numbering in the thousands and tens of thousands. They were ruled by royal lineages, in some of which the king married his sister, and religion was controlled by a class of priests. Lying midway between the two continents, this area was a crossroads for trade, goods and ideas going in both directions.

This completes the identification of the culture areas which serve as a framework for organizing information in the chapters that follow. The aim of this book is to describe Indian cultures as they were before they were disturbed by European colonization, but because the Indians left no written records other than the difficult to decipher pictographs and glyphs of Meso-America, this must be done from the writings of early missionaries, army officers, traders, and colonial officials.

Anthropologists employ a wide variety of terms to indicate time periods. Pre-Columbian, pre-European, precontact, prehistoric, native, aboriginal, and indigenous all refer to the culture of the Indians before its disturbance by Europeans. Post-Columbian, post-European, post-White, postcontact, historic, modern and recent all refer to the period after A.D. 1492, or after whatever later date

19

contact between Indians and Whites in a given locality first took place.

For Spanish-America the record begins in the early sixteenth century, for the eastern United States not until the seventeenth, for other less accessible areas not until the eighteenth, and for most Indians in the western United States and Canada, not until the nineteenth century. Because much of the information on Indians refers to the nineteenth century, when changes due to European contact had already taken place, no claim is made that everything said about them in this book represents pure Indian culture. However, such things as iron tools, which are certain to be of European origin, have been weeded out, and Indian life has been reconstructed as carefully as possible. Because some tribes became extinct, as a result of European colonization, before others were discovered, most of the maps in this volume do not refer to a single century. They telescope information from the sixteenth to the nineteenth centuries. Sometimes the map itself depicts temporal changes where they are well known, but more often the time element is mentioned in the text. Now and then the findings of archeology have added historical depth; where the evidence overwhelmingly points to one conclusion, some historical speculation has been admitted.

REFERENCES

Driver and Massey, 1957; Kroeber, 1939; Wissler, 1938.

3: Subsistence Patterns

Most of the food consumed in the modern world is derived from cultivated plants; smaller amounts are produced by milking and slaughtering domesticated animals and by fishing; only a very small amount of the modern diet is obtained from wild animals and wild plants. Indians of North America also depended principally upon domesticated plants; wild animals, wild plants, and fish were of secondary importance, while domesticated animals probably provided less than 1 per cent of the total diet. This chapter will offer a classification of the principal ways in which Indians obtained food, as well as a description of the major subsistence activities in each culture area.

Cultivated plants supplied nearly all the dietary in Meso-America, where population was greater than in all the other cultures areas combined. The domestication of the llama, alpaca, and guinea pig in the Andean region of South America supplemented the predominantly vegetable diet in that area from about 1000 B.C., but these animals were absent in North America and the dog, which was widely distributed on both continents, was only rarely eaten.

In the Americas farming probably began a little later than in the Old World. The earliest certain dates for farming in the Old World are about 8000 B.C. in the Middle East, though some specialists believe that peoples of southeastern Asia farmed at a still earlier period. In the first chapter we cited 7000–5500 B.C. as the period for first farming in the Americas. Because there was probably no trade or traffic between the two hemispheres at that early time, except across Bering Strait, where none of the domesticated plants can grow, and because the earliest genera and species of plants are different in the two hemispheres, except for the gourd,

21

the only conclusion to draw is that the American Indian independently invented farming. In other words, he had the same amount of intelligence or inventive genius as the first farmers in the Old World. Furthermore, most anthropologists believe that the first farmers in both hemispheres were women, not men. While this point cannot be proved, women almost everywhere in the world gather more wild plant foods than do men, and women are more often the farmers among those primitive peoples whose agriculture is little developed.

What determines the kind of food economy that a given people will follow? This depends on many things which, however, may be divided into two classes of factors: availability of the raw material in the environment; and knowledge of how to obtain the raw material and how to prepare it for food. Few foods are eaten without any preparation whatsoever. Because our knowledge of agriculture today far surpasses that of the American Indians, we can and do raise many foods in the United States which were totally unknown to them. Most of these were brought over by the colonists from Europe and many came ultimately from the Middle East or southeastern Asia.

Nonetheless, many of the plants first domesticated by American Indians were imported into the Old World, after the discovery of America, and continue to play an important part in the diet of Europeans, Asians, and Africans. Of these, maize is probably the most widespread. As we shall see later, in the section on food preparation and preservation, a number of foods eaten by Indians contained poisons which had to be extracted before they could be consumed. The amount of experimentation necessary to acquire the vast knowledge of plants and animals that they possessed was enormous. This took many millenia, because knowledge came slowly to peoples without writing or other adequate means of keeping records or conveying information other than by word of mouth.

Once food habits are established, change comes slowly. People the world over prefer one food to another because of taste, not as a result of carefully calculated nutritional values or production costs. Most of us today leave all that to the dietitians and often fail to eat the things our doctors advise. During the Second World

War, when canned combat rations first became common, many men complained about the taste, although these foods had been proved by dietitians to be superior to normal diet as most people choose it for themselves. So it was with the Indian. Conditioned from childhood to like certain foods, he continued to seek them because he preferred them. Conditioned to prefer hunting activity and meat to farming and cereals, the Plains Indians of the nineteenth century continued to hunt the buffalo until it was almost exterminated, and then starved in considerable numbers before they turned to farming. They considered beef too "sweet" to be palatable, and sometimes attributed to beef-eating the epidemics of diseases introduced by the White man. Today some of the Plains Indians have returned to raising buffalo on the range, much as we do with cattle. While a number of correlations of food habits with geographical environment will be pointed out in this chapter and those that follow, these will never be a complete explanation because of the role played by taste and preference for one kind of fare and one way of life as opposed to another. Such preferences are learned and are included in the crucial core of what anthropologists call "culture."

The inhabited regions of North America were the same in A.D. 1492 as they are today. They extended from the home of the Polar Eskimo in northwest Greenland to Panama. Within this vast area there are sharp differences in topography, soils, climate, fauna, and flora, which in turn have greatly influenced native subsistence patterns and their geographical distributions. These patterns may be classified in terms of the dominance in the diet of fish, game, wild plants, or cultivated plants (Map 3). Fish was the staple food on the Northwest Coast, part of Alaska, and in a number of smaller areas shown on Map 3. Game predominated in a huge triangular area which includes most of the Arctic, Sub-Arctic, Plains, and Prairies. Wild plants were the principal article of diet in California, the Great Basin, and probably Northeast Mexico. Cultivated plants predominated in the East, sporadically on the Prairies, in the Oasis area, Meso-America, and on to Panama. Two areas in the west were difficult to classify and were finally assigned to a category of their own labeled "balance of animal and wild plant

23

foods." These include a portion of the Plateau and Great Basin in the far west, and most of the Apache territory in the Southwest.

The five categories of Map 3 may be further subdivided into the twelve shown on Map. 4. These twelve units are of a magnitude more comparable to that of the culture areas on Map 2. They do not correspond exactly to the culture areas because no single aspect of culture ever matches culture areas exactly. Culture areas are composite units based on all major aspects of culture, and each separate aspect of culture, as represented by the various chapters in this book, fits the culture areas to a greater or lesser degree. In some regions the dependence was mainly on a single species of animal, such as the buffalo, while in others there was a great variety of food resources used. A description of the subsistence patterns of each of the culture areas in turn follows.

AREAL SURVEY

Arctic.—Beginning in the north, we see that almost the entire Arctic Coast, from the Alaska Peninsula on the west to Greenland and Newfoundland on the east, depended mainly on sea mammals for food. The only exception to this generalization is the small area at the mouths of the Yukon and Kuskokwim rivers, on the Bering Sea, where fish predominated. The inhabitants of this vast sea mammal area were all Eskimos except for a few Aleuts on the Alaska Peninsula and the Aleutian Islands. Second in importance to sea mammals was probably the caribou, hunted during the summer, while fish of various kinds were perhaps third. This seems to have been true of most of the sea mammal area, but would have to be reversed in some localities such as Alaska, where fish were more important than caribou.

Of the various kinds of sea mammals and their importance in the diet, seals would certainly be first, with walruses second and whales third. This rank varies inversely with the size of the animals partly because of the fact that walruses and whales did not inhabit the shallow, land-locked waters of the central area west from Hudson Bay to Coronation Gulf. Here the seal was the only one available.

Birds were a staple article of diet in a few localities in the sea mammal area in the summer, especially in Greenland. A little vegetable food was consumed, particularly by women, while men more often confined their vegetable intake to the sourish contents of the herbivorous caribou's stomach.

While game was plentiful at times, the vicissitudes of weather seriously limited the supply at other times, or made the sea too rough for navigation, or the trails impossible to negotiate in pursuit of game. The result was periodic starvation, as the folklore abundantly bears out. At the time of European contact Eskimo population had probably reached the limit that could be supported by means of the hunting methods known to the natives.

Because the Eskimos ate at least half of their meat raw, and included the fat and internal organs as well as the muscle meat, the diet contained every vitamin and mineral salt necessary for human nutrition plus an abundance of protein, which is insufficient in the diets of many more civilized peoples. It was only in times of scarcity that malnutrition occurred.

Sub-Arctic.—The people of the Sub-Arctic area, from interior Alaska on the west to the Atlantic Ocean on the east, subsisted primarily on caribou and moose meat. While both animals are found together in many localities, caribou predominates in the north and moose in the south. The nine species of caribou are likewise often divided into the barren ground types occupying the treeless tundra in the summer, and the woodland types confined all year round to the forested area farther south. Other animals which were commonly hunted for food were bear, beaver, porcupine, deer, and rabbit.

Second only to mammals in this area were fish, which were the primary food in the Yukon drainage and a few scattered localities; but they were of secondary importance over the remainder of the Sub-Arctic. On the Atlantic Coast shellfish were everywhere eaten. Birds were obtained in many localities, especially in the summer, but constituted only a minor part of the diet. Plant foods were very limited, with berries outranking greens, roots, and seeds, all of which were occasionally eaten.

Famines were common, especially in winter, and sometimes took the form of fat starvation which resulted from eating mainly lean meat. This happened when the animals had difficulty finding sufficient food and failed to put on a normal layer of fat. Like the

25

Eskimo, these people sometimes resorted to cannibalism when faced with otherwise certain death from starvation. While at its best the diet was adequate, famines were an annual threat to existence and a great deal of anxiety over food characterized this area.

Northwest Coast.—Salmon of five different species was the chief article of diet from the Eel and Klamath rivers of northern California to the Alaska Peninsula. Salmon are hatched in small streams, which form the headwaters and tributaries of the larger rivers, but migrate to the sea where they live for three or four years and grow to maturity. When the females are ready to lay their eggs, they return to the river in which they were hatched and swim upstream to the place of their nativity, or as near to it as possible. There the females lay thousands of tiny eggs which the males fertilize soon afterward. The urge to negotiate this reproductive journey is so powerful that a fish will leap over waterfalls twice as high as its own length. It is during such a "run" that they are taken by the thousands, dried, and stored for winter use.

Peoples on the Northwest Coast commonly obtained at least a dozen species of salt-water fish of which halibut and cod were the most important. Those living on islands or peninsulas whose streams were too small to attract large numbers of salmon depended more on halibut and cod. This was true of the Haida of the Queen Charlotte Islands, the Kwakiutl and Nootka of Vancouver Island, and the Makah of Cape Flattery. The candlefish, so oily that it will burn like a candle when a wick is inserted, was the most common source of oil, which was used as a sauce to go with meat and fish.

With the dozen species of shellfish and the sea mammals which were obtained everywhere along the coast, it is easy to see that salt-water dwellers had a more bountiful supply of aquatic products than the peoples on the inland streams. As among the Eskimos, the smaller sea mammals were most frequently obtained, so that the order of importance would be: seals and sea lions; dolphins and porpoises; and whales. The coastal peoples also gathered sea plants which were dried and pressed into cakes for future use. That land plants were not neglected is shown by an exhaustive list of sixty species used for food in western Washington (Gunther,

1945). Salal berries, blueberries, and camas roots were commonly eaten throughout this area.

This diet was entirely adequate, both qualitatively and quantitatively; there are no reports of famines from coastal dwellers. The fish, shellfish, and mammal components in the diet furnished an excess of protein and an abundance of fat, while the roots provided starch and the berries sugar. Recent biochemical analyses of these foods show that the drying methods universal in the area do not appreciably diminish vitamin content, and that while vitamins A and D vary from species to species, their amounts in some of the fish oils come up to that of cod liver oil, which has long been a standard source of these nutritive elements in our culture. One species of berries, Saskatoons, was found to contain three times as much iron and copper as prunes and raisins.

Plateau.—The subsistence pattern of the Plateau area was mixed. In the north it was similiar to that of the Sub-Arctic with chief dependence on moose and other large game. In the west fishing dominated all other food-getting activities, as it did on the Northwest Coast. In the east a number of large animals, such as the moose, elk, and deer, combined to make meat the staple diet. And in the corridor running south through Oregon to California, wild plant foods seem to have furnished about as much nourishment as meat and fish combined. The Plateau peoples of Washington and Idaho also ate considerable quantities of wild plants, especially the camas, a close relative of the hyacinth. The roots of the camas were the most important food furnished by any single plant species on the Plateau.

Plains.—On the Great Plains of North America, which extend from the North Saskatchewan River in Alberta nearly to the Gulf of Mexico in Texas and from the Rocky Mountains on the west to about the hundredth meridian on the east, the buffalo was the staple source of food. More than in any other area in North America, the Indian here depended on a single species for his livelihood. This extreme specialization was accentuated by the acquisition, in historic times, of the horse, which greatly facilitated buffalo-hunting. Buffalo were supplemented by elk, antelope, bear, and occasionally smaller game. The only plant food eaten in any quantity was berries, which were a standard ingredient in the pemmican made by all the tribes. A few roots were obtained by women with the aid of a pointed digging stick. Tribes adjacent to the agricultural areas to the east and to the southwest sometimes obtained a little corn in trade or in predatory raids on their more sedentary neighbors.

As long as the buffalo held out, Plains diet was adequate, as the superb physiques of the people proved. Until this animal was exterminated, food was seldom a serious problem. Fish were to be found in all the streams on the Plains but were not eaten, more often because they were considered not worth bothering with than as the result of a definite taboo.

Prairies.—In a relatively large part of this area hunting was dominant, with farming definitely secondary. Agriculture certainly furnished less than half the diet in most of this area and in many localities a fourth would be a better estimate. Maize, beans, squashes, and a few sunflowers were the crops raised. In the early nineteenth century most tribes as far east as Lake Michigan traveled westward on annual hunting excursions for buffalo while the crops were growing or after they had been harvested. In the seventeenth century in Illinois, one observer stated that buffalo were obtained in greater numbers locally than any other species of large game. Tribes adjacent to the buffalo area depended as much or more on that animal than they did on agriculture, and those farther east spent most of the year hunting other large game, of which the deer was the most frequently taken. Archeological sites east of the Mississippi consistently yield more bones of the deer than of any other mammalian genus. Wild rice was more important than maize in a small area in Wisconsin and was perhaps the first-ranking food for the Menomini. Around the Great Lakes in general, fishing rivaled hunting for first place in food economy.

Farming was more important than hunting for a few tribes on the southern edge of the Prairies area, and this may also have been the case on the western edge of this area before the horse was acquired in large enough numbers to shift the economy toward buffalo-hunting. By the nineteenth century the western tribes were living about half on the maize, beans, and squashes they raised. But with fewer horses in the eighteenth century they could not have obtained as many buffalo.

East.—In the eastern United States it is difficult to say whether agriculture furnished even half of the diet. At any rate, early historical observers report larger and more permanent towns with greater maize acreage than in the Middle West. In the Southeast, men as well as women were compelled by the chief and other public officials to work in the town fields. That hunting was still far from a lost art, however, is shown by the fact that many of these eastern tribes fled their villages when attacked by superior forces and managed to get a living from the woods after their supplies of corn, beans, and squashes had been appropriated or destroyed. Again archeological evidence shows that the deer was the most frequent single genus of animal taken. Wild plant foods, especially nuts, were of tertiary significance in the eastern United States but were used more than is generally known. Fish were caught in considerable numbers everywhere east of the Mississippi, but were no more important in this area than wild plant foods except on the coast and in the Great Lakes region. Shellfish were much in demand along the coasts and archeologists have found them in huge quantities on a number of inland rivers, where they date from some time before agriculture was known. The diet of the East satisfied every nutritional need, and famines were rare because there were plenty of wild foods to fall back on when crops failed or were destroyed by enemies.

California.—In most of California the acorn was the staple article of diet. It was ground into a meal, from which the tannic acid was leached out with water, and then it was boiled to make mush or baked into an unleavened bread. A wide variety of smaller seeds was prepared similarly after first being parched. Secondary to plants in the diet, small game, such as rodents and birds, plus a fair number of invertebrates such as earthworms, grasshoppers, and caterpillars, probably furnished more food the year round than did deer and other large game. On the coast, seafood of all kinds formed the staple diet wherever sufficient quantities were obtainable. Fish were evidently of tertiary significance in the interior streams, although in aboriginal times salmon frequented the Sacramento and San Joaquin drainages in modest numbers. The wide variety of food resources and the mild winters made California relatively free of famines.

Great Basin.—In the Great Basin there was a large area where wild plant foods predominated over animal foods. The piñon, from which pine nuts were obtained, was the most common single species used for food, but seeds of many other plants were also eaten, and a few roots were obtained with the aid of the digging stick in the northern part of this area. There was no single food that could be regarded as a staple because even the pine nut crop failed frequently. Deer inhabited the mountains of the Great Basin, where they were probably the most common large animal, and mountain sheep were to be found on the higher crags and summits over most of the area. Antelope became more frequent toward the north and, because they lived in open country in large herds, were usually hunted communally. These hunts were led by medicine men who were supposed to be able to attract antelope by their magical powers. Compared with other areas, however, large game was scarce and probably furnished a smaller part of the year-round diet than did rodents, reptiles, and insects. Rabbits in particular were hunted in communal drives similar, except for the absence of the medicine man, to those for antelope. Famines were common in the Great Basin and people were hungry much of the time, according to old Indian informants.

Northeast Mexico and Baja California.—In Northeast Mexico there was emphasis on mesquite pods and cactus fruits although many other plants were also eaten. Mesquite is a tree which bears a pod full of seeds resembling our string beans. These were eaten green or were gathered when dry, ground in mortars, and boiled. Several parts of the cactus were consumed: the fruit was eaten fresh or dried for preservation; the seeds were dried or roasted and then ground; the leaves and the pulp of the stalk were also edible; and the juice was drunk. Other food plants utilized in this area include the mescal or agave, yucca, tule (cattail), and the piñon. Large game was about as scarce as in the Great Basin; rodents, reptiles, and insects were eaten more often than the deer. On the Gulf Coast fish and shellfish were eaten in quantities. Hunger was a chronic condition, famine a constant threat, and malnutrition widespread in the interior of Northeast Mexico.

On the peninsula of Baja California and in southern California it seems that at inland localities desert plants, such as the agave, mesquite, and, in the south, pitahaya (a cactus) were the staples, with rabbits and deer furnishing supplementary diet, while on the coast seafood ranging from shellfish and fish to stranded whales was the main bill of fare. Hunger must have been common, but access to seafood made it far less serious than in the Great Basin and the interior of Northeast Mexico.

Oasis.—All of the Oasis peoples farmed but in varying degrees. Intensive agriculture was the pattern of the Pueblos, who live on the Colorado Plateau in northern Arizona and New Mexico. One author has estimated that maize constituted 80 per cent of the diet. If this is true, agricultural products as a whole must have accounted for 85 or 90 per cent of their food, because beans, squashes, and sunflowers were also raised in aboriginal times. Wild plants were much less important than agricultural ones, but a great many species were eaten. One writer (Underhill n.d.: 58–63) lists 9 species of roots, 29 of greens, 26 of fruits, 20 of seeds, 3 of nuts, and 3 of fungi, not to mention 14 species used as herb flavorings, 8 as delicacies, 11 as chewing gums, 7 as beverages, and 7 species of leaves for smoking. Since game was scarce, meat was seldom obtainable and formed as small a fraction of the diet as did wild plants. Deer, antelope, and mountain sheep were occasionally taken by all the Pueblo peoples, as were buffalo by the easternmost, but small game furnished more meat the year round. The rabbit was the most common single species eaten. A few fish were obtained in the Rio Grande, but they were a negligible factor in the diet and were not eaten at the other pueblos. Famines were a real threat to the pueblos, where drought seriously affected population density and movements. Diet was also probably deficient in protein, although the bean offset this to some extent.

The Navaho acquired agriculture from the Pueblo people, probably in the seventeenth century and by the nineteenth century were relying more on maize and other crops than on hunting or wild plant gathering. The Apaches of the nineteenth century seem to have relied almost equally on game and wild plants, with farm crops of tertiary rank.

As for the River Yumans, farm crops furnished about half of the total diet of the Mohave, perhaps 40 per cent for the Yuma, 30 per cent for the Cocopa, and less for the Maricopa. Wild plants were of first rank for the last two tribes. The Desert Yumans relied principally on wild plants, with game second and farming third.

31

Fish were generally scarce in the Oasis but they were of tertiary importance among the River Yumans who lived on the Colorado River.

Meso-America.—Southward down the west coast of Mexico, the role of agriculture in the subsistence pattern increased, until in central and southern Mexico it was more intensive than among the Pueblos of the Southwest. While maize was by far the most important single species in both areas, southern Mexico cultivated a much greater number of other species, as we will see in the next chapter. Wild plants, wild game, and domesticated animals (dogs, turkeys, geese, ducks, quail, bees, maguey slugs) competed with each other for second place, each achieving secondary importance in restricted areas. Many parts of Meso-America were capable of supporting a large and varied assortment of animals, but with the increase of human population accompanying the development of maize agriculture, game was reduced to a fraction of its former density. Hunting was a sport reserved for the nobility among the Aztecs. Fish and other seafood certainly outranked land game on the coasts but were every bit as inconsequential as game in most localities in the interior. Fish was also an important trade item for coastal peoples. Famines were rare, but it seems likely that the diet was deficient in protein, although the bean bolstered this nutritional element to some extent.

Circum-Caribbean.—Manioc, the starch of which is known as tapioca in the United States, was the leading crop on the Caribbean side of Central America and on Hispaniola and eastern Cuba. In these areas maize was also raised but was of secondary importance. Manioc was undoubtedly derived from South America, as were a number of other tropical species which were raised here. Wild plants probably took precedence over both hunting and fishing in the area as a whole although certainly not in every locality. Fishing was dominant over hunting along the coasts and possibly everywhere on the islands because only one land mammal, a rodent, was to be found on the Antilles. The manatee, a sea mammal, was an important source of food all around the Caribbean. Famines were unknown in this area as there were plenty of other foods to fall back on when one source failed.

NATURAL VEGETATION AREAS

Natural vegetation areas provide a good summary of total geographic environment because plants reflect rainfall, humidity, temperature, soils, and other essentials of geography. Without citing every detail of agreement or disagreement between culture areas (Map 2) and natural vegetation areas (Map 5), one can see at a glance that the correspondence is close. Therefore culture, at the developmental level achieved by North American Indians, is heavily dependent on geographical environment, although nowhere near wholly determined by geography. The poorest match is in Meso-America, where four natural vegetation zones occur. This reflects the generalization that as culture becomes more and more complex it becomes less and less geared to geography. Irrigation canals make farming on deserts possible, and extensive trade makes products available many miles from where nature provides the materials from which they are made. As civilization advances, man gains more and more control over nature and becomes less and less dependent on the raw materials nature provides; he constructs more and more of his environment as his knowledge of how to do so increases. The Meso-Americans were far in advance of the peoples of any other culture area in North American and had managed to adjust their culture to several geographical environments.

Subsistence areas (Map 4) also show a substantial, though far from perfect, agreement with natural vegetation areas (Map 5). Again the correspondence is poorest in Meso-America and also in the Oasis. In other words, in areas where farming was most intensive, man's way of life was least dependent on what nature provided. He had learned to maneuver nature to his own advantage.

DOMESTICATED ANIMALS

Domesticated animals provided only a very small percentage of the diet and were much less a part of the North American Indian bill of fare than they were in the Old World. Turkeys were domesticated in the Oasis, Meso-American, and Central American areas, where they were actually bred in captivity. The Athapaskan-speaking peoples and the Tarahumara in the Oasis

33

area took wild turkeys alive and caged or leashed them. The chief use of the bird in Meso-America and in Central America was for food, although the Mixe in southern Mexico confined the eating in recent times to ceremonial occasions. In the Oasis area, on the other hand, the turkey was kept principally for its feathers, which formed a part of sacred costumes and other ritual objects. Among the Pueblos, it has been eaten in this century only at Isleta and Taos. Some of the Apaches kept turkeys merely as pets, without eating them or using the feathers, and still other Apaches hunted them and ate them as wild game.

Dogs were raised for eating in the eastern United States, in the central Plains, in California, and in Meso-America (Driver and Massey, 1957: Map 6), but were probably eaten only on special occasions or in ceremonies. On the Northwest Coast they were eaten by cannibal impersonators in secret society performances. In the northern Plains, Prairies, and Great Lakes regions, they were eaten in ceremonies associated with warfare, at secret society performances, or at sib festivals. In the single known Eskimo occurrence, a boy at one year of age was fed a part of a dog's head so that he would have a strong head. Nowhere was the dog a regular part of the diet. The ceremonial eating of dogs seems to have spread in historic times; at least the Haida, Blackfeet, and Crow say it is recent. The general attitude toward dog flesh was that it was poisonous, but, like other poisons, it could convey supernatural power. Eating it was either an act of defiance of natural law on the part of one in rapport with supernatural law, or a means of building up resistance to evil by partaking of it in modest doses. Most of the Eskimos ate dog flesh for food only when starving; but since they ate human flesh under the same conditions, this should not be equated to the ceremonial eating of dogs above.

Horses were eaten by many Indian tribes when first obtained, but on the Plains their greater utility for hunting and transportation soon removed them from the dietary. Where buffalo were available, a single horse could run down a large number of buffalo in a hunting season and thus provide a great deal more meat than could be obtained from its own carcass. In parts of the Oasis and Great Basin, where the rabbit was the principal game animal and the horse was of no aid in its hunting, and where at the same time life was less migratory than on the Plains, horses continued to be eaten occasionally. As late as 1850 these Indians were stealing horses for food from parties of Whites who had joined the California Gold Rush.

Bees were kept for their honey by a few Meso-American tribes, and quail and maguey slugs were raised for eating in some localities. Ducks and geese are reported for the Aztecs, at least. The ducks seem to have been derived from Peru in early historic times, while the origin of the geese is still more problematical. Ducks were also kept on the island of Hispaniola, where they may have been pre-Columbian. Fish were impounded by peoples of the West Indies and also by the Aztecs. Several of these instances are to be regarded as borderline domestication, if indeed the fish impounding can be regarded as domestication at all. None of these animals made any significant contribution to the diet. The stocking of small streams with salmon by depositing their eggs near the headwaters, as was practiced on the Northwest Coast, is certainly closer to domestication than is mere impounding.

POPULATION

It is impossible to determine exact population statistics for tribes or areas at the time of first White contact, and totally out of the question to obtain them for 1492. Although we have some census material for individual tribes or communities during the colonial period, we are forced to rely on mere estimates for most of the continent. There is a fair amount of agreement for the areas north of Mexico, where it is estimated by Mooney, Kroeber, Rosenblat, and Steward that population totaled about one million at White contact. Sapper (1924) estimated two to three and a half million for the same area. Cook (1954, 1955) has raised Kroeber's earlier estimates in two areas of California. This suggests that one million for the areas north of Mexico is too low and that the true figure might lie somewhere between one and two million.

South of the Mexican border, including Central America and the West Indies, the picture is more confused. The lowest estimate in this area is that of Kroeber which, with Central America added, is about four million. Rosenblat's and Steward's estimates were approximately five and one-half million, while Sapper's earlier (1924) figure is twenty to twenty-five million. Cook and Simpson (1948), on the basis of detailed tribute and census figures, estimate the aboriginal (1519) population of only a portion of our Meso-American area, that from about Nayarit to the Isthmus of Tehuantepec, to have been 11 million. This figure suggests a total population for North America south of the Mexican border (including the West Indies) as great as that given by Sapper. Therefore, we conclude that population south of the border was somewhere between Sapper's figure and those of Rosenblat and Steward.

From the cultural point of view, the interesting thing is the correlation of population with types of subsistence and other aspects of culture. The relative density of native population is shown on Map 6. Even though the absolute figures are uncertain, the relative density can reflect the essential facts. Several generalizations are apparent at once: population was heavier in the south than in the north, heavier on the coast than in the interior, and heavier on the Pacific Coast than on the Atlantic Coast. Although areas where farming was practiced generally show a denser population than areas where farming was unknown, it is interesting to note that the non-farming regions of the Pacific Coast were more heavily populated than the farming areas of the eastern United States. Kroeber has estimated that eastern Indians cultivated less than 1 per cent of the available land suitable for horticulture by modern standards. Nowhere in the East did cultivated plants seem to have furnished much over half of the total diet, and on the Prairies they provided less than half. On the North Pacific Coast, fish and marine mammals supported a denser population than occurred anywhere on the eastern coast of the United States, and even in California, where food resources were less specialized than in most other parts of North America, population density topped that of the East.

The difficult conditions of human habitation are reflected in the population figures of the Arctic, Sub-Arctic, and parts of the Great Basin and Northeast Mexico. Although many non-farming tribes in the deserts of the Great Basin and Northeast Mexico must have been familiar with the farming of their neighbors in bordering

36

areas, the environment checked the diffusion of domesticated plants. It is noteworthy that these same areas remain sparsely populated to this day. The modern population picture differs from the aboriginal one most strikingly in the eastern United States, where first intensive plow farming and later industrialization have brought about the heaviest population on the continent. In Mexico and Central America, areas which held the greatest population densities in North America in aboriginal times, the situation has changed only slightly. The uplands of central Mexico still dominate the population picture, but recently there have been significant increases in population in northern Mexico as agriculture with irrigation and industries has increased.

REFERENCES

COOK, 1954, 1955; COOK AND SIMPSON, 1948; DRIVER AND MASSEY, 1957; GUNTHER, 1945; KROEBER, 1939; ROSENBLAT, 1945; ROSTLUND, 1952; SAPPER, 1924; SAUER, 1935, 1939; STEWARD, 1938a, 1948b, 1949; SWANTON, 1946; UNDERHILL, n.d.; WISSLER, 1938; YANOVSKY, 1936; YANOVSKY AND KINGSBURY, 1938.

4: Horticulture

THE IMPORTANCE of farming can scarcely be overestimated. Although the total area where farming was practiced constituted less than half of the entire North American continent (Map 7), the native population (Map 6) was much heavier in those regions. In relation to total Indian population and total diet, horticultural products probably furnished about 75 per cent of all the food consumed by North American aborigines. The greatest culture development, which occurred in Meso-America, was made possible in part by the increased food production in this area of intensive cultivation.

Before considering the field practices, techniques, and tools used in agricultural North America, we shall discuss the important crops, their uses, history, and distribution in pre-Columbian times. The total number of species cultivated in aboriginal North America comes to about 86, but only 21 of these were raised in the territory that is now the United States.

MAIZE

Indian corn or maize (*Zea mays*) was the most important and widespread cultivated food plant in the entire New World (Map 7). It was grown from the upper Missouri River in North Dakota and the lower St. Lawrence River region, 47° north latitude, to Chiloé Island in Chile, 43° south latitude. This span is roughly the middle 90 degrees of the 180 between poles. With the possible exception of Northwest Coast tobacco, no other plant was raised by Indians beyond these limits—certainly no other food plant. In the Andean region of South America maize was grown from sea level to 12,700 feet above sea level at Lake Titicaca in the Peruvian Andes, the difference in altitude here causing as much variation in climate as is found at sea level along the entire latitudinal range from Chiloé to the St. Lawrence.

Maize was probably first domesticated in southern Mexico. The oldest maize so far discovered is that from southern Puebla, Mexico, which has been dated at about 5000 B.C. By 4000 B.C. it had spread to other localities in southern Mexico and north to Bat Cave, New Mexico. This most ancient maize is a popcorn with each kernel inclosed in a little separate pod, so that it may also be called a pod corn. This same type of maize has also been found in Romero's Cave, in southwest Tamaulipas, Mexico; the date there is 2770 B.C. Since no wild close relatives of maize have ever been found in New Mexico, we may assume that this pod-popcorn at Bat Cave was introduced as a cultivated plant, no doubt from Mexico. At later levels in Bat Cave, corn showing evidences of crossing with *teosinte* (*Euchlena mexicana*) appeared. *Teosinte* is a "cousin" of maize which grows wild in southern Mexico and Central America. Actually it is intermediate between maize and *Tripsacum*, a wild "second cousin" of maize. *Tripsacum* flourishes in the most tropical regions in Central America and Colombia, and extends as far north as the state of Indiana in the United States. Most forms of maize grown today exhibit relationship to *Tripsacum* or *teosinte*. Maize and *Tripsacum* have been crossbred in laboratory experiments, and maize and *teosinte* cross in nature.

More varieties of maize are to be found in Mexico than in any other area of comparable size. Recent research on Mexican maize has resulted in the collection of thousands of specimens and a classification of all the variants into 25 "races." Like the races of man, which are all regarded as belonging to a single species, the 25 races of corn belong to *Zea mays*. These races of corn do not exist as pure races anywhere, because there is considerable variation within each race, and boundaries between races are not always clearly defined. They do serve, however, to induce some order in what would otherwise approach chaos. Once a large number of specimens is available for experimentation, it is possible to crossbreed them in many combinations and eventually to work out the history of the domesticated corn plant. This is what botanists are doing.

The races of maize in Mexico may be divided into four main

39

groups: Ancient Indigenous, Pre-Columbian Exotic, Prehistoric Mestizos, and Modern Incipient.

Ancient Indigenous races are those believed to have originated in Mexico from the kind of primitive pod-popcorn found in Puebla, Mexico. There are four races in this group, all popcorns, with two of them showing weak development of pods. The earliest corn from South America also seems to belong to this group.

The Pre-Columbian Exotic races are believed to have spread by diffusion from Central or South America to Mexico in prehistoric times. All four of the races in this second group have South American counterparts, and all but one (*maíz dulce*) have been the parents of later hybrid races.

The Prehistoric Mestizos are races which are believed to have resulted from the crossing of Ancient Indigenous with Pre-Columbian Exotic races, plus hybridization with *teosinte*. Thirteen races of this type have been identified so far. Some of these are related to the dent corns found in the eastern United States.

The Modern Incipient races consist of four types which are definitely post-Columbian, some less than a century old, and all somewhat unstabilized.

North of Mexico less is known about races of maize, and varieties from these areas cannot always be equated with those from Mexico. Nevertheless, it is clear that Indian corn in the Southwest is of four kinds which have as many distinct origins. The oldest is the pod-popcorn of 4000 B.C., mentioned above. The second oldest is a flour variety which diffused up the west coast of Mexico to Arizona as early as 200–100 B.C. It is called Hohokam–Basket Maker after the archeological cultures with which it is found. It is probably derived from the Mexican Pre-Columbian Exotic group, which in turn stems from South America. It survives today among the Pima, Papago, and River Yumans. In northern Arizona, among prehistoric Basket Maker peoples, this type of corn was modified from A.D. 200 to 1200 in the direction of that from the Mexican Plateau, creating a third kind. Between A.D. 1200 and 1300, the third variety developed into a fourth as the result of hybridization with flint corn, so called because of the hardness of its grain. This flint corn was derived from the eastern United States.

On the Prairies and in the East there were at least four major varieties of maize grown by Indians. The first is popcorn, which may be presumed to be the oldest in these areas. Even though its priority is definitely established in the Southwest, it could have diffused to the Southeast from either the Southwest or Mexico at a much later date.

The second oldest variety is apparently flint corn, which is characterized by a full-bodied and hard kernel. This is the only kind of corn found archeologically in the East, and it is also common in archeological sites on the northern half of the Prairies. The oldest sites date from the first millennium of the Christian Era. The source of this flint corn is not positively known, but because flint corns farther south center in the Circum-Caribbean area, this is the most likely derivation for these kinds in the United States. Because the northern flint corns have few knobs on the chromosomes, and such knobs seem to be a trait derived from *teosinte* and ultimately *Tripsacum*, these flint corns probably spread north before *teosinte* or *Tripsacum* admixture had progressed very far.

The third variety to appear on the scene is closely related to the Basket Maker corn from the Southwest, and presumably spread from there to the Prairie area in the first millennium of the Christian Era.

The fourth and apparently latest major variety to appear on the Prairies and in the East is a kind called dent corn because of the dents in the tops of the kernels. This flour variety has been found in prehistoric and protohistoric archeological sites on the Prairies but not in the East. The earliest reference to dent corn in the East is in Beverley's *History of Virginia,* published in 1705. The dent corns, therefore, appear to have arrived in the Southeast from the Prairies in historic times. They are closely related to the dents of Mexico, which belong to the Prehistoric Mestizo group. The relatively late appearance of this group in Mexico explains the even later appearance of its derivatives in the United States. The Mexican Plateau influence on Basket Maker corn, A.D. 200–1200, resulted in an increase in denting, among other changes. The modern commercial corn raised in the corn belt of the United States is a cross between Indian flints and dents.

Figure 1 summarizes our historical reconstruction of the diffusion of maize in North America. If more were known about it, the picture would probably be much more complicated, but as it is, it conveys some idea of the intricacies of maize history. Thus the Southwest received at least three waves of diffusion from Mexico and at least one from the Prairies. The Prairies and East apparently received influences from the West Indies, Mexico, and the Southwest. Diffusion was multiple with respect to a single direction and also was multidirectional. When the South American picture is

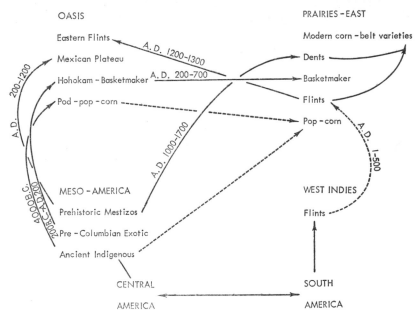

Fig. 1.—Diffusion of Maize. Driver and Massey

better understood, it will probably reveal a complicated series of reciprocal influences between North and South America.

OTHER PLANTS

The history of domesticated plants is a fascinating subject but much too lengthy for this volume. Table 1 is a checklist of plants raised by the North American Indians and gives their geographical distributions in terms of the four major areas of their occurrence: Mexico and Central America; the West Indies; Southwestern United States; and Eastern United States (Prairies and East culture areas).

TABLE 1

CHECKLIST OF PLANTS CULTIVATED BY NORTH AMERICAN INDIANS

	Mexico or Central America	West Indies	Southwestern United States	Eastern United States
Seeds, grain:				
Amaranthus cruentus	X			
Amaranthus leucocarpus	X		X	
Amaranthus paniculatus				X
Ambrosia sp., Ragweed			X	
Chenopodium nuttaliae, Pigweed	X			
Echinochloa crusgalli, Barnyard grass	X		X	
Helianthus annuus, Sunflower	X		X	X
Helianthus tuberosus, Jerusalem artichoke			X	X
Iva sp.			X	
Panicum hirticaule, Panic grass	X		X	
Panicum sonorum, Panic grass	X		X	
Phaloris sp.			X	
Salvia hispanica, Chia	X			
Zea mays, Maize, Corn	X	X	X	X
Fruits:				
Achras zapota, Sapodilla	X			
Ananas comosus, Pineapple	X	X		
Annona cherimola, Chirimoya	X	X		
Annona muricata, Soursop	X			
Annona reticulata, Chirimoya	X			
Byrsonima crassifolia, Nanchi	X			
Calocarpum mammosum, Zapote	X			
Carica papaya, Papaya	X	X		
Casimiroa edulis, White zapote	X			
Chrysophyllum cuimito, Caimito, Star-apple	X	X		
Cocos nucifera, Coconut	X			
Craetegus mexicana, Tecojote	X			
Cyclanthera explodens, Pepino hueco	X			
Cyphomandra betacea, Tree tomato	X			
Diospyros ebenaster, Black zapote	X			
Gonoglobis edulis, Cuayote	X			
Guilielma gasipaes, Pejibaye	X			
Guilielma utilis, Peachpalm	X			
Lucuma salicifolia, Yellow zapote	X			
Lycopersicon esculentum, Tomato	X			
Mammea americana, Mamey	X			
Musa paradisiaca, Banana	X			
Opuntia sp., Nopal cactus	X			
Persea gratissima, Avocado	X	X		
Physalis aequata, Husk tomato	X			
Prunus serotina, Capuli, Black cherry	X			
Psidium guayava, Guava	X	X		
Sechium edule, Chocho	X			
Spondias sp., Plum, Ciruela	X			
Legumes:				
Canavalia ensiformis, Jack bean	X		X	
Inga feuillei, Tree legume	X			
Pachyrhizus sp., Jicama	X			
Phaseolus acutifolius, Tepary bean	X		X	
Phaseolus lunatus, Lima bean	X		X	X
Phaseolus multiflorus, Scarlet runner bean	X			
Phaseolus vulgaris, Kidney bean	X	X	X	X
Prosopis edulis, Pod mesquite	X			

TABLE 1—*Continued*

	Mexico or Central America	West Indies	Southwestern United States	Eastern United States
Root crops:				
Arachis hypogaea, Peanut................		X		
Colathica allonia......................	X			
Ipomoea batatas, Sweet potato............	X	X		
Manihot aipi, Sweet manioc..............	X	X		
Manihot utilissima, Bitter manioc.........	X	X		
Maranta arundinacea, Arrowroot..........		X		
Pachyrhizus sp., Jicama, Yam bean.......	X			
Tigridia pavonia, Cacomite..............	X			
Xanthosoma saggittifolium, Yautia.........	X	X		
Narcotics, stimulants:				
Agave atrovirens, Agave.................	X			
Erythroxylon coca, Coca.................	X			
Jatropha acomtifolia, Chicasquil..........	X			
Nicotiana rustica, Tobacco..............	X			X
Nicotiana tabacum, Tobacco.............	X	X		
Cloth, fiber:				
Agave lechugilla.......................	X			
Agave sisalana, Sisal...................	X			
Gossypium hirsutum, Cotton.............	X	X	X	
Miscellaneous vegetables:				
Capsicum sp., Red pepper, Chile..........	X	X		
Chamaedorra bifurcata, Pacaya...........	X			
Chayote edulis, Chayote.................	X			
Crescentia cujete, Calabash-tree..........	X			
Cucurbita ficifolia, Malabar gourd........	X			
Cucurbita mixta.......................	X	X		
Cucurbita moschata, Crook-neck squash....	X		X	
Cucurbita pepo, Pumpkin, summer squash..	X		X	X
Cyathea arborea, Tree-fern (buds eaten)....	X			
Erythrina edulis, Coral bean (blossoms)....	X			
Lagenaria siceraria, Bottle gourd.........	X		X	X
Phytolacca decandra, Calahi (spinach)......	X			
Yucca elephantipes, (flowers eaten)........	X			
Miscellaneous:				
Bromelia pinguin, Pinula (hedge).........	X			
Cereus sp., Hedge plant.................	X			
Nopalea coccinellifera, Cochineal cactus....	X			
Polakowska tacaco, Tacaco..............	X			
Theobroma cacao, Cacao (chocolate).......	X			

Of the total number of 86 plants listed in Table 1, 79 were grown in Mexico or Central America, 17 in the West Indies, 19 in the southwestern United States, and only 9 in the eastern United States. In the Southwest there were four species raised which are not known to have been grown in Mexico. They were all seed producing plants and contributed only trivial amounts to the diet. They do prove, however, that Southwestern Indians took a little initiative in plant domestication and were not wholly dependent on plants derived from Mexico, although most of them came from

44

there. In the eastern United States only one species raised is not reported for at least one of the other areas, and it too was inconsequential in the diet. Of the few plants apparently domesticated in the territory that is now the United States, the two species of sunflowers (Helianthus) were the most important in Indian diet, but they were much less eaten than maize, beans, and squashes. There are no plants in the eastern United States which are shared only with the West Indies and suggest derivation from those islands except possibly flint corn. Therefore, the peoples of the Southwest, Prairies, and East were heavily dependent on Mexico for their food plants.

Beans (*Phaseolus*) of one species or another were grown everywhere that maize was raised (Map 7), usually in the same field, and in most localities were the second most important plant. The oldest domesticated beans so far discovered in the Americas are those from the Ocampo Caves in southwest Tamaulipas, Mexico, dated by radiocarbon at 4000–2300 B.C. (Whitaker, Cutler, and MacNeish, 1957) and those from Puebla, dated at about 3500 B.C. (MacNeish, 1960). All the species of beans were probably first domesticated in Mexico or Central America and were carried by man to the southwestern and eastern United States.

The squashes (*Cucurbita*) were also about as widespread as maize, and were often raised in the same field along with maize and beans. The oldest evidence of squash is the remains of the *pepo* species found in the earliest level of the Ocampo Caves in Mexico, dated by radiocarbon at 7000–5500 B.C. (Whitaker, Cutler, and MacNeish, 1957; Crane and Griffin, 1958). Most species of squash were first domesticated in Mexico or Central America. Squash was third in importance to maize and beans for North America as a whole.

The plants most important to the Indians were domesticated by them at early dates, but other plants of less consequence seem to have been imported from overseas before A.D. 1492. One of these is the coconut (*Cocos nucifera*). It was cultivated along the Pacific Coast of Central America and southern Mexico. Its home is southeast Asia or the neighboring islands, and it was dispersed to America either by ocean drift or by men in boats from South Pacific islands.

Another case for transoceanic travel is that of cotton (*Gossypi-*

um). New World domesticated cottons are crosses between domesticated Old World species and wild New World species. Each of the parent species has 13 chromosomes, while the half-breed plants have 26 chromosomes. It is difficult to date the first appearance of Old World cotton in the New World because plant geneticists must have living cells in order to count chromosomes and make other microscopic observations. The fibers in cotton textiles recovered by archeologists do not give the plant geneticist all the data he needs. The oldest cotton so far discovered in North America is that in the same Ocampo Caves, but in higher levels dated at 1800–1400 B.C. (Whitaker, Cutler, and MacNeish, 1957). Cotton found in Peruvian sites has been dated at 2300 B.C. Although we cannot prove that this early cotton has 26 chromosomes, it otherwise possesses the characteristics of the half-breed *hirsutum* species and suggests that Asiatic cotton had found its way to the Americas by that date. Because the Old World domesticated species did the traveling, it seems to have been brought to the New World by men in boats.

The gourd (*Lagenaria*) also has a fascinating history. Its recent discovery in the earliest levels of the Ocampo Caves, dated at 7000–5500 B.C., makes a revision of its history necessary. It seems likely that nature dispersed it by ocean drift across the Atlantic or the Pacific to the Americas, where Indians domesticated it without any help from Old World farmers. From its point of first American domestication in tropical or subtropical latitudes, it spread north and south to the limits of maize, and rattles made from it were traded even farther. It was used also for water bottles, dishes, and floats for nets and rafts, but not for food.

Bananas and plantains both belong to the single species *Musa paradisiaca*. There is little doubt that this domesticate originated in southeastern Asia and was introduced by man as a cultivated plant to other tropical regions. The only argument is whether it arrived in the Americas in pre-Columbian or post-Columbian times. By the second half of the sixteenth century, the plantain was reported all the way from southern Brazil to Jalisco, Mexico, and was regarded as a native crop by everyone who described it.

The sweet potato (*Ipomoea batatas*) was grown all the way from Valparaiso, Chile, to just north of the Tropic of Cancer in

Mexico. Its nearest wild relatives center in the Caribbean area, so that it was most likely domesticated on the north coast of South America bordering on the Caribbean Sea. It was propagated by cuttings rather than from seeds. The sweet potato was carried west to Polynesia by boat or raft in pre-Columbian times, as the native word *kumara* in both Peru and Polynesia helps to prove. The white potato was native to the Andean region of South America and was not raised in North America until after A.D. 1492.

The examples cited above are the strongest cases for overseas travel of plants. Some of them were probably carried by men in boats from South Pacific islands to America, and at least one, the sweet potato, seems to have been carried from South America to Polynesia by the same method. Such apparently intermittent overseas contacts do not seem to have had much influence on native American cultures, which remained largely independent of those of the Old World until A.D. 1492.

DOMESTICATED PLANTS AND CULTURE HISTORY

In the sections above on various domesticated plants a little has been said about the spread, dispersal, or diffusion of plants from a place of origin to the limits of their distributions, sometimes thousands of miles away. How is this kind of history proved and what caused these plants to spread? To understand this, it is necessary to introduce the botanist's principle of monogenesis. When two plants found in different localities on the earth's surface are classified by the botanist as belonging to the same species or genus, they are regarded as having sprung from a single ancestor at a single place at a single period of time. This is true also of more remotely related plants, such as those belonging to the same family, order, class, etc., but because these more remote relationships are less pertinent to the problem of domestication, this discussion will be confined to species and genera. Granting that two specimens of the same species or genus of plant found hundreds or thousands of miles apart have sprung from a common ancestral plant, how did the two specimens become separated? Although the details are seldom known, it is certain that one or both of the specimens was carried from the place of origin by man or by nature. Carried by nature means that the seeds of the plant were carried by the wind, by water, or by some species of animal. Birds sometimes spread seeds considerable distances by ingesting them and excreting them later, or by inadvertently carrying them along on the mud sticking to their feet. The wind in California has spread the oats raised by the Spanish along a fifty-mile strip of coast to almost all parts of the state. Floods sometimes uproot plants, carry them downstream, and then cast them onto the bank where they take root in a new locality. Ocean currents, as suggested above, may carry plants long distances. Granting now that nature can disperse plants, why would man bother to do such a thing? He would bother to carry a plant from one place to another only if the plant were of some utility to him: if he intended to use it later for food or clothing, or if he could trade it to another person for something of value. Furthermore, he would only bother to carry it along if it were not available in the locality where he was going.

There is abundant evidence on the transportation and trading of wild plants, and foods made from them, by Indians and other primitive peoples, but that on domesticated plants is more pertinent to this problem. Corn was traded by the farming Indians on the Missouri River to the nomads of the Plains living farther west where it was too dry and cold to farm. The Pueblo peoples of the Oasis also traded corn to the nomads. And the nomads of both areas often stole corn when they raided the farming peoples. In fact, most cultivated plants are carried by man some distance beyond the localities where they are raised.

How is it known whether a particular domesticated plant has been dispersed by nature or by man when there is no documentary evidence? Science cannot give an infallible answer in every case, but when the plant is so dependent on man that it will not survive without his care, it is quite certain that it was dispersed by man, not by nature. Most cultivated plants will not survive very long, in most of the areas where they are raised, without the help of man. This is especially true of plants raised from cuttings, such as potatoes, sweet potatoes, and bananas. No animal except man knows how to cut the potato up into pieces with a bud (eye) in each and plant them in properly cultivated soil at the right depth. Even seed plants, such as corn and beans, would be choked out by weeds

48

after a few years in most localities where they are raised today if they were not tended by man. Therefore when a plant such as corn is found to be cultivated by the Indians over about half the area in the New World, anthropologists infer that it was not dispersed by nature but rather by the Indian.

In reference again to Figure 1, the question may be asked whether each of the lines on the figure represents a single trading expedition by a single party of traders? Almost certainly not. Local trade was much more common than trade over long routes. Tribes without farming normally visited neighboring tribes engaged in farming and were acquainted with the technique. After trading hides or other products of the chase for cultivated plant foods for decades or centuries and acquiring a taste for the latter, some ambitious person of the nomadic tribe might eventually try to farm. If the climate and soil were right and he or she got a good crop, the project might be continued indefinitely and, if others of the same tribe followed suit, the whole society might become agricultural. Finally, after the people had acquired a little surplus, they might be glad to trade some of it to a nomadic tribe a little farther out from the agricultural fringe. Such seems to have been the process of dispersal not only for plant products but also for many other items of culture. This relay process, with one tribe passing an item on to the next, and the next to still another, is most commonly called diffusion.

In the chapters that follow it will frequently be assumed that all the occurrences of some feature of culture, such as the bow and arrow, have sprung from a single origin. This means that one tribe invented the bow and arrow and that the others all derived it from the original tribe or some intervening tribe by this relay process. When geographical distributions are continuous, that is, when all the occurrences are clustered into a single limited and continuous area, anthropologists generally agree that one origin is sufficient to account for all the occurrences.

TOOLS AND TECHNIQUES OF FARMING

The plow was totally unknown in the New World until it was introduced by Europeans, and draft animals were not used in farming. Cultivation with hand tools, as was done by the Indians,

49

is frequently called horticulture (garden cultivation). All the farming tribes used a straight pointed stick for some part of the routine. This was shaped like the digging stick used to obtain wild
roots and bulbs, and often the same individual implement was used
for both purposes. The pointed stick was used most frequently to
make a hole for the grains of corn, beans, or squashes at planting,
although it might also be used to break up the ground for planting.
In areas where precipitation was adequate, a hole a few inches deep
would suffice, but in the dry Oasis area the planter sometimes made
a hole as much as eighteen inches deep. The stub of a forking
branch was left on the stick by the Pueblos and Navahos to serve
as a footrest and thus facilitate the making of the deep holes which
the dry soil demanded.

A number of tribes used an end-bladed implement made of a
single piece of wood. In the Northeast this tool resembled a modern spade with a footrest on one side but, because it was reported
by Champlain, it appears to have been aboriginal. This tool was not
always distinguished from a swordlike weeding tool which was
limited to the Southwest. Throughout that area, the end-bladed
wooden implement lacked a footrest, and this difference suggests
that the end-bladed feature in the two areas is best explained by
independent histories.

The northern Missouri River tribes employed a rake of wood or
antler to handle brush when clearing land, and in the Southwest the
Hopi, at least, used a similar wooden tool. Whether either or both
instances are aboriginal or modern is unknown, but it is certain that
there was no direct contact between the two areas.

Hoes were probably universal on the Prairies and in the East.
They seem to have been used much less frequently in the Oasis and
Meso-America and were apparently entirely absent around the
Caribbean. One of the most common materials for the blade was
animal bone, most often the shoulder blade. On the Prairies this
was invariably derived from the buffalo, but in the East, deer and
perhaps other Cervidae furnished the material for the blade. Hoes
with wooden blades were also common, especially where the buffalo shoulder blade was not available. Hoes with copper blades are
reported only for the central Mexican area of Meso-America,
where wooden ones were also used, and do not seem to have been

common there. Hoes with shell, stone, and fishbone blades were common in the East, where they have also been unearthed in quantity by archeologists. It is quite apparent that the hoes of the Prairies and East stem from a single origin, and possibly those in the Southwest are derived from them. Those in Mexico, however, may even be post-Columbian. Hoes were most often used to hill up the soil around the growing corn, but sometimes they were used to clear land or to dig holes for planting.

Irrigation was limited to Meso-America, the Oasis, and the Circum-Caribbean area. Complete irrigation systems with ditches were fairly common in the Oasis, the oldest on record being that at Snaketown, on the Gila drainage, A.D. 800–900. The largest and longest canals were to be found in that part of southern Arizona; those on the Colorado and Rio Grande drainages to the north were less pretentious. The huge irrigation canals and dykes in the Valley of Mexico were the largest irrigation operation in Meso-America, and North America as well. The dense population of central Mexico was made possible by the intensive farming which demanded irrigation.

In the Oasis area the custom of planting in soils which were naturally irrigated by floods of overflowing streams was widely distributed. This floodplain agriculture was important to the Yuman tribes of the lower Colorado River and to the Cáhita tribes of the lower Yaqui, Fuerte, and Mayo rivers in Sinaloa. The overflow, which was the key to Cáhita economy, usually occurred in winter and summer, making possible two crops a year. The Indians planted in the rich alluvial mud deposited by the streams. Any other kind of farming would have been impractical because the annual rainfall is only about five inches. In other parts of the Oasis, where large streams were absent, crops were planted at the foot of mesas or in washes where the runoff from an occasional shower provided the precious moisture. Here and there wing fences, dykes, or dams were constructed to control this natural runoff. In one locality in Nevada, some sort of irrigation short of ditches was practiced on wild plants, but details and time of origin are unknown.

Grass, brush, and trees were cleared from farm land by burning in most localities where agriculture was practiced in aboriginal

51

North America. The purpose was threefold: to get rid of the vegetation, to fertilize the soil, and to make the soil more friable. The northern Missouri River farmers spread brush evenly over the entire plot, including barren spots, before burning, because the ashes loosened the soil and made it more workable. In areas of heaviest rainfall, in southeastern Mexico and the Circum-Caribbean region, the soil possessed only the minimum of essential minerals because these were continually leached out by the torrential rains. Some of this land was so poor that it had to be abandoned after a single crop. In one Maya locality, land was cultivated only one or two years out of seven. In more favorable localities, it might be farmed for several years in a row. Among some Cáhita groups living in mountain basins, fields were abandoned every one to three years, in contrast to conditions of floodplain agriculture where continual replanting was possible. Among the Iroquois of New York State, a town was moved about twice in a generation because of exhaustion of the soil, scarcity of firewood and timber for building, and depletion of game. For the Prairie-East area as a whole, about ten years was the maximum length of time a plot could be continuously farmed in any locality.

In the tropical forest, farming was done in the woods because the entire landscape was overgrown with vegetation and there was no other choice. On the Prairies and in the East, however, farming was done in the woods even where open meadows or prairies were available. This held also for the Indians living in the savanna lands of Central and South America. The meager tools used by the Indians and the absence of the plow and draft animals made the softer soils in the woods more attractive. The prairies of Iowa, which constitute the best land for corn today, could not have been worked with the pointed sticks and hoes of the Indians. These implements could not have broken up the tough sod which the heavy grasses produced. It was, therefore, more profitable to clear woods than to till the tough soils of open country. Large trees were not felled but were simply girdled by pounding with a stone axe. This treatment was sufficient to kill the tree and permit the sun to shine through its bare branches. Another way was to pile brush around the trunk and set it on fire. Burning to produce a better wild crop the next season was practiced over a large area in the Great Basin and California. This treatment was applied to grasses and to small plants such as tarweed and wild tobacco. This method is especially effective for perennials because the roots beneath the surface are unharmed and the elimination of surface coverage gives the new sprouting crop the maximum of sunlight and the minimum of competition from other species.

Wild seeds were sown in a few localities, but this is hardly to be called farming, because the varieties sown were identical with endemic wild forms. In the area from Lake Winnipeg to Lake Superior, wild rice (*Zizania aquatica*) was sometimes sown in the swamps. In California, Nevada, Utah, and north Mexico, a few wild grasses were occasionally planted. It was on the Colorado and Gila rivers, however, that this activity attained its greatest importance. A recent analysis by Martínez del Rio of the historical documentation on the Laguneros of north Mexico indicates that reports of agriculture among those people refer to possible cultivation of seeds which were probably wild.

Fertilizers, other than the ashes from burned-over land, were rarely employed. Fish heads and ground shell were applied to corn hills in New England and Virginia. The references to manure among the Seneca and Arikara, however, may be questioned in regard to aboriginality. The same is true of the Zapotecs, the mountain Maya, and the Taino on the island of Hispaniola. Informants from many other tribes on the Prairies and in the East emphatically deny the use of manure. In the areas where fertilizers were most needed, the tropics, there was no adequate source available, and soil exhaustion has often been mentioned as a partial explanation of the fluid political fortunes of these people.

The sexual division of labor for farming activities presents a clear picture (Map 8). Women did most of the farm work everywhere in the Prairie-East area except among the Ojibwa and a few tribes in Maine and New Brunswick. These exceptions to the rule were on the northern periphery of horticulture and these peoples may have adopted the White pattern by the time their customs got on record. The men of the Prairie-East normally helped with the clearing of the new land and also with the harvest, although on the western Prairies, where buffalo hunting was important, young and active men might disdain farming entirely. Women also bore the

53

brunt of farming among the Apaches of the Southwest. This pattern seems to stem from the Plains through which the Apaches might have passed on their migration southward a few centuries before White contact, and where some of them lived in the early historical period. Both sexes among the Jicarilla farmed, at least in the nineteenth century, but among the Navaho the men have done most of the horticultural labor as far back as the record goes. This is not surprising because, of all the Athapaskans, the Navaho have become most acculturated to Pueblo ways.

Among the Pueblos, the men everywhere do most of the farming, although early accounts mention the help of women more often than recent reports do. Men also dominated horticulture among most of the Yuman-Uto-Aztecan peoples in the Oasis and on down the west coast of Mexico to Meso-America. It is only when we reach the Circum-Caribbean area that women do most of the farming in some localities, and here the men help them by clearing the land.

To sum up, in the areas most intensively farmed, Oasis and Meso-America, men were the principal farmers. In areas where farming was secondary in importance to some other subsistence activity (Map 4), women were the principal farmers. The East superficially appears to be an exception to this rule, but we must remember that although farming seems to have dominated subsistence, it is problematical whether it provided over half the total food supply in this area. Therefore, we may say that for North America as a whole there is a positive correlation between the importance of farm products in the dietary and the amount of time men devote to farming.

CONCLUSIONS

Although a few food plants raised by Indians seem to have been derived from the Old World via the South Pacific islands, the staples, such as maize, beans, squashes, manioc (tapioca) and sweet potatoes, are all endemic to the Americas. Because these staple plants were probably all domesticated in the New World by the time the first imports seem to have arrived from the islands of the Pacific, the American Indian has demonstrated his ability to invent agriculture without external assistance. He possessed the same intelligence, perseverance, and imagination as the first farmers of the Old World.

Maize, beans, and squashes are primarily temperate zone plants grown from seeds, while manioc and sweet potatoes are tropical species raised from cuttings. These facts, combined with the particular areas where domestication of each form probably first took place, suggest that horticulture was invented at least twice by the Indians. The seed plants seem likely to have been cultivated first in the highlands of southern Mexico or Guatemala; the root plants in the tropical lowlands of South America. Once large numbers of Indians began to farm, it was easier to domesticate new species locally in the areas where the wild forms occurred because the people were already sedentary and possessed the necessary tools and habits to clear the land and cultivate the soil.

By the time Columbus discovered America, maize was being raised about as far north and west in North America as climate permitted (Map 7). In Canada, except for a narrow strip along the St. Lawrence, the frost-free season in the summer is too short to raise a good crop of maize. The western boundary of the maize area in the Plains states is at about the hundredth meridian, which is also the approximate boundary between regions with more than 20 inches of average rainfall and those with less than 20 inches. West of this line there is less than 20 inches of rain, which is too little rain for maize unless it is irrigated or grown in the best-watered spots. In the Great Basin region, maize was formerly grown about as far west and north as Great Salt Lake, but the abandonment of this region by the farmers long before America was discovered by Europeans is probably an indication that the climate was not very favorable for agriculture. In the Southwest, the area west of the Colorado River in California is desert, averaging only a couple of inches of rain each year. This served as a barrier to the spread of maize into California, but even where rainfall in that state is adequate in quantity, it comes at the wrong season for maize. Maize demands summer rains during its growing season, but in northern California most of the moisture falls in the winter months. The absence of maize in Northeast Mexico is also to be explained partly by climate. Here it was also too dry to grow a good crop consistently. Geography, therefore, was an important limiting factor in the distribution of the maize plant, and other plants as well.

Although horticulture was practiced over less than half the area of the North American continent, it should be remembered that population was much heavier in farming areas on the average. Horticulture contributed to the diet of at least 90 per cent of the population in native North America and perhaps as much as 95 per cent. It will be seen in the following chapters that many other important developments of culture were made possible by horticulture.

REFERENCES

AMES, 1939; ANDERSON, 1952; ARMILLAS, 1949; BENNETT AND BIRD, 1949; BROWN AND ANDERSON, 1947, 1948; CARTER, 1945, 1950; CARTER AND ANDERSON, 1945; CASTETTER AND BELL, 1942, 1951; CRANE AND GRIFFIN, 1958; DRIVER AND MASSEY, 1957; HEISER, 1951; JONES, 1949; KROEBER, 1939; LOWIE, 1954; MC-CUE, 1952; MACNEISH, 1960; MARTÍNEZ, 1936; MARTÍNEZ DEL RÍO, 1954; MEIGHAN AND OTHERS, 1958; SAUER, C. O., 1950, 1952; SAUER, J. D., 1950; SCHERY, 1952; SWANTON, 1946; WEATHERWAX, 1954; WELLHAUSEN, ROBERTS, HERNANDEZ, MANGELSDORF, 1952; WHITAKER, 1948; WHITAKER, CUTLER, AND MACNEISH, 1957.

5: OTHER SUBSISTENCE TECHNIQUES

THE EARLIEST dates of archeological sites where actual remains of domesticated plants and animals have been found are 7000 B.C. in the Old World and 7000–5500 B.C. in the New World. This seems a long time ago, but man hunted, fished, and gathered wild plants hundreds of thousands of years before he learned to farm. The first Indian immigrants to the New World knew nothing of farming and could not have raised crops in the Arctic climate of Siberia and Alaska if they had wanted to. These people lived solely on the wild animals, fish, and wild plants that nature provided. The abundance of spear points in the early archeological levels, mentioned in the first chapter, is mute but incontestable evidence that the earliest immigrants to North America were hunters.

In over half the area of aboriginal North America at European contact the Indians did not farm but lived exclusively by hunting, fishing, or gathering wild plants. Complete inventories of all species of animals, fishes, and plants consumed as food by the Red man of North America have never been compiled, but they would probably total more than 2,000 species. This suggests tremendous knowledge of the habits of the animals and fishes and an equally vast acquaintance with the nutritional qualities of the plants. Such knowledge could be acquired only by thousands of years of experimenting and some casualties from sickness or death. As we shall see below, some of the plants eaten contain poisons in their raw condition and must be cooked or otherwise treated before they can be consumed by human beings.

HUNTING

We saw in chapter iii that hunting was the dominant means of obtaining a livelihood in seven out of seventeen culture areas. The hunting regions cover at least half of the total area of the continent: nearly all of Canada and Alaska, and the middle half of the United States (Map 3). This area is wedge-shaped, with the point of the wedge in southern Texas. It falls almost entirely to the east of the continental divide, and the near-linear character of its western boundary is determined by this great divide. Hunting of wild game was also practiced to some extent in all other areas of North America, even in those regions where farming supplied 80 per cent or more of the diet.

Sea mammal hunting.—Sea mammals were hunted chiefly with the harpoon, which consisted of a detachable head with retrieving line attached, a foreshaft, and a main shaft. The significant feature of the harpoon is that the head remains in the hide or flesh of the animal, which is then played like a fish. The flexible line absorbs the swiveling and thrashing about of the animal, while a shaft with a fixed point would break in two. The larger sea mammals could never have been taken with fixed-pointed spears alone, because no man or small group of men could have held such animals even if the spear shaft did not break. With the aid of inflated floats made of bladders and seal hides and with mechanical drags of several varieties, even whales could be taken. Inflated floats and drags were indispensable to whaling, because the boats used were too small to withstand the pull of a diving whale and would have been submerged if the line had been attached to them; but floats were also used for capturing smaller sea mammals. The seals were small enough to be played with a hand line if the hunters wore mittens for protection from rope burns or the loss of a finger.

Land animal hunting.—Land animal hunting methods show almost endless variation in details from locality to locality and species to species. The bow and arrow was almost everywhere the chief weapon used. The thrusting lance was likewise nearly universal. The sling, which could be effective only against small game, is reported for about half the North American tribes. The spear-thrower is reported by European observers only in the far north and extreme south with a huge gap in the middle, and the blowgun is found only in the south. The javelin, hurled with the hand without spear-thrower, was extremely rare. Clubs of some kind were fairly common but were used more in warfare than in hunting.

Co-operative drives involving a number of hunters were almost universal, being absent only in restricted localities where artiodactyls (split-hoofed animals) and rodents were absent, or nearly absent, in the environment. The driving of land mammals into water or the pursuit of them in water is most characteristic of the Arctic and Sub-Arctic areas, where it is most often associated with the hunting of caribou and moose. Driving game with fire probably was practiced almost everywhere in the United States in aboriginal times, but was rare in other parts of North America. The surround appears to have been most common in the Prairies, Plains, Great Basin, and Oasis, although it is reported from other areas as well. After the acquisition of the horse by the Plains tribes, the surround became much easier and replaced other methods such as driving over cliffs or into man-made inclosures. Driving animals along a fence or barrier, or between a converging pair of them into a corral made of timber, was common in the northern two-thirds of North America. Another variant of the fence and inclosure was the long flat net, like a tennis net, but higher. Nets were used to catch deer and elk in British Columbia, and farther south deer or antelope were occasionally caught in them, but most often in the west they were employed in rabbit drives.

Pitfalls, concealed traps into which animals may fall, are reported in every major area of North America but not for every tribe. Deadfalls appear to have been known to about three-fourths of the tribes, being absent, little used, or not reported in the southeastern quarter of the continent. A deadfall is any sort of trap with a triggered weight which falls when sprung by the victim, pinning it fast or killing it instantly. Snares or nooses were almost universal, but were probably absent among most of the Plains tribes where the dominance of buffalo-hunting and the dearth of trees made them impractical.

Deceptive techniques were common in hunting and may be divided into visual disguises and auditory decoys. Visual disguises, consisting of the horns, head, and sometimes the entire hide of an

59

animal, were worn by the hunter, who stalked his quarry from the down-wind direction, so that he would not be detected by his body odor until he was within bow shot. A considerable variety of auditory decoys were employed by North American Indians. The conical bark trumpet was used to imitate the call of the moose, and smaller models of the same type for caribou as well. The blowing on a leaf or piece of grass held in the hands employs the principle of the ribbon reed. It was used more often for deer than for any other genus and imitated the cry of a fawn which might attract a doe. Whistles used as auditory decoys are fairly widespread but seldom described in detail. A number of tribes struck antlers together to imitate the sound of fighting bucks in the rutting season, or rubbed a scapula against a tree to produce a noise like a female in heat rubbing her horns to call a buck. The Shoshoni of the Great Basin struck stones or sticks together to produce a sound like the clashing together of mountain sheep horns. Hunters in the Sub-Arctic in the rutting season sometimes poured water out of a container, held a few feet above a stream or lake, to imitate the sound of a urinating female moose in order to attract a male animal.

Dogs were probably used in hunting by the majority of North American tribes, but on the Plains, Prairies, in the Great Basin, and in Meso-America only a minority of peoples seem to have followed this practice. In general, it appears that dogs were of little utility for large animals running in herds, which were easy for man to locate, but were of greater utility in hunting animals which were solitary or lived in small social groups and were, therefore, more difficult to find.

Nutritional value of meat.—Some idea of the food value of game can be obtained by comparing analyses of the meats of modern domesticated animals. For example, beef averages more than half protein, by dry weight, somewhat less than half fat, and contains in addition a small percentage of carbohydrates, minerals, and vitamins. Most other domesticated animal products conform to this picture, except pork, which contains over half fat. However, the meat of wild animals is usually leaner.

In order to be absorbed by the human animal, proteins must first be broken down into their constituent amino acids, and then synthesized again to form tissues in the body. Meat proteins provide all the essential amino acids, and over 90 per cent of the total protein in meat can be absorbed by human beings. In spite of the vegetarian bias of our monkey and ape ancestry, man today is well adapted to a meat diet.

Of the vitamins, A, B_1 (thiamine), and B_2 (riboflavin) occur in substantial quantities, especially in the internal organs, which were universally eaten by Indians. Vitamin C (ascorbic acid) is lost in cooking but is obviously present in raw meat, including blood, as the scurvy-free Eskimo proves.

Generally, meat contains more calories than fish, and the fatter the meat, the more calories per pound. Seal blubber, however, approaches the figure for butterfat, which is about 3,500 calories per pound. Lean cuts of meat may run as low as 400 calories per pound.

FISHING

Although fishing as a dominant subsistence activity was the rule mainly on the Northwest Coast, it was an important source of food in several other areas which total about half of the continent. The rank of fishing in native production economy depended, of course, on the quantity of fish available, the fishing skills, equipment, and knowledge possessed by the Indian, and the other kinds of food resources available in the area. The mere presence of quantities of fish in nature is insufficient to bring about their extensive utilization as food by man.

Fish were obtained by Indians in every major manner known to modern commercial fishermen: by means of weirs and traps, nets, spears, and hooks. They were also poisoned, shot with the bow, snared, and raked in.

The net is one of the most generalized of fishing devices and all species of fish are obtainable with it. At the same time it is among the most efficient of devices to operate, although it may take many hours to manufacture. Small hand nets, dip nets, and scoop nets were widely used in native North America, but seines and gill nets were of more limited distribution.

A weir is any sort of fence or barrier sufficient to block a fish yet permit the passage of water. The majority of weirs were built in streams, but some were built on the tidelands of the coasts to impound fish when the tide ebbed and flowed. They consisted normally of stakes or posts, driven into the bottom of the stream or tideland, with cross members attached to form a fish-proof latticework. In areas where wood was scarce or absent, such as the Arctic, weirs were made of stones; sometimes both wood and stones were used. Although nets were highly efficient fish-taking devices, weirs and traps probably caught more fish per year than any other method. Weirs and traps were especially effective for migrating fish such as salmon and shad. On the Northwest Coast, where fishing most completely dominated all other subsistence pursuits, more salmon were taken with these devices than with any other.

Fish spears were used in all regions except, of course, the deserts and semideserts, where streams and lakes were few and fish scarce. Harpoons were less common. Fish-spearing and harpooning are most effective in relatively shallow water which is clear or heavily stocked with fish. Attracting fish by means of a torchlight or a bonfire on the prow of a boat or raft is associated with spearing and was known in both eastern and western North America but not in the Arctic or most of the Sub-Arctic. This method is so efficient that it is forbidden by law in most civilized areas lest the numbers of fish become seriously depleted.

On the whole, fishhooks were much less effective than nets, weirs, and spears. Many species of fish will not take bait at all and others, such as salmon and shad, will not do so when ascending rivers to spawn. The fact that civilized nations today generally limit freshwater fishing to hook and line, in order to conserve their fish resources, is conclusive evidence of the relative ineffectiveness of hooks.

Catching fish with poisons was limited to the Plateau, Great Basin, California, Baja California, the Mexican Oasis, Meso-America, around the Caribbean, and in the East. This method was much less important than angling, for the continent as a whole. Not only was it a minor technique in the areas where it was used, but most of these areas made relatively little use of fish. It is noteworthy that fish-poisoning areas made considerable use of plant resources for both food and other purposes. Optimum conditions for fish-poisoning, in addition to the presence of poisonous plants, include sluggish streams and a high concentration of fish. The latter requirement was enhanced by communal fish drives which might extend for several miles in a stream. The poisonous part of the plant was usually pounded up before being thrown into the water, and the physiology of the fish converted such poisons into compounds harmless to human beings.

The food value of fish shows little variation in protein and minerals from species to species or season to season, but considerable variation in fat and water are found. Protein content of edible portions of fish varies from 15 to 20 per cent when water is included. By dry weight, however, protein almost always runs over 50 per cent and sometimes as high as 90 per cent. The balance is almost all fat. Carbohydrates are almost totally lacking in fish. Essential elements such as calcium, potassium, phosphorous, and iodine are found in adequate quantities in fish. Iodine content is ten to twenty times as great in salt-water fish as in fresh-water species. As is generally known, fish livers are excellent sources of vitamins A and D. Thiamine (B_1) and riboflavin (B_2) are also found in fish flesh in about the same amounts as in mammal meat, and fish roe and liver also contain large amounts of these indispensable items. Even ascorbic acid (C) occurs in small amounts in fish roe.

Averages of calories per pound, including moisture, for various species and genera of fish range from 250 to 1,000. The fattest fishes with the highest calorie content per pound are found in areas where the greatest numbers of fish are taken. Thus the salmon averages 1,000 calories per pound.

It is significant to note that fresh-water streams and lakes in North America constitute only about 5 per cent of the surface of the continent. Therefore, it is certain that fishing was more productive per acre than hunting or wild plant gathering. It was second only to agriculture in this respect. The relatively sedentary way of life on the Northwest Coast was made possible by the abundance of food available within a small territory.

WILD PLANT FOODS

Wild plants dominated subsistence in California, the Great Basin, Northeast Mexico, and a small part of the Oasis (Map 3). Before the time of agriculture, they were probably either dominant or much more important in the areas which later became agricultural. A combined list of both wild and domesticated native American plants north of Mexico, dating from 1936, gives 120 families, 444 genera, and 1,112 species. About 2 per cent of these species were cultivated plants; the other 98 per cent were wild. While considerable work in ethnobotany has been done since 1936, the above figures on numbers of families, genera, and species probably have not been increased very much. However, if Mexico and Central America had been included, the list would contain the 63 domesticated species grown only south of the Mexican border (Table 1), plus a number of wild species, bringing the total to at least 1,200 species.

The nutritional elements which occur in greatest quantities in plant foods are carbohydrates: sugars and starches. Fats are dominant, however, in nuts. While carbohydrates are not necessary to sustain life if one has sufficient fat, witness the Eskimo, they become essential where fats are not obtainable in adequate quantities. The sugars and starches of wild plants were indispensable in areas where game was scarce and farming absent or little developed, as in the Great Basin and Northeast Mexico.

Because protein content in vegetable foods rarely exceeds half that of meat and fish, and usually runs much less than half, it becomes a critical element in evaluating vegetable foods. Analyses of nutritional ingredients in 66 species belonging to 28 families of wild plants eaten by Indians yields an average of 8 per cent protein by dry weight, with a range of total absence to 25 per cent and a standard deviation of 5 per cent. Modern maize in the United States averages about 12 per cent protein, but some varieties consumed by Indians probably had a higher protein content. Beans contain around 25 per cent protein, and squashes (*Cucurbita*) approximately 10 per cent. Wild plants, therefore, average less protein even than maize or pumpkins-squashes, and contain only about a third as much as beans. Unless supplemented by considerable quantities of meat or fish, a wild plant diet would be inadequate.

Of those wild plant foods which contain about the same percentage of protein as beans (which is relatively high), the only one which was anywhere near a staple item of diet is the California

64

buckeye (horse chestnut). This was widely eaten in California but was considered inferior to the acorn by the Indians and was eaten in quantity only when acorns were scarce. It contained a poisonous ingredient (hydrocyanic acid), also used for poisoning fish, which had to be leached out before it was fit for human consumption. Although we know less about the quantities of the cow-parsnip eaten in Utah, it appears to have been of lower rank than the buckeye. The other plants in Table 2 come from areas where meat was the main diet and plant foods minor in compari-

TABLE 2

HIGH PROTEIN WILD PLANT FOODS

(After Driver and Massey)

Percentage of Protein	Popular Name	Genus and Species	Family	Part Analyzed	Area
19.....	American Lotus	*Nelumbo lutea*	Nymphaceae	Seeds	Minnesota
25.....	Hog-peanut	*Falcata comosa*	Fabaceae	Tubers	Michigan
18.....	Potato-bean	*Glycine apios*	Fabaceae	Underground fruit	Michigan
23.....	California Buckeye	*Aesculus californica*	Aesculaceae	Nuts	California
18.....	Cow-parsnip	*Heracleum lanatum*	Apiaceae	Leaves and stems	Utah
23.....	Buffalo-gourd	*Cucurbita foetidissima*	Cucurbitaceae	Fruit and roots	Texas

son. The conclusion from this evidence agrees with what was suspected in the beginning: that plant foods did not provide an adequate amount of protein in the Indian diet. Those areas which depended most on plant foods appear to have been most deficient in this respect. Therefore it seems probable that native diet was short of protein in at least parts of California, the Great Basin, Northeast Mexico, Oasis, and Meso-America. While the bean helped out in agricultural areas in the Oasis and Meso-America, it was offset by the even smaller consumption of meat in the regions intensively farmed. The increased population made possible by agriculture had long since killed off most of the game. Furthermore, less than half of bean protein can be digested by human beings without the presence of animal proteins which aid its absorption. Animal proteins, on the other hand, are at least 90 per cent digestible. Indians in the Prairies and East also ate cultivated plant foods in large quantities, but had plenty of meat and fish to supplement them. Their diet was superior to that of other agricultural areas.

The dominance of wild vegetable foods in California, the Great Basin, and Northeast Mexico is heavily channeled by geographical environment. The flora of these areas was richer than the fauna at the level of exploitation known to the Indian. While agriculture supplanted wild plants in parts of the Oasis, its spread into Northeast Mexico, the Great Basin, or California was limited by climate and other environmental factors. It is notable that the population in California, which utilized only wild plant foods, was heavier than that of the Prairies and East, which were farming areas (Maps 4, 6).

FOOD PREPARATION AND PRESERVATION

Every Indian tribe prepared and preserved its food in some way and stored away some of it for future use. Recipes are well reported in many localities and run into the thousands. For the Kwakiutl alone there are 150 recipes on record. We have already noted that about 1,200 species of plants were eaten, and if we add to this the lists of mammals, birds, fishes, and invertebrates consumed by Indians, the total might exceed 2,000 species. Now if we combine these by twos, and threes, into food recipes, we get an enormous number of dishes. No attempt will be made to give even an abbreviated list here; instead, a description of some of the widespread ways of preparing and preserving food follows.

Boiling.—Indians boiled food in all culture areas except possibly in Northeast Mexico and Baja California, where boiling is not mentioned in early sources. Boiling techniques are of two major kinds: direct-fire boiling, or placing a vessel containing liquid near a fire; and stone boiling, or immersing heated stones in the liquid. Both methods were known to Indians and each is about equally widespread. Direct-fire boiling is almost the exclusive method in the Arctic, where stone vessels were the rule; and in the Prairie, East, Oasis, Meso-America, and Circum-Caribbean areas, where pottery vessels were known. Stone boiling is the dominant type in the western Sub-Arctic, Northwest Coast, Plateau, and California, where only burnable vessels of wood, bark, basketry, or hide were used. In the middle regions there are huge areas where both types were known and used, especially on the Plains, in the Great Basin, and in the Eastern Sub-Arctic. Because the early Indian immigrants into the Americas were without pottery and do not seem to have had other adequate containers for direct-fire boiling, it is almost certain that stone boiling was once a general practice, except in the Arctic and possibly part of the Sub-Arctic. As pottery became more and more common it tended to replace stone boiling with direct-fire boiling because the latter required less labor on the part of the housewife. But the change was slow and stone boiling continued to be used on certain occasions. For example, when hunters were a long way from home and had nothing to cook in except the body of the animal they had slain, they stone-boiled in the paunch, hide, or thorax.

For the world as a whole, as of about A.D. 1500, there was a high positive correlation between pottery and agriculture. The same was true of North America. Although pottery in North America was more widespread than farming, it was little used in areas which lacked farming, except in Alaska. It is only the sedentary peoples that can make full use of pottery, because pottery is difficult to transport.

Earth oven.—The earth oven, a kind of Indian fireless cooker, was known to some tribes in all culture areas except the Arctic. It was simply a hole in the ground into which hot stones and food were placed. It was covered with the earth from the hole so that the heat and steam would be confined long enough to cook the food, normally overnight. The food was wrapped in leaves, bark, and other handy materials to keep it clean. Sometimes a fire was built on top to add to the heat from within, and the contents might be moistened beforehand or water might be poured into the hole after it was covered, to make more steam. The earth oven could not have been used extensively in the Arctic because the ground was frozen solid most of the year and there was insufficient wood for fuel to heat the stones. In most areas both animal and plant foods were cooked in the earth oven, but plant foods certainly more often.

Broiling and roasting.—Although meat was boiled in vessels and baked in the earth oven, it was broiled or roasted more frequently in areas with little or no pottery and only the laborious stone boiling technique. In areas where pottery vessels occurred, on the other hand, meat was most commonly boiled. This was certainly true of the Prairies and East, where the Indians boiled most of their meat, often mixed with plant foods which were also cooked chiefly by boiling. The pepperpot of the Circum-Caribbean area and tropical South America was a perpetual meat and vegetable stew which was constantly added to and dipped into, but seldom eaten wholly or removed from the fire. In stone boiling areas of North America, meat was more often broiled or roasted. The Arctic is the only area where meat was always boiled, when it was cooked at all; it was never broiled or roasted, because the oil lamp and lack of wood made boiling the only practical cooking method. In other areas, meat was broiled on single sticks stuck into the ground and inclined toward the fire, and on horizontal frames over the fire; or it was roasted on hot stones beside the fire, or in the ashes. Small animals, from mice to porcupines, were most often roasted unskinned and whole in ashes.

Acorn preparation.—Many foods are indigestible or poisonous in their raw condition and must be processed before they can be eaten in quantity. One of the best-known examples is the acorn, which is normally unpalatable without special preparation. It was probably of greater importance in Indian diet before Christ, when farming was less known, than it was after Christ, when about half of the tribes farmed. There are some 60 species of oaks in North America, most of which are grouped under a single genus, *Quercus*. Of these, acorns from 27 species are known to have been eaten by Indians. Acorns from all these species are known to contain tannic acid in varying amounts. The majority contain enough of this acid to prevent large quantities being eaten without first removing at least some of it. The main nutritive elements of acorns are starches and fats, with the former predominating in most species.

Although acorns were eaten by at least half the Indian tribes in the United States, they were a staple food only in California, where they were eaten in greater quantity than the product of any other genus, animal or vegetable. The acorns were first cracked open with the aid of a small elongated stone for a hammer and a heavy flat slab of stone for an anvil. The nut meats were then ground with a mortar and pestle. When the meal was ground sufficiently fine, it was taken to the bank of a stream for the leaching process. Most frequently the meal was placed directly on the sand in a shallow depression or basin which had been prepared for the purpose. Then water was dipped from the stream and poured over and through the meal in the manner of making drip coffee. This leaching process was repeated until the bitter taste of the tannic acid was eliminated. The meal was then ready for cooking.

Grinding and pounding.—Many foods, both animal and vegetable, were prepared for eating by grinding, pounding, pulverizing, mechanical tenderizing, hulling, and shelling. Vegetable foods were more consistently treated in this manner than animal foods, and seeds more often than any other part of the plant. Equipment used for grinding and related processes is generally divided into mortars, which are operated by pounding, and milling stones, to which a rubbing motion is applied. A mortar is usually hollowed out like a vessel, but also may be a flat slab. A milling stone is usually flat, but may also be grooved or troughed. Mortars and the pounding technique were used to pulverize and tenderize meat as well as to grind plant foods, but milling stones and rubbing technique were usually limited to plant products. Our definitions, therefore, are based as much on how the mortar or milling stone is used as on its appearance in a museum showcase. Furthermore, milling stones and their hand stones often served a double purpose. Although designed for the grinding of seeds with a rubbing motion, they were also used to crack nuts or to tenderize meat by pounding. The mortar and pestle was less versatile, but might be used to mash berries or fruits as well as to grind or hull nuts and grains. Grinding equipment of all kinds was little used or absent in much of the Arctic, Sub-Arctic, Northwest Coast, and Plains. This emphasizes its primary association with plant products.

For both North and South America there is an east-west contrast in climate which affects both wild and cultivated plant ecologies. West of the continental divide, the climate is drier and frequent deserts and semideserts are found. The edible wild plants in deserts must be drought resistant and able to get along on a mini-

69

mum of moisture. Seeds from such plants tend to be hard and dry and require the thorough grinding which is possible with stone and a rubbing technique. East of the continental divide, except for the Plains near the Rockies and Northeast Mexico, climates are much more moist, and seeds tend to be replaced by fruits, nuts, and tubers which are fuller-bodied and softer. These may be adequately ground with wood and a pounding technique. Therefore it appears likely that these two contrasting grinding patterns were somewhat differentiated before cultivated plants were known. Milling stones date from 9000 B.C. at Danger Cave in the Great Basin (Jennings, 1957:212) and outnumbered projectile points in Cochise Culture in the Oasis by 5800 B.C. (Wormington, 1957:169–73). Mortars are probably of equal age.

After maize became domesticated, its varieties were selected partly for keeping qualities. The hard-grained flint corn would keep better in the humid areas of the Caribbean and eastern United States, while the soft-grained flour corns were adapted to the dry regions of the West. Because it would have been impossible to grind dried flint corn in wooden mortars, it was first soaked and then merely hulled with the wooden equipment. Flour corn, on the other hand, could be ground on the milling stones in the West which had originally been designed for wild seeds. In the Oasis, most of the maize was ground dry, as were wild seeds in former times. The bulk of the maize among the Pueblos was consumed in the form of a thin wafer called *piki* bread. This was prepared from finely ground corn meal, which was first made into a batter and then toasted or grilled on a hot stone. The other Oasis peoples in the United States, however, ate most of their corn in the form of a boiled mush or gruel, made from corn meal previously ground on the milling stone. The appearance of grooved and troughed milling stones in the northern Oasis at about the time that maize became common is probably no accident, but due to diffusion through the southern Oasis area from Meso-America. Corresponding to the *piki* bread of the Pueblos was the *tortilla* of Meso-America. This thin pancake was made from corn that was soaked in hot lime water, ground wet on the three-legged milling stone, and finally baked on a pottery griddle.

Although some primitive peoples, such as the Australians of

the western deserts, lived literally from hand to mouth without preserving or storing any food for the future, we have no indication of such an extremely precarious way of life from accounts of North American Indians. Probably all tribes preserved and stored food in some manner.

Smoking and drying.—The majority of peoples north of Mexico fire-dried or smoked meat. The fire and the smoke not only hastened the drying process but also kept away flies and other insect pests. The majority probably also dried meat in the sun and wind when the weather permitted, but as an exclusive method this would have been inadequate for most of the continent. It was only in parts of the Plains, Great Basin, California, and Oasis that meat was exclusively sun and wind dried. These climates were dry the year round and hot in summer, making a fire unnecessary. The term "jerky" is derived from an Indian word *charqui*, which means dried meat. Jerky was merely dried, not jerked.

Meat was dried or smoked on anything from a bush to the huge frames hung above the house fires on the Northwest Coast. Most tribes employed a simple rectangular frame of poles with a fire beneath. Smoke houses were common in the western Sub-Arctic and on the North Pacific coast. They hastened the drying process in these cool or damp regions.

Dried meat on the Plains, and in parts of neighboring areas, was pounded with the stone-headed maul to make pemmican. The dried meat was first softened by holding it over a fire, then pulverized, mixed with melted fat and marrow, and finally with berry or fruit paste to give it the desired taste and texture. The whole mess was then packed in a folded rawhide container called a parfleche. With proper care such pemmican would keep for years, although most of it was consumed within a single year.

Fish were also preserved in a number of ways. They were sun and air dried exclusively in most of the Arctic, Plateau, Great Basin, California, and probably Meso-America. Fish were buried in pits and allowed to decay in the Arctic, on the North Pacific Coast, and less frequently on the Plateau. In the East the Micmac, Huron, and Iroquois Indians suspended fish and allowed the flesh to decompose partially. Possibly the action of micro-organisms on the fish produces some ingredient beneficial to human nutrition,

71

because European explorers in the Arctic grow quite fond of rotten fish.

Fish-smoking is mentioned less often than the smoking of meat. It is reported consistently only on the Northwest Coast, Sub-Arctic, northern Prairies and East, although it has been noted sporadically in other regions.

The preservation of fish by freezing was a common method in the Arctic and Sub-Arctic, and no doubt was occasionally resorted to elsewhere. The use of salt for preserving fish is mentioned only for the East, California, and Meso-America and is probably modern, although some form of native salt was known to these areas. Salting, roasting, and sun-drying are all reported for the Yucatan Maya.

Fish was pulverized after drying in California, on the Northwest Coast south of the Columbia River, on the Plateau, sporadically in the Sub-Arctic, and in a small area in the East among the Iroquois and their neighbors. Lewis and Clark estimated that about 30,000 pounds of dried and pulverized salmon were prepared annually for the Indian trade in the area of the Dalles on the Columbia River. The addition of berries, the storage in hide bags, and the sealing of the bags with fat suggest a common origin with the making of pemmican on the Plains.

A great variety of vegetable foods, both wild and domesticated, was preserved by drying. The only area where plant foods were not dried was the Arctic, where practically no plant foods were eaten. The natives of the Sub-Arctic and Plains made use of little dried plant food except in pemmican, and the North Pacific Coast peoples not much more. On the Plateau, however, the camas was first cooked in the earth oven, and then dried in large quantities for winter use. In the areas where plant foods predominated, including agricultural areas, their drying for winter use was indispensable.

In the United States west of the Rockies, occasionally east of the Rockies, and south through Meso-America, seeds, including maize where cultivated, were dried and cooked by parching. In Mexico parched and ground corn is known as *pinole*. The popping of corn is primarily a cooking rather than a preserving technique, but is obviously related to parching and was done in a pottery vessel heated to the necessary temperature. Ordinary corn will not pop in an open vessel, but the Indians of the Oasis and Meso-America raised popcorn which was cooked in this way.

Ordinary varieties of maize dried sufficiently in the sun and air in the Oasis and highland Meso-America, and required no other drying method; but in the Prairies, East, and lowland tropics, the humidity was sufficient, in many localities, to necessitate drying on a scaffold over a fire.

Salt.—Sodium chloride is a biological necessity without which a human being cannot live. It is found in normal human blood in a concentration of three-tenths of 1 per cent, which is far greater than that of any other mineral salt. It helps control the osmotic pressure in body fluids which in turn determines the amount of water retained in the body. Vegetable foods contain a high concentration of potassium, which tends to replace sodium in the blood. In order to overcome this sodium deficiency, vegetarians require additional sodium chloride. Meat eaters, on the other hand, get adequate amounts of mineral salts of all kinds from the meat and blood of the animals they eat. The amount of salt required by a human being is further determined by the amount he loses in perspiration. Therefore, dwellers in warm climates need more salt than those in cool climates.

The distribution of intentional eating of sodium chloride is given on Map 9. A comparison with Map 4 shows a close correspondence between the predominance of vegetable food, whether wild or domesticated, and the eating of salt. Thus in California, the Great Basin, Oasis, parts of the Prairies and East, Meso-America, and the Circum-Caribbean areas, salt was eaten. In Northeast Mexico refined sodium chloride was lacking except near the Meso-American border, where a little was obtained in trade. However, the Northeast Mexicans ate crude salts obtained from dry lake beds and such natural sources.

Salt was eaten by a few tribes which relied mainly on fish or meat; but in all cases these areas of salt-eating were minor extensions from adjacent regions where vegetable fare predominated.

The correlation between salt-eating and temperature is also apparent. Salt-eating peoples are those in the southern half of the continent. The chief exception to this generalization is the salt-free corridor in the southern Plains and Northeast Mexico. The predominance of hunting in the southern Plains accounts for the discrepancy in that area, but Northeast Mexico is again anomalous. Possibly salt was eaten more often than is reported there.

In the Southeast and Meso-America, salt was obtained principally by evaporating salt water. The water might be from a salt spring or from the ocean, and the evaporation might be facilitated by exposure to the sun or by boiling over a fire. Shallow pottery vessels used for making salt, called salt pans, have been excavated in large numbers by archeologists in the Southeast. The Great Basin, in contrast, obtained most of its salt dry from the surface of the land in and around dry lake beds. Indians in California and the Oasis employed both methods; they gathered it in dry form on the surface or from shallow mines, and also evaporated the moisture from salt water.

Salt was an important trade article in the Southeast, Oasis, California, and Meso-America. In Mexico it approached the status of a currency and, with cotton, was the major trade item. The Aztecs demanded as tribute from their conquered neighbors 2,000 loaves of salt of a standard size and shape. These were divided among the nobility. Salt was even involved in economic warfare by one community of Maya, who refused to sell salt to one of their traditional enemies. The enemy, in turn, refused to trade any *cacao* (chocolate) beans to the Maya. In the Oasis, salt was obtained in greatest quantity by tribes living near the source of supply and traded to those at a distance, although long journeys were also made to obtain it. In the Southeast salt was widely traded, especially on the Mississippi, where De Soto's men obtained it from the natives. In California it was traded from the east side of the Sierras, where it was plentiful, to the west side where it was less common, and in one area a dispute over a salt deposit was the cause of a local war.

In the Oasis and Meso-America salt played a prominent role in religion, mythology, and ceremonies. The Oasis peoples engaged in elaborate salt-gathering expeditions for which the choice of leaders, dietary restrictions, sexual continence, and the precise manner of gathering and refining salt were all prescribed by ritual. This was all done to propitiate a female deity who was supposed to be the guardian of the salt supply. The Aztecs of Mexico had a still more elaborate ceremony in honor of their salt goddess, who is described as having golden ears, and wearing yellow vestments, an iridescent green plumed mitre, a wave-shaped embroidered bodice, a fishnet skirt, and woven cotton sandals. This goddess was impersonated in the ceremony by a maiden who was sacrificed to her as the climax of the ten-day rite.

CONCLUSIONS

Some generic hunting techniques, such as harpoons for sea mammals, driving animals over a cliff, pitfalls, deadfalls, snares, animal head disguises, and auditory decoys were probably known in Paleolithic times and, therefore, known to the first Indian immigrants to the New World. Although Red men probably did not invent these major hunting methods, a more detailed analysis of them would reveal many minor details absent in the Old World and, therefore, invented by the American Indian. The same is true of fishing; the generic techniques were probably brought in from the Old World, but specific details were invented in the New World. Because the earliest immigrants to the New World came by way of Bering Strait into Alaska, they could not have survived in that region without expert knowledge of hunting and fishing.

The wild plant picture is different. There were few edible wild plants in the Arctic, and the knowledge of wild plants in more southern latitudes in the Old World would have been lost in the slow trek of centuries through the Arctic made by all early immigrants to the New World. Therefore, practically all American Indian knowledge of the more than one thousand species of wild plants eaten by them was acquired after arrival in the New World. This demonstrates that the early Red men were capable of patient experimentation with plants and were able to pass on this knowledge to future generations.

Techniques of preparing and preserving food likewise must be divided into those associated with animals and fish, wild plants, and domesticated plants. Methods of processing meat and fish must have been known, at least in part, to the earliest immigrants to the New World, because they lived principally on these foods.

Ways of preparing and preserving wild plants, in contrast, must have been invented after immigrants reached the regions where edible wild plants were common. The processing of domesticated plants was likewise developed independently by the Indians, except possibly for a few techniques associated with the small number of species derived by way of Pacific islands from the Old World.

REFERENCES

AGUILAR, 1946; BARTLETT, 1933, 1936; BEALS, 1932a; BIRKET-SMITH, 1929, 1936, 1945, 1953; BIRKET-SMITH AND DE LAGUNA, 1938; COOPER, 1938; DAHLGREN, 1954; DRIVER, 1953a; FLANNERY, 1939; GODDARD, 1945; HAWLEY AND GARDEN, 1941; HEIZER, 1953; HILL, 1938; HUNTER, 1940; JENNESS, 1932; JENNINGS, 1957; KROEBER, 1925, 1939, 1941; LOWIE, 1954; MARTIN, QUIMBY, AND COLLIER, 1947; MARTÍNEZ, 1936; MASON, O. T., 1901; MENDIZÁBAL, 1930; ROE, 1952; ROSTLUND, 1952; ROYS, 1943; SAUER, 1939; STEWARD, 1938a, 1948b; SWANTON, 1946; UNDERHILL, n.d.; WEYER, 1932; WISSLER, 1938, 1941; WORMINGTON, 1957.

6: SOCIAL AND RELIGIOUS ASPECTS OF SUBSISTENCE

SINCE the desire for food is one of the most basic biological drives and one on which the life of every animal of every species depends, it is no wonder that food-getting is inextricably enmeshed in other departments of man's culture, particularly the social and religious ones. Man the world over lives in social groups which range in size from a single family to the huge cities and nations of modern times. He is everywhere a participant in a co-operative economic venture, even though the unit may include only two persons, a man and wife. Such a unit nowhere exists independently of other such units. More remote kindred are everywhere recognized, and couples everywhere have social obligations and privileges which involve food. In our own society, where money economy and its chain stores make it possible for two persons (or even one) to lead a separate existence as far as purchase and consumption of food is concerned, this independence is more apparent than real. One has to work with or for somebody to earn the money to buy his groceries, or must inherit a fortune from a relative. He normally does not eat alone and, if married, not always only with his spouse. He sometimes invites guests to meals and in turn is invited by them.

Food is hedged by religion in all cultures, probably more so among so-called primitives than with civilized peoples. Spirits and magical forces everywhere are thought to determine one's success in his food-getting venture whether it is hunting, fishing, gathering, farming, or stock-breeding. One must propitiate these spirits or forces in the proper way and at the proper time if he is to be a successful provider. Although primitive man's knowledge of ethnobotany and zoology is often impressive, it is invariably linked with a maze of religious notions which almost defy analysis.

One example of the way the mind may work will suffice for these introductory remarks. A generation ago an anthropologist was cruising down a Canadian river with Indians in a canoe. Half a mile or so downstream they saw an object that they all thought was a bear. It went out of sight as they rounded a bend in the stream, and when it reappeared at much closer range, the anthropologist saw that it was only a stump and remarked about his mistaken perception. Not so for one of the Indians, who insisted that it had been a bear in the beginning and had somehow been changed into a stump while out of sight. Indian religion bristles with notions of this kind which pyramid onto one another in a manner hard for us to understand.

A few simple generalizations on sexual division of labor will be offered here. Almost all hunting was done by men. Women, however, occasionally hunted birds or small game, and frequently helped butcher and bring home game. They also participated in communal drives in some areas. While fishing was likewise chiefly a man's job, women generally did more fishing than hunting. The gathering of wild plant foods was largely a task for women, but men helped in areas where plants were indispensable or where tree-climbing was required. For horticulture there is a rather neat cleavage between east and west: on the Prairie and in the East, farming was mainly the work of women, with men concentrating on hunting, fishing, and fighting; in the Oasis and Meso-American areas farming was mainly the work of men, who did relatively little hunting, less fishing, and not much fighting. Women normally did the cooking in all areas, and also the bulk of the processing of food short of cooking. Other aspects of economics, such as trade and property concepts, will be discussed in chapters xiii and xiv.

HUNTING

Although a hunter sometimes hunted alone, he normally shared his kill at least with the members of his family. While he made his own weapons, as a rule, his wife usually had a hand in making his clothing. In the Arctic, where a wife prepared all the hides and made all the clothing, a man could not have hunted at all without the co-operation of his wife.

Boys in all areas were given toy weapons with which to play until they were old enough to hunt small game. Each received constant instruction from an older relative, usually his father, in the habits of game, the use of weapons, the manufacture of weapons and traps, and in the ever-present religious aspects of hunting. The average North American Indian boy progressed through a series of stages of learning, beginning first with birds and small game and then gradually working up to the more elusive, more dangerous, but also more valuable large animals such as the seal, caribou, deer, bear, or buffalo. Each time the lad killed his first of a new species he had to carry his game back to camp and stand by while the others of the family or band cooked it and ate it. He was not allowed to eat a single bite. His reward came in the form of direct praise and the social recognition of his enhanced status in the community. It was not until after he had demonstrated his ability to obtain a major game animal that he could even consider getting married. Some form of special attention to a youth's first game was probably a universal practice in areas where hunting was of importance.

Even when a mature hunter went out alone and brought home game unassisted, he usually shared it with other families in the community if they were in need. While such families were often related by blood or marriage, unrelated members of the same community were treated in the same way. Furthermore, whenever a visitor made a social call he was always offered food. A good hunter could therefore expect plenty of visitors in time of need, and in all hunting areas there was a tendency for mediocre men to attach themselves to a more skilled individual. This was the lowest level of leadership and political organization.

For a group of hunters going out together, there was invariably a series of rules governing the disposition of the meat. The one who killed the game usually got the lion's share, but he who was first to touch a fallen animal often got a sizable portion. Under these conditions, a man who was a poor shot with the bow or who was unskilled in stalking or locating game, could profit by being alert when a more capable person dropped an animal.

There was a rigid regulation of the buffalo hunt by the men's societies of the Plains. One society served as a police group to force every hunter to take orders from the leader of the communal hunt, instead of engaging in individual hunting at the risk of frightening off the entire herd. The penalty for failing to conform to the rules was destruction of personal property and a severe beating which sometimes resulted in death. In the Oasis there is little mention of punishment for failure to co-operate in communal hunting. This is to be expected in an area where people depended more on plant than on animal foods and where they hunted mainly the rabbit in communal fashion. In Meso-America, where the nobility controlled most of the game, rules were probably stricter, but few of them have come down to us.

The belief in animal souls is probably universal among North American Indians. This in no way interfered with the parallel belief in human souls, which was likewise found everywhere. Animals and human beings were spiritually equated by the Indian as they are physically equated by biologists today. Every animal, then, had a soul which survived after its death and was able to report on the manner in which it had been killed, butchered, and consumed and on the disposal of inedible parts. If the hunter did not follow the proper procedure, he offended the spirit of the slain animal, which did not hesitate to inform other animal souls of its indecent treatment. Souls of living game, as well as dead ones, got wind of such cases and refused to allow their bodies to be slain by such an unkind hunter. The hunter, therefore, failed to get any game.

The taboos surrounding hunting have never been catalogued or classified, but it is certain that they run into the hundreds. Some are shared by many tribes and others only by a few. One of the most widespread beliefs is that menstruating women are offensive to game animals. When a hunter's wife is menstruating, he often must not hunt at all, or he must at least take care that she does not touch any of his hunting gear or drip any menstrual fluid on the meat of previously slain game. In northwestern California, meat was taken into the house by removing a wall board instead of through the normal entrance for fear that a menstruating woman had dripped fluid in the entrance way. A hunter usually abstained from sexual intercourse for one or more nights before a hunt.

Anyone who was ill or associated with illness was thought to be potentially dangerous to hunting luck and was required to refrain from eating meat, particularly fresh meat. This applied to menstruating women, medicine men acquiring power or practicing their arts, warriors who had slain an enemy, mourners for a recently deceased kinsman, and the like. In some areas a hunter who had killed a major animal, such as a whale, had to go into mourning the same as he would for a dead relative. An entire Eskimo community occasionally starved to death because of the rule forbidding anyone to hunt until several days after the death of a member of the community. When one of a number of persons on the verge of starvation died, the others got no food for several days, which was sufficient to cause the death of another, and so on until all were dead.

In every culture every animal could be ranked according to the number and severity of its associated taboos. The rank of common species differed from tribe to tribe, some Indians concentrating on one species, others more on another. Therefore it cannot be said that any one animal was any more revered and tabooed than another for the entire continent. However, the bear was among the group of most highly venerated and propitiated beasts. It was frequently addressed by a kinship term, as if it were a relative, and told in advance that it was going to be killed. After the killing it was offered a long harangue by way of apology for being forced by necessity to be so rude as to kill it. It was sometimes even cried over, as was the custom for a deceased relative. Its head and other inedible parts were placed in trees out of the reach of dogs and other lowly beasts. In some areas there were bear cults or classes of medicine men whose souls were thought to dwell within bears' bodies and to activate the bears. Bear ceremonialism is probably universal in the northern half of the continent, and is no doubt more common than reported in the United States. Similar attitudes toward the bear are widespread in northern Asia. While most anthropologists believe that many of these attitudes and practices have a single origin for Asia and North America, it is impossible to say precisely which item originated where, because similar beliefs and rites are associated with many other species of animals.

FISHING

The social aspects of fishing resemble those of hunting in that one normally shared his catch with others and in turn obtained a share of another's fish. The fishing education of a boy also closely resembled that for hunting, including special attention to the first fish he caught. Because the best fishing places were small areas at the falls of streams, these were more often owned by kin groups than were hunting territories. Furthermore, fishing was hedged with less ceremonialism than hunting. The reason is probably twofold: fish were less important in the diet for the continent as a whole; fish are farther removed from man biologically than mammals and resemble man much less in both appearance and behavior. Nevertheless the first salmon ceremony of the Northwest Coast and Plateau was an elaborate affair which topped all other subsistence rituals in these areas. It is no accident that such was the case here, because these were the two areas which relied most heavily on fish for food, and the salmon was the most frequent fish.

The following details give some idea of the content of this ceremony. The first fish must be caught by a ritualist who is acquainted with magic verbal formulas and other secret fish lore. It must not be allowed to touch the ground after being taken from the water, but must be laid on a mat or some leaves. It is butchered with an antiquated knife of mussel shell, but the tail, which is ordinarily cut off, must be left on. It must be cooked in some prescribed manner, such as being placed head up on the roasting sticks. It must be eaten by a prescribed group which varies from tribe to tribe, in some cases everyone present, in others only the ritualist, only the men, or only the children present. After the fish is eaten, the bones are thrown back into the water so that dogs or wild carnivores cannot eat them. Finally, there is singing and dancing by those who know the proper songs and dance routines.

The psychological attitude of the Indians includes the belief that the salmon has a soul, and that, if the first one is captured, killed, and eaten in the most formal and correct manner, its soul will tell other salmon about the event and they will swarm up the stream to be killed and eaten in the same respectful manner. The first fish is usually thought to be a leader whose word is a command to others. The major first-fish ceremonies of the Pacific drainage suggest that many of the beliefs and practices spread from one tribe to another from a single point of origin somewhere in the area.

GATHERING OF WILD PLANTS

The gathering of wild plants was principally the work of women. While a woman sometimes gathered alone, she was more often accompanied by other women who were either relatives or friends residing in the same camp or village. Women seem to have gathered in groups more consistently than men hunted in groups, probably for mutual protection against men of hostile tribes. At any rate, the woman gatherer shared her plant produce with the other women of the group and, in the form of prepared food, with the other members of her family. Husbands probably contributed less to wives' gathering ventures than did wives to husbands' hunting forays. Nevertheless, the manufacturing of the digging stick and gathering poles was usually the work of men. Seedbeaters and basketry containers, however, were made by women, as were most other articles of basketry.

A girl was almost always taught plant lore, gathering techniques, and food preparation by her mother. Special attention was given to the first plant products gathered by a girl much less often than a boy's first game. We find such individual rites for girls reported in a few widely scattered and isolated localities in the Alaskan Arctic, Eastern Sub-Arctic, Northwest Coast, Plateau, Great Basin, and Prairie. The theory behind a girl's rite was the same as for that of a boy: that she should be encouraged to be a good provider by the praise and publicity she acquired at this time. She also was not allowed to eat any of her first gatherings. The plant products to which the rite applied varied according to the locality: berries in the north; berries or roots on the Plateau; seeds in the Great Basin. No doubt this custom was more widespread than the meager data indicate.

Rites for the first plant food of the season are much more frequent. They are characteristic of the Northwest Coast, Plateau, California, Oasis, Meso-America, Prairies, and East. The following example from the Plateau will illustrate this type of ceremony for wild plants. When about half the berry crop is ripe, the chief calls the people together to pick them. The people assemble before their chief with all exposed parts of their bodies painted red for the occasion. The chief presents a birch-bark tray, filled with previously picked berries of every variety, to a mountain and utters this prayer or formula: "Quailus, we tell you, we are going to eat fruit." He addresses each mountain in turn in a like manner and, walking sunwise around the assembled throng, gives each person a single berry to eat. Then all the women go out and gather berries. The appeal of this simple ritual is to the personalities or spirits of the mountains. Its purpose is to assure a good berry crop.

On the whole, first-fruits ceremonies are found in areas where other kinds of public ceremonies are well developed. In the west, first-fruits ceremonies are distributed in close conformity to major first-fish rites. In the rest of the first-fruits area they conform closely to the distribution of maize. These facts suggest that all these subsistence ceremonies are interrelated, that one has been stimulated by another. As a matter of actual fact, some tribes combine all of their subsistence rites into a single major ceremony. This was true in the East among the Iroquois and the Creek, was also common in the Oasis and Meso-America, and occurred in northwestern California in the form of World Renewal Rites. Tribes with first-fruits rites belong to the more sedentary half of those on the entire continent. Those leading a more nomadic life seldom found time for such cultural elaboration. To say that tribes with elaborate public subsistence ceremonies possess them because their anxiety over food is greater than that of tribes which lack them is certainly missing the mark. Anxiety over food was universal in native North America. The areas where population was thinner because starvation was more frequent are the very ones which lacked such major ceremonies. While some sort of psychological necessity must be present to give rise to such rituals, it is far from sufficient to produce them. Many other factors must be taken into account.

HORTICULTURE

Farming was a highly socialized activity with a myriad of rules and regulations. Two reasons for this are the great importance of agriculture in the economy and the relatively small amount of acreage devoted to it for each family. When a large amount of a person's time and effort is concentrated in a few acres of land, he is bound to be concerned about the rules of tenure and of consumption of the products of his handiwork. Farm plots were usually assigned to a family or an individual by a leader of a larger social unit such as a sib or a community. A family or individual normally kept a plot for years or even a lifetime, except in the Prairies, East, and Circum-Caribbean areas, and other localities where the clearing of new land was a necessity. At any rate, if land was not used or the owner died, it reverted to the sib or tribe. Normally it would be reallocated to an heir of the deceased, but in native theory farm land belonged to the group, not to the individual.

Girls were taught to farm by their mothers on the Prairies and in the East, and boys most often by their fathers in the Oasis and Meso-America. There is nothing in farming rites comparable to the first-game rite for a boy or the first wild plant product ceremony for a girl. Such minor rituals associated with a child's education seem to have been submerged by the huge public ceremonies which lasted for days.

In the Southeast, there were special public fields, called either town fields or the chief's fields. While there were a few tribes whose chief was in complete authority, among the majority of eastern Indians he was more like an elected official subject to impeachment. He or his lieutenants gave orders for all able-bodied men and women to work in the public fields, and criers walked through the towns and villages to call out the man and woman power. The produce from these fields did not become the personal property of the chief, but was stored in a public granary. While the chief's immediate family subsisted on the results of this community enterprise and did no physical labor themselves, they were also obligated to feed foreign guests as well as needy local families from the public stores. Food for public ceremonies also came from the same storehouses. The role of the chief, then, was that of a custodian of a public reserve of food.

In the agricultural areas there was more ritual associated with maize than with all other cultivated plants combined. There were planting rites, Green Corn rites, and harvest rites. Such rituals were more complicated and formalized in densely settled Meso-America, where ceremonies were in the hands of the priesthoods. Local village observances were also important there, just as they are today. Ceremonial emphasis varied in the agricultural cycle; in the Oasis and Meso-America planting and rain rituals were pre-eminent, while in the Prairies and the East the Green Corn harvest ceremony was the greatest ritual occasion and was frequently in the nature of a new year celebration. Rain-making rites are sporadically reported in the Prairies and East, but are usually performed by a single shaman. Such individual activities are also widely distributed among tribes without agriculture, where the bringing of rain was as much a stunt to prove the power of the shaman as it was an economic necessity. Not so in the much drier regions of the Oasis and Meso-America where periodic droughts sometimes brought actual starvation. Here the most elaborate group rituals were concerned with rain-making and, conversely, rain-making was the most recurrent theme in all public ceremonies. Prominent in the rituals of both Aztecs and Mayas were vigils and ceremonies honoring the rain gods. The Aztec god Tlaloc controlled the rain so necessary for Indian survival. Similarly the Chacs, rain gods of the Mayas, received offerings of *balche* (fermented honey) and child and bird sacrifices. For both peoples, as elsewhere in the Oasis and Meso-America, imitative magic was an essential aspect of the ritual; this included ceremonial weeping, blood-letting, and attention to associated phenomena such as thunder, lightning, and frog croaking. The sacred numbers seven, nine, and thirteen play an important part in all of these ceremonies. Rain ceremonialism must be ancient throughout these areas. This is to be expected where agriculture furnished a very large per cent of the annual diet and all adults, at least, had experienced severe droughts at some time in their lives, particularly in the northern Oasis. Environment, therefore, can be a partial determinant of religion and ceremony.

REFERENCES

BIRKET-SMITH, 1929, 1936, 1945, 1953; BIRKET-SMITH AND DE LAGUNA, 1938; BONNERJEA, 1934; EWERS, 1955a; FLANNERY, 1939, 1946; GODDARD, 1945; GUNTHER, 1928; HALLOWELL, 1926; JENNESS, 1932; JUEL, 1945; KROEBER, 1925; LANTIS, 1938, 1947; LOWIE, 1954; McILLWRAITH, 1948; MENDIETA Y NUÑEZ, 1949; PARSONS, 1939; PETTITT, 1946; SPECK, 1935; SPECK AND EISELEY, 1939; STEWARD, 1938, 1948; SWANTON, 1946; THOMPSON, 1954; TOOR, 1947; UNDERHILL, 1948, n.d.; VAILLANT, 1941; WEYER, 1932; WISSLER, 1938, 1941; WITTHOFT, 1949.

7: NARCOTICS AND STIMULANTS

NARCOTICS and stimulants were common in the New World before European discovery. South America was well in advance of North America in this respect, the total list of drugs and the frequency of use in the southern continent far exceeding that of the northern continent. Nevertheless, drugs were used to a considerable extent by North American natives in Mexico and the United States, although they were not used in the Arctic and Sub-Arctic. Some of the North American drugs, particularly tobacco, are known to have originated in South America; and others common to both continents, whose place of origin is veiled in mystery, may also stem from South America. The principal narcotics and stimulants used in aboriginal North America were tobacco, peyote, Jimson weed, and alcoholic beverages. Probably all were used as medicines. Many modern drugs, for example cocaine and quinine, are derived from South American Indian narcotics and medicines.

TOBACCO

Our word "tobacco" comes from the Spanish *tabaco*, which in turn is derived directly from the Arawak term for cigar. Christopher Columbus brought the first knowledge of tobacco to Europe. Members of his crew observed natives on Cuba or Hispaniola smoking huge cigars. The Indians claimed that it comforted the limbs, made them sleepy, and lessened their weariness. Other European explorers found tobacco being used by Indians almost everywhere except in the Arctic, Sub-Arctic, and part of the Northwest Coast.

From America, tobacco was taken to Europe: to Portugal in

1558; from Portugal to France in 1560; from Portugal to Italy in 1561; to Spain probably directly from the New World about the same time; and to England directly from the West Indies in 1565. By 1600 it was grown and widely used in Europe. European colonists in the eighteenth century took tobacco to the Arctic and Sub-Arctic, where it could not be raised and had been unknown aboriginally: the Danes to Greenland; the British and French to most of the Sub-Arctic; the Russians to Alaska. By the end of the nineteenth century it had penetrated almost everywhere in North America.

Tobacco has been much studied by botanists, who have found over a dozen species, almost all of which are native to the New World. At least two forms are cultigens, plants which have been modified by man by selection or hybridization, and which are cultivated by man in areas where the wild ancestors are absent. The cultigen tobaccos are *Nicotiana tabacum* and *Nicotiana rustica*. These were the plants taken to Europe and spread by Europeans over the world. *N. tabacum* won out in most localities and is today the tobacco raised commercially. A large number of varieties of this single species have been intentionally produced by the tobacco industry to satisfy everyone's taste and thereby stimulate sales.

Nicotiana tabacum has been found to be a hybrid of two wild forms: *Nicotiana tomentosum* and *Nicotiana sylvestris.* The wild *N. tomentosum* is found in Peru and Bolivia, the wild *N. sylvestris* in northern Argentina. After its origin in one of these localities, *N. tabacum* seems to have spread by diffusion or migration down the Amazon drainage to the Atlantic, thence north to the West Indies, where it was discovered by Columbus. *Nicotiana rustica* is also a hybrid, having been derived from two wild species growing on the west side of the Andes near the border of Ecuador and Peru. *Nicotiana rustica* spread by diffusion and migration over a much larger territory than did *N. tabacum;* south to the limits of agriculture at Chiloé Island off the coast of Chile, and north to the limits of agriculture in New Brunswick. Its distribution in North America (Map 10) closely follows that of maize (Map 7).

While it is next to impossible to determine a species of tobacco archeologically, pipes give us a clue to the first appearance of tobacco. The proof is not final, because we are seldom able to determine conclusively what was smoked in the pipes and because some pipes were not used for smoking. However, in area after area and site after site, pipes appear at about the same time as maize agriculture. This temporal correlation, when combined with the spatial one just cited, yields overwhelming evidence that *Nicotiana rustica* spread from south to north in North America along with other cultivated plants, especially maize. Because its wild ancestors do not exist in North America, it could not possibly have originated there. Its absence in the West Indies makes it highly probable that the eastern United States Indians received the plant from Mexico. The *N. tabacum* of the West Indies did not reach North America until post-Columbian times, when the British began raising it on their Virginia plantations. Here it soon superseded the local *N. rustica*, which was the first species to be raised commercially there.

Probably the next most widely distributed species is *Nicotiana attenuata*, which grows wild in the Great Basin, the Oasis, and the southern Plains. It was used by Indians in these areas, both as a wild plant and as a cultivated one, and extended north as a cultivated plant into western Canada (Map 10).

Tobaccos of the *bigelovii* group (*bigelovii, quadrivalvus, multivalvus*) have a curious distribution (Map 10). They are native to the West, where they are also sometimes cultivated, and *quadrivalvus* seems to have been introduced from the West into the northern Plains as a cultivated plant in pre-Columbian times. The same native term, *op* or *ope*, is found all the way from southern California to Montana and North Dakota.

Nicotiana trigonophylla is much more restricted in area. We have found only a few occurrences, in the Oasis. This plant is also known to have been used by the Hopi, along with *N. attenuata*. The Tarahumara used a wild form, probably *N. trigonophylla*, along with *N. tabacum* in recent times. On the northern Northwest Coast, an unknown or unnamed species of *Nicotiana* was cultivated and chewed with lime by the Indians.

A majority of North America Indians mixed other plants with their tobacco. This was done partly for economy among tribes which had little tobacco, partly to improve the flavor, and partly to dilute the strength of the tobacco. It is agreed that *N. tabacum* is much the mildest species, and that all the others have a much more pronounced narcotic effect. Tobacco mixtures in the eastern United States and Canada were called *kinnikinnik* from an Algonquian word meaning "that which is mixed." Two common adulterants in this area were sumac leaves and the inner bark of a species of dogwood.

Tobacco was cultivated more widely than any other North American plant (Map 11). It was raised nearly everywhere that maize was grown and, in addition, on the northern Plains, in California, on the Oregon coast, and on the northern Northwest Coast. The species grown outside the maize area are all indigenous to western North America, although some individual species were grown outside the more restricted regions where they occurred in wild forms. Where maize was cultivated, tobacco was always raised in a separate plot and more often by men than by women. This latter point is noteworthy because women were the chief farmers of food plants north of Mexico. In the west where food plants were not grown, men also raised more tobacco than did women. Tobacco-farming technique consisted of burning off wild vegetation, loosening the soil, sowing tobacco seed in the ashes, weeding, and sometimes pruning. It is interesting that tribes which lacked true cultivation of tobacco frequently burned over a wild tobacco patch (after gathering the harvest) to increase the next year's crop. This burning tended to discourage trees and shrubs and to encourage perennials such as tobacco.

Tobacco was smoked everywhere it was known in North America except on the northern Northwest Coast, where it was only chewed with lime. There the leaves were pulverized, mixed with shell lime, and made into pellets which were allowed to dissolve in the mouth. A similar practice, better labeled eating, was followed in California and Nevada. Tobacco leaves were ground in a stone mortar with lime and water and the concoction licked off the pestle, or the tobacco was less often eaten straight, or mixed with an infusion of *Datura* and drunk. Sometimes the stupefying effect was all that was desired, while on other occasions the mixture served as an emetic. In the Southeast tobacco was eaten with lime from mollusk shells and, among the Creek, was an ingredient of the famous "black drink," which was definitely a ceremonial emetic. The Aztecs also ate the tobacco leaves, apparently not in combination with other narcotics.

The snuffing of tobacco was common only in the Circum-Caribbean area, where it was drawn into both nostrils simultaneously through a Y-shaped tube. The Aztecs also snuffed, but without the fancy tube. Snuffing is more characteristic of South America, where other narcotics were also snuffed, and it most likely originated there.

Because tobacco was not smoked in the areas of South America where *N. tabacum* and *N. rustica* originated by hybridization, chewing or snuffing is likely to have been indulged in earlier than smoking.

Smoking can be accomplished with cigars or cigarettes on the one hand, and pipes on the other. It is impossible to distinguish between cigars and cigarettes other than to say that a cigar is tobacco wrapped in its own leaves while a cigarette consists of tobacco wrapped in a burnable material of another sort. The cigar was smoked most often in the Circum-Caribbean area, although cigarettes encased in bark cloth are known in Central America. Cigarettes with corn husk wrappings predominate in Meso-America and the Oasis. We are not certain that they are aboriginal in the Oasis, because the earliest Spanish settlers may have brought them north from Central Mexico. At any rate they have been the common smoking device in the Southwest in the historic period. Cigarettes or pipes made by filling short pieces of cane with tobacco do date, however, from Basket Maker times in the American Southwest. True pipes predominated in all other areas where tobacco was smoked.

Pipes occur in a bewildering number of shapes, which, fortunately, can be classified as either straight or elbowed; the materials are mainly wood, pottery, and stone, although hollow cane was also used. Some anthropologists believe that the cane tube was the link between the corn husk cigarette and the straight pipe of wood, and that stone and pottery materials and the elbow shape came later. Archeology proves that straight pipes are older than elbowed in the United States (not in Mexico), but the sequence from wood to stone or pottery is less demonstrable because wood often decays without leaving a trace.

Tobacco was used religiously as well as secularly. Most shamans used tobacco, both to establish rapport with their spirit-helpers and to drive away disease from a patient's body. Tobacco was a part of almost every public religious ceremony whether the occasion was a puberty rite, funeral, war expedition, or harvest festival.

Not all tobacco used for religious purposes was smoked, chewed, or snuffed. A considerable amount was burned as incense, was cast into the air or on the ground, or was buried. Speculation suggests that tobacco was consumed by people prior to its being offered without human consumption because, until its narcotic effect had been experienced, the Indian would have no reason to consider it sacred. Such a sequence might be inferred for small areas, but once the sacred character of tobacco became established, the plant and multiple uses could diffuse as a unit. Tribes acquiring tobacco for the first time might smoke it and also use it for offerings. The two methods of use would, therefore, be of equal age in such localities.

On the Plains, Prairies, and in the East, tobacco was an important part of the culture. Medicine bundles nearly always contained a pipe and tobacco. The pipe was smoked as a part of the bundle ritual whenever the bundle was unwrapped and put to its religious use. On the Plains, bundles were frequently owned by individuals, who established rapport with the supernatural with the aid of the sacred objects they contained. Possession of a bundle meant success in life, and one proved effective by being in the possession of a prominent man brought a high price. On the Prairies and in the East, bundles were more often regarded as belonging to the sib or tribe. The individual in charge of the bundle was a custodian or priest who had been taught the rituals which were thought to benefit every member of the sib or tribe. Such a custodian could not sell the bundle, but taught the secret ceremonies associated with it to a younger man who was ultimately to fall heir to the office. All such bundles contained sacred pipes and tobacco, and the manner of smoking the pipe was an important part of almost all rituals. A pipe was passed around at council meetings and was especially prominent at peacemaking ceremonies.

Although uses of tobacco were as numerous in Meso-America as to the north and south, there are few mentions of pipe-smoking. Montezuma, emperor of the Aztecs, was reported to have smoked an after-dinner pipe. Southward in the Circum-Caribbean area pipes were all but unknown.

The most famous term for pipe in early American records is calumet, which centered in the Prairies. The name itself is not Indian, but is derived from a Norman-French word meaning reed or tube. However, all calumets in early historical times consisted of a hollow tube of reed or wood to which an elbowed stone bowl had been attached. Except for the unusual length of stem, it was a typical elbow pipe. It was employed in many ways: by ambassadors and other travelers as a passport; to secure favorable weather for journeys; to bring needed rain; in ceremonies designed to placate foes and hostile tribes; to ratify alliances between friendly tribes; and to make binding any sort of contract or treaty. A breach of such a contract or agreement was thought to bring the wrath of the gods down on the violator. Its most important use was in peace ceremonies in which representatives of both sides smoked the pipe of peace amidst the singing and dancing of a formal character in keeping with the gravity of the occasion.

ALCOHOLIC BEVERAGES

The distribution of alcoholic beverages (Map 12) falls almost wholly within the bounds of horticulture (Map 7). However, there was a sizable area in Northeast Mexico which was without agriculture and where wine was made from wild plants. For the world as a whole there is a definite correlation between alcoholic beverages and agriculture, although negative instances can also be found in the Old World. The explanation is a simple one; the liquors were made principally from domesticated plants. It is commonly assumed either that knowledge of the fermenting of these plants spread with the plants, or that the making of the liquor from the plant could spread only as far as the plant was known. There are also a number of examples of alcoholic beverages being made only from wild plants in an area where agriculture was known, for example the persimmon wine of the Southeast. These American data suggest that alcoholic drinks were sometimes made aboriginally in areas which lacked agriculture, or even made before agriculture was introduced in regions that later learned farming.

Agave and Dasylirion.—Two distinct plants, *Agave* (maguey)

93

and *Dasylirion* (sotol), were widely used in the Oasis, Meso-America, and Northeast Mexico for the production of alcoholic beverages. They were even more widely used as food. It has been conjectured that before the time when agriculture was common, say in the second or third millennium B.C., these plants were a staple food or even *the* staple food of a large part of this region. They were baked in the earth oven, as described in chapter v, and some idea of the age of the cooking method and plant can be obtained from archeology. Recognizable fragments of *Dasylirion* fibers have been recovered from pits in a Basket Maker horizon in Brewster County, Texas. This horizon cannot be dated exactly but goes back to about A.D. 500. There is every reason to believe that the utilization of these plants for food is considerably older, but there is no sure way to date the first appearance of the alcoholic drink made from the plant.

In the Oasis, the wine was usually made from the cooked juice of the agave, not the fresh juice as in Meso-America. The exact boundary between cooked and fresh juice is not known, but the Tarahumara and all tribes to the north cooked the agave. The part of the plant most often processed in the Oasis was the bud, although the leaves were also used. The plant was first pit-roasted, exactly as it was for food, then cut up and pounded to obtain the pulp. The pulp was sometimes allowed to ferment first before water was added, or in other localities was added to water at once. The same containers were used over and over again so that each new batch responded rapidly to the yeast from the last.

For Meso-America the process of making agave wine (*pulque, neutle*) is very different. When the plant is ready to sprout a flower shoot, the heart of the plant is cut out, and the juices which collect in the hole are removed. The heart is baked in the earth oven and eaten; the raw juice is used for wine. Although use of the maguey for food was probably primary in central Mexico, pulque has a long history.

The juice is removed from the same plant every day for a few months until the plant is exhausted. A large specimen will produce four to seven quarts of sap daily for three to six months, totaling over 1,000 quarts. The principal nutritional element is a sucrose sugar. When this juice is allowed to stand a few days, it ferments and then sours. To obtain the desired quality, the juice is usually seeded with "mother of pulque" from a previous batch so that the proper micro-organisms are set to work. It should be consumed within a day after it is ready as it quickly undergoes decomposition and acquires an objectionable stench. The alcohol content is only 3 or 4 per cent. Besides sugar and gums, pulque is a rich source of vitamin B$_1$ and also contains considerable quantities of vitamin C. It probably also induces the formation of beneficial colonic flora which tend to check dysenteries. Its 88 per cent of water makes it a significant source of comparatively safe drinking water in the areas where water is scarce or contaminated.

Cacti.—Other wines were made from the fruit of cacti, such as the saguaro, pitahaya, and nopal. The Pima and Papago process will serve as an example. The wine was made once a year and played an integral role in the rainmaking ceremony, which was the most important ritual occasion known to the tribe and was held on their New Year's Day. When the cactus fruits were gathered the previous season, they were boiled in water until the juice was about the consistency of molasses. In this condition it was stored in pottery jars which were covered and sealed with clay or gum. To make the intoxicant for the ceremony, every family in a village contributed a jar of the stored syrup to the brewing operation held in the council house. The syrup was poured into a huge pottery jar, made and kept especially for the purpose, and four times the amount of water was added. A low fire under the receptacle kept it at the right temperature for fermentation, which took about seventy-two hours. Everyone drank, believing that as men saturated themselves with the liquor so the earth would be saturated with rain.

Maize.—Maize beer was made in the Oasis south of the Mexican border, in Meso-America, and around the Caribbean. There were three principal varieties: that made from grains which were chewed to start fermentation; that made from sprouted maize grains; and that made from the stalks. Chewed grains were employed mainly in the Circum-Caribbean area, where the process forms a continuous distribution with that of South America, from which it probably stemmed. Sprouted maize beer, *tesgüino* of the Tarahumara, was characteristic of western Mexico, while corn-stalk beer was most common in Meso-America.

The first step in the preparation of the sprouted maize beer was
naturally to sprout the corn. The grains were moistened, shielded
from the light, and allowed to produce sprouts an inch or so in
length. As a result of the enzymes in the grain which become ac-
tivated when it sprouts, a large proportion of the starch is converted into fermentable sugars. After this malt is ready, it is ground,
boiled for many hours, diluted, and then fermented. The final fermentation takes only twenty-four hours. The alcohol content runs
to 4 or 5 per cent, which is about that of modern beer. This kind
of maize beer has spread northward to the San Carlos, Chiricahua,
Mescalero, and Lipan Apaches within the memory of old Indians.
It was unknown there a century or more ago.

Cornstalk wine was made from the juice squeezed from green
cornstalks. The unfermented juice was boiled down and used as a
syrup in both Mexico and Peru. The wine, however, was most
often made from the raw juice as it came from the press.

Beer from chewed maize is made by simply chewing the grains
and spitting them into a container of water. The enzymes in the
saliva start the fermentation process, which takes only a few days
in the warm climate of the Circum-Caribbean lowlands.

Mesquite and screwbeans.—The alcoholic beverage made from
mesquite and screwbeans was prepared simply by mixing the dried
or baked cakes, or the flour, with water and allowing the mixture
to ferment. The production of alcohol obviously stemmed directly
from the production of food and did not require any special technical knowledge. This drink was widely imbibed in the Oasis and
Northeast Mexico.

Tapioca.—Liquor was made from tapioca in the part of the Circum-Caribbean area where the manioc plant was the staple food. In
Central America, at least, part of the tapioca was chewed to start
fermentation.

Persimmons.—A kind of wine made from persimmons seems to
have been enjoyed by a few Southeastern tribes. It is mentioned by
Captain John Smith, which indicates that it was of Indian origin.
All data except those from Virginia date from the eighteenth century but, because the tribes involved are all neighbors of one another, it seems likely that we are dealing with an aboriginal custom.
Corn liquor is mentioned for a number of tribes in this area, but all

the references are eighteenth century or later, so it may be the result of European influence. Many other fruits were used in the making of alcoholic beverages in colonial times in the Southeast by both Indians and Whites but, like corn, the aboriginality of their use for alcohol is not established.

Other alcoholic beverages.—The wide variety of plants used for liquors in Mexico is amazing. For agricultural Meso-America there were several times as many alcoholic beverages as for the rest of the continent. Following the Conquest, Spanish preference for distilled liquors, particularly brandy and tequila, added to the number. The addition of Old World plants increased the opportunities for making both fermented and distilled drinks. Although we have space to list only a few of them, one study (Bruman, MS) describes forty distinct alcoholic beverages in use among the Indians of Mexico. Fermented honey, *balche*, was found particularly among the Mayan-speaking peoples. Wine from the sap of the wine palm was made among Central American groups, the Aztecs, and the Chinantecs at least. Other common sources of drinks in Meso-America include wild plums, pineapple, mamey, and the sarsaparilla root.

Alcoholic drinks played only an informal and secular role in the Southeast and among the Yumans, Apaches, and Zuñi of the Oasis; but from the Pima and Papago southward, they were also associated with religion and ceremony. A number of Mexican sources tell us that the women hid the weapons of the men during these drunken orgies to avoid trouble. In other localities half of the men remained sober so that they could maintain order when the other half became intoxicated. The dreams and emotions associated with intoxication in Mexico were thought to have supernatural potency and to be necessary to success in meeting the many problems of daily life. An example is the Papago belief, mentioned above, that getting drunk would bring rain. However, among the Aztecs drunkenness was regarded as the root of most evils. Public drunkenness on the part of students, nobles or priests was punished with death. A commoner would receive only a beating for the first offense, but would be killed if found drunk a second time. Few cultures in the world have placed such a heavy penalty on inebriation. However, on a few ceremonial occasions, old people were allowed to get drunk without penalty.

MAJOR NARCOTICS

Peyote.—The plant peyote, known botanically as *Lophophora williamsii*, belongs to the cactus family. It is unique among the cacti in having no spines. It ranges from carrot-like to turnip-like in size and shape, and grows mostly below ground. The rounded top surface, which alone appears above the ground, is cut off, dried, and becomes the peyote "button," which is the part eaten. Chemical analyses of the plant reveal as many as nine alkaloids which fall into two classes: strychnine-like, which are stimulants; morphine-like, which are sedatives. The most studied of these alkaloids is mescaline. The considerable variation in the amounts of these two kinds of drugs apparently accounts for the wide range of reactions to peyote.

The effect of peyote on the individual is difficult to isolate from its varying cultural contexts. However, it is generally true that the first stage of the reaction after eating is one of physical or mental exhilaration. There is no desire or ability to sleep for ten or twelve hours. The pupils of the eyes become dilated and salivation is increased. In this first stage, the drug allays hunger and thirst on the march or out hunting, gives courage in war and endurance in dancing and racing. This is followed by a second stage of depression and hallucinations, in which the individual may feel fear or hostility to the point of becoming dangerous or, on the contrary, experience euphoria and partial anesthesia. Among the hallucinations which appear, color visions are the most frequent, with auditory sensations next, and taste and smell somewhat less common. Because peyote is not habit-forming, it is not a true narcotic.

Peyote was taken in two ways: it was simply eaten, or a concoction was made of it and drunk. Eating was the universal method in the United States, but in Mexico it was often drunk, sometimes mixed with alcoholic beverages. It was also worn in Mexico as a charm without eating or drinking and was even kept in powdered form.

Its many cultural associations may be divided into ritual and non-ritual uses. It was used non-ritually by natives in all parts of its area of distribution (Map 13) for many purposes. It was used to allay hunger, thirst, and fatigue in strenuous tasks such as carrying loads, hunting, and making war. It was also taken to find lost or stolen articles, to discover secrets such as adultery, to make the eater able to detect the approach of the enemy, and to predict the outcome of a battle. Prediction of the weather was another one of its virtues. When worn on the body, it was thought to ward off disease and all manner of danger. Shamans performed magical tricks under its influence. Perhaps its most frequent function was in the curing of disease. It was taken as a cure for toothache, headache, rheumatism, cramps, fainting spells, colds, tuberculosis, hiccoughs, skin disease, snake bite, bruises, and wounds. A powdered form was sprinkled on any kind of cut or wound and was thought to check hemorrhage.

Its ritual uses can be classified into two main areal types: Mexican and Plains. Some of the elements common to both are: ceremonial trip to obtain peyote; meeting held at night; peyote regarded as a fetish; use of feathers and symbolisms associated with birds; ritual circuit; ritual fire and incense burning; water ceremony; concept of the "Peyote Woman"; morning curing rites or baptism; abstinence from salt; singing; tobacco used in ceremony; public confession of sins; Morning Star symbolism; and ritual breakfast of parched corn in sugar water, boneless sweetened meat, and fruit.

At the same time there are a number of contrasts between the Mexican and Plains peyote ceremonies. In Mexico the ceremony was participated in by the whole community and was for the benefit of all, while on the Plains it was confined to a society of more restricted membership. The Mexican rite served to allay anxieties associated principally with the food quest: hunting, gathering, and especially agriculture, where the emphasis was on rainmaking. The Plains rite, in the beginning at least, revolved around success in warfare. Dancing was a conspicuous part of the Mexican performance, but was totally lacking in the Plains area. The Mexican rite was seasonal because of its association with the food quest, but the Plains tribes held their peyote meetings the year round. Both men and women participated in Mexico, but on the Plains the ceremony was originally limited to men. The Mexican affair was held outdoors, that of the Plains in a tipi. Ritual racing and ball games were associated features in Mexico but were absent from the Plains ceremony. The Mexicans used a wooden drum, while the Plains Indians beat a hide-covered kettle drum, partially filled with water, which they derived from the Southwest. The notched rasp was the next most frequent musical instrument in the Mexican rites, while it was absent on the Plains, where the gourd rattle and eagle-bone whistle were universal. Ceremonial drunkenness was an indispensable part of the Mexican affair but was unheard of on the Plains. Christian elements were rare in Mexico, in spite of centuries of contact with the Spanish monks, but were common in the Plains ritual.

The history of peyote is fairly well known, especially in the United States. The geographical range of the plant, which was never domesticated, is limited to the Rio Grande Valley in the United States and to Mexico (Map 13). Its aboriginal use in Mexico is beyond question since it is mentioned by a number of observers in the sixteenth century. By the early seventeenth century in Mexico it was so obtrusively employed in native religious ceremonies that the Spanish officials in charge of the Mexican Inquisition attempted to stamp it out. That they failed is demonstrated by the many reports of it from later dates. The Aztecs and their neighbors imported the plant from Northeast Mexico, as did the tribes in the highlands of western Mexico.

By the eighteenth century there are vague references to Texas Indians drinking peyote in connection with their dances. The first definite evidence of United States Indians taking peyote is that from the Mescalero and Lipan Apaches who visited Mexican natives at the Coahuila mission in Northeast Mexico and attended peyote meetings in 1770. Between 1850 and 1900, peyote was acquired by the southern Plains tribes, and in the twentieth century it has spread to Canada on the north and California on the west. A word of caution about Map 13 is in order. Most of the tribes in the United States acquired peyote while on reservations in Oklahoma or from Indians residing there. For example, all tribes shown as peyote-using in the East culture area on the map obtained the plant after settling in Oklahoma. The plant did not diffuse eastward beyond the Mississippi except in the Great Lakes region. Indians at the extreme northern and western limits of our distribution, however, did receive peyote in this century while living in areas approximating those indicated. Thus the Cree of Canada did not learn of the drug until shortly before 1936, the Indians of Nevada between 1929 and 1936, and other Canadian tribes in the 1950's. Peyote meetings are still being held by most of the United States tribes shown on the map. Their organized peyote religions are called the Native American Church.

Anthropologists are not in complete agreement on the reasons why peyote spread where it did when it did. However, one explanation recurs again and again in the literature. During the last hundred years in the United States, the Indians have been fighting a losing battle against the encroachment of our culture. Anxieties have multiplied to the point of despair. A new drug associated with a new religion which promised to improve the individual's plight had strong appeal.

Why was peyote received so enthusiastically by Plains tribes and not by the Pueblos? Plains tribes suffered greater shock from their complete defeat by Whites in the last half of the nineteenth century than did the Pueblos in any period of equal length in their history. The change from the free hunting Plains way of life to the confinement of the reservation with its insistence on farming was severe indeed. The Pueblos had been farmers for centuries before the Spanish arrived. Although many were forced by various pressures to abandon their homes, the majority remained where they were and continued to farm and otherwise carry on much as they had in the past. Furthermore, the Pueblo Indian, by culture rather than nature, was a more introverted and conservative personality than the Plains Indian. Pueblo religion was highly socialized; every act of ritual was for the benefit of the entire community, and most of the ceremony was in the hands of societies whose members performed as a group. Personal experiences were almost completely submerged in group activities. Not so on the Plains. There religion centered around the individual vision quest. Those who experienced new illusions and hallucinations were regarded at least as minor prophets. The Plains area was, therefore, a much more fertile field for a new religion based primarily on individual emotional experience. After the 1890 Ghost

101

Dance movement played out, it was replaced by peyote cults in many cases.

The spread of peyote westward was checked by the presence of another narcotic, the Jimson weed. A comparison of the distribution of peyote (Map 13) with that of Jimson weed (Map 14) shows that the two are almost mutually exclusive in the United States. Actual testimony from recent Indian informants in the Great Basin reveals the fact that Jimson weed users did not want to take up peyote and did not want peyote competition to move in on them. If this is true of Great Basin tribes, it probably applies also to other Jimson weed users, although the occurrence of the two drugs together in a few localities proves that this principle cannot account for every single instance.

The role of the individual in the spread of the peyote religion was obtrusive when a person with exceptional powers of persuasion became a proselyter. What were the rewards which the individual received for his efforts? That there were "spiritual" rewards in the form of feelings of satisfaction at having furthered a noble cause cannot be denied. At the same time, there were mundane rewards in the form of money: cash from the sale of peyote buttons; fees for curing the sick; cash from taking up collections, as in European religions; and even a charge for a handshake with a prophet. The sale of peyote buttons was estimated at $20,000 per year in the depression thirties. It is probably much more at the present time. One proselyter is reputed to have realized $700 from his introduction of the religion in one locality. Compared to the sums accumulated by White leaders of new religions in present day southern California, these figures are modest indeed. The individuals concerned do not seem to have realized much more income than the average Indian they converted. Although monetary gain may be regarded as one of the incentives to spread the new religion, it was undoubtedly secondary to the prestige factor.

Jimson weed.—Plants of the genus *Datura*, called Jimson weed or Jamestown weed in English and *toloache* (from the Aztec *toloatzin*) in Spanish, were taken for their narcotic effect by a considerable number of tribes (Map 14). The name Jamestown weed is derived from the fact that a troop of soldiers stationed at

Jamestown in 1676 cooked and ate the leaves of the plant without anticipating its narcotic effect. The results were startling enough to be reported in the historical record. There is no proof that the plant was eaten or drunk by Indians in that area, or for that matter in any part of the eastern United States.

Datura was used intensively in aboriginal California. The leaves, stems, and sometimes even the roots of the plant were pounded and soaked in water to make a concoction which was drunk. The drug produced visions and dreams which were thought to foretell the future or to make supernatural beings visible. Clairvoyance was also believed to result; a person was able to see things hidden from ordinary view, events happening at a distance or in the future. The acquisition of a personal spirit-helper, so dear to the Indian, was facilitated by drinking *Datura*. In California the drug was usually taken at the age of puberty or later by a group of young people under the supervision of elders. Only men were allowed to drink it in some localities, but both men and women imbibed the concoction in other regions. Where definite male puberty initiations existed, the drinking of *Datura* was a part of these rites. Where such initiations were lacking, a group of both sexes often took it in a more informal manner, and sometimes repeated the act in later years. A considerable number of California tribes used it as an anesthetic for setting broken bones or otherwise treating the injured. Medicine men also took the drug in order to "see sickness." Other minor purposes for which it was consumed were to obtain hunting luck, to improve the food supply, to detect witchcraft, and to talk with spirits of the dead.

In the Oasis it was most often taken individually and for a number of reasons: to bring success on a deer hunt, to alleviate vomiting and dizziness, to induce the drinker to utter prophecies, or simply for the pleasure derived from the accompanying dreams and visions. At Zuñi, *Datura* was believed to be one of the medicines derived from the gods, and its use was limited to rain priests and directors of the Little Fire and Cimex fraternities. The plant was addressed in a respectful manner while being gathered. To make rain, the rain priests offered the powdered root to certain rain birds or induced a man of good heart to eat a bit and dream of ghosts. If a man had been robbed and wished to discover the thief, the priests gave him a dose of *Datura*. Here also it was used as an anesthetic to set fractured bones or perform surgery on a patient.

Although widely used and known in Mexico, our fullest information is for the Aztecs, who used the drug for both religious and medicinal purposes. Here again *Datura* was regarded as holy. There were special officials who took *Datura*, along with peyote, to discover cures for illness, lost or stolen property, and the cause of chronic illness due to witchcraft. Sometimes the patient was given the drug instead. *Datura* was also one of the ingredients in an ointment made of venomous insects, burned to ashes, and tobacco. The priests who were anointed with this salve are said to have lost all fear and to have become bold and cruel enough to kill their sacrificial victims. This ointment was also used to cure the sick, who came from all parts of the land to be treated by the priests, and as an anodyne to set fractured bones. It was also used in the Andean region of South America as far south as Peru, and in the Old World as well.

MINOR NARCOTICS

A narcotic mushroom, *teonanácatl* (*Paneolus campanulatus*), has been used in central Meso-America since before the time of the Conquest (Map 14). When eaten, the *teonanácatl* produces a sensation of euphoria and well-being very similar to that of peyote. Aztecs present at the ceremonies surrounding the coronation of Montezuma II were said to have intoxicated themselves with the mushrooms. The modern Mazatec medicine men find lost objects and divine the future under the intoxication of *teonanácatl*.

The seeds of another narcotic plant, *ololiuqui* (*Rivea corymbosa*), are widely used in the same area (Map 14) for divining purposes and as a "truth drug." Although the plant was known to the Maya, they were unaware of its narcotic effects.

The "mescal bean," *Sophora secundiflora*, grows wild in Mexico from Coahuila to San Luis Potosí, and in the United States in western Texas and southern New Mexico. It is a member of the bean family, *Fabaceae*, and is not to be confused with the term *mescal* used to designate the genus *Agave*, which belongs to the amaryllis family. The mescal bean contains a highly toxic alkaloid called sophorine which resembles nicotine in physiological action. It is said to produce nausea, convulsions, and even death by asphyxiation if taken in sufficient quantity. It was eaten by a number of tribes and was also worn as a charm. At least a dozen tribes had organized cults centering around the eating of the bean in a group ritual. It was acquired earlier than peyote by tribes in the United States but never attained as wide an appeal as did peyote.

The leaves of a tree, *Ilex cassine*, were the principal ingredient in the "black drink" of the Southeast (Map 14). This drink produced immediate vomiting. It was most often used as a form of ritual purification before setting out on a war expedition. The Creek, however, drank the concoction before important council meetings and in connection with most of their sacred ceremonies. It was especially prominent in their annual harvest ceremony called the "busk." The plant grows wild from the Carolinas to the Rio Grande and continues across the Antilles into South America. Emetic drinks were commonly employed in the Antilles and South America, but botanical identifications are too few to establish indisputably the use of *Ilex* there.

REFERENCES

ABERLE AND STEWART, 1957; ARISS, 1939; BEALS, 1932*a*; BELL AND CASTETTER, 1937; BENNETT AND ZINGG, 1935; BRANT, 1950; BRUMAN, MS; CARR, 1947; CASTETTER, 1935, 1943; CASTETTER AND BELL, 1937, 1938; CASTETTER AND OPLER, 1936; FLANNERY, 1939; GAYTON, MS; GUERRA AND OLIVERA, 1954; HEIZER, 1940; HOWARD, 1957; JAEGER, 1940; JOHNSON, 1939*a*, 1939*b*; JONES, 1944; LABARRE, 1938*a*, 1938*b*, 1960; LASSWELL, 1935; LEONARD, 1942; LINTON, 1924*a*; LOWIE, 1954; MCGUIRE, 1897; MARTÍNEZ, 1936; MARTÍNEZ DEL RÍO, 1954; MASON, 1924, 1948; PORTER, 1948; ROJAS, 1942; SAFFORD, 1916; SAUER, C. O., 1950; SCHULTES, 1940; SETCHELL, 1921; SLOTKIN, 1952, 1955, 1956; SOUSTELLE, 1956; STEWARD, 1948; STEWART, 1944; SWANTON, 1946; THOMPSON, 1954; WEST, 1934; WISSLER, 1938.

8: Housing and Architecture

Every tribe of North American Indians constructed some form of dwelling. Caves were used temporarily for habitations and travelers sometimes slept outdoors, but everyone occupied a house at least part of the year. Many tribes used more than one kind of dwelling, the particular type at any given time depending on the season of the year, the building materials available, and sometimes on the amount of wealth of the occupant family. For example, a number of tribes along the Missouri River lived in large multifamily earth-covered lodges arranged in villages about half the year during the farming season, but when hunting buffalo they changed to hide-covered conical tipis. Some of these same tribes occupied bark-covered dome-shaped wigwams part of the time, in emulation of their Algonquian neighbors to the east and north, where this kind of house was more common. A detailed description of each type of dwelling possessed by every tribe would fill several volumes. In order to simplify this vast amount of information we have selected a single representative variety for each tribe. The kind of dwelling used by the largest part of the population or for the greatest part of the year has been chosen as the type. The geographical distributions of these structures are shown on Map 15.

DOMINANT HOUSE TYPES

Arctic.—The domed dwelling built of snow blocks was the typical house of the central Eskimo, although it was used to a lesser extent by almost all the Eskimos (Fig. 2). The builder had first to locate snow packed to the right consistency, neither too hard and icy nor too soft and powdery. He then cut the first rectangular block, which he placed on edge to form the beginning of

106

the base of the wall. Next he cut another block which was set adjacent to it, and continued until the circle was completed. Working from the inside, he added the next upward spiraling row of blocks, each one being tipped inward a trifle to narrow the circle which was to end in a dome. As progress was made, the snow blocks became a continuous spiral which was less likely than separate rows to cave in during the process of construction. This is the only type of dome known to architecture which can be constructed out of blocks without first building a scaffold to support it. When the last block was put in place at the top, the builder cut a hole for an entrance and exit and let himself out. To complete the house, he constructed a low passageway or tunnel of snow, in front of the entrance. This tunnel had to be negotiated on hands

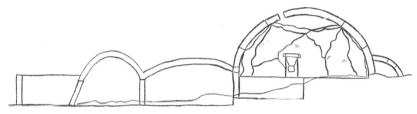

FIG. 2.—Domed snow house (Eskimo). Driver and Massey

and knees. A double door consisting of two suspended hides kept out the cold.

A snow platform was made or left at the rear half of the floor plan, as well as on both sides. The family slept on the rear platform, which was amply provided with hides to serve as mattresses and bedding. On the side platforms the women of the house cooked and sewed. A small hole was left in the top of the roof, and an ice window was sometimes placed in the front wall over the passageway. Snow houses were normally occupied by single families, but sometimes two or more families might live in an unusually large one.

The dwelling of the eastern Eskimo is labeled domoid, or domelike, because its ground plan frequently had rounded "corners" which made it transitional between circular and rectangular shapes, and its walls usually rose almost vertically and then turned in rather abruptly to form the roof (Fig. 3). The walls were made of sod or

107

stones laid to a height of four or five feet. The roof was bridged with whale ribs, or large slabs of stone laid in the manner of a crude corbeled arch. The tunnel entrance and the arrangement of the interior were similar to that of the snow house. In contrast to the snow house, which melted every summer, the stone-earth-whalebone house remained to be reoccupied the next winter. Ownership, however, was only for a season; even the builder was obliged to relinquish claim on the house if another family occupied it first after the return of the villagers from their summer excursions.

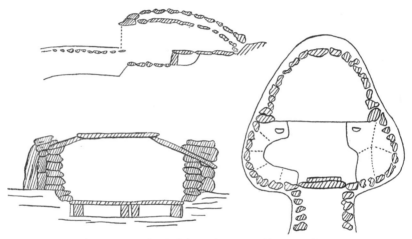

Fig. 3.—Domoid stone-earth-whalebone house (Eskimo). Driver and Massey

The permanent or winter house of the Alaskan Eskimos and their Athapaskan Indian neighbors consisted of a rectangular framework of horizontally laid logs, about five feet high, over which was a four-pitched pyramid roof of logs (Fig. 4). At the top center, eight or nine feet high, a hole was left for smoke and light. Another hole, at ground level, connected with a tunnel-like passageway of logs which formed the entrance. The entire structure and its passageway were covered over with several feet of earth, which made it almost airtight and insulated it from the cold. Raised log platforms a foot or less in height occupied three sides of the room. These were sat on by day and slept on at night. Commonly three families occupied such a house, each appropriating one of the platforms. The space on each side of the doorway was used for storage, but the third platform might serve as storage space if only two families occupied the dwelling. The floor was covered with planks, or half-round logs with the flat side up, so that its surface would be smooth. Sometimes half-round logs with the flat side inward were also used for the walls. On the earth floor directly under the roof hole was the fireplace, which served for cooking, heating, and lighting. Fuel consisted of wood or, where wood was scarce, of seal oil burnt in a lamp. In southern Alaska, where wood was plentiful, the lamp was not needed for cooking but provided illumination.

Northwest Coast.—The large plank houses of the Northwest Coast were supported by a framework of logs to which planks

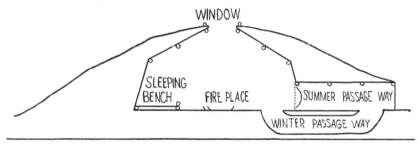

Fig. 4.—Rectangloid earth-covered Alaskan house (Eskimo). Driver and Massey

were attached vertically or horizontally to complete the structure (Fig. 5). The framework remained for generations in the same spot, but the planks which formed the walls and roof might be transported to other localities when subsistence pursuits demanded a change of residence. The planks also tended to warp and split and otherwise disintegrate sooner than the huge logs of the frame and required more frequent renewal. These dwellings varied in size from about 15 by 20 feet to 50 by 60 feet. They were occupied by several families which collectively made up one extended family. Each constituent family had its own allotment of space and cooked over its own fire, although obtaining food was often a group enterprise in which all the families participated and shared in the results. These houses stood with a gabled end facing the sea. In this end was the doorway, consisting of an oval hole in a large plank. On the inside around the walls were built platforms of poles and planks on which to sit and sleep; the same effect might be achieved by excavating the center of the house and leaving one or two terraces around the edges. All floors and terraces were covered with planks.

A number of peoples in the center of the area built houses with a one-pitch roof, the so-called shed-roof type. One such house ran to 520 feet in length, although most were within the range of the gabled houses described above. Sometimes the high sides of two shed-roofed structures were joined to form a two-pitched-roof gabled house, a combination which suggests one way in which the latter may have originated. In the extreme southern part of this

Fig. 5.—Rectangular plank house (Kwakiutl). Driver and Massey

area, in northwest California, a few peoples built a house having a roof with three pitches. Since it had no separate log frame, the roof was supported by the vertical planks which formed the walls. These houses averaged smaller than the other two types.

Sub-Arctic.—The dominant house in this area was a crude conical tipi covered with hide or bark (Fig. 6). Both kinds of covering were sometimes used together on the same structure, and hides were never sewn together as on the Plains in the nineteenth century. Additional poles laid on top of the many pieces of bark or hide held the covering in place in windy weather. Smoke escaped through a hole at the apex, and the covering was left loose in one place for a doorway. These houses were only about half as large in linear dimension as the Plains tipis of the nineteenth century.

In a part of the western Sub-Arctic, double lean-tos with gables at the ends appear to have been the most common type of habitation (Fig. 7). Single lean-tos were also used but were inadequate for permanent winter occupancy. These lean-tos were made of a framework of poles covered with bark, hides, or brush. Sometimes these structures had vertical sides, on top of which rested a gabled two-pitch roof, but these are probably derived from European log cabins or from Alaskan or Northwest Coast houses in historic

FIG. 6.—Crude conical tipi (Ojibwa). Driver and Massey

FIG. 7.—Double lean-to (Slave). Driver and Massey

111

times. The double lean-to was occupied by a single family or an extended family, depending on its size or the type of family which built it. There were no bed platforms or other furnishings.

Plateau.—The most typical dwelling consisted of a circular pit, four or five feet deep, over which a conical or pyramidal roof was built (Fig. 8). The roof was supported by one to four posts erected near the center of the pit. Rafters were laid with one end on these posts and the other on the ground near the edge of the excavation. On the rafters smaller poles were laid, then thatch, and finally the earth which came from the pit. The fireplace was in the center of

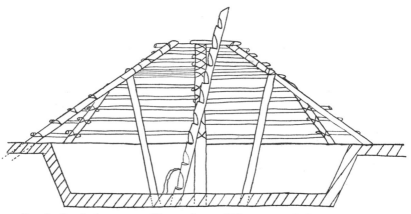

Fig. 8.—Semisubterranean Plateau house (Thompson). Driver and Massey

the earth floor. The smoke hole, located usually at the top center, served also as entrance and exit, and was reached by means of a notched log ladder. These houses were occupied by one or by several families, according to size and to local or individual preference.

Plains.—The conical tipi of the Plains was a carefully constructed portable dwelling with a tailored buffalo hide cover (Fig. 9). A foundation of three or four poles was made by tying the ends together and standing them up; additional poles up to about twenty were leaned against the tripod or tetrapod. After the covering was put in place, it was staked down or weighted down with stones around the bottom edge and the top "ears" fastened to two poles so that the wind could be kept from blowing smoke back down into the tipi. The fire was built near the center, and the beds were placed on the ground around the circle except in front of the doorway. Nineteenth-century tipis were often 10 or 12 feet high, 12 or

15 feet in diameter, and were covered with fifteen or twenty buffalo hides. Sometimes a hide lining covered the floor and ran up the sides four or five feet. This prevented drafts from creeping in from under the edges of the outer covering. Buffalo hide is much more windproof than canvas, and while these Plains tipis were not as warm as modern buildings, they could be kept above the freezing mark in the coldest weather. The erection and dismantling of the tipi was the work of the women, as was also the tanning of the

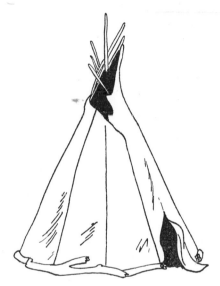

FIG. 9.—Plains tipi (Crow). Driver and Massey

hides and the cutting and sewing of them to form the tailored cover. Men might obtain the poles, however. The dragging of the poles by dogs, and later by horses, which the treeless character of the Plains made necessary, seems to be an adequate explanation of the origin of the travois.

Prairies.—This area is one of the most mixed with respect to house types. There were no less than four distinct kinds of dwelling, each dominant in part of the area: the Dakota tribes lived most of the time in hide-covered tipis simliar to those of the Plains; an earth lodge was the rule in the Missouri River drainage, a grass-thatched house in the extreme south, and a low domed dwelling around the Great Lakes.

113

The earth lodge of the Missouri River area consisted essentially of a cylindrical base on which rested a conical roof and from which projected a tunnel-like entrance passage (Fig. 10). The whole structure was covered over with earth, hence the name earth lodge. These dwellings, by inside measurement, varied from 30 to 40 feet in diameter, from 10 to 15 feet in height in the center, and from 5 to 7 feet high at the eaves. The ground was often dug down a foot or more in order to find compact earth to serve as a good floor. Peripheral posts, 5 to 7 feet high, were planted at intervals around the edge of the circular pit. Four center posts 10 to 15 feet in height were placed in position. Then rafters were laid

Fig. 10.—Prairie-Southeast earth lodge (Pawnee). Driver and Massey

from the center posts to the peripheral posts, and on the rafters were placed smaller poles, brush, thatch, and finally earth to complete the structure. In the center of the earthen floor a round hole was dug for a fireplace. A low platform of poles around the outer wall served as a bed by night and a bench by day. A number of families of related persons, collectively making up an extended family, occupied a single such dwelling.

The thatched house with Gothic dome is found among the Caddo, Wichita, and their neighbors on the southern Prairies (Fig. 11). A number of long, flexible poles were set in the ground in a circle and the tops bent over and joined in the center. The ends of the poles protruded above the top of this structure in the manner of a tipi; they did not form a continuous arch like those of typical domed dwellings. Horizontal poles, encircling the house, were tied on at intervals and the whole was covered with grass thatch, each layer of which was held in place with pole binders on the outside. The fireplace, as usual, was in the center, and the smoke found its way out through the thatch without the aid of a smoke hole. Bed platforms were placed around the sides. These houses were occupied by a number of families which collectively formed an extended family. They were larger than the nineteenth-century tipi, averaging about fifteen feet in height and perhaps a little more in diameter.

FIG. 11.—Gothic dome thatched house (Wichita). Driver and Massey

The domed houses around the western Great Lakes are labeled "wigwam" in the Algonquian languages (Fig. 12). Pairs of poles were set vertically in the ground at the proper distance and bent over to form a series of arches. Encircling horizontal poles were firmly lashed to the arches to strengthen the frame, which was covered with woven or sewn mats, pieces of bark, and sometimes hides. When moving camp, the covering materials were normally taken along but the frame was left standing. Single families occupied small domed structures of this type which were approximately round in ground plan; extended families lived in elongated houses which were elliptical in ground plan. Bed platforms were some-

115

times built in these dwellings in historic times, but their aboriginality is doubtful.

East.—The famous longhouse of the Iroquois Indians of New York State dominated the northern part of this area (Fig. 13). These averaged 60 feet in length, 18 feet in width, and 18 feet in height. Poles were set in the ground at proper intervals around the periphery of the building. These were braced by horizontal poles across the tops of paired poles, and by other horizontal poles along

FIG. 12.—Domed bark, mat, thatch, or hide house (Ojibwa). Driver and Massey

FIG. 13.—Rectangular barrel-roofed house (Iroquois). Driver and Massey

the walls. The roof was made by bending over a series of pairs of flexible poles so that it formed a half cylinder, hence the label barrel-roofed. The entire frame was covered with bark, most often elm bark, which was perforated and sewed on in overlapping layers like shingles. Pole binders on the outside made the covering windproof. Like other Indian dwellings, it had no windows, but light entered through the doorways at the ends or the smoke holes in the roof. A central hallway 6 to 10 feet wide ran the length of the interior. On both sides was a series of booths, each occupied by a separate family. They were on platforms about 18 inches high, 5 to 6 feet wide, and 6 to 12 feet long. A second level of platform around the sides of each booth served as a bed, and a third level about 7 feet above the ground was used for storage. Down the center of the hallway was located a series of fireplaces, each shared by pairs of families in opposite pairs of booths. These families were related, the whole constituting an extended family.

Dominant house types on the Atlantic Coast from Cape Cod to the Savannah River were of the same essential variety as that of the Iroquois except that they were smaller.

FIG. 14.—Rectangular gabled house, thatched (Middle Mississippi). Driver and Massey.

Summer houses of the Southeastern tribes were similar in shape to those of the Iroquois except that the roof was two-pitched and gabled instead of barrel-shaped (Fig. 14). They were rectangular, with four vertical walls of poles plastered over with mud to form mud wattle, or of a pole frame covered with thatch. The roof was covered with either bark or thatch, and smoke holes were left at the apexes of the gables. The doorway was normally in one side and was a rectangular opening flush with the wall. The fire was built in the middle of the earthen floor and bed platforms were placed around the walls. Shakes or shingles were used for house covering in the third quarter of the eighteenth century, but this appears to be the result of European influence. Such dwellings were normally occupied by a single family, but those of a number of related families were built close together in extended family clusters.

117

The eaves were a little higher than a man's head, the length fifteen or twenty feet, and the width somewhat less.

The winter house of the Southeast was a semisubterranean earth-covered structure with a tunnel entrance, identical in its essential features to the earth lodge of the Prairies.

California.—In this area the most common type was the domed house, made with a framework of poles bent and tied in the proper shape over which was placed a thatch of grass, tules, or other plant materials. The thatch was held in place by horizontal pole binders on the outside. The second most popular dwelling was a crude conical tipi covered with slabs of bark or with thatch. Semisubterranean earth-covered structures with tunnel entrances were also to be found but usually functioned as men's sweathouses or as religious assembly houses rather than as family dwellings.

Great Basin.—In this arid region the dominant dwelling was a conical tipi covered most often with thatch held down by pole binders, but sometimes the covering was of hide or bark. This structure was much smaller than nineteenth-century Plains tipis. The second most popular house was a domed affair covered with thatch or brush. Many Basin houses were crude, hastily assembled and soon abandoned in the wandering in search of food.

Oasis.—There were six kinds of houses in the Oasis, each dominant in its special area. The Pueblo peoples lived in rectangular, flat-roofed rooms, built flush against one another to form a continuous large village unit comparable to an apartment house (Fig. 15). The western Pueblos built principally of stone, while those on the Rio Grande in the east generally used adobe (clay); but because the western peoples plastered over their stone walls, the appearance of the houses in the two localities is very much the same. In aboriginal times lower-story rooms had no doorways or windows but were entered by means of notched log ladders through a hatchway in the roof. Pueblo rooms were about a dozen feet square and were grouped together in apartment houses of three or four stories which accommodated about two hundred people on the average. Each family lived mainly in a single room, although it might possess other rooms used for storage and sacred rites. The roofs of these habitations were supported with logs, over which were laid successive layers of poles, thatch, and earth. Such a roof was practical only in a dry climate. The roof of one story served as the floor of the next above. Furnishings were few—the most conspicuous article was a built-in bench of logs or stone along one or two walls. Wall niches served as cupboards. The boxed-in milling stones occupied one side of the room, and the fireplace the center, with the smoke going out through the hatchway. Today Pueblo Indians build a chimney and fireplace in a corner.

Fig. 15.—Rectangular flat-roofed house (Zuñi). Driver and Massey

The Colorado River Yumans had a distinct kind of house called Mohave type, after one of the tribes. It had a frame of logs and poles, a thatch of arrow weed, and on top of that a covering of sand (Fig. 16). The ground plan was rectangular and nearly square, dimensions averaging about 20 by 25 feet. The door was in the middle of one side and always faced south. The roof was nearly flat, sloping only about 10 degrees, and had four pitches. Sand covered the roof and three sides, so that the house itself was visible only from the front. The fireplace was near the door, perhaps because there was no smoke hole, but also because the warm climate made heat unnecessary during most of the year. Such habitations were built and occupied by a number of related families which formed an extended family.

The non-Pueblo peoples of the northern and eastern part of the Oasis lived in a crude form of conical tipi, made of poles leaned together and covered with thatch, brush, or slabs of bark or wood, and sometimes with earth piled as high up on the sides as possible.

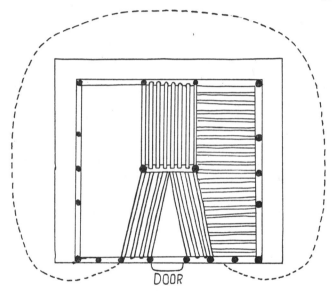

Fig. 16.—Mohave type four-pitch roof house (Mohave). Driver and Massey

The Navaho hogan was originally such a structure, but today it is an octagonal structure with walls of horizontal logs.

Other non-Pueblo peoples in the Oasis occupied domed huts covered most often with thatch but sometimes with other materials. In a few localities the domed hut became blended with the rectangular house to produce a half-breed type consisting of four rectangular walls covered with a domed roof (Fig. 17).

There were rectangular houses with flat roofs in the Mexican part of the Oasis, but they tended to be set apart and not clustered into apartment houses like Pueblo dwellings.

Finally, the peoples in the southern part of the Oasis nearest

Meso-America lived in houses with four rectangular walls topped by a four-pitched roof, either hipped (Fig. 18) or pyramidal.

Northeast Mexico.—The Chichimecs of this area probably lived in crude domed huts or double lean-tos in pre-Columbian times, but they slept in the open so much when traveling that more than one Spanish priest thought they had no houses at all. The rectangular gabled house, shown on Map 15 and in Figure 14 is probably post-Columbian in this area.

Meso-America.—This complex region had at least three major types of houses. The rectangular flat-roofed house was the dominant variety in western Mexico and highland central Mexico (Fig. 15). Its walls were of stone cemented together with adobe, of adobe plastered against poles (mud wattle), adobe supported be-

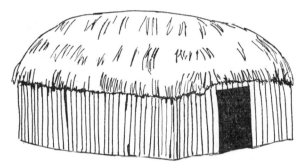

Fig. 17.—Rectangular domed-roof house (Opata). Driver and Massey

Fig. 18.—Pyramidal or hip-roof rectangloid house (Guaymi). Driver and Massey

121

tween walls of poles, or adobe mixed with little stones. The Aztecs and their neighbors lived in such dwellings. They were grouped in small clusters, most often one story, occupied by patrilocal extended families.

Among the many house types found in Meso-America the rectangular gabled house was particularly common among peoples along the Gulf of Campeche and with the Lacandones. In pre-Conquest times most of the commoners among the Totonac lived

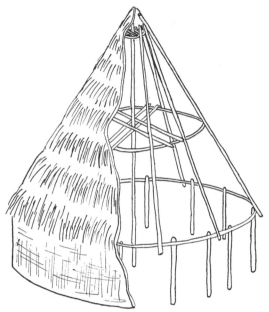

Fig. 19.—Conical roof on cylinder thatch house (Cuna). Driver and Massey

in such houses with pole walls and thatch or grass roofs; similar houses are general in the area today. The Popolocas of southern Veracruz and the Lacandones of the Guatemalan lowlands have such houses. The rectangular, gabled house was probably an alternate form among neighboring peoples. Today in Mexico this house type is widespread but its dispersal was due to Spanish influence.

The rectangular houses with hip roof (Fig. 18) or pyramidal roof of Meso-America and Central America invariably had thatched roofs, but the walls were more varied; they consisted of

122

poles or canes without adobe, of mud wattle, of adobe bricks or puddled adobe, and sometimes of stone, especially at the base. The four pitches of the roof were relatively steep, the better to shed the downpours to which much of the area was subject. Sometimes the ends of such houses were rounded. Doorways were rectangular openings in end or side, and the floor was of earth. Shakes for roofs and horizontal interlocking logs appear to have been introduced by the Spanish in early historic times. Some of these houses were large enough to accommodate extended families. Wooden platforms, carved stools, and sleeping mats were common, although there were regional variations in the household furniture.

Circum-Caribbean.—There were two major house types in this area: the first is the rectangular structure with hip roof or pyramidal roof, just described in the paragraph above; the second is a conical roof perched on a cylindrical wall. This second dwelling consisted of a circular wall of poles, forming a hollow cylinder, on top of which was built a conical roof of thatch (Fig. 19). This type was also common in northern South America, from which it has apparently been derived. Furnishings consisted of built-in bed platforms, hammocks, and wooden stools carved from a single block of wood. Some of these houses were large enough to accommodate several families which were undoubtedly related and formed an extended family.

COMPARATIVE ANALYSIS

Ground plans.—Houses with round or oval ground plan are almost universal in North America, although not the dominant type everywhere. The distribution of those of conical shape is shown on Map 16. Domed shapes are even more widespread, because the water vapor sweathouse (Map 20) was nearly everywhere of this shape. It was only in Mexico and Guatemala that it was consistently rectangular. In many areas where other shapes were dominant, domed houses were used as temporary or secondary dwellings. Because the round ground plan is so nearly universal, its distribution does not give us any historical clues.

Not so for rectangular ground plans. These are definitely limited in distribution. They occur in the western Arctic, Yukon Sub-Arctic, Northwest Coast, and adjacent parts of the Mackenzie

123

Sub-Arctic and Plateau. They also are found in the United States east of the Mississippi, and continuously from the northern Oasis to Panama and the West Indies. The northwestern rectangular houses are probably derived from Asia. They show a generic similarity to dwellings in Siberia, China, and Japan, although there is argument about the details. They appear in the Old Bering Sea Culture, about A.D. 100 to 500, and also in early Aleut Culture about 100 B.C. to A.D. 500. These early forms were semisubterranean and were made of logs rather than planks. They are the direct ancestors of the Alaskan houses described earlier in this chapter. Plank houses apparently developed later, although the exact date is unknown.

Houses of rectangular ground plan east of the Mississippi, in the Oasis, Meso-America, and Circum-Caribbean areas are closely correlated with agriculture (Map 7). If we add archeological data, we find such structures extending as far west as the hundredth meridian on the Prairies and Plains and all the way across Texas to unite the Oasis and Southeast. The archeological association of rectangular houses in these areas is overwhelmingly with agriculture. Temporally the relationship also holds. Both traits appear together at about the same time in both the Southwest and the Southeast. Because maize and other domesticated plants were diffused from south to north, it seems very likely that rectangular houses in farming areas have the same history.

It is, therefore, evident that rectangular houses in North America have a dual origin and history: those in the northwest seem to be derived from Asia; those in other areas apparently stem from Meso-America or the Caribbean area.

Conical and subconical houses.—The term subconical is introduced to take care of shapes which are intermediate between conical and domed forms and which sometimes have projecting entrance passages and other features which depart from a true cone. Conical dwellings may be classified according to the number of poles tied together and erected as the foundation against which the remaining poles are leaned (Map 16). Three is the minimum number that will stand without the butts being planted in the ground. A glance at the map shows that many tribes, especially in the West, use four poles as a foundation. The choice between three and four, being an arbitrary one, since both are equally efficient, is a matter of group habit or custom. Because four poles are more frequent in the West and three in the East, there is some indication that diffusion within each of these major areas has taken place. At the same time, the irregularities also suggest a certain amount of independent invention. Some of the irregularities can, however, be explained in terms of migrations. For example, the Comanches in A.D. 1600 were indistinguishable from the northeastern Shoshonis and lived in Wyoming and Colorado. About A.D. 1700 they migrated southward to the southern Plains, retaining the four-pole tipi foundation of the northeastern Shoshonis.

It is probably significant that the area of most elaborate development of the tipi, the Plains, is one in which the number of foundation poles is most consistently patterned. In much of the Sub-Arctic and Great Basin, where crude conical dwellings predominated, there was apparently no specified number of foundation poles, or informants were not aware of it. The limited number of foundation poles is associated with the frequent setting up and taking down of the tipi and the transportation of the poles. In wooded areas, such as the Sub-Arctic, where fresh poles were available, the used poles were often left standing and only the hide and bark covering moved. Where the poles were not at a premium, their use was less patterned.

Conical dwellings are distributed continuously across northern Eurasia to Lapland, and occur as far south as Tibet. They are rare or absent in Africa, southern Eurasia, Oceania, and South America. These facts suggest a single origin in the north, more likely in Asia than North America, because the bulk of cultural features shared by these two continents seem to have originated in Asia. It is probably no accident that the conical house in the Southwest stops at the southern boundary of the Athapaskan territory. Linguistic evidence of the northern origin of Southwest Athapaskans is indisputable. The conical dwelling was apparently carried to the border of Mexico by their migration, not by diffusion. Diffusion, however, may explain its occurrence in southern California and the southern Prairies. Apparently both historical processes were at work.

125

Semisubterranean houses and tunneled entrances.—The majority of the houses covered over with unprocessed earth were semisubterranean or had tunnel entrances, and about half had both (Map 17). Although the correlation of these three elements is not perfect, it suggests that these features are of northern origin. Alaskan houses consistently have all three. In other areas one or the other drops out here and there. Nevertheless, when these distributions are viewed from an over-all point of view, the compactness of the North American data is overwhelming. These elements of house construction are found to be associated also in Eurasia, but are apparently absent as a complex everywhere else in the world. Eurasia and North America therefore constitute a single area for these features of house-building, with a single origin somewhere in Eurasia.

The earliest evidence for semisubterranean houses dates from the early Upper Paleolithic period (Gravettian, Aurignacian) in southern Russia. The age in years has been estimated at about 25,000 years ago. These were oval in ground plan and varied from 18 feet to 108 feet in greatest diameter. The larger ones were obviously multifamily dwellings as the nine to eleven fire hearths of one house indicate. In the same area but in late Upper Paleolithic (Magdalenian) times, the oval shape of the earlier semisubterranean houses changed to rectangular, the entrance passageway appeared, and the stone lamp replaced the wood-burning hearth.

Small semisubterranean rectangular huts with entrance passage have been found near Lake Baikal in Siberia. These are also dated as early Upper Paleolithic. This type persists with little change down to modern times, as finds in the Ob River drainage dated in the second millennium B.C. and the first millennium A.D. indicate. Modern Paleo-Asiatic peoples of northeast Siberia still occupy essentially the same kind of dwelling as do the neighboring Alaskan Eskimos.

The semisubterranean, earth-covered, tunnel-entranced structures of the Southeast were called the winter house or "hot house." They were round in ground plan and were occupied mainly in cold weather. The men's council house, which was located in the center of the town, was of the same construction but much larger. The largest of these reported is said to have accommodated several hundred men and to have had 47 posts supporting the roof. In the Southwest, houses with the same three features date from Basket Maker II period, A.D. 100–500. They ultimately developed into the ceremonial men's house called the *kiva,* which did away with the entrance passageway and flattened the roof, but retained the circular ground plan.

Multifamily dwellings.—Large houses occupied by two or more families were widespread in North America (Map 18). In most cases the families were related, so that the household aggregates they formed were extended families. The areas indicated on Map 18 are those in which the bulk of the population lived in such groups most of the year. In other areas, such as that of the central and eastern Eskimos, two or more families might live together for a time, but the arrangement was not very definitely patterned. In areas where conical dwellings predominated (Map 15), they were occupied almost exclusively by single families. They were too small in aboriginal times to have regularly accommodated more people. However, small dwellings do not necessarily preclude the development of extended family organization as is shown by the Apaches, who pitch their tipis in extended family clusters which are united economically and socially.

The relation of multifamily dwellings to nomadic, as opposed to sedentary way of life, is marked. The more sedentary peoples tend to have multifamily houses, the more nomadic tribes to live in single family structures. Before the appearance of the horse it was impossible for the nomadic Indians to transport a large dwelling.

The earliest reported multifamily dwellings are those of the early Upper Paleolithic in Russia, mentioned above. They were semisubterranean structures which may be ancestral to houses of similar construction in northern North America.

Division of labor.—Map 19 shows the areas in which each sex dominated the bulk of the work or the most indispensable tasks connected with building the dominant types of houses shown on Map 15. Where a single tribe erected more than one type of dwelling, one sex might build one and the opposite sex the other. For example, among the central Eskimos the men built the snow houses, but the women erected the summer tents. In general it

127

was the women who erected and dismantled the conical and dome-shaped portable structures of the Sub-Arctic, Prairies, and Plains. Large dwellings supported by heavy timbers were usually constructed by both sexes, but it was the men who performed the most indispensable task, which was the cutting and erecting of the timbers. It is also true that in areas where women erected the houses, the men provided most of the food through their hunting activities. The converse, however, is less true.

On the Northwest Coast, the building of the plank house was exclusively the work of men as was all other woodwork. The stone and adobe structures of the Oasis and Meso-America were built almost entirely by men, but Pueblo women, at least, plastered the walls with adobe. Where thatch was used, women usually gathered the plant materials because gathering of plant foods was also their job; where earth covering was employed, women usually helped collect and place the earth on the house. Women also made the mats for mat-covered dwellings, but these were nowhere the dominant type.

SWEATHOUSES

Special sweathouses were used by the vast majority of North American aborigines (Map 20), except the central and eastern Eskimos, a few tribes in the southern Great Basin, the Yumans (except Diegueño) and Pimans, and the north Mexican peoples. Sweating was induced in two ways: by direct exposure to a fire and confinement inside a building with the fire; by first heating stones in a fire, then pitching a portable structure over them or rolling the stones inside a nearby structure, and finally pouring water on the hot stones to produce water vapor.

The buildings used for these two sweating techniques differ considerably. The direct fire sweathouse of Alaska was a semi-subterranean earth-covered log house with tunnel entrance, very much like the Alaskan dwelling. It served as a men's clubhouse in which bachelors or male travelers might sleep and in which married men might spend considerable time. It was owned collectively by all men of the village. The direct fire sweathouses of California are surprisingly similar. The majority of these were also semi-subterranean, earth-covered, and with tunnel entrance. They dif-

fered in being round in ground plan while those of Alaska were
rectangular. In both Alaska and California sweating was a daily
group affair, indulged in simply to "feel good" more often than
for a specific reason.

The kivas of the Pueblo Southwest share the same three features, except that the tunnel entrance has contracted to a mere
draft hole. They were formerly all round in ground plan like those
of nearby California. Archeological evidence conclusively shows
that the kivas developed from the more primitive California model.
In fact, the sweathouses in all three areas are probably derived
from a common circular ancestral form. Archeological evidence
from Alaska indicates that the earliest houses there were round
in ground plan. Like the dwellings mentioned above, all of these
men's houses seem to stem from a common ancestral house of
round ground plan in northern Asia.

Water vapor sweathouses were of a very different character.
They were almost invariably small, domed structures with round
ground plans. Although they were sometimes permanent structures, the majority were hastily assembled for a particular occasion and not used daily. They consisted of a light framework of
poles or withes over which hides, pieces of bark, or mats were
thrown to confine the water vapor. Often they were so low that
the occupant had to stoop to enter. They were used most often
for a purification rite by those seeking supernatural power or by
the sick seeking relief from infirmities. Usually only a single person
sweated in such a structure, whereas in the direct-fire type all
the men of a village might join together in a contest to see who
could withstand the most heat. Women were usually permitted
to sweat by the water vapor method, but almost never in the
direct-fire manner. The water vapor technique is found all the
way across Asia to Scandinavia and to Turkey, whence it diffused
to North Africa and Europe, where it is known as the Turkish
bath. It was also employed in ancient Rome. Therefore, a single
origin in northern Asia and subsequent diffusion to Europe on the
west and to North America on the east seems likely.

In the Southeast the winter dwellings, called hothouses, are
reminiscent of direct-fire sweathouses. Men, women, and children
slept together in them with a fire going all night, arose together

in the morning dripping with perspiration, and rushed out the door to the nearest stream for a cold bath. Among the Delaware each village apparently had an earth-covered sweathouse entered through a hole in the roof, and a crier invited the entire populace to come and sweat.

One of the most interesting problems connected with the distribution (Map 20) of sweating lies in the gap between Meso-American and other occurrences. In this area, where the practice is absent, there is an environmental correlation; the climate tends to be hot and dry. This undoubtedly discouraged the practice of sweat-bathing.

ARCHITECTURE

Although some would like to dignify the building skill of the Pueblo Indians with the label architecture, the term is here reserved for the much more spectacular achievements of the peoples of Meso-America. This region was a densely populated area with many cities and towns. In central Mexico alone, from Nayarit to the Isthmus of Tehuantepec, the Spanish have left us names of 1,600 communities. From the Isthmus of Tehuantepec to the Bay of Honduras, a territory which includes the Maya, there must have been nearly as many more. The total might have reached 3,000. These communities varied in size from Tenochtitlán, estimated at 300,000 souls, to mere villages. At least one hundred of these centers of population were large enough to be called cities. They differed from our modern cities in being less compact and congested. They were scattered over a wider area, which was more suburban than urban with its garden plots intermingled with dwellings. In the centers of these cities were courts and plazas around which public buildings such as temples, sanctuaries, palaces, pyramids, monasteries, ball courts, dance platforms, and astronomical observatories were assembled. Near these public buildings were the houses of the nobles, priests, and the wealthy, while on the outskirts of the town were located the dwellings of the lowest and poorest class. Public buildings were made of, or at least faced with, stone and, although the Spanish wrecked untold numbers of them to obtain the stones for their Christian churches, a large number still survive as ruins.

130

The true arch is generally regarded as absent in the New World, although the domes of the Eskimo snow house and the Meso-American sweathouse (Clavigero, 1945: 348) could be regarded as examples of the true arch. The corbeled arch, on the other hand, was much used by the Maya and their neighbors for public buildings and has been found by archeologists to date as far back as A.D. 317. Because of the limitations of this arch, there were no large rooms in which hundreds of people might assemble. The

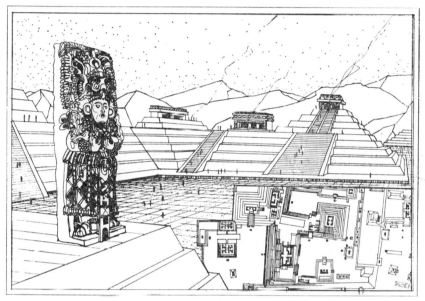

Fig. 20.—Sculpture, ground plan, and elevation from Copan, Honduras

total volume of the walls of such buildings about equaled the room space within. Flat roofs of lime-concrete or adobe supported by logs were probably more common than the corbeled arch. They were similar in all essentials to the flat roofs of dwellings.

The principle of the post and beam is involved with the flat roofs supported by logs but becomes more conspicuous in door-ways or on the façades of buildings. Columns were both round and square and were normally of several blocks of stone, but those employed for mere decoration on the front of the structure were sometimes in the half-round.

Most public buildings in Mexico were built on substructures

which varied from terraces a few feet high to the huge pyramid at Cholula which is 1,150 feet square at the base and rises to a height of over 210 feet. Although this pyramid is less than half as high as the largest in ancient Egypt, its greater base gives it a volume 15 per cent greater. These substructures were ascended by broad, steep stairways on one or more sides.

Buildings in the early centuries of the Christian Era were almost devoid of decoration, but those erected after about A.D. 1000 were embellished with elaborate sculptures. Although geometric designs were common, conventionalized figures of men and animals also abounded. One of the most frequently represented characters was the feathered serpent, Quetzalcoatl, who was a prominent member of the pantheon. He first became obtrusive on the temples and pyramids at Teotihuacán, was later incorporated into Aztec architecture, and still later into that of the Maya. Sculptures consisted of carvings in stone and of modeled figures in baked clay.

On the whole, the architecture of aboriginal Meso-America is impressive because of its massiveness and elaborate sculpturing. Some compare it with the massive and ornate architecture of Hindu origin in Southeast Asia at such famous sites as Angkor Wat and Borobudur.

REFERENCES

Arreola, 1920; Beals, 1932*a;* Beals, Carrasco, McCorkle, 1944; Birket-Smith, 1929, 1936, 1945; Birket-Smith and de Laguna, 1938; Bushnell, 1919, 1922; Clavigero, 1945; Cresson, 1938; Daifuku, 1952; Douglas, 1932; Fairbanks, 1946; Flannery, 1939; Judd, 1948; Krickeberg, 1939; Kroeber, 1925; Linton, 1924*b;* Lowie, 1954; Marquina, 1951; Martin, Quimby, and Collier, 1947; Morgan, 1881; Olson, 1927; Pollock, 1936; Ray, 1939; Sanford, 1947; Satterthwaite, 1952; Smith, 1940; Steward, 1948; Swanton, 1946; Vaillant, 1941; Waterman, 1924; Wissler, 1908, 1938, 1941.

9: CLOTHING

CLOTHING in aboriginal North America exhibits a wide variety of styles and materials which are definitely correlated with geographical environment. The sharp contrasts between the cold of the Arctic, the heat of the tropics, the dampness of the rain forests, and the dryness of the deserts have all had their effect on dress. At the same time, these correlations are far from perfect, because fashion has also played a part. Styles and materials change with the times, and fashions spread from one tribe to another. Clothing is also dependent on other facets of culture, for example, subsistence economy. If a tribe subsists mainly on the flesh of large mammals, it is likely to make its clothing out of hides, which are readily available. The acquisition of the horse increased the efficiency of hunting and encouraged the spread of hide clothing to areas where it had been less common formerly. On the other hand, in areas where people lived mainly on agricultural products seldom were there sufficient hides from which to manufacture clothing for everybody. They more often made clothing of plant materials.

MAJOR STYLES OF CLOTHING

Arctic.—The principal clothing material of the Eskimo was caribou hide, which is warmer, lighter, and more flexible than sealskin. The winter upper garment of both men and women was and is the well-known parka, which consists of two hides sewn together at the sides, with sleeves and hood (Fig. 21); it must be pulled on and off over the head. The length varies, according to locality, from the hips to below the knees. The woman's parka differs from the man's in being cut much fuller so that the infant

133

child may be carried inside it or inside the wider hood. Most of the time the child rides naked, except for its cap, in a hide sling on the mother's naked back. The garment is full enough so that the child may be moved around to the front to nurse without being removed from it. Toilet training begins early under such circumstances.

Men sometimes wore clothing of polar bear fur while waiting

Fig. 21.—Arctic clothing

at breathing holes for seal because exercise was impossible and maximum warmth a necessity. Fox skins were worn in some localities by women.

Both sexes wore fur trousers which seem to have originated by sewing together two leggings. They were made of two pieces with the joining seam running down the middle in front, between the legs, and up the middle in the rear, exactly like modern men's trousers, which are derived from the same Asiatic source. Men's trousers reached to the knee, but women's were much shorter. Both sexes also wore inner garments similar in cut to the outer ones but made of lighter fur. The upper garment lacked the hood and the lower was the length of shorts for men as well as women. In the summer only these inner garments were worn.

On the feet and lower legs both sexes wore fur stockings and fur boots, the stocking being of lighter material than the boot. Grass was sometimes stuffed into the boots for added warmth, either with or without the fur stocking. The sole of the boot was a separate and heavier piece than the upper, which extended nearly to the knee. Women's boots were longer than the men's in order to meet their shorter trousers. Fur sandals were tied on over the boot when the occasion demanded, for instance, in smooth ice hunting when added traction was needed. Mittens with thumb stalls were worn everywhere by both sexes and were necessary to protect the hunter's hands from rope burns and more serious injury from the sealskin thongs used to land sea mammals, as well as against the cold. Gloves with separate finger stalls were unknown aboriginally.

A combination suit all sewed together in one piece like modern coveralls was worn by Greenland whalers. It was made of waterproof sealskin, had parka, mittens, and boots attached, and was put on through a round hole in the abdomen. This hole could be closed tight enough with the drawstring to be waterproof, as could the opening for the face. In case the open whaling boat capsized, the whaler could float in the water, buoyed up by the air within his suit. A similar combination suit was worn by men in Alaska and by children over most of the Arctic.

Snow goggles of wood, or more rarely ivory, with one or two slits to see through, were a necessity in the spring and were used

135

everywhere to prevent snow blindness. Eye shades were also used by men in kayaks in the Hudson straits region, in Greenland, and in Alaska.

The making of clothing fell entirely to the women. Thread was of split sinew, the eyed needle of bone, the thimble of thick skin worn on the index finger, and the sewing direction from left to right. The stitches were the same as ours; for example, running stitch, overcasting, and "blind stitch" in which the needle is run only halfway through the hide. Each article of clothing was owned by the wearer, although it might be loaned to another on occasion.

Skins were colored only in Greenland, where they were dyed red by immersing them in a concoction of driftwood bark, but in other areas banded designs were made by using skins of contrasting natural colors. Women's parkas in the central regions were fringed, and their under garments are elaborately beaded at the present time, the beadwork being most certainly in imitation of other Indians to the south. In the eastern part of the area the lower edge of the woman's parka has a fur border, and the inner garment has a huge collar of trade cloth beautifully embroidered with trade beads. Necklaces and bracelets of fish vertebrae, seal and bear teeth, or fox tarsal bones were worn more often by women than by men. At the present time trade beads on bands of skin have replaced these native items.

Women consistently allowed their hair to grow full length but were careful to do it up close to the head, or to part it in the middle and braid it. Men, on the other hand, always cut their hair in some manner, usually leaving bangs in the front even though the back might be full length. It was not braided and seldom tied up. Tattooing was practiced by all groups and is nearly everywhere confined to the faces of women. This anatomical limitation correlates with the type of clothing where the face is the only visible area. The most widespread tattooing technique is the sewing of lines just under the skin with a sooted thread. This demands the presence of the needle and aboriginally was limited to the Eskimos and the Indians of northwest North America, who probably learned it from Siberia. The pricking method, which is the prevailing one in the rest of North America, and among the

South American marginal cultures, as well as in civilized countries today, is found in the central Eskimo region where the influence of other Indians has been found to be greatest.

Northwest Coast.—The clothing of this area is illustrated in Figure 22. Men sometimes went entirely naked in summer but also wore tunics of woven plant fiber. In winter and on ceremonial occasions a rectangular robe of animal skins or woven plant fiber ex-

FIG. 22.—Northwest Coast clothing

137

tending to the knees was worn. It might be thrown over both shoulders but might also be worn under the left arm and over the right shoulder. The most highly prized fur to Indians and Europeans alike was that of the sea otter, which was nearly exterminated in the first century of European contact. As protection against rain, conical hats of woven plant fiber were worn on the head, and waterproof mats of woven or sewn plant materials cut like a poncho were worn on the body. Moccasins and leggings were known and were worn occasionally when the Indians were traveling to the interior. They were ill-adapted to the damp climate and to boat travel, however, because when wet they were less comfortable than bare legs and feet and stiffened on drying.

Women never went naked in public, except on rare ceremonial occasions, but wore a plant fiber skirt. The upper part of the body, including both shoulders, was covered with a robe of the same material. A woman of rank or wealth might wear a fur robe, but such garments were more often the exclusive possession of the men. Rain hats were sometimes worn by women, but less often than by men because women spent more time indoors. Footgear was also worn less often by women than by men because they traveled less.

A wide variety of bodily ornamentation characterized both sexes. Necklaces, belts, arm and leg banks of shells, teeth, and claws were commonly worn. The ears of both sexes were pierced and the same articles were worn as earrings. Only men pierced the nasal septum and attached ornaments to it. Both sexes were tattooed on the face, chest, front of legs, or back of arms. The designs were often inherited crests which only the owners dared use. Paint of red, black, and white pigments mixed with grease was applied to the bodies of both sexes on gala occasions, and might also depict the inherited crests. Men plucked their beards and women their eyebrows.

Intentional head deformation was practiced in the central part of the area and was of two types: compression of the forehead and back of the head by binding to a cradle board; compression of the entire head in a ring above the ears by binding with hide or flexible plant material. The heads of slaves were not deformed, and this provided a ready way to distinguish them from free men.

In the northernmost part of this area head-binding was not practiced, but slaves who had been obtained by capture from the south usually had deformed heads. Thus the rules of identification were reversed.

Northern Plains.—The styles of clothing worn on the northern Plains at White contact also extended over much of the Sub-Arctic. The Plains is chosen as the type merely because it is better known (Fig. 23).

Fɪɢ. 23.—Northern Plains clothing

There were two articles of clothing which represent the minimum of costume for a Plains man: the breechcloth and moccasins. The former was a strip of buckskin which passed between the legs and under the belt before and aft, or possibly at an earlier time only a small apron which hung down in front. The moccasins were more often the kind with a separate piece of heavy hide for the sole, although those with a continuous piece of buckskin for both sole and upper were also worn. When a man was at home in the summertime he might wear only these items. However, he always kept a buffalo robe on hand to wear when appearing in public or in cold weather. When traveling, a man wore full-length leggings tied at the top to his belt. The breechcloth, leggings, and

139

moccasins combined covered practically all the body from the waist down and gave the appearance of trousers from a distance. A buckskin shirt with flaps for sleeves was worn on the upper part of the body in winter or on gala occasions. This was normally made of two deerskins. The head was left bare most of the time, but a fur cap might be worn or the robe pulled over the head in winter.

Plains women wore more clothing than the men. The main garment was a dress made of two deer or elk hides sewn together with the tail ends up. The tails of the animals and part of the skin of the hind legs folded downward to form a yoke. Such dresses reached to the calf and were fringed at the bottom. Women's leggings reached only to the knee, and their moccasins were of the same types as those of the men. Fur robes were worn primarily by men, but women sometimes wore them in winter.

Both sexes wore the hair in two braids. Men sometimes artificially lengthened their hair by gumming on extra strands until it dragged on the ground. Men wore feathers in the hair aboriginally, and these culminated in the nineteenth-century war bonnet familiar to every schoolboy. Claws, teeth, and shells were worn as beads around the neck or as ear ornaments. There was little tattooing and noses were seldom pierced. The hair on the face and parts of the body was pulled out with small tweezers. A porcupine tail was used for a hairbrush.

Southeast.—The clothing of this area is illustrated in Figure 24. The one indispensable article of clothing for men was the buckskin breechcloth which went between the legs. It was about a yard in length and was held in place by a belt around the waist. The ends hung down in both the front and the rear, giving the appearance of two aprons. Men wore untailored robes or mantles over the upper part of their bodies in winter or on formal occasions. These were made of furs, either of a whole hide of a large animal such as the buffalo or a patchwork of small animal hides, of feathers thatched on a netted foundation, or of woven inner bark. Such a robe might cover both shoulders but often was worn under the left arm and knotted on the right shoulder. When traveling, men wore full-length leggings, fastened to the belt, and moccasins.

Women in the Southeast wore a wrap-around skirt reaching

from the waist to the knees. It was of buckskin, woven inner
bark, or woven bison hair. Most of the time they went naked
above the waist, as did the men, but in winter and on special
occasions they wore robes of the same materials and in the same
manner as the men. Women's leggings were only half-length and
were fastened by a garter just below the knee. The wealthier
women sometimes wore moccasins, but not regularly.

Neither sex habitually wore any form of headgear, although
priests and officials decorated their heads with symbols of their

FIG. 24.—Southeastern clothing

supernatural powers and offices. Women allowed their hair to grow full length and parted, braided, or put it up on top of the head. Men shaved their hair, except for a scalp lock from the crown, or allowed enough to grow to form a longitudinal ruff which stood up like a crew haircut. Both sexes plucked out all body hair with tweezers of clam shells.

Both men and women pierced the ears and wore ear ornaments of shiny stones, pieces of shell, or feathers, all of which were later replaced by trade metal. Men, at least, pierced the nasal septum and wore similar kinds of ornaments in the nose. Both sexes were tattooed by pricking the skin and rubbing in soot. The most elaborate designs were worn by warriors and chiefs, who recorded their valorous deeds in this symbolism. Face, trunk, arms, and legs were all tattooed. The head was intentionally deformed by pressure from a bag of sand or a buckskin-covered block of wood applied to the heads of infants. The cradle board was hollowed out slightly to receive the back of the head, and the infant lay on its back on this board with its head lower than its body and bag or block pressing on its forehead.

Painting in a wide variety of colors and designs all over the body was resorted to for war, mourning, ball games, and other ceremonial occasions, mostly by men. A great variety of necklaces, arm bands, leg bands, and belts were also worn: strings of pearls, and manufactured beads of bone, stone, or shell, for instance. Garters and belts of woven bison and opossum hair were also common. Women wore turtle shells containing pebbles and bunches of deer hoofs on their legs to produce a rhythmic rattle when dancing.

Although sharply defined social classes did not occur everywhere, differences in rank were reflected in dress. The quantity and quality of clothing was some indication of rank, whether acquired by noble deeds or by amassing wealth. Chiefs' families were consistently better dressed than the average citizen.

Oasis.—The Pueblo Indians of Arizona and New Mexico were the only Indians, living wholly within what is now the United States, who wore garments made of cotton cloth in pre-Columbian times. Skins were also used for clothing, but cotton predominated. Pueblo clothing is illustrated in Figure 25.

The men wore between the legs a piece of cotton cloth which

was held in place by passing the ends over a belt. A second piece of the same material was wrapped around the waist to form a kilt from seventeen to twenty inches in length. A few kilts were made of buckskin, for instance those worn in the Hopi snake dance. A sash of braided cotton cords was worn on top of the kilt. A cotton shirt, which was nothing more than a rectangular piece of cloth with a woven-in hole for the head in the middle, was sometimes worn. It was tied at the sides rather than sewn, and sometimes smaller rectangular pieces of the same material were tied on at the

Fig. 25.—Pueblo clothing

143

shoulders to form half-length flaps or sleeves. Moccasins had a separate stiff piece of buffalo hide for the sole but the upper, which covered the ankle or reached halfway to the knee, was of buckskin. Full-length leggings, like those of the Plains, were worn by men of the easternmost Pueblos. Blankets woven of twisted strips of rabbit fur were thrown over the upper part of the body in cold weather, and a garment of feathers thatched on a net foundation was sometimes worn in the same manner.

Women wore a kind of dress which was nothing more than a rectangular piece of cotton cloth worn under the left arm and tied over the right shoulder. It was not sewn together or fastened at the right side except by a belt of the same material. An additional piece of cloth of about the same size may have been worn on top of the dress as a shawl. On the feet and lower half of the leg a combination moccasin and legging was worn. The sole was of buffalo hide, to which was sewn a piece of buckskin large enough to fold over the toe and instep. A strip of buckskin three or four feet long was wound around the moccasin proper and on up the leg to just below the knee, where it was tied fast. The legging part resembled a First World War puttee.

Both sexes cut their hair just above the eyes in front, just below the ears at the sides, but allowed it to grow full length in back. The long hair was gathered together with a cord or done up in a cylindrical knot at the back of the neck. The hairbrush was a cylindrical bundle of plant stems tied together in the middle. Men wore most of the jewelry, which consisted of beads of turquoise and other precious stones as well as shells. These were worn as necklaces and ear ornaments.

Meso-America.—There is no doubt that in this area clothing attained a greater degree of elaboration and distinction than elsewhere on the continent. The descriptions from the Conquest, native codices and murals, as at Bonampak, all attest to the colorful and varied nature of the costumes (Fig. 26).

The preferred clothing material was woven cotton cloth; in many parts of the area, as among the Aztecs and the Mixtecs, only the nobility could use this material. Commoners wore clothing woven of *ixtle* (maguey fiber). Prohibitive laws enforced this class distinction. Dog hair was the only form of wool and, because of its scarcity, was used more for decoration than for the body of any cloth. Occasionally, twisted strips of rabbit fur were interwoven with cotton to produce a heavier and warmer fabric. Mantles of feathers, attached to a cloth base by threads or by paste, were also worn. The cheaper ones were covered with feathers of the domesticated turkey, but the finer were overlaid with the multihued and brilliant plumage of tropical wild birds.

FIG. 26.—Meso-American clothing

145

The common man wore sandals of hide or woven agave fiber (*cactli*) on the feet, a woven breechcloth (*maxtlatl*) between the legs and around the waist, with the ends hanging down the front, back, or both, and a knee-length cloth mantle tied over a shoulder and running under the opposite arm. Sometimes the mantle covered both shoulders and was fastened at the neck in front. In cold weather a man might add a sleeveless tunic (*xicolli*), which was naturally worn under the robe. Men banged their hair at the forehead, allowed locks resembling sideburns to extend down the sides of the face, and cut the hair behind the ears to shoulder length.

Women wore a wrap-around skirt (*cueitl*) of cloth from waist to calf and on the upper part of the body a sleeveless blouse which was similar to the tunic worn less often by men. There were two distinct types of these blouses. In the south and west of Meso-America the *huipil*, a straight sleeveless blouse, was worn; whereas in the north and east of the area the *quesquemitl*, a capelike blouse, predominated. Women went barefoot a greater part of the time than did men but might don sandals for a special occasion or a long walk. Women's hair was cut like that of men in front and at the sides, but was allowed to grow full length in the back. Sometimes they braided the hair or braided ribbons into it and then wrapped the braids around the head.

Both sexes pierced the ears and wore conspicuous cylindrical plugs in them, but only the men pierced the nasal septum and the lower lip and wore ornaments in these orifices.

Clothes reflected social status among the Meso-Americans. Costumes of renowned warriors, priests, and chiefs bristled with symbols of their offices. They were decorated with copper, gold, silver, jade, turquoise, emeralds, and opals. Elaborate headdresses of the colored feathers of wild tropical birds and body painting in a half-dozen hues added to the glamor of these important personages.

GEOGRAPHICAL DISTRIBUTIONS

Dominant clothing materials.—Hide was almost the exclusive clothing material in a huge area which included the Arctic, Sub-Arctic, Plains, Prairies, and the northeastern United States (Map 21). This area corresponds closely to that in which hunting was the dominant subsistence economy (Map 3). The relation of the two is obvious. Where animals were slain in quantity, hides were always available for clothing. The severe winters of the Arctic and Sub-Arctic also made fur clothing a necessity for hunters who spent most of their time in the open in pursuit of game. The few plants available in these areas could not have furnished adequate material for clothing. Animal hair or wool was used for minor articles of clothing or as decoration on clothing by many of the tribes in this area of dominant hide clothing, but the nomadic way of life followed by the vast majority discouraged the development of loom weaving of wool cloth in pieces large enough for entire garments.

Hide, fur, and wild plant materials were used jointly on the Northwest Coast, the Plateau, in California, the Great Basin, Northeast Mexico, part of the Oasis, and in the East as far north as Cape Cod (Map 21). Bast (inner bark) was probably the most important plant material. It was woven on the North Pacific Coast, in the Southeast, and to a lesser extent in other parts of this large area. So fine was the weave and so white was the color of mantles of this material in the Southeast that the Spanish mistook it for cotton. Unwoven grasses, mosses, rushes, and leaves were also widely used for clothing, especially by women. Skirts or aprons of such materials resembled the palm fiber skirts of the South Pacific, which are familiar to everyone as the costume of Hawaiian hula dancers. Mats of whole stems of rushes and cattails, woven or sewn together, were worn as raincoats, especially on the Northwest Coast and Plateau. Hide and fur was worn to some extent elsewhere in this mixed area. For example, fur robes were common on the Northwest Coast, Plateau, California, and the East. They were absent or little used in areas where large game was scarce such as the Great Basin, Northeast Mexico, Oasis, and Meso-America. However, garments woven of twisted strips of rabbit fur served as a substitute in these areas.

Cotton was the dominant or preferred clothing material in much of the Oasis, most of Meso-America, and part of the Circum-Caribbean area (Map 21). It was the 26-chromosome domesticated cotton. Where it was not raised, it was obtained as woven cloth in trade. Its distribution in these areas closely follows that of other cultivated plants (Map 3). It was not raised at all in the present-

147

day cotton belt of the southeastern United States. It was even traded in limited quantity outside its area of dominance. For example, cotton cloth and turquoise were observed by De Soto's expedition in Caddo territory in 1542. The natives there said they had obtained these articles in trade from the west, which probably meant the Pueblos. Although the area of cotton dominance or preference is smaller than the other two areas shown on Map 21, its population was much larger, so that cotton clothed considerable numbers of people. In Meso-America the poorer classes often wove their cloth for garments out of the fiber of the agave, which was both a wild and a domesticated plant. Because the poor outnumbered the rich, this fiber may have clothed greater numbers of people than any other material in aboriginal North America. Fur, especially that of the jaguar, was worn as part of the costumes of officials and priests but was a negligible item in the clothing of the population as a whole in Meso-America.

Historically, domesticated cotton in North America is a clear case of a single origin with subsequent diffusion, as was pointed out in the chapter on horticulture.

Fur-strip clothing.—Furs of small animals were often sewn together to form a patchwork robe large enough to cover the human figure. For example, furs of the sea otter were combined in this manner on the Northwest Coast to produce the most valuable single article of clothing known to the culture. Another technique, most often applied to rabbit skins, was also widely used. These skins were removed without a longitudinal cut, resulting in a fur in the shape of a hollow cylinder. This was cut spirally into a single continuous strip of fur an inch or so in width. A number of these were joined together at the ends and twisted or braided to form a fur rope which was finally woven, netted, or sewn into a rectangular or circular shape. The resulting blanket was used for bedding or worn as a mantle. This technique was common in the Sub-Arctic, Plateau, California, Great Basin, and Oasis and was practiced by the Aztecs, at least, in Meso-America. It was probably more common in these areas than the patchwork technique before the appearance of trade needles. The fur-strip technique was laborious enough but probably more efficient than sewing without a needle.

There were at least three separate techniques for joining the fur strips to form a blanket. First there was the knotless netting of most of the Sub-Arctic, which was usually done in a circle without fastening the strips to a frame. Second, among the Ingalik, the strips were first braided together and then sewn into an oval shape in a clockwise direction as in making coiled baskets. Third, in the rest of the area, from the Plateau to Meso-America, the strips were fastened to a two-bar frame and were woven together by finger methods. The result was a rectangular blanket. Too little is known of these techniques to provide reliable historical inferences. However, parts of such blankets have been found in the Oasis and Great Basin at archeological levels dating from the beginning of the Christian Era.

Feather clothing.—Feathers were thatched onto a foundation of netting or cloth, working from the bottom upward. The result was a garment which was water repellent, less warm than fur and, above all, decorative when made from brightly colored feathers. Such garments were common in California, Meso-America, and the East. This is the familiar reversed Y distribution, suggesting southern origin. These feather garments were probably worn more frequently for show than for warmth or protection from rain. They were often worn in ceremonies or by special persons such as shamans, priests, or officials. Being less warm and lighter in weight than fur was an advantage in the areas in which they were used.

Aboriginal uses of wool or hair.—Large garments of woven wool or hair were characteristic of only three areas: Northwest Coast, Prairies, and Southeast. On the Northwest Coast the hair of the wild mountain goat was most frequently used in the northern half of the area, while that of a domesticated dog was added to it among the Salish tribes farther south. Wild mountain sheep hair was used to a lesser extent here and there, as was the inner bark of the cedar, which was combined with wool to form the warp elements. In the north, members of the Chilkat tribelet, a subdivision of the Tlingit, were the most industrious weavers and traded their blankets to many other tribes. In 1779, Captain Cook found such blankets among the Pacific Eskimos, who said they had obtained them in trade from the Tlingit. Woolen garments consisted entirely of rectangular blankets which were draped around the body. There was no tailoring.

On the Prairies and in the Southeast the most common animal fiber was buffalo hair, although opossum hair was also used to some extent. As on the Northwest Coast, the only shape of these garments was the rectangular shape of the woven material itself, but they seem to have been made in more sizes because some are called kilts instead of blankets. Nevertheless, the word blanket is used much more frequently than any other term to describe them. In addition, a number of small articles of wearing apparel, such as bands worn around the head, neck, waist, arms, and legs, were also woven of buffalo and opossum hair.

In a vast area across the Sub-Arctic, probably stretching continuously from Bering Sea to New England, moose hair was embroidered on hide clothing. It was often dyed several colors so that the effect produced was superficially similar to that of dyed porcupine quills.

In the Middle West bags were woven of buffalo hair, and on the Plains ropes were made of the same material. All of the ropes used to bridle and picket horses were made of buffalo hair. In Meso-America the hair of the domesticated dog and of wild rats and rabbits was occasionally used for embroidery on cotton clothing.

Other clothing materials.—Porcupine quill decoration on hide clothing was widespread in aboriginal North America and, except for its absence in the Arctic, conformed closely in distribution to the area where hunting was the dominant food pursuit (Map 3). The quills were dyed a variety of colors and were sewn onto buckskin with sinews. They were also woven into bands which were attached as a unit to costumes. In historic times quills were largely replaced by glass trade beads. Many of the elaborate designs so plentiful in nineteenth-century beadwork were formerly made with porcupine quills. Most tribes employing porcupine quill decoration hunted the animal locally, but in the Plains area, where the porcupine was absent, some tribes obtained the quills in trade, while others made special trips to the mountains to obtain porcupines.

Unwoven bark cloth competed with cotton in Central America and adjacent Mexico as a clothing material, but seems to have been less used than cotton. Pieces of inner bark were beaten with a wooden mallet into pieces of material large enough for breech-cloths or wrap-around skirts. The place of origin of bark cloth is undoubtedly South America, where it was more extensively used. Inner bark was also used for papermaking in Mexico.

Tailored hide clothing.—Strictly tailored clothing, with hood attached to upper garment, full-length sleeves, trousers, moccasins, and mittens, was limited to the Eskimos and their immediate Indian neighbors in Alaska and on the Labrador peninsula. In the historic period, many imitations of European clothing were worn in the Sub-Arctic and East.

The history of tailored clothing is an interesting one. It probably goes back to Upper Paleolithic times when the eyed needle first appeared. The climate of Europe at that time was cold, and the bones of animals slain by man have been found in sufficient quantity to suggest that hides were plentiful. Tailored hide clothing apparently originated somewhere on the Eurasian continent at this early time. Although northern Asia is often given as the place of origin, we must remember that it was under a solid ice sheet much of the time in the Upper Paleolithic. Tailored clothing, therefore, was probably first used in the middle latitudes of Eurasia and spread north and east as the glaciers retreated. Because Eskimo culture in North America goes back only about 2,000 years, we can be quite certain that the Eskimos derived their tailored clothing from Siberia.

Semitailored clothing, like that described above for the northern Plains, was also worn over most of the Sub-Arctic. Leggings were cut to fit, and moccasins were sometimes sewed to them. Sleeves, however, usually consisted of half-length flaps, except in the Eastern Sub-Arctic where separate fur sleeves were worn. The upper garments of men and the dresses of women were cut a little to conform to the human body although the shape of the hide of the animal was still discernible. No very close counterpart of this style of clothing is reported for Asia. It has either been replaced by more modern garments in Asia or has originated in North America. In the historic period the Plains type of clothing spread south to the Apaches on the Mexican border, east to the Iroquoians, southeast to the Chickasaw and the Natchez in Mississippi, and west to the

Pacific Coast. These imitations of aboriginal Plains clothing often showed minor differences from the earlier forms; for example, the man's shirt might be made of a single deerskin instead of two. At the present time Plains type clothing has replaced most other kinds of Indian clothing for occasions in which Indians appear in costume. Its diffusion accelerated after the acquisition of the horse, about 1750, and even today, Indians of both the Southwest and the Northwest are still adding more and more Plains items to their costumes worn on gala occasions.

In much of the Sub-Arctic, tailored coats with an opening in front, like European garments, were worn. Although the European origin and post-contact time level of these garments cannot always be proved for each locality, this explanation is the best one for almost all of these coats. Some of the trousers in the same area may also have been derived from European models.

Headgear and haircutting.—Headgear was continuously worn outdoors only by the Eskimos in winter; in summer these people often went around with the parka hood removed from the head. In other areas utilitarian headgear was confined to winter or to the rainy season. Fur caps, separate from the upper garment, were sometimes worn by the Eskimos, but were more characteristic of Sub-Arctic, Plateau, and northern Plains peoples. Buckskin caps were worn on the Plains, in the East, in the Great Basin, and in the Oasis, but mainly as war bonnets. They served as foundations to which feathers and other showy articles might be attached. Women seldom wore fur caps in northern areas and never the buckskin caps of the more southern latitudes.

In the Far West, utilitarian hats and caps, woven like basketry from plant materials, were regularly worn. On the North Pacific Coast, from Kodiak Island to the Columbia River, broad-brimmed rain hats were worn by both sexes in rainy weather. These are surprisingly similar to the "straw" hats of China and Japan. On the Plateau, in the Great Basin, and in California and Lower California, a smaller-brimmed or completely brimless basketry cap was worn principally by women to protect the forehead from the carrying strap, but here and there was worn almost continuously. Although the history of basket hats and caps is not indisputably known, the two types seem to go back to a common origin, but their more recent histories represent two different adaptations to two different physical and cultural environments.

Hairdressing shows a great deal of variation from tribe to tribe and area to area. Nevertheless, a few generalizations are possible. Over much of North America both sexes allowed the hair to grow full length. Exceptions were the Eskimo men, who cut their hair in some manner, peoples of the Oasis and Meso-America, where the men wore a long bob, and the men of the Prairies and East, who cut their hair in a number of styles. In the latter two areas, the scalp was often shaved so that the remaining hair formed a pattern, and the most common pattern was a longitudinal roach or ruff. Sometimes a ruff of animal hair—often the white hair of a deer's tail dyed a brilliant red—was worn like a wig. This wiglike ruff was worn in all those places where a natural ruff was the fashion, except in the Southeast. At present the aboriginal manner of headshaving is not practiced, but many of those who participate in costumed dances or ceremonies wear the roached headdress of animal hair.

Stockings and leggings.—Almost all the Eskimos wore hide stockings or grass socks inside their boots, and about half the Sub-Arctic peoples either wore hide stockings or sewed their moccasins to the bottoms of leggings or breeches. Thigh-length leggings were worn by men over most of the continent north of Mexico, although many of the instances west of the Rockies and a number in the East are probably historic. European influence is discernible in those in the East. Long leggings were everywhere associated with the breechcloth which, when the two were combined, approached the completeness of trousers. In the Far West men wore only knee-length leggings or none at all, and a few instances of knee-length leggings are reported from other areas. Leggings were worn less continuously than moccasins.

In the Arctic, women's stockings were similar to men's except that they were sometimes longer in order to meet the shorter trousers. Over most of the area where men wore thigh-length leggings, women wore them only knee length and fastened them with garters just below the knee. Women's dresses or skirts usually extended below the knee, making a longer legging unnecessary. In the Far West, where men's leggings were knee length, women

153

wore them the same length or dispensed with them entirely. Because men traveled more, leggings were more common among them than among women.

Moccasins.—There were as many kinds of moccasins in North America as there were tribes wearing them. The moccasins of each tribe differed in some detail from those of all the other tribes. On the Plains and Prairies, it was said that a man's tribal affiliation could be determined from his tracks. Where the cut of the moccasin showed no tribal specialization, the decoration of porcupine quill work or moose hair embroidery (later of glass beads) exhibited a particular tribal style.

Fortunately, the fundamental construction of the moccasin falls into two major types: the soft-soled, made from a single and continuous piece of buckskin for both sole and upper; and the hard-soled, consisting of a buckskin upper sewed fast to a heavier and stiffer piece of hide for the sole. The hard-soled variety predominated in the Arctic, the Great Basin, the Oasis, and Plains (Map 22). In the areas depicted as having both types, the hard-soled seems to have been more frequently worn. The soft-soled type was characteristic of the Sub-Arctic, Plateau, northern Prairies, and East. The soft-soled type is generally regarded as more efficient for use with snowshoes, and the area of its exclusive occurrence correlates fairly well with the distribution of snowshoes. However, the soft-soled moccasin has spread all the way to the Gulf in the Southeast and to the Mexican border in the Southwest, far beyond the limits of snowshoes.

The distribution of the hard-soled moccasin is more difficult to explain. Its Oasis, Great Basin, and Plains occurrences favor derivation from the hide sandal. However that may be, a hard and stiff sole is good protection from the thorns and stones of the deserts and plains of the West. In the wooded East, the soft-soled type was sufficient. The hard- and separate-soled Eskimo boots appear to have developed independently of the hard-soled forms of footgear to the south. The Eskimo boot is apparently of Asiatic origin, and may even be historically related to the riding boots of Asia.

Sandals.—Sandals have a strange distribution. Those worn by the Central and Eastern Eskimo and Chipewyan were usually pieces of fur tied on over the regular boot to give added traction on slippery ice or make it possible for a hunter to tread silently from one seal breathing hole to another. The hide sandals used by the Lillooet and Shuswap on the Plateau were worn only by those so poor that they did not have enough skin for a moccasin. Although it has been proposed that Eskimo sandals are remotely related historically to hide sandals in the Southwest and Mexico, this relationship seems unlikely. The true hide sandals of the south are made from dehaired skins and are associated with a hot dry climate, as they are in the Old World. They are characteristic only of Mexico and Central America. Sandals made of plant fibers were also worn in the same areas but extended farther north into the Oasis and Great Basin in the United States.

Footgear frequency.—Footgear was worn most of the time in a huge area which corresponds closely with that of the dominance of hide and fur for clothing (Map 21). It is also significant for the continent as a whole that moccasins were the kind of footgear which was worn daily. Warmth, as well as protection, was a factor, especially in the north. Sandals were worn less regularly and seem often to have been reserved for trips or gala occasions. Because they provided no warmth, there were no marked seasonal differences in frequency of use. In the Southeast, both the heavier rainfall and warmer climate discouraged the daily wearing of moccasins, and even when traveling, a group of men would often stop to take off their moccasins when it began to rain. Footgear seems to have been totally lacking in the West Indies, or at least was little worn. The combination of heavy rainfall and much time spent in boats and on the beach made footwear impractical, just as it did on the Northwest Coast.

Hand and arm covering.—Mittens with thumb stalls were regularly worn in winter in the Arctic, Sub-Arctic, on the Plateau, and northern Plains. They were a necessity without which a hunter could not function with top efficiency. This was especially true of the Eskimo, for the sudden jerk of a powerful sea mammal on a line held in the bare hands might sever a finger. In other areas, mittens kept the fingers warm enough to permit accurate shooting of the bow and arrow and the manipulation of other weapons as well.

In the western United States, more specifically in California, the Great Basin, and the Oasis, hunters carried a fur muff in winter to keep their hands warm enough to shoot the bow effectively. This muff was generally a cased skin turned wrong side out so that the fur was on the inside. Because quivers were frequently made of such skins, the origin of the muff is not very puzzling.

In the eastern Sub-Arctic and the adjacent northern fringes of the Plains, Prairies, and East, detachable sleeves of fur were worn in cold weather, especially by women. One or two such sleeves might be worn; in the latter case they were usually held on by a cord across the shoulders connecting the two. These were apparently worn with sleeveless dresses or tunics which were held up by shoulder straps, but may have also been added to the more typical Sub-Arctic upper garment which at least covered the shoulders.

DIVISION OF LABOR

The sexual division of labor in clothing manufacture depends partly on the materials from which the clothing was made. For most of North America north of Mexico, where hide material predominated, women made most of the clothing. In California and the Great Basin, where both hide and plant materials were worn, no definite division of labor prevailed. In the northwestern Oasis, men made most of the clothing, although it consisted of both hide and woven plant materials. In Meso-America women made most of the clothing out of the cloth they wove, but in urban centers men specialists sometimes wove textiles and fashioned them into clothing.

REFERENCES

BEALS, 1932a; BIRKET-SMITH, 1929, 1936, 1945; BIRKET-SMITH AND DE LAGUNA, 1938; CARR, 1897; CONN, 1955; DAHLGREN, 1954; DEMBO AND IMBELLONI, 1938; DIENES, 1947; DINGWALL, 1931; FARABEE, 1921; FLANNERY, 1939; GODDARD, 1945; HATT, 1916; JACOBSON, 1952; JENNESS, 1932; JOHNSON, 1953; KINIETZ, 1940; KRIEGER, 1929; KROEBER, 1925; MARTIN, QUIMBY, AND COLLIER, 1947; ORCHARD, 1929; ROEDIGER, 1941; SINCLAIR, 1909; DU SOLIER, 1950; SPECK, 1911, 1928; STEWARD, 1948; SWANTON, 1946; UNDERHILL, n.d.; WISSLER, 1916, 1926, 1938, 1941.

10: CRAFTS

THERE was much variation in crafts from one area to another, as in other aspects of Indian culture. The crafts to be described in this chapter have been selected on the basis of widespread occurrence, except for metallurgy, which was confined to Meso-America and the area around the Caribbean. There is a high correlation between the number of distinct crafts practiced by a people and their general level of cultural achievement. Meso-America attained by far the highest standards of craftsmanship and is universally regarded as having possessed the most advanced total culture in North America; indeed it ranks as an equal with Incan Peru. At the same time, areas of modest general achievement might become expert in single crafts. For example, the basketry of the California Indians is ranked among the finest in the world.

As an introduction to basketry and pottery, let us first discuss containers in general. In chapter v we gave descriptions of the more common kinds of boiling vessels. The dominant forms of containers used for other purposes are shown on Map 23. Thus the Eskimo used hide containers for water pails, for storing and transporting meat, and for many other purposes about the household. The dominance of hunting in the subsistence economy provided an ample supply of hides for every use. Dishes were carved out of wood but, because of its scarcity in most of Eskimo territory, wood was used less often for containers than was hide.

The other area where hide predominated was the Plains. One of the most common articles of hide there was the parfleche, which was simply a piece of rawhide folded together like an envelope to form a container. Food especially was carried in the parfleche, but other articles might also be included. In historic times a horse carried two parfleches, one on each side. Other common hide containers were quivers, tobacco pouches, berry mashers, cases for sacred objects, and medicine bundles. As among the Eskimos, hunting was the basis of subsistence.

Bark, especially birch bark, was the dominant material for containers in the entire Sub-Arctic from Alaska to Nova Scotia. The bark was curved or bent into the desired shape and sewed where necessary with strands made from roots. Such vessels served as water pails, carrying containers, food storage receptacles, berrying baskets, dishes, trays for winnowing wild rice, and troughs for making maple sugar. They could be made much more rapidly than woven basketry but wore out sooner.

Wooden containers predominated on the Northwest Coast in Canada and Alaska. They were of two main types: dugouts and boxes. The dugouts were made by hollowing out a solid chunk of wood. Dishes, ladles, and oil storage vessels were commonly made in this manner. Box containers were made by bending and sewing boards together. They were thinner-walled and lighter than dugouts. They were used for water pails and as storage containers for a wide variety of things from food to sacred objects, and even as coffins. The Northwest Coast was the area where woodwork reached its highest development.

Woven basketry containers predominated on the Plateau, the Northwest Coast of the United States, in California, the Great Basin, Northeast Mexico, part of the Oasis, a small fraction of the Prairies, and in the East. Baskets were put to dozens of uses in these areas. They were used by women for gathering plant foods, for carrying loads on the back, as water pails and dishes, and as storage containers for all materials stored in and around the house. Special shapes were used for winnowing, sifting, gambling, and even for housing rattlesnakes. In the western half of this basketry area, pottery was absent or scarce. In the deserts of the Great Basin, drinking water was carried in a jug-shaped woven container, plastered on the outside with pitch to make it completely waterproof. In the eastern half of the basketry area, on the other hand, pottery was universal and served for water pails as well as cooking vessels. There was no point in making baskets watertight, and indeed they were far from it. As we shall see later, the weaves and materials also differed in east and west.

Pottery vessels were the dominant non-cooking (as well as cooking) containers among the more sedentary tribes of the Oasis, in Meso-America, and in the Circum-Caribbean area. Basketry was also known but was less common about the household. Besides their use as cooking pots, pottery vessels were used for dishes, water jars, storage of food, as incense burners, and even for burial urns. The total number of uses would probably exceed that for basketry. The area of pottery dominance corresponds closely to that of greatest dependence on agriculture and most sedentary mode of life.

WEAVING

Basketry, bags, and matting.—Basketry, bags, and matting are treated as a unit because the technique of manufacture is often the same. Mats, by definition, are always flat and essentially two dimensional. They were used most commonly as floor coverings, house coverings, mattresses, and raincoats. Baskets, on the other hand, were made in a wide variety of three dimensional shapes, and the number of different uses to which they were put was as great as the number of shapes. Bags are intermediate between basketry and matting in that they are essentially two dimensional when empty and three dimensional when filled. They are more flexible than basketry and more finely woven than mats. The artistic embellishment of basketry far exceeded that of matting, and probably also that of bags. Most of the basketry made by North American Indians was decorated in some way, with design elements running into the thousands. Because basketry, bag, and matting weaves are fewer in number than shapes, uses, and decorations, this brief survey will be restricted to weaving techniques.

There are three major kinds of basketry weaves: coiling, twining, and plaiting (Fig. 27). Although each in turn may be further divided into a number of varieties, the three categories are mutually exclusive. Even when two are employed in the manufacture of a single basket, it is easy to see where one weave leaves off and the other begins. In coiling, the warp or foundation element is horizontal and its coils are sewn together with a flexible vertical weft

159

element; in twining, the vertical warp elements are fastened together with pairs of horizontal wefts which are twisted between each adjacent pair of warps; in plaiting, there is no distinction between warp and weft, because both elements are of equal size, shape, flexibility, and activity in the weaving process. The two principal kinds of plaiting are checker and twill.

Mats are commonly twined or plaited, but rarely, if ever, coiled. Mats of whole plant stems may also be held together by sewing: piercing each stem at intervals with needle or awl and inserting

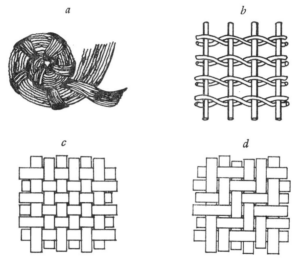

Fig. 27.—Basketry weaves, coiling (*a*), twining (*b*), checker (*c*), and twill (*d*)

cords which bind the stems in a parallel row. This sewing is, of course, not true weaving. Bags also are normally twined or plaited, rarely coiled.

The geographical distributions of coiling and twining are given on Map 24. Coiling is the dominant basketry technique in the Arctic, although baskets there were rare or unimportant in most localities. Mats and bags were still less numerous. Although actual specimens have been collected from all the localities indicated on the map, some of those from the western Arctic were not manufactured locally but were obtained in trade from neighboring Indians in the Sub-Arctic. Coiling was the exclusive technique in the Plains area, where it was limited to gambling trays. In a third area in the

160

western Sub-Arctic, from the Han tribe to the Carrier, coiling was the only technique known. Here woven baskets were more numerous and more important than among the Eskimos, but they still seem to have been dominated by birch-bark vessels. The other area of exclusive coiling is Lower California, where basketry was the dominant type of container.

Twining reaches its maximum development on the North Pacific Coast, where basketry rivals wooden containers in importance in the culture. Coiling and twining occur together in Alaska, where coiling is the more frequent, and again in a much larger area farther south which includes the Plateau, Great Basin, Oasis, and most of California. In all of these latter areas except the Great Basin, coiling is more frequent than twining.

Baskets used for stone boiling were either twined or coiled. Both techniques employed fine materials which were woven so tightly that when wet they would swell enough to make the basket practically watertight. The bulk of the materials employed in the manufacture of twined and coiled baskets were whole stems or whole roots of small plants. The bark was usually removed, although sometimes the bark was the part used. The stems or roots were also sometimes split to make a finer or flatter weaving material.

Coiled baskets were almost always tightly woven, but the twining technique was well adapted to both close work and open work. As a result, baskets used to carry or store coarse materials were more often twined than coiled in areas where both techniques were known. Basketry fish traps, most characteristic of the Pacific Coast, were also twined.

The twining on the Prairies is confined to buffalo-hair bags and mats of whole plant stems, and that in the East to mats. The stems were laid parallel to one another and fastened together with pairs of cords which were twined around each stem at intervals of a foot or so.

Plaiting is the dominant basketry, bag, and matting technique in the East, the Mexican part of the Oasis, Meso-America, and the Circum-Caribbean area (Map 25) but is a minor method in all other areas of its occurrence. It was employed principally in mat-making on the Northwest Coast and the Plateau, although in these areas it was also commonly used in starting the bottoms of baskets

161

which were otherwise twined. Occasionally it was employed in those areas in the manufacture of an entire basket. Plaiting, however, could not produce watertight containers. It is significant that its greatest development occurred in areas where cooking vessels and water containers were consistently made of pottery.

The materials used in plaiting were rarely whole stems of plants but consisted usually of strips of material cut and prepared in a uniform manner. It was important that the material be flattish in cross section, not round as for coiled and twined weaves. In the Southeast, strips were cut from pieces of cane, and farther north, where cane did not grow, "splints" were cut from solid woods such as hickory and oak. Among the Hidatsas, Mandans, and Arikaras of the upper Missouri River, strips of rawhide were plaited together to form containers. Materials used in plaiting were consistently coarser than those employed in twining and coiling, with the result that a plaited basket could be made in a fraction of the time required to make other types. Splints from solid woods were larger than those from cane, and the speed with which these baskets could be made was sufficient to give rise to the manufacture of quantities of such baskets for trade to Whites. These are still being made to this day by Indians from Minnesota to Maine.

Women made most of the baskets, bags, and mats in all areas north of Mexico. The exceptions consisted of fishing baskets and other types used exclusively by men, and baby cradles, which men sometimes made. In Meso-America, by way of contrast, baskets and mats were often made by male specialists who devoted a considerable portion of their time to this craft. In historic times in the eastern United States, splint basketry for the White trade was often made by men, but in pre-Columbian times women seem to have made all the basketry and matting.

Twining and plaiting are both found at the earliest levels of the Ocampo Caves in southwest Tamaulipas, Mexico, where the time range is about 7000–5500 B.C. (Whitaker, Cutler, and MacNeish, 1957). Another early date for twining is about 7000 B.C. at Danger Cave, Utah (Jennings, 1957:93, 257). Coiling has not yet been found at such early archeological levels but appears in association with other materials dated at about 2500 B.C. from the same area of Tamaulipas (MacNeish, 1955:111). Coiling has also been found in level three in Danger Cave, Utah, but that level has not been dated by radiocarbon technique; interpolation betweens levels two and four suggests about 4500 B.C. Plaiting is the dominant technique in most of South America and covers a continuous area with the North American data presented on Map 25. It seems likely that plaiting in the eastern United States, Meso-America, and the Circum-Caribbean area has a common origin with that in South America. The plaiting on the Northwest Coast, Plateau, and in northern California does not lend itself to this interpretation, because it is separated by a considerable geographical gap from that of the other areas. We can leave determination of its origin to weaving specialists.

Splint basketry in the eastern United States is known to have been diffused to the northernmost areas of its occurrence in very recent times. The Abnaki of Maine received it about 1890 and the Micmac of New Brunswick and Nova Scotia as late as 1900. The Lake St. John Montagnais learned this craft at about the same time. It has gained ground against birch-bark containers among these tribes. On the other hand, splint basketry is known to be pre-Columbian in the Middle West at least as far north as Wisconsin because it has been found there by archeologists. It may be post-Columbian, however, among coastal Algonquian tribes as far south as the Carolinas, because it is not reported in the earliest sources. However, matting made by plaiting unspun strips of cedar bark was found wrapped around a burial in New Brunswick, where it was associated with a brass trade kettle. Although the kettle proves that the matting belongs to the historic period, the material employed is certainly indigenous and so may also be the weaving technique.

Knotless netting.—A curious technique analogous to weaving is knotless netting or knitting. In the Sub-Arctic, this technique was employed in the manufacture of rabbitskin blankets from twisted strips of fur. These blankets were used for bedding and worn as robes. The Yavapai of the Oasis is the only tribe outside the Sub-Arctic which is known to have made rabbitskin blankets in this manner. Bags or nets for carrying were made with knotless netting technique in all major areas. More restricted uses to which this

163

technique was put include the manufacture of caps, leggings, and sandals in California and the Oasis.

Knotless netting is common in South America, Oceania, and probably other major areas of the world. Archeological specimens from North America mostly fall within the Christian Era. Although this degree of antiquity is insufficient to account for the entire world-wide distribution, it conclusively establishes the indigenous character of the North American evidence.

Spindle whorl.—The joining together of individual sections of basketry and matting material to form continuous elements offered no particular problem. Additional whole stems or split sections of plant materials could be added whenever one already incorporated in the object being woven came to an end. The rigid nature of baskets, at least, made it unnecessary to join, for example, a new element in a coil to the old elements; the sewing of each new turn to the adjacent old turn automatically made fast the new segment of the coil. When working with finer and shorter fibers, such as cotton and wool, it is impractical to handle each minute fiber individually. The only practical method is first to join thousands of such fibers into a continuous thread or yarn. This process is called spinning.

Spinning is known to nearly all peoples in the world. The rolling of fibers between the palm and thigh is a very widespread and presumably old method of spinning. This was done by many tribes to make cordage for a variety of purposes short of weaving. Some weaving peoples still clung to the old palm and thigh method of spinning: for example, the Tlingit of the Northwest Coast and a large number of tribes east of the Rockies who spun and wove buffalo hair. However, most peoples who spin and weave cotton and wool extensively use a spinning device called the spindle whorl. It consists of a shaft over which is slipped a perforated disk of wood, stone, or clay which acts as a flywheel to keep the spinning shaft in motion longer. The weighted end of the spindle whorl is commonly placed on the ground, and from the other end the instrument is twirled, either vertically between the fingers or horizontally along the thigh. The free hand of the spinner manipulates the cotton or wool which, when spun, is wound around the spindle. In North America the spindle whorl was used on the Northwest Coast and the adjacent part of the Plateau, by the Illinois and Cherokee, and generally in the Oasis, Meso-America, and Circum-Caribbean areas. Spindle whorls received their greatest elaboration in Meso-America, where pottery whorls were decorated with stamped and incised designs. They are frequently found in archeological excavations in this area.

Weaving frames and looms.—The number of weaving techniques is so great, especially in Meso-America, that no attempt will be made to describe them all. Instead, we shall rest content with a brief treatment of frames and looms. The weaving of flexible material is differentiated from basketry by the use of a support of some kind. A few North American tribes (Aleut, Tlingit, Haida, Virginia Indians) wove twined baskets upside down with the basket suspended from a stake. This represents a transition between basketry and true weaving. Another group, consisting of the central Algonquians and southern Siouans of the Prairies, suspended the radial warps of twined buffalo-hair bags from a stake in similar fashion to facilitate weaving.

A still more advanced technique is the suspension of warps in a linear arrangement from a cord or bar (Map 26). This was characteristic of the Northwest Coast of Canada and Alaska, of the Algonquians of the Prairies, of a few scattered tribes, and doubtless many others for which we have no information. The weaver twined with her fingers from top to bottom in a manner as time-consuming as that for basketry, except that the materials employed for the mats and blankets made in this fashion were generally coarser than those used for twined baskets. The famous Chilkat blankets of the Northwest Coast, made principally of mountain goat wool and beautifully decorated, were made in this crude manner, as were also mats of the inner bark of the cedar. Inner bark seems to have been the chief material thus woven on the Prairies. A single California tribe is reported to have twined together rabbitskin blankets in this manner.

The next step toward loom weaving was the attachment of both ends of the warp to a two-bar frame. Frames of this kind were used on the Northwest Coast and the adjacent part of the Plateau, in California, the Great Basin, the Oasis, and the Southeast (Map 26). All such frames on the Northwest Coast and the adjacent strip of the Plateau were upright; one bar was directly above the other and the fixed warp ran vertically. Weaving was done with the fingers and from top to bottom, the weaver rotating the finished work on her side of the frame in an upward direction periodically, until the entire circuit of warp was negotiated. Then she pulled out a stick which held the warp ends together and the result was a rectangular piece of material.

In California a number of interesting variants of the two-bar frame are to be found. In some cases the bars consisted of two vertical stakes around which the continuous warp was wound, resulting in a warp which was horizontal but a weft which was vertical. In other instances both bars were attached to stakes close to the ground so that both warp and weft were horizontal and parallel to the ground. In the Great Basin and the Oasis, the majority of heddleless frames were of this latter variety. They were used chiefly to weave rabbitskin blankets. In the Southeast, the same type of horizontal frame supported by stakes in the ground is reported for the Creek. Such weaving frames which hold the warp rigid are a necessary step in the development of the loom, because without them the heddle would have been impossible.

The bow "loom" (Map 26) is a curious variant found principally in the Sub-Arctic. It was used to weave bands worn on the body. These were decorated with porcupine quill and moose hair embroidery. The warp elements were held rigid by the tension of the flexed bow.

The true loom may be defined as a two-bar, fixed warp, weaving frame to which heddles have been added. A heddle is simply a stick to which only a part of the warp strands are attached. If the weaver desires a checker weave he attaches each alternate warp strand to the heddle so that a single pull on the stick will separate every other warp strand from the remainder. He is then able to thrust a ball of weft in a single motion all the way across the material being woven. By releasing the tension on the heddle after the weft ball has traversed its course, a checker weave results. A second heddle, attached to the remaining warp strands, separates them for the return journey of the ball. Thus, with the aid of the heddle, the worker can weave a row many times faster than by working the weft with the fingers over and under each alternate warp.

Modern machine weaving is made possible by the principle of the heddle.

Two-bar frames with heddles are indigenous from the northern Oasis to Panama and probably also in the West Indies (Map 26). True shuttles seem to have been unknown. Weaving was always from bottom to top when the looms were upright. Two other weaving tools commonly associated with these looms are the comb and the batten, both of which were used to beat down the weft elements in order to increase the closeness of the weave. The

FIG. 28.—The true loom

comb, with its teeth, could be applied at any time in the weaving process, but the batten could be used only when the warp was separated by the heddle.

The warp threads of true looms may run horizontally, diagonally, or vertically. The diagonal or slanting position is associated with the waist or belt loom, so called because one bar is attached to a house post or tree several feet off the ground and the other bar to a belt around the waist or hips of the weaver (Fig. 28). The waist loom was used among the Pueblos of the Oasis area, in Meso-America, and in Central America. The vertical loom also is definitely known to have been used among the Pueblos. For this we have archeological evidence, namely, holes in dwellings and kivas (sacred men's houses) for the insertion of weaving bars. Cloth

167

too wide to have been woven on a waist loom has also been interpreted as evidence of the vertical loom, but it could just as easily have been woven on the horizontal loom, which is also known to have been used by the Pueblos. Horizontal looms are, in addition, to be found in the Oasis area from the Pima to the Huichol, and sporadically in Meso-America and Central America.

In the Oasis, Meso-America, and Central America, men sometimes did the weaving. In all other areas women were the weavers. This is another example of the adaptation to sedentary and urban life which characterizes these southern areas. Men in these areas were not predominantly hunters and warriors, but were farmers, craftsmen, and tradesmen instead.

The indigenous character of true looms in the Southeast (Map 26) is problematical. Descriptions of looms for the Creek, Cherokee, and Chickasaw date from the last half of the eighteenth century, and that for the Osage from the first half of the nineteenth. The earliest of these descriptions is more than a century later than permanent White contact. Therefore, derivation from other American areas or from Europe should not be ruled out. On the other hand, the inner-bark mantles observed by the De Soto expedition were woven so finely that they were sometimes mistaken for cotton. Work of such high quality suggests the true loom.

The entire history of weaving is too controversial to be settled here. Suffice it to say that every feature described here for North America occurs in South America and the Old World as well. It was the Peruvian Indians who surpassed all other peoples in weaving, for not only did they practice every technique known in the rest of the world, but they possessed methods not duplicated elsewhere. The similarities from the Oasis to Chile in South America suggest a common origin for many features of true loom weaving. With a little imagination the Southeast might be drawn into this orbit. The Northwest Coast, because of its isolation from both Middle American and Asiatic weaving, presents a problem of origin which will be difficult to solve.

POTTERY

Pottery has already been mentioned in chapter v and in the beginning of this chapter (Map 23). Its combined ethnological and archeological distribution is presented on Map 27. The majority of American anthropologists believe that many peoples of North America derived their knowledge of pottery and its making from Asia in pre-Columbian times. Except in Alaska, peoples of the Arctic and Sub-Arctic have not made and used pottery in post-Columbian times, or at least the data have not been reported in the historical record in these areas. In light of this fact, the case for diffusion from Asia must be strengthened largely by archeological evidence. Continuity of geographical distribution is one of the diagnostic features of diffusion. In our present state of knowledge there is a geographical gap of about seven hundred miles between the pottery sites of the central Arctic and those of the central Sub-Arctic (Map 27). With this exception, the distribution of pottery in North America is practically continuous or follows routes where contact between tribes is well established.

The study of pottery is primarily a task for archeology, since the total amount of available evidence of that kind is at least a hundred times as great as in ethnology. The total number of variations in pottery is almost unbelievable. Pots can differ in the kind of tempering added to the clay, in shape, in size, in decoration, and in use. Add to these a chemical analysis of all the materials that go into the pot, and the result is a classification so detailed that the pottery of each tribe or locality can be distinguished from that of every other tribe or locality. This kind of analysis would fill many volumes and cannot be attempted here. Instead we shall concentrate on pottery-making methods, which are few in number and fairly well known.

Pottery-making.—There were only three major methods of manufacturing pottery in aboriginal North America: coiling, modeling, and molding. Probably more pots were made by coiling than by any other method. The potter shaped the base of the pot in his hands and then built up the side by coiling on ropelike pieces of clay made by rolling a lump of clay between the palms. After each additional coil, the potter kneaded the point of contact of the new coil with the previous one to insure a complete fusing of the two. She might also slap with a paddle the outside of the pot, which was prevented from caving in by an "anvil" held by hand against the inner wall of the pot.

169

Modeling means shaping the entire pot in the hands without coiling. The base was made in the same manner as for coiling, but the sides were built up with slablike sections of clay which were pinched or patted into place with the hands. A paddle was sometimes used to manipulate the clay, as in coiling.

Molding refers to the shaping of the clay around a previously constructed mold of some kind. This might be a fired pot, a basket, the end of a log, a hole in the ground, or a specially constructed mold of fired pottery made exclusively for the manufacturing of pottery vessels.

Coiling is dominant in the southern half of the North American continent. Because it is also the most common method of making pottery in South America, there is good reason to believe that coiling had a single origin in middle America, and subsequently diffused to other areas. There is a high positive correlation in space between coiling and horticulture in North America. Add to this the fact that pottery and horticulture appear at about the same time in many North American localities, and the case for diffusion from the south looks fairly good. Coiling apparently replaced other pottery-making techniques in some localities as it spread north. For example, the earliest pottery in the Southeast is definitely modeled.

Modeling and molding are the principal pottery-making techniques in the northern half of the continent and extend southward in the Plains and Prairie areas in the familiar wedge-shaped distribution so commonly assumed by predominantly northern culture elements. The only exception to this statement is a small Eskimo area on the Bering Sea where coiling apparently prevailed. In spite of this one case of coiling, it seems that early far northern pottery was modeled or molded and that instances of these techniques in North America, north of Mexico, were derived from Asia. The coiling on Bering Sea therefore appears to be a more recent diffusion from Asia.

In Meso-America and Central America, pottery was apparently sometimes made in pre-Columbian times by molding and modeling. The simplest form of mold was a previously made pot, which was turned upside down and plastered over with fresh clay to form the new pot. Because most shapes of pottery have a constricted neck or mouth, only about half of the new pot could be formed in this manner. It then had to be removed from the mold and completed by coiling or modeling. Fired clay molds, in the shape of a mushroom, were also employed in making pottery in these areas. Some of these molds were so shallow that only the base of the pot was shaped from them, while others were deep enough to produce about one-third of the vessel. In a smaller number of localities, pots were molded in two vertically bisected halves which were then fused by kneading and rubbing before the pot was fired. Small pots were sometimes made exclusively by modeling, but more often the handles, legs, and decorations were modeled on after the body of the pot had been made by coiling, molding, or a combination of the two.

The relationship between these Mexican pottery molds and the wide variety of cruder molds used north of Mexico is problematical. Archeologists have found a fair number of fragments of rude, fabric-impressed pottery in southern Mexico which seem to have been molded in baskets of twined weave. Insofar as these can be dated, they belong to early and middle temporal horizons. Perhaps molding was a more common pottery making method here than is generally known.

The paddle and anvil technique, employed to produce a complete fusing of the separate pieces of clay used to build up a pot, was most highly developed among the Yumans and Uto-Aztecans of the Oasis in association with coiling. Their anvils were made of pottery and resemble the pottery molds of southern Mexico so closely that there can be little doubt that they were derived from Mexico. In one case at least, the base of the pot was molded around the anvil. Paddles and anvils were lacking among Pueblos and Athapaskans, who joined their coils by kneading and rubbing. Paddles and anvils seem also to have been widely used in the Prairies and East, although much of the evidence is indirect. The quantities of ware with stamped or cord-marked designs on the exterior must have been decorated by striking with a paddle or similar device to which the design was affixed. A fair number of paddles and anvils have been found by archeologists. Paddles and anvils may have been associated with modeling and molding as well as coiling in these areas.

171

Potter's wheel.—The true potter's wheel, rotated on a pivot, was unknown in the New World in pre-Columbian times but was adopted from the Spanish by Latin American Indians. It was most enthusiastically received by those peoples who molded pottery, because it offered a quick method for completing the upper section of the vessel. However, a number of twentieth-century observers have reported the making of pots on rotating bases without pivots in Meso-America. Such bases are often wooden cylinders or discs rotated on a baseboard by the feet as well as the hands. Sometimes the rotating base is made of pottery. In one locality in Oaxaca the rotating platform on which the pot is shaped is spun at speeds as great as those of European-derived true wheels, from sixty to ninety revolutions per minute. We do not know for sure whether such turntables were used in pre-Columbian times or whether they are post-Columbian imitations of European-derived true potter's wheels. It seems likely that slowly rotating bases are pre-Columbian, but that speeds of sixty to ninety revolutions are post-Columbian.

The sexual division of labor in pottery-making corresponds to that of many other crafts. North of Mexico it was exclusively the task of women, but in central Mexico it was also the work of men who were specialists in the craft.

SKIN-DRESSING

True tanning by means of tannic acid was unknown to natives of North America in spite of the fact that a large number of tribes ate acorns which contained the acid. Skin-dressing by other means, however, met the needs of all peoples, including the Eskimos, whose lives depended on the quality of their skin clothing.

In order to dress a hide in any manner it must be held stationary in some way. In the central and eastern Arctic, where trees were scarce, large hides were most often laid on the ground or snow, and held in place by stakes driven through holes near the edge. This held the skin firm and allowed the worker to scrape the flesh off the inside or the hair off the outside with both hands. Buffalo hides were staked down also on the Plains. Ground support is characteristic only of these two areas, although it was practiced occasionally elsewhere. There is no reason to suppose that the Plains Indians learned it from the Eskimos or vice versa, because there was no direct contact between the two areas. It was probably independently invented in the two areas as an adaptation to a treeless environment.

In other areas hides were fastened to a rectangular frame of poles by means of thongs run through holes around the periphery. The frame was most often placed in an upright position so that the worker could stand up at her task. This kind of support is characteristic of the Alaskan Arctic, the entire Sub-Arctic, the Northwest Coast, Plateau, Prairies, and East. It was used especially for large hides. Small hides might simply be laid on a log or plank to be worked.

Small hides were fleshed, dehaired, and softened by being pulled back and forth over the upper end of a post or stake in the ground. The end was often sharpened so that the post actually constituted an end-bladed tool. This device is reported in all major areas except the Arctic, Meso-America, and the Circum-Caribbean area. In the latter two regions information on skin-dressing is meager.

The scraping of the flesh off the inside of the hide with an end-bladed tool was characteristic of all areas north of Mexico except California, the Great Basin, and the Yuman-Uto-Aztecan Oasis, where edge-bladed fleshers predominated. On the Plains and Prairies, plus a few tribes in neighboring areas, the end-bladed tool had an elbowed handle. It was used something like a hoe. The worker bent over the buffalo hide staked out on the ground and cut away the useless flesh with a two-handed pulling motion toward her body. In the Arctic and among a few neighboring tribes in the Sub-Arctic, hides were fleshed with the woman's semi-circular stone knife called *ulo* by the Eskimo. This was done with a one-handed motion away from the body.

Fleshing tools were sometimes used in dehairing after the skin had been soaked a while, often in ashes, to loosen the hair. This was done on large hides such as that of the buffalo. However, edge-bladed tools, held at the ends and pulled toward the body like a drawknife, were used more commonly for this purpose. They were usually made of a single long bone which had a longitudinal

173

section removed so as to produce two scraping edges. They are reported for every culture area north of Mexico and seem to have been nearly universal. They are sometimes called beamers, especially by archeologists. The hide to be dehaired was most commonly laid across an inclined pole or log to facilitate the operation of this tool.

After the hide was fleshed, and dehaired if this was desired, it was treated with a skin-dressing agent which perhaps acted chemically as well as physically on it. By far the most common agent was brains, normally those of the same animal which furnished the hide. They were apparently rubbed into hides in all areas north of Mexico except in the Arctic. The exact effect of the brains is unknown, but they seem to have softened the skin and to have increased its flexibility. The second most widespread skin-dressing agent was human urine, in which the hide was soaked for a time. This practice was limited to the Arctic and Northwest Coast, except for one tribe in the Alaskan Sub-Arctic. In the Arctic human beings bathed themselves in urine; women especially washed their hair in it. As a detergent it has a reputation for dissolving grease, so that we can assume that it dissolved the excess grease on sea mammal hides. Other agents less commonly used in North America were the spinal cord, liver, marrow, ashes, vegetable materials, and in modern times, eggs. In spite of the claims made by natives for the efficacy of these skin-dressing agents, one gets the impression that the physical manipulation of the skin by the worker was the most essential part of the process. This was normally continued after treatment with the agent.

Two more kinds of physical manipulation may be barely mentioned: the chewing of the hide by the Eskimos; the pulling of the hide back and forth across a rope of sinews on the Plains. Both practices are localized within their respective culture areas.

Skins were sometimes smoked over a wood fire in all major areas except the Arctic, where the oil lamp was the only kind of fire available. Bark of a certain kind was usually thrown on the fire to give the skin the desired color. In the Arctic, skins were occasionally colored with vegetable or mineral dyes.

Among the vast majority of tribes, women prepared the hides. Since men did practically all the hunting, and fighting as well, this was equitable enough. There is a fairly close correlation between the dominance of hunting in the subsistence pattern (Maps 3 and 4) and the dressing of hides by women. It is only in California, the Oasis, and Meso-America that hides were characteristically dressed by men. In these areas women were occupied with obtaining plant foods or processing them when obtained by men, and hunting was of secondary importance at best. The few hides that were obtained could be prepared by the hunter without interfering with the sexual balance of labor. In central Mexico, however, skins were dressed by professional male specialists, as was the case for so many tasks in this area.

The dressing of hides by women in the northern Plains played a prominent role in the change of family structure in the first half of the nineteenth century. At that time the demand for buffalo hides was at its peak. Because women prepared the hides, the more wives a man had, the richer he became. A single hunter, with the aid of the horse and gun, could kill enough buffalo to keep many women busy. As a result of this combination of factors, the maximum number of wives possessed by one man skyrocketed from five or six to as many as twenty or even thirty.

METALLURGY

In most of aboriginal North America, true metallurgy was unknown; the majority of Indians merely cold-hammered chunks of native copper produced in almost pure form by nature. There were no true mines with underground tunnels and subterranean caverns north of Mexico. Copper used by Indians in this area was obtained on the surface or from shallow pits which were dug to recover metal which at first had been seen from the surface. The largest deposits of native copper were on the southern shore of Lake Superior, and from this locality the metal and the objects made from it were traded hundreds of miles. There were other copper deposits, however, in the Appalachian Mountains and here and there on the Atlantic Coast from New Jersey to Nova Scotia. Farther north, the source of copper centered in two regions: southeast Alaska, and the central Arctic on the Coppermine River, which flows into the Arctic Ocean. There were many other local deposits of less magnitude.

Early observers have left us many accounts in many localities of indigenes beating out lumps of copper into desired shapes with nothing more than a stone. One enterprising museum curator demonstrated conclusively that all of the types of copper objects from the eastern United States could be made in this crude manner. However, some specialists believe that Indians north of Mexico might have used an additional technique known as annealing. This is merely heating the metal to the point where some of the brittleness produced by the pounding is eliminated.

The majority of objects made from native copper north of Mexico were body ornaments: beads, ear ornaments, head and breast plates, necklaces, bracelets, anklets, and even copper embroidery on hide clothing. There is some argument about the utility of the head and breast plates. Although some of these might conceivably have deflected a missile, most were too thin to have been really effective as armor. At the same time a fair number of tools were made of native copper, especially near the source of supply, where large quantities of the metal were available. As distance from the source of supply increased, the value tended to rise until ultimately the copper was regarded as a precious metal suitable only for jewelry. The list of utilitarian objects includes knives, ax blades, adz blades, spear points, arrowheads, chisels, hooks, ice-picks, needles, and drinking cups. On the Northwest Coast a large copper plate of stylized shape and design came to be an object of great value and a symbol of great prestige attainable only by chiefs and rich men.

A single band of Eskimos, the Polar Eskimos, who are the northernmost people on earth, hammered out meteoric iron, obtained locally, into spear points and knives. Arrowheads were made of the same material after the bow was reintroduced to them in the nineteenth century. In the historic period, natives on all coasts eagerly sought timbers from wrecked European ships for the iron bolts and nails which could be easily extracted by burning the planks. Such iron was worked principally by cold hammering.

A few copper objects have been mentioned by early observers and found by archeologists in the Southwest. They consist mostly of body ornaments, which were much less numerous than those in the Prairies and East and first appeared at a later date. The most complex type of copper object was a "sleigh" type of bell of thin-walled copper with slits and a copper pellet inside. All of these objects except the bells seem to have been made by cold hammering. The bells, on the other hand, are regarded by experts as having been cast by the lost wax method. It is generally thought that they were obtained in trade from Mexico and not made locally. The earliest of these date from A.D. 900–1100, but they were not common until the thirteenth and fourteenth centuries. Just how far north in Mexico this technique was practiced remains a problem, because the bells have been found all along the West Coast route from southern Mexico to northern New Mexico.

The oldest evidence of metal-working in the New World dates from about 300 B.C. in Peru. At this time nuggets of gold were cold-hammered into jewelry. Cold hammering into sheets, embossing, and annealing appeared between this early period and A.D. 700. Then by A.D. 700 copper and silver had been discovered, and casting, soldering, and gilding invented. By about A.D. 900 three alloys appeared on the scene: gold-silver, gold-copper, and silver-copper. About A.D. 1100 bronze was discovered or invented in the Bolivian highlands, and the smelting of ores became known.

While this development of metallurgy was going on in Peru and Bolivia, a partially independent movement arose in Colombia. The Colombians concentrated on a gold and copper alloy, which served as a model for Peru at a later date, and they were also familiar with gold and platinum combinations. Almost every technique known to Peru was also a part of the Colombian repertoire.

Meso-American metallurgy was a combination of that from Peru and that from Colombia, in addition to a few Mexican inventions. The oldest pieces of metal found in Mexico are the legs from a cast copper-gold figurine of Panamanian style. It dates from A.D. 782, but is regarded as a trade article rather than one of local manufacture. True metallurgy was unknown in Mexico until a late Toltec period, A.D. 968–87. A copper-lead alloy, unknown to South Americans, was invented by the Mexicans, but bronze was never achieved by them. The Mexicans were also familiar with the gilding of copper. Copper and gold were cast into bells and ornaments by the lost wax method. The shape of the casting was modeled in clay, over which was dusted finely ground charcoal, followed by an even layer of wax. This wax coating was also dusted with charcoal, and then the whole object was encased in clay, which was perforated at top and bottom. The entire mold was then heated to the point that the wax melted and ran out, and the clay became sufficiently hardened. Then the bottom hole was plugged and the molten metal poured in at the top. When the metal cooled, the mold was broken and the finished casting was removed. The metal filled the space previously occupied by the wax. Although Mexican metallurgy stemmed from South America, the best work of the Mexicans is generally regarded as superior.

Nearly all of the metal objects produced in Mexico were ornamental in character, but a few were utilitarian. Copper axes, picks, blow pipes, chisels, helmets, and needles, at least, are mentioned by the chroniclers and have been found in excavations. Metal tools and weapons failed to make much headway among the Aztecs not only because copper was soft but also because there was an abundant supply of obsidian, from which razor-sharp blades and points could be manufactured.

Compared to Old World metallurgy, which began thousands of years earlier, New World metal-working was in its infancy. Bellows in any form were unknown. The heat necessary for smelting and casting was generated by nothing more than the human breath blown through a reed or copper tube into a charcoal fire. This could not have produced enough heat to smelt or cast iron. Whether the American Indian would ever have invented an adequate bellows and discovered the superior properties of iron, if the Spanish had not arrived with their iron weapons to end forever his freedom of action, will always remain a mystery.

DIVISION OF LABOR

Division of labor according to age was universal in North America and the rest of the world as well. Children were incapable of performing the tasks of adults, and the older adults often worked at different occupations from the younger. Among the Papago, for example, a young man concentrated on hunting and warfare, and helped a little with agriculture and house-building. When he became middle-aged, he substituted weaving, skin-dressing, and weapon-manufacture for the more arduous tasks of hunting and fighting. In similar fashion, young women gathered wild plant foods, ground maize, and fetched wood and water, while middle-aged and old women did more sedentary work such as cooking, basket-making, and pottery-making. Where sedentary crafts were highly valued, old age meant little or no diminution in status; where sedentary crafts were few, as in the Arctic, and much strenuous outdoor activity was demanded of men, they either died young or suffered a definite loss of rank in old age.

Sexual division of labor is also practiced by all human societies. The classic picture of the lazy Indian brave and the industrious squaw, however, applies only to certain culture areas, and even there demands considerable qualification. In regions where hunting and warfare loomed large, as on the Plains, the Prairies, and in the East, a man performed his most strenuous duties away from home. Partly because of the violent nature of these activities and partly because of the religious fasting which usually accompanied both, a man often arrived home exhausted and needed a few days of leisure in which to recuperate. Most of the early historical observers in those areas saw only village life, where the women actually were doing most of the work. The result was a distorted picture.

Not so among the Meso-Americans. Here both men and women labored almost constantly, although perhaps at a more leisurely rate than our forty hours a week workers. Men did most of the farming and sometimes engaged in crafts such as pottery-making, basket-making, and even weaving. They marketed their products in neighboring towns. Women stayed in their home village. The grinding of maize alone, as fine as the culture demanded, might take as much as six hours a day when the family was large. Add to this the cooking, weaving, child care, and other household tasks, and women probably worked as long as men. Although the tasks assigned to the sexes differed, both sexes spent practically all of their waking hours working at the prescribed occupations.

If we had enough quantitative information, we might scale other cultures along an imaginary work line between the Meso-Americans and the peoples of the Plains, Prairies, and East. For example, the Pueblos of the Oasis would fall rather close to the Meso-Americans. Peoples of California and the Great Basin might be intermediate. Those of the Arctic, Sub-Arctic, and Plateau might be a little closer to the Plains, Prairies, and East. The Northwest Coast is difficult to classify but would probably fall into the intermediate group.

In other parts of this volume, the sexual division of labor has been discussed comparatively for the following topics: horticulture, Map 8, pages 53–54; house-building, Map 19, pages 127–28; clothing-manufacture, page 156; basket-making, page 162; weaving, page 168; pottery-making, page 172; skin-dressing, pages 174–75. A few additional generalizations will be attempted here.

Where hunting was the chief source of subsistence (Map 3), men devoted considerable energy to it, and women tended to perform all the other tasks listed in the paragraph above if they were carried on at all in the culture. In the area where fishing was most dominant, the Northwest Coast, women relinquished the building of the huge plank houses to men, shared skin-dressing with them, but otherwise did all the other jobs in the list which were present in the culture. In the East, where horticulture dominated subsistence, women were the principal workers in the fields, but men bore the brunt of building the large frame houses, and sometimes helped with skin-dressing. Women performed the other jobs. When we turn to the Pueblos of the Oasis, where horticulture was even more important, we find men doing not only most of the work in the field, but also most of the house-building, clothing-manufacturing, weaving, and skin-dressing. In Meso-America, where horticulture was most dominant, men might share all the other tasks with women or become specialists in them and perform them to produce goods for the market.

In areas where wild plants formed the mainstay of the diet (California and the Great Basin), the sexual division of labor was less sharp than in the rest of the continent. Although women may have obtained the bulk of the food, they got considerable help from men. House-building was done principally by men or shared by both sexes, clothing-manufacture was rather evenly divided, and skin-dressing was mainly the work of men or was shared by both sexes. Basket-making, pottery-making, and weaving were exclusively feminine tasks, however.

It seems likely that, before horticulture was known in the Oasis and Meso-America, the main reliance was on wild plant foods. The sexual division of labor presumably was somewhat flexible like that of California and the Great Basin. After horticulture arrived and improved the efficiency of the subsistence pattern, more time was available for greater specialization in crafts. Because men were already working at crafts which would have been disdained in hunting societies, it was entirely consistent for them to take up more of the tasks formerly limited to women.

What would have happened in the East if European contact had not put an end to its Indian history is by no means obvious. However, the prehorticultural basis of subsistence seems to have been hunting, and, with the great emphasis placed on warfare, the male personality was an ultramasculine type who took little interest in crafts, which he considered to be feminine. Horticulture remained primarily a woman's occupation even though its first appearance may have been almost as early as in the Oasis and Meso-America. While the division of labor seems to rest primarily on the total economy, it may also be determined by other aspects of culture. Whether horticulture in the Oasis and Meso-America was originally women's work, no one knows, but if so, the shift to men had been accomplished in most localities by the time of European contact.

Specialization of labor.—Specialization of labor is less fully known than sexual division of labor. Nevertheless, craft specialization on the part of individuals of the same sex is of vital importance in the growth of culture as we know it today in Europe and America. It is one of the measuring sticks which may be applied to a culture to determine its degree of complexity. Another perhaps still more advanced criterion is the amount of craft specialization by community. If one community specializes in pottery-making and exports considerable quantities of the ware to other communities, and each of them in turn pursues its own specialty, the total economic system differs decidedly from one in which every community makes practically everything it uses.

An impressionistic summary of craft specialization is offered on Map 28. In the Arctic, Sub-Arctic, about half the Great Basin and Northeast Mexico, and a few smaller areas, there was either no craft specialization or only a few part-time specialists. A man in

181

these cultures tended to be a jack-of-all-trades, and a woman had to be just as versatile. Often a single family functioned as a complete economic unit for a considerable length of time. While it is true that shamans and headmen among the Eskimos were sometimes distinguished from other men, their special activities were concerned with the supernatural and with group leadership, which can hardly be called crafts. Probably the nearest approach to a craft specialist in this culture was the whale harpooner. Whales were hunted by a group of men in the large open boat called the *umiak*. One man of the group had to be selected to cast the harpoon. Repeated success, thought to be due to supernatural sanction, was enough to place this man in a special category. Furthermore, there were some raw materials, such as copper and soapstone, which could be obtained only in limited localities. The fact that these were traded great distances is proof that the individuals who first obtained them from nature had acquired a surplus which, in turn, implies at least a minimum of specialization.

The Sub-Arctic is about as devoid of craft specialists as the Arctic. No doubt hunters who were thought to be able to locate game or attract it by supernatural means were somewhat in a class by themselves. From a western tribe in this region, the Ingalik, we learn that wooden dishes and bowls were sometimes manufactured for trade to other individuals. This indicates some specialization.

The Great Basin presents a comparable picture. Antelope shamans, thought to be able to attract antelope by supernatural means, were held in high esteem but can hardly be called craft specialists. In a few instances certain men may have produced extra bows and arrows which were traded to others, or certain women a few extra baskets to be disposed of in the same way, but there were no regular surpluses and no regular trade channels in most of the Great Basin. Northeast Mexico and the other smaller regions shown in fine stippling on Map 28 are less well known but seem to have functioned in about the same way.

Definite part-time specialists are reported for about half of the continent (Map 28). Beginning with the Plains-Prairie area, we find men specializing in the manufacture of pipes, bows, arrows, and lariats. A few women specialized in house-building. Cutting the buffalo skins for the tipi cover and sewing them together so that they would take the shape of a cone when fastened around the tipi frame required unusual skill. Women specialists also directed the building of the earth lodge, even though men obtained the heavier logs and lifted them into place. Sacred objects used in ceremonies were always made by specialists familiar with the rules of manufacture and usually thought to be in rapport with the supernatural. These are hardly to be classed as economic goods, however.

Specialization was probably more advanced in the East, although it is less often reported in the literature. The rich and variegated material culture of a tribe like the Iroquois is proof of craft specialization. The lively trade which occurred in pre-Columbian times and continued after Europeans settled America is further evidence of specialization. In the Southeast, salt was a common article of trade and the persons connected with its making by evaporation in pottery salt pans were most certainly specialists.

On the Plateau, there was probably less specialization than on the Plains, Prairies, and in the East, but it was present. Men made all articles of stone, bone, and wood, and those most skilled in the manufacture of a single article, such as a canoe or bow and arrows, traded some of their surplus to other men. The definitely documented intertribal trade in parfleches, buffalo robes, shells and beads, rope, baskets, and the like, is indirect evidence of individual specialization.

In central California part-time specialists were associated with a wide variety of tasks: hunting, fishing, bow-making, arrowhead-making, pipe-making, bead-making, salt-making, fire-making, and the making of ceremonial regalia. Often esoteric knowledge of the supernatural was thought to be required for success in these activities, so that a young man would not attempt a trade without adequate instruction from a successful older man. With respect to a single tribe, the Patwin, it is reported that such activities were professional monopolies which ran in lineages from father to son. While this has not been confirmed elsewhere, it at least demonstrates the considerable amount of specialization in the area. Turning to the Circum-Caribbean area, we know only that men specialized in basketry and women in pottery- and hammock-making. The paucity of information is almost certain to be due to inadequate reporting, because the occurrence of markets in the majority of communities is proof of considerable part-time specialization.

The Northwest Coast was characterized by part-time specialists and perhaps even an occasional full-time specialist. House-building and canoe-building were largely under the supervision of acknowledged experts, even though every man knew enough to assist in the operation. Woodcarving of totem poles and less conspicuous objects likewise fell to the more skilled individuals. Hunting, both of land and sea mammals, and fighting were specialities of men in some localities. The considerable amount of trade reported on the Northwest Coast also is evidence of surplus goods and, in turn, of some degree of specialization on the part of the makers. One of the most highly specialized professions was that of whale harpooner. Success in whaling was thought to be possible only with the co-operation of the supernatural, and a novice was trained for years before he actually cast a harpoon. Normally only one man in a community was a whale harpooner. Basketry and weaving were the most common specialties of women.

Among the Pueblos of the Oasis, there were also some part-time specialists, even though every individual could perform most of the tasks assigned to his sex. Men tended to specialize in the skin-working, weaving, turquoise work, and, in the historic period, in silver work. Women sometimes specialized in the making of pottery and basketry. The expert was fed by his employer while on the job and received an additional gift of food when the article was completed. The hiring or commissioning of experts seems to have been more common in the Oasis than in other culture areas north of Mexico. However, the great amount of specialization in things pertaining to the supernatural far exceeds that in purely economic tasks.

In Meso-America the picture changes. Here we encounter cities with populations up to 300,000, ruled over by nobility and graced with elaborate public architecture. Many full-time craftsmen were required to construct and maintain the quarters of the nobility alone, and large numbers of others found it profitable to specialize in a single craft and sell their goods or services to others. Besides farming, hunting, and fishing, men worked full time at manu- facturing such things as stone tools, pottery, jewelry, featherwork, and woven textiles; they also engaged in masonry, sculpture, paint- ing, mining, metallurgy, woodworking, and weapon-making. Women specialized in spinning, weaving, and featherwork but did not work full time at such occupations after marriage.

Not everyone in Meso-America lived in a city. Communities were of all sizes, from those of 300,000 just mentioned to villages with only a few hundred persons. In the more rural areas where only small villages existed, specialization of labor was more like that north of Mexico; full-time specialists were rare or absent and part-time specialists not very common.

Specialization of labor on the part of whole communities was probably more common than the ethnographic record shows. The most conclusive proof of specialization consists of the wealth of information on trade, some of which will be assembled in chapter xiii. When a commodity is produced by a limited number of com- munities in surplus quantities and traded to other communities which do not produce it, community specialization is indicated.

Community specialization reached its greatest development in Meso-America, where dozens of products were made locally in sufficient quantities for export. Export often consisted of nothing more than the maker back-packing his wares to the market of a neighboring town. Specialists who made and marketed articles for export were always men; the household duties of women kept them near home. Certain villages specialized in pottery, others in basketry, still others in obsidian points and knives, textiles, cochi- neal dyes, and almost every other commodity that was widely traded. Under such circumstances the beginnings of mass produc- tion were realized. Pottery was made with the aid of molds, textiles with the aid of true looms, and buildings were constructed with quantities of adobe brick and faced with pieces of stone of uniform size and shape. For better or for worse, the signs of an industrial age were beginning to be manifested. The vast difference in total economy between Meso-America and the rest of North America is reflected in the size of the population, which was greater in this area than in all other culture areas combined.

REFERENCES

AGUILAR, 1946; AMSDEN, 1932; BEAGLEHOLE, 1937; BEALS, 1932*a*; BIRKET-SMITH, 1929, 1936, 1945; BIRKET-SMITH AND DE LAGUNA, 1938; CUSHING, 1894; DAVIDSON, 1935; FEWKES, 1944; FLANNERY, 1939; FOSTER, 1948, 1955, 1959; GIFFEN, 1930; GIFFORD, 1928; GOGGIN, 1949; GRIFFIN, 1935; GRIFFIN AND KRIEGER, 1947; HAURY, 1947; HERSKOVITS, 1952; KELLEY, 1943; KING, MS; KROEBER, 1925; DE LAGUNA, 1940; LINTON, 1944; LOTHROP, 1952; LOWIE, 1954; MACNEISH, 1955; MARTIN, QUIMBY, AND COLLIER, 1947; MASON, 1891, 1904; MENDIZÁBAL, 1942; MILLER, 1950; NELSON, 1899; RICKARD, 1934; RIVET AND ARSANDAUX, 1946; SAVILLE, 1920; SPECK, 1920*a*, 1931, 1937; STEWARD, 1948; SWANTON, 1946; TAX, 1953; UNDERHILL, 1939; VAILLANT, 1941; WELTFISH, 1930; WHITAKER, CUTLER, AND MACNEISH, 1957; WILSON, 1917, 1924, 1934; WINTENBERG, 1942; WISSLER, 1938, 1941

11: Art

ALL NORTH American Indian peoples possessed some kind of visual art, although there was a great deal of variation in the
quantity and quality of artistic expression. Probably every tribe
had some artistic specialty which distinguished it from every other
tribe, but most tribes shared much of their art style with neighbors.
In other words, examples of art may be classified and grouped into
areal types in the same manner as other aspects of Indian culture.
The art areas delimited by Miguel Covarrubias (1954: 135) match
very closely the culture areas of this volume (Map. 2).

AREAL SURVEY

Arctic.—Eskimo art shows considerable variation from east to
west. That in Alaska is the most showy because of the greater
amount of wood carving, which is often accented with paint. The
art of the Greenland Eskimo is second in complexity to that of
Alaska, while examples from the central Arctic are fewer in number as well as more modest in appearance.

The art of the Eskimo consisted almost entirely of carving and
engraving in wood, bone, horn, and ivory. The only exception
would be the decoration of clothing with borders of hide and fur
of different color or shade from the rest of the garment, and the
moderate amount of tattooing on the face. Because work in wood,
bone, horn, and ivory was done exclusively by men, practically all
art was produced by men. There are few examples which were
executed wholly to satisfy the aesthetic impulse and were without
any other utility. Most art consisted of the decoration of a primarily utilitarian article such as a knife handle or a harpoon head.
Some Eskimo art was naturalistic; it depicted human beings, ani-

mals, boats, sleds, houses, and other natural and cultural objects. But it was just as often geometric, consisting of designs made up of a variety of lines and abstract two-dimensional figures which were not supposed to represent anything in nature or culture. Sometimes the two styles were combined on a single object (Plate I).

Animal carvings in the round are known from all archeological and nearly all contemporary Eskimo cultures; the whale, walrus, seal, bear, dog, and bird are the most common animals represented (Plate II). Human figures in the round are less frequent but probably occurred everywhere. They were mostly used as dolls by children, but some at least are known to have been shaman's puppets supposedly endowed with supernatural power. They were originally armless and invariably sexless, with no attempt to depict either primary or secondary sexual characteristics. Twentieth-century human figures distinguish sex by clothing, however (Schaefer-Simmern, 1958). In addition to these animal and human carvings, objects such as hair ornaments, beads, ivory plates, and toy kayaks might be said to approach the status of pure art objects.

Animal engravings on flattish objects were common and included the caribou in addition to the animals listed above. These engravings were invariably in silhouette and the internal space was filled with parallel or cross hatching or in solid black or brown. To show a number of animals in a composition, the Eskimo either repeated similar figures, or hatched a horizontal band to represent the bodies from which legs were extended below and heads above.

Carved and painted Eskimo masks, made mostly of wood, were worn in spirit-impersonating ceremonies. They were made only in Alaska and Greenland. Those in Alaska show influence from the Northwest Coast, as do the religious cults with which they were associated. To such masks were frequently attached feathers, imitation hair, and other appendages which were set in motion by the movements of the dancer. Masks were the largest art objects produced by the Eskimo. The art displayed on small surfaces, such as that on implements used in daily life, was neat, precise, and able to convey meaning with a minimum number of lines. What was lacking in size was made up in liveliness, humor, and fidelity.

Northwest Coast.—The Northwest Coast area from the Columbia River north to the Arctic was characterized by a single major art style which is easily recognizable in museums today. Figures of animals, mythical monsters, and human beings were carved or painted on totem poles, house fronts, canoes, wooden boxes, and other objects (Fig. 29). Carving was in the round, in high relief, and in low relief; and the painting was applied in red and black to all forms of carving as well as to smooth surfaces. The animal, monster, or human forms depicted represented supernatural beings

Fig. 29.—Northwest Coast (Kwakiutl) house front depicting a thunderbird lifting a whale. Boas, 1897.

who had revealed themselves to the ancestors of those persons permitted to carve, paint, or display them at a later date. All art was thus geared to religion and social organization, and the production, ownership, and display of objects of art was proof of the noble descent of an individual as well as of his rapport with the supernatural. Sometimes the supernatural personality was thought to have transformed himself into a human being and to have become the original procreator of the line of descent. These art motifs have sometimes been called crests because of their universal association with particular lineages, sibs, and extended families. They were

189

markers of status, rank, wealth, and social class, as were the crests of Europe in the past. The same art motifs were occasionally carved in stone, bone, horn, and ivory, cold-hammered into copper plates, painted on hide, or woven into baskets and blankets; but decorated wooden objects probably outnumbered all other kinds of art objects combined.

Artists were always men, but not all men were artists. In the old days, however, few, if any, of the artists worked full time at their profession. Most of them worked at the food quest, at house- or canoe-building, and carved undecorated utilitarian objects out of wood as well as decorated objects of both art and use. Although women were nowhere regarded as artists, they sometimes wove art motifs into baskets (especially hats), blankets, and dance costumes. However, it was the male artist who designed the pattern board which the female craftsman followed in weaving a Chilkat blanket, and men may also have designed the patterns woven into less important objects.

Northwest Coast art may be divided into two major stylistic divisions: the Tlingit, Haida, and Tsimshian in the north; the Kwakiutl, Nootka, and Salish in the central part of the area. The art of the northern division was the most distinctive and the most highly stylized, and may be characterized by the following features.

It was essentially an applied art. Practically all of the work of the artist was the decoration of utilitarian objects, such as houses, canoes, boxes, backrests, cradles, rattles, cups, ladles, and clothing. Even the appurtenances of the medicine man and the totem poles had utility or function other than as ways of displaying artistic achievement. Paintings and statues to hang on the wall or place on pedestals as objects of "pure" art did not exist. Therefore the artist had to adapt his figure to the cylindrical form of the totem pole, the flat angular surface of a house front, the round flat surface of a plate, or the curved line of a ladle or paddle.

Naturalism was forced to give way to conventionalization in the northern area. There was a passion for lateral symmetry. This was accomplished on flat surfaces by "splitting" the animal figure longitudinally and exhibiting two profiles instead of one (Fig. 29). On a round surface, such as that of a dish, two profiles were shown, wrapped around the outside of the dish, so to speak. Certain parts of

190

interest, such as the head and face, were emphasized more than other parts of the figure. Certain features of each species of animal served as markers to distinguish it from all other species, and mythical monsters were sometimes identified by combinations of features from two or more species. Thus the bear was characterized by a short snout, large teeth, and protruding tongue, while the wolf was depicted with a long snout and large teeth. The beaver was given protruding upper incisor teeth, a wide flat tail marked with crosshatching, and was always shown holding a stick in its forepaws. The raven had a long straight beak, while the eagle was given a heavy downcurved beak.

There was a strong tendency to fill up all available space, approaching an artistic agoraphobia. The naturally rounded lines of an animal figure were squared to fit a rectangular surface (Plate III), or they were forced into a cylindrical shape to fit a section of a totem pole or handle of some implement. Figures on totem poles were interlocked to avoid vacant space, and the internal organs of the body were sometimes indicated for the same reason.

The art of the Kwakiutl, Nootka, and Salish exhibits enough difference from that of the northern peoples to make most examples of the two styles distinguishable. Figures of the central peoples were more naturalistic and less conventionalized. For three-dimensional carvings, this was accomplished by cutting deeper into the log, to the point that the statue approached naturalistic proportions, rather than a high relief carving on the cylindrical shape of the natural log, as was done in the north. A closer approach to naturalism was also achieved by adding appendages to a figure carved from a single piece of wood. Thus the wings of the thunderbird on a Nootka chief's grave were assembled by fastening together fifty or sixty boards, each one of which represented a feather (Inverarity, 1950; Pl. 265); and the dorsal fin of the killer whale was always a separate piece of wood protruding from the principal log from which the body of the animal was carved. On a Kwakiutl dance costume depicting an eagle, cedar wood slats were used to represent feathers on the wings and upper legs, and overlapping pieces of caribou hide served the same purpose on the upper body and lower legs (Plate IV). The elaborate masks, which reached their peak of development among the Kwakiutl, were decorated with

191

feathers when they represented bird spirits, and with vegetable fiber hair when a human figure was portrayed (Plate V). These masks were intended to be interpreted naturalistically by the naïve, who were supposed to believe that they were actually the physical forms assumed by supernatural personalities taking part in the dance. By the dim light of the fire at night, this illusion was often achieved.

The absence of strictly unilateral organization in the form of lineages and sibs, the greater premium placed upon direct rapport with the supernatural in visions, and the generally more individualistic ethos of the culture of the Kwakiutl and their neighbors were reflected in the boldness, vigor, and greater individualism of their art. However, the art of the Tlingit, Haida, and Tsimshian remains the most distinctive for the Northwest Coast as a whole and represents the most specialized achievement of that area in the graphic and plastic arts. The sheer size of carvings and paintings on houses, canoes, and totem poles produces a dramatic effect not equaled by any other art style north of Mexico.

Plains.—Plains art may also be characterized as a decorative or applied art because all objects on which it was displayed had use or function in the culture other than for the exhibition of the art itself. Almost all Plains artwork was applied to hide, which was the most common material available in this hunting culture where the buffalo was the principal animal taken. Of the two techniques of hide decoration, painting and porcupine quill embroidery, painting was the more frequent. Glass bead embroidery became increasingly more common after trade beads were obtained from Europeans in the historic period, and today has almost replaced the pre-Columbian quillwork. In addition to the decoration of objects made of hide, the Plains Indians decorated stone pipes, rattles, and other wooden ceremonial objects with painting and by attaching feathers, quills, and beads.

Painting and embroidery were applied to buffalo robes, men's shirts, women's gowns, moccasins, tipi covers, tipi linings, rawhide containers (parfleches), drums, medicine cases, quivers, and shields. All of these objects were made wholly or principally of hide, and the decoration was always applied to the hide part of compound objects such as drums and shields. The colors used in painting were brown, red, yellow, black, blue, and green. Most of them were obtained from clays, but charcoal was a ready source of black. Paint materials were ground to powder in a shallow stone mortar and mixed with a thin animal glue for a base. Brushes might be made of horn or wood, but the favorite material was the spongy, porous part of a buffalo's leg bone.

There were two distinct styles of painting associated to some extent with the sexes. Men generally painted naturalistic figures of horses, men, buffaloes, and, more rarely, other animals (Plate VI). Women painted only geometric figures and designs (Plate VII). The two styles were kept separate for the most part on buffalo hide robes, but occasionally both appeared on the same robe when painted by a man.

The naturalistic forms of men, animals, and objects were usually painted in profile, in flat color and without background. Horses and men were the most frequent figures depicted, appearing together on 90 per cent of the painted hides. This association is explained by the fact that most such paintings portrayed war exploits. The men were generally armed and many wore war bonnets with feathers streaming down their backs. Perspective was lacking; there were no highlights and shadows and a more distant figure was placed partly behind or above a closer one without any reduction in size. Composition was limited to small scenes, such as a pair of men engaged in combat or a single man riding home with stolen horses. The painting on a single hide showed a number of such scenes as well as a number of isolated figures scattered around.

Parfleches were decorated only with geometric figures and patterns by women. Tipi covers generally had geometrical borders at top and bottom, between which the adventures of the male owner were portrayed in the naturalistic style. On shields were painted both geometric and naturalistic figures. The latter represented the forms of guardian spirits obtained in visions and were thought to protect the bearer of the shield from harm. Men's shirts were also painted with religious symbols thought to protect the wearer in battle. The heads of skin drums were decorated with both geometric and lifelike elements.

Porcupine quill embroidery was the only kind known before glass beads of European manufacture were received in trade in the nineteenth century. As might be anticipated, it was the work of women. The quills were softened with water, flattened, and dyed a variety of colors. After they were sewn onto dressed hide, they presented a smooth, glossy surface like that of straw. Angular geometric designs predominated in quill embroidery among the older specimens (Plate VIII). More naturalistic floral designs and human and animal figures became more common after European contact. Beadwork reached its florescence at the end of the nineteenth century after the Plains Indians had been rounded up and confined to reservations (Hunt, 1951).

Geometrical design elements were frequently named, but the name used for a single element, such as a triangle, varied from one tribe to another in the Plains area. Although some of the designs might be correctly named by a novice, names of the majority seem to be quite arbitrary and not self-evident at all. Lowie (1954:150) comes to the conclusion that the association of a particular name in the language of a particular tribe with a particular design was probably secondary. The design was probably first invented or acquired from a neighboring tribe and later named to facilitate reference to it when speaking about art.

There was some color symbolism in Plains painting and embroidery but, like the names of designs, it varied from tribe to tribe. To the Dakota red suggested the sunset or thunder; to the Arapaho it signified blood, man, paint, earth, sunset, or rocks; while to the Crow it represented longevity, the ownership of property, and figured prominently in the Tobacco Society. There was at the same time some uniformity within groups of a few tribes, as is suggested by the sharing of red for sunset by the Dakota and Arapaho above, and the association of black with victory for the Crow and Arapaho.

Oasis.—Pueblo art manifested itself on pottery, basketry, woven cloth, jewelry of shell and stone, walls of religious structures, ceremonial objects and in sand paintings. No one material dominated the art as did wood on the Northwest Coast and hide on the Plains. Because of the dry climate and intensive archeological investigation in the Southwest, our knowledge of the pre-Columbian art there is much surer and fuller than that for any other area north of Mexico. Because women made the basketry and pottery, they executed the artwork on these receptacles. Men created almost all other objects of art.

Basketry was most often decorated by staining some of the materials black or red before weaving them into the basket. Basketry designs were overwhelmingly geometrical, but a few suggested animals, birds, and possibly the human figure. Symmetry, repetition, and contrast were established early in basket decoration and continued as fundamental principles of Pueblo art down to the nineteenth century (Fig. 30).

The art displayed on Pueblo pre-Columbian woven cotton textiles is richer than that on baskets, as might be anticipated, but it remained entirely geometrical and seems to have been derived in part from basketry designs. Although weaving did not appear until A.D. 700, five hundred years after basket-making, textile art reached its florescence at the same time as that of basketry, in the Pueblo III period, A.D. 1000–1300.

A type of decoration limited in the pre-Columbian Oasis to the Pueblo people is the stripe twill, in which the primary pattern consists of transverse stripes extending the entire width of the cloth. Secondary diagonal lines following the twill ribs are added to the heavier transverse stripes. Such patterns were woven with red, white, brown, and black wefts.

Patterns on tapestry are more complex. A tapestry weave is defined as one with wefts battened so closely together that the warps are completely concealed and patterns built from different colored wefts, no one of which extends the entire width of the material. The limitations of this technique necessarily fragment the design elements and encourage the invention of a large number of such units. These elements are combined to form a variety of patterns.

Designs on cloth were also made by a technique called tie dyeing. The cloth was folded in a prescribed way at certain points and tied firmly with string. When it was dipped momentarily in dye, the dye did not penetrate the tied areas, which formed a white pattern against a colored background.

Cloth was also decorated by painting designs on it after the weaving was completed. Such designs were sometimes the same as those woven into tapestry or made by tie dyeing. But the Pueblo artist did not fail to take advantage of the greater freedom which

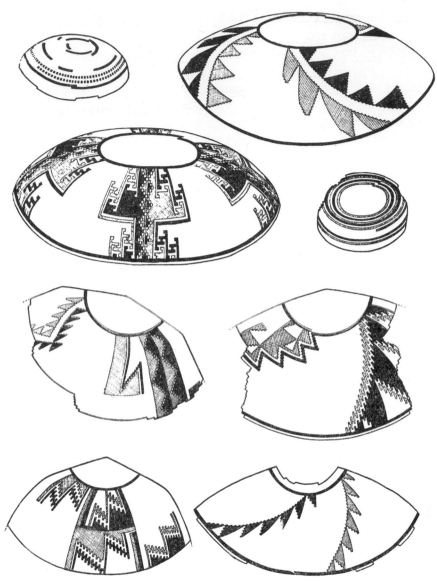

FIG. 30.—Pueblo basket designs (Basket Maker III). Earl H. Morris and Robert E. Burgh, 1941. Courtesy of the Carnegie Institution of Washington.

painting permitted and to employ curved design elements similar to those painted on pottery. Colors used on pre-Columbian cotton fabrics were predominantly inorganic kinds made from minerals, and were largely limited to three colors: red from iron oxide; yellow from yellow ochre; and blue-green from copper sulphate. Organic dyes from plants were used for black, dark brown, and light blue.

Modern Pueblo textile designs are a blend of pre-Columbian designs from all over the Oasis area, as well as a retention of designs from the Pueblo III period. All but one of the modern design elements are of Indian origin. Although changes have taken place over the centuries, they have been gradual and have not disturbed the fundamentals of the art style. Today aniline dyes are in common use.

Pueblo pottery decoration is principally geometric. However, a few conventionalized natural forms and occasional truly naturalistic forms were employed (Fig. 31, Plate IX). As might be anticipated, curves are common in pottery designs, in contrast to the straight lines and angles which the basketry and weaving techniques impose upon the artist. Practically all the pottery was decorated in some way. In the "golden age," Pueblo III, the most common decoration was black lines and other geometric elements on a whitish background. In later prehistoric times the variety of colors and design motifs increased. Three colors on the same vessel became common, and occasionally four were used together. Negative painting—the background was painted and the design left in the original color of the pot—was also known. Along with this increase in number of colors came an increase in naturalistic forms, especially conventionalized bird and feather symbols, which originated among the Hopi and Zuñi Indians of the west. The shoulder and neck of the pot were the areas most often decorated, but sometimes designs covered the entire vessel. Like decorations on basketry and weaving, those on pottery show only gradual changes over the centuries, reflecting the artistic conservatism of the Pueblo Indians. (Mera, 1937, 1939).

Designs on basketry, textiles, and pottery are predominantly geometric but not necessarily lacking in symbolism. Lack of knowledge prevents saying for the Pueblos as a whole exactly which designs are symbolic and which are not, or what percentage of the total number of design elements are symbolic. However, in the light of the abundant symbolism in the more distinctly religious arts to follow, we may assume that there is probably much more symbolism present in the geometric designs on basketry, textiles, and pottery than the ethnologist or archeologist is aware of.

Mural paintings on the walls of underground religious structures, called kivas, reached a florescence in late prehistoric and early historic times. They are almost certain to have been parts of altars around which religious ceremony rallied, because most of the nineteenth-century Pueblo peoples painted murals for their altars. The two most famous examples of Pueblo murals are those in the Jeddito Valley of northern Arizona and those at the Pueblo of Kuaua, near Albuquerque, New Mexico. The subjects represented in these

Fig. 31.—Pueblo "Rain Bird" design on pottery (Tsia). Harry P. Mera, 1937. Courtesy of the Laboratory of Anthropology, Santa Fe, New Mexico.

murals are: human beings, mostly men in ceremonial costumes, with masks, quivers and staffs, buffaloes, rabbits, fishes, birds, snakes, corn, clay vessels, netted gourds, and clouds giving forth rain. A great variety of colors were used: red, blue, maroon, pink, orange, yellow, green, gray, white, and black. Although perspective was attempted rather than achieved, life forms were rendered with a high degree of fidelity. This unusual art seems to have evolved from simpler drawings and paintings on kiva walls and to be wholly of Indian origin (Tanner, 1957: 9–15, facing p. 8).

The art of the sand painting is the most distinctive form of Pueblo art because it is restricted to the Oasis area and a small region in southern California. Sand paintings were part of the sacred altars in the kivas and were made on the floor in front of the fetishes and wall paintings associated with the altars. Sand or ochre of various colors, corn pollen, pulverized flower petals, and pulverized green leaves were employed as dry pigments in "painting" the religious symbols. Handfuls of the dry material were carefully sprinkled from between the thumb and forefinger to form the lined and solid figures of the painting. These figures were conventionalized representations of the sun, moon, stars, earth, mountain lion, snake, or kachina; or of something associated with spirits, such as clouds, a cornfield, the house of the sun or of a kachina. The purpose of these sand paintings was to influence the spirits to bring rain, plentiful crops, good health, and other good things to man. Although the Navaho learned the sand painting art from the Pueblo, the finest and most elaborate examples today are made by the Navaho (Covarrubias, 1954: pp. 231–34 and Plate facing p. 248).

Another aspect of Pueblo art is the ceremonial costumes which are worn in the great religious dramas valued above all else by the Indians. Practically all colors of the spectrum are represented in these elaborate costumes, due in part to the acquisition of sheep and wool from the Spanish as well as modern dyes from the United States. Colors are associated with the six cardinal directions: yellow with north, turquoise with west, red with south, white with east, many colors with the zenith, and black with the nadir. The most important color is turquoise, made from blue-green copper ore.

Pueblo art may be divided into two major varieties: the modest geometric designs that predominate on basketry, textiles, and pottery; the more naturalistic motifs that characterize the religious art in murals, sand paintings, fetishes, and ceremonial costumes. The latter variety ranges from truly naturalistic figures to conventionalizations of naturalistic forms which may appear geometric to the naïve unfamiliar with Pueblo symbolism. Nevertheless every element of religious art is symbolic and thought to be of benefit to the society producing and displaying this art in the manner prescribed by the spirits.

Parallels between Pueblo art and that of neighboring culture areas point principally to Meso-America to the south, although the number of similarities suggesting common origin of art motifs in the two areas is not great.

All the Pueblo arts just described persisted well into the nineteenth century but are declining in the twentieth century. However, silversmithing, introduced by the Spanish, has increased in quantity in the twentieth century and is economically important in the tourist trade of the Pueblos today (Adair, 1944). To this has been added modern painting in the last few decades (Tanner, 1957).

East.—The art of the southeastern United States was probably as rich and varied as that of the Southwest, but European contact disturbed the Southeast peoples much more, and most of their art vanished before it was described or collected by literate observers. We shall first review accounts of early European observers and then turn to the archeological record.

A considerable range of artistic endeavor was involved in the ornamentation of the human body. Objects made of wood, stone, shell, pearls, and copper were worn on the body as head bands, bracelets, necklaces, etc. Paint was applied to the bodies of men for all public occasions, and in preparing for ball games and war. The most common colors in order of mention are red, black, yellow, white, and blue. Figures were geometric although at the same time probably symbolic. The most famous warriors were tattooed from head to foot with mementos of their successful war exploits (Fig. 24). The following account is from observations in the eighteenth century.

But the most beautiful painting now to be found among the Muscogules [Creeks], is on the skin and bodies of their ancient chiefs and micos, which is of a bluish, lead, or indigo color. It is the breast, trunk, muscular or fleshy part of the arms and thighs, and sometimes every part of the surface of the body, that is thus beautifully depicted or written over with hieroglyphics: commonly the sun, moon, and planets occupy the breast; zones or belts, or beautiful fanciful scrolls, wind round the trunk of the body, thighs, arms, legs, dividing the body into many fields or tablets, which are ornamented or filled up with innumerable figures, as representations of animals or battle with their enemy, or some creature of the chase—and a thousand other fancies. These paintings are admirably well executed, and seem to be inimitable. They are performed by exceedingly fine punctures, and seem like *mezzotinto*, or very ingenious impressions from the best executed engravings (Bartram, 1909: 19).

The most decorated article of clothing was the cloak, which was worn principally in winter. The following description comes from the Carolinas in the first decade following A.D. 1700.

The Indian men have a match coat of hair, furs, feathers, or cloth, as the women have. . . . Their feather match coats are very pretty, especially some of them, which are made extraordinary charming, containing several pretty figures wrought in feathers, making them seem like a fine flower silk shag; and when new and fresh, they become a bed very well, instead of a quilt. Some of another sort are made of hair, raccoon, beaver, or squirrel skins, which are very warm. Others are made of the green part of the skin of mallard's head, which they sew perfectly well together . . . (Lawson, 1860:310–12).

The canoes which De Soto's expedition encountered on the Mississippi were said to have been painted in a variety of colors. The front posts of the council buildings in town squares were carved to represent snakes, alligators, and the garfish, and the walls of such structures were painted with a great variety of animal, bird, and human figures some of which had animal heads and human bodies, or vice versa. While some of these may have had totemic significance, others, like the opossum, were not venerated.

Wood carvings in the round of humans, animals, and birds were common in, on, and around the buildings in the central area of the towns, including the winter council house, the ossuary, where it existed, and the four structures forming the square. Birds, especially the eagle, were perched on the tops of the buildings like weather cocks, and also housed inside. Human figures, life size or

201

even larger, stood impressively at attention, some bearing arms. Alligators, serpents, and frogs were also carved in the round. Images in stone were even made, but averaged much smaller, probably due to the difficulty of working stone. Many of these figures were not representations of gods or other important religious personalities but seem to have been art for art's sake. Almost none of these carvings and paintings have survived to find their place in museums. The above descriptions are all from literary sources.

The one art which has survived into the twentieth century with comparatively little change is that of basket decoration. This was most elaborate on the lower Mississippi, and a number of specimens made by women of the Chitimacha tribe have found their way into museums. Baskets were decorated by plaiting and twilling in elements previously colored black, yellow, or red by vegetable dyes. Designs are all geometric but include a few curves along with the more common angled motifs. Some design elements bore unimaginative names such as dots, crosses, and plaits, while others were given animal names. It is impossible to tell whether the inventor of each "animal" design wove the design first and named it at a later date, or deliberately tried to invent a design to represent an animal or some part of its anatomy. At any rate, the designs with animal names are just as geometric as the others and could scarcely be called conventionalizations of naturalistic forms.

Much Southeast pottery seems to have been undecorated, but decoration increased from about the beginning of the Christian Era to the time of European contact. This was due in part to influence from Meso-America, which reached its peak at the time of European contact. The most common technique of pottery decoration was by incising the soft surface before firing or engraving the hard surface of the finished pot after firing. Second to incising and engraving was the impressing of the unfired soft clay with a stamp on which the design had already been produced in the negative. Square holes, round holes, and other small and simple figures were punched into the clay with blunt-pointed instruments, and more rarely little bumps called nodes were added to the pot to form designs. Small indentations and bumps were even made by pinching the clay with the fingers, as a baker does to the edge of a pie crust. The outsides of vessels were also marked with cords tied around the paddle used in shaping the pot, and a few pots seem to have been intentionally decorated by pressing a woven textile against the outer surface when the clay was still soft.

Effigies of people, animals, and even plants were commonly modeled on pottery vessels or pottery pipes, and sometimes non-utilitarian works of art took the form of effigies modeled in clay. Human beings appeared more often than any other in these effigies, but birds, mammals, reptiles, fishes, invertebrates' shells, gourds, and squashes were not lacking.

Only a few of the pottery vessels recovered by archeologists in the Southeast were painted. Red seems to have been a common color; it was frequently associated with white, and sometimes was used against a buff background. Black on white was also employed, and all black or all brown vessels were not uncommon. Even the technique of negative painting was used. A design was first painted on the vessel with wax or some other material resistant to paint; then the paint was applied to the entire surface, leaving unpainted only the areas covered by the wax.

Designs made by stamps, punches, and textiles were always geometric, but those incised or engraved on pots were occasionally naturalistic or at least recognizable conventionalizations of life forms. Painted designs were likewise predominantly geometric and only rarely naturalistic. Modeled effigies were either naturalistic forms or easy-to-recognize conventionalizations of naturalistic forms. Sometimes the head of an animal appeared at one end of an oval bowl, the tail at the other, while the profile appeared twice, once on each of the sides. A large number of vessels with long bottle necks have been found in the Southeast, and also a few pots possessing three legs or a stirrup neck. All three of these features are reminiscent of Meso-American forms. Geometric pottery designs in the Southeast exhibit many more curves than those in the Oasis, although curves are not lacking in the latter area. What the Southeast lacked in color, as compared to the Oasis, it made up for in its intricately engraved scrolls and other curvilinear designs (Griffin, 1952).

Sculpture in stone was much more developed in the Southeast than in the Oasis. Effigies of many kinds of animals, as well as humans, appeared on stone pipe bowls, beautifully wrought and polished to perfection. Stone statuettes of men up to two feet in height have been unearthed by archeologists in a few localities. The best examples of Southeast stone carving in the round compare favorably with those from Meso-America (Plates IX–XII).

Elaborately engraved shell disks a few inches in diameter were worn on the body as chest ornaments. The combinations of life figures and geometric designs strongly suggest Meso-America again. A number of these ornaments depict a warrior with a knife in one hand and a severed enemy head in the other (Plate XIII), and eagles and snakes are common. Ornaments made from sheets of copper and mica are common in the graves of chiefs and other important persons (Kelemen, 1956: Plate 193). These reflect the same fundamental art style as other objects described above. The cold-hammering of copper, which was the only technique applied to this metal, is the highest achievement in metals north of Mexico.

Meso-America.—Meso-American art easily surpasses that of all other culture areas in both quality and quantity. With a population that exceeded that of all other culture areas combined and a large number of full-time artists and craftsmen, the quantity of art objects produced may have exceeded that of all other areas combined. Meso-American art was displayed in basketry, textiles, pottery, metal work, sculpture in stone and stucco, carving in jade and other precious stones, and in murals and manuscripts.

Meso-American pre-Columbian basketry is not well represented in collections and has not been carefully studied. Post-Columbian basketry is often undecorated and uninteresting to the art collector. Meso-American artists apparently did not consider basketry to be a very adequate outlet for their talents and left basket-making to the craftsmen. Weaving, on the other hand, seems to have been a well-developed art, but few examples of pre-Columbian weaving exist today. However, the nineteenth- and twentieth-century weaving in Guatemala gives us some idea of the complexity of the weaving art in Meso-America, although O'Neale (1954:87) believes that most of the designs have been strongly influenced by pressures from the outside since the Spanish conquest.

Modern Guatemalan weaving designs are both stylizations of living forms and abstractions unrecognizable as life forms. In addition, the weaver often includes his own signature, initials, or other

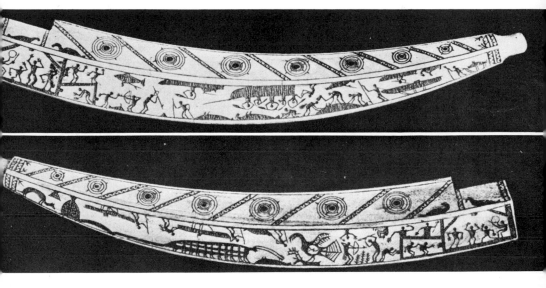

Plate I.—*Eskimo ivory pipe stem. After W. J. Hoffman, 1897. Courtesy of the Smithsonian Institution, U.S. National Museum.*

Plate II.—*Eskimo ivory seal carved by the "Mystery People," buried city of Ipiutak, Alaska. Courtesy of the American Museum of Natural History.*

Plate III.—Northwest Coast carved and painted wooden chest (Haida). Courtesy of the Washington State Museum (photo by Carroll Burroughs).

Plate IV.—Northwest Coast dance costume (Kwakiutl) representing an eagle. Courtesy of the Museum of the American Indian, Heye Foundation.

Plate V.—Northwest Coast mask (Kwakiutl) depicting a sculpin. The wearer covers his head with the hide at the bottom. Courtesy of the Washington State Museum.

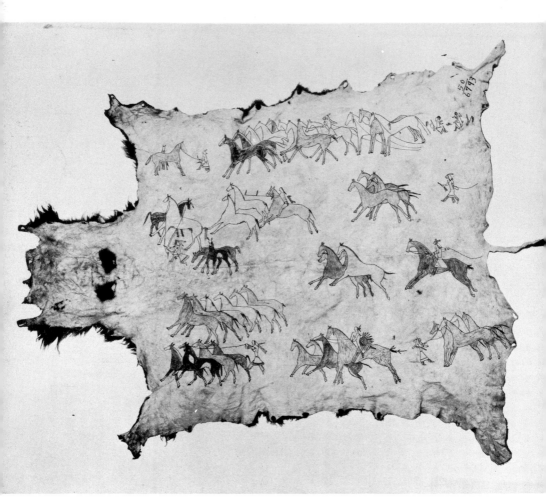

Plate VI.—Plains man's painting on buffalo robe (Oglala Sioux). Courtesy of the American Museum of Natural History.

Plate VII.—*Plains woman's painting on buffalo robe (Dakota). Courtesy of the American Museum of Natural History.*

Plate VIII.—*Plains quill-decorated band for a man's blanket or robe (Blackfoot). Courtesy of the American Museum of Natural History.*

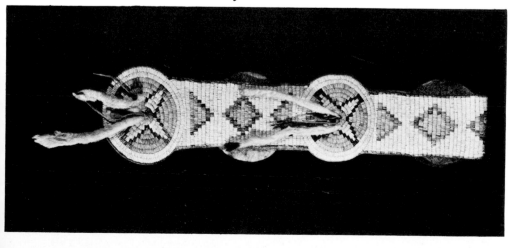

Plate IX.—Pueblo pottery vessels; left, Tularosa black-on-white jar (ca. A.D. 1100–1200); right, Reserve black-on-white duck effigy (ca. A.D. 1000–1100). Courtesy of Paul S. Martin and the Chicago Natural History Museum.

Plate X.—Eastern stone pipe from the Tremper Mound, Ohio. ($3\frac{7}{8}$ inches long, $2\frac{1}{2}$ inches high.) Courtesy of the Ohio State Museum.

Plate XI.—*Eastern flourspar figurine from Angel Mounds, Indiana. ($8\frac{3}{4}$ inches high.) Courtesy of Glenn A. Black and the Indiana Historical Society.*

Plate XII.—*Eastern stone pipe from the Adena Mound, southern Ohio. (8 inches high.) Courtesy of the Ohio State Museum.*

Plate XIII.—Eastern stone face from Gallatin County, Kentucky. (9½ inches high.) Courtesy of the Museum of the American Indian, Heye Foundation.

Plate XIV.—*Eastern shell gorget from Sumner County, Tennessee.
(3⅞ inches in diameter.) Courtesy of the Museum of the American
Indian, Heye Foundation.*

Plate XV.—*Meso-American naturalistic weaving designs. Modern
Huipil from San Pedro, Sacatépequez, Guatemala. Photograph by
Hilda Schmidt de Delgado; courtesy of the Museo Nacional
de Etnología.*

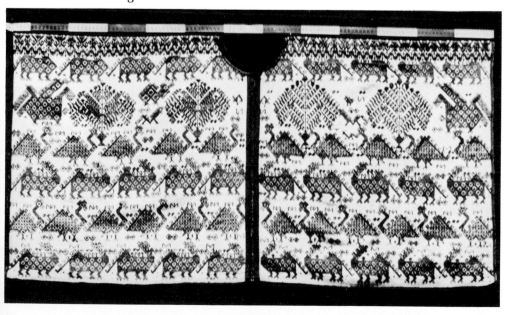

Plate XVI.—Meso-American sculptured pottery jar from San Augustin, Acasaguastlán, Guatemala. (7¼ inches high.) Courtesy of the Museum of the American Indian, Heye Foundation.

Plate XVII.—Meso-American pottery head from Vera Cruz, Mexico. (11 1/16 inches high, 10⅜ inches wide.) Courtesy of the Cleveland Museum of Art, J. H. Wade Collection.

*Plate XVIII.—Meso-American pottery head from
Vera Cruz, Mexico. (6 inches high.) Courtesy of
the American Museum of Natural History.*

Plate XIX.—Meso-American seated clay figure from Vera Cruz, Mexico. (13½ inches high.) Courtesy of the American Museum of Natural History.

Plate XX.—Meso-American baked clay figure from Chiapas, Mexico. (About 6 inches high.) Courtesy of the American Museum of Natural History.

Plate XXI.—Meso-American baked clay group of dancing women (Tarascan). (About 9 inches high.) Courtesy of Instituto Nacional de Antropología e Historia.

Plate XXII.—Meso-American sculpture in stone. Mayan stela from Copan, Honduras. Courtesy of the American Museum of Natural History.

Plate XXIII.—Meso-American metal work. Mixtec cast gold chest ornament depicting Jaguar-Knight as God of Death, from Monte Alban, Oaxaca, Mexico. (4½ inches high.) Courtesy of Instituto Nacional Antropología e Historia.

Plate XXIV.—Meso-American manuscripts

Plate XXV.—Meso-American painting. Scene from Mayan temple at Bonampak, Chiapas, Mexico. Courtesy of Instituto Nacional Antropología e Historia.

identifying trade mark. In O'Neale's illustrations of design motifs abstract forms outnumber conventionalized life forms, but not by a wide margin. Abstract forms are mostly geometric and some may be stylizations of former natural figures and, therefore, possess symbolism. Bird representations are the most frequent and varied class of naturalistic designs, but figures of humans, other mammals, and plants are also numerous (Plate XIV). Naturalistic and abstract design elements are often used together on the same piece of cloth. The colors employed in decorative designs are more varied than in pre-Columbian times because of the wool and aniline dyes introduced since the Spanish conquest; but the blood of the cochineal insect has been the chief source of red up until the last few decades. It seems clear from illustrations of Guatemalan weaving that Meso-Americans probably excelled the weavers of all other North American culture areas in the complexity and variety of decoration on textiles.

Meso-American pottery easily surpasses that of any other North American area in its variety of shape and decoration. Polychrome painting, handles, legs, lids, and effigy forms burst forth in great profusion. What appear to be purely geometric patterns are present, but conventionalized symbols and definitely naturalistic forms are more frequent than in the Southwest and Southeast. The Mayas made fresco vases on which they painted important personages clothed in the garments and decorated with the symbols of high rank. Some are seated on thrones, some ride in litters, and others walk or stand. Glyphs often accompany such pictures, presumably to explain what life drama is being enacted. In addition to painting, pottery vessels were decorated by incising, by engraving, and by relief which is deep enough to be called sculpture. Many naturalistic forms were modeled on vessels, often to represent important mythological deities such as the eagle, the jaguar, and the plumed serpent; but the human figure, particularly the head, was the most common (Plate XV). In addition to the many human figures appearing on pottery vessels as appendages, there were many human heads and statuettes made of baked clay and untold thousands of figurines of the same material (Plates XVI–XX). The baked clay human figures of the Olmecs are the largest and sometimes attained life size. The variety in posture and dress of these human figures is

205

indeed great, and those which seem a bit crude, when compared to the treatment of the human body in the classical art of the Old World, may still possess a bold quality that commands attention. Meso-American pottery is amply illustrated in Kelemen's excellent work (1956: Plates 110–49).

Meso-American sculpture in stone is the most impressive work of its kind in the entire New World. It varied in size from figurines small enough to be held in the palm of the hand to the huge stone heads of the Olmecs which, without any body, are up to seven or eight feet in height and thirty tons in weight. Like the stone statues of the ancient Greeks, those of the Aztecs, Mayas, and their neighbors were lavishly painted in many colors and, in association with architecture, created a striking spectacle. Kelemen (1956:106–7) believes that none of these statues and relief carvings can be regarded as portraits of particular individuals; there is too much stylization and not enough attention to idiosyncratic detail for actual portraiture. But the fact that it was not achieved does not mean it was not attempted. At any rate, the Maya sculptors featured the high-bridged convex nose, the receding chin, and the sloping forehead achieved in life by binding the head. The art styles approximated the different physical types in the various areas.

Sculpture took three forms: carving in the round, carving in relief, and modeling with clay or stucco. Carving in relief was more common than in the round. On Maya stelae, carving in relief and modeling with stucco sometimes appear on one and the same stone. As on painted pottery, human and other figures carved in relief or modeled with stucco are often accompanied by glyphs, which give the date and apparently other explanatory data about the historic event being depicted. The dates are the only parts of the glyph writing that can be translated with any degree of certainty. In addition to the glyphs, other conventionalized designs were crowded around the principal figure or figures to fill up all available space (Plate XXI). Most stone carving was displayed on and in palaces and religious structures, but these Maya stelae stood apart from such buildings. These huge monoliths, up to a height of thirty-five feet and a weight of fifty tons, were erected periodically to commemorate important dates and events associated with the ceremonial calendar. Each portrays the figure of a religious or political leader, well adorned with the regalia of his high office and surrounded with glyphs. The body faces front, with feet spread and pointing outward, but the head is turned in left profile. The dates on these stelae are important to the archeologist because they are the principal source of chronology in the Mayan area.

The most lifelike examples of the sculptured human figure seem more natural than those of the ancient Egyptians and Babylonians but much less so than those of the ancient Greeks. It is possible, however, that Meso-American sculptors were not attempting naturalness any more than many modern carvers of today and that an evaluation of their artistic achievement on that score misses the mark.

The metal work of Meso-America is known, from the archeological record, to have been largely derived from that of Andean South America. Objects made from precious metals were perhaps ten times as numerous in Peru as in Mexico, yet the metal jewelry made by the Mixtecs and Zapotecs of Oaxaca, southern Mexico, is the most elaborate in the pre-Columbian New World. Therefore, although Mexico derived most of its metallurgical techniques from South America, it developed its own idioms of expression. Jewelry in the form of finger rings, bracelets, necklaces, lip plugs, chest ornaments, and masks was beautifully designed and wrought (Plate XXII).

A number of semiprecious stones were worked by Meso-American artists. The principal ones were jade, turquoise, rock crystal, serpentine, amber, onyx, jasper, and agate. Of these stones, jade was the most valuable in the eyes of the Mexicans and their finest stonework was done with jade. When Montezuma saw how delighted the greedy Spaniards were with his gifts of gold, he promised them even more valuable presents the next day and brought forth some of his best jade, only to find them disappointed with the "green stones." Jade jewelry was worn only by the nobility and took the form of bracelets, anklets, masks, figurines, and other ornaments, some of which were regarded as amulets possessing supernatural power. Jade was carved in the round and in relief, both in about equal proportions (Kelemen, 1956: Plates 253–54). The human figure, or some part of it, predominates over other subjects.

The Meso-Americans also possessed books or codices in which

207

they displayed their art. The covers were of wood or hide and the "pages" of dressed hide, inner bark, or "paper" made from the maguey plant. The "pages" were a continuous sheet of material as much as thirty-four feet long, folded up like the strings of photographs in tourist shops. The human figures, glyphs, and other symbols were painted in the same style as similar compositions on pottery, murals, and stone carvings. The profusion of color was great, Mexican glyphs alone being painted in red, blue, green, black, white, yellow, orange, brown, and purple. These books contained all the official codified religious lore of the societies they served. From them the tremendous round of ritual, all geared to the calendar, was taught to young men dedicated by their parents to the celibate life of the priest. Those outside the priesthood were not allowed to see these sacred books and would have been unable to read them. To this day only 40 per cent of the glyphs have been deciphered (Plate XXIII).

Similar human figures, glyphs, and other symbols were painted on the inside walls of temples and palaces, and were viewed only by the priests, their students dedicated to the priesthood, and the nobility. Some of the most famous of these murals were found at a place called Bonampak ("the painted walls") in Chiapas, Mexico, near the border of Guatemala. On the inner walls of a Mayan temple are a set of murals depicting a raid for prisoners and the subsequent sacrificial ceremony. Among these is a dramatic scene showing the arraignment of a group of captives before a group of chieftains standing above them on a platform (Plate XXIV). The chieftains are elaborately decked out in headdresses crowned with the heads of animals, including the jaguar; and the highest-ranking chief, standing in the center, is wearing quetzal feathers on his head. This central figure is about four feet tall, including his plumes. The bodies of the chiefs are clothed in the skins of the jaguar or in body armor decorated according to their rank. In addition, all the chiefs carry weapons in their hands. Each of these chiefly figures differs in some detail from all the others, emphasizing their individuality which the artist does not submerge by exact repetiton of costume or body posture. The captives, in contrast, crouch on a terrace below, wearing nothing but breechcloths.

Some show blood dripping from their fingers, and in the left foreground are a head, a leg, and an arm from a dismembered body. Several of the captives crouch with upturned palms and eyes directed toward the head chief as if begging for mercy. The central captive, half-reclining and with eyes closed, is painted with an unusual degree of naturalness and grace of line. Various chiefs and attendants occupy the lowest terrace. Although the figures of the chiefs above and in the rear are not reduced in size, one nevertheless gets some feeling of depth in this remarkable mural. On the whole the figures are less stiff and distorted than those on other murals, stone carvings, vases, and books produced by the Meso-Americans.

The wood of utilitarian objects, such as suits of wooden armor, helmets, shields, canoe prows, lintels over doors, and the large cylindrical drums, was normally decorated by carving. Since wood rots rapidly in soil, few examples of wood-carving are preserved in museums. Their quality and style, however, compare favorably with that of carvings in stone.

Stone mosaics, consisting of small pieces of precious stones set in wood or stone, were also made by Meso-Americans. A beautiful mosaic plaque composed of more than three thousand bits of stone was found in the Temple of the Warriors at Chichén Itzá, a famous Mayan site in Yucatan, Mexico. The most common material used in mosaics was turquoise; but jade, other semiprecious stones, and shell were also employed.

An inventory of Meso-American art must include mention of the feather mosaics overlaid on cloaks, shields, and decorative objects. Feathers on cloaks were fastened to a cloth base, while those on shields were attached to the hide covering. Four different kinds and colors of feathers are arranged in horizontal bands around the neck and shoulders of a royal cloak, while on a shield the figure of a coyote is done principally in turquoise blue, with the belly, feet, and facial features set off in purple, against a red background (Kelemen, 1956: Plates 286–87). Both the cloak and the shield were given by Montezuma to the King of Spain.

Although the art of the Aztecs, Mayas, Toltecs, Mixtecs, and Zapotecs is better known than that of the earlier Olmecs of the first millennium B.C., Olmec art on the whole is subtler, gentler, freer, and more naturalistic than that of the others. It compares favorably with the best of Old World art of its time, except that of the ancient Greeks, which surpassed it.

GENERAL REMARKS ON VISUAL ART

In this survey of American Indian art we have omitted entirely the curvilinear floral motifs incised, painted, and stamped on the birch bark of the Sub-Arctic, the unsymbolic but intricate basketry designs of California and the Great Basin, and other more localized art styles of aboriginal North America. Nevertheless our inventory of the artistic achievement of the Red man reveals a great variety of techniques and styles of expression. Although the innovation of the individual artist obtrudes itself here and there, most work in the visual arts conforms to localized styles which the specialist can recognize at a glance and allocate to the proper place or time level. Innovations are more often in small details than in totally new conceptions. Where we have the most archeological documentation, in the Southwest, we find a definite continuity between the art of adjacent time periods and of neighboring localities.

Until the last few decades, American Indian art has been given very little attention by the art critics and connoisseurs of Europe and its derivative cultures. This has been due more to ignorance of native American art than to the culture-bound snobbery of some members of this group. Most examples of the art of the Red man were destroyed by the Spanish and other European invaders. It was only after archeology came of age and implemented a program of field investigation that enough exciting specimens appeared in museums to attract modern artists and their camp followers. Now that the scarcity of many of these art objects has become known to collectors, their value has increased enormously and has encouraged the smuggling of specimens over international boundaries. Although researchers on the American Indian are pleased at the present stampede of interest toward this art, they hope that most of the great and inimitable artistic achievements of the Indian will find their way into universities and public museums where they can be seen by every interested person and studied by all qualified scholars.

REFERENCES

BARTRAM, 1853; BUSHNELL, 1908; COVARRUBIAS, 1954; DOUGLAS AND D'HARNONCOURT, 1941; DRUCKER, 1955; EWERS, 1939; GRIFFIN, 1952; HOFFMAN, 1897; HUNT, 1951; INVERARITY, 1950; KELEMEN, 1956; KENT, 1957; DE LAGUNA, 1932–33; LAWSON, 1860; LORM, 1945; LOWIE, 1954; MERA, 1937, 1939; MORRIS AND BURGH, 1941; O'NEALE, 1945; ROEDIGER, 1941; RUPPERT, THOMPSON, AND PROSKOURIAKOFF, 1955; SCHAEFER-SIMMERN, 1958; STEVENSON, 1904; SWANTON, 1909, 1911; TANNER, 1957.

12: MUSIC

By Wilhelmine Driver

NORTH American Indian music, like other aspects of Indian culture, exhibits great variety. It is far from conforming to the usual stereotype in the mind of the general reader. The average intelligent listener, if asked to describe American Indian music, would think it easy to reply in a few sentences. He would mention the prevalence of drums and rattles, and the harshness of the singing tone. He might add, as exceptions to prove the rule, the use of the flute in courtship, and a few sweet songs like the "Indian Love Call" or the "Land of the Sky-Blue Waters," written by non-Indian composers on partially Indian themes.

A student of ethnomusicology would go into more detail concerning musical instruments. He might also describe the technique of voice production in terms of great tension in the vocal organs, strong accents, and pulsations of intensity on the longer notes. If he attempted to analyze the actual melodies, he might characterize them as predominantly descending from higher to lower pitch, either in a gradual progression or "terraced" or "cascading" downwards.

All of these features were formerly thought to make up the general type of North American Indian music, following the analysis by E. M. von Hornbostel. They can, in fact, be found in a number of areas, but only in the Plains, Prairies, and Oasis are all of them present in the majority of songs. Early collectors obtained more music from these areas than elsewhere and scholars like Hornbostel assumed that these samples were representative of the whole continent.

Nowadays, on the basis of wider and more thorough research,

it is possible to make more valid generalizations about North American Indian music as a whole. It consists, for the most part, of songs, which may last (including repetitions) from about 20 seconds to about three minutes. Larger forms, where they exist, are produced by stringing together a series of brief songs. In most areas the range of the melodies lies between a fifth (e.g., C to G) and a twelfth (e.g., C to G an octave higher). About 60 per cent of the samples studied by Nettl (1954) are pentatonic (containing five tones separated by intervals of major seconds and at least one minor third, e.g., C D F G A). Most of the intervals in Nettl's samples approximate, he says, those of the Western tempered scale. This resemblance may, however, be partially due to European influences in the music which has been recorded, or to faulty notation. Nearly all songs are monophonic, including only a single melody; that is, at a given moment only one pitch is sounded. In some areas women sing along with the men, but in the higher octave. Instruments are used mainly to provide a rhythmic accompaniment. Melodic polyphony (the simultaneous singing of two or more rather independent melodic lines) is practically absent, except for some occurrence of the "drone" type, in which a melody is accompanied by sustained notes on a single pitch. Harmony is absent, except in American hymn tunes sung by Christian congregations. Instruments are used mainly to provide a rhythmic accompaniment; there is very little purely instrumental music, and solo drumming does not occur. The only melodic instruments are flutes or flageolets, which are employed in many areas for love charms and less often in ceremonies. Most of these instrumental melodies may also be sung. Simultaneous combination of two or more flutes, or flute and voice, is unknown.

Consistent measure or bar lengths are apparently less common than uneven bar lengths and asymmetrical rhythmic patterns. Rhythms are, in general, relatively complex. Songs in most areas are strophic. A strophe consists of between two and twelve separate sections or phrases; these last several seconds each and are often of unequal length within an individual song, tending also to become longer toward the end of the song.

The most common musical instruments in North America are idiophones. These are represented by rattles of various types; less

213

frequently by planks or rods beaten, sticks beaten together, and the like. Membranophones, that is, drums with skin heads, are also found in most tribes. Of the aerophones, or wind instruments, whistles and flutes or flageolets have a wide distribution, and simple reed instruments occur in a few areas. Chordophones, stringed instruments, have a very limited distribution and only one, the musical bow, may possibly be native to North America.

Song texts very frequently contain entirely or partly meaningless syllables. Texts may also include archaic words or phrases, loanwords, or special phonemic alterations. These devices, in certain areas, make the song text style rather different from the spoken prose style, and tend to obscure the meaning.

American Indian music is, for the most part, functional, that is, used as an integral part of the other, non-musical activities. It is indispensable to all rituals and ceremonies. Since most of these are performed by men, it is men who predominate in music-making. Men lead the singing and compose or learn the ritual songs; they also make and play the instruments. The fact that women in North America are mainly relegated to a passive role in ritual may account, to some extent, for the lack of polyphonic music. Songs are also interspersed in tales, though true narrative songs are rare. There are special gambling songs and songs for other games as well. Dances of all sorts are accompanied by singing and percussion instruments. Marching songs, however, were absent in North America, except possibly in Meso-America, before the Spanish conquest. Work songs are rare. Women sing various types of songs including, of course, lullabies. Both group and solo singing are common everywhere. In some areas certain songs are individually owned as property which can be inherited or even sold. Songs may also be used for love-making, for ridicule, or for boasting.

Music is valued principally for its magical or personal power rather than for its aesthetic component. If well performed it is "good" rather than beautiful. Not all music, however, is functional; some of it is produced simply for the pleasure of making music, individually or in groups.

Music has attained its most complex development on the Northwest Coast, in the Oasis, Meso-America, and possibly the Southeast. It is in these areas that we find the most complex musical styles and forms, theories about types and origins of songs, some musical instruction, and musical specialists or semiprofessionals.

Study of North American Indian music is not yet advanced enough to permit a satisfactory division of the entire continent into musical areas. Three significant attempts have been published so far: the first a brief survey by George Herzog in 1928; the second, stressing the distribution of musical instruments, by Helen Roberts in 1936; the most recent, based on technical aspects of musical style, by Bruno Nettl in 1954. Since none of these presents a comprehensive picture, we shall rest content, in this volume, with a brief non-technical description of the music of several of our major culture areas. More detailed discussion of such technical matters as melodic contour, intervals, and rhythmic patterns may be found in the sources listed in the bibliography.

Arctic.—The Eskimo singing technique is characterized by considerable vocal tension and rhythmic pulsations on the longer notes. Accents and stressed grace notes are common. In most of the Arctic, however, these features are less intense than in Plains or Oasis music. Melodies are undulating in contour. Antiphonal singing, with alternation of solo and chorus, occurs, but melodic polyphony is unknown.

Eskimo songs are usually in slow tempo. Rhythms tend to be asymmetrical and complex. Most of the songs are accompanied by the beating of drums or of a part of the body. In some areas this is in indefinite rhythmic patterns, producing a complex rhythmic polyphony between voice and accompaniment. The drums are of the tambourine type, a single hide stretched over a hoop, that is, a disc-shaped variety of single-headed drum. This type of drum was probably derived from Asia. Rattles, flutes, and whistles are absent in the Arctic.

Music in the Arctic serves chiefly religious purposes. Shamans deliver incantations to the spirits for good weather, success in hunting, health, and the like. Individuals own, inherit, and buy charms which include magical songs. Disputes are sometimes conducted in song. Two men, instead of fighting, may compete with each other in songs of ridicule, with the audience acting as court. There are no professional music specialists, but certain individuals

215

are considered particularly good singers. Some of these evince great love of music and devotion to their art.

Northwest Coast.—The musical style of the Northwest Coast resembles that of the Arctic but is more complex. The vocal technique is similar. Melodic contours are undulating or descending. Here, in addition to some antiphonal singing, we find a few instances of the drone type of melodic polyphony, one voice sustaining a single tone while another sings a moving melody. Rhythmic polyphony between the melody and the percussion accompaniment is often quite intricate.

Percussion instruments include clappers made of split sticks, foot drums of a plank over a pit in the floor, and rattles. The rattles are of the container type, holding small pebbles, and are made chiefly of wood, often carved in bird or animal form. Logs, planks, or boxes are beaten. The tambourine was acquired in the nineteenth century. Here we also find wind instruments. True flutes are rare, but single-note whistles occur. The Northwest Coast is one of the few areas in which reed instruments, on the order of clarinets and oboes, were played by some tribes. They reach their most elaborate development in this area and include tubes with single, multiple, or ribbon reeds, but without fingerholes. These instruments may have been derived, in part, from Asia.

Here also the principal function of music is religious. Individuals, both men and women, own songs as property which may be inherited or sold, and many of these songs are correlated with their individual spirit dances. There are no musical professionals, but music is taught and rehearsed, and musical errors may be punished. A fairly well-developed musical terminology exists here.

Great Basin.—The simplest musical style on the continent is found in this area and among the Modoc and Klamath on the Oregon-California border. The singing technique is smooth, without much vocal tension or pulsation. The range of the melodies is usually small. Many of the songs are performed without any percussive accompaniment.

Percussion instruments used include drums, rattles, and musical rasps. The only kind of drum was the tambourine, which was derived from the Plains and Plateau area in the nineteenth century. Both container rattles, made of rawhide filled with pebbles, and jingler rattles, usually made of deer hoofs, were common. The musical rasp, a notched stick a couple of feet long, rubbed back and forth with a smaller stick, was much used in the Great Basin. In the twentieth century two instruments have spread to this area from the Plains with the Peyote religion: the gourd rattle and the kettle drum. The latter consists of a hide stretched over a pottery vessel partly filled with water.

Other instruments used include whistles, true flutes capable of producing a melody, and the musical bow. The last-named is the only stringed instrument which may possibly be pre-Columbian in North America. In its simplest form it consists merely of a hunting bow, of which one end is held between the teeth, and the string is struck with a stick. The pitch and quality of the sound was varied by the player's changing the shape of his mouth which served as a resonator. The tone was feeble and the range so limited that the instrument sounded more percussive than tonal. It was used more often for musical doodling than for a more serious musical effort.

The songs of the 1890 Ghost Dance, a religious movement which spread from the Great Basin to the Plains area, carried with them the musical style of the Great Basin. Music has both religious and non-religious uses in the Great Basin area. A few of the non-religious uses of music include songs in animal tales, songs connected with gambling games, and lullabies. For these three purposes very simple music is widespread and is thought by Herzog to represent archaic layers in North American Indian music.

California.—The musical style of this area extends also through the Yuman-speaking peoples of Arizona, but excludes a few of the northern California tribes. The vocal technique is smooth and relaxed like that of the Great Basin. The Yuman melodies contain a section of higher pitch, called the "rise," somewhere in the body of the song. Percussion instruments provide a brief introduction and conclusion for the song, in addition to rhythmic accompaniment. In the rise section the instruments often play tremolo.

Rhythm instruments include foot drums, baskets beaten or scraped, split-stick clappers, musical rasps, and rattles. The tambourine was introduced here in the nineteenth century. Container rattles were made of gourds, turtle shells, or cocoons filled with

217

pebbles. Deer hoof jingler rattles were also common. Wind instruments include flutes, tubes with reeds, and whistles. Two whistles are sometimes bound together to produce a two-tone instrument. Most of the Yuman songs are organized into long series with a set order of songs. The religious function of music is important here, as elsewhere in North America.

Plains-Prairies.—This musical area includes the Plains, the Prairies, and the Western Great Lakes region. Its singing technique is characterized by loudness, great vocal tension, strong accents, glissandos, and heavy pulsation on the long tones. These vocal practices tend to produce fluctuating pitch or intonation. Melodies cover an average range of a tenth, but may even exceed two octaves. Melodic contours are mainly descending, of the terraced or cascading type in which each section is lower in pitch than the preceding section. Song rhythms are usually complex and asymmetrical. The most common rhythmic accompaniment, however, consists of regular pulse beating. Songs are usually introduced and concluded by drum beats or rattle tremolos. The great majority of songs have instrumental accompaniment.

Percussive instruments include the tambourine and a few double-headed hide drums which may be of modern introduction. The pottery kettle drum spread through this area with the Peyote religion in the late nineteenth and twentieth centuries. Pieces of rawhide were sometimes scraped to provide rhythmic accompaniment, and musical rasps made of wood, and less often of bone, were also used. Rattles include jingler animal hoof rattles and container rattles made of rawhide filled with pebbles. Gourd rattles probably diffused to the Plains from the adjoining farming areas. The musical bow is absent in this area. Wind instruments include one-note whistles, flageolets, and true flutes. The latter were played principally by youths courting their ladyloves and were not used in ceremonies.

Most of the Plains music is functional, and a large proportion of it is connected with dancing. Both performers and audience are predominantly masculine, since much music serves such male activities as religious ritual, cult societies, warfare, military and other sodalities, curing ceremonies, gambling, the vision quest, and serenading. Women's sodalities, however, also have music. Music is also used for entertainment, in social dancing, games, and story-

218

telling, and for education in the form of story-songs. Women, of course, sing lullabies to their children.

There are no professional musicians, but there is some informal specialization. In large group activities usually a few individuals, medicine men or song-leaders, perform the music while the others listen. Plains Indians have few theories about music and little musical terminology. However, boys' vision quest songs are thought to be given by the spirits.

Songs may be owned, sold, or inherited. They may be individual property, such as the songs pertaining to a medicine bundle, or may be owned by a social group such as a sodality.

Throughout the Plains four types of music differ radically, in both singing and instruments, from the characteristic Plains style. Two of these result from diffusion in modern times: the 1890 Ghost Dance music from the Great Basin, and the Peyote cult music from the south and southwest. The third type, for lullabies, animal tale songs, and some gambling songs, is of the archaic style mentioned above. The fourth, for love songs, is probably also the result of diffusion.

Oasis.—In this area we find three principal musical styles, represented here by the Pueblos, the Pima-Papagos, and the Navahos. In the Pueblo style, the vocal technique resembles closely that of the Plains, except that many of the Pueblo Katchina songs begin at a very low pitch. Melodies are also of the Plains style, though much more complex and of greater range. Rhythmic accompaniments range from steady beats to definite rhythmic designs independent of those of the melody. Pueblo musical style is the most complex in North America in post-Columbian times.

Pima-Papago musical style combines Pueblo with California-Yuman musical traits. The singing technique is smooth and relaxed. Melodies seldom exceed an octave in range. Rhythms and melodic patterns are comparatively simple. Melodies are mainly descending, but the terraced or cascading contours of the Plains and Pueblo songs are not common. The Pima-Papago style appears among the Pueblos in the women's corn-grinding songs.

Much of the Navaho ritual music has been learned, with the rituals, from the Pueblos. However, the basic musical style of the Navahos and their linguistic relatives, the Apaches, seems to be connected with that of areas farther northwest. The vocal technique resembles that of the Pueblos and Plains. Melodies cover a fairly wide range, and are often arc-shaped in contour. Large intervals, with almost acrobatic jumps from low to high notes, sometimes occur. Rhythms are simpler than those of Pueblo music, and the accompaniments are usually even, pulsating beats. The songs of the Peyote cult, wherever it is found in the United States, are somewhat similar in musical style to those of the Navahos and Apaches. Peyote songs have usually, however, a smoother singing technique, more like that of the Great Basin or of European folk singing.

In the Oasis area as a whole, a wide variety of instruments is used. Drums include double-headed hide drums, which may be comparatively modern, pottery kettle-drums, and foot drums consisting of a plank over a pit. Baskets are also beaten, and musical rasps are used. Rattles made from the domesticated gourd, filled with pebbles or seeds, are used here, as in all other farming areas. Other container rattles include turtle shells and sections of hollow horn. Handled pottery rattles contain stones, seeds, or clay pellets. Rattling material was also built into hollow parts of pottery vessels, and a few "sleigh bells" of pottery with rattling pottery pellets have been reported. The last may have been imitations of copper "sleigh bells" which were traded to the Oasis from Meso-America. Animal hoof jingler rattles are also used. In the Oasis, as in California, the musical bow may be used in religious rituals. Whistles are common and tubes with ribbon reeds are found in some tribes. True flutes are played not only for love-making but also in sacred ceremonies.

All of the uses of music in the Plains, by individuals and by groups, have their parallels in the Oasis. In addition there are work songs, namely the corn-grinding songs of the Pueblos. Oasis music is, however, predominantly religious. Even the gambling songs of the Navaho are used to contact spiritual power. The most striking difference in musical function between the two major areas, however, reflects the contrasts between the character of their sodalities. Whereas the social groups of the Plains are usually loosely organized and are formed for a variety of purposes, some being merely social clubs for entertainment, those of the Pueblos consist of permanent cult groups with complex religious ceremonial. Ritual music must, of course, meet the needs of these ceremonies,

Therefore songs are organized into set, invariable series, from short suites of a few songs to elaborate song cycles to accompany ceremonies lasting several days.

Such song series are usual also among the Pima-Papagos, as for instance in the harvest festival, and in Navaho curing ceremonies such as the Night Chant or the Enemy Way. Since any mistake or omission in performance may invalidate the entire ceremony, the ritual leaders may have to spend months in learning a single song cycle. Certain cult group officials are also, therefore, music specialists. Among the Navaho, where permanent cult organizations are lacking and groups are formed for specific curing ceremonies, we find semiprofessional singers. A young Navaho Singer pays a tuition fee to the older Singer who teaches him the text and music of one of the longer ceremonial song cycles, as well as all the accompanying lore of the ceremony. To learn and be able to perform several such cycles is the accomplishment of a lifetime.

The texts of these chants are often obscure to the audience, though better understood by the performers or by the older men. Among the Pima-Papago phonemes may undergo changes from speech to song, *b* becoming *m* or *mw*, *d* becoming *n*, and the like. Archaic religious words, or words borrowed from another language, are frequent and are sometimes described as "old language."

In the Oasis there is little interest in theories about music. The Pima-Papagos, however, distinguished between "picked-up songs" learned from other tribes or from White people, "dreamt songs" obtained from the spirits, and songs "given in the beginning," that is, dating from the creation of the earth. To the Navaho, on the contrary, all songs were "given in the beginning," even those which they are known to have learned from the Pueblos.

East.—Information about the music of this culture area is derived partially from recordings in the last fifty to sixty years and partially from descriptions given by early writers and travelers. The modern musical style is fairly consistent throughout the area. Its singing technique has a moderate amount of vocal tension and pulsations. Melodic contours are mainly undulating and gradually descending. Song series consist of six or eight or less songs performed in fixed cycles. Rhythms are fairly simple. Rhythmic accompaniment, when present, is usually a steady beat, though rattle tremolos are also used. The most distinctive feature of this area

221

is antiphonal singing, between two individuals or leader and group. This, by overlapping of the end of one phrase with the beginning of the next, may give rise to some rudimentary polyphony. Early writers reported polyphony of the round or canon type, and also drone polyphony.

Percussion instruments include the tambourine, the double-headed hide drum (which may be modern) and pottery and wooden kettle drums. Container rattles were made of gourds, turtle shells, hollow horn, or, around the Great Lakes, of cylinders of bark. Deer hoof jingler rattles were also common. Musical rasps were used, but the musical bow is not reported for the area. Whistles were common, and some tribes played tubes with reeds.

True flutes were used on official occasions and in sacred ceremonies. For instance, De Soto encountered chiefs and other high-ranking officials in Florida playing cane flutes as a sign of peace and good will on greeting him. In the Southeast trumpets like those of Meso-America and the Caribbean, made of marine conch shells, were used as bugles in war. The presence of music specialists seems likely on the Southeastern coastal plain where hereditary kings and full time priests were the rule in the most complex societies. The music associated with religious ceremonies was an important part of the knowledge of these priests, who taught it to the students in the schools for priests.

Meso-America.—The aboriginal music of this area was almost completely wiped out by the conquering Spaniards, who were fully aware of its powerful religious influence. The Spanish priests, in Mexico at least, immediately taught their converts the ritual of the Catholic Church. The Latin singing of some of the Indian choirs soon compared favorably with that of Spain. Indians also adopted Spanish popular songs and dances, and the use of the mandolin and the guitar. It is, therefore, impossible to know much about Meso-American musical style. Mexican musicologists and composers, exploring remote areas in search of native music, have recovered only a few traces of aboriginal melodies and instruments. Even these may represent only the music of less civilized tribes rather than that of the high Meso-American cultures.

The pottery kettle drum probably originated in this area, but was replaced by a one-headed tubular type of drum open at the bottom. Hollow, so-called log drums were also common. One type of these had an H-shaped slit, and the two inwardly projecting wooden tongues thus formed were tuned to different pitches. Turtle shells were also used as percussion instruments.

Gourd rattles were used, and are still a standard instrument today in Latin-American popular music. Other container rattles used include turtle shells, wooden tubes, and hollow pieces of horn, as well as handled pottery rattles and pottery vessels with rattling material built in. Copper "sleigh bell" rattles were also common and were traded to the Oasis area. Animal hoof jingler rattles were infrequent in Meso-America although they were used in Northeast Mexico. Musical rasps were used, and the musical bow may have been pre-Columbian in Meso-America and around the Caribbean. Tubes with reeds were lacking, but whistles and true flutes flourished, the latter playing an important part in official and religious ceremonies. Marine conch shell trumpets functioned as war bugles.

Sahagún and other sixteenth-century writers report the close association of music with religious ritual and daily musical rehearsing in the boarding schools for youths. We may assume that Meso-American music must have been more complex than any music north of Mexico, and priests must have acted as semiprofessional music specialists.

Circum-Caribbean.—All of the musical instruments mentioned for Meso-America are reported also around the Caribbean, except the beaten turtle-shell, horn or turtle-shell rattles, and animal hoof jingler rattles. We find here, in addition, the true "Pan-pipes," consisting of three or four tubes of different pitch, bound together. This instrument was obviously derived from South America.

Since the more complex cultures around the Caribbean were destroyed by the European invaders, we have scarcely any knowledge of their aboriginal musical style. We know, however, that music played a conspicuous role in sacred ceremonies, which were performed principally by the men.

REFERENCES

DENSMORE, 1926; DRIVER, 1953*b*; DRIVER AND RIESENBERG, 1950; HERZOG, 1928*a*, 1928*b*, 1934, 1935*a*, 1935*b*, 1936, 1938, 1949; IZIKOWITZ, 1935; McALLESTER, 1954; MERRIAM, n.d.; NETTL, 1954; ROBERTS, 1936; SAHAGÚN (Anderson and Dibble), 1950–58.

13: Exchange, Trade, and Transportation

IN THE discussion of craft specialization in chapter x it was pointed out that such specialization must be accompanied by the exchange of surplus goods, at least within a single community. If each family lived in isolation, there would be no point in producing a surplus because there would be nobody else with whom to exchange it for some other desirable product. Probably every family in aboriginal North America exchanged something of value with another family at least a few times a year. There is no record of any culture in which the nuclear family, consisting of parents and children, was the only social group. Each family had some contact with other families and was combined in some way to form a larger social grouping at some season of the year. The Canadian Algonquians of the Eastern Sub-Arctic probably lived in the smallest and most isolated family groups in all of North America, but only during the winter season. In summer, these families joined others at fishing places on rivers and lakes and formed aggregates up to several hundred persons. Exchange of everything from material goods to brides and folktales took place at these summer rendezvous. Other small and relatively isolated populations, such as the Eskimos of the Arctic and the Shoshoni of the Great Basin, also formed larger aggregates at least once a year.

GIFT AND CEREMONIAL EXCHANGE

The process of distribution in non-industrial societies may be inextricably blended with facets of culture ordinarily not regarded as economic. There is a wide range of exchange behavior varying all the way from informal giving to a friend to elaborately stylized reciprocal exchange by large groups of kindred. Practically every major North American Indian ceremony is accompanied by feasting, which is a form of distribution. For example, the rites performed for an individual at birth, puberty, marriage, and death are often of this character. There is usually a host group consisting of the relatives of the individual for whom the rite is performed and a guest group of non-relatives who have been invited to attend the celebration. The hosts provide the guests with food as long as the ceremony lasts, which may be for days. Then at some later date the roles are reversed—the guests become hosts and the hosts become guests.

Probably the one occasion on which gifts were most often exchanged was that of marriage. Among the majority of North American tribes, the families of the bride and groom mutually exchanged gifts. While it is true that the amount of goods "paid" by the groom's relatives for the bride was sometimes negotiated in a business-like way, this practice was characteristic only of the Northwest Coast, although occurrences in other areas have been reported. Even in this area, the bride's family was expected to make reciprocal gifts. The strong bride-purchase ideas of the northern Plains in the nineteenth century were at least partly the result of White contact and the fur trade, which placed a premium on women skin-dressers.

The most elaborate ceremonial exchange of economic goods is that of the famous potlatch of the Northwest Coast Indians of British Columbia and southeastern Alaska. One person (or at most a few who are closely related) assumes the role of donor by declaring his intentions, inviting guests, and acting as host. At the same time he is assisted by his kinsmen, or by village mates who are principally kinsmen. In the north they are his matrilineal kinsmen, while farther south relationship is reckoned bilaterally (Map 32). These kinsmen either engage in a series of minor distributions of gifts at the same assemblage or join with the major donor by making contributions, which are publicly acknowledged, to his pool of property which will then be disposed of at one larger session. Every freeman, then, is related to someone important enough to give a potlatch or to receive at one and may, therefore, participate in the system. Even women and children may take part; only slaves are excluded.

In order of their rank the host seats his guests, serves them food, and presents them with gifts to take home. The value of the gift is also correlated with rank; the more important one's rank, the more expensive is the gift he receives. The result is that every time a potlatch is given all who attend are ranked in a series from high to low and everyone sees exactly how everyone else is rated by the host. A given person's rank may be raised or lowered by the lavishness of his own giving when he is host at his own potlatch. The more he gives away and the more impoverished he is at the end of the ceremony, the greater is his social prestige.

Northwest Coast culture is replete with titles equivalent to offices in churches, lodges, and clubs. When it is desired that a title he passed on from an older to a younger relative, a potlatch is given. Thus, there are birth, puberty, marriage, and death potlatches, to mention only the most obvious occasions. With the title goes the right to recite certain myths, sing certain songs, wear certain crests on clothing and carve them on houses and canoes. In a culture without legal documents, newspapers, radio, or television, the potlatch serves to publicize a change in status of an individual. Potlatches may also be given as a demonstration of wealth and prestige to outdo a rival, or to compensate for the death of a relative or personal injury to oneself.

The potlatch of the Kwakiutl Indians of British Columbia was probably the most ostentatious and dramatic of all and has been studied in most detail. There were altogether 658 titles or positions in all the thirteen local subdivisions of the Kwakiutl. The translations of the names of some of these positions are: "creating trouble all around"; "giving wealth"; "throwing away property"; "about whose property people talk"; "envied"; "satiating"; "getting too great." A man who had received property at a potlatch was expected to make a return, of double the value received, at another potlatch in about a year. He thus "paid" 100 per cent "interest" on the "loan." Preparatory to every potlatch, however, there was a series of small "loans" at smaller "interest" rates. The following "interest" rates were customary: under six months, 20 per cent; six months, 40 per cent; 12 months, 100 per cent; 12 months under circumstances where the borrower has poor credit, 233 per cent. Codere (1951, Fig. 5), gives a schematic presentation of how a boy gets his start in Kwakiutl culture. The gist of the scheme is that he borrows blankets from friends, loans them out to other friends at a higher rate of interest, and uses the profit as capital for his first potlatch.

It is obvious that if everyone returned gifts or "loans" received with these amounts of "interest," the total wealth of the tribe would have to double every year. Although Kwakiutl material possessions did show a phenomenal increase in the historic period, which probably surpassed anything of the kind in pre-European times, the total wealth did not increase at such a rate. The one feature which served as a check on this annual doubling of wealth was the destruction of wealth. Canoes were sometimes destroyed and slaves killed in aboriginal times, but in historic times the destruction of copper plates was the highest level of attainment. These plates were cold hammered from native copper into rectangloid sheets about two feet long and half as wide. The top half was engraved in black lead (of European origin) with the face of the crest animal of the owner. Like a rare art object today, the value of the copper depended on the amount of property that had been paid for it in the potlatch in which it had last changed hands. The destruction of a copper, by breaking it into bits and tossing them into the fire or into the sea, demonstrated that a man was so wealthy he could afford to lose a fortune. A rival of a copper-destroyer might feel compelled to destroy another copper of even greater value, as indeed he would have to do to surpass the first man's act of destruction.

Potlatches were of all degrees of magnitude. The maximum number of each material item exchanged at any single Kwakiutl potlatch from 1729 to 1936 will give an idea of the immensity of some of these affairs: six slaves; fifty-four dressed elkskins; eight canoes; three coppers; two thousand silver bracelets; seven thousand brass bracelets; thirty-three thousand blankets. As many as fifty seals were eaten at the accompanying feast.

Anthropologists in the past have attempted to justify the potlatch by saying that it was a legitimate form of investment analogous to life insurance. A more recent and convincing justification, however, is that it became a substitute for physical violence. Disputes or rivalries which would have led to feuds a century or more ago were settled by potlatching in later times. This change was due in part to the firm stand of the Canadian government, which on one occasion burned an entire village as punishment for the killing of a war captive in connection with a winter ceremonial. Regardless of the cause of the change, the destruction of property is to be preferred to the loss of lives, and the outlet for aggressions provided by the potlatch made it desirable, at least in the stage of transition from aboriginal to Canadian culture.

TRADE AND TRANSPORTATION

Trade was engaged in to some extent by all but one North American local group or tribe. This exception is the Polar Eskimos, who had no contact with other tribes and thought they were the only people on earth when discovered by John Ross in 1818. Every tribe but this one possessed at least some objects which could not be obtained locally but which had to be obtained in trade from the outside. Data on trade are of theoretical importance because they demonstrate the process of diffusion, which is so powerful a determiner of cultural growth. We need not speculate how customs or ideas traveled from one tribe to another when we realize that every locality had some contact with the outside through trade.

Transportation was a daily problem for all Indians, whether it involved a group of men with trade goods to be taken hundreds of miles or a single woman carrying home the food she had gathered within a few miles' radius during a single day. The greatest amount of tonnage was carried on the backs of human beings, mainly because of the absence of suitable beasts of burden. Back packing was universal in aboriginal North America and was the principal method known to the most heavily populated area, Meso-America. Although dugout canoes and balsas were also known in this area, they dominated human carrying only on lakes and on the coasts. In the Oasis, Northeast Mexico, and the Great Basin, the picture is about the same, with the human back being relieved only occasionally by balsas and log rafts, which were makeshift structures, hastily assembled from whatever materials were at hand, and abandoned as soon as a stream was crossed. Women consistently carried heavier loads than men, except in Meso-America where specialized male craftsmen usually carried their own wares to market. While this seems inequitable at first blush, it must be remembered that much travel was in search of food, and that a man had to be prepared at any moment to pursue game as well as to defend his family against enemies. Therefore, he traveled lightly laden but heavily armed.

The wheel was never put to any practical purpose by Indians and has appeared only on a few wheeled toys made of pottery which were unearthed by archeologists in Mexico. There was no wheeled vehicle of any kind, nor was the true wheel used in making pottery. Both of these revolutionary inventions were made in the Middle East of the Old World about 4000 B.C. which means that in this respect the New World had lagged behind 5,500 years by the time of the European conquest. Indian methods of land transportation were inferior to those of the Old World because of the absence of the wheel. The importance of the wheel in our own machine age can scarcely be overestimated.

Arctic.—The Copper Eskimos obtained copper from the Copper-mine River, which empties into the Arctic sea in their territory, and traded it to both the west and the east. They also possessed the largest supply of soapstone in the entire Arctic. Neighboring Eskimo bands sometimes traveled hundreds of miles to mine this soapstone. Those at greater distances, as far west as Alaska and east to Labrador, obtained the finished lamps and pots in trade. The Copper Eskimos and their closest eastern neighbors made journeys south to obtain wood. This was a valuable article of trade as far east as Baffinland, because driftwood was extremely scarce in the central Arctic. Wood was more valuable than ivory in much of this territory because it was the best material for sleds and was indispensable for boat frames.

Probably more tonnage was transported by dog sled in the Arctic than by any other means; but in the summer months the large hide-covered open boat, called the *umiak*, was much used. During the summer hunts for caribou, inland away from the coast, baggage was carried on the backs of both human beings and dogs.

Northwest Coast and Plateau.—On the Northwest Coast, the

Plateau, and the adjacent Sub-Arctic there was a lively trade in pre-Columbian times. Dentalia shells, obtained principally on the west coast of Vancouver Island, were widely traded and served as a medium of exchange over a considerable part of the area where they were known. At White contact they were found in the western Arctic as far east as the Mackenzie Delta, in the Yukon Sub-Arctic, on the Northwest Coast and the Plateau, on the northern Plains as far east as the village tribes on the upper Missouri in the Dakotas, and among the northernmost tribes of central California. Copper, from the Copper River in southern Alaska, was traded as far south as the Columbia River. It was exchanged for dentalia, other shells, and sharks' teeth.

The trade articles brought by European ships, and the new demand for furs by the European traders from about 1775 on, greatly stimulated Northwest Coast trade. In the south, the Chinooks soon dominated the Columbia River route and exacted a toll from other tribes who paddled their wares up or down the river. At the Dalles, where huge falls make portaging necessary, the aboriginal trading center grew to great proportions. Much of the goods from the interior was obtained at this point by the Chinooks and taken downstream to the mouth of the Columbia River, where European vessels awaited it. A trade language called Chinook jargon was used in this region as far north as Alaska and as far south as northern California. It was composed largely of Chinook, Nootka, and Salish words.

Farther north the coastal tribes became the middlemen in the exchange of furs from the interior for European and American goods on the coast. At trading rendezvous near the coast, the buyers and sellers spent days in feasting, singing, dancing, and otherwise enjoying themselves, much as our businessmen do at a modern business convention. These prolonged contacts between coast and interior peoples were conducive to the diffusion of non-economic elements of culture. Some of the interior tradesmen who had become wealthy could afford to "buy" wives from the coast people. As a result of such intermarriages, many features of the coast social organization spread to the interior.

The social repercussions on the coast were equally revolutionary. Surpluses of blankets and metal utensils soon arose as a result of the unprecedented amount of goods pouring into Indian hands. There was plenty to give away at potlatches, which became larger, more frequent, more competitive, and more destructive of physical property. The carefully graduated scale of social rank began to come apart at the joints. Energetic young men who acquired a few sea otter furs or worked a while on a fishing schooner could save enough to give an impressive potlatch. Furthermore, a considerable number of titles went begging because of the decline in population from European diseases, such as measles and scarlet fever, to which the Indian had less immunity. The result was that new social climbers appropriated the unclaimed titles.

Dugout canoes were the dominant means of transportation everywhere on the Northwest Coast and on the major streams of the Plateau. Peoples living on islands some distance from shore, such as the Haida, had to have ocean-going canoes capable of withstanding heavy seas. In the historic period after steel tools arrived from Europe, Haida dugouts reached a length of sixty to seventy feet and were paddled and sailed as much as 700 miles from home. Loads were also back-packed by human carriers from coast to interior, but the individuals who did this legwork were nearly always interior peoples.

Oasis.—Marine shells, worn as beads and pendants, were derived from two sources: the coast of southern California in the vicinity of Los Angeles and the Gulf of California (64 species); the Gulf of Mexico (9 species). Pacific Coast shells were traded as far north as southwestern Colorado and as far east as the Texas panhandle. Pacific Coast shells reached the Oasis over two principal trade routes: (1) from the Gulf of California to the middle of the Gila, thence north and east; (2) from the vicinity of Los Angeles across the Mohave Desert to northern Arizona. The Mohave were the middlemen along the second trade route across the Mohave Desert. On the Pacific Coast they obtained shells, fishhook blanks, beads, and other manufactured shell objects from the Angelinos and traded them to Pueblo Indians in Arizona for pottery and textiles.

Fine cotton textiles and cast copper "sleigh bells" reached the Oasis from Meso-America. Cotton textiles were also woven locally, but it does not seem likely that the Southwest Indians were familiar with the lost wax technique by which the bells were almost cer-

231

tainly cast. An extraordinary trade item from Mexico was macaw birds, which were apparently transported alive the entire 1,200 miles from their nearest habitat in Mexico to northern Arizona and New Mexico. They seem to have been highly valued, which was fortunate because their careful burial preserved their bones for archeologists.

In historic times, Plains Indians visited the eastern Pueblos to trade buffalo hides and jerked meat for corn and other farm products. The Navaho in early historic times, and the Apache well into the nineteenth century, traded products of the chase for those of the farm with all the Pueblos at one time or another.

Back packing was almost the only means of transportation in the Oasis. Rafts were used a little on the larger streams, especially on the Colorado River, but more often to ford the stream than to navigate it. Horses were extensively used for both riding and transportation by the Navaho and Apaches after the Spanish brought this animal to the Southwest, but other Oasis peoples made little use of the horse.

Plains and Prairies.—On the Plains and Prairies, trade consisted mostly of the exchange of products of the chase by the hunting tribes for the agricultural products of the farming tribes. The nomads offered horses, dried meat, fat, prairie-turnip flour, dressed hides, tipis, buffalo robes, other furs, shirts and leggings of buckskin decorated with quillwork, and moccasins. The sedentary village tribes offered in return corn, beans, melons, pumpkins, and tobacco. After trade goods began to arrive from Europe and the Atlantic Coast of America, it was the agricultural tribes which first received most articles. After about 1800 these agricultural peoples were trading quantities of guns, powder, bullets, metal kettles, axes, knives, awls, glass beads, and mirrors to the nomads.

The way of life of the Plains Indians was changed a great deal by the acquisition of the horse. It was from the Spanish colonists in northern Mexico and New Mexico that the Plains tribes obtained their horses. As was customary in Spanish colonies, the herding of the horses, cattle, sheep, and goats was often done by Indians. It was a common occurrence for these Indian wranglers to become disgruntled over the discipline of the more civilized life and return home to their people. What could be simpler than to drive off a herd of cattle or horses at the same time? When a man of average Indian status returned to his people with a herd of animals, he was welcomed as a hero and a public benefactor. The cattle were normally eaten in short order, and sometimes the horses, at this early stage, but gradually the Indians on the Plains realized that a horse could supply many times its own weight in meat if it were used to hunt buffalo. The horse fitted in ideally with their roving, predatory way of life, and those tribes who first acquired it had a tremendous advantage, in both the chase and warfare, over their neighbors who lacked it.

The Indian demand for horses skyrocketed to unbelievable dimensions. They were stolen at every opportunity, not only from the Spanish, but from other Indians. The horse rapidly became an important motive behind the perpetual raids which the Plains tribes made on each other. By the nineteenth century, stealing a picketed horse from within the camp of an enemy became one of the highest-ranking war deeds. While the rank of the deed was determined by the danger involved, the picketed horse was also a rare prize because it was usually the best of a man's string and was kept close at hand for its safety as well as for its availability in an emergency. Probably a hundred times as many horses changed owners by theft as by trade. Horses as far north as the Canadian border often bore Spanish brands. Members of the Blackfoot and other northern Plains tribes journeyed all the way south to Santa Fe to obtain horses. By 1800 all the Plains tribes were fully equestrianized.

The great demand for furs had a decided effect on the marriage structure of the northern Plains. Although a man actually killed the buffalo, the sexual division of labor ruled that his wife should dress the hide and dry the meat. As the demand for furs grew, men who were successful hunters purchased more and more wives to do the skin-dressing and meat-jerking for them. The maximum number of wives possessed by a single man of the Blackfoot tribe rose from six in 1787 to twenty, or possibly thirty, by 1840. Because wives were purchased with horses and horses were essential to buffalo economy, this extreme polygyny could not have arisen without large numbers of horses. Therefore, it arrived late, and came to an abrupt end when the buffalo became practically extinct in 1880.

Effects of the fur trade on material culture were less startling

233

but quite numerous. Buffalo corrals, into which the animals were driven, were enlarged. Tipis grew from small structures covered by a half dozen buffalo hides, and accommodating as many people, to huge structures requiring twenty skins for covering. One exceptionally large tipi made of forty skins and housing nearly one hundred persons was actually observed about 1840. Pottery was abandoned early in favor of the metal trade kettle which was not subject to breakage. Trade tobacco replaced the native tobacco which had been raised by some of the nomadic tribes. Woven rabbitskin robes and basketry became extinct, being replaced by buffalo robes and trade dishes.

The policy of the Hudson's Bay Company was to trade with chiefs. As long as this company had a monopoly of trade the authority of chiefs increased, but when other trading firms or independent tradesmen arrived, business was done directly with any Indian. The chief, who had served as a middleman, was no longer necessary and his authority declined.

Even religion was affected by the fur trade. The most obtrusive religious symbol in northern Plains culture was the medicine bundle, which gave the owner control of supernatural power. He might sell his services to others much as does a priest in modern organized religions. The wealth brought by the fur trade encouraged men to buy, as an investment, medicine bundles which might later be turned over at a profit or kept as symbols of prestige. Bundles changed hands oftener, became more numerous, and sold for higher prices.

Along with the fur trade came the gun and the horse. Guns reached the Plains from the Northeast and horses from the Southwest. Those tribes who acquired one or the other had an advantage in warfare over those who had neither, but those who got both were superior still. In the eighteenth century, before horses and guns were common, battles were fought with massed infantry armed with lances, bows and arrows, shields, and a little hide armor. Fighting was accompanied by considerable ceremony and casualties were few. War parties were large, often numbering hundreds, and were led by war chiefs, some of whom were permanent officers. However, other leaders were elected by tribal councils to lead in only one engagement. After horses and guns arrived, casualties increased, war parties became smaller, war chiefs disappeared, and the element of surprise often determined the outcome.

Trade on the Plains was facilitated by the famous sign language, which was the most elaborate means of silent communication in the New World. The multiplicity of languages would have made trade difficult, if not impossible, without this lingua franca.

Northeast.—There were well-established water routes in the Northeast along which the Indians, in birch-bark canoes, plied their trade. The copper from the southern shore of Lake Superior found its way east, where it was exchanged for tobacco and wampum. One tribe specialized in raising tobacco and trading it to neighbors in quantities sufficient for it to be labeled the Tobacco tribe. Brown pipestone from the Chippewa River and red pipestone from Minnesota were taken east on the Great Lakes as far as the Iroquois country in New York State and thence north into Canada. Flint from Ontario traveled west and north in unfinished "blanks" to Saskatchewan and Alberta. Obsidian from the Rocky Mountains, in the form of raw material and in finished points and knives, has been found in Hopewell mounds in Ohio in deposits up to several hundred pounds.

Next to the Great Lakes, the St. Lawrence River was probably the most important trade route, with the Hudson not far behind. Farther inland the Ottawa River was much used, and an Algonquian tribe residing at some dangerous rapids, around which it was necessary to portage, exacted a heavy toll of all other tribes using the river. Another Algonquian group, residing on Lake Nipissing in eastern Ontario, traveled forty-two days west and forty days north on trading expeditions. Canoes of the Ottawa tribe on the lower Ottawa River traveled as far west as Green Bay, Wisconsin, and as far east as Quebec.

Probably no tribe in the Northeast participated in as much trade as did the Huron, whose territory lay astride the St. Lawrence and also bordered on Lake Ontario and Georgian Bay of Lake Huron. In the winter of 1615, Champlain observed the women grinding quantities of maize for trade the following summer. This was exchanged for furs with tribes to the north and west. Although this was probably the aboriginal pattern, it was already beginning to be stepped up by the insatiable European demand for furs. Men spent more time trading than hunting or fighting in 1615, and most of them seem to have been away from their home villages for this purpose during the summer.

From the beginning of European contact, the Hurons acquired a monopoly on trade with the French at Montreal. The Hurons acquired the entire crops of maize, tobacco, and hemp raised by two weaker tribes, the Tobacco and the Neutral, and traded the crops to non-agricultural tribes for furs and fish. The furs were passed on to the French. The Hurons traveled nearly as far as James Bay to the north and to the mouth of the Saguenay River in the Gulf of St. Lawrence on the east. Although the Hurons obtained beaver furs in their home territory around 1600, these resources were exhausted by 1635, and they were forced to acquire them from tribes to the north and west.

The strongest rivals of the Hurons in the first half of the seventeenth century were the Iroquois, who dominated the trade with the Dutch in New York State. By 1641 the Iroquois were in a predicament. Their own beaver supply had run out and the Dutch had passed legislation forbidding the sale of firearms to the Indians. This left the Iroquois without the two most important items in the Euro-Indian trade. It was at this time that they began seizing the fur-laden canoes of their Huron rivals on the St. Lawrence. They also attempted to improve their lot by means of treaties with the French, Hurons, and Algonquians in 1645, in which they requested that the two Indian tribes come to trade with them. Nothing came of these agreements.

In 1649, a party of one thousand Mohawks and Senecas attacked a large Huron village at night. As the village was almost without guards, their success was swift and before sunrise they attacked a second village which was stormed and fired by 9:00 A.M. A Huron counterattack a few days later turned back the Iroquois, but irreparable damage had been done. Panic seized the rest of the Hurons, who burnt their fifteen remaining villages and fled in numbers between six thousand and eight thousand to an unproductive island which had the sole virtue of being easily defended. A smaller number sought refuge with neighboring tribes but, although their lives were saved, they were adopted by these other nations and lost their tribal identity. During the next winter, most of the Hurons on the island starved. By the following June only about five hundred were left, and they made their final retreat to Quebec, where their descendants remain to this day. Within the next ten years the Iroquois found excuses to attack and annihilate or adopt their neighbors, the Tobacco, Neutral, and Erie.

The trade which they had so eagerly sought never materialized. After the defeat of the Hurons, the Ottawas seized most of the trade along their river and many tribes feared the Iroquois so much that they refused to trade with them. The Iroquois were able to blockade the Ottawas but did not succeed in acquiring the volume of trade formerly realized by the Hurons. About all they gained was the territory formerly occupied by the Hurons in which to trap and hunt furs themselves. As this was practically depleted by this date, the gain was slight.

The last independent conquest of the Iroquois was the unsuccessful attempt against the Illinois in 1684. A few years later, in 1688, they signed a treaty with the French in Montreal. From this date on, the fortunes of the Iroquois were even more closely geared to those of the French and the British. They took the side of the winner, the British, in the French and Indian War, but were divided in their allegiance in our own successful Revolutionary War.

Southeast.—Trade in the Southeast was principally between contrasting geographical environments: coast with interior; uplands with lowlands. The Mississippi River became a trade artery in historic times and probably served in that capacity in prehistoric times as well. Perhaps the most important single trade item was salt, which was peddled by itinerant merchants throughout the area but especially in the Mississippi drainage. Most of it was made by evaporating saturated solutions of salt, obtained at salt licks, in shallow pottery pans set over a fire. West of the Mississippi, at least, salt was made into cakes of two or three pounds each, as in Meso-America. Copper obtained in the Appalachians, and possibly a little from the south shore of Lake Superior, was also a common article of trade. It was used mainly for ornaments. Catlinite pipes from the same area penetrated the Southeast but not until historic times along with the calumet peace ceremony.

Fairs or markets were held periodically and drew people from towns within fifty or sixty miles radius. Although they were reported as late as the eighteenth century, there is no reason to doubt their occurrence in earlier times.

The fur trade had its ultimately disastrous effects here as elsewhere. The acquisition of the gun made hunting so easy that large numbers of animals were killed just for the hides, the meat being left to rot or to be devoured by carnivores. Game eventually became scarce and dependence on corn increased. As in other areas, European and American trade goods rapidly replaced many Indian articles.

Transportation was by dugout canoe for large shipments going considerable distances, but back packing was common everywhere for local trade.

Meso-America and the Circum-Caribbean Area.—Meso-America differed from areas to the north in having a greater amount of community craft specialization and along with it a greater amount of intercommunity trade. One town might have access to a superior clay bed and be able to make better pottery than its neighbors. Another might be close to a supply of obsidian, which was the preferred material for points of weapons and tools and for knives. A third might be near deposits of metal which could be cast into ornaments in quantity. As technical knowledge grew, specialization and trade increased and markets grew in number and in size. Women normally went to market only in their home towns, but men sometimes back-packed their wares a hundred miles. Markets in small villages were held at regular intervals, while those in large towns and cities were often daily affairs. Those in the great commercial centers were attended by merchants from distant nations who brought their wares to be exchanged.

Barter was the only means of exchange, and scarcity affected price. True money did not exist, but the chocolate bean was used in making "change" and approached the status of money. The beans were of fairly uniform size, were scarce enough not to be subject to damaging inflation, were portable, and had universal utility as food. In the more sophisticated cities, quills of gold dust and copper knives were sometimes used as mediums of exchange. Jade, being worth much more than gold, was the most precious substance among the Aztecs.

Differences in geographical zone had their effect on trade here as elsewhere. The Aztecs of the temperate highlands obtained chocolate, vanilla, pineapples, rubber, and bitumen from the tropical lowlands of Veracruz; serpentine, porphyry, and jade also had to be imported from the southeast. In exchange, they offered obsidian, cloth, salt, jewelry, pottery, and rope from the Valley of Mexico. Shells from both oceans found their way to inland cities. The extension of the Aztec "empire" can largely be understood in economic terms, as this people sought to control the source areas of both necessities and luxuries. The Spanish conquerors moved along Aztec trade trails.

The Aztecs sponsored a class of itinerant merchants, called *pochteca*, whose members traveled widely in armed bands over Meso-America, exchanging their goods for foreign products. They had their own god, trappings, and insignia and lived in a special quarter (*barrio*) in the cities. Like fifth-column agents of modern governments, they served as spies and made estimates of the amount of tribute a given town could pay if conquered. They also passed on secret information about its military establishments. Their security of body and property, which at first had been preserved because of the desirability of their wares, later became guaranteed by the force of arms of the Aztec government. They ultimately grew to be a sort of commercial corporation which controlled the entire trade of the country. They had their own laws and courts of justice and, with this protection, became a threat to the nobility. Full-time professional traders are also reported for the Otomí, Zapotec, Popoloca, Zoque, and Maya, but they were less organized among these tribes than with the Aztec.

In highland central Mexico among the Aztecs and their neighbors, human porters carried practically everything on their backs. It was only on lakes and the larger streams that dugout canoes served as the chief means of transportation. Canoes were indispensable to the largest concentration of population at Mexico City (Tenochtitlán), which was founded on an island in a lake and continued to be dependent on water transportation until after the Spanish conquest.

Maya trade in general was as well developed as that of the Aztecs, and probably more so in respect to sea trade. Maya trade was also handled by a class of professional merchants who often traveled with their goods. There was no competition with the nobility here because these merchants belonged to the nobility. The chocolate bean was a medium of exchange all the way from the Valley of Mexico to Nicaragua, although stone beads, copper bells, copper axes, and shell beads approached the same status.

Christopher Columbus encountered, at the Bay Islands in the Gulf of Honduras, a huge Indian trading canoe operated by a crew of twenty-five paddlers and transporting colored cotton blankets, shirts and breechcloths, obsidian-edged wooden swords, copper axes, copper bells and ornaments, crucibles for melting copper, and many chocolate beans used as money. No one knows the nationality of the sailors or the destination of the canoe. However, other sources mention regular sea trade on the Caribbean side of Mexico and Central America.

In the West Indies almost all transport was by canoe. There was a brisk internal trade in tapioca, pepper, wooden stools carved from one piece of wood, wooden bowls, pottery, gold, carved stone objects, stone axes, and cotton. Gold was mined and cold-hammered into ornaments on Hispaniola and exported to the other islands. The most valuable item of outside origin was the gold-copper alloy neck pendants obtained from Colombia via Trinidad and worn by chiefs and nobles. Rare stones for beads were also imported from the mainland of South America. In exchange, nephrite from the West Indies was shipped south. There seems to have been no regular trade between the West Indies and Florida, although the island people knew of the continent to the north. Neither is there evidence of any regular trade between the West Indies and Yucatán, although each of these lands was also known to the inhabitants of the other.

In the United States today, few things we consume are produced locally; the majority are obtained in trade. No American Indian community approached this level of commerce. In Meso-America, where trade reached its highest development, most trade goods fell into the hands of a wealthy minority. The average individual continued to consume principally local products and to produce many of them himself.

MONEY

Definitions of money are legion because of the difficulty of arriving at one which characterizes the wide variety of exchangeables which have been called money. We shall define money as material which possesses homogeneity, portability, divisibility, durability, and which serves as a medium of exchange, as a store of value, and as a standard of deferred payments.

Perhaps the nearest approach to this definition were the dentalia shells of the Yurok Indians at the southern end of the Northwest Coast culture area. The value of a shell depended on its length; the longer, the more valuable. Five grades of shells were recognized, and both the individual shells and the strings of them were designated by as many terms in the language. From their source on Vancouver Island, these shells were traded north to Alaska and east to the Missouri River, but nowhere were they as carefully graded and evaluated as among the Yurok.

In central California, disk beads were made of clam shells and strung. Values were in terms of the lengths of strings, which were measured by wrapping them around the hand in a prescribed manner. Such valuations, however, were less precise than those for dentalia and the beads themselves were regarded less highly.

Throughout most of interior Alaska and Canada the beaver fur was the nearest approach to a standard of value, in historic times at least. It can scarcely be labeled money, however. On the Plains the horse became the standard of value but most certainly was not money.

A much closer approach to money was the shell beads called *wampum* in the eastern half of the United States. These beads have been called tubular because the length of each cylindrical bead is normally greater than the diameter, unlike the California disk beads, whose diameter was greater than the length. Wampum was made of marine shells obtained on the coast of New England and the Middle Atlantic States. At first European contact, these beads were confined to this area plus the Iroquois and possibly a few other inland tribes. As European trade grew, they became accepted as a standard of value by Indians and Whites alike and spread west to about the hundredth meridian. Their manufacture was greatly facilitated by metal tools, but eventually they became worthless owing to an oversupply. This is another example of how White contact stimulated and crystallized Indian culture at first, only to shatter it at a later date.

From the Valley of Mexico to Nicaragua, the chocolate bean (*cacao*) was the nearest approach to money. It was relatively homogeneous, definitely portable, definitely divisible, and fairly durable although subject to spoilage in time. The beans were sometimes kept in bags of 24,000 each. They had the advantage of being consumable as food and were regularly taken in the form of a drink. Perhaps their most useful function was in making change when articles of unequal value were being bartered. Cacao was grown on the west coast from Colima southward; the Soconusco area of Guatemala was particularly famous for its plantations.

Although we have applied the word money to a few media of exchange in Indian North America, it is important to bear in mind that nearly all of the trade goods in pre-Columbian times were exchanged by barter. The Yurok tended to hoard his money at home rather than to carry it on his person. It was used mainly to purchase wives, or as treasure to be displayed in ceremonies, or as compensation for personal loss or injury. Wampum in the East was associated with an even greater amount of formality and ritual. The chocolate bean was a much more commercial money, but run-of-the-mill trade goods were not consistently priced in terms of these beans. Money, therefore, had barely obtained a foothold in North America by the time of European discovery.

CONCLUSIONS

The above summaries on trade have been given to demonstrate the tremendous amount of contact between the many distinct tribes of native North America. Some trade objects traveled only a few miles, but others were traded hundreds and occasionally thousands of miles from point of origin. What was the mechanism of their dispersal?

In the chapter on horticulture we pointed out that corn was not carried from its point of origin in the tropics all the way to the St. Lawrence River by a single trader or by a single trading expedition. It was relayed from one locality to the next, and the time it took to negotiate this great distance ran into thousands of years. Because corn does not survive in nature but must be cared for by man, each people who received corn kernels for seed for the first time had to have learned how to farm in advance. This meant some exchange of personnel between the donor and recipient peoples. This could occur in a number of ways. A man of the recipient tribe might obtain a wife who knew how to farm from the donor tribe; or a member of the recipient tribe might have lived for a time

242

as a spouse or captive among the donor tribe, to return later to his or her own people with corn seed and knowledge of farming. Then at a later date the recipient tribe would change its role to that of donor and pass on its seed and knowledge of farming to another locality beyond the periphery of the farming area. As this process was continued, corn became consciously or unconsciously selected for the cooler climate and shorter growing season in the north. The development of special varieties of corn, adapted to the many environments in which the plant was raised by A.D. 1492, took a great deal of time.

Many trade objects moved much faster than corn, but they were normally dispersed by the same relay process, called diffusion by anthropologists. It is true that a few trading expeditions traveled some hundreds of miles, but these were the exceptions rather than the rule. A man with a surplus traded most often with one of his immediate neighbors, who in turn might relay some of the goods received to another neighbor a little beyond.

After European contact there was a tremendous increase in trade and in the number of full-time professional traders, many of whom were Europeans. Individuals and expeditions traveled greater distances than were negotiated in pre-Columbian times. This marked increase in trade was accompanied by an equal increase in the diffusion of elements of culture other than trade goods, with the result that the contemporary culture historian is able to reconstruct the pre-European picture only with difficulty. Nevertheless, we can be sure each pre-Columbian Indian society made regular contacts with other societies which were independent politically and spoke different languages.

REFERENCES

Acosta, 1945; Alexander, 1939; Beals, 1932a; Chard, C., 1950; Codere, 1951; Colton, 1941; Denhardt, 1948; Driver and Massey, 1957; Einzig, 1948; Ewers, 1955b; Haag, 1948; Haines, 1938a, 1938b; Haury, 1947; Herskovits, 1952; Hunt, 1940; Jablow, 1951; Lewis, 1942; Lowie, 1954; Martin, Quimby, and Collier, 1947; Mason, O., 1896; Olson, 1927; Quimby, 1948; Ray, 1939; Roe, 1939, 1955; Roys, 1943; Slotkin and Schmidt, 1949; Speck, 1919; Steward, 1938, 1948; Swanton, 1946; Vaillant, 1941; Waugh, 1919; Wilson, 1924; Wissler, 1914, 1938, 1941; Wormington, 1957.

14: PROPERTY AND INHERITANCE

ALL PRIMITIVE peoples in the world have some concept of property rights, and North American Indians are no exception. Their ideas on this subject differ considerably from our own, as we shall see, and show great variation from one tribe to another. To begin with, property may be owned by a single individual, two or more individuals, an entire community, or a tribal group. The number of joint owners may vary all the way from two persons to thousands. Joint owners are seldom randomly chosen; they normally belong to a definite social group such as a family, clan, deme, lineage, sib, phratry, moiety, or sodality. These terms will be defined later in the chapters on social organization; all we need to know here is that there can be as many kinds of joint ownership as there are kinds of groupings of human beings.

Property may also be fixed (real estate), or it may be movable (chattels). In our culture, buildings on real estate are considered to be part of the real estate, and sale of a plot of land usually includes the buildings on it. Dwellings of Indians were seldom bought and sold, but where they were immovable, they also were regarded as belonging to the land and were, therefore, real estate. Where dwellings were portable, they were regarded as movable property or chattels. Thus the Plains Indian recognized individual or family ownership of tipis but not of the land on which they were pitched.

Property may also be divided into corporeal and incorporeal forms. Both real estate and chattels are usually regarded as corporeal property, while patents and copyrights are examples in our culture of incorporeal property. Indian cultures abound in examples of incorporeal property. Songs, dances, family or clan crests, cur-

244

ing rites and many other intangibles were owned and exclusively used by certain individuals or groups of individuals.

Property may be transferable in a variety of way: by gift, barter, sale, inheritance, appropriation; or it may be inalienable. Many examples of transfer were given in the last chapter; others will be discussed in this chapter. The method of transference is often correlated with other aspects of ownership. Thus, chattels were frequently individually owned and tended to be disposable by gift, barter, or sale. Real estate, in contrast, was often owned or used by a kin group and might be inherited by succeeding generations of kindred without being disposable by sale or barter. Land which had not been used for some years might be appropriated by anyone who chose to use it, or might be reapportioned by a tribal official.

At the outset, we should also keep in mind the difference between nominal ownership, that is, ownership in name or speech, and use ownership or usufruct, as it is technically called. Often a single person was said to own a house or a tract of land, but he was normally compelled to share it with certain kindred, such as the members of his immediate family. He could not dispose of it or refuse to share it with his relatives. Land was often said to belong to the tribe, yet in practice it might be used exclusively by a single family or lineage segment.

In discussing land tenure it is important to separate the various uses to which land may be put and also to distinguish between productive sites and continuous tracts of land. As we shall see below, different uses of land were shared, inherited, or transferred in different ways, just as we may sell mineral rights to land without relinquishing title to other rights.

The variation in property rights which surround a single person's activity may be great. Thus a man may own his weapons individually, own a fishing station jointly with relatives, share hunting territory with the whole tribe, share the meat he obtains with other families in his community, share the fish he catches only with his own household, and earn the right to sing a bear song at a public ceremony by having slain a bear.

Ownership may also be regarded as having three main aspects: privilege of use, privilege of disposal, and privilege of destruction. These represent a scale of increasing control over the property in

245

question. For example, a slave among the Yuroks could be used in the sense that he could be compelled to perform work for his master, but he could not be bought or sold, nor killed. Farther north a slave could be used for labor, could be bought and sold, but could not be killed. When we reach the Kwakiutl, the slave was completely owned because he could be compelled to work at labor, could be bought and sold, and could also be killed. For North America as a whole, however, this privilege of destruction was rare. Privileges of use were certainly most frequent, privileges of disposal next, and privileges of destruction least common.

LAND TENURE

Land tenure in aboriginal North America shows much variation from tribe to tribe and area to area, depending not only on the kind of exploitation of the land, but also on the political and social organization associated with it (Map 29). One of the most obtrusive features is the differentiation of land tenure rules for the various uses of land within a single tribe. For purposes of this summary, we shall distinguish between unimproved hunting land, improved hunting sites, fishing sites, wild plant gathering tracts, and farm plots. Improved hunting sites are those at which game fences, traps, pitfalls, and any other devices to facilitate the taking of game have been constructed.

A lot of discussion has arisen over nominal ownership and use ownership. If the nominal owner is a specific individual, sib, or official in a culture, this distinction is of some significance, but if the nominal owner is the whole tribe, this does not tell us much. More often than not, land was used by smaller groups of individuals who co-operated in its exploitation and shared in its products. The relationship of the members of these work parties to one another has important bearing on social organization.

The kinship relations among groups of owners or users and modes of inheritance of land are often poorly described. I have, therefore, created a few broad terms to designate certain fundamental distinctions. By "patricentered" I mean that a tract of land or site is owned or used by a group of persons residing together patrilocally or belonging to the same patrilineal descent group, or that it is owned or used by a single individual who will pass it on at his death to another individual belonging to his patriresidential or patrilineal group. The term "matricentered" applies likewise to matrilocal and matrilineal groups of kinsmen. It is important to remember that in matrilineal societies land may be exploited by males and inherited from mother's brother to sister's son. To the best of our knowledge, there are no instances of land in patrilineal societies being shared or inherited by father's sisters and brother's daughters. "Bicentered" refers to the same concept applied to bilocal or bilateral groups of kin. "Kincentered" is used for those cases in which it is known only that a group of relatives owned, used, or controlled a tract or site, without knowing whether the group was patri-, matri-, or bi-centered. There are still other instances of improved sites owned by the person or persons who improved them, but there is no information about the relationship of the joint owners, or the disposal of the property at death or abandonment by one or more of the owners. These cases have been placed in a residual category of their own.

Where residence was patrilocal and descent patrilineal, it was a common thing for title to land to be vested in the oldest male or all the mature males in the paternal lineage, lineage segment, or patrilineal sib, yet for the land or its products to be used by patrilocal extended families or patriclans. The lineage or sib was never the land-using unit because it would require married brothers and sisters to use the same land. The patrilocal residence rule and the rule of lineage or sib exogamy demanded that the sisters marry men from the outside and go elsewhere to live with them. The men who belonged to the lineage or sib stayed at home and, after acquiring wives on the outside, brought the wives home with them. The land-using unit was, therefore, composed of the male members of the paternal lineage or patrilineal sib plus their wives. Such units are called patrilocal extended families and patriclans.

Where residence was matrilocal and descent matrilineal, the title to land was likewise often vested in the oldest female or all the mature female members of the maternal lineage, lineage segment, or matrilineal sib. The land was used, however, or the products were shared almost always by these women and their husbands, who constituted matrilocal extended families and matriclans. In similar fashion, where avunculocal residence and matrilineal descent were

247

paired, the title might be vested in the males of the maternal lineage or matrilineal sib but the land was used by avunculocal extended families and avuncuclans. Most ethnographers have failed to distinguish adequately between the family-clan type of unit and the lineage-sib concept. Because of the garbled nature of most of the source material, the loose terms patricentered, matricentered, and bicentered have been coined as a matter of expediency.

Land and productive sites may be owned or used by individuals (at least nominally), by a group of kin, by a group of unrelated persons, by a community consisting of two or more groups of kin, by a tribelet or tribe consisting of two or more communities, and by any and everyone who comes along. This last unit is the equivalent of our international one to which the oceans in the modern world have been allocated. In the Prairie and East areas, where tribal organization was well developed in the historic period, most of these land-owning units might exist even in the same tribal area. In the far west, where true tribal organization was lacking, the largest land-holding unit was often the kin group, the band, or the village community. In a considerable number of localities the kin group was the largest territorial unit; it was not aggregated into larger units. Statements about communal ownership of land have little meaning until we know the size and socio-political structure of the community unit.

A summary of the facts is given on Map 29. Here every instance of even a tendency for land to be used and inherited by the various kinds of kin groups is shown. In the detailed descriptions to follow the products of these tracts or sites, as controlled by kin groups, and their importance in the total subsistence or economic picture will be discussed.

Arctic.—Among the central Eskimos the landscape and seascape, as well, approached an international status. Any central Eskimo could hunt sea or land animals anywhere he chose. The Eskimo "tribes" shown on our maps were mere aggregations of people at various localities. They had no real political organization and no conception of boundaries between "tribes." When Eskimos and Indians met in the summer, they sometimes fought, but always over the particular product they were seeking at the time, never over boundaries. It was only when a caribou fence or a trap of some

248

sort had been built that any group of individuals claimed hunting land, and this was only for a short time or at most a season. Whoever got there first the next season could appropriate the spot.

In the western Arctic, the most productive places for setting salmon nets were regarded as personal property and handed down from father to son. If an outsider put a net in one of these places, the owner removed it and put his own in its place. Sometimes these sites were rented for a fixed sum but more often on a percentage basis, the renter giving the owner half his catch. The best spots to set seal nets were also owned and operated by patricentered groups of relatives, and inland hunting tracts or sites were controlled in the same manner.

In Greenland seal breathing holes and favorable places to set seal nets were owned and operated by families. The mode of inheritance, if any, is unknown.

Sub-Arctic.—The Algonquians of the Eastern Sub-Arctic recognized ownership of hunting and trapping territories by patrilocal families. This system was remarkably uniform all the way from about Lake Winnipeg to Labrador and Nova Scotia (Map 29). Such tracts were delimited by natural boundaries such as rivers, lakes, forests, and mountains, and in historic times by ax marks on trees. Trespass might be punished with death or, more commonly, witchcraft. Permission might be given to a man to hunt in the territory of another family if he and his family were badly in need of food, but the hides were always given to the owner of the tract. Such permission was always reciprocated. Not only was each family territory carefully guarded from without, but game was consistently preserved from within. Pregnant females or those with young were preserved and quantities of other animals taken were regulated so as to prevent depletion. Although inheritance was not sharply crystallized, it more often followed the male line.

One of the remarkable features of this system is the smallness of the land-holding unit. In one region these families averaged only six persons, and in one of the more favorable areas only fifteen. In former times families like these spent every winter in isolation except for an occasional visit to or from a neighbor. When the spring thaw came, however, each family left its winter hunting territory and congregated with others at fishing places on lakes and rivers.

249

Then when winter came again everyone returned to winter quarters.

There has been much discussion in anthropological writings about the aboriginality of these family-owned hunting territories. Some authors believe they are an adaptation to the European demand for furs. In keeping with the latter view is the fact that rules regarding fur-bearing animals, particularly the beaver, are more strict than those applying to meat-producing species such as the caribou. However, small animals, of which the beaver is again typical, tend to restrict their movements to small areas, while moose and caribou migrate. Conservation of small animals in a small area would have direct bearing on the numbers available in future years, while the same principle applied to large animals would be ineffective because they might be killed while wandering in another man's territory.

When we compare the western Sub-Arctic, where environment is similar but European contact later, we find several examples of tribes adopting the concept of individual or family-owned trapping territories in the historic period. Adaptation to the European fur trade is thus established by documentary evidence in the west. It appears likely that the family hunting territory system of the northeast Algonquians, as observed in the nineteenth century, is partly a post-contact development. Leacock (n.d. and 1955) elaborates this view of the facts, and even goes so far as to say that these cultures were originally bicentered and that whatever patricentering they achieved was a result of European contact. However, the European fur trade in the Northwest did not consistently produce patricentered concepts of land tenure; a number of societies there retained their matricentered or avuncucentered systems. This suggests that patricentered rules would not have arisen in the Northeast if the culture had not already had a bias in that direction. Therefore, it seems clear that the Eastern Sub-Arctic possessed a patricentered bias aboriginally and that this merely became crystallized into small hunting territories as a result of the fur trade. The system was most rigid in the southern part of the territory nearest European colonists.

In the Mackenzie Sub-Arctic most territorial rights were controlled by loose and fluid bands rather than by individuals or families. The kinship structure of these bands followed no regular pattern and they seem to have included members from a number of unrelated families. Trap lines, however, were owned and operated by individuals and families in the western part of the area. Both matrilocal and patrilocal residence occurred, with a corresponding matrilineal and patrilineal inheritance of the trap lines. The patri-centered system seems to be the older, with the matricentered pattern a later derivation from the Tlingit and Tsimshian on the Northwest Coast.

In the Yukon Sub-Arctic, kinship groups owned fishing places as well as trap lines. Such ownership was patricentered in the north and matricentered in the south where the amount of contact with the Tlingit was greatest. The hunting of the caribou and other animals for food was controlled by the band in some localities, while the concept of open territory for all comers prevailed elsewhere in the area. It seems likely that in the Mackenzie and Yukon Sub-Arctic the kinship control of trap lines was largely a post-European development, as it was in the Eastern Sub-Arctic.

Northwest Coast.—On the Northwest Coast, and to some extent elsewhere, it was seldom the entire landscape which was parceled out to groups of kindred but only the most favored sites. These were nominally owned by rich men, each of whom granted permission to his house or village mates, most of whom were his relatives, to exploit the land. That permission was never refused proves that the use of the land belonged to the entire group of kindred rather than to a single individual. What at first passes as individual ownership turns out to be a sort of stewardship, the right to direct the economic exploitation of the tract by the local group. Over most of the area, from the Wiyot to the Bella Coola, such usufruct was patricentered; but in the north, from the Haisla north to the Tlingit, it was matricentered. Such private ownership applied to fishing, hunting, trapping, and wild plant gathering rights.

Rules and regulations surrounding fishing sites were strictest on the Northwest Coast, where the rich man held title to the weir but could not refuse permission to members of his household or village to fish there. Sometimes sharing was accompanied by dividing up the twenty-four-hour period so that the weir was used by different men at different times. Where this system prevailed,

251

the nominal owner managed to retain the time period which was likely to yield the most fish. At the southernmost extension of the Northwest Coast culture area, among the Yuroks, fishing stations were owned by individual men, sometimes jointly with a non-relative, and they were rented to outsiders for a share of the catch. Rights in such locations might also be bought or sold. It was forbidden to establish a new fishing place or to fish below a recognized one, thus providing a monopoly for the owners. At a man's death, his fishing rights passed to his son. In addition to those privately owned fishing stations, there were communally owned weirs which were constructed annually at certain places in the river. Rights to fish at certain sections of these weirs were privately owned, however. During the feasts which accompanied the building of these weirs, food was served to all comers, even to members of alien tribes.

Although some of the land was free to hunt over, the best places for snaring and trapping land animals were owned in the same manner as places to gather roots and berries, that is, nominally, by rich men who could not refuse to grant permission to their house and village mates to exploit these tracts.

Plateau.—On the Plateau the large weirs at the most profitable fishing places were owned or shared by everyone in a community, and even outsiders who chanced along were commonly given a share of the catch. It was only the small weirs or scaffolds, built and operated by single men or small groups of relatives, which may be said to have been patricentered. In the minority of cases, where post-nuptial residence was reported as bilocal, the ownership of small fishing stations should likewise be regarded as bicentered. If the communities on the Plateau could be shown to be demes, which they apparently were in some cases, one might argue that the ownership of even the large weirs was in the hands of groups of kindred. Because of the general looseness of Plateau social organization, this point should not be pushed too far.

Traps, pitfalls, game fences, and other improvements at hunting sites were owned by the builders, but the relationship of the builders is vague or unknown and the duration in time of their tenure equally obscure. It also seems likely that some localities for gathering camas bulbs were habitually used or owned by restricted groups, some of which may have been kinship groups.

Plains.—On the Plains, where band and tribal organization existed, hunting territory was controlled by the band or tribe. The boundaries between bands or tribes are difficult to establish, and neighboring tribes often shared a large territory. It was only when enemies were encountered that disputes arose, and these were less concerned with boundaries than with establishing dominance (in the prehistoric period) or eliminating competition (in the historic period). Vague as knowledge of tribal or band territories is, we know for sure that no individual or small group of individuals within a Plains tribe owned any hunting land. During the summer buffalo hunts, individuals were forced by a specially chosen group of police to co-operate with the tribe as a whole. However, it was a communism only of the hunt, as we shall see below. Before the appearance of the horse, on the northern Plains, pounds or corrals with wing fences were more common than in later times. The territorial group which built and operated such pounds was smaller and is better labeled band than tribe. Some of these were apparently patridemes, which are technically kinship groups. Because fishing and wild plant gathering were very minor activities on the Plains, there were no restrictions on streams or places to gather berries and roots.

Prairies.—On the Prairies, control of hunting lands was similar to that on the Plains, with tribal, village, or band ownership the rule. Individuals or kinship groups did not own unimproved hunting territory, and if traps, fences, or pounds were so owned, other than for a season, it has not been reported except for eagle pits. Eagles were highly regarded by many Indians and were captured for their feathers by many tribes, including those on the upper Missouri River in the Dakotas. The hunter lay in the pit covered with a light frame of poles and brush on which he placed bait. When the bird alighted to take the bait, the hunter grabbed the eagle by the feet and wrung its neck. Such pits were owned by maternal lineages and lineage segments among the Hidatsa and Mandan, and probably by other kinds of kinship groups elsewhere on the Prairies. Some of the Prairies tribes, villages, or bands engaged in communal buffalo hunts which were in every way identical to those on the Plains. In the wild-rice area around the western Great Lakes, each family gathered wild rice in its own tract, which was marked by tying the rice plants in a particular manner. Apparently the same spot was returned to year after year, the family making its camp nearby. Most of this wild-rice area is labeled patricentered because residence was preponderantly patrilocal and descent mostly patrilineal.

Turning to farming, we find the Hidatsas and Mandans on the Missouri River divided into maternal lineages, lineage segments, and matrilocal extended families, the women of which owned their own farm plots. There was a tendency for the same field to be cultivated by these maternal kin groups year after year although exhaustion of the soil necessitated some changing about. When a woman died, her female relatives did not work her garden for a couple of years but, after letting it lie fallow for that length of time, a sister or a daughter would cultivate it the following year. If the relatives of the deceased woman failed to farm the plot for several years, it could be appropriated by any woman in the community who cared to make use of it. However, it was considered proper for her to ask permission of the heirs first. This change of title came about informally without any official passing judgment on it. Although title to a particular plot might technically be vested in an individual, it was normally cultivated by work parties of matrilineally related women, who worked each other's gardens in a group. Boundaries were seldom disputed but were sometimes marked with sticks or stones.

East.—In the East, restricted ownership of hunting land is reported only for the Delawares and Powhatan. Among the Delawares, hunting land was owned by maternal lineages, matrilineal sibs, matrilocal extended families, or matriclans. At any rate, it was a matricentered kin group of some sort. Although such land was hunted on principally in winter, ownership seems not to have been seasonal but permanent. Powhatan information is less complete and was obtained at too late a date (1900) to provide satisfactory answers. Nevertheless, individual men were the nominal owners of tracts of land, as among the northeastern Algonquians, and we may presume these were shared by kin or inherited in some manner. For the better-known tribes, such as the Iroquois and Creek, the emphasis is always on the tribal ownership of hunting territory. However, if we accept the matriclan as an aboriginal social unit,

254

we may assume that it was associated with its own hunting territory at some time in its history.

Ownership of fishing sites by kinship groups is reported for the Powhatan and Iroquois. Fishing as well as hunting rights were included in the ownership of tracts of land by individual men among the Powhatan. Details about the Iroquois system are few, but apparently some of the best places to fish were owned by maternal lineages and sibs in the same way that farm land was. Such ownership of fishing places was probably not general in the East or it would have been reported more often.

Among the Iroquoians, cultivated lands were parceled out to maternal lineages, or lineage segments, and the women members occupied a single longhouse with their husbands and children. The oldest woman, who was the lineage head, directed the work party of women members. Some individual women may have had the individual right to cultivate a certain part of the plot and to control its produce, but most of the ownership and operation was on the lineage segment level. When the fertility of the land waned and firewood became scarce, the whole village moved. On arriving at a new village site, plots of fresh land were allocated to each household.

The picture in the Southeast is essentially the same, except that there were also fields nominally owned by the chief but more properly called town fields, which were worked by everyone and from which some or all of the produce was kept in a public storehouse to be served to out-of-town guests or to be doled out to the needy. Even men were required to help with the planting and harvesting of these fields, although women seem to have done most of the cultivating, weeding, and watching. It is not possible at this date to determine the relationship of these public fields to the private ones which surely existed along with them. We do not know for sure whether maternal families or lineage segments were assigned separate plots in the town fields or whether each kin group cleared land of its own, or whether both systems prevailed.

California.—California exhibits a few instances of hunting land being owned privately. Among the various clans of the Chumash, unimproved hunting land was divided, as well as among the equally small but less definable local units of the Owens Valley Paiute.

With the Yokuts, pigeon-snaring blinds were owned by individual men and probably passed on to sons or brothers. Outsiders had to ask permission to use such blinds, but apparently the permission was usually granted. Farther north we find that certain Maidu families erected fences for deer-drives in certain favored spots and controlled their operation. Among the neighboring Nomlaki all land of any productive value was divided among the various villages, and the chiefs were the nominal owners of such tracts. These village communities seem to have been patrilocal extended families and patriclans. In the northern part of the state the patri-centered ownership of the Northwest Coast appears.

In California about half the peoples seem to have recognized ownership of wild plant tracts by groups of relatives. Most of these were patricentered, but a few were bicentered or even matri-centered. The small area with stippled pattern in central California (Map 29) refers to an interesting incipient matricentered system which never fully matured because of conflict with other facets of the culture. Among some local groups, a newly married daughter continued to gather wild plant products from fields owned or exclusively used by her mother. This might continue for a year or two, which was the normal length of the initial and temporary matrilocal residence prevalent in the area. If, when the couple later joined the groom's parents, the distance was too great for the bride to continue gathering on her mother's land, she stayed at home and did the housework for her mother-in-law and unmarried or newly married sisters-in-law while they gathered in their own family wild plant plots. Because of the preponderance of final and more or less permanent patrilocal residence and the dominance of men in socio-politico-religious affairs, this incipient matrilineal succession to tracts of land never developed into permanent matrilocal residence, much less matrilineal descent. It is significant that this matricentered system coexisted in the same locality with the patrilineal use and inheritance of pigeon-snaring booths.

Great Basin.—In this desert region we find no ownership of hunting territory by individuals or groups of kin, except for eagle nests, which were owned by individual men. Eagles were not eaten but were caught for their feathers, which were considered sacred. A few bands in the Basin recognized ownership of wild plant tracts by vague groups of bicentered relatives, but this was not the general rule. The few fishing sites were apparently not owned by kinship groups.

The picture of Basin subsistence is one of almost continual wandering about by family groups in search of the meager wild fare that nature provided. Rainfall was too spotty and amounts of wild foods too variable from year to year to make it possible for a family to limit itself to a single territory.

Northeast Mexico.—What little we know about this area suggests that there was no ownership of natural resources by kinship groups. As in the Great Basin, there was much wandering about by families in search of the uneven natural food supply. A family which limited its gathering and hunting to a restricted area would have had more than it could eat one year and would have starved to death another.

Oasis.—For the most of the Oasis area, the ownership of hunting tracts by kin groups was apparently lacking. Among the Chiricahua Apache, however, all land was controlled by bands which were endogamous demes. Although the membership was somewhat fluid, most members of a single band were related in a vague bilateral manner. This may also have been true of the Mescalero. The Walapai and Papago had a patricentered system of land tenure in which the patrideme was the territorial unit. While the system was not rigid, the patrilocal residence practiced by the majority kept together lines of males who hunted over the same territory generation after generation. The clans of the Navaho and Western Apache suggest separate hunting territories at an earlier time, but the literature does not state the fact specifically. As for the Pueblos, hunting land was either international or controlled by an entire pueblo, which was an autonomous political unit. Such pueblos consisted of a considerable number of kin groups, each of which owned agricultural land separately but never hunting land. This is explained in part by the fact that the most efficient way to hunt rabbits, which were the most important single species of game, was for all the men of the pueblo to join in a great drive. Smaller groups of relatives, limited to a fraction of the territory, would have accomplished little.

Farm plots in the Oasis were limited to the small fraction of the total area which received sufficient water and therefore were cultivated for an indefinite period of time. Among the Hopi the matrilineal sib was the most important land-controlling agent. Within the sib, fields were assigned to lineage segments, which lived in separate households, and these in turn were divided so that each woman had her own plot. She had the right of usufruct and also the right of disposal subject to the veto of the sib expressed either by mass opinion or as a decision of the sib mother. The lands of a given sib were not continuous but were distributed in patches so that a flash flood in a single wash, or a sand storm, would not destroy all the fields of a sib. In addition, a certain amount of arable land was held in reserve so that a household whose fields had been destroyed would have a place to plant again. In spite of the fact that women held title to farm plots, men did most of the agricultural work. Women's title to the land is believed by many anthropologists to be evidence of former dominance of women in farm work.

The Navaho system was more individualistic and lacked control over land by sibs or community officials. Farm land was formerly inherited matrilineally, however, although at the present time inheritance is often patrilineal. The first person to farm a plot, whether man or woman, automatically acquired and subsequently retained possession of the plot, although relatives and even friends might be allowed to cultivate a part of it. Boundaries were carefully set, and, once established, rights to a particular field were permanent. Even though the owner abandoned his farm for a number of years, he or his heirs might evict anyone else who had appropriated it during their absence. A sure way to retain title was for an owner to arrange for a relative to farm the plot while he was away. Ownership applied only to the agricultural products raised on the land; wild shrubs or trees, roots or berries, and springs were free to everyone, and the entering of a field to obtain these natural resources was not considered trespass. Only trees which were planted were privately owned. Apache concepts of land tenure were looser and are characterized as matricentered and bicentered.

Among the Yumans of the Colorado River, farm lands were restricted to the bottoms which were annually flooded. Plots were marked by boundaries and were inherited patrilineally. They were also bought and sold, a successful warrior often purchasing land with the spoils of victory. If a man wanted more land he could obtain it by clearing off the natural vegetation which grew thickly near the river. An individual's holdings were usually in a continuous strip, although sometimes they were scattered within a narrow radius. Boundary disputes not settled by arbitration were settled by force: first by a pushing contest; but if the results of this did not satisfy both parties, then by a battle with sticks and staves. Land was normally inherited from father to son, the theoretical claims of daughters being waived when they married and went to live on their husbands' land. A widow had a right to some of her deceased husband's land, which was cultivated for her by her nearest male relatives. Often, however, she lived with a son, who worked the farm, or son-in-law who owned another plot sufficient to support her along with the rest of his family. At the death of an owner, his land was left to lie fallow for a year or two. If it was not refarmed after a reasonable length of time, anyone might appropriate and cultivate it.

Meso-America and Circum-Caribbean.—In Meso-America and around the Caribbean, where agriculture dominated subsistence, hunting territory seems to have been international or controlled by the tribe or state. An exception to this was the control which chiefs and kings, such as Montezuma, exercised over hunting preserves which were set aside for royalty. The common man, however, never belonged to a kinship group which owned hunting land. In many parts of Meso-America hunting was in the hands of specialized groups which hunted for the nobility. The presence of clans and demes in some parts of these areas suggests that these kin groups may have controlled tracts of hunting land at some time in the past.

Among the Aztecs of Mexico, all land nominally belonged to the state. The state council divided the land among the demes, and the leaders of these units, in turn, further allocated it to extended families or their heads. Certain sections were reserved for members of the political and religious staffs who were full-time specialists and did not farm. These sections were worked by volunteers or conscripts from the entire community, and no doubt also by slave labor. This is reminiscent of the town or chief's fields in the Southeast. Family plots were nominally owned by males, and, when a man died, title passed to his son. If the son died without offspring or failed to cultivate his land for two years, it reverted to the deme for redivision. The deposed owner was demoted to the ranks of the propertyless proletariat who worked as hired hands for farm owners or at crafts.

As population increased in the Valley of Mexico, land became scarce. New land was made by scooping up mud or soil from the borders of the lakes and holding it in place with barriers of reeds and later by roots of trees planted for the purpose. Thus were created the famous floating gardens, *chinampas*, which exist near Mexico City to this day. Large areas of unproductive marsh were converted into valuable truck gardens in this manner. Fresh mud was added each year to maintain the high level of soil fertility. New land was also taken from conquered neighbors. Successful warriors were granted portions of conquered land, which was worked by the vanquished people. These lands were inherited from father to son or, if an heir was lacking, reverted to the Aztec state organization for reallotment.

From the above evidence it is clear that property concepts did not apply uniformly to all uses made of land. Peoples which had agriculture generally recognized the right of exclusive use of tracts of farm land by individuals and groups of relatives, but very few agricultural tribes divided up hunting, fishing, or wild plant sites in the same manner. The northeastern Algonquians were fussy about hunting and trapping rights but not about any other land uses. The Northwest Coast exhibited the most comprehensive system of land tenure, restricting hunting, fishing, and wild plant sites alike. Even sections of beach and seascape belonged to groups of relatives. No other area of comparable size was as thorough.

The other obtrusive fact about land tenure is the consistency with which a single tribe is patri-, matri-, or bi-centered with regard to two or more uses of land. With few exceptions the same alignment of relatives controlled multiple uses of land when they were controlled by groups of relatives at all. For example, on the Northwest Coast, hunting, fishing, and wild plant sites were all three matricentered in the north and patricentered in the remainder of the area. The fact that men exploited the first two kinds of sites and women the third did not interfere with a consistent matrilineal or patrilineal bias. Sexual division of labor did not cause ownership to descend in two different lines.

OWNERSHIP AND INHERITANCE OF DWELLINGS

A sample of facts on the ownership and inheritance of dwellings have been assembled on Map 30. Houses were occupied by kinship groups and inherited within these groups in the western Arctic, western Sub-Arctic, North Pacific Coast, East, Meso-America, and parts of the Plains, Prairies, and Oasis. In general, dwellings which were large or substantially built to last a number of years tended to be inherited rather than destroyed at the death of an inmate or owner. These dwellings were usually occupied by a number of related families (Map 18). Small, hastily constructed houses, in contrast, were normally destroyed or abandoned at death so that there was nothing left to inherit. The picture is complicated by the existence of several kinds of houses among single tribes and by seasonal considerations but, by and large, tends to follow these generalizations.

The social structure of the groups of relatives occupying large permanent houses and the inheritance of such dwellings conforms closely to rules of land tenure. In other words, housing behaves like other real estate. Where land was owned tribally or internationally, dwellings were portable, in keeping with the nomadic way of life. Such dwellings were often destroyed at the death of an inmate, or at least torn down and moved. The parts which were movable (poles, hides, mats, bark) are best regarded as chattels. The large, sewn hide tipis of the Plains in the nineteenth century were not consistently destroyed at a death, and in this respect conform to the pattern of large, permanent housing. Although their portability groups them with other tipis and simple, dome-shaped structures, their size puts them in the class of large, permanent dwellings.

A comparison of Map 30, on the ownership and inheritance of dwellings, with Map 31, on post-nuptial residence, shows substan-

261

tial agreement between the corresponding traits when the cases where houses were destroyed at death are eliminated On the other hand, correspondence between the dominant house-building sexual division of labor, Map 19, and ownership and inheritance of dwellings, Map 30, is low. One obtrusive difference is on the northern Northwest Coast and adjacent interior, where men dominate house-building and ownership is matricentered. However, this discrepancy is only apparent: men are the nominal owners and title passes from a man to his sister's son on the coast. Among the Kaskas of the interior, title passes from a man to his son-in-law, who may not be a genetic relative. We have labeled this matricentered also because title is held nominally by the husbands of a maternal lineage segment. Another area where a difference appears consistently is the East. Here the men do most of the work of house-building, but the women own the houses and inherit them matrilineally. The same is also true in part of the Oasis. The female ownership of houses constructed by men is a common feature of matrilineal societies in other parts of the world and demands no special explanation in North America. These are examples where the sex of the maker and sex of the user and owner of material possessions do not correspond. There are many other examples of this kind which need not be cited.

OWNERSHIP AND INHERITANCE OF CHATTELS

Movable property of all sorts is called chattels, a term which has the same root as the word cattle. Chattels were often owned by single individuals, although canoes and other things requiring a crew for operation might be jointly owned by the whole crew or several of its members. Tools, weapons, household articles, and any other objects used exclusively or nearly exclusively by a single individual were generally regarded as the property of that individual with the right of disposal and destruction. Ethnologists purchasing museum specimens from Indians have often found a husband refusing to sell anything belonging to his wife. Even children owned a few things which their elders would not dispose of. At death the chattels of the deceased were often buried with the corpse or burnt, sometimes so extensively that there was nothing left to inherit. In other societies, only a part of a person's chattels were destroyed or buried at death, the remainder being inherited in some fashion. Disposal of property before death by willing it to certain individuals was also known to some North American Indian societies but seems to have been less common than inheritance.

Movable property may be divided according to sex. A comparison of the rules of inheritance for men's chattels shows high correlations with the corresponding modes of inheritance for land (Map 29). In the same areas where land tenure was matricentered, men inherited chattels matrilineally, that is, from a man to his sister's son. Likewise, where land tenure was patricentered, inheritance of chattels tended to be patrilineal; where land was bicentered, chattels were bilateral.

Women's chattels show a striking difference; inheritance is either matrilineal or bilateral, never patrilineal. Not a single instance of women's chattels' being inherited from a woman to her brother's daughter was found. This was anticipated in patrilineal societies but never appeared. The fact that women's household articles, clothing, and the like are commonly inherited from mother to daughter in societies where most other kinds of property descend from father to son is a significant point. It shows that there are conflicting lines of inheritance coexisting in single societies. The type of lineage or sib descent which a society subscribes to apparently depends on which line of descent receives the most emphasis in that society as a whole.

INCORPOREAL PROPERTY

Incorporeal property, such as songs, dances, magic formulas, myths, crests, and membership in sibs and sodalities, was universally recognized by North American natives. Such material has never been systematized, but a few examples will suffice here. Medicine men often possessed magic formulas or songs which were owned and used by individual practitioners in curing the sick. A fee was charged for their employment on a patient, and they were sometimes bought and sold. On the northern Plains, medicine bundles, which were a combination of corporeal and incorporeal property, were normally bought and sold. Along with the sale went the teaching of the songs and ritual, without which the

263

bundle would have been ineffective. These bundles were not the exclusive property of a class of medicine men but were owned by every man of any importance. Prices rose in the nineteenth century, in keeping with the general inflation brought by the fur trade, to the point that some individuals bought medicine bundles just to hold them a while and sell them later at a profit.

Membership in sibs involved a number of incorporeal rights such as the right to participate in sib ceremonies, to wear sib insignia, and to be protected legally by one's sib mates. In fact, the whole sib system is an outstanding example of ownership and inheritance of a wide range of intangibles by the membership. The fact that sibs might also own corporeal property should not obscure the fundamentally incorporeal nature of these unilateral institutions.

The area of greatest elaboration of incorporeal property concepts is probably Meso-America, although the Northwest Coast was not far behind. Other examples of such ownership may be found in chapters xix, xx, and xxiii.

REFERENCES

COOPER, 1939; DRUCKER, 1939; EGGAN, 1950; FLANNERY, 1939; GOLDSCHMIDT AND HAAS, 1946; HALLOWELL, 1949; HARRIS, MS.*b;* HERSKOVITS, 1952; HICKERSON, MS; KROEBER, 1925; LEACOCK, n.d., 1955; LINTON, 1942; LOWIE, 1948; MURDOCK, 1949; ROYS, 1943; SPECK, 1915; SPECK AND EISELEY, 1939; SWANTON, 1946; VAILLANT, 1941.

15: Marriage

and the Family

NORTH American Indians exhibit an amazing variety of ways to acquire a mate, of structural forms of marriage such as polygamy, of incest taboos, of post-nuptial residence customs, of parent-in-law relations, and of family structure. In fact, almost all of the principal variants of these phenomena known to the entire world are found in North America alone. In comparison, European marriage and family practices were almost uniform. This wide range of variation indicates great historical depth as well as meticulous adaptation to natural and cultural environments.

The sex act itself may be called mating, whether done within or without wedlock. Marriage, on the other hand, is usually defined as both an economic and a sexual union known to other members of the society, accepted by them, and considered to be permanent. The secret marriage of today, made legal by a marriage license and ceremony obtained without publicity, was unheard of in Indian societies. In the absence of written records, every marriage had to be known to everyone in the community; otherwise, there would be no adequate regulation of sexual activity.

Another point which cannot be over-emphasized is that the parents and other elder relatives of a bride or groom normally had more to do with the selection of a marriage partner than did either of the principals. Marriage among most primitive peoples is regarded as a contract between two groups of kin rather than between two individuals. In general, a bride and groom had more voice in the matter among the economically less advanced tribes such as those in the Arctic, Sub-Arctic, Great Basin, and Northeast Mexico. Those areas which were economically more advanced or possessed sib systems tended to give more weight to the opinions of elders.

INFANT OR CHILD BETROTHAL

The authority of the parents in choosing a mate for their offspring is reflected in the custom of betrothing an infant or a child. At first blush this practice would seem to belong in cultures of considerable economic and social stability, but such is not always the case. The Eskimo commonly betrothed infants or children, even though the vicissitudes of their way of life often made consummation of these agreements impossible. Among the central Eskimos, where the incidence of female infanticide was greatest, it was said that only betrothed female infants were spared. If we are to take this statement at face value, it means that all brides were betrothed in infancy. Whether or not this is literally true, it emphasizes the importance of infant betrothal in this culture.

Infant or child betrothal is reported from some tribes on the Northwest Coast, Plateau, western Sub-Arctic, California, Great Basin, Oasis, East, and Meso-America. On the Northwest Coast, at least, a partial payment of the bride price was made at this time. Elsewhere some gift exchange may have taken place at the time of betrothal, but it should hardly be labeled bride price.

PREMARITAL MATING

Mating prior to marriage was practiced in the majority of North American Indian societies although it was far from universal. Even where condoned or taken for granted, there might still be a premium placed on virginity. Thus among Plains tribes, where unchastity was everywhere condoned except among the Cheyenne, we find the higher-ranking families attempting to instil standards of virtue in their daughters. With the Crow, a certain ceremonial role could be performed only by a woman who had been a virgin bride and remained faithful to her husband, which proves that premarital chastity was valued. On the Northwest Coast, young women were sometimes confined in a boarded-off room in the house from the time of first menstruation until marriage, so that their virginity plus an unusually light skin would not only command a higher bride price but would also facilitate a union with a higher-ranking family.

By and large, premarital sexual relations were less a problem in Indian societies than in our own, partly because of the younger age at which marriage took place. Young women were normally considered marriageable after first menstruation, which might take place at twelve or thirteen years of age (we have no adequate figures on the average age). Men tended to be older, but probably married at less than twenty years of age on the average. Carefully compiled modern statistics tell us that young women near the age of first menstruation are much less fertile than they will be even a few years later. Illegitimate pregnancies must have been less common in Indian societies than in societies with later marriage age. This fact, coupled with the more permissive attitude taken by some Indians, contrived to make premarital intercourse a somewhat less traumatic experience than in our society today.

In the Southeast, attitudes about sex were especially liberal. Both young men and women were allowed premarital sexual experience, which was taken for granted and was nothing to be ashamed of or kept secret. The only restriction was that they should not violate the rules regarding incest, exogamy, or adultery. It was even legitimate for unmarried young women to sell themselves for a price, subject to these same restrictions, and this was carefully distinguished from professional prostitution on the part of adulteresses who had been cast off by offended husbands. Prostitutes were looked down on but were tolerated. Premarital pregnancies were fairly common, and the children were reared by the mother's family, extended family, or sib as a matter of course. While the child was apparently always kept within its mother's sib, it might be adopted by some family other than the mother's; or, if the unwed mother preferred, she had a right to put her infant to death within one month after birth. There was little or no stigma attached to the mother or the offspring of a premarital sexual union.

WAYS OF ACQUIRING A SPOUSE

Most of the ways and means of acquiring a bride reported for primitive man the world over are also known for aboriginal North America. One of these is called marriage by purchase or by bride price. Such purchase does not give the right to dispose of the bride either by sale to another or by renting her out as a prostitute. Neither does it carry the right to injure or to kill her. All the husband purchases is the right to share with her the type of sexual and economic life permitted and approved by the society in which he lives. Furthermore, the bride's family often repays or makes return gifts to the groom's family of a value equal to that of the gifts received. Because of these qualifications, many anthropologists prefer the phrase bride wealth to bride price. Where bride wealth was obtrusive in the culture, as on the Northwest Coast, the social prestige of a woman, and that of her offspring and husband as well, were positively correlated with the amount "paid" for her. In this same area, the bride price was often negotiated as in a business transaction. In spite of this bargaining feature, the return payments or gifts from the bride's family to that of the groom were commonly of a value equal to that of the bride price. Therefore, it is best to regard this whole process of exchange of wealth at marriage as a means of establishing social rank and position rather than as a business transaction.

On the northern Plains in the nineteenth century, bride price and polygyny became involved in a truly economic competition brought on by the fur trade. In this culture women dressed the buffalo hides, a task which took far longer than for a man to kill an animal with a horse and gun. Men purchased wives, largely in exchange for horses, in order to acquire more hands to work at the skin-dressing trade. This highly commercial brand of bride purchase was unknown before European contact.

Bride service or suitor service was another way in which a man could qualify as a husband. The prospective groom went to live with his future bride's parents and worked for and with her father. If, after a year or so, he had demonstrated his ability to hunt and otherwise earn a living in the way prescribed by the culture, he was given the daughter as a bride. This custom often resulted in a temporary matrilocal residence for a year or so after the couple was married, or until the first child was born. At that time the marriage was regarded as fully consummated, and the groom often took the bride to his own community to live.

Exact distributions of bride price, bride service, and related customs have not been worked out. In general, it may be said that the concept of bride price or "purchase" was strongest on the Plains, Prairies, and Northwest Coast. However, among the northern matrilineal peoples on the Northwest Coast, where residence was avunculocal and cross-cousin marriage preferred, a boy as young as ten years went to live with his future father-in-law, where he served for his bride but remained to inherit the estate. Bride service was most dominant in the Sub-Arctic and Great Basin areas. A mixture or balance between bride price and bride service characterized all other areas. For example, among the Creek Indians of the Southeast, gifts of about equal value were exchanged by the families of the bride and groom, and the groom often helped his wife's relatives farm, or built the house on their land which he and his bride were to occupy in the near future. For the Aztecs of Mexico, no bride service is mentioned, but the wealth exchanged by the families of the principals was of about equal value.

Marriage was sometimes effected by two families exchanging daughters, each of whom became a wife of the other family's son. This is called interfamilial exchange marriage. It eliminated bride wealth and suitor service. Although the distribution of this custom is not well known, it seems to have been comparatively rare in North America. It is reported mainly in areas where formalities were at the minimum, such as the Great Basin and Sub-Arctic.

The frequency and importance of marriage by capture or abduction of the bride was vastly exaggerated by nineteenth-century anthropologists. In aboriginal North America, the majority of tribes sometimes captured women in warfare and kept them as wives. On the Northwest Coast, however, women were enslaved rather than married when they were taken in a raid. Some tribes in Mexico and Central America enacted a mock capture as part of the marriage ceremony, and a few abducted a minority of brides against their will. On the whole, however, the percentage of wives acquired in this fashion was small and had little effect on the customary marriage practices.

Still another means of acquiring a spouse is called adoptive marriage. Where patrilocal or patrilineal families lacked a son to inherit the family property and perpetuate the line of descent, they sometimes adopted a young man who married one of their daugh-

269

ters. The third generation inherited from him in the same manner that they would have from a true member of the line. The entire distribution of this custom is unknown, but it was practiced in the Eastern Sub-Arctic, the Prairies, the patrilocal part of the Northwest Coast, and no doubt in other patrilocal or patrilineal areas. Matrilocal and matrilineal societies seem to have adopted daughters less often, although among the Haisla on the Northwest Coast a man who had no sister's son adopted his own daughter to inherit his title. Among the Mandan of the upper Missouri River, a family without a daughter adopted a daughter-in-law to carry on the line. Some maternal lineages and sibs among the western Pueblos have become extinct because of the lack of female heirs, which is evidence that adoption was absent or at least rare in that area.

A custom known as fictive marriage was occasionally practiced by the Kwakiutl of the Northwest Coast. Among these Indians, chieftainship and other statuses tended to pass from a man to his son-in-law and then to his daughter's son. When a chief had no daughter, he acquired a legal son-in-law by means of a sham marriage between his son and the man who was to be the son-in-law. The fictive son-in-law produced children through a real wife of another family, normally one of lower rank, and carried on in the role of the chief.

Elopement was practiced now and then by almost all North American tribes but was rarely the approved method of acquiring a bride. A man without the usual family connections, having difficulty in raising an adequate bride price alone, might resolve his predicament by elopement. If a love match was frowned upon by ambitious elders trying to arrange an economically or socially advantageous marriage, the lovers might settle matters by elopement. When this happened in the Southeast, a posse of the bride's relatives often pursued the couple with an eye to breaking up the affair. If, however, the eloping pair were able to hide in the woods until the annual harvest ceremony, all they had to do was to appear as man and wife at this public ritual in order to win approval of the society. All offenses short of murder were annually forgiven by this culture at this time, and elopement was less serious than many other wrongs.

INCEST TABOOS AND EXOGAMY

Mating with any person regarded as a genetic relative is called incest. Incest was universally tabooed in Indian North America. Nowhere was mating or marriage between father and daughter or mother and son allowed, and brother-sister unions were tolerated only among royalty around the Caribbean. Marriage with certain first cousins was permitted and even preferred among a small number of tribes, but, as we shall see later, these cousins were not regarded as genetic relatives.

Incest taboos were often automatically extended by the meaning of the terms for kin in the many Indian languages. For example, if the word for sister included all of a man's female cousins, as it actually does for many tribes, marriage with cousins would normally be forbidden by extension of the incest taboo from sister to cousin. The same principle applies to other relationships. To take another example, if the term for sister is extended to some of a man's cousins but not to others, it often follows that he may have sexual relations with or may marry the cousins not called sisters, but must behave like a brother to the ones designated as sisters. Where sibs exist, an individual has a large number of fictitious or traditional relatives who may actually be unrelated to him. Nevertheless, such traditional relationships are a bar to marriage and a man must look for a mate outside of his sib. The rule requiring a person to marry outside a defined social group is called exogamy.

Where does the incest taboo leave off and exogamy begin? There is no agreement among anthropologists on the limits of these two terms. A simple rule of thumb is to designate the ban on marriage or mating with actual genetic relatives as the incest taboo, and to reserve the term exogamy for the prohibition of sexual relations within the larger kin group which recognizes traditional relationship. Exogamy may also apply to a locality; a man may be compelled to seek a mate outside the locality or community in which he lives. This is called local exogamy. Normally this rule is applied only to small communities in which most members are genetically related or are so considered by tradition. Incest taboos or exogamy may be extended three ways: bilaterally, patrilineally, or matrilineally. By bilateral extension is meant an equal extension to relatives of both the father and the mother. Patrilineal extension means a greater extension among relatives in the father's line than in the mother's. Matrilineal extension refers to a greater extension in the mother's than in the father's line.

COUSIN MARRIAGE

First-cousin marriage was permitted or preferred by a small minority of peoples. Before describing particular areas or tribes, we must first consider the different kinds of first cousins commonly distinguished by Indians. From the point of view of a man looking for a wife, there are four kinds of female cousins: (1) his father's brother's daughters; (2) his father's sister's daughters; (3) his mother's brother's daughters; (4) his mother's sister's daughters. The first and the last types of cousins are sometimes grouped together by Indians as well as by anthropologists and, by the latter, are called parallel cousins. This refers to the fact that the sex of the two connecting relatives in the parental generation is the same. The second and third types are called cross-cousins because the sex of the two connecting relatives in the parental generation is different.

On the northern Northwest Coast, cross-cousin marriage was the preferred kind of union. If no first cross-cousin was available to a man, he chose a more remote cousin designated by the same word in the language. Among the Haida, a boy of ten years of age ideally went to live with his mother's brother, who gave him his education in the lore of the sib as well as in practical matters. When the boy reached marriageable age, he ideally married his mother's brother's daughter and continued to live in the house of his mother's brother. When the latter died, the boy, who was now the deceased's son-in-law and also his sister's son, inherited his house, land, and chattels, as well as his social position and prestige. If no mother's brother's daughter were available to a young man, he might substitute a father's sister's daughter, who was designated by the same kinship term in the language. As we shall see later on, one's cross-cousins always belong to a different sib or moiety than oneself, and because of this fact, are regarded as non-relatives for marriage purposes. For the world as a whole, there is a positive correlation between unilateral descent with exogamy and cross-cousin marriage. The same is true of North America, but there are many exceptions to the rule.

Among the Kaska, inland from the Northwest Coast, the only first cousin a man was permitted to marry was his mother's brother's daughter. This was the preferred marriage, although many men had to be content with cousins further removed or with unrelated wives. At Lake Teslin, between the Kaska and the coast, and among the Chipewyans farther east, a man could marry only his father's sister's daughter.

Proceeding farther east to the Cree and Ojibwa, we find a different picture. Although marriages with both kinds of first cross-cousins were permitted, they were not preferred over more remote cousins designated by the same kinship term. First-cousin marriages were less frequent than those with more remote cousins. Almost any distant relative about one's own age would be called by the term for cross-cousin, even though the exact relationship was unknown, hence some of such marriages were not with persons we would call cousins. Double cross-cousin marriage sometimes occurred; a man married a woman who was both his mother's brother's daughter and father's sister's daughter at the same time. This could happen only when two men in the older generation had exchanged their sisters, each marrying the other's sister. The offspring from these unions would be double cross-cousins. Figures on the frequency of single cross-cousin marriage show that the mother's brother's daughter was married more often than the father's sister's daughter. The pattern of the Montagnais-Naskapi of the Labrador Peninsula was similar to that of the Cree and Ojibwa.

In California and Oregon cross-cousin marriage was permitted or preferred only by a small minority of tribelets, and in every case the mother's brother's daughter was singled out. In the Great Basin, four bands allowed father's sister's daughter marriage and three permitted union with the mother's brother's daughter. There is no obvious explanation for this difference. Nine other bands permitted step-cross-cousin marriage. A person's step-cross-cousin is the stepson or stepdaughter of his father's sister or mother's brother. Such persons were designated by the same kinship term as that for cross-cousin.

Some anthropologists believe that cross-cousin marriage was formerly permitted among some of the Pueblo peoples of the Oasis, but it cannot be proved. However, the nearby Walapai permitted a man to marry either variety of cross-cousin. The Maya of Yucatan appear to have had both kinds of cross-cousin marriage at the time of first Spanish contact, although the evidence is indirect. The Misumalpan tribes on the Caribbean side of Central America also practiced the custom.

North American instances of cross-cousin marriage are remarkable for the wide variety of other social traits associated with them. Thus descent may be patrilineal, matrilineal, or bilateral; post-nuptial residence may be patrilocal, matrilocal, avunculocal, or bilocal; kinship terminology may be Crow, Omaha, Iroquois, Hawaiian, or Eskimo. These facts, added to the scattered appearance of the geographical distribution of cross-cousin marriage, suggest a multiple origin of the phenomenon as well as a multiple causality.

If everyone married his cross-cousin it would not be necessary to have any kinship terms for in-laws because they would also be genetic (blood) relatives. Such is actually the case in most of the Eastern Sub-Arctic. Special terms for in-laws do not exist in the language. Wherever in-laws are thus lumped with genetic relatives, we may suspect marriage or former marriage of genetic relatives. All the kinship terminologies of the Algonquians of the Plains have features suggesting cross-cousin marriage. The same is true of the Santee and Teton Dakota. All of these tribes seem to have had cross-cousin marriage at some time in the past when they were living farther east where their territories probably adjoined those of the Ojibwa and Cree, who have continued to marry cross-cousins down to the present time.

Parallel cousin marriage was tolerated in a very few localities but was nowhere a preferred form. Because parallel cousins were most often designated by the same terms used for brothers and sisters, marriage with such relatives would not be anticipated.

AFFINAL MARRIAGE

There are two major kinds of relatives: genetic or "blood" relatives; affinal or relatives by marriage. Affinal relatives include all the genetic relatives of one's wife or husband, commonly designated as in-laws. Any marriage with an in-law is an affinal marriage.

Affinal marriages are always secondary marriages, because there are no in-laws before a first marriage.

The marriage of a woman to her deceased husband's brother is called levirate. This form of marriage was nearly universal in Indian North America; at least there are few reports of its being forbidden. Each party to such a marriage may be regarded as an asset or a liability by the other according to circumstances. A widow with children to support would be in need of a husband, and an attractive younger brother of her deceased husband would definitely be an asset. If, on the other hand, he was an unattractive person, or was already married so that the widow became a second wife who took orders from his first wife, then he might appear to be a liability. Similarly, an attractive widow would be an asset to a man without a wife, especially if the bride price demanded by a first marriage were high; but if she were considerably older or had many children to support, he might regard her as a liability. A widow was generally obligated to accept her husband's unmarried brother as a mate, and the latter was equally obligated to care for his sister-in-law and her children. The near universality of this custom reflects the attitude that a marriage is a contract between two families or lines of descent, and not binding merely to the two principals.

The marriage of a man to his deceased wife's sister is called sororate. As in the case of the levirate, there was an obligation as well as a benefit involved for both parties. The sororate was also nearly universal, and little evidence of its being forbidden is reported.

Some field reports distinguish between optional and obligatory levirate and sororate, and contrasts of this kind are not hard to find. However, we suspect that if more detailed information were available, every degree of compulsion would turn up and that the representation of these differences as points along a scale would be more correct.

The levirate and sororate are often extended to relatives of the deceased more remote than a brother or sister, in cases where the latter are unavailable. For example, a man might marry his deceased wife's cousin or niece if she had no sister. Similarly, a woman might marry a more remote relative of her deceased husband if he did not have a brother. Such extensions are the rule in primitive cultures

275

and may be taken for granted except where they are specifically denied.

POLYGAMY

Any marriage with multiple husbands or wives is called polygamy. It may take two forms: polygyny, the marriage of one husband to two or more wives simultaneously; polyandry, the marriage of one wife to two or more husbands simultaneously.

The vast majority of North American peoples practiced polygyny. It was probably most frequent in the northern part of the Plains and Prairie areas. We have already mentioned the prodigious increase in numbers of wives on the Plains in the nineteenth century as a result of the fur trade. This could have happened only in an area where the institution was well established in early times. Actual figures obtained from the records of priests among the Crees and Ojibwas indicate an incidence of polygyny in former times well over the 20 per cent mark. Another area of common occurrence is the Northwest Coast. Although polygyny was limited to the wealthier class in this area, mainly because of the great amount of the bride price, it seems to have exceeded the 20 per cent figure in the majority of localities.

Exclusive monogamy was the rule among the Iroquois and a few of their neighbors. This is to be expected in cultures in which matrilineal descent and matrilocal residence were coupled with female ownership and control of agricultural land and houses, not to mention the unusual authority of women in political affairs. Here the men literally moved in with their wives, who could divorce them merely by tossing their personal effects out of the door of the longhouse. Even sororal polygyny, which was the only form conceivable under these conditions, was lacking.

The only other area where female dominance approached this level was that of the western Pueblos in the Southwest. Here the picture was similar and exclusive monogamy prevailed. The other instances of exclusive monogamy are scattered and occurred in both bilateral and patrilineal societies. They do not lend themselves to any ready explanation.

Sororal polygyny, that is, the marriage of a man to two wives who were sisters, probably occurred wherever polygyny was to be found. A number of Plains tribes had no other form. A man in this society was especially anxious to acquire an eldest sister as a first mate, with an eye to acquiring her younger sisters if and when he could afford them. Although it is not the purpose of this volume to justify Indian behavior, it is easy to see that polygyny had more utility in societies where male mortality in hunting and warfare was high. The Plains was one of these areas. Among the Eskimos, where a man had more difficulty in supporting multiple wives, the terrific male mortality was offset by female infanticide. This partially explains the more modest amount of polygyny present in the Arctic.

Polyandry as a preferred form of marriage is extremely rare in the world, and its existence in North America may be questioned. It is true that many instances have been reported, but closer examination of the facts reveals many qualifications. In the first place, the husbands were often brothers or other close relatives. The older brother normally began with a monogamous union and at a later date allowed his younger brother to come to live with him. Often the younger brother had access to the wife only when the elder brother was away from home. This was certainly true in California and the Great Basin, where isolated cases have been reported. Polyandry was nowhere the preferred kind of union, was probably never lifelong, and is best regarded as an expedient solution to the sex problem.

Among the Eskimos, polyandry was complicated by that form of northern hospitality called wife-lending. Any man would lend his wife for a night to a total stranger, and to a friend or relative for longer periods depending on circumstances. In theory, at least, wife-lending eventually terminated. In some cases the wife lent was a second wife from a polygynous marriage. At the same time, cases of two brothers sharing one wife are widely reported. While details are often wanting, the general pattern is that of a younger brother moving in with his married older brother and playing a secondary role. The common procedure in wife-lending was for the visitor to go to bed with the wife of the host in the one room hut where the host also slept. The only privacy was darkness. Such being the case, we may presume that two brothers shared their wife at home with each other present. The length of time such multiple

277

unions lasted is seldom reported. However, it is generally agreed that they did not continue for a lifetime. The arrangement is best regarded as an expedient in cases in which one of the brothers had no wife.

It has been argued that female infanticide has been a cause of polyandry, that the killing off of too many girl babies has produced a sex ratio of more males than females. Population figures available for the Eskimo show that forty-two communities out of seventy-six (55 per cent) had fewer women than men. Because male mortality was higher than female mortality among all the Eskimos, these figures appear to reflect female infanticide. Where female infanticide eliminated half the girl babies, as it did near the magnetic pole in the central Arctic, it definitely encouraged polyandry, but where the sex ratios show only slightly fewer females, infanticide alone was hardly a sufficient cause. The other factor was polygyny. The strongest and most capable men appropriated more than their share of wives. Polygyny, polyandry, and of course monogamy, all existed side by side. Monogamy was much the most frequent, but polygyny was the preferred form of marriage and was generally more common than polyandry. Polygyny may, therefore, be regarded as a partial cause of polyandry.

POST-NUPTIAL RESIDENCE

When a couple married, they had to decide where they were going to live, whether with or near the groom's relatives, the bride's relatives, or somewhere else. Patrilocal residence means living with or near the groom's parents; it is also called virilocal. Matrilocal refers to residence with or near the bride's parents; it is also called uxorilocal. Avunculocal is applied to residence with the groom's mother's brother's family, neolocal to residence in a new house or locality where neither the groom's nor the bride's parents are present, bilocal to residence with either the groom's or the bride's parents, or a shifting back and forth from one to the other. Matri-patrilocal residence refers to initial and temporary matrilocal residence, usually for a year or until the first child is born, followed by permanent patrilocal residence.

Initial and temporary matrilocal residence, combined with a certain amount of bride service, may precede all other types of later and more permanent residence. Thus it preceded bilocal residence in the Great Basin, neolocal residence on the Prairies, avunculocal residence with the Haislas on the Northwest Coast, and patrilocal residence in most of the Sub-Arctic and California. Because of its ubiquitous association with other forms of residence and its temporary character, it is not shown on a map. Map 31 gives only the final or more permanent forms of post-nuptial residence.

A second source of confusion in residential data is the frequent failure to distinguish between house and community. It is one thing for a newly married couple to set up housekeeping in a new dwelling located a dozen feet from that of the groom's or bride's parents, and quite another for them to sever ties with both sets of parents and move to a new community miles away. When the facts are given, and there is a conflict between dwelling and community, we have chosen the latter. Thus for the Chiracahua Apaches, among whom newlyweds usually live in a new house close to the bride's genetic relatives, matrilocal residence has been tabulated. In cases of data referring only to the dwelling, they have been recorded as given. Thus in the Middle West neolocal residence has been recorded when the source material merely said that the newlyweds moved into a house of their own. Whether any aboriginal North American tribe regularly followed a rule of neolocal residence with respect to community is problematical. The majority of young couples everywhere seems to have lived in communities with at least some genetic relatives present. The choice between a separate house and living in the same house with parents is also dependent on the size of the prevailing house type in the culture; cultures with small houses more often have new-house residence, those with large houses, old-house residence. Parent-in-law avoidances have probably also tended to increase the frequency of new-house residence.

A third source of difficulty in dealing with post-nuptial residence is the absence of adequate information on frequency of occurrence within single cultures. Few, if any, North American tribes appear to have followed any rule of residence 100 per cent of the time. For the vast majority, a rule of residence was merely a preference or a tendency subject to change according to a variety of disruptive circumstances. If adequate census material existed, it would be

279

a simple matter arbitrarily to assign statistical boundaries between patrilocal, bilocal, and matrilocal residence, for example. But in lieu of such data, preferred or most frequent forms, according to sources, have been recorded and the alternatives eliminated.

A fourth factor which complicates the picture of residence is seasonal variation. Most of the Canadian Algonquians, to choose a well-known example, followed a pattern of predominantly patrilocal residence in relation to hunting and trapping territories in winter, but in the summer, when they congregated in large numbers at fishing places, the residence may have been bilocal. Because the combined evidence would show a patrilocal bias, we have characterized this area as patrilocal. The Omaha also exhibit an interesting seasonal shift of residence. During the farming season they resided matrilocally in the large earth lodges; during the rest of the year, patrilocally in the smaller tipis. In general, we have chosen the kind of residence practiced in the majority of cases, even though the majority was small.

Patrilocal residence is the most widespread type—the dominant form in the Sub-Arctic, northern Prairies, northern Plains, Plateau, southern Northwest Coast, California, the Mexican Oasis, and Meso-America. Matrilocal residence is characteristic of the East, central plains, Ute, Southwest Athapaskans, western Pueblos, the western part of the Athapaskan Sub-Arctic, and Central America. Bilocal residence is the most frequent form in the Great Basin and the Arctic. Neolocal residence occurs only sporadically and may be partly the result of European contact. Avunculocal residence is limited to the Northwest Coast, perhaps extending all the way to the Aleut.

THE FAMILY

Before describing the different family units of aboriginal North America, let us first review the general terminology of family structure. The family is a social group consisting of adults of both sexes, at least two of whom maintain a socially approved sexual relationship, and one or more children produced by this relationship or adopted by the adults. It is also characterized by common residence, economic co-operation, and responsibility for the education of children. According to Murdock, families may be classified into three major types: (1) the nuclear family, consisting of parents and offspring; (2) the polygamous family, which is an aggregate of two or more nuclear families brought about by plural marriages; (3) the extended family, which is also an aggregate of two or more nuclear families, but produced by joining three or more generations of genetic relatives.

Family structure can best be described with the aid of diagrams. In anthropological genealogies, it is customary to use triangles to

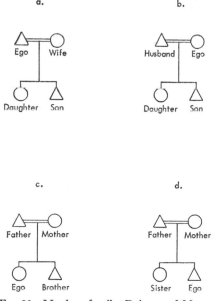

Fig. 32.–Nuclear family. Driver and Massey

represent males and circles to represent females. Marriage is indicated by double horizontal lines which contact the two principals in mid-section, brother-sister relationships by a single horizontal line which contacts these relatives by means of a short vertical line from above. Relationship must always be reckoned from a single individual called the "ego" or "I."

Figure 32 illustrates the simplest kind of family, called the nuclear family, from the point of view of the husband and father, *a*, the wife and mother, *b*, the daughter, *c*, and the son, *d*. There may be, of course, a larger number of children, but it is necessary to indicate only one of each sex.

281

Figure 33 represents the polygynous family in which the wives are unrelated, *a*, and the polygynous family where the wives are sisters, *b*, as well as a polyandrous family in which the husbands are unrelated, *c*. As an accepted and permanent form of family, type *c* does not exist in North America, and possibly not in the entire world. Figure 33 shows the fraternal polyandrous family, *d*, which was accepted as a temporary arrangement in a few localities but never became a permanent or preferred family type in North

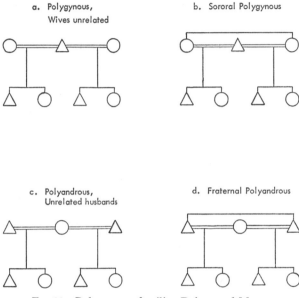

FIG. 33.—Polygamous families. Driver and Massey

America. The various kinds of polygamous families are composed of two or more nuclear families which share a common member. All more complex types of family structure may be said to be aggregates of nuclear families.

Extended families are classified according to the rule of postnuptial residence. Thus extended families may be patrilocal, matrilocal, bilocal, or avunculocal. Figure 34 illustrates these types. In the patrilocal extended family, the sons continue to live with their fathers and bring their wives to their father's house or locality; married daughters live elsewhere, but unmarried daughters belong to this group. For the matrilocal type it is the daughters who stay at home; their husbands must come to live with them. In the bi-local variety either sons or daughters may stay at home, or either may go to live with the spouse's family. We have diagrammed it arbitrarily to show one son and one daughter remaining under the family roof. For the **avunculocal** extended family, the groom takes

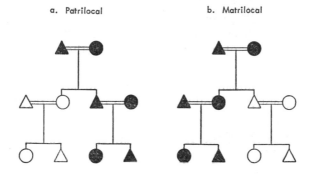

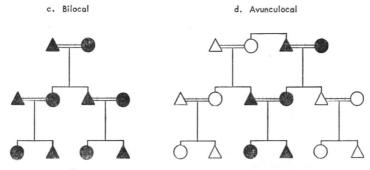

Fig. 34.—Extended families. Driver and Massey

his bride to live with his mother's brother, and the son of the next generation stays with his father until about ten years of age, or until married. The minimum number of relatives required to define each type has been shown, but in actual practice there were often four generations and about fifty persons in all.

Because nuclear families were combined to form polygamous and extended families, and also occurred where these more complex forms were absent, they were universal in North America. Because polygyny probably nowhere constituted more than a minority of cases in a given locality, less than half the families in any society were polygynous. Polyandrous families were never permanent social units in any North American culture and probably nowhere reached even the 10 per cent mark. They were everywhere dominated by monogamy.

Extended families would appear to be widespread if we noted low frequencies. Practically every tribe had at least a few three-generation groups of relatives living together at a given time. While we do not have adequate statistical evidence to prove this statement, the abundant references to grandparents and grandchildren in biography and folklore indicate plenty of three-generation propinquity. However, the history of such a group of relatives may be necessary to classify it. If each younger generation continues to reside with older generations and forms a functioning economic and social unit, then the term extended family would seem to be applicable. But when younger generations set up independent households and economies which they operate for years, and take in the older generations only after the latter are unable to care for themselves, this is not properly termed an extended family. Extended family organization implies a certain amount of authority and leadership in the older generations. It can be said to be dominant only where it is the preferred form as well as the form actually achieved by the majority of the population.

The extended family is the dominant type for the western Eskimo as far as the Mackenzie Delta. In chapter viii we pointed out that the dominant house type of this area was a substantial, semi-subterranean, earth-covered, rectangloid structure large enough to hold several nuclear families. Everyone spent the winter, which was well over half the year, in these houses. While it is certainly true that some nuclear families lived alone part of the time, the cultural pattern was overwhelmingly one of multiple family housing. The men of these large-house groups hunted together as a team, especially when they went whaling, because it required a sizable crew to manage the *umiak*. They also co-operated in fishing and land mammal hunting. Although the wife in each nuclear family owned her own household utensils, there was considerable sharing of food within the household. There was sometimes wife-lending or exchanging on the part of the husbands in the group. There was certainly mutual babysitting and mutual aid in educating children. If we consider in turn the four main characteristics of the family, namely, common residence, economic co-operation, reproduction, and education of offspring, we find that the house group in this area performed all four functions. There is no important function of the nuclear family which was not also taken care of by these extended families.

Extremely little information is available on the kinship relationships of the occupants of these houses. About the only clue to this important aspect is information on post-nuptial residence (Map 31). While this leaves much to be desired, it seems probable that young couples normally lived with relatives rather than with unrelated persons. This is not meant to imply that newlyweds had no choice in the matter or that there were no exceptions to such a rule. Where residence was patrilocal and inheritance of real estate and chattels patrilineal, there can be little doubt that many of the house groups were patrilocal extended families. Where the residence rule was bilocal and inheritance less definite, the household unit seems to have been the bilocal extended family, as Robert F. Spencer (1959) has confirmed for the north Alaskan Eskimos.

Proceeding to the central and eastern Eskimos, we find the independent nuclear family the predominant unit except in the part of the central region where the independent polygynous family is indicated. Houses were smaller than in the West and nomadism more pronounced. The fact that even the earth-stone-whalebone house was owned only for a season, and was the property of the first family to occupy it the following year, is certainly an indication of the looseness of the social structure.

The Sub-Arctic offers many difficulties of classification. Perhaps the most controversial part of this area is the east, where the family hunting territory system prevailed. Although these family groups in one area averaged only six persons, and 70 per cent of them had only a single hunter and trapper, the land tended to pass from father to son. The patrilocal extended family existed potentially. In another locality, where families averaged fifteen persons including three hunters and trappers, there is little question about the reality of the patrilocal extended family. Partly on the assumption that White contact and the fur trade, with its emphasis on individualism, tended to reduce the size of families as well as the tracts of land they occupied, it is safe to assume that the patrilocal extended family was formerly the rule in most localities. In the Mackenzie and Yukon Sub-Arctic, the picture is too complicated to permit any simple generalizations.

On the Northwest Coast we find definite extended families with clear-cut functions, especially in the north, where avuncular residence and matrilineal descent prevailed. Among the Haidas, for instance, each avunculocal extended family occupied a large plank dwelling. It was the unit of common residence, of primary economic co-operation, of trade, and of chattel accumulation, but reproduction was by the constituent nuclear or polygynous families. To the south the pattern shifts to the patrilocal extended family, which shows little variation all the way to California. This patrilocal area was bilateral in descent, and the residence rule was much less strict than in the north. Some of these extended families owned or used productive sites jointly (as we have mentioned in the chapter on property), engaged in trade, and accumulated chattels for the potlatch.

In central and southern California patrilocal extended families were again the rule. These families sometimes were housed in a single structure but, more often than not, seem to have occupied several adjacent small structures, each with its nuclear family. Life was a little more nomadic than on the Northwest Coast, especially in southern California. The larger extended families merge into patriclans over a part of the area. Productive sites were exploited either by extended families or patriclans, or by both, indicating that these social groups were important economically. The Pima-Papago pattern differed only in detail; in addition to sites productive of wild foods, their patrilocal extended families also owned farm land, and the members formed work parties to accomplish the most necessary economic tasks. Even money obtained from the sale of articles made by single individuals in recent times was placed in a common fund or divided up among the entire adult membership of these extended families. The Colorado and Gila River Yumans conform to the same general pattern but again differ in details. Here it was only farm land which was owned by individuals or families and worked jointly by family members, with the products shared within the families. The substantial house of the River Yumans, called Mohave type in the chapter on housing, sheltered several nuclear families related most often through males, thus constituting a patrilocal extended family.

In the Great Basin, the independent nuclear family was the most characteristic type. Although these were often aggregated into larger units possessing some of the earmarks of bilocal extended families, these larger units were of such a temporary and unstable nature that they have never been so labeled. Much of the time, food was so scarce that it was more advantageous for each nuclear family to go it alone. Larger aggregations of related nuclear families neither owned productive sites or houses, nor possessed any other exclusive functions. The extended family was the most common family unit among the northeastern Shoshoni after the acquisition of the horse, when Plains influence penetrated this region.

The Plateau is difficult to classify. Three types of families occurred in different parts of the area: patrilocal extended, bilocal extended, and independent polygynous. The extended families here seem to have had a looser integration than those on the Northwest Coast. The frequency of polygynous families certainly increased after White contact, as on the Plains, so that they may reflect as late a time period as that for the northeastern Shoshoni.

On the northern Plains it is difficult to choose between independent polygynous and patrilocal extended families. Both were present among all tribes, and any differences among them can at most be a matter of emphasis. Probably the larger unit was more typical before the horse, and later gave way to the more individualistic polygynous unit when the fur trade changed many features of the socio-political organization. The Cheyennes and Arapahoes possessed matrilocal extended families which dated from the time when they lived farther east, on the Prairies, and farmed. The Cheyennes gave up farming as late as about 1830, so that their matrilocal organization easily survived until anthropologists came along. Comanche culture was dominated by the independent polygynous family. The Kiowa family type is probably bilocal extended because of that trend in the residence pattern.

On the Prairies the most widespread and dominant family type

287

was the patrilocal extended family, which correlated with the patrilineal descent of the area. The men of these families co-operated in hunting and other essential economic activities. The picture is complicated by the fact that most of these tribes also farmed and that women did most of the farming. Among the Omaha, matrilocal extended family organization seems to have prevailed during the farming season, when everyone lived in the large earth lodges. During the rest of the year, when hunting dominated subsistence, tipis were the universal house type and they were grouped according to patrilocal and patrilineal alignment. This may have been true of other tribes which occupied both types of dwellings. One gets the impression that the matrilocal bias may have been more obtrusive at an earlier date, and that the shift has been toward the patrilocal, perhaps again aided by the fur trade, the horse, and the buffalo.

Matrilocal extended families were dominant among tribes on the extreme western edge of the Prairie area: Hidatsa, Mandan, Arikara, Pawnee, and Wichita. All of these peoples lived in permanent houses large enough to accommodate an entire extended family. The first three tribes occupied these structures almost all the year round, while the last two spent more time in tipis. Besides the house, these families owned, in common, farm land, chattels such as mortars and pestles and dogs, but not horses, which belonged to individual men. Because polygyny was principally, if not wholly, sororal, it fitted into the matrilocal picture.

Among the Iroquois in the Northeast, the matrilocal extended family also prevailed. It occupied a longhouse, with each constituent nuclear family partitioned off in a room by itself, but sharing its fire with the nuclear family opposite it. Leadership was vested in the oldest matron, who directed farm work, kept peace within, and appointed a man in the same maternal line to represent the group in council. Husbands were expected to hunt, and thus provide meat for their families, but had little to say about management of the household. Compared to the extended family, the nuclear family amounted to little. Although monogamy was the only form of marriage tolerated, the practice was highly elastic because of the high mortality of men in warfare and the ease with which a disgruntled wife could divorce a husband. The nuclear family was, therefore, unstable and, aside from reproduction, performed no important functions that could not be more effectively taken care of by the extended family. Individuals came and went, were born and died, but maternal lineage segments, which formed the core of the extended family, went on indefinitely.

The same matrilocal extended family organization prevailed in the Southeast, although by the time literate observers arrived, it was already on its way out. Non-sororal polygyny was one of the disruptive factors. A man could not reside matrilocally with two wives who were unrelated and hence from two different families. He had to break the residence rule and set up an independent establishment of his own. The fact that the chiefs and other officers were all selected by a male council is evidence of the weaker authority of women as compared to Iroquois women. All offices were filled by men, although descent of offices usually remained in the female line. Under these conditions, the functions of the matrilocal extended families were mainly limited to the sphere of economics. Each extended family occupied a "block" in a town, among the Creeks, with each constituent nuclear family having its own house and yard. If a man married two sisters, they might share the same house and yard.

The western Pueblos in the Oasis possessed a matrilocal extended family organization which approached that of the Iroquois in its importance. It was the maternal lineage segment which constituted the core of the extended family, owned the farm land and houses, and functioned as a stabilizing force in the society. As among the Iroquois, monogamy was insisted upon, and strict matrilocal residence was formerly observed. Because everyone in a pueblo shared a large apartment house with everyone else in the community, separate housing for extended families did not exist. However, nuclear families commonly occupied separate rooms, and those which collectively made up a matrilocal extended family lived in adjoining rooms. Female members often worked together, especially when grinding maize. The extended family section was also a center for ritual activities, not of the husbands, but of the brothers and mother's brothers of the women. This was really a lineage of sib function, but the location was in the household. The more obvious economic functions of the extended household have already been described in the chapter on property.

Of the Athapaskan-speaking peoples of the Southwest, all had matrilocal extended families. The Navaho family structure was most like that of the western Pueblos, with that of the western Apache next, and that of the other Apaches still further removed. It is possible, although not proved, that this family type was acquired from Pueblo II peoples before the Athapaskans arrived in the Southwest proper; some anthropologists believe it even stems from the Sub-Arctic. Whatever the explanation, it is the universal family type among these peoples. Although the modern Navaho hogans are large enough to accommodate an extended famliy, earlier and more widespread Athapaskan house types were small and geared to the nuclear family. Such small dwellings were grouped in clusters to form the extended family unit. The functions of these extended families were mainly economic; the women worked together at wild plant gathering and farming, the men at hunting. However, in some localities a man hunted with the male members of his maternal lineage, who did not constitute a residential group.

The patrilocal extended families of the Aztecs of Mexico occupied walled courtyards, within which there were several separate houses for as many constituent nuclear families. Although farm land nominally belonged to the tribe, it was parceled out by officials to families, and the use of a certain plot often passed from father to son, thus staying within the extended family as well as the lineage. Such family units probably manufactured some surplus goods to be exchanged at markets or traded to distant towns. The picture for the Maya is similar but somewhat looser because of the geographical environment. The heavy rainfall in most of the Maya territory leached out minerals from the soil, resulting in land of inferior quality. A field could be used for only two or three seasons, after which it was allowed to be reclaimed by the jungle and a new field cleared. This constant shifting of farm plots discouraged strict inheritance. However, it seems likely that in pre-Columbian times extended family members co-operated in agricultural labor and that, when a man died, his fields or share from common fields went to a son. Patrilocal extended families had similar economic functions among other Meso-American peoples.

The matrilocal extended family of the Cuna Indians offers some interesting details. It occupied a large house, without partitions, theoretically owned by the female occupants. Farm land, like that of the Maya, was subject to no strict inheritance because new fields had to be cleared every few years. Coconut groves, however, were permanent and belonged to both the women and the men of the household; they were inherited bilaterally. However, the authority in the household was vested in the oldest husband who had married into it. The husbands formed work parties under his direction. When traveling by canoe, the oldest husband sat in the rear and steered, the youngest paddled in the bow, and the others were arranged according to age and rank between the two extremes. When walking on land as a group, the oldest husband led the file and the youngest brought up the rear. Coconuts, which today are the chief export item, are picked and sold by the husbands. Each husband, however, divides the cash received with his wife. In planning a marriage, a young man must consider not only the bride and her female relatives but also the hierarchy of resident husbands he will have to live with the rest of his life. Women's affairs were in the charge of the male leader's wife, who directed common household tasks such as preparing food and washing clothes. The Cuna matrilocal extended family differs vastly from those of the Iroquois or western Pueblos because it is dominated not by the lineage segment of females or their brothers, but by the husbands who have married into it. These husbands are not a kin group but only a residential group.

George Peter Murdock, in his book *Social Structure* (1949), stresses the role of the nuclear family when he says, "Whatever larger familial forms may exist, and to whatever extent the greater unit may assume some of the burdens of the lesser, the nuclear family is always recognizable and always has its distinctive and vital functions—sexual, economic, reproductive, and educational . . ." (p. 3). In contrast Ralph Linton, in his book *The Study of Man* (1936), says that the nuclear family plays "an insignificant rôle in the lives of many societies" (p. 153). In an attempt to evaluate North American family structure in the light of these opposing statements, the extended family may be regarded as playing a socially more important role than the nuclear family among

291

about half the tribes of the continent. The matrilocal extended families of the western Pueblos, Hidatsa-Mandans, and Iroquois play an especially dominating role. The position of women is particularly strong in these societies where women own the houses and farm land and are the sex through which descent is traced. The position of the husband in the nuclear family in these cultures is consistently weak; he has little to say, has little control over his own children, and can be divorced at the drop of his hat outside the dwelling door. The average man and woman in these cultures have been a member of three or four different nuclear families in their lifetimes, as a result of death, divorce, and remarriage, but membership among the core of women in the extended family has remained stable. The sexual and reproductive roles the males play are absolutely necessary to biological and cultural survival, but one individual is readily replaced by another. In such matrilineal societies, the nuclear family is relatively insignificant.

REFERENCES

DRUCKER, 1939; EGGAN, 1950, 1955; GAYTON, 1945; GIFFORD, 1916, 1926, 1944; GOLDSCHMIDT, 1948; HALLOWELL, 1937, 1949; HARRIS, MS.*a*; HOEBEL, 1939, 1949; KELLY, 1942; LEACOCK, n.d., 1955; LEWIS, 1942; LINTON, 1936; LOWIE, 1948, 1954; MURDOCK, 1949, 1957; SPECK, 1915, 1917, 1918, 1920*b*; SPECK AND EISELEY, 1939; SPENCER, 1959; STEWARD, 1938; STRONG, 1929; SWANTON, 1946; WEYER, 1932.

16: LARGER KIN GROUPS AND KINSHIP TERMINOLOGY

IN ADDITION to the family units described in the last chapter, there are six other kinds of kinship groups known to North American natives: lineages, sibs, moieties, phratries, clans, and demes. All except the lineage are normally larger than the extended family. All are generally regarded as kin groups, but relationship in all but the first may rest partly on tradition, and moiety affiliation is sometimes determined by factors other than kinship.

LINEAGES, SIBS, MOIETIES, PHRATRIES

The extended family groups described in the last chapter are residential groups; all the members reside together in a single large dwelling, or in several small dwellings close together. They all include husbands and wives and unmarried children. The kinship bonds which link the members are in part genetic and in part affinal. In contrast to families, "lineages" are bound together exclusively by genetic ties. Lineages as functioning kinship units do not exist in the United States among Whites, but our patrilineal inheritance of surnames is undoubtedly a vestige of a former lineage system in Europe.

Lineage structure may be illustrated by the following hypothetical example. Suppose that all women in the United States retained their maiden surnames after marriage and that everyone was compelled to marry a person with a different surname. Assigning the name "Smith" to the senior male, his patrilineal descendants inheriting the same name would be: son, daughter, son's son, son's daughter, son's son's son, son's son's daughter, and so forth. These relatives are shown in Figure 35*a*. They constitute a paternal lineage, or patrilineage, and all members are genetically related to each other. Brothers and sisters always belong to the same lineage, but husbands and wives never do, because the rule of exogamy requires everyone to marry outside of his own name group. A lineage, therefore, is not a residential group (except for a few deviant peoples in the Old World). Brothers and sisters reside together only in childhood; they part company at marriage.

a. Patrilineage

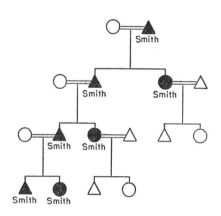

b. Matrilineage

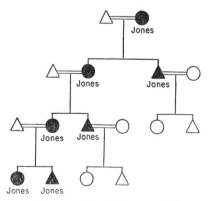

FIG. 35.—Lineages. After Driver and Massey

A maternal lineage may be illustrated by a hypothetical example in which everyone inherits his surname, Jones, from his mother instead of his father. If everyone is required to marry a person with a different surname and women retain their maiden surnames, as above, those who possess the name Jones are aligned as in Figure 35*b*. These genetic relatives form a maternal lineage, or matrilineage for short.

In actual life, multiple sons and daughters frequently appear in the same generation, so that in succeeding generations cousins belong to the same lineage. A patrilineage with multiple males in all but the first generation is illustrated in Figure 36. In the third generation the two males belonging to the lineage are first cousins;

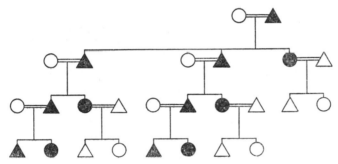

FIG. 36.—Patrilineage with multiple males in all but the first generation

in the fourth generation they are second cousins. A matrilineage may also be ramified by the presence of multiple females in any or all of its generations.

When two or more lineages are thought to be related by a fictitious or traditional bond, such as belief in common descent from a mythical ancestor, and when marriage between persons in these lineages is forbidden on the same grounds, the group of lineages constitutes a "sib." A minimal patrilineal sib consisting of two minimal patrilineages is shown in Figure 37. A matrilineal sib is formed by combining two or more matrilineages according to a principle which prohibits marriage between the member matrilineages.

Historically, lineages probably arose before sibs, and sibs appear to have been formed most often by a lineage forking and reforking, as in Figure 36, until the cousins were so remote that it was impossible to trace their ancestry back to a real progenitor. In the absence of written records, this might occur in as few as six or seven generations. Sibs are normally larger than lineages, although a sib recently decimated by war or disease might be smaller than a lineage which escaped these ravages. The largest sibs in native North America probably had about a thousand members, although some of those of the Maya may have been larger. North of Mexico there were few towns with populations as high as a thousand, so that when sib membership approached this figure, the members usually were distributed among a number of villages or towns. For example, the Creek Indians of Alabama and Georgia possessed about 40 sibs, 50 villages, and a population of about 18,000. Although the sibs averaged about 450 members, some were much larger than others and may have had a thousand members. Each village, on the average, was occupied by people from half a dozen different sibs. Rules of sib exogamy were extended to all of the 50 villages: for example, a man of the deer sib could not marry a woman of the same sib even though she lived in another Creek village more than a hundred miles distant from his place of residence.

The difference between an extended family and a lineage is further illustrated in Figure 38, where a matrilocal extended family and a maternal lineage are shown together. Note that immature children in the last generation belong to both. When the boy marries, however, he will go to live with his bride's family and will no longer be a member of the family in which he was born.

Belief in descent from
common mythical ancestor

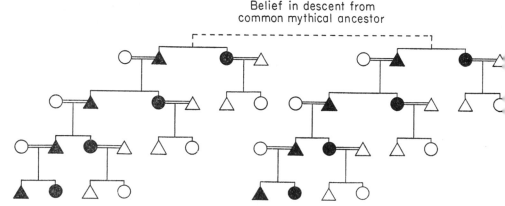

Fig. 37.—Minimal patrisib

Figure 39 illustrates all four types of unilocal extended families and lineages in one figure: the maternal lineage; the matrilocal extended family; the paternal lineage; the patrilocal extended family. The opposed patrilocal and matrilocal systems could not exist in the same society; but there are a few societies in the Old World where both kinds of descent, but in respect to different attributes, coexist. Again it should be pointed out that large numbers of

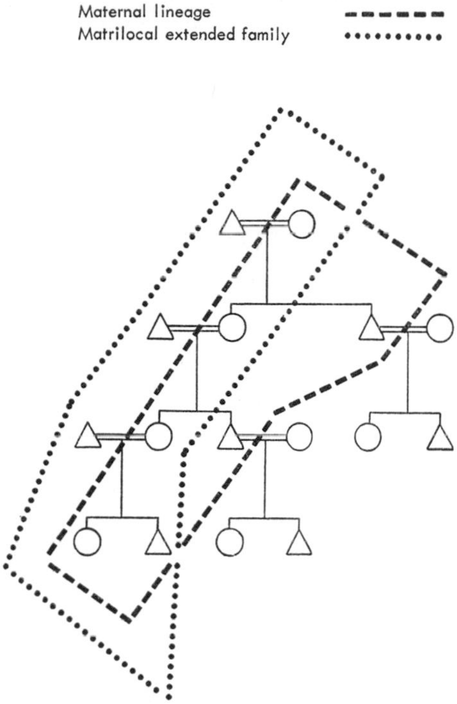

FIG. 38.—Matricentered lineage and extended family. Driver and Massey

children can swell such kin groups to several times the size indicated on the diagram.

When either lineages or sibs, or both, exist in a society, the society is said to possess unilineal, unilinear, or unilateral descent. These three terms are synonymous in anthropology, and the thing that descends is affiliation in a kinship group. Such descent may be marked by a name or crest and reinforced by mythology. When lineages and sibs are absent, descent is said to be bilateral. The term bilineal is rarely used for this concept, and bilinear has been assigned to double descent systems by Murdock (1949). The term multilateral or multilineal is occasionally used to describe descent in non-unilineal societies, because the number of one's actual genetic ancestors doubles with each ascending generation. One has two parents, four grandparents, eight great grandparents, and so on. Where unilineal descent prevails, only one person in each of these generations is singled out as the significant ancestor, although the others, of course, are known to exist. It is possible

Maternal lineage	- - - - - - - -
Matrilocal extended family	• • • • • • • • • •
Paternal lineage	– – – – – –
Patrilocal extended family	▬▬▬▬▬▬

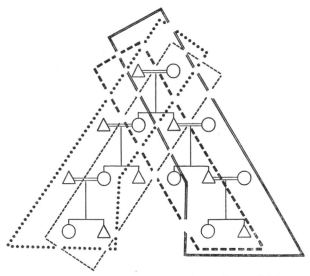

Fig. 39.—Lineages and extended families. Driver and Massey

to have lineages without sibs, but not sibs without lineages. Where both exist together, native terminology sometimes recognizes one without the other, designates both by the same term, or has a separate word for each.

Map 32 gives the geographical distributions of the three kinds of descent. Matrilineal descent is found in a large area in the northwest which includes part of the Sub-Arctic as well as the Northwest Coast. It appears again in a small part of the Oasis, and among three tribes on the northern Plains and Prairies; it covers almost the entire East, and is the most common kind of descent in the

298

Circum-Caribbean area. Patrilineal descent and patrilineages were present in California and adjacent Baja California and Oasis, were of rare occurrence in southwest Mexico, apparently universal for the Mayas of southeast Mexico, and general on the Prairies and the adjacent part of the Sub-Arctic occupied by the Ojibwa. Almost all the remaining territory of aboriginal North America lacked lineages and sibs and traced descent bilaterally.

A term related to lineage and sib is "moiety," from the French; it means simply "half." Applied to social structure it means one of two organizations into which a tribe or community is divided. Moieties may be unilineal and exogamous kin groups, or unilineal but not always exogamous kin groups. They may be patrilineal and consist entirely of male members. They may not be kinship groups at all, but membership may be determined in some other way, as will be shown below. When only two sibs exist, they may be called sibs, moieties, or moiety-sibs. However, some anthropologists designate all twofold kinship groups moieties and reserve the term sib for three or more. The former usage will be followed here.

Another related term is "phratry." A phratry is two or more sibs which are linked in some way. When a man cannot marry a woman of a certain other sib, the two sibs which form the exogamous unit may be said to constitute a phratry. Phratries may contain three or even more sibs. When there are only two phratries, they are the equivalent of moieties and may be so labeled. Phratries occurred among a majority of tribes on the Prairies and in the East, and also on the northern Northwest Coast.

A large majority of North American Indians with unilineal descent had multiple (three or more) sib systems. Exceptions to this generalization are the following: (1) the Bering Sea Eskimo had only lineages; (2) most of the Sub-Arctic Athapaskans with matrilineal descent had only two moiety-sibs; (3) lineages were the largest unilateral unit on the Oregon coast and in most of California except on the Colorado River. All, or nearly all, other unilateral North American tribes possessed three or more sibs. Some idea of the wide variation in numbers of sibs can be gathered from Map 34. The range of reported sibs is from three to sixty. In most cases of large numbers of sibs, they were not all present in the same community. Thus the sixty sibs of the Western Apache are a summation of the sibs in each of the five subdivisions and, within these smaller territorial units, each sib was not present in every band. This great variation in numbers of sibs suggests local independent history and considerable fluidity for the sib as a social unit. Some of the sibs consisted of only one lineage, and some were extinct by the time the anthropologist arrived. There is no areal patterning in the number of multiple sibs; each of the three major areas, Northwest, Oasis, and Prairies-East, shows much internal variation.

Information on moieties has been assembled on Map 34. In the Northwest, the matrilineal exogamous moieties were most often called Wolf and Raven. They were further subdivided into sibs on the coast, but the interior tribes possessed only the two units. The moieties of the neighboring Haisla were non-unilineal and non-exogamous. They were nothing more than boys' rivalry groups in which membership was determined by place of residence in the village. An imaginary line running through the center of the village separated the two groups. Boys who crossed the line were stripped of clothing or otherwise mistreated by their rivals, and sometimes sham battles with toy weapons or stones were engaged in. The nearby Mackenzie Eskimo possessed two informal moieties called Raven and Crane. Everybody could join one of the groups—children usually chose that of their father—but they had no function other than rivalry in jesting and hurling derogatory remarks at one another. The name Raven suggests derivation from matrilineal exogamous moieties to the southwest, although the history of the name may be independent of that of the kin alignment and functions.

The patrilineal exogamous moieties of California were made up of constituent lineages, but sibs were lacking in most localities. The moieties functioned in practically every ceremony known to these cultures, and were especially obtrusive at death rites. The Pomos and their neighbors possessed patrilineal but agamous moieties, which did not regulate marriage but functioned in the competitive group sweating of men, in men's athletic games, and in public ceremonies participated in by both sexes, including the Kuksu cycle. Social groups are called agamous when marriage is random with respect to one's in-group and out-groups; agamous groups are neither exogamous nor endogamous. The Washo moieties were similar to those of the Pomos, functioning in men's athletic games and, with slight modification, in ceremonies of both sexes. The dual organization of the western Mono and eastern Yokuts was also patrilineal and agamous and had like functions: games, feasts, ceremonies. All of these peripheral systems seem to have had a common origin with the more central patrilineal exogamous systems.

In the Oasis, exogamous moieties are lacking. The patrilineal, agamous, twofold divisions of the Pima and Papago functioned in ceremonies and athletic games and influenced a man's dreaming and choice of guardian spirit. Those of the eastern Pueblos show much internal variation but are generally agamous and non-unilineal, but with some patrilineal leaning. Multiple kivas (religious organizations) are divided into two moietal groups; political officers are dual, one set for each moiety; and moieties function in racing and dancing at public ceremonies.

A considerable variety of moieties occurred in the Prairies and East. Among the Prairie Sioux, multiple sibs were grouped into two moiety-phratries which functioned in athletic games, tribal councils, and religious ceremonies. Those of the Pawnee are unique: the endogamous demes were divided into north and south divisions for the chief's council, the camp circle, and the ceremonial circle of practically all ceremonies. With the Hidatsas and Mandans, moieties owned game pits and served as units for the division of the products of the hunt. In the Southeast, the Chickasaws and Choctaws had moieties which were dedicated to peace versus war but which also buried each other's dead. The Creek possessed two sets of moieties: phratry-moieties and town-moieties. Both sets were called peace (white) and war (red). The phratry-moieties divided the sibs nearly evenly between them and were both present in every town. The town-moieties divided the towns into two groups, there being thirty-one peace towns and eighteen war towns among the forty-nine for which moiety affiliation is known. There was only one town-moiety in each town because the whole town belonged to it. The phratry-moieties tended to be exogamous, the town-moieties endogamous. Among

301

the Iroquois, multiple sibs were grouped into two moiety-phratries which opposed each other in athletic games. Around the Great Lakes, a number of tribes had non-unilinear agamous moieties where membership in some cases was determined by order of birth or season of birth. These units competed in athletic contests.

The eastern Eskimo had weak moieties, the membership in which was determined by season of birth. Those born in the winter belonged to one, those born in the summer to the other. The men competed in a tug-of-war at a public festival in late autumn.

Many aboriginal Mexican towns were divided into two or more sections which are known in the source material by the Spanish term *barrio*. Wherever two such divisions exist, they may be called moieties. Among the Mixe, membership in the moiety-barrios was inherited from the father. The town was divided into two halves by an imaginary line through the plaza. As regards marriage, these moieties were agamous, but a woman joined that of her husband at marriage if her father had belonged to the opposite one from her husband. If a widow married a man from the opposite moiety of her deceased husband, her children did not go with her but lived with their father's relatives in order to remain in the patrilineal moiety. The highest officials in the town, the major and judge, had to be of opposite moieties, and each year each office rotated to a man of the opposite moiety. The police force also had to be chosen from the two moieties, and its leadership rotated weekly from one moiety to the other. All of this strongly suggests the town organization of the eastern Pueblos.

This cursory survey of moiety organization shows amazing variety. In general, it may be said that the distribution of moieties conforms fairly closely to the distribution of unilateral descent, whether the moieties are unilateral or not. This suggests some historical relationship between the two, as Olson (1933) suggested.

CLANS AND DEMES

The term "clan" has been used in anthropology for about a century, but a new meaning, which is used here, has been assigned to it (Murdock, 1949). The new meaning introduces a new concept, which clears up earlier confusion and fills a vacuum left in previous systems of kinship structure. We have seen that families are residential groups and that lineages, sibs, moieties, and phratries are unilineal genetic groups. The clan has been called a compromise kin group because it is both residential and unilineal. It is composed of persons of one sex who are members of the same sib, the unmarried members of the opposite sex, and the spouses of the married members. Thus a matriclan consists of the women of a matrisib, their unmarried sons, and their husbands. A patriclan is made up of the men of a patrisib, their unmarried daughters, and their wives. An avunculan is composed of the men of a matrisib, their unmarried sons and daughters, their married daughters where

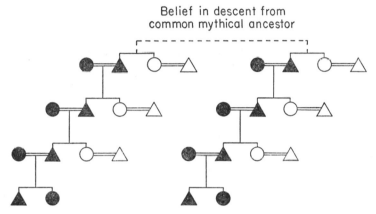

FIG. 40.—Minimal patriclan

cross-cousin marriage prevails, and their wives. Each clan which is also a village apart from other clans may be called a clan community, whereas a clan which comprises a section of a town or city is called a clan barrio.

The clan is made up of two or more unilocal extended families and also must be associated with a formalized rule of unilineal descent with sib exogamy. A patriclan is illustrated in Figure 40; it consists of two patrilocal extended families joined by a traditional bond of unilineal descent connecting the males. Unilocal extended families may exist with or without strict unilineal descent, but clans occur only where unilineal descent is present. Not every society with unilineal descent has clans, however, because it is possible to have a number of lineages or sibs in the same villages or section of a town. Avunculans are found on the northern

303

Northwest Coast, where avunculocal residence and matrilineal descent prevailed. Most of these clans were separate villages, hence they are properly called avunculocal clan communities. Each was a land-owning unit, a political unit, and a warring unit against other clans.

Patrilocal clan communities or extended family communities are found among almost half the tribes in California. Each normally had a separate territory and was a separate entity. Here and there they were aggregated into larger political units. In the Oasis, the Navahos and Western Apaches had matriclans which formerly owned farm land which was worked by both sexes, with men doing more than women in recent years. There is no conclusive evidence for matriclans among the Hidatsas of the upper Missouri River, but for the Mandans it is said that there was a tendency for related families to select adjacent quarters in the village and, in another passage, that lineages were closely associated with lodge groups. These statements may refer to clans. The Prairie tribes with patrilineal descent may have possessed patrilocal clan communities in the early historical period. It is difficult to prove their existence, however, because of the disruptions caused by White contact. When the Deghia Siouan tribes assembled considerable numbers of their members, each clan camped in a certain part of the camp circle and became, for the time being, a clan barrio. These units were ceremonial rather than economic, however.

In the East, both the Iroquois and the Southeastern tribes seem to have possessed matriclans. Among the Iroquois in historic times these seem to have been principally clan barrios in villages up to 3,000 persons. The Mohawks, however, are reported to have had three villages, each a matriclan community. In the Southeast there were both matrilocal clan communities and matrilocal clan barrios. The former predominated among the Chickasaws, the latter among the Creeks. The matrilocal clan communities, at least, were farm land-owning units and political entities. The matrilocal clan barrios were politically part of a town unit. Whether they had separate fields is uncertain, but it seems likely in light of what we know of extended family organization.

In Mexico, patrilocal clan barrios seem to have occurred on the western coast of Nayarit and Colima. Patrilocal clan communities may also have been present among some of the Maya groups. The paucity of information makes it impossible to give a complete distribution.

Another territorial and political kinship unit is the "deme." Demes may be endogamous or exogamous. Seldom do we find 100 per cent endogamy or exogamy. The endogamous deme is a community (village or band) which is not further segmented by unilineal descent and which is small enough so that all members are aware of their bilateral genetic relationship to all or most other members of the group. Such genetic relationship is often not traceable in cultures without writing, but if the members regard themselves as being genetically interrelated, that is sufficient to label their group a deme. Marriage within the endogamous deme is the rule, providing the bride and groom are not too closely related.

Exogamous demes fall into two classes according to rule of residence: patrilocal and matrilocal. These may be abbreviated to patridemes and matridemes. Patridemes are communities in which residence is mainly patrilocal and most of the marriages are locally exogamous. Technically, all of the marriages may be locally exogamous, but actual data show that this seldom happens. Complete exogamy is associated with unilineal kin groups such as lineages and sibs. If a patrideme were completely exogamous, its structure would be identical with that of a patriclan. It would differ only in lacking a formalized rule of exogamy and a belief in common descent from a mythical ancestor. If the broken line at the top of Figure 40 were eliminated, it would depict a patrideme. Patridemes, however, are usually regulated by looser rules of behavior. Matridemes are communities in which residence is principally matrilocal and most of the marriages are locally exogamous. The majority of the population is genetically related through females. If there were 100 per cent conformity to these rules, the matrideme would be identical in composition to the matriclan, except for the unilineal traditional tie at the top.

Demes tend to be clustered near areas of unilateral descent rather than randomly scattered about. This suggests that the kind of geographic and cultural environment conducive to lineages and sibs, or the contact with lineages and sibs, encourages demes.

Patridemes are found on the Northwest Coast from the Bella

305

Coola or Bella Bella in the north to about the California-Oregon line in the south. Throughout this area, incest taboos are extended bilaterally, not patrilineally. In other words, marriage with matrilineal relatives is just as much forbidden as with patrilineal relatives, the incest taboos being extended to the same distance in both lines. Among some tribes in this area, however, marriages to distant kin were not only approved, but were preferred. This feature smacks of the endogamous deme or perhaps of social stratification. However that may be, it was not powerful enough to override the dominance of men in the culture and patrilocal residence. These patridemes appear to be a local development not dependent on contact with the outside. Surely the avunculocal, matrilineal organization of the more northern Northwest Coast was not their inspiration. The resemblance to the patrilocal clan communities of California is superficial. There was no direct contact between Oregon tribes and the Nomlaki and Patwin of California. The cultural boundary between these two groups is one of the sharpest in all of North America.

Patridemes crop up again in the Oasis and in western Mexico. They occur among the Walapais and Papagos in the form of villages or bands, depending on the season. Patrilocal extended families were often aggregated into larger units which can only be called patridemes. Exogamy was less strict among the Walapais but was practiced in the majority of instances among the Papagos. Political authority of these patridemes was weak, and neither tribe was able to stand up to the warlike River Yumans.

In western Mexico, patridemes have been mistaken for clans and sibs. Unilateral descent with strict exogamy seems to have been lacking in most of this area. Kinship terminologies were consistently of the kind associated with bilateral descent in other areas. This suggests that the majority of tribes probably possessed patridemes.

Endogamous demes are found among the Chiricahua Apache and probably the Mescalero, Lipan, and Jicarilla as well. The so-called bands of these tribes, which are the demes, were both territorial and political units.

In Mexico, the *calpulli* of the Aztecs were apparently endogamous demes. In Tenochtitlán these demes were barrios, each occupying a section of the city, but in less populated areas they may have been village communities. They were, therefore, territorial units, which parceled out farm land to extended families and nominally to individuals, but they were politically subservient to the Aztec state.

The endogamous demes of the Maya-speaking Chorti of Guatemala were village communities which averaged between two hundred and three hundred souls. They had title to hunting, fishing, and gathering lands, the larger irrigation ditches, and a ceremonial house. Bilocal extended families owned most of the other kinds of real estate. Demes have had no chiefs, councils, or any other political machinery or authority in modern times, but may have had something of the kind formerly. Today the demes are combined into municipios, which are the smallest units of the Guatemalan government.

The Cuna, who inhabit the islands off the north coast of Panama, are divided into endogamous demes, each of which is a village on an island. Each deme holds an assembly of all adults, in which men freely discuss public affairs and elect officers. Once elected, the officers have lifelong tenure. Besides the chief, there are officers in charge of public funds, policemen to preserve order and collect food among the villagers for feasts, and men in charge of community enterprises such as house-building, canoe-building, farming, path-building, and girls' puberty ceremonies.

Endogamous demes were present in the southern Plains-Prairie area among both the nomadic and the agricultural tribes. They are best called bands among the nomadic tribes, while with the agricultural tribes they were either bands or villages according to whether it was the hunting or the farming season. A man was required, or at least strongly encouraged, to marry a woman from his own deme, so that he would not go elsewhere to live with his wife's people. This was especially important for the Pawnees and Wichitas, who practiced matrilocal residence. The necessity for good hunters and brave warriors to compete successfully with those of other demes provided an ever present reason for endogamy. The demes were thus economic and political units. All of the tribes in this group, except the Comanche, had a tribal organization which outranked and controlled the political activity of its

307

constituent demes. However, the tribe assembled in its entirety for less than half the year, so that for most of the time the deme was the only political unit. Each deme did not have a well-defined territory among the nomadic tribes, but with the agricultural peoples its territory was fairly definite.

The Arapaho and Cheyenne in the central Plains, and probably also some of the Ute, are the only North American tribes to possess exogamous matridemes. These demes were bands during most of the nineteenth century, but, because the Cheyenne farmed until 1832, the demes of this tribe must have been villages before this date for at least part of the year. The rule of matrilocal residence helped produce the matrilocal extended family, which had only to expand until it attained the size of a deme. There is a suggestion in the history of the Cheyenne and Arapaho that the matridemes were formerly matriclans when both tribes lived farther east and farmed. The nomadic life of the Plains seems to have changed the earlier more rigid matrilineal scheme into the more plastic matrideme.

On the northern Plains, the majority of tribes were divided into patridemes which were nomadic bands. These have often been confused with patriclans or sibs, and with good reason. Many of the tribes which had them may have possessed true patriclans and sibs when they lived farther east at an earlier date. In other words, these patridemes may represent a breakdown of a clan-sib system rather than an incipient clan-sib system. Some older accounts, such as those of J. Owen Dorsey (1897), categorically describe these bands as patriclans and insist that exogamy was adhered to. Even some of the later accounts tell us that exogamy was formerly adhered to. However that may be, these bands seem to have been patridemes in the last half of the nineteenth century, to which most of our data refer. They functioned as economic and political units even though they were aggregated into larger political units which had tribal organization.

In the Eastern Sub-Arctic north of the Ojibwa, patridemes may have prevailed but information is not conclusive. Southeast of the St. Lawrence River, among the Micmacs, Malecites, and Abnakis, the picture is also confused. Sibs have been attributed to these tribes by some researchers, while others have denied their existence. Possibly some of these social units were patridemes,

KINSHIP TERMINOLOGY

Kinship terminologies of foreign languages are sometimes confusing because of insufficient knowledge of English kinship terms. Therefore, we shall begin this discussion with English terms. Figure 41 assembles the basic English words. It is noted immediately that some of the terms, such as cousin, appear more than once in the diagram. As anthropologists, we need a more specific term for each of the relatives not distinguished by English words. If we begin with English terms for primary relatives, that is, the relatives closest to oneself, we can string these together with apostrophes to designate more remote relatives. Thus mother's brother refers to an uncle, and mother's brother's daughter to a cousin. The length of these terms can be taken care of by using the following two-letter abbreviations: *Fa*, father; *Mo*, mother; *Si*, sister; *Br*, brother; *So*, son; *Da*, daughter; *Hu*, husband; *Wi*, wife. To express a more remote relationship, these abbreviations may be strung together without apostrophes. For example, *MoBrDa* may be used to signify one's mother's brother's daughter.

Figure 42 presents the same relatives as Figure 41, but gives them a more precise set of labels in terms of these abbreviations. If we list the terms in both diagrams for comparison, as in Table 3, we find that there are twenty-three basic English terms which designate forty-six specific relatives which anthropologists keep separate in their thinking. On the average, each English term takes care of two relationships. In more detail, we find that ten basic English words include only one relative, another ten include two relatives each, two others include four relatives each, and one basic word, cousin, includes eight relatives. The twenty-three basic English terms may also be divided into fifteen words for genetic relatives and eight for affinal relatives.

In addition to the twenty-three basic English terms, there are a number of others in common use: parent, child, grandparent, grandchild, stepfather, stepmother, stepson, stepdaughter, stepparent, stepchild, stepbrother, stepsister, half-brother, half-sister, and, in cases of adoption, foster father, foster mother, foster son, foster daughter, foster parent, foster child.

Every language not only has its own words to designate kin,

309

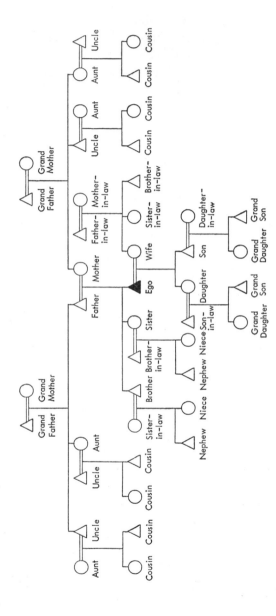

Fig. 41.—Basic English kinship terminology. Driver and Massey

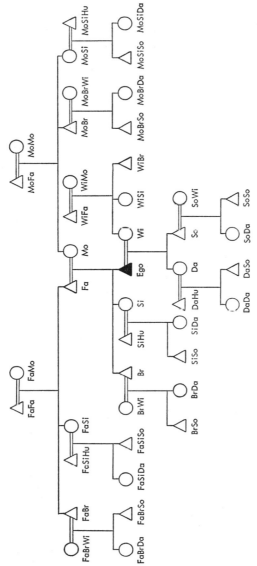

FIG. 42.—English abbreviations of anthropological terminology. Driver and Massey

but it normally employs a classification of kin specifically different from that of every other language and culture. The result is a bewildering amount of detail which anthropologists have not succeeded in analyzing completely. However, by narrowing down to a few relatives and to a few principles of classification, it is possible to exhaust the data. Let us first consider terms for genetic aunts and their relation to terms for mother. Altogether there are three relationships involved: mother, mother's sister, and father's sister.

TABLE 3

BASIC ENGLISH KINSHIP TERMS, WITH
ANTHROPOLOGICAL MEANINGS

Aunt.	FaSi, FaBrWi, MoSi, MoBrWi
Brother.	Br
Brother-in-law.	SiHu, WiBr
Cousin.	FaBrDa, FaBrSo, FaSiDa, FaSiSo, MoBrDa, MoBrSo, MoSiDa, MoSiSo
Daughter.	Da
Daughter-in-law.	SoWi
Father.	Fa
Father-in-law.	HuFa, WiFa
Granddaughter.	DaDa, SoDa
Grandfather.	FaFa, MoFa
Grandmother.	FaMo, MoMo
Grandson.	DaSo, SoSo
Husband.	Hu
Mother.	Mo
Mother-in-law.	HuMo, WiMo
Nephew.	BrSo, SiSo
Niece.	BrDa, SiDa
Sister.	Si
Sister-in-law.	BrWi, WiSi
Son.	So
Son-in-law.	DaHu
Uncle.	FaBr, FaSiHu, MoBr, MoSiHu
Wife.	Wi

In English we designate mother by one term, but we lump mother's sister and father's sister under a second term, "aunt." This is called *lineal* terminology because the lineal relative (mother) is distinguished from the collateral relatives (aunts). In some languages there is only one word for all three of these relatives; this is called *generation* terminology. In still other languages there are three separate terms for each of the relatives; this is labeled *bifurcate collateral* terminology to emphasize the fact that the two forks of one's ancestry are distinguished as well as the lineal from the collateral. In still other languages there is one word for both mother

312

and mother's sister, and a second word for father's sister; this is called *bifurcate merging* because it distinguishes both ancestral forks but merges the mother and the mother's sister on one fork. Figure 43 illustrates these four types of mother-aunt terminology. Each different shade stands for a different word in the language.

A considerable number of North American tribes have pairs of kinship terms which are not exact duplicates but which overlap. An example from English is the term for one's first cousin's child.

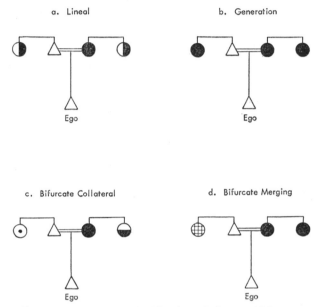

FIG. 43.—Mother-aunt classifications. Driver and Massey

This relative is called first-cousin-once-removed by some persons and second cousin by others. The phrase second cousin may also be applied to one's parent's first cousin's child. This sort of confusion is to be found in the classification of mother-aunt terms among North American Indians. Wherever two ways to refer to these relatives occur for the same tribe, this evidence has been plotted with overlapping or special symbols.

The distinction between the term used to address a relative when he is present and the term used to refer to him when he is absent must also be made. The vast majority of kinship terms are employed in both address and reference, in Indian languages as well as our own, but a minority are limited to one or the other usage. For example, in English we refer to our spouse's mother as mother-in-law, but we address her as mother. In address we classify her with our true mother; in reference we put her in a class by herself. In general, experience has shown that terms of reference are more specific than terms of address. For this reason, terms of reference have been selected over those of address wherever they differed.

Map 35 gives the geographical distributions of the four ways of classifying mothers and aunts for terms of reference. It can be seen at a glance that bifurcate collateral is the most frequent for the continent as a whole. It is the dominant type in the Eastern Sub-Arctic, on the Plateau, in California, the Great Basin, and the Oasis. It coexists with bifurcate merging on the northern Northwest Coast, in the Southeast, and among isolated tribes in other areas. It is positively correlated with bilateral descent (Map 32) in conformity with functional theory, although there are a fair number of instances where it is associated with either matrilineal or patrilineal descent. In the majority of these unilineal instances, bifurcate collateral classification coexists with bifurcate merging. The inference naturally drawn from these facts is that bifurcate collateral is probably the oldest type of mother-aunt classification in aboriginal North America, or at least older than bifurcate merging. After unilocal residence and unilateral descent arose, bifurcate collateral seems to have lost ground to bifurcate merging. The process of change, however, was not abrupt; on the contrary, both systems coexisted for a time during the transitional period. After White contact, the process was reversed; bifurcate merging lost ground to bifurcate collateral. The fairly common coexistence of the two systems among a number of tribes, as shown on Map 35, is to be explained in this historical manner.

Lineal mother-aunt terminology is much more restricted than bifurcate collateral and overlaps it in only one instance. Nevertheless, it (lineal) is also positively correlated with bilateral descent (Map 32). Lineal and bifurcate collateral combined, however, yield a higher correlation with bilateral descent than either taken alone. What determines a people's choice between lineal and bifurcate collateral is difficult to say. Furthermore, lineal shows much less overlap with bifurcate merging than does bifurcate collateral. One is almost forced to conclude that bifurcate collateral is more compatible with unilateral descent than is lineal.

Bifurcate merging mother-aunt terms (Map 35) exhibit a definite positive correlation with unilateral descent (Map 32), although this correlation is far from perfect. Murdock has previously established this and the other correlations from his world-wide sample of 250 tribes. The explanation is a simple one. In a system of unilateral descent with exogamy, one's mother's sister is always in the same lineage and sib as one's mother, while one's father's sister always belongs to a different lineage and sib. This is true regardless of whether descent is matrilineal or patrilineal.

The Plains area bristles with negative instances. Here most tribes have bilateral descent along with bifurcate merging mother-aunt terms. A possible explanation of this discrepancy is that most of the Plains tribes formerly possessed unilateral descent or cross-cousin marriage when they lived farther east and were more sedentary, but that they lost one or both when they adopted the nomadic life of the Plains. Linguistic evidence favors eastern origin for all the Plains tribes known to have had bifurcate merging terminology except the Sarsi, Wind River Shoshoni, and Comanche.

Generation mother-aunt classification is much the rarest of the four and overlaps each of the other three in at least one instance. It coexists with patrilineal, matrilineal, and bilateral descent, all three. It is too rare, however, to be satisfactorily explained by correlation theory.

What about correlations with language? It is generally agreed that any possible correlations which might exist between kinship classification and systems of phonology and morphology would prove no causal relationships. The aspect of language that is relevant to kinship problems is the historical relationships revealed by language family classification based primarily on vocabulary. Map 37 gives distributions of the language families of native North America. A comparison of major language units with mother-aunt terminologies reveals no startling high correlations. However, there are a few language families in which all or nearly all the member languages possess the same mother-aunt classifications. Thus the Yuman languages of the Southwest are all bifurcate col-

315

lateral; the Salish of the Northwest are predominantly lineal; the Plains-Prairie Sioux are all bifurcate merging. In spite of the fact that all three of these mother-aunt classifications occur among languages in many other families, their near universality within these particular language families would yield a significant positive correlation between them and the language family. This suggests that these ways of classifying mothers and aunts may possess considerable antiquity. While they may not go back to the time when each language family consisted of only a single mother tongue, they may date from a time when there was much less linguistic differentiation within these families. If such is the case, the present uniformity or near uniformity of mother-aunt categories within each of these families may be *partially* explained as a linguistic heritage—*partially* explained with emphasis because, unless the social structure remained fairly stable, we should not expect the kinship classification to remain stable.

Another example of a correlation between language family and mother-aunt terminology is that of the Algonquians, most of whom have bifurcate collateral terminology. Only those who are neighbors of Sioux and Iroquois employ bifurcate merging terminology. The historical inference from these facts is that the older variant among Algonquians is bifurcate collateral and that those tribes which later contacted Sioux and Iroquois acquired a more sedentary economy, unilateral descent, or some other cultural feature which encouraged the shift to bifurcate merging terminology. In such cases the classification for mothers and aunts may be acquired by contact with languages of another family, even though the words themselves are not transferred. This is called stimulus diffusion (Kroeber, 1940*a:* 1–20). The acquired culture, which goes with the new verbal classification, seems to be the principal cause of the change. Language classification gives us clues to historical priority and direction of change.

An exhaustive study of the relationship of kinship terminology to language and culture demands analysis of the words themselves used to designate kin. Demitri Shimkin has done this for Uto-Aztecan languages. After making a careful reconstruction of the original Uto-Aztecan terms for relatives, he found that, on the average, each language retained about half of the list. The origin of the new terms, which replaced the half that were lost, is still un-certain. In order to show that words from neighboring language families were acquired by the Uto-Aztecans, it would be necessary to reconstruct prototypes of the kinship terminologies of these lan-guage families. This has not been done completely. In regard to the mere classification of kin, only about one-third of the original classificatory elements seems to have been lost. Classificatory cate-gories, therefore, are more stable than the words used to label them in this language family. When we look to neighboring language families for possible sources of classificatory categories, the search is rewarding. Those tribes which have had most contact with alien language families have not only lost the most Uto-Aztecan ele-ments, but they have replaced them with the largest number of foreign elements. The processes of change have also involved shifts in economy and social organization, often facilitated by in-termarriage. Language and culture therefore changed together; one did not cause the other to change.

Kinship terminologies for sisters and female cousins are a little more complicated. There are six principal ways of classifying sis-ters and cousins in native North America, as shown in Figure 44. The Eskimo or lineal type has one word for all female cousins but a separate term for sister. The Hawaiian or generation type uses a single term for sister and for all female cousins as well. The Iro-quois type designates sister and female parallel cousins by one word, and female cross-cousins by a second word. The Omaha type merges sister and female parallel cousins under a single term, calls MoBrDa and MoSi by a second term, and FaSiDa and SiDa by a third term. The Crow type follows suit by merging sister with female parallel cousins, but calls MoBrDa and BrDa by a sec-ond term, and FaSiDa and FaSi by a third term. The Descriptive (Sudanese) type uses separate descriptive terms for MoBrDa and FaSiDa, and for each of the parallel cousins as well, in the few in-stances reported for North America. In Figure 44d, Crow type, we have added an extra generation on the left side to bring out the fact that FaSi, FaSiDa, and FaSiDaDa, are all referred to by the same word. These relatives form a maternal lineage which may be extended in a descending direction indefinitely. The significant point about the Crow kinship system is that persons of the same sex

317

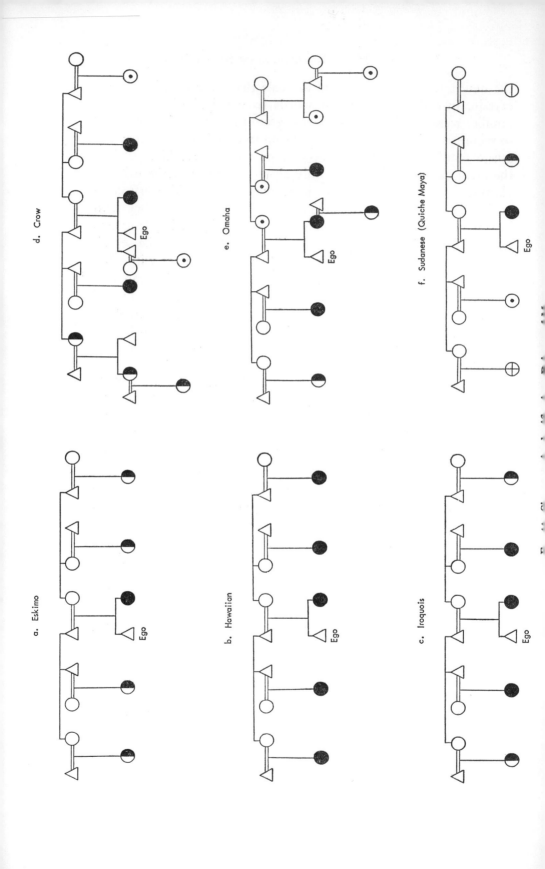

a. Eskimo

b. Hawaiian

c. Iroquois

d. Crow

e. Omaha

f. Sudanese (Quiche Maya)

in certain maternal lineages are designated by a single kinship term. For the Omaha type, Figure 44*e*, a paternal lineage may be observed on the right side of the diagram. The Omaha type agrees with the Crow in being a lineage system, but it features the paternal line while the Crow stresses the maternal line. Geographical distribution of types of classification of sisters and female cousins have been given by Driver and Massey (1957: Map 161).

THE ORIGIN OF UNILATERAL DESCENT

The origin of unilateral descent has been a favorite topic for speculation by anthropologists from the time of Lewis H. Morgan (1871, 1877) down to the present. There are two extreme points of view which may be regarded as the poles between which all others range. The first is the extreme diffusionist explanation of Morgan and others. All of this group have argued for a single origin and subsequent world-wide diffusion of unilateral descent, or a dual origin with patrilineal and matrilineal descent originating independently of each other and subsequently spreading over the world. The second extreme point of view is that of certain evolutionists who do not always deny diffusion but who stress the repeated independent origin of unilateral descent from certain relatively uniform antecedent conditions. The most recurrent evolutionary sequence begins with a unisexual division of labor in subsistence pursuits, from which unilocal residence is derived, and proceeds from unilocal residence to unilateral descent. No evolutionist has argued, however, that there are as many separate origins of sibs as there are tribes known to have possessed them. Evolutionary hypotheses, therefore, have not been pushed to the extreme that marks some of the diffusionist explanations. Almost all of the evolutionists have also recognized the role of diffusion or acculturation.

Because Murdock's discussion of evolution versus diffusion in *Social Structure* is among the most recent and at the same time the most comprehensive, we can use a quote from him as a point of departure:

The evidence from our 250 societies supports the contention of the American historical anthropologists, against the evolutionists, that there is no inevitable sequence of social forms nor any necessary association

319

between particular rules of residence or descent or particular types of kin groups or kinship terms and levels of culture, types of economy, or forms of government or class structure. On the other hand it supports the evolutionists, against the several schools of historical anthropology, in the conclusion that parallelism or independent invention is relatively easy and common in the field of social organization, and that any structural form can be developed anywhere if conditions are propitious (p. 200).

It should be emphasized that evolutionary and diffusionist interpretations are not necessarily mutually exclusive, even with reference to a single society. For example, agriculture may diffuse to a hunting and gathering economy and initiate a sequence of evolutionary changes. It may also carry some social correlatives along with it, for example, a unisexual division of labor and a unisexual property concept. Where diffusion is facilitated by intermarriage, involving an introduction of foreign personnel, it is conceivable that changes in economy, residence, and descent might all get a foothold at about the same time and gain ground in the new home at about the same rate. Finally, no matter how extreme the diffusionist point of view, it does not explain how unilateral descent arose in the first place. The diffusionist needs the economic determinist to account for the first instance of unilateral descent even though he believes all subsequent instances are derived from it by diffusion.

Detailed information on subsistence has already been presented in chapters iii to vi. Here we are interested only in the dominant sexual division of labor in obtaining food. The sexual division of labor for subsistence pursuits behaves consistently for three out of four of our major activities. Hunting and fishing were nearly everywhere chiefly the work of men. Women sometimes participated in communal drives and even carried home the game their husbands had killed, but nowhere did they dominate hunting. Women seem to have fished more consistently than they hunted, but again their efforts were almost always secondary to those of men. Wild plant gathering, in contrast, fell mainly to women, with men assisting most often in obtaining tree crops such as acorns and pine nuts.

It is only for agriculture that an areal difference in sexual division of labor is marked. In the eastern half of the United States women consistently did most of the farming, with men co-operating by clearing new land or by helping with the planting and harvest. In the Southeast, men were required to work in the community fields along with women, but this also appears to have been confined to planting and harvesting. Even where such public fields existed, each woman usually cultivated a separate allotment of her own and, in addition, farmed a small plot near her dwelling.

Turning to the Oasis and Meso-America, we find men doing most of the farming although women frequently helped. There is a statement by Beals (1932b: 100) that the division of labor in agriculture in north Mexico was "more or less equal," but his table heading for the localized information (1932b: 160) reads "women help in fields." Perhaps women helped more in the sixteenth and seventeenth centuries than in the nineteenth, from which most of our information comes. It is true that women among some of the Apaches of the Southwest did most of the farming, but agriculture was of tertiary significance in the diet of most of these tribes. They depended more heavily on wild plants and game. Among the Colorado River Yumans, where agriculture was of more importance, there was no clear sexual division of labor, the whole family of men, women, and children sometimes working together.

The results of an attempt to determine sexual dominance in subsistence pursuits are shown on Map 36. The selection of subsistence activity is limited to the actual procurement of food, thereby eliminating cooking and all other kinds of food-processing between the delivery of food to the dwelling and its final consumption. This seems to be the kind of thing the economic determinists have in mind, or at least it has the virtue of being specific enough to provide an answer of sorts from the source material. Any attempt to decide which sex does the most total labor in each culture would be likely to result in endless controversy.

Men seem to have procured more food than women among the vast majority of North American tribes. Thus men dominated food-getting activities in all hunting and fishing areas, plus the intensive farming areas of the Oasis and Meso-America. Women seem to have obtained more food than men in the East, among a few tribes on the Prairies, in the deserts of the Great Basin and part of the Oasis, and in the regions around the Caribbean dominated by root crop agriculture. A considerable area in the western

321

United States shows no very clear sexual difference. Where there was a balance in rank between animal foods and wild plant foods, no sexual dominance would be anticipated. However, in most of California, where almost every authority agrees that wild plants dominated animal foods, the division of labor is still not precise. Men everywhere climbed oaks and pines to knock down acorns and pine cones to their women below, and sometimes helped carry home the gatherings or assisted in the hulling of acorns or the firing of pine cones to get at the nuts.

Although men assisted in gathering pine nuts in the Great Basin and parts of the Southwest, they certainly did not use the seedbeater and conical basket to help gather wild seeds. Among the Papagos, men gathered no wild plant foods of any kind (Underhill, 1939: 99) and, because wild plants probably provided more food the year round than agriculture and hunting combined, we have characterized this tribe as female dominated. Game was scarce in all of the desert areas and supplied a much smaller fraction of the diet than did vegetal products.

The areas depicted as patridominant are perhaps less controversial. Where hunting and fishing furnished most of the diet and agriculture was absent, there is no question about the greater contribution of men to the dietary. Where agriculture was present, but secondary to hunting, the picture is more complicated, but, because men helped a little in agriculture, their dominant role in the total subsistence pattern can scarcely be questioned for the areas so indicated on Map 36.

When the areas for sexual dominance in subsistence pursuits (Map 36), post-nuptial residence (Map 31), descent (Map 32), and kinship terminology (Map 35; Driver and Massey: Map 161) are compared by correlation method (Driver and Massey, 1957: 425–34), a threefold classification tends to emerge. Societies in which women dominate subsistence tend to have matrilocal residence, matrilineal descent, and Crow kinship classification. Societies in which there is a balance of men's and women's subsistence activities tend to have bilocal residence, bilateral descent, and Hawaiian kinship terminology. Societies in which men dominate subsistence tend to have patrilocal residence, patrilineal descent, and Omaha kinship terminology. This evidence lends support to the theory of economic determinism of descent. However, although the relevant correlations are significant, most of them are low. This means that there are many exceptions to the three general trends. Therefore there must be other causes involved in addition to the dominance of one sex over the other in the procuring of food.

Changes in economy and social organization may come about in at least three major ways. The first is innovation within a single society without direct stimulus from neighboring peoples. The second is the introduction of new culture elements from the outside. For example, the introduction of the maize plant with women doing the farming might bring about matrilocal residence and initiate an evolution toward matrilineal descent and Crow kinship terminology. This may well have been the case in parts of the Oasis, Prairies, and East. The third major cause of change is the migration of a people from one geographical environment to another, necessitating a change in economy. For example, the Crow Indians probably lived on the Missouri River in North or South Dakota and farmed several centuries ago. When they moved west to Montana, they were forced to abandon farming because of geographical factors and to concentrate on buffalo-hunting. The dominant subsistence activity changed from farming by women to buffalo-hunting by men. Residence followed suit and became predominantly patrilocal. Descent and kinship terminology, however, were slower to change and remained matrilineal. Thus the Crow Indians seem to have gone halfway through the cycle of change from dominant division of labor to kinship terminology by the time the ethnographer arrived to describe their way of life.

The second and third classes of causes of change, introduction of new culture elements or patterns from the outside and migration to a new geographical environment, are accompanied by contact with alien peoples. This contact may be brief and involve the exchange of only a modest amount of the total cultural inventory, in which case the word diffusion may be applicable. Such contact may also be prolonged and continuous and, by means of intermarriage and other exchange of personnel, may engender the transfer of a relatively large amount of the cultural inventory. In this case the term acculturation would be more appropriate. Diffusion and acculturation seem to have been neglected in favor of internal factors confined to single tribes or peoples in recent theories of social change.

On the other hand, diffusion and acculturation should not be viewed as mechanical processes which proceed everywhere at a uniform rate. Both are highly selective. Although all societies are exposed to the different ways of life of neighboring peoples, they acquire only the culture elements or patterns which have value to them and can be fitted into their own manner of living. If all societies rapidly acquired every alien cultural feature to which they were exposed, Indian cultures would be much more uniform than the many maps and descriptions in this volume show them to be.

REFERENCES

BEALS, 1932*a*, 1932*b*; DORSEY, 1897; DRIVER AND MASSEY, 1957; EGGAN, 1950, 1955; FOSTER, 1949; GIFFORD, 1944; GOLDMAN, 1941; GOLDSCHMIDT, 1948; HALLOWELL, 1937; HOIJER, 1956*a*, 1956*b*; HYMES, 1957; KELLY, 1942; KROEBER, 1937, 1940*a*; LEACOCK, n.d., 1955; LID, 1948; MORGAN, 1871, 1877; MURDOCK, 1949, 1957; OLSON, 1933; PASSIN, 1944; SHIMKIN, 1941; SPECK, 1917, 1918, 1920*b*, 1938; SPIER, 1925; SPOEHR, 1947; STRONG, 1929; UNDERHILL, 1939.

17: Government
and Social Controls

Political organization is generally regarded as synonymous with territorial organization and is concerned with the manner in which those people who occupy a particular territory are integrated internally with respect to each other and at the same time are organized to present a united front to the outside. Although the territorial tie has been stressed in all discussions of government, the territory may be a shifting one, as among Plains Indians. At a given time, however, the members of a nomadic band or tribe are occupying a common territory, even though the precise locality may change from week to week or month to month.

Each political unit always includes a number of families, and sometimes is made up of a number of larger residential kinship groups. In the chapters on marriage, family, and kinship above we distinguished two kinds of kinship groups: genetic (consanguineal) and residential (territorial). Residential kin groups, such as families, clans, and demes, always bring together husbands and wives but usually not married brothers and sisters. Residential kin groups reside in separate territories or in distinct subdivisions of villages and towns, but they are generally dependent on their neighbors for wives or husbands, the only exception to this rule being the endogamous deme. Because clans and demes can be enlarged to include hundreds of members by the extension of fictional or traditional bonds of kinship, there is no universally accepted line of demarcation between kinship organization and political organization. However, for our purposes it is best to draw the line between residential kin groups within which all the members are bound to-

325

gether by actual or traditional bonds of kinship, and larger residential entities united by other common ties and concepts. Societies which have no territorial organization larger than the residential kin group will be classed as lacking true political organization, while those with territorial ties based on non-kinship factors, will be classed as possessing it.

AREAS WITHOUT TRUE POLITICAL ORGANIZATION

Most peoples in the Arctic, Great Basin, Northeast Mexico, and Baja California lacked true political organization at the time of first European contact. In these areas the largest permanent unit was generally the family. Clans and demes were absent, unreported, or rare, population was sparse (Map 6), and band organization was weak and fluid. These areas were the least productive economically at the level of exploitation known to the Indian inhabitants, and even today they are thinly populated and underdeveloped. None of these Indians farmed (Map 4); they were all nomads on the move almost daily in search of a meager living. Their failure to develop political organization is generally attributed to the impossibility of maintaining a permanent local group of sufficient size in the face of such adversities.

Arctic.—Among most of the Eskimo the nearest approach to a permanent residential unit was the nuclear family, but even this was frequently broken by the high mortality and by wife-exchange. Polygynous and polyandrous families also existed but were less common than the nuclear family. In the west a bilocal extended family may have occupied the larger and more permanent log houses which were owned by the occupants and returned to each winter. In the Central and Eastern Arctic the snow houses melted away entirely in the summer and even the place of residence might be obliterated. Where walls of earth, stone, or whalebone remained, they could be appropriated by the first family who came along when the icy blasts of winter drove them indoors; ownership of dwellings was only seasonal. Nevertheless, the Eskimo family lived in a larger group most of the time, especially in winter. These winter settlements averaged less than a hundred persons for the Eskimo as a whole, and less than fifty for those in the central region. The composition of these settlements was fluid because the same families did not return to the same locality every winter. In spite of such instability, most settlements enjoyed a minimum of leadership by a headman and a medicine man.

The headman was the best hunter and most capable individual in the village, as translations of epithets applied to him show: "he who thinks"; "the one to whom all listen"; "he who knows everything best." His status was achieved wholly by his performance; there was not a trace of hereditary transmission of this position, nor was there any mechanism for election or appointment to it. As the first among equals, he continued to be the acknowledged leader in the relentless pursuit of game animals. A man of mediocre skills got along much better by co-operating with such a leader because every hunter obtained a share of the game killed by any member of his hunting party, and also because the rules of hospitality required those with any food at all to serve it to visitors. A man or family with nothing to eat could get by for a time by visiting friends, especially the friend who was a good hunter. In this way the best hunter attracted the most people and became the accepted leader of the group. What the headman gained from this relationship was the manpower at his disposal when he wanted to go whaling or walrus-hunting in the big *umiak* boat, or to attack the ferocious polar bear.

The Eskimo shaman also enjoyed a role of leadership because he was thought to be able to locate or to attract game animals in time of need, and it was also his responsibility to ferret out confessions from those who had broken taboos and thus jeopardized the hunting luck of the entire group. For instance, if a person ate caribou and seal meat at the same meal, he was thought to have insulted the sensitive souls of both species, which would then retaliate against the entire settlement by no longer permitting themselves to be taken in the chase. Such a sinner, therefore, was a public liability and the shaman able to locate the sinner and prescribe atonement became a public benefactor. Penance for wrong-doing usually required avoiding certain foods and observing sexual continence for a time. Punishment for failure to do penance was banishment from the community, often resulting in death from freezing or from the attack of hungry wolves or polar bears. The shaman who had the

327

power to mete out this fate to an individual ranked along with the headman in authority.

Great Basin.—In the deserts of the Great Basin in Nevada and Utah, man struggled against the heat instead of the cold and against the drought instead of angry seas, but the margin of life over death was just as narrow. Among the western Shoshoni, and many of their Northern Paiute and Southern Paiute neighbors, the largest permanent residential unit was the family. This was nearly always the nuclear family, but there were also a few polygynous families and fewer polyandrous families. Permanent extended families were absent, although temporary aggregations of related nuclear and polygamous families might rally around one another for a time. The nuclear and polygamous families often wandered about independently in search of food in the summer, but tended to group themselves into small villages in the winter. Reliable figures on the size of these winter villages are lacking, but they seem to have ranged from two to ten families and probably averaged less than fifty persons. Families comprising a village were often related but need not possess any kinship ties. The larger of these villages, at least, had a headman called a "talker." He gave periodic orations to the group, telling them about the ripening of plant foods in various localities, planning the trip to these productive areas, and allocating to each person or family a particular spot in which to obtain food. He had little actual authority and any family so inclined might leave the group and wander off on its own.

Organization larger than the village was only temporary among the Western Shoshoni and their neighbors. The most common occasion for the assemblage of the members of several villages was the rabbit or antelope drive, which rarely lasted more than two or three weeks and was normally held only once a year. One group of 150 people could round up more game per capita than say five groups of 30 operating independently. Such drives were led by skilled hunters thought to possess supernatural power and to be able to attract rabbits and antelopes. The "talkers" of the various villages harangued the people from time to time, exhorting them to behave properly, enjoy themselves, get out and rustle food, and prepare it for a feast. Food was so scarce over much of this desert area that it would have been impossible for a group of a hundred or more to stay together without emphasizing game drives and other food-getting ventures. At the same time there was some time and energy left over from necessary tasks to permit a little dancing and singing under the direction of a dance specialist. Just as an individual family might shift from one village to another at will, so might each village realign itself with a new group of villages for the occasional communal game drive. None of the leaders had any authority to maintain the composition of the amorphous groups they led.

Northeast Mexico and Baja California.—Northeast Mexico is less known than the Great Basin but seems to have been as devoid of true political organization. Because winters were milder, there was less tendency to settle down in winter villages, and family groups continued to wander about in search of food at all seasons. Band affiliation was fluid and temporary except along the southern border where there was contact with Meso-America. Baja California is even less known, but probably had no permanent social unit larger than the family.

AREAS WITH BORDERLINE AND MIXED SYSTEMS

The Sub-Arctic, Northwest Coast, Plateau, California, and Oasis areas exhibit borderline and mixed systems of territorial organization which range all the way from family groups to true tribes of several thousand.

Sub-Arctic.—In the Sub-Arctic of eastern Canada among Algonquian-speaking Indians we find, in the nineteenth century, a twofold system geared to the two principal environments, barren grounds and forest. On the barren grounds in the northern part of this region the people were grouped into bands with more or less mutually exclusive territories. They relied chiefly on the caribou for sustenance. The caribou herds could be more effectively taken by a number of hunters than by a single individual. It was only when caribou were scarce that those bands split up, with each family reduced to hunting smaller game on its own. In the forest, on the other hand, each family occupied its own trapping and hunting territory in the winter and subsisted to a greater extent on the beaver and other small animals taken principally with traps. Such families congregated during the short summer season at lakes and

329

streams where fish were available in quantity, or joined one another in a communal caribou or moose hunt. Thus the barren ground families lived most of the time with the band, while the forest families lived most of the year alone, each isolated on its own tract of land. The forest pattern of ecology is largely a post-European development. The huge increase in the demand for furs following European contact gave rise to this family trapping territory system. Beaver furs brought the best price and encouraged the Indians to concentrate on beaver-trapping on family-owned tracts wherever this animal could be found. Every forest Indian, however, joined a band in the summer and regarded himself as belonging to a band.

The first extensive figures on band size in this area date from 1857 when H. Y. Hind (1863: 336) estimated 3,910 persons in twenty-four bands, averaging 163 persons per band. The size of these bands and their patrilocal composition suggest that they may have been patridemes. Each band had a headman who was an excellent hunter and a man of high ethical standards willing to lead and help his fellow bandsmen. It was he who did most of the bargaining when his group traded at the summer rendezvous, both with other bands and with the Hudson's Bay Company. It was ideal for a son to succeed his father as headman, but ability was stressed much more than heredity. The headman was sometimes aided by an informal council of the older men. As a mark of his position in the historic period he wore a special headdress with feathers and a richly decorated coat on public occasions, but at other times his dress was indistinguishable from that of other men. Within the band he was often asked to settle disputes involving violations of family rights to trapping territories and, if a family died out, he might distribute their land among other families of his band. He was also obligated to help those in need, even by allowing them to hunt or trap in his own territory. There was no mechanism for enforcing the headman's wishes or those of the informal council, which was consulted when a serious problem arose, except in the case of murder; but other offenders were brought to justice by being ostracized from society if they refused to conform. If a murderer was not killed or seriously injured by the relatives of the person he had killed, he was tried before the headman and council.

If found guilty he would be told to leave camp and would be followed by armed members of the council. At a given signal the three or four men chosen in advance as executioners would shoot him in the back.

The shaman also enjoyed a position of authority in the Eastern Sub-Arctic, especially in the forested areas where the family trapping territories prevailed. If a man came to him with a complaint over infringement of territorial rights, he would accept a gift from the plaintiff and, after the latter had gone, would investigate the details of the case. If the shaman thought the plaintiff had been wronged, he would warn the offender, either in person or by supernatural means. According to native belief, the shaman might send his spirit in the form of a dog, gigantic bird, or bear to warn the guilty one. If the offender failed to right his wrong, he might be injured or even killed by this mechanism, according to Indian belief. What we would call accidents were often interpreted by the Indian as manifestations of divine wrath. Warning by the shaman, therefore, helped to maintain the social order.

The Mackenzie Sub-Arctic area possessed loose band organization comparable to that just described, although family trapping territories were much less frequent. Because of variable residence rules, the presence of the deme is less probable than in the Eastern Sub-Arctic.

The Yukon Sub-Arctic presents a somewhat deviant picture because of contact with the Northwest Coast. Bands had a little more cohesion and their leaders tended to inherit their positions patrilineally, in spite of the presence of matrilineal moieties in most localities. Leadership was also associated with the prestige acquired from success in predatory raids against outside groups. Such raids brought material possessions, which increased a man's wealth, gave him extra wives, and provided proof of physical superiority.

Northwest Coast.—Population in this area was much more dense than in the Sub-Arctic (Map 6), and life depended mostly on fishing (Map 3). Therefore the population was concentrated at the mouths of streams, where fishing was best, in villages numbering in the hundreds of persons. Before European contact there was probably no territorial unit that exceeded a thousand souls. These large villages were often clans and demes, but some were aggregations of a number of clans and demes. Sometimes the villages were combined into larger territorial units which might be called tribelets, but the population of such tribelets was often no larger than that of one of the larger autonomous villages in another locality. After European trading vessels arrived and trading posts were established, there was an increasing trend toward larger villages at or near these trading centers and also wider territorial organization. Everywhere on the North Pacific Coast headmen and chiefs were men of wealth. They were the nominal owners of houses, canoes, lands, and a vast assortment of social and religious statuses more highly valued than material goods.

Among the matrilineal and avunculocal peoples in the north (Maps 31, 32), there was a hierarchy of residential units from the single plank house inhabited by an avunculocal extended family, to a village representing an avunculocal clan community, to a larger village with a number of avuncuclans, and finally to a tribelet comprising a number of villages. The headmen or chiefs in these societies inherited their positions matrilineally from their mother's brothers.

The Tlingit, for instance, are estimated to have numbered ten thousand at European contact, and in the late nineteenth century were divided into fourteen named territorial districts or tribelets averaging about seven hundred persons each. Each district possessed from one to eight villages, which may formerly have been distinct avuncuclans. While the people in each district were aware of common mutual interests and co-operated occasionally to repel invaders or to conduct an offensive campaign against them, there was no district chief nor any other form of district government. Each clan had its own headman, exclusively exploited its own lands, and was under no compulsion to co-operate in any way with other clans. There is no instance in the historical record of all fourteen of the districts ever uniting for any purpose.

The relation of kinship units to political units is well illustrated by the Haida, who lived on the Queen Charlotte Islands directly south of the Tlingit. The smallest residential unit was the nuclear family which occupied only a part of a plank house. Its functions were principally those of sex, reproduction, and elementary education of offspring. Each nuclear family was a part of an avunculocal

332

extended family which occupied an entire plank house. This was the unit of use of chattels, such as canoes, hunting and fishing gear, and the household articles used in common by the women. Each house had a male leader who inherited his authority from his mother's brother, not his father, and directed the economic activities of his following. Most houses were grouped in villages which were avunculocal clans, each with a headman who also inherited his position matrilineally. The clan was the real-estate-using unit; each clan had title to and exclusive use of its share of the more productive areas in the neighborhood, both on land and in the sea for several miles from shore. Such clan villages varied from one to a dozen houses and from forty or fifty to several hundred people. Often the clans were grouped into larger villages, especially after European contact. The clan and the multiclan village were the unit of warfare against outsiders. Incorporeal property, on the other hand, was owned by the sibs and moieties which were genetic kin groups, not territorial groups. Thus personal names, house titles, canoe titles, songs, dances, and totemic crests were all confined to the sibs and moieties. The multiclan villages, however, had no distinct form of government; the headman of the largest or highest-ranking clan tended to assume the leadership when an occasion demanded concerted action.

The Nootka of Vancouver Island had a system as complex as that of the peoples just described, except that it lacked strict unilateral descent. Nuclear families were combined into extended families in the large plank house, and the houses were aggregated into villages which appear to have been patridemes. These villages were named and each was led by a headman who inherited his position. Each owned land, houses, and many incorporeal privileges as well. Each village was formally united with several others nearby, and all lived together in a larger, named winter village in which the headmen of the smaller member villages were ranked in order of wealth and prestige. This unit we shall call a tribelet. These tribelets were sometimes still further combined into a third unit which we shall call a tribe. The tribe possessed a still larger town on the ocean, where all the member tribelets might assemble in the summer for the taking of salt-water fish and sea mammals. Such towns were named, and the headmen or chiefs who assembled there were carefully ranked as in smaller territorial units. There was a very real feeling of solidarity within these tribes, which were united in war as well as in peaceful ceremonies. Wars between factions within these tribes were almost unheard of, although one or two are reported in old traditions.

Thus we have three distinct territorial units among the Nootka: patridemes, tribelets, and tribes. The leaders of each were not three separate sets of officials like those of our cities, states, and federal government. The leader of the most important deme in a tribelet was the highest-ranking man in the tribelet, and the leader of the most important tribelet in the tribe was likewise the ranking man in the tribe. This would be comparable to the mayor of New York City being simultaneously the governor of New York State and the president of the United States. The other mayors of the other cities in New York State would sit in ranked order as a sort of advisory group to the governor to help him settle state affairs, and the governors of all the states would assemble and sit in ranked order to help the president decide national issues. A similar hierarchical arrangement also applied to the officials of the Tlingit, Haida, and their neighbors.

The total population of the Nootka has been estimated at 6,000, suggesting that the tribal unit may have embraced 1,500 or even 2,000 persons. In light of the fact that most of the Nootka data were obtained from informants in the 1930's, the tribe may be a post-European development, and may not alter the generalization so often made that true tribes were lacking on the Northwest Coast.

The Yurok of northwest California, who fall within the Northwest Coast culture area, were totally devoid of true political organization, as were their neighbors. The largest residential unit was the patrilocal extended family which occupied a plank house. A number of such extended families normally lived close together in what superficially appeared to be a village, and a census taken in 1852 shows that these villages ranged from under 50 to a maximum of 165 inhabitants. However, there was not a shred of village organization. All property, both real estate and chattels, belonged to the extended families, nominally to the single headman of the family. All wrongs were against individuals, and when disputes arose, it was the extended families who quarreled, fought, paid compensation, and made peace. However, many extended families would join each other for the great annual religious festival called the "world-renewal ceremony." There was, then, some feeling of solidarity as well as a common language, but there was no true political organization. These examples give us some idea of the wide range of variation in government encountered on the Northwest Coast.

Plateau.—A small minority of peoples in this area possessed only village organization, almost half were grouped in tribelets or aggregations of villages with slight tribal tendency, and the remainder acquired tribal organization from the Plains area in the historic period. The village unit was probably predominant before European contact and was rather small, those of the Sanpoil averaging only seventy-five persons. Fishing rights on rivers were jealously guarded, but the hunting territory between streams was normally shared by neighboring villages. After the eastern peoples acquired tribal organization, they tended to exclude speakers of foreign languages from their entire territories.

The office of headman or chief over most of the Plateau was passed on from father to son if the son also had the personal qualifications. If the son did not possess qualities of leadership, the office might shift to the most capable man available. This has been called a loose heredity. Among the peoples with the greatest amount of Plains influence, however, the premium was placed on war record, not on heredity. Over most of the Plateau, where loose heredity prevailed for civil chiefs, the war leader was a separate officer. In the central part of the area there was also a chief's spokesman or crier who conveyed to the public the wishes of the chief. The majority of peoples in this area also had councils of men to support the chief, and in a few localities in the central region women occupied seats on councils. Even female chiefs are reported for three central peoples where loose heredity prevailed, apparently in the absence of a suitable male heir.

California.—This area offers two distinct types of territorial organization. The smallest unit was the extended family, which possessed its own territory, a small winter village, and a headman. Over more than half the California culture area, however, these

335

extended families were combined in groups of two to perhaps a half-dozen to form tribelets. The tribelets sometimes had definite territories, a rallying point at the largest village, and chiefs with limited authority. Patrilineal inheritance of chieftainship was the general rule. Occasionally these tribelets defended their territories against outsiders. Those peoples with no organization larger than the extended family lacked true political integration, while the tribelets had achieved the rudiments of government.

The Miwok formerly possessed no territorial unit larger than the patrilocal extended family, but each of these families had its own territory and a headman. The aggregation of several such families into tribelets seems to have been the result of Spanish pressure in the historic period.

The Yokuts, however, possessed the most definite tribelet organization of any people in the California culture area. With a total population of fifteen to twenty thousand, they were divided into about fifty tribelets, averaging three or four hundred persons each. Most tribelets possessed a single permanent village and several more transient ones of smaller size. Each tribelet had a number of male officers: a chief, a chief's messenger, a ceremonial leader, and a village crier. Each of these offices was confined to a single lineage, was inherited patrilineally, and functioned principally at social and religious ceremonies. Most tribelets were on friendly terms with some of their neighbors and mutually shared each other's territories, but they also had Yokuts enemies whom they repelled by force of arms when the latter poached on their lands. Marriages might be either exogamous or endogamous with respect to tribelet, but the former predominated. Each tribelet also had a name which was a pure ethnic term with no other meaning in the language. This was rare in the California area, where most names of tribelets were also place names.

Large festivals were held from time to time, and outsiders were invited as guests. Because there was no system of taxation, it was necessary for every man of means to contribute his share of the food and other goods to be consumed. If a man failed to meet this obligation, the medicine man would inflict illness upon him and charge an exorbitant fee for a cure. Since the chief's consent was required before violent reprisals could be leveled against the doctor, the chief could procrastinate on the grounds of insufficient evidence and keep the victim dangling indefinitely. Public opinion normally sided with the chief and medicine man because the responsible citizens did not approve of dodging social obligations by refusing to contribute to a feast. In this way the medicine man helped enforce the wishes of the chief and the majority of citizens as well.

Oasis.—This area exhibits every kind of organization from small weak bands to true tribes. The desert-dwelling Yumans were grouped in loose bands which averaged about 135 persons each, but part of the year these broke up into extended families of about 25 persons each. The bands were led by headmen who had good war records and were bold enough to speak to the others and advise them about economic and military matters. This organization was little more stable than that of the Western Shoshoni and is, therefore, at the borderline between absence and presence of government.

The Athapaskans, both Navahos and Apaches, never attained political units larger than loose and fluid bands until they were forced onto reservations by the United States government. The matrilocal extended family was the basic residential unit shared by all the Athapaskans, and these were combined into bands of from perhaps one hundred to several hundred persons. Some of these bands seem to have been clans and demes. From late nineteenth-century figures for the Western Apaches, the bands of this group averaged about two hundred persons each, but this was after they had been somewhat reduced by warfare with the United States. These bands were grouped in five ecological zones most of the year and in three desert valleys in winter, but these larger units were not political. Leadership of the band was weakly developed until war with the United States gave rise to chiefs such as Geronimo. Before that time the band had a chief who attained his office principally by achievement as a speaker and war leader, although heredity also played some part. The chief consulted with an informal council of extended family heads, before which anyone might speak, including women.

The Pueblo peoples, who live in the compact apartment-house villages, never achieved any unity beyond that of the village with

337

a population numbered only in the hundreds. Although Zuñi has been much larger in the historic period, it is the Spanish consolidation of the "Seven Cities of Cibola," which could not have numbered more than a few hundred each. A Spanish system of officials can be found today at all Pueblos except those of the Hopi, which lie farthest west. At the same time all the Pueblos still retain a second set of preconquest officials. Because the preconquest system is so closely geared to religion, it is frequently called a theocracy. Every pueblo had a number of religious organizations, comparable to our churches, lodges, fraternities, and faith-healing groups. Each chapter of each type of religious society had its own officers. These positions tended to be inherited, although which one of a man's sister's sons or own sons would succeed him depended on the interest the young man took in religious affairs and his ability to learn and perform the ritual correctly. All, or nearly all, such officers in a particular pueblo sat on its council, the number of council members varying from ten to about thirty among the various pueblos. The council was the highest authority in the pueblo and functioned principally as a judiciary body. It decided the fate of citizens accused of crimes, such as witchcraft, betrayal of religious secrets, and disloyalty to the pueblo. Theft, adultery, and even homicide were regarded as torts by Pueblo standards, and did not reach the council unless they became too violent to be handled by the proper officials. Tort-handling officials were the leaders of the warrior society, present in some form among all the Pueblos, and the members of this society served as police within the pueblo as well as an army without. On most Pueblo councils there were two individuals who served as executive officers for the pueblo. They may be called the civil priest and the war priest, and their orders were enforced, if necessary, by the warrior society led by the war priest or his lieutenant. Most of the concern of the council centered around deciding what course of action would be most in harmony with the supernatural, from which all blessings flowed. It is clear from this brief description that the Pueblos possessed true political organization at the village level.

The Yumans living on the Colorado and Gila rivers were organized into tribes of two thousand to three thousand persons each. Each had multiple chiefs, who supposedly controlled as many areal subdivisions, but these smaller territories have never been mapped. The chief was a versatile man who kept peace within his following, led them in economic pursuits and religious festivals, and often inherited his position from a paternal relative. Warfare was the national sport for these River Yumans, and again and again tribes fought with traditional enemies, most often other Yumans. Sometimes two or three of the tribes formed an alliance against another group, but national identities were never confused and warriors normally returned to home territory after the campaign. Boundaries between tribes were rather definite along the rivers but were vague out on the deserts, which were much less frequented. Each tribe spoke a different language or dialect, and each had a distinct name. In spite of a fairly heavy concentration of population on the rivers, most of the Yumans did not live in definite towns of known size, but rather on little farms scattered about on the floodplain of the river.

In the Oasis area on the Mexican side of the border, towns become larger as one proceeds southward. These towns differed from those of the Pueblos not only in the greater size of their populations but also in the absence of apartment-like clusters; they were more spread out and had more space between houses. Sixteenth- and seventeenth-century writers mention towns ranging in size from one hundred to six hundred houses. The populations of most of these towns were obviously larger than those of the Pueblos of the United States and the largest towns must have possessed several thousand inhabitants. Although little is known of the pre-Spanish government, it seems clear that the political unit was at least as large as the town, which makes it larger than that of any people discussed so far in this chapter except the River Yumans. Possibly several towns were united at times. All the towns had chiefs who most often inherited their positions patrilineally, although the particular individual chosen from a lineage also had to have sufficient ability. In the very southernmost part of the Oasis area we find regular markets, nobility, the collecting of tribute by large towns from small, and other manifestations of Meso-American culture, but these are not typical of the Oasis.

339

AREAS WITH TRIBAL ORGANIZATION IN THE HISTORIC PERIOD

On the Plains, Prairies, and in the East, some Indians, but not all, had tribal organization in the historic period, although it seems probable that band and village organization was much more common before White contact. The populations of the historic tribes ran into the thousands, and all tribes had chiefs and other officers. These are the classic tribes mentioned most often in United States history. The number of political units does not always correspond to the linguistic names on the large map at the end of the book, however. The Crow and the Shawnee, for example, were divided into three and five subdivisions respectively, each of which was a separate political unit. These subdivisions were of sufficient size and possessed enough integration to be labeled tribes, however.

The distinction between civil chiefs and war leaders was general throughout these areas. A man could not be both a civil chief and a war leader at the same time. All young men went to war to obtain scalps and other war honors which were necessary before they could be accepted as full citizens in the society. Only after success in war was a man likely to be selected for membership on the council and from there to civil chieftainship. Civil chiefs were obligated to stress peace within their own societies, as well as to discourage hot-headed young men from stirring up too much trouble with other tribes, and they had to resign their positions as chiefs before they could go on the warpath. Because chiefs were generally mature or old men, this was seldom done, but there are enough cases on record to establish the principle involved.

Plains.—Most of these peoples achieved tribal organization in the historic period, but a few, such as the Shoshoni-speaking Comanche, never got beyond the band stage. The Plains tribes occupied fairly well defined territories which, although sometimes shared with friendly neighbors, were at the same time defended against enemy tribes. Each tribe assembled at least once a year, and sometimes oftener, for a communal buffalo hunt, and each was further integrated by tribal religious ritual and beliefs. Each also was led by chiefs, and the will of the leaders was enforced by a police group. Chieftainship was acquired by achievement, particularly in warfare, but once having gained this high status, the chief became a peacemaker within his own society and often advocated a peaceful course of action in disputes with other tribes.

The political structure of the Cheyenne, who numbered about four thousand, has been more completely described than that of any other Plains tribe. The Cheyenne were governed by a civil council of forty-four chiefs, divided into five priestly chiefs, two doormen, and thirty-seven others. The priestly chiefs, who outranked the others, conducted tribal rituals, including the chief-renewal ritual performed every year when the group assembled. One of the five priestly chiefs presided at the meetings of the council of forty-four chiefs and manipulated the sacred medicines in the chiefs' medicine bundle; he was called the Prophet and represented the mythical culture hero. The doormen were sometimes called upon to sum up the essence of the discussion and to render a decision for the group. When one of the five priestly chiefs retired, he chose his successor from the remaining thirty-nine members of the group or, if he died so suddenly that he could not choose his successor, the surviving four priestly chiefs chose one for him. A priestly chief, on retirement, stepped down only to the rank of the undifferentiated thirty-seven chiefs; he did not have to leave the council. If an undifferentiated chief died without choosing his successor, the entire council chose one for him. Each ordinary chief could serve only ten years, which explains why the rules of succession are so complicated. New chiefs were chosen on the basis of merit, and it was considered bad taste for a man to choose his son. The personal qualities which constituted merit were control of temper and generosity.

None of the forty-four chiefs ever exerted any force to carry out the will of the civil council. Force was applied by the members of one of the six men's societies which the council selected on two important occasions: moving camp, and the tribal buffalo hunt. Moving camp was a military venture because there was always some danger of encountering an enemy. The tribal buffalo hunt was the most important economic occasion of the year and teamwork was necessary to kill the maximum number of buffaloes.

The two headmen and the two doormen of each of the men's

341

societies formed a council of twenty-four war chiefs. A man could not be both a civil chief and a war chief. If a war chief were chosen as a civil chief, he must first resign his position of war chief before accepting that of civil chief. The council of war chiefs chose the war leader for each military raid, but once the campaign was ended his authority terminated.

There were only three crimes among the Cheyenne: homicide, disobeying the rules of the tribal buffalo hunt, and repeated theft of horses. The punishment for homicide was banishment from the tribe for a period of five to ten years. Although this seems light to us, a banished man might be killed or captured by enemies before he could achieve asylum with a friendly tribe. The punishment for disobeying orders on the hunt was a severe beating, sometimes resulting in broken bones, and the destruction of the offender's personal property, such as horse, bow, and tipi. For repeated horse-theft the punishment was the same. All these punishments were meted out collectively by the members of one of the military societies selected in advance by the council of civil chiefs. If the Cheyenne were scattered about in winter camps when a murder occurred, riders were dispatched to notify each of the civil chiefs to assemble to hear the case. Thus, even though the tribe was not assembled in one locality, the law was still in force and was marshaled in whenever a crime was committed.

Prairies.—Some of the Siouan tribes of this area had intricate systems of government in the historic period comparable to that of the Cheyenne, who were a Prairie tribe before abandoning farming and moving farther west onto the Plains in the early nineteenth century. The Algonquians, on the other hand, tended to be less well integrated. A most interesting account of Fox government illustrates how elusive and tenuous the role of leadership can be without actually being absent.

Fox concepts of power in religion and government are closely related. Supernatural power, called *manitu,* is impersonal, like atomic energy, but it must be possessed by both human beings and spiritual beings if they are to achieve any outstanding success. The possession of *manitu* is thought to be temporary and contingent on many things, so that the only proof that one person possesses more power than another is successful performance at a given time and place, such as success in battle. Since supernatural power is temporary and contingent, success in one venture does not insure success in the next, so that success in one battle, or even in several, does not tend to raise a man to a permanent position of success and leadership. Because religious power was dangerous, it was considered both hazardous and immoral for one individual to exercise much control over another. Individualism was extreme in comparison with other Prairie tribes.

There were three principal leaders in Fox society: the civil or "peace" chief, the war leader, and the ceremonial leader. The civil chieftainship was a permanent position, inherited patrilineally by a member of the Bear lineage. This chief was supposed to encourage harmonious relations within the group and to act as arbiter in the event of dissension in council meetings. The war leader's position was the result of *manitu* acquired in a vision and was limited to a single campaign. Any warrior in the tribe who, according to his own testimony, had acquired supernatural power in this manner could become the leader of a war expedition. As is general for the Plains, Prairies, and East, membership in a war party was voluntary, the number and ability of the volunteers being correlated with the amount of incitement which the relating of the vision brought. The war leader, therefore, merely suggested what the group should do and, if the majority dissented, he might be forced to come up with a fresh suggestion. The ceremonial leader was anyone who had memorized one or more of the many religious rituals of the Fox. His role did not include the initiation of the ritual, he did not serve as an intermediary between another person and the supernatural, and his activity was limited to the duration of the ritual in which he played the principal part.

In addition to these three kinds of weak leaders, there was a village council composed of the headmen of each of the extended family groupings. This was presided over by the civil chief. No action was taken unless the decision of the council was unanimous. Public opinion, therefore, was almost automatically followed because every family was represented on the council. Any person not an actual member of the council might attend a meeting and plead any cause he chose.

How did such concepts of authority and power work out in

343

practice? When Father Allouez contacted the Fox in 1667 he told them that Jesus Christ, as represented by the cross, was a powerful *manitu*, and at once attracted a large following. In 1671 a group of warriors painted crosses on their bodies and shields, thus putting themselves under the protection of the cross *manitu*, and won a decisive victory over their traditional enemies, the Sioux. They returned victorious, proclaiming to the skies the White man's religion. The following year, when they painted themselves as before and went out again to fight the Sioux, they were disastrously defeated. On returning home, the enraged warriors repudiated the White man's *manitu*, tore down the cross Allouez had erected, and refused to let the priest re-enter the village.

On the whole, Fox government was a weak village system, and did not attain the level of true tribal organization. This was true of other Prairie Algonquians.

East.—In the East the League of the Iroquois, embracing a population of ten to seventeen thousand, was the largest and best-organized political unit; yet its lack of cohesion is easily shown by its part in the Revolutionary War when the Oneida and half of the Tuscarora sided with the colonists while the others took the side of the British. This was the only confederacy north of Mexico at the time of European contact, soon after 1600, and the traditional date of its founding is about 1570. Many others came and went at later dates as Indians and Whites clashed in the contact period.

There was a limited strip of territory along the coastal plain from Louisiana to Florida, thence north up the Atlantic Coast to Virginia, where the political units were true tribes and the rulers had absolute authority, including the power of life and death, over their subjects. This is the only area north of Mexico where such absolute power existed. The best-known examples of this system are the Natchez and the Powhatan, whose populations are estimated at 4,500 and 9,000 respectively in the seventeenth century. Among the Natchez the chief was regarded as a descendant of the sun god and traveled in a litter, the bearers running in relays and changing over without slackening their pace. His subjects were required to keep at least four paces away from his person and to speak to him with reverence. When the chief died, his wives and servants were killed to serve him in the afterlife, and his body was disemboweled and laid to rest in a temple near those of his predecessors. This reminds us of the Incas of Peru and the Circum-Caribbean peoples.

Matrilineal descent was the prevailing form in the East and leadership in all its forms tended to be inherited matrilineally. The clan and sib organizations were the units which made up the towns and tribes, and normally both religious and political offices were confined to particular lineages and sibs which were matrilineal.

Since the League of the Iroquois has been described so often in books, let us choose the government of the Creek Indians of Alabama and Georgia as our typical example for this area. The territorial unit among the Creeks was the village, of which there were about fifty among a total population of about eighteen thousand, averaging about 360 persons per village. Some villages or towns, as they were often called, were much larger than others, the largest single one possessing five hundred houses, according to Garcilaso de la Vega. But Garcilaso obtained his information second hand in Spain from a member of the De Soto expedition years after the town had been visited. However, the largest Creek towns may have reached a thousand inhabitants. The highest officer in the town was the chief, and each of the fifty towns had its own chief. The position was not strictly hereditary because the chief was chosen by the town council, but normally the council selected the chief from a single sib such as the bear sib. It was thus hereditary within the sib. Chiefs of Red ("war") towns were usually chosen from one of the Red sibs, and chiefs of White ("peace") towns from one of the White sibs. The council might also impeach a chief any time they felt he was unsatisfactory, and there are actual cases of this on record. The chief's duties were many: he was in charge of the public area in the center of the town, including the public granary which stored part of the harvest from the town fields, and after a successful hunt in which he participated, he might invite the whole town to a feast followed by an all-night dance; he presided over council discussions, maneuvering the members so as to reach a decision; he designated the time for the annual harvest ceremony, distributing invitation sticks to heads of families; he received embassies from other towns and tribes and represented his town in foreign affairs. Chiefs were all called "peace" chiefs, meaning civil chiefs, even though some were from "war" sibs and served "war" towns. Policing of the town and actual warfare were in the charge of officers and members of a warrior group to be described below.

Each Creek town also had a second or vice chief who might be nominated by the chief but also had to be approved by the council. He always belonged to one of the White sibs, and usually it was the Wind sib. He was the highest authority when the chief was absent and might rise to first chief. Each town had another official who was a spokesman for the chief, sitting beside the chief in council and orating the latter's wishes. His main qualification was being a good speaker, but he also usually belonged to the same sib as the chief.

There was in addition a group of officials whom we shall designate as cabinet members. They belonged to the same sib as the chief and assisted the chief in executing his desires. They directed the planting, cultivating, and harvesting of the town fields, also the gathering of leaves for the black drink, which was the emetic and purge used on all ceremonial occasions.

Another similar group was that of the "beloved men," the ceremonial leaders who actually conducted the harvest ceremony. They knew every verbal line and every act of non-verbal behavior that made up this complex ritual. They were veteran warriors, too old to go to war, but held in high esteem.

There were three classes of warriors, who had a certain amount of political authority. Their statuses were wholly achieved by valorous deeds of war. The highest class served as town police, punishing those who acted contrary to the will of the council or failed to attend the harvest ceremony. The intermediate class were less distinguished in war, but far enough along to have a voice in the council. The lowest warrior class included anyone who had killed an enemy and had brought back a scalp to prove it.

There was also an official, called the war speaker, chosen by the warriors from their highest class. He was the chief of police, orator for the cause of war, and announcer of a war campaign to the public. We are not told whether he actually led a war party.

All of the above officials and classes of officials, except possibly the lowest class of warriors, were members of the town council. Often their personal names were bestowed on them as new names when they accepted office or membership in a group of officers. Because the names were sometimes hereditary within a sib and were always associated exclusively and successively with the offices, they amounted to titles. To this extent, then, the Creeks recognized differences in rank, and the council members were seated according to rank and were served the black drink in rank order. The significant point, however, is that all of these ranks were based on the achievement of the individual. Even though a minority were limited to certain sibs, and were thus hereditary within the sib, the particular individual chosen from the sib had to have merit. While we are not always told so, it seems certain that every officer, including the "peace" ones, got his start up the ladder of fame as a warrior. Once he had attained one of the more modest civil offices, he could progress to higher ones on the basis of oratorical ability, knowledge of tribal lore and law, administrative ability, and other such civil qualifications. It also seems likely that every officer could be impeached by the council.

The existence of any sort of Creek confederacy in De Soto's time or earlier is doubtful. White pressure against the Creeks in the eighteenth century encouraged them to attempt centralization for mutual protection. All they ever achieved was a loose confederation led by from two to four of the most influential and largest towns. National council meetings were held from time to time in these towns, but they never became regularly scheduled. The purpose of the meetings was to settle internal strife between constituent towns and to present a united front against Indian enemies and Whites. They were more successful in the former than in the latter but failed in both. There is not a single instance where all Creek towns contributed warriors to wage a common battle. A little later, 1813, when the Creek War (United States *vs.* Creeks) took place, some towns fought against the Whites, some assisted the Whites, and some remained neutral. In other words, they were divided in every possible manner.

THE STATE

Meso-America and the Circum-Caribbean are the only areas where territorial units are large enough and well enough integrated to be called states, and even in these areas there were also small, autonomous villages, tribelets, and tribes. Here intensive farming made a large concentration of population possible and tens of thousands of people were often integrated under a single government. The largest territorial organizations embraced hundreds of thousands.

Meso-America.—The Aztecs, Tarascans, and Totonacs, at least, were organized into political units with populations of more than one hundred thousand, and the Aztec confederation had some control over millions. The Mayas of Yucatan were divided into at least a dozen territorial units with as many separate governments in the early sixteenth century. With a total population of 250,000 in 1549, these little Mayan states averaged about 20,000 persons each, but they were surely considerably more populous in 1520. The Mixtecs' political unit was generally the town, but one ambitious ruler conquered a stretch of Pacific coastline 120 miles in length and subjected the entire population to his rule. Since the total population of the Mixtecs has been estimated at an even million in 1520, this largest Mixtec state may have reached one hundred thousand.

Because the Aztec system of government was dominant in Meso-America when the Spanish arrived, it will be described in more detail. Every individual was a member of a patrilocal extended family and a patrideme. Each deme had three principal officers: a secretary-treasurer, who was in charge of economic affairs; a war leader or sheriff, who maintained order within the deme in time of peace and led the deme's military force in time of war; and a speaker, who represented his deme on the council of state which, in turn, controlled the entire nation. There were twenty demes in Mexico City (Tenochtitlán) and apparently the same number in the other large towns and cities of the Aztecs. The officers of the deme were selected by the deme council, composed of heads of extended families and other elder male citizens. There was no formal ballot, voice vote, or standing vote; all selections of officers and other decisions as well were, in theory, unanimous. In addition to the three principal officers, there were many petty positions open to men who had distinguished themselves in civil, religious, and martial affairs. These include those who policed the markets, members of tribunals to settle disputes within demes, teachers of young men, and the keepers of the records of tribute and wealth in the deme's storehouses.

The speakers from each of the twenty demes formed the council of state and it, in turn, selected four officials from among its twenty members. Each of these officers represented one of the quarters into which a city was divided and, derivatively, five of the demes. Their duties were generally to lead the military forces and settle disputes between demes. Two were concerned principally with judicial affairs, a third was an executioner, and the fourth served as a liaison officer between civil and military affairs. A "chief of men" was chosen by the four officers just described. He represented the nation in foreign affairs involving war and alliances and, when Cortez arrived, it was Montezuma who held this position. A second official who shared top honors with the chief of men was the "snake woman," who was a man in charge of internal affairs of the nation. All of these officials selected by the council of state or the four special councilors could be impeached by action of the council and removed from authority. In practice, however, the council tended to choose successive chiefs of men from a single lineage, so that the office came to be inherited within the lineage. It did not go automatically from father to son because merit was a consideration. A brother, half-brother, or paternal nephew who showed more ability than a son might be the next in line.

The chief of men, however, was treated as a king. If any lesser chief wished to speak to him, he approached him with downcast eyes, wearing the clothing of a commoner, and barefoot. Montezuma was carried on a litter borne on the shoulders of four chiefs, and under no circumstances were his feet allowed to touch the earth. Four additional chiefs held above the litter a canopy of green feathers, fringed with gold, silver, pearls, and jade. At home, Montezuma was served food seated behind a screen so that no one could watch him eat. Even his closest relatives approached him in humble manner and remained standing in his presence. His palace had one hundred rooms and one hundred baths and, with attached buildings, was large enough to accommodate the more than two thousand soldiers of Cortez and his Tlaxcalan allies.

About a century before Cortez arrived the Aztecs of Tenoch-titlán formed a triple alliance with two other city-states in the Valley of Mexico. They soon dominated the alliance and continued to do so until the Spanish conquest. It was during this period that they conquered most of the important peoples in central Mexico and even some as far away as Guatemala. They collected tribute from all these subject peoples, occasionally by force of arms, but never welded them into a single "empire" or nation. Small, insignificant, and poor minority groups within this huge territory were often bypassed. The state organization of the Aztecs never became larger than the city of Tenochtitlán, but, with a population estimated at 300,000, this was easily the greatest political achievement of aboriginal North America.

Circum-Caribbean.—In this area the village was often the governmental unit, but federations of villages into tribes and states were also common. Because the populations of villages and tribes sometimes numbered thousands, the states often ran into the tens of thousands. Like the Aztecs, the dominant state would often exact tribute from weaker neighboring states or tribes and thus build up an economic "empire." The chief or king, as he is sometimes called, possessed more power than the Aztec leaders and generally obtained his position of authority by matrilineal inheritance. In some localities he had the power of life and death over his subjects, and his wives, concubines, and slaves were sometimes sacrificed at his death. He lived among much pomp and splendor: he occupied the largest house in the town, never worked at labor, wore special kingly dress, rode in a litter, and, in at least four instances, married his sister to keep the royal blood line pure.

SUMMARY AND CONCLUSIONS

Our survey has shown that the family was the largest permanent residential unit over most of the Arctic, Great Basin, and Northeast Mexican areas. The Sub-Arctic, with its weak bands of a hundred or two, was only slightly more integrated politically. On the North Pacific Coast and in California the territorial unit was generally the village or tribelet, with population numbered in the hundreds. The Plateau formerly seems to have had only village and tribelet organization throughout, but in the eighteenth

350

and nineteenth centuries Plains influence brought true tribes to the eastern part of this area. In the Oasis we found all degrees from small bands of less than a hundred to true tribes numbering several thousand. On the Plains, Prairies, and in the East, integrations of a thousand or more persons into tribes were common in the historic period. In Meso-America and the Circum-Caribbean we found much larger territorial units which we labeled states, with populations in the tens and hundreds of thousands.

How are these differences to be explained? The largest political entities were in the areas where farming was the principal source of food: Circum-Caribbean, Meso-America, Oasis, and East (Map 3). The Plains tribes are an exception to this rule, but, because most of them formerly lived farther east and farmed, their government can easily be demonstrated to be of eastern derivation. The size of the political unit is also correlated with population density (Map 6), although this relationship, too, is far from perfect. It was in Meso-America, with more people than in all the other culture areas combined, that the largest states developed. In the areas of sparsest population, the Arctic, Sub-Arctic, Great Basin, and Northeast Mexico, political integration was either absent or at the minimum. In areas of intermediate population density, however, we find our relationship reversed. On the Northwest Coast and in California population is generally more dense than on the Plains, Prairies, and even in the East, yet the political units in the former areas are generally smaller than those in the latter.

At this point we must again introduce the historical factor. The tribes in the southeastern United States unquestionably derived some of their social and political organization from Meso-America or the Circum-Caribbean area, as Kroeber long ago (1928:392–96) pointed out. The Natchez, Powhatan, Timucua, and other Southeastern peoples show a great deal of similarity in their entire sociopolitical structure to the peoples around the Caribbean. Many archeologists believe that these tribes are the remnants of the mound-builders whose earthworks extend north to the Great Lakes. It therefore appears that most of the Indians in the United States east of the Rocky Mountains were exposed to forms of government originally derived from the Circum-Caribbean or Meso-American areas. Why the Oasis peoples failed to acquire more of this interest in political organization is not obvious. Population per square mile in the Pueblo part of the Oasis is greater than that of the East and presumably it would have been no more difficult to form a permanent federation among the Rio Grande Pueblos than among the five or six Iroquois tribes. But the fact remains that it was never done. Thus, there appear to be differences of a subtle nature, perhaps in personality, which determine in part how far a given people will proceed in the direction of a larger governmental integration.

REFERENCES

BEALS, 1932; BIRKET-SMITH, 1936; DAHLGREN DE JORDAN, 1954; DRIVER AND DRIVER, MS.; FISHER, 1939; GAYTON, 1930; GIFFORD, 1932, 1936; GOODWIN, 1942; HIND, 1863; KROEBER, 1925, 1928, 1935, 1939, 1955; LIPS, 1947; LLEWELLYN AND HOEBEL, 1941; LOWIE, 1951, 1954; MILLER, 1955; MURDOCK, 1957; OPLER, 1941; OSGOOD, 1936, 1937; RAY, 1939; ROYS, 1957; SPECK AND EISELEY, 1942; SPIER, 1928; STEWARD, 1938, 1948; THOMPSON, 1940; VAILLANT, 1941; WEYER, 1932.

18: Violence, Feuds, Raids, and War

Few indigenous peoples in the world at the same level of culture have fought so valiantly against European intruders as did the Indians east of the Rocky Mountains in the United States. Man for man, bow for bow, and gun for gun, they were at match for the best troops sent against them and were overwhelmed only because of the greater numbers and superior armament of the English and French colonizers. The more civilized and settled peoples of Meso-America and around the Caribbean fell an easy prey to the Spanish for a number of reasons, among them the fact that the rank and file were so overregimented that it never occurred to them to resist after their leaders were slain or captured.

The arrival of Europeans in the Americas produced many indirect changes in Indian ways of life, largely in the nature of adaptations to the changing conditions. Without these changes the end of the Indians as independent cultures would have come much sooner. Patterns of warfare were no exception to this rule. In pre-Columbian times war parties in the area that is now the United States were smaller, just as the political units they represented were smaller. After the European invasions, small villages or bands tended to unite with one another to form tribes and ultimately confederations. Although the cohesiveness of these larger political entities left something to be desired and many were only temporary, they were able to offer more resistance to the Whites collectively than individually. The pressure of White settlement on the East Coast pushed the eastern Indians toward the west and stirred up a host of conflicts between them and those tribes already located in the new land. Although the Indians did not use their land as intensively as did the colonists, the forcing of two tribes onto land formerly occupied by one stirred up trouble between them. Competition for beaver and other fur-bearing animals became extreme. Probably as many Indians were killed fighting each other after White contact as were killed in wars with the Whites.

The weapons of war will be mentioned only incidentally here, except for the gun. The first trade guns from Europe were so deficient technically that their superiority over the bow and arrow was debatable. As late as our own Revolutionary War, George Washington and other military leaders had considerable discussion on whether the bow and arrow should be a part of the armament of the thirteen colonies. Washington had been present at Braddock's defeat and had seen with his own eyes what the Indians could do with the bow and arrow. While an English soldier was reloading with powder and shot through the muzzle, an Indian could shoot at least half a dozen arrows, and sometimes the flint failed to produce a spark or the powder became too wet to fire. When breech-loading guns and ammunition in cartridges appeared, however, the superiority of the gun became obvious, and this improved weapon was a factor in the final defeat of the Indians.

"Violence" is the broadest word in the title of this chapter. It refers to bodily injury or killing whether resulting from an encounter between two persons, two families, two bands, two lineages, two sibs, two tribes, two confederacies, or any other social and territorial units. It may terminate with the death or injury of one party, continue in a series of reprisals, or go on indefinitely. "Feud," on the other hand, is limited to conflicts between two families, lineages, clans, sibs, or other kinship groups. Feud also suggests a protracted series of reprisals without any mechanism for settling the dispute but, because concepts of law and order show much variation, one cannot always draw a sharp line between feud and law. The term "raid" will be used to designate a single small military engagement of short duration. "War," on the other hand, will be reserved for conflicts between two factions with true political organization, each of which possesses definite leadership, some kind of military tactics, and at least the hope of being able to weather a series of battles.

ABSENCE OF TRUE WARFARE

Because we have defined war as a military encounter between two political units, those areas which lacked true political organization lacked true warfare. Therefore, most of the peoples of the Arctic, Sub-Arctic, Great Basin, Northeast Mexico, and probably Baja California lacked true warfare before European contact. None of these had any permanent military organization, special fighting regalia, or associated public ceremonies. However, violence occurred in these areas in the form of duels and raids by small groups, and feuds were common.

Arctic.—Murder apparently occurred from time to time in every Eskimo settlement. Disputes over women were the most common immediate cause of murder. One anthropologist carefully canvassed every Eskimo man in a certain settlement in northern Canada on this question and found that every mature man of about thirty or older had killed at least one Eskimo man at some time in his life. Even a peace-loving man would be compelled to fight to prevent a more aggressive personality from absconding with his wife. The sex urge was not the only motive in these encounters, because the custom of wife-lending made every woman available to any man as long as he asked her husband first. The husband was socially obligated to give his consent to such a proposal, which was usually for a single night or at most a few days. It was only when one man sought to appropriate permanently another's wife that trouble arose. The fact that a married man sometimes acquired a second wife by killing her husband suggests that the issue was not exclusively sex but was combined with a desire to conquer another man. A man's status in the society was enhanced by an occasional murder of another under these circumstances. It was only when he killed too many men too close together in time that he was socially disapproved of and in danger of losing his own life at the hands of a group of vigilantes.

Feuds were also present among the Eskimo. For example, an anthropologist's chief informant among the Caribou Eskimo had killed his wife's entire family when he appropriated her, because they disapproved of him. If he had left a single man or boy alive, the latter might have taken revenge on him at a later date. A more complicated example from the central Arctic will illustrate the blood feud further.

355

In 1905 a Netsilingmiut couple moved over to settle among the Asiag-miut, with their three grown sons. Of those sons, the eldest had an Asiagmiut wife. A local native declared he would have regular sexual intercourse with the woman. The husband did not want to acquiesce, but was not strong enough to prevent the aggressor, and in consequence, he speared his own wife. Immediately, the husband was seized and killed by his father-in-law and some henchmen. In defending his brother, a younger son of the Netsilingmiut family stabbed the avenging father-in-law in the back, killing him. The boy was then seriously wounded himself. The Asiagmiut, considering the situation, decided that wisdom counselled the complete eradication of the killer's family in order to forestall blood revenge. The remaining son, sensing the danger, escaped, though the father was brought to his doom. (Hoebel, 1941:674–75.)

Sometimes, however, the community might rise up to enforce justice. A series of unprovoked murders might be punished by a group of able-bodied men who banded together and killed the offender. One who was reputed to kill by sorcery might also be gotten rid of in this way. Such groups of justice-dispensers were not appointed or elected in any way nor had they any leader.

Even when the desire to acquire a woman was not the cause of a murder, the murderer was nonetheless expected to provide for the murdered man's wife and children. This meant that a man normally reared the son of a murdered victim, a boy who might later exact blood vengeance upon his foster father. Revenge was more often accomplished by a surprise attack on the unsuspecting victim, but might take the form of an open challenge to a wrestling match with the loser forfeiting his life.

When small bands of Eskimo met their Indian neighbors to the south, as they sometimes did in the summer, they often fought them over the hunting and fishing rights at a particular locality. These were not planned punitive expeditions and did not involve large enough, permanent enough, or sufficiently well integrated social groups to be labeled war. Nevertheless it is significant that intergroup encounters on this scale happened much more often with Athaspaskan and Algonquian bands than with other Eskimo bands.

The Alaskan Eskimo carried on a series of raids and feuds with their Athapaskan neighbors. The motivations included the desire to appropriate the material possessions and young women of the vanquished, as well as to avenge an injury or death from an earlier engagement. The prestige of the victor was always enhanced also.

Sub-Arctic.—Among the Naskapi of the Labrador peninsula, murders sometimes occurred but they were not common. Murder in self-defense went unpunished, but an unprovoked murder brought retaliation from the male relatives of the slain man. If these relatives failed to act, the band chief might remind them that they had a social obligation to do so. Retaliation for murder usually took the form of shooting or drowning. If a man were incapacitated by an injury unjustly inflicted by another, the latter had to give food to the injured party as long as he remained incapacitated. If a murder occurred at the summer rendezous with the band chief and informal council present, the chief would call a hearing. If the majority of the old men of the council thought the murderer guilty, the chief would pronounce the death sentence. The condemned man would start walking away with the armed council members following. When they reached an appropriate spot, three or four men previously designated as executioners by the chief, shot the offender in the back. His corpse was left to lie where it fell without burial.

Among the northern Ojibwa just east of Lake Winnipeg, murder by physical encounter is unheard of. Wrongs are avenged by witchcraft, sometimes performed by the injured man, but also by a shaman employed for the purpose. These people occasionally fight when drunk, but are normally completely non-violent. Witchcraft serves as a substitute for physical violence and is thought to be capable of killing a person as well as making him severely ill.

Peoples of the Eastern Sub-Arctic who had contact with the Eskimo occasionally fought with them, but there is no record of an entire band of Montagnais, Naskapi, or Cree fighting against another speaking the same language. The southernmost Montagnais, who contacted the Iroquois, learned some of the tricks of organized warfare from the latter, but it was generally the Iroquois who were both the aggressors and victors. When the Cree moved west in the early nineteenth century, they often fought with the more timid Athapaskans and stole their material possessions and women.

In the Mackenzie Sub-Arctic the Athapaskans sometimes fought each other, as well as the Eskimo. The Chipewyans, Slaves, Dog-ribs, Yellowknives, Kaskas, and Beavers fought one another regularly, more often for material goods and women than for any other reason, although revenge was also a motive. However, the number of persons involved was too small and their organization too little to call these encounters war. There were also raids and feuds between bands speaking the same language, although these seem to have been less common than interlingual disputes. The surprise attack early in the morning was the principal tactic employed, whether the encounter was between two bands speaking the same language or between those of different languages. Membership in such raiding parties was voluntary, and any man might persuade others to join him in such an attack, since there was no permanent military organization.

In the Yukon Sub-Arctic the Athapaskans fought principally with the Eskimo. Here the economic prestige motives loom larger than elsewhere in the Sub-Arctic because of contact with the Northwest Coast, but revenge was also a factor. The spoils that went to the victor were weapons, boats, clothing, hides, and any other goods of value, as well as women. The proof of physical superiority, added to the gain in personal wealth, raised the prestige of the winner in his society. As elsewhere in the Sub-Arctic, these encounters were in the nature of small raids, or occasionally feuds, initiated by any individual.

Great Basin.—The Western Shoshoni and their neighbors in the heart of the Basin area lacked definite warfare. With the family the largest permanent residential unit, there was no government to carry on a true war. Violence, raids, and feuds were not totally lacking, however, although they were normally carried on without any special organization, regalia, or ritual. Such hostilities were more frequent between speakers of different languages: Shoshoni versus Northern Paiute, Southern Paiute, Ute, or even Mohave. Woman-stealing is the most frequently reported motivation for such attacks, although economic motives were not lacking. On one occasion an apparently unprovoked attack by Northern Paiute on Shoshoni, resulting in the death of several Shoshoni women and children, was settled by compensation in the form of shell money (probably imported from California). The Shoshoni of Death Valley once killed some intruders without bothering to determine their identity. Horse-stealing became a motive for raids in the eastern part of the Basin after the acquisition of this animal in the historic period. "Legal" procedure for settling disputes within a band seems to have been totally lacking or at least is unreported. The Western Shoshoni, therefore, appear to have had less law even than the peoples of the Arctic and Sub-Arctic.

Northeast Mexico.—The Chichimecs of this area apparently lacked true warfare in pre-Columbian times except in the south, where they made contact with the peoples of Meso-America. Later, when the Spanish invaded their territory in the middle of the sixteenth century to mine silver, the Chichimecs became very aggressive against the intruders and formed bands for mutual defense. However, the temporary and expedient nature of these bands is shown by the fact that after winning a victory, they sometimes fought among themselves over the spoils. In the early sixteenth century, the same writers who characterized them as lacking fixed settlements and band organization mentioned at some length their skill and courage as fighters. These writers give the impression that the Chichimecs murdered strangers on sight, which may have been generally true, but at least one Otomí trader was allowed to go among them unmolested and to exchange salt and cloth from Meso-America for hides and bows.

Although the aboriginal Chichimecs lacked the political organization to carry on true wars, their geographical position between Meso-America on the south and the Plains-Prairies-East on the north and northeast gave them a number of traits which they share in common with these more advanced cultures. For instance, they took scalps, tortured prisoners, mutilated corpses, ate the flesh of slain enemies, and each man kept a record of the number of his victims by carving a notch for each on a human arm or leg bone. Gonzalo de las Casas, writing in 1574, gives one of the most graphic accounts of Chichimec violence.

When they take a captive they dance around him and also make the prisoner dance. . . . They are not horrified at the death of men, but kill them for pleasure and pastime, just as one kills a hare or deer.

They are extremely cruel and brutal. To a person they capture, whether man or woman, the first thing they do is to scalp him, leaving the entire crown bare, like the tonsure of a friar. . . . They also remove the sinews, which they use to tie the flints to their arrows. They take

359

out the long bones of the arms and legs, while the victim is still alive, and also sometimes even the ribs, and perform a hundred other tortures until the victim finally dies. They wear, hanging at their backs, the scalps which they have taken, and some of these are from beautiful woman with long blond locks; they also wear arm and leg bones as trophies. They show no mercy even to the corpses, on which they inflict every imaginable torture, hanging them from trees. They use them as targets, shooting arrows into their eyes, ears, tongue, and even genitals. . . .

They fight nude, with bow and arrow, very skilfully and boldly; if they happen to be wearing clothes, they undress for fighting. They always wear their quivers full of arrows, and carry four or five arrows in the bow hand to supply themselves more quickly. . . .

As I have said, they are cruel to the utmost in war, without regard for sex or age, killing and scalping both mother and child. . . . Although they take a few women and children as captives and make use of them, they never spare the life of a man. Their women seem to be more merciful, and have been known to give food to captives and weep over them, which the men never do.

They use no arms but the bow and arrow. With these they are so quick that one has been seen to shoot an arrow through both hands of a soldier holding an arquebus in his face, before the soldier could disarm him. . . . They shoot with such force that when they shot at the head of the horse of one soldier . . . the arrow passed through the horse's crownpiece, made of a double thickness of cowhide and a sheet of metal, and through the head and chest of the horse. . . .

They dance at night, around the fire, linked arm in arm . . . in a way which seems confused, though there must be some order to it. . . . In the center of this dance they place the captive whom they intend to kill, and each one who enters the dance shoots an arrow into the victim. (Las Casas [1574] 1944:28–36.)

WEAK OR MIXED PATTERNS OF WARFARE

On the Northwest Coast, Plateau, in California, and in the Oasis, at least some of the peoples possessed a more definite form of warlike behavior. Territorial units were a little larger, and those with true political organization tended also to have more military organization. At the same time all these areas included some peoples with little in the way of violence, raids, or feuds, and no hostilities pretentious enough to be labeled war.

Northwest Coast.—In this area kinship was of much greater importance than in the areas described in the section above, and all the more productive pieces of real estate were owned and used by kin groups, such as extended families, lineages, sibs, clans, and demes. Competition and rivalry in the accumulation of wealth and prestige was keen, along with an almost paranoid sensitivity to criticism and slander. Under these circumstances disputes between kin groups were common enough to have been reported for almost all the peoples on the entire Northwest Coast.

After a physical injury or a killing, the relatives of the victim sometimes retaliated by injuring or killing a member of the kin group which had initiated the violence. If the retaliation succeeded, the two sides were even, but the affair did not stop there. Each side demanded compensation from the other in tangible goods or "money." Sometimes there was no retaliation and the original wrong was settled by an indemnity. Regardless of the number of casualties involved, each person had to be paid for by the kin group of the person who had committed the violence. The amount of damage was negotiated by an intermediary, who was not a member of either of the disputing groups. In northwest California among the Yurok and their neighbors, the valuation placed on a life was exactly the amount of the bride price that had been paid for the victim's mother. Elsewhere in the area the price for a life was not fixed in any manner, and often the aim was to demand enough weregild to embarrass and humble the opponents. Sometimes among the Tlingit, when the amount of compensation for a life could not be agreed upon, the headman or chief of the slayer's kin group would give his own life to keep the peace. Dressed in his finest ceremonial regalia and dancing one of the formal hereditary dances of his lineage, he approached the posse of the enemy waiting outside his house. They courteously allowed him the dignity of continuing his act until he was within a few yards of them, at which point they killed him. All the peoples on the Northwest Coast, except the Kwakiutl and Nootka, settled grievances by compensation. The Kwakiutl and Nootka were openly aggressive and defended their aggressions with a renewal of hostilities if necessary.

Should this system be labeled feud? The fact that physical retaliation for an injury or life was common suggests the concept of the feud, but the further fact that compensation had to be paid eventually for every injury or life is evidence that there was a mechanism for settling such disputes. The system therefore stands astride both law and feud, with some of the aspects of both.

The Northwest Coast peoples of British Columbia and Alaska also carried on campaigns aimed at robbing, driving out, or annihilating another kin group in order to appropriate its lands and movable possessions. Although these were not usually disputes between true political units, the economic motivation is clear and the aggression just as deadly. Most of such economic conquests were between kin groups speaking different languages, such as Tlingit against Eskimo, Haida against Tlingit, Tsimshian against Xaihais, and Bella Bella against Xaihais. The Haida, for example, made raids as far south as Puget Sound, which is about seven hundred miles from the Queen Charlotte Islands. Among the Nootka, however, these economy-motivated raids of extermination took place between speakers of the same language. Here there was true political organization, at least in the historic period, so that the larger encounters of this nature involving this people may be labeled war.

Slaves were a further reason for conducting a raid or, rather, they were another kind of movable property to be acquired along with canoes, furs, food, and clothing. Most of the peoples on the Northwest Coast from Alaska to the Columbia River, and then southward inland to the Klamath of southern Oregon, captured people, as well as movable property, in raids. Some of the people may already have been slaves, but most were free persons, who were sold or kept as slaves after being captured. Sometimes they were ransomed later by relatives, but often the stigma attached to the slave status was so marked that the relatives did not want to have a freed slave in their midst and, therefore, took no steps to recover their kinsman. Children of slaves, if any, became slaves. This is the only area in North America where slavery was sometimes hereditary.

Heads were taken by most of the Northwest Coast peoples in Canada and Alaska, but only the Tlingit scalped, and this was done on the way home at leisure, from the whole head that had been previously acquired. The heads were mounted on tall poles erected in front of the village.

362

With all this fighting there was no separate military organization. The same wealthy men who were the headmen and chiefs of their kinship groups, tribelets, and tribes normally accompanied the fighting force and claimed the lion's share of the spoils.

Supernatural sanction was required of at least the leader of a raiding expedition among the Salish-speaking peoples of southern British Columbia, Washington, and Oregon, as well as others in Oregon and northern California. This usually took the form of a vision or a dream which the visionary interpreted as support from the supernatural. This was coupled with a dance of incitement before the raid on the Oregon and northern California coasts.

There was also a connection between aggressiveness and other psychological states. A man who had lost a relative by death, including natural death, or one who had been defeated in a potlatch or suffered some other kind of economic misfortune, would often go to war to even up the score. If an important man, he might lead an expedition; if not, he could join that of another. As mentioned above in chapter xiii, the converse was also true in the nineteenth century, when the potlatch became a substitute for physical violence in the settling of rivalries and disputes.

Plateau.—The raids, feuds, and wars on the Plateau have been much influenced by the practices of neighboring culture areas in the historic period. What appears to have been formerly the predominant pattern is most in evidence in the center of the area in the state of Washington. Hostilities were limited to raids and occasional small scale feuds in this region. The principal motives for raids seem to have been plunder, adventure, and revenge. When captives were taken, they were regarded as slaves in the beginning but might later become free citizens, often by marrying a member of the group that had captured them. Raiding parties were small, normally two or three canoes full of men representing only their own selfish interests. Volunteers made up the entire party, and anyone who wished could lead a party. Headmen and chiefs of villages and bands disapproved of such raids and went to great lengths to maintain peace, sometimes risking their lives in negotiations with hostile outsiders. Feuds between kin groups were known but not common, and chiefs served as arbiters of such disputes, which were

363

often settled by blood money. The rudiments of a legal mechanism were, therefore, present.

Hostilities among the Salish-speaking peoples on the Canadian side of the Plateau area were more pronounced. Here raiding parties numbered all the way from five or six individuals to several hundred. Although participation was voluntary, a man who refused to join such expeditions lost the respect of his fellows. The motives, therefore, were multiple: plunder, adventure, revenge, and prestige. Such parties were made up of men from a single village, or at most a band, never from all the speakers of a given language. However, they more frequently raided a village where a different language was spoken, as elsewhere in North America. These expeditions were led by a war leader who acquired his position by his proficiency as a warrior and who was often the one initiating the enterprise. The civil chief was always a distinct individual who devoted his efforts to peace, as in most other culture areas, and only joined in defensive efforts. The larger war parties exhibited considerable organization: scouts were sent ahead and sentries were posted at night; secret communication was maintained by bird and animal cries and by sign language; messages were made of sticks and left behind for other members of the party to find. Scalps and heads were sometimes taken, but not often. Every large war party was accompanied by a shaman, whose duty was to control the weather, prophesy the outcome, ward off the evil influences directed at them by the enemy, and conjure up debilitating spells against the enemy.

The peoples on the Canadian side of the Plateau also had blood feuds between kinship groups. The most trivial quarrels and insults often precipitated hostilities, and no man went unarmed. Such disputes were sometimes settled by blood money, again demonstrating the presence of the germ of law and order.

The Plateau peoples with the most Plains influence acquired the Plains pattern of warfare in the eighteenth and nineteenth centuries. It will be described in the section on the Plains below.

California.—On the whole, these Indians were among the most mild-tempered and peace-loving on the entire North American continent. Most hostilities were between small parties representing a kinship group or a village, but tribelets also clashed at times, and, because these conflicts were between political units, they may be labeled war. Again, motives were multiple as the following list in frequency of reporting shows: revenge of witchcraft; revenge of violence; disputes over economic rights in productive areas; retaliation when women and girls were kidnapped. As compared to other areas, witchcraft looms large but, because witchcraft is probably universal for the whole continent, this impression may result from unevenness of reporting. On the other hand, witchcraft can be met with counter-witchcraft, and if the California Indians met it more often with physical aggression than peoples of other culture areas, this is a significant difference. Land-grabbing was not a common thing; yet boundary disputes between tribelets were fairly common, and in a few instances the aggressor took land by force and held it permanently.

Clashes between speakers of different languages were probably more common than between those who spoke the same language, but the latter did occur. Some of the intralingual conflicts were feuds between kinship groups, but because these were often settled by blood money in the northern half of the area, at least, the germ of law was there.

There is great variation in the leadership of these raiding parties. In some localities the civil chief was the leader; elsewhere there might be a more or less permanent war leader; in still other localities war leadership was only temporary, and here and there a shaman might be a leader or coleader of a raiding party. Supernatural sanction in some form was a prerequisite to every punitive expedition, as is general for the continent. Scouts are reported for about half the tribelets.

As elsewhere on the continent, surprise attacks were the general rule, but occasionally one tribelet challenged another to a pre-arranged battle. These formal encounters did not take many lives and were often stopped when a single prominent man on one side had been killed. Scalps or whole heads were taken more often than other body parts, and weapons or other valuable objects were frequently stolen too. The individual who seized the plunder always kept it for himself. Membership in raiding parties was on a voluntary basis, as in all areas described so far in this chapter. In the northern part of California, women participated in ceremonies at home during the campaign or in a victory celebration after the men had returned home, but this may be due to recent Plains influence. A dance of incitement before the fight was also a common practice and may be native. Women and children were sometimes taken captive, but they were normally treated well and adopted into the tribelet.

Oasis.—The Pueblo peoples have been characterized as unemotional, co-operative, and peaceful by Ruth Benedict in her famous book, *Patterns of Culture*, but she has overstated her case. While the Pueblos were less warlike than their neighbors, they could not have survived without military activity. All of the Pueblo villages had a war priest who was ranked with the head civil priest in executive authority, and the two were responsible to a council whose unanimous decision controlled the affairs of the pueblo. In some pueblos the war priest led the fighting force, while in others they were led by his lieutenant. The warrior sodality served as a police force within the pueblo and a military force without. Participation in offensive hostilities was determined by membership in this sodality, not by the voluntary action of the individual as in the areas discussed so far in this chapter. The war priest and the warriors' sodality formed a permanent group ready to cope with violence at any time. Each pueblo embraced people from a number of internally related but externally unrelated kinship groups, so that conflicts between pueblos can scarcely be called feuds. In size they fit the term raid, yet their organization suggests the term war.

The Spanish put a stop to interpueblo warfare at an early date, and the United States later pursued the same policy, but there is good evidence to indicate that all the Pueblos at one time or another fought with other Pueblos as well as with Navahos, Apaches, and Utes. Sometimes two or more pueblos would unite to make war on a third and, under the yoke of the Spanish in 1680, nearly all joined together and succeeded in driving out the Spanish. When the latter returned in 1693, however, the confederation had come apart at the seams and was further split asunder over the issue of loyalty to the new Spanish regime.

Fear of witchcraft was sometimes a cause of hostilities between pueblos. Evil supernatural power leveled against one pueblo by another could precipitate an armed clash between them, as in Cali-

fornia. However, reprisals against raids initiated by enemies probably account for more Pueblo forays than any other motivation.
The weakness of the Pueblo military position, as compared to that
of the Navahos and Apaches, was that the Pueblos usually waited
until they were attacked before they fought. They were like sitting ducks for the mobile Athapaskans, who were mounted on
horses for the most part after Spanish contact. The Navahos and
Apaches had so little in the way of material goods that the Pueblos
had little desire to rob them. The Pueblos, on the other hand, possessed a great deal more material wealth, including food, than the
Navahos and Apaches and were repeatedly preyed upon by the
latter. From a combination of archeological and linguistic evidence
we are sure that the Pueblo villages existed when the Navahos and
Apaches first arrived in the Southwest from the north, so that the
pattern of the nomads raiding the settled people had probably been
going on for several centuries before the Spanish showed up.

The predatory character of the Navaho and Apache bands can
be seen in their relations with the Pueblos. The economic motive
behind their raids on the Pueblos, and less frequently on each
other, dominates all other causes of hostilities, although revenge
and prestige were involved, too. The Athapaskans stole anything
they could lay their hands on and run off with: food, clothing,
jewelry, livestock, and women and children, who were adopted
into the band. The war leader was generally a different individual
from the civil leader and attained his position solely on the basis of
his achievement as a fighter. The informal band council and civil
leader had to approve an offensive foray of any size before it could
be undertaken, but any man could initiate the raid and participation in it was voluntary. A shaman usually accompanied the expedition to maintain contact with the supernatural at all times. A
combination dance of incitement and religious ceremony was held
before the fight to work up enthusiasm and a sufficient number of
volunteers, as well as to obtain the sanction of the supernatural. If
a raid was successful, a victory celebration, with women participating, was held when the party reached home. Scalps, often consisting of the entire skin on the head, were taken and were placed
on stationary poles at the home camp or danced with in the victory celebration. Those who had slain an enemy were secluded for

367

a few days, required to avoid eating meat and certain other foods, and compelled to drink water through a tube and to scratch themselves only with a stick provided for the purpose.

The Desert Yumans lived in smaller family groups or bands than the Athapaskans, were more timid, and lacked horses. Their raids were smaller and less frequent. The Yuman tribes on the Colorado and Gila Rivers were more warlike than other Oasis peoples on the United States side of the border, and fighting took on some of the character of an international sport. They fought principally among themselves, that is, with other River Yuman tribes, only occasionally raiding one of the weaker desert peoples. There is one instance in the historical record of a River Yuman tribe being defeated and driven out of its territory, but the intent of the aggressors was to win in a fair fight with this tribe, not to cause them to flee. Plunder and captives were sometimes taken but were never a major incentive to fight. Warfare was an obsession among the young men of these tribes and war power was acquired in dreams, which were interpreted as contact with spiritual personalities who conferred upon the dreamer the supernatural power to insure success in war.

Any River Yuman man who had acquired war power in this fashion could lead a small raiding party of a dozen or so men, but the larger campaigns involving hundreds of participants were planned by the war chief, who was a permanent officer of the tribe. A shaman normally accompanied a war party to maintain contact with the supernatural and to fend off the evil magic of the enemy. If the journey to the home of the enemy took several days, speeches were made at the nightly camps to keep up the morale of the warriors. The warriors ate only parched corn and drank little water en route to battle. They were divided into two groups according to weapons: those with bows, who projected their arrows from a distance; those with short clubs used in hand-to-hand fighting. Although surprise attacks were considered legitimate, as was general in North America, it was difficult to conceal the approach of a large force, and the defenders were often prepared when the aggressors arrived. The result was a pitched battle. Slain enemies with long hair were scalped by a special scalper who had acquired his power in a dream. The skin of the entire head, including the ears, was removed. Those who had killed an enemy or taken a scalp had to observe food and drink taboos for several days afterward. When a successful war party returned home, a victory dance was held around the scalps mounted on poles, with women participating. A special custodian of the scalps kept them in a sealed pottery vessel or gourd container and took them out to wash them at intervals.

The River Yuman emphasis on war is reminiscent of the Plains region to be described below. Two details, not described so far, link the River Yumans with the Plains Indians: the round shield of hide; and the feathered stave, planted in the ground and defended at all costs. Only a very brave man carried one of the feathered staves, but, once he plunged it into the ground, he was pledged not to retreat from his position but to defend it with his life. However, because there was no direct contact between River Yumans and Plains peoples, and these traits were also found in Mexico, the River Yuman and Plains tribes probably derived them from Mexico, not from each other.

In the Oasis area in Mexico the political units were comparable to the tribes of the River Yumans, and the pattern of warfare also shows resemblances, although it is much less fully reported. Armies were larger than any reported for the areas described so far in this chapter, were divided into definite squadrons with a commander for each, and fought pitched battles. Beals (1932: 190) lists two squadrons for the Pima Bajo; one thousand men in four squadrons on the Rio Fuerte; four hundred to five hundred men in three squadrons for the Ocoroni; definite squadrons in Sinaloa and among the Chiametla; three thousand men under a chief at Tepic (according to one writer); and eight to ten squadrons of men in an army at the same town (according to a second writer). Some of these armies apparently maintained their ranks on the march as well as in battle formation. With some allowance for exaggeration of the numbers of fighting men, these armies are still much larger than any fighting force north of Mexico at earliest White contact.

The taking of both scalps and whole heads was common in the Oasis below the Mexican border, as was also the preserving of the skulls and other bones of enemies. Such bones were kept in special buildings or displayed on poles in the plaza. Victory celebrations were general, with the participants dancing around the scalp or

369

head mounted on a stationary pole. Cannibalism was also practiced on the bodies of slain enemies, the idea no doubt being to obtain supernatural power for war from the departed. We know little about the motives for warfare in this area, but the desire for economic gain was probably not wholly lacking. The round hide shields and feathered staves with non-flight obligations link these peoples with the River Yumans and the Plains Indians.

WELL-DEVELOPED WARFARE

On the Plains, Prairies, and in the East, warfare was a more integral part of the total culture than in any other region of equal size north of Mexico. Features shared by all three areas will be described first.

Although tribal organization was common in all three areas, fights between whole tribes seem to have been rare before White contact. Small raiding parties of four or five to fifty men were far more common than larger "armies." And even when numbers were large, as in an engagement of Cree and Blackfoot versus Shoshoni about 1725, when eight hundred men took part, casualties were few. After White settlement on the East Coast, clashes of both Whites against Indians and Indians against Indians became much larger and more deadly. The largest war parties in the seventeenth century were probably those of the Iroquois, which ran up to about one thousand fighting men. If we define war as a clash between territorial units with true political organization, war was less frequent throughout the Plains, Prairies, and East before White contact, because political organization, also, was less frequent in the pre-White period. White contact stirred up the Indians in many ways and brought about many irreversible trends in their cultures. The European demand for trade goods, especially furs, created a general economic competition which, when added to previous causes of fighting, vastly increased the number and size of armed conflicts. The economic motive was, therefore, paramount in this area in the historic period.

In all these areas, fighting was a means of acquiring prestige for the individual. No young man ever thought of getting married or of being accepted as an adult citizen until he had slain an enemy and brought back a scalp to prove it. So important was this

370

achievement to the individual that, when war parties failed to contact the enemy and to obtain the necessary scalps, they sometimes killed members of their own tribe, whom they accidentally encountered on their way home, rather than return empty-handed and in disgrace. If none of the innocent victims lived to tell the tale, the murders might go down on the verbal record as valiant war deeds, but if the story got out, blood money or a life for a life would be demanded by the kinsmen of the murdered persons.

Motives for violence, therefore, were always multiple and mixed. The individual wished to enhance his personal prestige in the social hierarchy, and the band, village, or tribe wished to maintain its unity and independence as well as to improve its economic position. In addition to these general motives, desire for revenge was always present, and mere adventure should not be ruled out entirely. Although plunder in the form of weapons, food, clothing, furs, and other movables was generally taken in raids, this was not a major cause of hostilities, except possibly on the Plains, where horse-stealing was general. On the Prairies and in the East, where villages were the rule, more movable goods seem to have been destroyed by fire and other means than were carried away by the victors. The taking of captives was common in the East but was never a major cause of conflicts.

Armed clashes were more common between speakers of different languages than between speakers of the same language, but the latter were far from lacking, for there was emphasis in the tribal and confederational councils on keeping the peace within such linguistic units.

Anyone could lead a raiding party and membership in the party was on a voluntary basis. Some peoples insisted that a raiding expedition must be approved by the band, village, or tribal council, but others had no mechanism for preventing a raid against an enemy. A permanent war chief to lead war activities is reported for the Prairies and East, but this official always coexists with lay leaders and probably did not exist before White contact in these areas. Supernatural sanction for at least the leader or a shaman, obtained through dreams, was necessary before even the smallest raid would be undertaken. The authority of the lay leader, little as it was, ceased when the raid was over.

Probably all war parties of any size employed scouts and sentries in these areas. They communicated with signs, such as animal cries and smoke signals. The men were not divided neatly into squadrons, as in Mexico, nor was armament definitely divided, as among the River Yumans. The premium was placed on individual fighting with full use of the natural protection afforded by trees and rocks. The close formation of the colonial armies, as in Braddock's defeat, made them an easy prey to the individualism and open fighting of these Red men. The greater mobility of the Indian, both on foot and on horseback, and his ability to live off the country and to go for long periods without food and water made him a formidable foe for colonial, or later United States, troops. Fasting, before and during a fight, was the general rule for Indians, and they were psychologically hardened to discomfort to a degree never attained by our soldiers. As elsewhere north of Mexico, the surprise attack was the preferred method of the aggressors. Pitched battles were fought only when forces were large and when deception had failed.

Ceremonies before departing on a raid, and victory celebrations after returning, were general throughout all three areas. Women took part in the victory celebrations, sometimes dancing with or around scalps or other trophies.

Those who were mourning the death of a relative or close friend often helped promote, or joined, a war expedition. Often the motive was to avenge a life lost in a previous encounter at the expense of the particular enemy group involved; but deaths from disease and other natural causes sometimes gave rise to punitive expeditions directed at the first enemy group encountered. Because material possessions of the relatives, as well as those of the deceased, were often destroyed at a death, the raid was also a chance to even up the economic score with a little stealing from the vanquished. When a victorious war party returned, the scalps were often given to mourners, especially to women, to dry their tears, both literally with the hair and psychologically with the feeling that revenge had been achieved.

Although the civil chief and most other officers were committed to a policy of peace, they would never have been selected for these high positions without successful war records. It was only by demonstrated worth as a warrior that one was regarded as qualified to smooth ruffled tempers, settle disputes between litigants, and decide whether war or peace was to be chosen for the group when a crisis arose. The brash and ambitious young men would never have taken the advice of an old man who had had no experience in the thick of battle.

A successful war experience was also an occasion for bestowing a new name, reminiscent of the brave deed, on the warrior.

Plains.—Many writers on the Plains Indians of the nineteenth century have described their warfare as a game, but, while this was a prominent aspect of it, it was not the whole story. Many men were killed and whole war parties were sometimes wiped out by superior numbers. As the buffalo became progressively scarcer, the competition for good hunting territory, horses, and guns became keener; and as European trade goods came more and more to be used, the desire for these modern conveniences, obtained in exchange for buffalo hides, drove men to greater efforts.

All the Plains tribes had a set of graded war honors, such as coups, killing, scalping, stealing a fine horse from inside an enemy camp, or stealing a gun or magic shield. A coup meant merely touching an enemy without harming him but was done at the risk of one's own life. It is interesting to note that this harmless act often rated higher than killing or scalping. At the scalp dance following the return of a victorious war party, each warrior who had performed one of the honorific deeds told about it in public. This is called counting coup. Thereafter, as a young man accumulated new war honors, he would recount the old ones on appropriate public occasions. It was only the old men, with well-known records of past war honors and no new ones to add, who refrained from recounting coup again and again in public. In the absence of newspapers, radio, and television, this was the only way to keep the public informed about its great men. If a man lied about his war achievements, he could be challenged by anyone who had been on war parties with him.

The reciting of war exploits also served a function in intertribal affairs. Sometimes when two war parties of equal strength were drawn up in battle array, a single warrior would ride out between the lines singing his war songs and calling out his names received in honor of his brave deeds. After he had finished, his performance might be duplicated by a number of famous fighters from both sides with the result that the tension released in this manner sometimes prevented tempers from boiling over and precipitating actual hostilities.

Horse-stealing was a part of most raids on the Plains, and war parties frequently set out on foot to give themselves a greater incentive to steal enemy horses. Probably a hundred times as many horses were stolen on the Plains as were obtained in legitimate trade. Horses with Spanish brands were observed as far north as the Canadian border. In the nineteenth century the horse became the principal symbol of wealth and prestige and was the most common commodity traded for a wife.

East.—The war between the Iroquois and the Huron over the fur trade has already been described above (chapter xiii). Economic causes were paramount here, the death toll amounted to thousands of lives, and the Huron were eliminated as an independent tribe. This war took place in 1649, less than half a century after European contact. This suggests that, even though White contact was an incontestable contributing factor to the catastrophe, the Indians in this area already possessed the political and martial mechanism to make such a war possible. It could not have happened on the Pacific Coast so soon after Europeans settled there.

The Iroquoians and their neighbors settled disputes between kin groups, and even between tribes, with blood money in the form of the shell beads called *wampum*. Champlain recorded such a settlement between a Huron and an Algonquian band as early as 1615–18 (Champlain, 1619: 101–3). At meetings of the council of the League of the Iroquois, much emphasis was placed upon the cessation of strife within the league in order to present a united front to the outside, and *wampum* was one of the principal means of arriving at peace within the league. Although blood money was probably known here and there on the Plains and Prairies, it seems to have attained its greatest development in the East.

The most distinctive feature of the warfare pattern in the East as compared to other areas north of Mexico was the emphasis on the torture of prisoners. Most instances of torture on the Plains and Prairies seem to have been derived from the East in the historic period. Generally the prisoner was tied to a stake, frame, or platform, and tortured with fire, blows, mutilation, stabbing, shooting with arrows, or dismemberment while still alive. Such orgies lasted from a few hours to a few days, and the remains of the victim were often eaten in a cannibalistic feast. The prisoner might also be required to run the gauntlet. Two parallel rows of warriors lined up with clubs and sticks and beat the captive as he ran between them. If he survived this ordeal he might be given his freedom. Men, women, and children were taken as prisoners, but normally only men were tortured, at least in the large public spectacles. Because the terrific mortality from warfare left many widows, a young man captive might be taken as a husband and eventually adopted into the tribe. Older men prisoners were likely to be tortured to death, especially if the tattooing on their bodies suggested many successful war exploits, as it did in the Southeast. Women and children seem generally not to have been mutilated, but they were treated as slaves until married or until they were formally adopted into the tribe.

Sadism was very obtrusive in the torturing of prisoners, although the element of sacrifice to the supernatural was also present. The following account, from Le Jeune's relation of 1637, in the *Jesuit Relations,* is one of the most detailed and horrible on record; it refers to the torturing of an Iroquois prisoner by the Hurons.

Meanwhile the sun, which was fast declining, admonished us to withdraw to the place where this cruel Tragedy was to be enacted. It was in the cabin of one Atsan, who is the great war Captain. Therefore it is called "Otinotsiskiaj ondaon," meaning, "the house of cut-off heads." It is there all the Councils of war are held; as to the house where the affairs of the country, and those which relate only to the observance of order, are transacted, it is called "Endionrra Ondaon," "house of the Council." . . . Towards 8 o'clock in the evening, eleven fires were lighted along the cabin, about one brass distant from each other. The people gathered immediately, the old men taking places above, upon a sort of platform, which extends, on both sides, the entire length of the cabin. The young men were below, but were so crowded that they were almost piled upon one another, so that there was hardly a passage along the fires. Cries of joy resounded on all sides; each provided himself, one with a firebrand, another with a piece of bark, to burn the victim. Before he was brought in, the Captain Aenons encouraged all to do their duty, representing to them the importance of this act, which was viewed, he said, by the Sun and by the God of war. He ordered that at first they should burn only his legs, so that he might hold out until daybreak; also for that night they were not to go and amuse themselves in the woods. He had hardly finished when the victim entered. I leave you to imagine the terror that seized him at the sight of these preparations. The cries redoubled at his arrival; he is made to sit down upon a mat, his hands are bound, then he rises and makes a tour of the cabin singing and dancing; no one burns him this time, but also this is the limit of his rest—one can hardly tell what he will endure up to the time when they cut off his head. He had no sooner returned to his place when the war Captain took his robe and said, "Oteiondi"—speaking of a Captain—"will despoil him of the robe which I hold"; and added, "The Atachonchronons will cut off his head, which will be given to Ondessone, with one arm and the liver to make a feast." Behold his sentence thus pronounced. After this each one armed himself with a brand, or a piece of burning bark, and he began to walk, or rather to run, around the fires; each one struggled to burn him as he passed. Meanwhile, he shrieked like a lost soul; the whole crowd imitated his cries, or rather smothered them with horrible shouts. One must be there, to see a living picture of Hell. The whole cabin appeared as if on fire; and, althwart [*sic*] the flames and dense smoke that issued therefrom, these barbarians—crowding one upon the other, howling at the top of their voices, with firebrands in their hands, their eyes flashing with rage and fury—seemed like so many demons who would give no respite to this poor wretch. They often stopped him at the other end of the cabin, some of them taking his hands and breaking the bones thereof by sheer force; others pierced his ears with sticks which they left in them; others bound his wrists with cords which they tied roughly, pulling at each end of the cord with all their might. Did he make the round and pause for a little breath, he was made to repose upon hot ashes and burning coals. . . . But God permitted that on the seventh round of the cabin his strength should fail him. After he had reposed a short time upon the embers, they tried to make him rise as usual, but he did not stir; and one of these butchers having applied a brand to his loins, he was seized with a fainting fit, and would never have risen again if the young men had been permitted to have their way, for they had already begun to stir up the fire about him, as if to burn him. But the Captains prevented them from going any farther, and ordered them to cease tormenting him, saying it was important that he should see the daylight. They had him lifted upon a mat, most of the fires were extinguished, and many of the people went away. Now there was a little respite for our sufferer, and some consolation for us. . . . While he was in this condition, their only thought was to make him return to his senses, giving him many drinks composed of pure water only. At the end of an hour he began to revive a little, and to open his eyes; he was forthwith commanded to sing. He did this at first in a broken and, as it were, dying voice; but finally he sang so loud that he could be heard outside the cabin. The youth assembled again; they talk to him, they make him sit up—in a word they begin to act worse than before. For me to describe in detail all he endured during the rest of the night, would be almost impossible; we suffered enough in forcing ourselves to see a part of it. . . .

As soon as day began to dawn, they lighted fires outside the village, to display there the excess of their cruelty, to the sight of the Sun. The victim was lead thither. . . . Meanwhile, two of them took hold of him and made him mount a scaffold 6 or 7 feet high; 3 or 4 of these barbarians followed him. They tied him to a tree which passed across it, but in such a way he was free to turn around. There they began to burn him more cruelly than ever, leaving no part of his body to which fire was not applied at intervals. When one of these butchers began to burn him and to crowd him closely, in trying to escape him, he fell into the hands of another who gave him no better reception. From time to time they were supplied with new brands, which they thrust, all aflame, down his throat, even forcing them into his fundament. They burned his eyes; they applied red-hot hatchets to his shoulders; they hung some around his neck, which they turned now upon his back, now upon his breast, according to the position he took in order to avoid the weight of this burden. If he attempted to sit or crouch down, someone thrust a brand from under the scaffolding which soon caused him to arise. . . . They so harassed him upon all sides that they finally put him out of breath; they poured water into his mouth to strengthen his heart, and the Captains called out to him that he should take a little breath. But he remained still, his mouth open, and almost motionless. Therefore, fearing that he would die otherwise than by the knife, one cut off a foot, another a hand, and almost at the same time a third severed the head from the shoulders, throwing it into the crowd, where someone caught it to carry it to the Captain Ondessone, for whom it had been reserved, in order to make a feast therewith. As for the trunk, it remained at Arontaen, where a feast was made of it the same day. . . . On the way [home] we encountered a Savage who was carrying upon a skewer one of his half-roasted hands. (Thwaites, 1897–1901, XIII, 59–79.)

HUMAN SACRIFICE AND CANNIBALISM

Southeastern coastal plain.—Along the Gulf from Louisiana to Florida and then up the Atlantic Coast to Virginia, chiefs had absolute authority over their subjects, including the power of life and death. In this area men were compelled to serve in the armed forces; they had no choice in the matter. The war leader was the chief himself or a lieutenant appointed by him. Scalps or heads taken in battle were treated primarily as sacrificial offerings by the tribe to the supernatural rather than as appeasers of individual grief or as symbols of individual war achievement. They were kept in or near temples. It also seems likely that true slavery existed in this area, that war prisoners were sometimes kept as slaves for the remainder of their lives. The tendons in the feet of captives were sometimes cut so that they could not run fast enough to escape.

Human sacrifice of members of the in-group, as well as the sacrifice of war prisoners, has also been reported for this region. Wives and slaves were also killed at the death of a chief so that they might accompany him to the afterworld. Such sacrifice was also thought to appease the wrath of powerful spirits. Men sacrificed their own children at public spectacles to gain favor of the chief and be raised to the rank of nobility. These sacrifices were generally independent of the fortunes of war; they were held annually by some tribes but only when catastrophe struck among others. They were more closely associated with religion than with war, although the two were interrelated. Sacrificial victims were not tortured, but were killed quickly and efficiently; nor was cannibalism practiced on their remains.

The Pawnee Indians of Nebraska were the only other people north of Mexico to practice human sacrifice. Although they were located outside the southeastern coastal plain in the historic period, they speak a language related to that of the Hasinai (the westernmost member of the coastal plain peoples) and show other evidences of having formerly lived in the Southeast. They used to sacrifice a maiden of their own tribe by tying her to a rectangular frame and shooting her with arrows.

Circum-Caribbean.—In the last chapter we noted tribes and states in this area numbering their populations in the thousands and tens of thousands, led by hereditary chiefs or kings with the power of life and death over all subjects. These political units had armies numbering in the thousands and even occasionally including women in the ranks. Warfare offered the individual four ways of increasing his rank: (1) the augmentation of the number of his wives with captive women; (2) the acquisition of prisoners of both sexes who became his slaves; (3) the furnishing of war captives for cannibalistic feasts to which important people were invited; (4) the acquisition of titles and the display of insignia associated with war. The titles usually reflected the number of enemy slain and the insignia in some localities showed to which of several graded military classes a man belonged, much as do insignia on our own military uniforms.

Cannibalism was sometimes limited to eating only a certain part of a victim, such as the heart, but elsewhere most of the body might be consumed. Body parts of slain enemies were often displayed as war trophies, either in the public square before or within a temple, or at the home of the slayer. Skulls, hands, feet, teeth, and the entire skin stuffed with ashes or straw were common trophies. At least one tribe made flutes of human arm and leg bones.

Human sacrifice was common in the Circum-Caribbean area. A few peoples sacrificed their own citizens, but the majority used prisoners of war. The purpose of these sacrifices varied from one religion to another: to honor or appease idols and sacred mountains; to insure success in war; to effect cures of the sick; to insure agricultural fertility by offering human blood to the fields; to provide hearts to be worshipped as gods; to appease the sun, especially during droughts; to obtain ghosts to guard family idols; and to supply the dead with servants in the afterworld.

Warfare was well integrated with social organization and religion, as in the Plains, Prairies, and East.

ECONOMIC CONQUEST AND HUMAN SACRIFICE

Meso-America.—This area, with a population greater than that of all other culture areas combined and states with citizens numbered in the tens and hundreds of thousands, possessed huge armies divided into a hierarchy of subdivisions and carried on military campaigns of far greater magnitude than those of any other area. Two motives for warfare stand out above all others: to enhance

379

the national economy by exacting tribute from the conquered peoples; to obtain prisoners for sacrifices to the gods. An individual's rank and wealth in the society was determined principally by the number of captives he took in battle, although as he grew older other qualifications played some part. Insults to or ill-treatment of the Aztec itinerant merchants (see p. 239) was a frequent precipitator of hostilities. Because the Aztecs were the dominant military power at the time the Spanish appeared, their war machine is subject to more detailed description.

Every able-bodied male over fifteen years of age, except civil officials and priests, was technically a member of the army, although it is not likely that the entire male population was ever mobilized at one time. They were all subject to call like our national guard or officer's reserve units. At an early age every boy was taught the use of the bow and arrow and the spear-thrower. At fifteen years of age all boys, except those training for the priesthoods, went to live in boarding schools, called houses of youth, where they were taught the art of war, along with other subjects. There were twenty such schools in Mexico City (Tenochtitlán), one for each deme. Every twenty days there occurred a religious festival in which the warriors appeared in full costume and engaged in sham battles. The youths were required to attend such performances to learn all they could about war.

Weapons were kept in arsenals called "houses of darts," the dart-thrower and dart being the principal weapon of the army. Stewards in charge of these arsenals handed out the weapons for sham battles and target practice as well as for actual warfare. In addition to the dart-thrower and darts, the bow and arrow and the sling were used to launch projectiles. The obsidian-edged sword and clubs were used for hand-to-hand fighting. For defense every warrior carried a shield made of quilted cotton over a cane frame and wore a tunic of quilted cotton on his body. Warriors of rank wore wooden helmets carved to represent ferocious beasts such as jaguars, wolves, and rattlesnakes, and the highest military officers added brilliant feathers to the tops of their helmets. Rank was indicated by the style of haircut as well as by regalia and insignia worn on the body.

The army was subdivided into a hierarchy of units of varying sizes, like modern armies. The largest subdivision, called the brigade by us, included the entire fighting force of one of the four quarters of Tenochtitlán. Each brigade was divided into regiments called minor quarters, and each minor quarter was divided into companies of two hundred to four hundred men, each company in turn into platoons of twenty men and, on the eve of battle, the platoons were further divided into squads of four to six men. Some of these smaller units were made up from kin groups, such as demes and patrilocal extended families. Each military unit was distinguished from the others by the color of the feather overlay on the tunics or by some other conspicuous mark.

There were two main classes of officers: the war chiefs and the lesser officers. The former commanded entire armies, brigades, and regiments; the latter led companies, platoons, and squads. All officers won their rank wholly on merit; heredity played no part. The chiefs were elected by the junior officers or the social units they represented, while the lesser officers won their positions by capturing the enemy in battle. Both classes of officers were apparently divided into three grades each, corresponding to the different sizes of units they commanded, making a total of about six grades of officers and six sizes of military units. The chiefs apparently did not fight regularly in the ranks, but the lesser officers, like our lieutenants, sergeants, and corporals, led their men in the thick of the fight. These fighting lesser officers were called "fierce cutters" or "beasts of prey," "strong eagles" or "old eagles," and "wandering arrows."

When a dispute arose between the Aztecs and a neighboring nation, the former sent a foreign minister (comparable to the Secretary of State in the United States) and other delegates to the neighboring nation to negotiate the amount of tribute to be paid. If the other nation agreed to the demands of the Aztecs, the delegates returned home laden with gifts and all was well. If the nation refused to pay the tribute requested, the Aztec delegates stepped up to the commander-in-chief of the enemy army, anointed his arms with white paint, placed feathers on his head, and gave him a shield and a sword. This was a formal declaration of war. After war was declared, the Aztecs notified their allies to muster troops and meet the Aztec army at certain localities and then advanced

381

against the foe. Sometimes, however, the Aztecs made surprise attacks without formal declaration of war.

Although the Aztecs possessed by far the most formidable military organization in North America at the time of the Spanish conquest of Mexico, they fell an easy prey to the Spaniards. The reasons for this are multiple. The purely military shortcomings of the Aztecs were their failure to concentrate sufficient numbers of men at a critical spot in a battle, inability to sustain an assault by sending in fresh troops when needed, and an armament inferior to that of the Spanish, who employed cross-bows with iron-pointed arrows, guns, and even cannon. Perhaps more important was the fear and awe which the Spanish inspired in the Aztecs. Their myths of White gods prevented them from understanding the true motives of the Spaniards, and their belief in the beginning that a man on a horse was a two-headed monster struck terror in their hearts. They had never before witnessed anything like the amount of slaughter that the Spanish inflicted on them. In their own system of warfare the taking of a prisoner far outranked killing him in battle, and casualties seem to have been light. And when Cortez' men killed Montezuma and other high-ranking leaders, there was no ready mechanism for replacing them. Men accustomed to obey did not suddenly begin to command. We must remember that the Spanish had been fighting the Moors almost continuously from A.D. 711 to 1492. Almost 800 years of military experience with the best armament and competition in the world at that time had made the Spanish a formidable foe for any force. The Aztecs were no match for them.

CONCLUSIONS

There is no connection between the size of military operations and the amount of human suffering and mortality from violence. Mortality by violence was apparently as high among the Eskimo as anywhere, and human suffering under torture was rampant among the simple Chichimecs. Both of these peoples lacked true political organization and their fights, raids, and feuds can scarcely be labeled war. The huge war machine of the Aztecs probably inflicted no more pain and death per capita than the duels of the simplest cultures, even though twenty thousand captives are said to have been sacrificed at the dedication of a single Aztec temple.

The correlation between size of political unit and size of military operation is too obtrusive to require more than mere mention here.

Population density (Map 6) shows some association with the size of the war operation. Areas with dense population had larger armies and bigger battles than those with sparse populations. However, for the areas north of Mexico, the Pacific Coast was more densely populated than the Atlantic Coast, and yet the size of the military machine was less on the Pacific Coast than on the Atlantic Coast. This was also true of the size of the political unit, as was pointed out in the last chapter.

Of the motives behind violence, raids, and wars, the economic factor seems to be more obtrusive than some text writers in anthropology admit. In order to call the attention of the reader to the game aspect of war, the function of war as a ranker of men and creator of social solidarity within the political unit, and the religious functions of war, some anthropologists have depreciated the economic aspect. Economic motives were probably most obtrusive in Meso-America and on the Northwest Coast, but they can also be found in most other areas. Although the desire for material wealth north of Mexico was stepped up by trade with Europeans, the response to the new opportunity would not have been so rapid if the Indian cultures had not already possessed a considerable interest in acquiring possessions. Even the least competitive individuals, bands, and tribes were forced to acquire steel traps, guns, or horses, in order to survive at all in the new system. Motives for violence and war seem normally to have been multiple and mixed. Although one or two appear to dominate the others in this or that area, the others were also present. The difference from one area to another seems to be a matter of frequency and, if fuller information existed, one might tabulate the frequencies of each principal cause of hostilities for each clash of each tribe and produce a sort of box score on the causes of war.

The pattern of warfare in a particular region is partly determined by contacts with peoples on the outside and by the ideas and values derived from these contacts. For example, the torture

383

of prisoners or their sacrifice to the supernatural, as well as cannibalism, occur in a continuous area from the Iroquoians in the northeast to the Gulf tribes in the southeast, thence south through Northeast Mexico to Meso-America and the Caribbean. For instance, both the Iroquois and the Aztecs adopted a prisoner before killing him, sometimes calling him by a kinship term. The methods of killing, as summarized by Knowles (1940), show much in common between the East and Meso-America. It is true that the Aztec sacrificial victim sometimes impersonated a god and lived in luxury before his death, but the religious facet of torture in the East was by no means lacking. The coastal plain in the Southeast is also reminiscent of the Circum-Caribbean in many respects, and its warfare pattern is no exception to this rule.

There is no reason to believe that the warfare syndrome of the Meso-Americans or, for that matter, the Incas of Peru, was derived from the Old World before A.D. 1492. Although there may have been some trans-Pacific contact between South America and Oceania, as postulated in the chapter on Horticulture, a few boat loads of people with samples of domesticated plants would not be likely to exert much influence on the political organization and warfare systems of the New World. Therefore, it seems likely that war could and did arise independently in the Old and New Worlds. However, the greed, cupidity, deceit, and utter disregard of Indian life on the part of most of the European conquerors surpassed anything of the kind that the Indian cultures had been able to produce on their own in their thousands of years of virtual independence from the Old World.

REFERENCES

BANDELIER, 1877; BEALS, 1932a; CHAMPLAIN, 1619; CODERE, 1951; COOK, 1946; DRUCKER, 1955; ELLIS, 1951; FARMER, 1957; HADLOCK, 1947; HOEBEL, 1940, 1941; HONIGMAN, 1946; HUNT, 1940; JENNESS, 1932; KNOWLES, 1940; KROEBER, 1925, 1932; LAS CASAS, 1944 [1574]; LINTON, 1944; LIPS, 1947; LOWIE, 1940, 1954; NADEAU, 1944; NEUMANN, 1940; NEWCOMB, 1950; OSGOOD, 1936, 1937; RAY, 1939; SAHAGÚN (Anderson and Dibble), 1950–58; SALAS, 1947; SECOY, 1953; SMITH, MARIAN W., 1938, 1951; SNYDERMAN, 1948; STEWARD, 1938, 1948; STEWART, 1947; SWANTON, 1946; THWAITES, 1897–1901.

19: Rank and Social Classes

Although American Indian societies were more democratic on the whole than those of Africa and Oceania, there were, nevertheless, marked differences in status and rank in some areas and true social classes in a smaller number. All societies in the world recognize the simple fact that some people can perform a certain task better than others, that one man is a better hunter than another, or that one woman is a better weaver than another. American Indians were no exception to this rule and were well aware of individual differences within societies.

The term "status" refers to the social position of an individual with respect to other members of his society. It may be based on a single attribute, several attributes, or on all the attributes of which a particular society is aware. In all societies each individual possesses a multiple number of statuses simultaneously. For example, in our own society a man may be an absent-minded professor, a golfer, a member of the masonic lodge, and a book salesman during the summer vacation period.

Statuses may or may not be ranked from high to low. Thus the carpenter, stone mason, plumber, electrician, and plasterer occupy different statuses in the building trades, but they all earn about the same wages and are of approximately the same rank in our society. The architect or the engineer, however, would out-rank the laborer in the building business as a whole. Among some Indian societies, statuses tended to be unranked, while in others they were very meticulously ranked from highest to lowest. The basis of rank might be proficiency, wealth, social heredity, supernatural sanction, or some combination of a number of such criteria.

Social classes are said to exist in a society when the entire population can be grouped, according to statuses and rank, into a limited number of units, such as nobles, commoners, and slaves. A society with social classes, then, must possess an explicit number of criteria for pigeon-holing individuals, and there must be breaks somewhere in the continuum where boundaries can be drawn between one class and another. Ideally, all statuses present in a particular society should be employed in allocating a given individual to one social class or another but, in practice, a few tend to be emphasized more than others. There must be a minimum of two social classes in a class society; a one-class system would not differentiate the members.

MINIMAL DEVELOPMENT OF STATUS AND RANK

There are several culture areas in native North America where differences in status, other than those based on sex and age, and differences in rank were at the minimum. These areas are Central and Eastern Arctic, Mackenzie and Eastern Sub-Arctic, Great Basin, and Northeast Mexico. These are the now familiar areas where life was hardest, the land least productive, and population (Map 6) sparsest. None of these peoples farmed. These areas also possessed no, or few, part-time craft specialists (Map 28), and certainly no full-time craft specialists. In these regions a man was a jack of nearly all masculine trades and a woman was equally experienced in nearly all feminine tasks. These areas also lacked true political organization and organized warfare.

At the same time, differences of ability within each sex were recognized; some men were regarded as better hunters than others and some women were admitted to be better at household tasks than others, but there was not the slightest notion that such aptitudes were hereditary. Leadership, weak as it was, tended to be vested in the most capable man, regardless of ancestry, and this man was followed only as long as he continued to demonstrate his superior skills and judgment. Social classes could not possibly develop in regions with so little differentiation in status and rank and, as might be anticipated, they were completely absent.

NORTHWEST COAST SYSTEM

All the peoples on the Northwest Coast shared a system of rank based on a combination of wealth and heredity. As pointed out in chapter xiv, the most productive parts of both the land and the sea were owned nominally by individuals but were exploited by kinship groups. On the death of the nominal owner, the title to the real estate always went to a surviving kinsman and the same kinship group continued to use it in the same manner as it had done before the death of the first nominal owner. Much movable property was also owned and used by kinship groups in the same way. Incorporeal property in all its forms was likewise shared and inherited. Social position, then, was based on the value of the corporeal and incorporeal forms of wealth and the hereditary titles that went with them.

Two distinct social classes were to be found everywhere on the Northwest Coast: freemen and slaves. The following account of the status of slaves refers to the dominant pattern over most of the coast, but does not apply to a small area in northwest California and southwest Oregon, which will be treated in a separate paragraph. Slaves were obtained by taking prisoners in raids, but once slave status was established, the slave could be bought or sold, either from one society to another or from one freeman to another within the same society. The owner had the power of life and death over his slave, and slaves were sometimes killed on the following occasions: at the death of the owner; at a potlatch, as destruction of wealth to show that the owner could afford it; at the building of a new house, in the form of a foundation sacrifice; and at performances of the cannibal society of some of the British Columbia peoples, who actually ate part of the corpse. Slave-killing was much more common in Alaska and British Columbia than in Washington and Oregon and was totally lacking in California. However, slaves were sometimes freed at the death of an owner in the same areas where killing was permitted, showing variation within societies in this respect. Slaves were released for ransom if their kinsmen could raise the price, although in a few localities the stigma attached to slavery was so great that even the slave's closest relatives did not want him around after he had been for a time in this lowest status, and they refused to redeem him. In the north, where matrilineal descent prevailed and kinship ties were strongest, slaves were generally ransomed by kinsmen and the stigma removed by a purification ceremony.

Slaves were treated almost as well as the lowest-ranking free-men in some localities, but in others they were compelled to do the most menial work, to eat inferior food, and at death were denied normal burial by being cast into the sea. Slaves could sometimes be distinguished by head shape (see pp. 138–39), by haircut, or by the presence or absence of items of clothing or bodily decoration. In general a man could have sexual relations with a female slave, and, in the parts of the area where rules were not so strict, he sometimes married her after a purification ceremony to remove her stigma. This would never have been done in the matrilineal area in the north, and elsewhere the children of such a union acquired some stigma. Slaves were allowed to marry each other in most localities, but their children usually remained slaves, thus showing that slavery was hereditary. However, such children were sometimes adopted by free people and thus raised to the rank of the free.

In a small area in southwestern Oregon and northwestern California only debt slavery prevailed. The master owned only the services of the slave, and could not kill or abuse him in any way, nor did he possess the right of concubinage over a female slave. Slaves were sold only rarely. The slave worked as a sort of serf or bond servant for his master at the same tasks as freemen and was fed and housed in the same manner as a member of his master's family, although he slept nearest the door in the lowest-ranking place within the house. Debts were incurred by such infringements of the legal code as striking another person, destroying his property, swearing at him, or speaking the name of one of his dead relatives. If a person were rescued from drowning, he owed a debt to his rescuer, and sometimes a gambling debt could not be paid. A slave, therefore, was a person who did not possess the money to meet his financial obligations, but since these were most often incurred for wrong-doing there was some stigma attached to the status. Normally the debt slave was ransomed by his own kinsmen whenever they could raise the money.

Debt slaves are also reported sporadically all along the Northwest Coast. Inability to repay a loan, as well as gambling debts, was sufficient to relegate a person to this status. As elsewhere, the debt slave was normally ransomed by relatives, and was never equated to the true slave described in detail above.

In respect to differences in rank of freemen, all anthropologists agree that most freemen were carefully ranked from highest to lowest according to wealth and heredity. The two always went hand in hand because the most valuable kinds of property were inherited. Freemen were carefully scaled according to rank at potlatch feasts in four ways: they were seated, served, and given presents to take home in order of rank, and the value of the present was correlated with the order of rank (see page 226). Because the same persons attended many potlatches every year, this carefully calibrated order of rank was confirmed publicly again and again.

Occasionally disputes arose over who outranked whom, and occasionally the order was changed by some sudden stroke of good or bad fortune befalling a person, but changes seem to have been few before White contact. The most productive parts of the landscape and seascape were all owned by kinship groups and nominally by individuals, so that there was no easy way to increase one's wealth and position. However, a man who was an unusually skilled canoe-maker, mask-carver, or warrior might be given a title and its associated privileges by his chief. Such privileges might include a title of "war chief," the right to use a special crest, or the exclusive right to some good fishing place. Sometimes the chief would give the title and privileges directly to a man's heirs. A man might also acquire titled status more directly by capturing real estate or killing a titled man in a raid, by accepting a title as repayment on a debt, or by receiving a title as repayment of a bride price.

After White contact, mobility in rank increased through two principal causes: increased economic opportunities which made the acquisition of wealth easier; and a sharp decline in population by death from European diseases and firearms. The value of sea otter fur skyrocketed to previously unheard of figures, and later the furs of land animals showed a parallel increase, with the result that an industrious man could get rich in a few years as an independent businessman or as a hired hand on a sealing schooner. With the wealth accumulated in this way he could return home to give a big potlatch to raise his rank or that of his heirs. Because titles had been vacated by the sharp increase in mortality, it was easy to find a title and to validate it at a potlatch feast.

389

At the present time anthropologists disagree on the question of the existence or non-existence of social classes among freemen on the Northwest Coast. This confusion is the result both of variation from one village or tribelet to another and of changes after White contact. Within some tribelets all free individuals seem to have possessed titles and privileges of some sort, so that no line can be drawn on this basis. However, there were other tribelets whose members formed two distinguishable classes: nobles, those who had titles, and commoners, those who did not.

In British Columbia and in southeastern Alaska there were secret societies of limited membership which divided freemen into members and non-members. Those of highest rank in the potlatch system were of highest rank in the secret society system. Every ritual act in the ceremonies performed by these societies was individually owned, and ceremonies could be witnessed only by members. This is in sharp contrast to the potlatch system in which every freeman was allowed to participate in some capacity. These secret societies also terrorized and even murdered non-members for inadvertently overhearing or seeing any part of the secret ritual, and even members who revealed secrets were killed. The society members, who were all regarded as shamans, sometimes engaged in sorcery against a non-member in order to make him sick, so that they could collect the fee for curing him. From these facts it seems clear that these native cultures drew a line of demarcation between freemen who were members and freemen who were non-members of these secret societies and that the members were the ranking group.

Another criterion for differentiating two groups of freemen is found in southwestern Oregon and northwestern California, where a custom known as half-marriage prevailed. A man who could not afford the full bride price made a substantial down payment on his wife and went to live with her family and worked for her father for the remainder of the payment. Those who could raise the full bride price took their wives to their own homes (also their fathers' homes) and were not required to undergo any period of work for their brides. A census taken in the early part of this century among the Yurok revealed that about 25 per cent of the marriages were half-marriages with matrilocal residence and 75 per cent were full marriages with patrilocal residence. In a culture which places as great an emphasis on wealth as that of the Yurok, no man who could raise a full bride payment would ever be content with an agreement for part payment and a servant's position among his wife's family. It is therefore obvious that the half-married men were of lower rank on the average than the full married men, although conceivably a part payment on an expensive bride might come to more than a full payment on a cheaper one. We thus have found a way of differentiating Yurok men into two groups according to wealth and rank, but the wives and children have a confused status because their value is determined by the total amount of the bride price, not whether it was paid in cash, or part in cash and the rest in labor. This twofold classification of men, therefore, is hardly sufficient to establish social classes for this region.

SYSTEMS ADJACENT TO NORTHWEST COAST

Plateau.—Most peoples on the Plateau took prisoners in war, but these were few in number and were more often women and children than men. Such so-called slaves lived like the poorer classes in these societies and were normally adopted or assimilated into the tribelet in due course. Women especially could gain full status quickly by marrying their captors, bearing children, and otherwise playing the role of a wife. However, the peoples from about the Columbia River south to the Klamath and Modoc on the Oregon-California border engaged in captive-motivated raids for the express purpose of obtaining prisoners to sell at the slave market at The Dalles. The Dalles is a fifteen-mile stretch of rapids on the Columbia River which blocks navigation in both directions and therefore became a trading center for all kinds of movable property. Some of these Oregon peoples got their first horses by exchanging slaves for them. Slaves sold at The Dalles were resold later to peoples living as far north as the Canadian border. Trade slaves were held in lower esteem than those captured in war, but they were rarely abused or killed and could still be ransomed by relatives. A trade slave was often exchanged for a wife, a good slave being regarded as of equal value to a wife. Slavery on the Plateau was, therefore, of a borderline variety which gave rise to a separate social class only in the part of the region where slaves

391

were traded. It was obviously derived from the Northwest Coast, and most of it was probably post-European.

Distinctions in rank and wealth among freemen were marked only in the western part of the Plateau adjacent to the Northwest Coast, and the evidence points also to the recency of such notions. On the whole, the Plateau was as democratic as any culture area in native North America, and nothing like social classes existed there. The eastern peoples likewise acquired in recent times the ranking system, based on war record, of the Plains tribes, but whatever status of this kind the individual acquired was not passed on to his descendants, and nothing remotely approaching social classes developed there. A more detailed description of the Plains system will be given below.

Yukon Sub-Arctic.—Only those peoples closest to the Northwest Coast possessed true slaves, which were obtained from the coast in trade. They were few in number but were sometimes sacrificed at the death of their owner, and their children tended to remain slaves. War captives were mostly women and children, who were assimilated into the society of their captors, but occasionally young men were also taken in raids and treated as menials until their loyalty to their captors was demonstrated by participation in a later armed clash on the side of their masters. As mentioned above in the chapter on war, plunder was a more obtrusive motive for raids than in the Mackenzie or Eastern Sub-Arctic, and the tendency to rank all men according to wealth was also stronger. This interest in wealth and rank was obviously derived from contact with Northwest Coast peoples. However, freemen were nowhere differentiated into social classes.

Western Arctic.—These Eskimo were strongly influenced by Northwest Coast cultures and shared with them considerable emphasis on wealth and rank. They captured women and children in raids but assimilated them into the society of the captors. Enemy men were killed, not enslaved, and trade slaves were unknown.

California.—In the California culture area there was a weak and vague ranking of men according to wealth, from the border of the Northwest Coast area south at least to the Yokuts. There was a little debt slavery in the extreme northwest, and those peoples nearest the Klamath and Modoc were captured by them and taken

392

north for sale at The Dalles, but these exceptions were the result of border contacts and did not amount to a system of slavery for the California area. In chapter xvii we mentioned that all the Yokuts tribelets had several officers including that of chief, each of which was confined to a lineage. In other words these were hereditary offices which passed from an incumbent to some lineage mate, normally a younger brother or a son. Those who belonged to one of these lineages enjoyed a little more prestige than those who did not, especially in the case of the chief's lineage. The word for chief, *tiya*, was applied not only to the chief but also to all the mature members of his lineage, sometimes including even women. As already mentioned in chapter xvii, chiefs and shamans sometimes colluded to force a recalcitrant citizen to chip in his share of the food and money needed for a festival. Thus there was a correlation between authority, prestige, heredity, and wealth, but it was much weaker than on the Northwest Coast.

It is obvious from these brief descriptions of status and rank in the areas adjacent to the Northwest Coast, that the tremendous emphasis on rank in that coastal area fades out rapidly in all directions as one leaves the area. In the Mackenzie Sub-Arctic, the central Plateau, and the Great Basin, it disappears entirely in favor of a sweeping egalitarianism. Another center of rank and prestige, which seems to be totally independent of that on the North Pacific Coast, is found in Meso-America.

COMPLEX SYSTEMS OF MESO-AMERICA

In Meso-America a number of native states possessed complex systems of social rank based on multiple kinds of achievement and, to a lesser extent, on heredity. The early Spanish chroniclers, saturated as they were with knowledge of the hereditary classes of Europe, described these systems with the same terms they applied to European class structure. Although hereditary monarchs and the royal lineages from which they stemmed emerge with some clarity, the hereditary character of the lower ranks is open to doubt. The acquisition of rank by achievement, especially in warfare, is much more obtrusive in the literature than are descriptions of hereditarily tight compartments ascribed to the individual at birth. Although modern scholars may be divided over the precise

393

number of social classes, they agree that the Meso-American systems of status and rank were based on many more criteria and were otherwise much more complex than those of any other culture area in native North America. The Aztecs, Huastecs, Totonacs, Zapotecs, and Mayas all possessed complicated systems of rank and social classes, and the Tarascans and Mixtecs had at least three social classes each. Because material on the Aztecs is fullest, they will provide the basis of description here.

The Aztecs had a system of slavery reminiscent of the debt slavery of the Northwest Coast, but certainly independent historically as well as geographically. Wrongs short of capital offenses might be atoned for by the offender's service as a slave, either to the person he had harmed or to the one who happened to discover him at some forbidden act. Thieves, minor traitors, and indigents who were hungry became slaves, and gamblers sold themselves or their children to pay gambling debts or to acquire a new stake to keep on gambling after they had lost everything. That this was not typical slavery is brought out clearly by the fact that a slave could himself own the services of another slave. Slaves normally owned their own homes and could not be sold to another master without their consent. Masters on their deathbeds often liberated slaves, but if this were not done, the slave was inherited by the deceased's heirs. Children of slaves were free, proving that the status was not ascribed to them at birth but was determined by behavior.

Often a family in financial distress would sell a boy as a slave and, after a certain period, send a younger brother as a substitute. If a slave died while working for his master the arrangement ceased and it was not necessary to send a substitute, but if he died on his own time at home, his family was compelled to provide a successor. Frequently a master or mistress married a slave, raising him to the ranks of the free. A slave could also be freed by being ransomed by relatives or by accumulating the price of the ransom himself. Freedom could also be gained by reaching the asylum of the royal residence.

Slaves worked at routine tasks, such as farming for men and housework for women, and seem to have been fed and housed as well as the lower classes of free men. What the slave lost was his opportunity to increase his rank by achievement in the society, because he became ineligible for public office, in both civil and military affairs. Slaves, therefore, may be regarded as a separate social class.

The four highest positions in the government were obtained by election from the council of state, but in practice the newly elected individual always belonged to the same paternal lineage as his predecessor, thus making the office partly hereditary. It is important to note that this heredity never crystallized into primogeniture, ultimogeniture, preference of son over brother, or any other precise system. We may concede, however, the presence of royal lineages at the top of the scale and label them a distinct social class.

The intermediate social classes between royalty and slaves are not as clear as the two extremes, but the following scheme has been worked out by Murdock (1934). Below the class of royalty stood a class of nobles (*tecutin*) who originally achieved their rank for outstanding service in warfare, trade (itinerant merchants, page 239), civil office, or the priesthood. These nobles were allowed to wear cotton clothing, as distinguished from the maguey fiber of the commoner, as well as ornaments of gold and precious stones and special insignia to denote their rank. Along with the royalty, these men received the major portion of the tribute pouring in from defeated neighboring nations as well as taxes from commoners within their own society. Because movable property was inherited patrilineally, these nobles passed on their wealth to their sons, who thus acquired at least some of the rank achieved by their fathers. Huge tracts of conquered lands were distributed to the most deserving nobles in high office as a reward for their services to the nation and, although the land was passed on to the next holder of the office, the tendency to elect a son to succeed his father increased to the point that land was virtually inherited from father to son.

Below the nobles stood the commoners, and below the commoners a propertyless proletariat class. The latter were the ne'er-do-wells who refused to marry and till their lands and had thereby forfeited their deme membership; they worked as porters, farm laborers, and at undistinguished routine crafts. The commoners were by far the largest group, and individuals within this class could raise themselves in rank by determined effort in war, crafts, or trade, even though their chances of moving into the class of nobles were less in A.D. 1500 than a century earlier. Each married male was apportioned a plot of land by the deme, and he could either till it himself or rent it to another until his death, when it passed to a son. He could not sell the land, however, and it reverted to the deme for reapportionment if he had no heirs. He also had to pay taxes in goods to the nobles in his deme.

The Aztecs thus appear to have had a system of about five major social classes, with an indefinite number of subdivisions of nobles and commoners, and with some mobility possible in either direction at the time of the Spanish conquest. A century earlier there were probably fewer social classes but more social mobility, especially in an upward direction. Because the Aztecs were latecomers to the Valley of Mexico from the northwest, where cultures were simpler, those peoples of longer residence in Meso-America seem to have had clearer concepts of hereditary kings and nobility. The Aztecs, therefore, appear to have acquired their trend in this direction partly from contact with earlier peoples in Meso-America rather than wholly from internal factors in Aztec society.

SYSTEMS DERIVED IN PART FROM MESO-AMERICA

Circum-Caribbean.—In chapters xvii and xviii we have already mentioned hereditary chiefs or kings, the means by which a man could acquire rank as a warrior, and the presence of a slave class around the Caribbean. There is little doubt that the hereditary chiefs or kings formed a separate royal class. In addition to the special privileges already listed, these monarchs were given elaborate burial rites not accorded other members of the society. Their bodies were disemboweled, drained of blood, and dried over a fire until sufficiently "mummified" to withstand the humid climate. Then they were buried in tombs, sometimes in mounds, seated on royal stools with the bodies of sacrificed wives and slaves nearby. Sometimes their bodies were kept in temples instead of being buried; and sometimes they were cremated and the ashes, mixed with *chicha* (native beer), were drunk.

396

Below the royal class was a group of nobles, made up of collateral relatives of royalty or of lesser chiefs of villages, tribelets and other units within the state organization. Some of these nobles had their statuses ascribed to them at birth, but others seem to have worked their way up from the commoners class by success in war ventures, which also brought wealth in slaves and other property. Priests probably also beloned to this group, which was more fluid than the royalty. Commoners were those of modest economic means who were too remotely related to royalty, too ineffective in war, or too young to have achieved enough to gravitate into the noble class. Slaves were war captives from which men were drawn for religious sacrifices and cannibalistic feasts; but the women were spared to become the extra wives and concubines of their captors. Women slaves certainly performed menial tasks around the household, but it is doubtful if men slaves contributed much to the economy as laborers. There is nothing to suggest that slave status was hereditary, because most of the children of slaves were from unions of free men and slave women. Slaves who were not sacrificed tended to become assimilated into the ranks of the free.

Oasis.—There may have been marked differences in rank and even social classes in the southern part of this area nearest Meso-America, as the size of political units, the magnitude and organization of warfare, the presence of markets, and the collecting of tribute from subjugated peoples seem to indicate. However, this system is obviously derived from the Tarascans or other Meso-American peoples and is not typical of the Oasis as a whole. Nevertheless, some of this Meso-American interest in warfare and the rank achieved by it extends as far north as the River Yumans, but with considerable attenuation. The peoples of Arizona and New Mexico were unusually democratic as compared to those south of the Mexican border and, although differences in rank were recognized, they were based generally on merit, not heredity. There was some tendency for chieftainship to be inherited, but the chief was always chosen from a lineage, so that it was possible to select from among the lineage group a man with some desirable qualifications. Just as frequently, chieftainship was non-hereditary or was almost devoid of authority, which remained vested in a council.

397

Among the Pueblos, seats on the council were hereditary because they were filled by the leaders of the many religious societies in which offices tended to be filled from within a certain lineage. However, no hereditary official or chief in Arizona or New Mexico was regarded as a member of a higher class. Slaves were totally lacking in most localities and, in the few places where they are said to have occurred, they were war captives who were eventually assimilated into the society as freemen if they were co-operative.

Ruth Benedict, in her *Patterns of Culture*, has given the egalitarianism and sobriety of the Zuñi Indians a great deal of publicity. Although later writers have challenged some of the ideas in her Zuñi pattern, this part of her characterization has withstood the criticism of the years. These people, and the other Pueblos as well, were as devoid of class structure as any people in the world; differences of rank were at the minimum, depending almost wholly on achievement in civil and religious affairs, and not at all on material wealth. All officials dressed in the same manner as other citizens and worked at farming and at the same crafts as the rest of the population. In council meetings it was considered bad form to become self-assertive and vociferous, and those who did so almost never gained the assent of the council to their proposals. Although many important features of economic culture in the Oasis, such as domesticated plants, houses, and clothing unite it with Meso-America, its social organization and ethos are very different. The democratic village government, minimization of war, and virtual absence of differences in rank among the Pueblos offers the sharpest possible contrast with the societies of Meso-America.

East.—A caste system is reported for the Chitimacha (Swanton, 1911: 348–49). The chief and his descendants were regarded as nobles and were addressed with special terms of respect by the commoners. Apparently the noble caste was endogamous because, if a noble married a commoner, he would have to live with the common people, and for that reason many refused to marry at all when no women of noble caste were to be had, and thus hastened the extinction of the tribe. If this account is true, we seem to have a caste system among the Chitimacha. However, the statement that, when a noble married a commoner, he lived with the com-

mon people probably refers to nothing more strange than matrilocal residence, whereby the noble husband would have to live in
his commoner wife's home. Therefore it seems that common men
would be only too glad to marry noble women in order to upgrade themselves into a home of the nobility, although we are not
told this was the case. Chieftainship, according to the manuscript
of Martin Duralde cited by Swanton, passed from father to son
regardless of the matrilineal sib affiliation of the son, but it seems
to be a confused document and no more to be trusted on caste
than on chieftainship and descent. There need be no doubt that
noble men preferred to marry noble women, but an aversion to
commoners as strong as Duralde implies is unlikely.

No book on North American Indians would be complete without reference to the Natchez system of so-called social classes. As
originally diagrammed by Swanton (1911) from French sources,
this is the scheme:

Nobility	Suns: Children of Sun mothers and Stinkard fathers. Nobles: Children of Noble mothers and Stinkard fathers, or of Sun fathers and Stinkard mothers. Honored People: Children of Honored women and Stinkard fathers, or of Noble fathers and Stinkard mothers.
Stinkards:	Children of Stinkard mothers and Honored men, or of Stinkard fathers and Stinkard mothers.

If this scheme is correct, there were three ranked groups of nobility and a single group of commoners called "stinkards." Everyone in all three nobility groups had to marry a stinkard, making
these groups exogamous. Only stinkards were allowed to marry
within their own social group. The suns were royalty, and this
status descended by strict matrilineal inheritance. One observer
reports only seventeen suns in A.D. 1700, and another only eleven
suns in A.D. 1730, after two wars with the French. It is probable
from these small figures that the suns were a single royal lineage.
They had absolute authority over all other citizens, and women
suns as well as men could order the death of any person of lower
rank including their stinkard husbands, who would in any case be

strangled to death at the demise of their sun wives. The nobles were a more numerous group, and from them were drawn war chiefs and other officials.

Hart (1943) has pointed out that, because stinkards must marry into the three upper groups, the population would eventually lose all its stinkards to the three upper ranks and could not function indefinitely. To meet this calamity Quimby (1946) has shown that the Natchez regularly replenished the stinkard class by assimilation of remnants of neighboring peoples whose ethnic independence had been destroyed by defeat in war.

The Natchez system, in sum, appears to consist of a royal lineage, two collateral lineages or groups of lineages ranked according to distance from the royal lineage, and a fourth group too remotely related to royalty to possess any rank, as well as a sprinkling of outsiders. These four ranked groups may be called social classes, but most certainly not castes.

Although nothing exactly like the Natchez system has been reported for other peoples on the southeastern coastal plain, royal lineages with matrilineal descent were the rule in this region, and war captives seem to have been kept frequently as slaves. The mutilation of the feet of male prisoners of war, so that they could not run fast enough to escape, is evidence that their prolonged captivity was desired. Slavery, however, does not seem to have been hereditary, so that the existence of a slave class is problematical. At any rate, royalty and commoners were distinguished everywhere in this area, so that a minimum of two classes existed, and this seems to have been the point of departure for the Natchez system.

The Creek of Alabama and Georgia recognized marked differences in rank, but did not have definite social classes. As mentioned in chapter xvii the chief was selected by the council but always from a single lineage, and individual merit was what gave one lineage member the edge over another. Some of the other civil officers and advisers of the chief belonged to the same lineage or to the same sib. There was, then, a tendency to rank lineages and sibs, but it was not carried far enough to produce social classes. Warriors were divided into three grades, but these statuses were based entirely on war record, not on heredity. The ceremonial leaders, called "beloved men," were also of high rank, but their position was achieved only after learning the long and complex rituals of the tribe. War prisoners were taken, but the men were generally tortured to death and the women and children assimilated. Prostitutes were known in historic times, at least, and formed a low-ranking group, but hardly a social class. Therefore, the Creeks had a rather well defined system of rank, based primarily on achievement and only secondarily on heredity, but there were no definite social classes.

Among the Iroquoians, the principal civil and religious offices were kept within maternal lineages, and the various lineages of a sib were ranked according to the offices they possessed. However, each officer was nominated by the matriarch or by a group of dominant women in the lineage, and he could be impeached any time his conduct displeased the women. Achievement, therefore, was necessary not only to become a chief or priest, but also to maintain an extended tenure of office. This system applied even to the fifty sachems who sat on the council of the league. The "pine-tree" chiefs were a small group chosen entirely on their achievement in war or in oratory at council meetings, irrespective of lineage and sib affiliation. Shamans, especially those organized in societies, also enjoyed high rank. Although men, women, and children were taken prisoner in warfare, the latter two were adopted, and the men who were not tortured to death were often taken as husbands by widows. A slave class never materialized, although captives normally performed menial tasks until trusted and formally adopted into the tribe. On the whole the Iroquois standards of status and rank were close to those of the Creek, with perhaps less marked differences in rank and more premium placed upon merit. There were no true social classes.

Plains and Prairies.—The peoples of these areas differed little from the Creeks and Iroquois with respect to rank and social classes. There were definite differences in rank, but these were not hereditary and did not crystallize into social classes. As in all other areas where distinctions of rank occurred, the children of distinguished men enjoyed certain advantages. Their goals tended to be higher, and their education in the ways and means of acquiring rank was better. In regions where public offices belonged to particular lineages and sibs, these social units tended to outrank the others, but the power of the officers was so limited that the advantage was slight.

All of the Plains and most of the Prairie tribes carefully graded war deeds and encouraged successful warriors to recount their military exploits on public occasions. But success in raids was, in turn, dependent on the sanction of the supernatural. This was realized in a dream or vision which was as likely to come to a man of low rank as to one of high. This individual religious experience, therefore, opened the road of success to all comers.

Wealth was also a means of grading men, especially after the appearance of the horse and European-inspired economic competition. Horses were the most common property exchanged for a bride on the Plains, and the giving away of wealth on other occasions was only topped by the Northwest Coast peoples. Next to the war record, generosity to the poor was the basis for high social standing among the Plains tribes. Medicine bundles, which aided the establishment of rapport with the supernatural, were privately owned among many tribes in these areas and were bought and sold. A man of means, therefore, was likely to be in possession of one or more powerful medicine bundles which gave him an edge over the poor man in dealings with the supernatural. On the Plains and Prairies, then, success in warfare and economic pursuits, and the good will of the supernatural which both demanded, were the basis for establishing differences in rank, but social classes did not exist.

CONCLUSIONS

The area with the most complex systems of status, rank, and social classes is most certainly Meso-America. It is no accident that this area also possessed the most efficient food production with its intensive farming and irrigation (Maps 3, 4) as well as the greatest concentration of population (Map 6), the most ramified specialization of labor (Map 28), the largest political units, the largest armies, and the most complicated religious organization. In sharp contrast, the Arctic, Sub-Arctic, Great Basin, and Northeast Mexico possessed the minimum of differentiation in status and rank and no social classes at all. These areas also had the least efficient methods of food production, lowest population density, practically no specialization of labor, no true political organization, no true war, and the minimum of religious organization.

The Circum-Caribbean area is second only to Meso-America in the complexity of its schemes of rank and social classes. The geographical propinquity of the two regions, as well as hosts of shared cultural details makes the historical unity of the two beyond question. Farther northward, in what is now the United States, there is little doubt that the development of distinctions of rank and social classes in the East, Prairies, and Plains owes some of its inspiration to the peoples of Meso-America and around the Caribbean. This comes out most clearly in the tribes of the southeastern coastal plain, but some influences appear to have reached most peoples in these areas. The similarities in patterns of government and warfare and the derivation of most of the plants raised by Prairies and Eastern Indians from Meso-America and the Circum-Caribbean have been pointed out in earlier chapters. It is no accident, then, that the fundamentals of economy, government, war, and society all match. The resemblance is far from perfect and details tend to disappear as one proceeds north and west of the southeastern coastal plain, but this is normal where diffusion is involved. After White contact, economic factors in rank and warfare became considerably augmented in these areas, as well as others, and have partly obliterated the earlier aboriginal patterns.

The Oasis patterns of status, rank, and social classes show much variation. The southernmost part of this area shares much with Meso-America, and a little of this pattern, as related to government and war, extends as far north as the River Yumans. But the other Oasis peoples, in Arizona and New Mexico, were as strongly egalitarian as any in North America. In spite of the derivation of domesticated plants, housing, clothing, and many other material things from Meso-America, the fundamental drives of these cultures were very different from those of Meso-America, or, for that matter, those of the Plains, Prairies, and East. The Southeastern Indians, especially, show a much closer relationship to Meso-America with respect to government, war, rank, and social classes than do the Pueblo, Navaho, and Apache of the Oasis.

The Northwest Coast stands apart from other areas with definite systems of rank and social classes. Here geographical environment provided a supply of fish and sea mammals that was inexhaustible by the techniques the Indians employed in taking them. The surplus of food, obtainable in favored spots as productive per acre as the best farms, made possible a relatively sedentary economy and an accumulation of a surplus of other material and nonmaterial possessions. Population was as concentrated as in any other area of equal size north of Mexico and specialization of labor may have been more developed than Map 28 shows. Although political units remained small, raids motivated by economy were common, and in a few localities land was actually taken by force. Religious organization, with its secret societies, was also relatively advanced. Distinctions of status and rank, based on a combination of wealth and heredity, were more marked on the Northwest Coast than in any area north of Meso-America, except possibly the coastal plain of the southeast. The slave class on the Northwest Coast was more clearly differentiated than in any other North American area and has been estimated to have varied from 10 per cent to 30 per cent of the population. Distinct classes among freemen are difficult to demonstrate, however, and controversy over the matter exists at the present time. All areas bordering on the Northwest Coast share some of its interest in rank based on wealth and heredity, but this fades away rapidly as one proceeds away from the coast. The historical as well as geographical independence of the Northwest Coast, as compared to Meso-America, is conceded by most anthropologists today. Its system of rank and at least two social classes seems to have developed on the spot in response to a bountiful geographical environment and an economy advanced enough to exploit it efficiently.

REFERENCES

BARNETT, 1938; CODERE, 1957; DRUCKER, 1939, 1955; EDMONSON, 1958; GAYTON, 1930; HICKERSON, MS; LOWIE, 1954; MURDOCK, 1934, 1957; OSGOOD, 1936, 1937; RAY, 1939; SAHAGÚN (Anderson and Dibble), 1950–58; STEWARD, 1948; SUTTLES, 1958; SWANTON, 1911, 1946; THOMPSON, 1940; VAILLANT, 1941.

20: SODALITIES

AND THEIR CEREMONIES

IN CHAPTERS xv and xvi genetic kin groups and residential kin groups were distinguished, and in chapter xvii larger residential subdivisions into which some societies are divided were described. Societies may be further divided into sub-groups not primarily determined either by kinship or by coresidence. Such subdivisions are called sodalities, from the Latin *sodalis*, meaning comrade, companion, friend, and associate (Lowie: 1948, 14: 294–316). Some examples from modern life are churches, lodges, fraternities, sororities, service clubs, social clubs, professional associations, boys' and girls' clubs, and political organizations. In all of these, memberhip is generally voluntary, although one's older relatives may exert a certain amount of pressure to persuade him to join what they consider to be the proper one. At least it can be said that membership in such social units is not irrevocably ascribed to every individual at birth as is membership in kinship groups and in most coresidential units.

The type of sodality embracing the largest part of a band, tribelet, tribe, or state is the so-called tribal sodality. In its most typical form it includes all mature males in a society, but excludes children of both sexes and women. Every young man at about the age of puberty undergoes an initiation ceremony which he enters as a boy and from which he emerges as a man. He generally receives some formal education at this time in the lore of the society; and religious secrets, known only to mature men, are also revealed to him. More rarely there are parallel initiations for pubescent females, all of whom must participate in the system, and the resulting group of mature women may also be called a sodality. Membership in tribal sodalities is not voluntary, but compulsory, yet where there are multiple chapters in a single locality, the initiate is often allowed to choose the particular chapter he wishes to join.

The term restricted sodality applies to an organization with membership restricted to only a part of the mature males, mature females, or some mixture of both short of the totality. Restricted sodalities may also have initiation ceremonies, as well as other rituals, with content and meaning unknown to the non-members in the remainder of the population.

A club is a more informal sodality of restricted membership without any secrets. Age classes are another type of sodality; these include any division of a population into organized age groups of a more or less permanent nature. Because a single society often possesses more than one kind of sodality and the relations of the two or three types may be quite close, they will be described for each culture area in turn.

INCONSEQUENTIAL SODALITY ORGANIZATION

Most of the peoples in the Arctic, Sub-Arctic, Plateau, Great Basin, and Northeast Mexico lacked all kinds of sodalities. Where such organizations occurred, they were invariably in the parts of these areas closest to a culture area supporting a sodality system. This suggests that the rare occurrences of sodalities in these areas are to be explained in part by influences from the outside.

There were no sodalities anywhere in the Arctic except in Alaska south of Bering Strait. These Alaskan Eskimo seem to have possessed a men's tribal secret sodality which included all mature males in these societies. Women and children were definitely excluded. The center of sodality activities was in the semisubterranean men's house where the men and boys slept. Women never entered this men's house except to deliver food and other necessities to their husbands, or when they were allowed to witness the dramas produced by the men. These dramas, centered around spirit impersonations, were enacted by a number of men, disguised by masks and grotesque costumes representing spirits, who would sing and dance in the manner associated with each "devil" or "giant." At times loud noises made by the voice, whistles, possibly bull-roarers, and blows on the wooden structure served to frighten and impress the women and children, who were supposed to believe that the performers were genuine and dangerous spirits, not their husbands and fathers in disguise. Although we know nothing about the initiation of the young men into such sodalities, fuller information from other areas suggests that such initiations facilitated the acquisition of supernatural power that was essential for success in hunting and all other important male activities.

One part of the performance is reminiscent of the secret sodalities of Northwest Coast peoples. At a ceremony given to appease the wrath of evil spirits, two men impersonating the spirits pretend to cut open the abdomen of a third actor and eat his intestines. What they actually do is cut open a seal's stomach, previously filled with seal's blood, and pretend to eat the seal's intestines. Blood flows freely over the reclining third party and creates a horrible spectacle sufficient to chill the spines of the innocents in the audience. Later in the ritual the third party supposedly killed is brought back to life again by the powerful skills of other members of the sodality. This death and resurrection theme is common to many primitive religions as well as to modern faiths.

In the Sub-Arctic, sodalities occurred only among the Ojibwa and Cree, and they were almost identical with those of the northern Prairie peoples. No sodalities of any kind have been reported for the Plateau, Great Basin, and Northeast Mexico, but they occurred in all other culture areas.

RELATIVELY IMPORTANT SODALITIES

Northwest Coast.—Most of the Northwest Coast peoples from the panhandle of Alaska to the mouth of the Columbia River possessed secret sodalities of restricted membership. Membership in these sodalities and participation in their dramas was limited to those persons of high rank who had inherited the right to play the various roles. Although kinship played a part, the restriction of the membership to those of high social position justifies the use of the term sodality for these organizations. Each drama re-enacted an ancestor's encounter with a spirit, who kidnapped him, whisked him away into the woods, bestowed supernatural power on him, and

407

then returned him to his village, where he demonstrated his newly acquired power to the people. The public was sometimes allowed to witness such ceremonies, but the knowledge of the religious secrets and the privilege of playing a role was limited to those of wealth and high rank.

Such rituals were most elaborately developed by the Kwakiutl-speaking peoples of British Columbia. Here as many as three separate secret sodalities flourished at the same time: the Shamans' Sodality; the Ones-Returned-from-Heaven; and the Nutlam (untranslatable). Each sodality possessed its own cycle of secret rituals which could be witnessed only by its members. Persons who were active participants in one sodality were barred from membership in the other two. Within each of these sodalities all members and participants were not equal, and the dances each performed were graded from high to low.

In the Shamans' Sodality of one tribelet there were eight roles which outranked all others: the cannibal dancer, the fire-throwing dancer, the grizzly bear dancer, the rat spirit dancer, the chewing spirit or destroying spirit dancer, the scalped spirit dancer, the woods spirit dancer, and the ghost dancer. In addition there were many minor dances that might be performed by men, and even women, of lower rank. In every case, however, the right to play a particular role must be inherited. Most of the eight higher-ranking dances had to be repeated annually every fall for four years in a row.

The Ones-Returned-from-Heaven also ranked their dances in the same way, and those of highest rank were on a par with the preferred eight of the Shamans' Sodality. The former performed their dances in the spring of the year. In this cycle the initiate is supposed to be taken up into the sky by his spirit, and to be returned to earth later after he has acquired supernatural power.

The myth of the Nutlam sodality relates that originally Wolf Spirits kidnapped the ancestors of certain extended families and that when these ancestors returned home they behaved like wolves, killing and eating dogs when angered. This was the definitive act of the Nutlam initiates.

Tribelets south of the Kwakiutl on Vancouver Island and on the mainland of British Columbia and Washington State possessed only a single secret sodality modeled on those of the Kwakiutl. Tribe-lets north of the Kwakiutl had one or two such sodalities, but not all three.

The principal actor in one of these spirit-seeking dramas might re-enact the myth in a variety of ways. He might slip quietly away from his village and hide in the woods, or he might be seized bod-ily by a few men disguised as spirit monsters and bundled off to a secluded spot. After hiding out for the proper length of time, he would return alone, or in the company of his abductors, so filled with spiritual power that he would be in a state of frenzy and likely to harm his fellow villagers. In this condition it was neces-sary to capture and restrain him. After the edge of his supernatural experience had worn off a bit, he would demonstrate the powers he had acquired from his ancestral spirit-helper to the members of a sodality or to the public. Sometimes he might pretend to be struck dead by a spirit and to be resurrected in a public ritual.

The Kwakiutl especially had a full bag of tricks comparable to those of our own vaudeville magicians. These were always per-formed by the dim light of the fire at night, when visual illusions were easy to put across. The elaborate costumes of the performers made good hiding places for stomachs or bladders of animals filled with animal blood which could be brought forth and pierced when a person was supposed to be stabbed. Spirit impersonators were disguised by carved and painted wooden masks which re-semble, to us, the conventionalized heads of animals and birds. Sometimes a second wooden mask would be hidden inside the first, so that the performer could open up the outer one by pulling strings, revealing only the inner one. This stunt was interpreted by the naïve as a metamorphosis on the part of the spirit.

The houses in which these seances were held were rigged in ad-vance for the occasions. Actors and puppets swung from ropes suspended from the roof to give the illusion of flying through the air. Tunnels with trap doors were dug in the floor so that the per-formers could miraculously diasappear and reappear. Hollow kelp stems were joined and buried under the floor to serve as speaking tubes so that the voices of spirits could be heard from unexpected places, such as under the fireplace, where it was too hot for a mere human being to survive.

Perhaps the most shocking illusion of all was the eating of a human corpse by the cannibal dancer, who was supposed to be so completely possessed by the cannibal spirit that he could not restrain himself from eating human beings. To prevent him from murdering his fellow tribesmen he was supposed to be fed on a diet of human corpses. A small black bear, or some other animal of proper size, was smoked to resemble a well-dried human body and masked to make its face look human. In the dim light of the fire, the cannibal impersonator ate a portion of such an animal. Sometimes he would dash among the spectators, biting or cutting off a piece of skin from someone's arm before his handlers could restrain him. Those he bit or cut were chosen for their roles in advance and were paid with special gifts for their co-operation.

These sodalities provided a mechanism for an individual to acquire supernatural power and at the same time to acquire high rank for himself and to maintain the high position of his extended family in the social hierarchy. The religious dramas sometimes went on almost continuously for several months. Such devotion to ritual was possible only in a society with a large surplus of food and other necessities to consume during this period when little work was done. The peoples of the Northwest Coast enjoyed by far the greatest economic surplus of any hunting, gathering, or fishing area, and in this respect compared favorably to those of Meso-America.

California.—The Indians of central California possessed three kinds of sodalities: tribal sodalities for all men, restricted sodalities for a limited number of men, and restricted sodalities for a limited number of women. Some tribelets had a second restricted sodality for men in place of that for women. Twentieth-century Indian informants refer to the initiation ceremonies of these sodalities as schools, comparing the tribal initiation to elementary school and the more restricted initiation to high school. This is a meaningful analogy, because the young were taught cosmology and general religious lore in all such initiations, and, in those restricted to the more talented offspring of the higher-ranking families, they were taught the art of curing the sick by supernatural means. The pupils in the elementary school were ten or twelve years of age, while those in the high school were a little older. These schools lasted from four days to about six months. The students were usually housed in the permanent religious structure which, in this area, was semisubterranean and earth-covered. Such initiations were annual events in some localities, while in other places they might be held at intervals as far apart as seven years. Frequency apparently depended on the number of eligible initiates as much as on a fixed calendar of events. All of these sodalities in central California are called Kuksu Cults, after one of the principal spirits impersonated.

The central core of the Kuksu initiations was the acquisition of supernatural power and knowledge by direct contact with spiritual personalities. When elderly Wappo Indian informants were asked if their religious leaders dressed up in masks and special costumes to impersonate spirits, they replied in the affirmative but hastened to add that real spirits also attended these ceremonies and helped instruct the younger generation. Such seems to have been the general belief. The initiates thought in the beginning that all characters in the drama were genuine spirits, but gradually learned that persons of their acquaintance possessed the regalia and wore them to impersonate spirits.

While secluded in the religious structure the initiates lay down most of the time, refrained from eating certain foods, drank little water, scratched their bodies only with a special stick, and otherwise observed the taboos associated with occasions heavily charged with the supernatural. The voice of the thunder spirit was represented by the noise of the bull-roarer. This was a thin piece of wood whirled around on the end of a cord so that it rotated in the air, making a noise resembling that of an airplane propeller. A prominent feature of these ceremonies was the reputed killing of the neophytes by shooting them with an arrow or by stabbing, and their subsequent resurrection by supernatural means. They were actually only slightly wounded by the shooting and stabbing, but feigned death until the resurrection ritual was performed. Another common stunt was to toss or swing the initiates over the fire, apparently to demonstrate their ability to withstand a great amount of heat. Some of the actors pretended to eat live coals, thus proving their possession of supernatural power. Others carried snakes, including rattlesnakes, for the same purpose, and some pretended to swallow the snakes.

411

Edwin Loeb (1933: Table 1) lists a total of twenty-five spirits impersonated for all the tribelets with Kuksu Cults. These were mostly animal spirits, but some were more human in appearance. Kuksu himself was represented by a large headdress of feathered sticks radiating out from the head of the wearer, and the player representing Calnis wore a long artificial nose. In addition to these twenty-five spirits, Loeb lists four supernatural personalities as gods: the creator, the culture hero, thunder, and coyote. These four figured more prominently in the mythology of the area and were held in higher esteem than the others.

This seems to be the mechanism for the education of the young in all important religious matters in the tribal initiations, with the emphasis narrowing to the curing of the sick in the "high schools" of the doctors' sodalities. Because serious illness was thought to be caused by spiritual beings, it could be alleviated only by those in rapport with the supernatural. The doctors' school conveyed a higher rank to its graduates, who were either chosen in the beginning from families of higher rank or from among the adolescents who showed the greatest aptitude for religious learning. So-called spirit possession is not mentioned in the source material on these cults, but it seems likely that some of the initiates, and some of the spirit impersonators as well, may have achieved such a psychological state.

In southern California there were quite different religious sodalities called collectively the Chungichnish Cults, after the name of the highest-ranking god in the area. These seem to have been tribal sodalities in some localities, because all boys were initiated, while in other tribelets participation in the rites was voluntary and seems not to have included all boys. Like those of northern California, the principal ceremonies of these cults were initiations, but the impersonation of spirits by masked dancers was totally lacking; the central theme was the obtaining of contact with the supernatural through the medium of a narcotic plant, the Jamestown weed or Jimson weed, genus *Datura*. The roots of this plant were crushed in a sacred mortar reserved for the purpose, and a concoction was made by adding hot water. Each of the initiates, boys of adolescent or preadolescent age, drank some of the drug directly from the mortar in which it was made. The potion was a powerful one that invariably produced hallucinations and sometimes resulted in a fatality. The hallucinations consisted principally of visions of animals, which often taught the initiate a song or dance. Such animals became the lifelong spirit-helpers of the boys and were regarded as essential to success as a hunter, ritualist, shaman, or any other male activity. Each boy was guided through the ceremony by his individual sponsor, who instructed him in the religious lore of the tribelet and in various sacred songs and dances.

Southern California peoples also had women's tribal sodalities, in which membership was achieved by undergoing an initiation similar to the one for boys just described. Rites at the first menstruation of each girl are small family affairs including the seclusion of the girl, dietary restrictions, and the like, but with no singing, dancing, or feasting. However, once a year an initiation ceremony is given for all the girls who have come of age within the last year. The character of this initiation ceremony is quite different from that of the first menstruation ceremonies described in the chapter on the Life Cycle. In fact, it resembles both boys' initiation ceremonies and birth rites of southern California more closely than it does the true puberty ceremonies of other areas.

The Cochimi of Baja California had ceremonies in which both a man from the sky coming to benefit the earth and the ghosts of the dead were impersonated (Kroeber, 1932: 414–15). Only the men knew that the characters in the drama were masked and disguised human beings; the women and children thought they were spirits. While little is known of these ceremonies, they seem very similar to the sodality initiation rituals of central California.

Oasis.—The Pueblo peoples in the northern Oasis possessed the largest number and most elaborate system of sodalities of any group described so far. All the Pueblos initiated all their youths into tribal sodalities called Kachina Cults. The Kachina Cults of each village were independent in organization of those of every other village, and there were as many as six such distinct cults within a single village. These are to be compared with six different Protestant churches in a town in the United States today. They shared much in common but at the same time had separate sets of officers and assembled in separate sacred structures called kivas. In addition to the Kachina Cults, which embraced all the mature

413

males, there were men's sodalities restricted to only a part of the mature males, sodalities restricted to only a part of the mature women in most of the villages, and also restricted sodalities with both men and women members. In the west, among the Hopi and Zuñi, about half the adults belonged to at least one restricted sodality in addition to the men's "tribal" Kachina Cults. Farther eastward on the Rio Grande, the numbers included in the restricted sodalities diminish to a small minority of the total population. At the Hopi villages and at Zuñi the number of members in each restricted sodality ranged from about thirty to sixty, while on the Rio Grande it was nearer six to twelve. Another difference between east and west is the greater emphasis on kinship in the west, where all or most sodality offices were matrilineally inherited.

Boys are usually initiated into the Kachina Cults at ten or twelve years of age. Up to that time they, along with the women and girls, are supposed to believe that the masked dancers are indeed supernatural visitors from the village of the spirits. Revelation of this and other secrets of the cults was formerly punished in some localities with death. The boys are severely whipped by the kachina spirit-impersonating priests to impress them with the gravity of the occasion, to inspire awe of the supernatural, and to remove sickness and contamination from their persons. Then they are told that they are the ones who will wear the masked costumes in the future, thus making it clear that the dancers are human beings in disguise.

Perhaps the most distinctive characteristic of Pueblo sodalities is their dedication to the welfare of the entire society of which they are a part, rather than the selfish interests of the members. We saw above that the sodalities on the Northwest Coast were principally concerned with maintaining or enhancing the high rank of the members, in some cases by advertising their shamanistic powers which, in turn, brought in fees for curing the sick. In California the tribal sodalities brought no special prestige because all boys, and less often all girls, were initiated into them, but sodalities of restricted membership were principally concerned with the training of shamans who also enjoyed a position of high rank as well as a superior income from curing fees. Among the Pueblos, members of restricted sodalities enjoyed none of these economic

414

advantages, although both civil and religious prestige were associated with membership and the holding of sodality office. Rainmaking was the most recurrent motivation behind sodality ceremonies, yet when the rain came it fell on the fields of members and non-members alike. The curing fraternities of the Pueblos performed cures on all comers, not just their members, and in most cases being cured of an ailment by the fraternity was requisite to membership in it. Likewise the Warriors' Sodality fought for the benefit of an entire village, not just its own members.

Among the Hopi each major religious ceremony is associated with a lineage within a sib, a sodality, and a kiva (rectangular underground religious structure). The head priest of a sodality selects for his successor a member of his own maternal lineage, ideally his sister's son, and trains him in the mythology and ritual. The costumes and other ritual apparatus are kept in the sib house where selected women of the same lineage as the head priest are entrusted with knowledge of the ceremony and the care of the ritual objects. If a lineage dies out, another lineage of the same sib carries on, and if a sib possessing an important ceremony becomes extinct, another sib of the same phratry normally takes over the ceremony. However, the members of a particular sodality do not necessarily belong to the same sib as the head priest, but may come from any sib. Each young person to be initiated into a sodality must be sponsored by a "ceremonial father" who belongs to an unrelated sib, and at a later date the initiate likewise plays the role of sponsor to a young person of a sib other than his own. This ex-sib relationship of sponsor and initiate continues indefinitely, mixing up the composition of sodalities to the point that the large ones may contain members from almost all the Hopi sibs.

There are two other common ways of achieving membership in a Hopi sodality: being cured by the fraternity, and "inadvertently" entering the kiva while a ceremony is in progress. The fact that most Pueblo sodalities put on ceremonies to cure the sick may strike us as strange at first, but when we remember that illness was thought to be caused by the supernatural, it was reasonable to expect those in close rapport with the supernatural to be able to cure it. Because non-members are supposed to know nothing of these secret ceremonies, anyone who trespasses and observes the rituals

415

must be initiated and taken in as a member. Any adult may also achieve membership in most sodalities by simply asking a member to sponsor him.

All boys and girls among the Hopi are initiated into the Kachina Cults, although those who participate in the dancing and other ritual activities are principally men. Each performer wears a mask and costume representing an ancestral spirit, and the dancing of a group of such impersonators is symbolic of the return of the ancestral spirits from the underworld with clouds and rain for the parched land. In the past many ancestral spirits took the forms of animals and birds, but more recently the costumes have converged toward a generalized type of anthropomorphic spirit. The kachina ceremonies are performed separately by four men's sodalities: two of these are primarily warrior societies, with ceremonies to weaken the enemy as well as to strengthen themselves; the other two are concerned mainly with fertility rites.

Each of the four men's sodalities engaged in kachina tribal initiations is associated with a kiva. These underground rectangular (formerly cylindrical) chambers symbolize the underworld from whence the Hopi people emerged in an earlier mythological period. A kiva is originally built and maintained by the sib mates of the head priest, but the members may belong to any sib, as mentioned above.

In addition to the four men's sodalities which put on the tribal initiations, there are eleven major Hopi sodalities with more restricted membership. All these restricted sodalities are concerned with rain-making and curing, while a smaller number concentrate on fertility, war, and clowning. Each of these restricted sodalities has its place of meeting, sometimes a sib house instead of a kiva, and produces group rituals designed to persuade or compel the ancestral spirits to aid their descendants on the surface of the earth. Three of the eleven are composed exclusively of women members, except that the brother or husband of the head priestess usually assists in ritual, and men may join temporarily after being cured of sickness by the group. Everyone who has analyzed Pueblo sodalities agrees that the men's organizations are more essential than the women's and probably of greater age. The women's sodalities seem clearly to be derived from the men's.

416

As noted above in the chapter on Government and Social Control, the village council, which was the seat of sovereignty among the Pueblo peoples, was composed of the head priests of the various sodalities. Sodalities, therefore, may have important political functions.

Other Oasis peoples on the United States side of the border seemed to have lacked sodalities, but they crop up again on the Mexican side in more than one locality. Beals (1943: 69–70) postulates a men's tribal sodality, several men's restricted sodalities, and one or more women's restricted sodalities for the Cáhita of Sonora and Sinaloa. So far as the scanty information goes, these sodalities are more like those of the Pueblo peoples than those of any of the other areas described so far. It seems likely that the Acaxee of Sinaloa and Durango, and other peoples to the south, also possessed sodalities.

Plains and Prairies.—These two areas share a system of sodalities which is an indisputable geographic and historical unit as compared to the sodalities of neighboring areas. Because these were largely confined to men and all men were warriors, they may be called men's sodalities, military sodalities, or police sodalities. They were more secular, informal, and less secret than the sodalities of the Northwest Coast, California, and Oasis described above. Membership was limited to men with good war records, was voluntary, and was not required of all males of a certain age, although in the early nineteenth century most men belonged to one such sodality. These organizations, therefore, were restricted sodalities, not tribal sodalities, and may simply be called clubs.

There were two principal types: graded and ungraded. The ungraded clubs of the Crow Indians are typical of that variety. When the death of a member caused a vacancy in the ranks, the club usually took the initiative in filling it by offering gifts to one of the relatives of the departed. Or if a man distinguished himself in war, he would be given gifts and asked to join one of these men's clubs. At the same time, a non-member could take the initiative by expressing his desire to join. There were no initiations or entrance fees.

Five tribes, the Hidatsa, Mandan, Blackfoot, Gros Ventre, and Arapaho, had a system of clubs graded roughly according to the

417

age of the members, with the oldest group being of highest rank. Boys at play would imitate the songs and dances of these clubs and, when old enough to have acquired some material possessions of value, such as hides, parfleches, and arrows, would buy the costumes, dances, and songs of the club with the youngest membership. The sellers did not remain without club affiliation, but jointly bought out the next older club and stayed together without change in membership but with a new set of costumes, dances, and songs. The second group of sellers, in turn, jointly bought out the next older age-group, and this exchange of club identification continued until the oldest group sold out entirely and retired from the system. Then after a few years another group of young men would enter the system by buying out the youngest club, and the turnover in regalia, songs, and dances would again continue until the oldest club had retired. Some tribes had as many as ten such graded clubs, suggesting that each covered about a four-year span of age. The names of the Hidatsa clubs, as recorded by Prince Maximilian of Wied in 1833, were as follows: Stone Hammers, Lumpwoods, Crow Indians, Kit-Foxes, Little Dogs, Dogs, Half-shaved Heads, Enemies (Black Mouths), Bulls, Ravens.

The transfer of the paraphernalia, songs, and dances took four or more successive evenings, since the vacating group had to teach the new purchasers their routines which, altogether, might last for hours. The purchasers not only had to offer substantial gifts such as pipes and weapons, but they had to provide sufficient food to feast the sellers during this training period. After the buyers had mastered their new roles, a public procession and dance performed by them on the final evening announced to everyone that they had acquired all the privileges of the club they had just purchased.

There was no difference in the functions of the graded and ungraded clubs in their relation to the tribes of which they were a part. To the individual member, his sodality served as a club, and at its lodge he could lounge, sleep, eat, dance, sing, and otherwise enjoy the company of his fellow members much as in fraternities elsewhere. Upon occasion these clubs paraded in public dressed in their best finery on their prancing horses, or put on a dance outdoors for all to see. But at the same time a club might be called upon to perform serious public duties associated exclusively with it, with all such clubs, or with each in rotation. There was variation in this matter from tribe to tribe. The most important of these duties was policing other members of the tribe on the collective buffalo hunt, on the march, or in camp on important occasions such as the Sun Dance. Wrong-doers were punished by a severe beating, in which bones were sometimes broken, and by the destruction of their horses, tipis, and weapons. Punishment was especially severe for a man who rode out against orders and frightened off a buffalo herd, leaving everyone without food for a time.

These clubs also entertained the public with their antics from time to time. Some of them possessed clowns who engaged in behavior contrary to the accepted norms and spoke in opposites, saying cold for hot, and good for bad.

Although the majority of these clubs had few religious features, those of some tribes, such as the Pawnee and Arapaho, were closely associated with the supernatural. Some had sacred bundles around which elaborate religious rituals revolved, and a man might found a new club as the result of a visionary experience in which a spirit instructed him to do so.

Among the Hidatsa, Mandan, and Arikara, on the upper Missouri River, there were several women's societies which had collective purchase features like those of the men but lacked, of course, the military and police duties. One such group, called the Goose Women, performed ceremonies to insure a good corn crop and also to attract the buffalo. Another women's club, called the White Buffalo Cow Women, also had a ritual to lure a buffalo herd within range of the hunters. Cheyenne women who had embroidered thirty buffalo robes with porcupine quills were eligible to join a club of robe-quillers.

The Crow Tobacco Sodality was of totally different character from the sodalities described above and included both men and women. Its activities centered around the raising of a special species of tobacco, different from the trade tobacco commonly smoked. There were a number of chapters of this sodality, each of which originated when an individual experienced a vision and received instructions from a spirit to found a new chapter. When the special

419

tobacco had been raised according to all the regulations of these cults, the stems and leaves were picked, cut up fine, and thrown into a creek to please the patron spirits.

Prairies and Eastern Sub-Arctic.—There was a secret sodality called the Grand Medicine Society or Midewiwin among the Indians of the northern Prairies and the adjacent part of the Eastern Sub-Arctic area. This sodality appears to have originated among the Algonquian-speaking peoples and to have spread from them to the speakers of Siouan languages. Because membership was on a voluntary basis and not everyone in a community belonged to it, at least in the past, it is best labeled a restricted sodality. The Ojibwa form of this sodality is well documented and typical of the area.

Secret meetings in a special elongated lodge built for the purpose were held at least once a year among the Ojibwa. The initiation of new members was the principal activity, although old members also renewed their contact with the supernatural at this time. The ceremonies were conducted by priests who instructed the candidates in the religious meaning of the rites as well as in the proper behavior during the initiation. In the old days initiation fees were high and candidates carefully screened; membership was small and limited to men. At the present time almost anyone can join, rites are no longer secret except to prying outsiders (including anthropologists), and the organization as a whole differs little from that of a church, which is the label the Indians give to it. In earlier days the purpose of the cult was quite generalized; it was thought to insure a long and successful life for the members, and at the same time to constitute a thanksgiving for benefits already received from the supernatural. A candidate normally had to have a proper dream interpretable as a visitation of a spirit, before he was eligible for initiation. Today, anyone who is ill may be initiated, in the hope of curing his ailment. This narrowing of purpose, from a panacea to take care of all life's problems to a mere cure for a specific ailment, has been going on for about a century.

The deity propitiated by the ceremony is none other than the Great Spirit or Great Force called Manido. The wishes of this supreme religious fountainhead were conveyed to man by the culture hero Manabozho, who traveled around on earth teaching the Indians how to put on the Midewiwin ceremony. This personage not only taught the Indians how to cure the sick, but also how to raise the dead. Along with such specific techniques went the moral notion that a good life would be rewarded and an evil life punished. The association of the cross with this moral dichotomy suggests Christian influence.

However, the cross was observed by some of the earliest French missionaries who arrived in the Western Great Lakes area. Whether this was the result of diffusion of the cross westward ahead of the missionaries or of the pre-European presence of the cross in the area is a debatable point. At any rate the wooden cross planted in the ground and bedecked with offerings of valuables and clothing to the Manido was an obtrusive symbol of the Midewiwin religion.

The most significant part of the ritual is the "shooting" of the initiate with a small white shell from the medicine bag of a member of the sodality. This shell is thought to convey supernatural power, which at first may shock the recipient into unconsciousness. When he regains consciousness he spits the shell from his mouth, and this is regarded as evidence that it had penetrated his vitals. The "shooting" is of a mystical sort because the shells are not physically projected in any way, and the initiates are obviously instructed to place a shell in the mouth, collapse at the proper time, and then spit out the shell a little later. After the initiates have been shot with supernatural power, the members shoot each other in the same manner, become unconscious and also regurgitate a shell as they regain consciousness.

The sodality was generally divided into four grades, each with its separate initiation rite and its associated myths, songs, herbal remedies, and Midewiwin bags. The essentials of each initiation ceremony were recorded in line drawings on bark scrolls. The animal and human characters on the scrolls were engraved with a bone stylus and the indentations filled in with vermilion. One writer compares these scrolls to the trestle board of the Masonic lodge, which is printed and available to a non-member, but is so esoteric that it does not convey any real meaning to the uninitiated. It serves essentially as a mnemonic device for those informed about its meaning, as do the Midewiwin scrolls of the Great Lakes Indians. Each candidate for membership is instructed from these scrolls by a member thoroughly familiar with their meaning.

A separate initiation fee is paid to the priests in charge of the rite for each of the four grades, the amount increasing as one progresses through the grades. One's rank in the system is shown by the design painted on his face and by the animal or bird skin out of which his Mide bag is made. Common materials for bags were weasel skins, mink skins, the skin from the paw of a wildcat or bear, the skin of a rattlesnake, and the skins of owls and hawks. Each material denoted one of the four grades.

Like other ceremonies described in this chapter, the Midewiwin provided a means for the individual to acquire the supernatural power necessary for a successful life, and at the same time gave him an enhanced status in the hierarchy of his society.

East.—Tribal initiations for youths occurred in the Southeast among the Virginia Algonquians, the Siouans of the Carolinas, the Chitimacha at the mouth of the Mississippi, and probably elsewhere along the coast. The Siouans, at least, had a separate tribal initiation for adolescent girls. The Chitimacha shut their youths up in the ceremonial house and forced them to dance and fast for six days. The Algonquians of Virginia kept their males of ten to fifteen years isolated in a special structure in the wilderness for nine months, not allowing them to speak with anyone during the entire period. They were instructed in religious lore by religious leaders at this time, and later some of them became "priests and conjurers." The fullest account from the Southeast, however, is that of John Lawson, on the Siouan peoples, with whom he lived from 1701 to about 1711.

There is one most abominable custom amongst them, which they call husquenawing their young men, which I have not made any mention of as yet, so will give you an account of it here. You must know, that most commonly, once a year, at farthest, once in two years, these people take up so many of their young men, as they think are able to undergo it, and husquenaugh them, which is to make them obedient and respective to their superiors, and as they say, is the same to them as it is to us to send our children to school, to be taught good breeding and letters. This house of correction is a large, strong cabin, made on purpose for the reception of the young men and boys, that have not passed the graduation already; and it is always at christmas that they husquenaugh their youth, which is by bringing them into this house and keeping them dark all the time, where they more than half starve them. Besides, they give the pellitory bark, and several intoxicating plants, that make them go raving mad as ever were any people in the world; and you may hear them make the most dismal and hellish cries and howlings that ever human creatures expressed; all which continues about five or six weeks, and the little meat they eat, is the nastiest, loathsome stuff, and mixt with all manner of filth it is possible to get. After the time is expired, they are brought out of the cabin, which never is in the town, but always a distance off, and guarded by a jailor or two, who watch by turn. Now when they first come out, they are as poor as ever any creatures were; for you must know several die under the diabolical purgation. Moreover, they either really are, or pretend to be dumb, and do not speak for several days; I think, twenty or thirty, and look so ghastly, and are so changed, that it is next to an impossibility to know them again, although you were ever so well acquainted with them before. I would fain have gone into the mad house, and have seen them in their time of purgatory, but the king would not suffer it, because, he told me they would do me or any other white man an injury, that ventured in amongst them, so I desisted. They play this prank with girls as well as boys, and I believe it a miserable life they endure, because I have known several of them run away at that time to avoid it. Now the savages say if it were not for this, they could never keep their youth in subjection, besides that it hardens them ever after to the fatigues of war, hunting, and all manner of hardship, which their way of living exposes them to. Beside, they add, that it carries off those infirm weak bodies, that would have been only a burden and disgrace to their nation, and saves the victuals and clothing for better people that would have been expended on such useless creatures. (Lawson, 1860:380–82.)

The loss of life in such initiations is emphasized even more in William Strachey's report on the Virginia Algonquians. Because the initiates in these rites later became "priests," these organizations appear to have been restricted sodalities. The Carolina Siouans, on the other hand, may have had tribal sodalities, because young people seem to have had difficulty in escaping the initiations. At any rate, the harsh character of the initiation ceremony comes out clearly in both localities. To the best of our knowledge, no other ceremonies of this character have been reported anywhere else in Anglo-America east of the Pueblos in New Mexico.

The Iroquois Indians of New York State and their neighbors speaking related languages possessed elaborate systems of sodalities whose activities centered around the curing of the sick. As elsewhere, illness was thought to be caused by the supernatural; therefore, it could be cured by appeasing the wrath of malevolent spirits or by soliciting the aid of benevolent ones, and also by maneuvering impersonal supernatural forces by magical means. These so-called "medicine societies" numbered eleven among the Seneca (Fenton, 1936) and nineteen among the Cayuga of Ontario (Speck, 1945). Because neither all the men nor all the women were compelled to join these sodalities, they were restricted in membership, but each had both men and women members. Among the Cayuga, eleven out of nineteen sodalities permitted anyone who wished to join by taking part in the curing ceremonies. The attitude was that an increased number of participants, each wanting the recovery of the patient, would augment the force of the appeal to the spirit-helpers of the sodality. For the remaining eight Cayuga medicine sodalities, membership was limited to those who had had the proper dream or visionary experience, or who had been cured of their own illness by the sodality. These organizations were somewhat secret, while those open to everyone who wished to join were not secret at all. All sodalities performed publicly in the longhouse at one time or another, and in these ceremonies the freedom of the entire town or tribe from disease and misfortune was sought. These sodalities, therefore, were concerned with the welfare of the entire town or tribe, as well as that of the individual they might be trying to cure or that of their own membership.

Each sodality possessed a myth explaining its origin and particular rites. The founder contacted animal spirits, was captured while observing their secret ceremonies, adopted into their group, and, after long study and many warnings, was sent back to his people to teach them the secrets of the animal spirits and how to obtain favor from them. Most of the rituals are chanted in unison by the entire company, and some contain archaic words, phrases, and even entire sentences which no member can translate.

424

The best-known Iroquois sodality is that of the False Faces. This name refers to the carved and painted wooden masks worn by all participants in the curing rituals of this organization. Each mask represented a benevolent spirit who was invariably ugly, apparently the better to frighten away the evil spirits causing disease amongst the people. The carving of a new mask was begun on the trunk of a living tree to keep within it the spirit of the tree, and later it was removed from the tree to receive its finishing touches. It was painted red or black, according to whether the carver began work in the morning or the afternoon, and fibers made from inner bark (or horse hair in historical times) were fastened to the top to represent hair. In addition to the masks worn over the face, performers shook hand-held hollow rattles made of turtle shells.

The False Face spirit-impersonators made several feints at entering the house of the patient they were asked to cure. They scraped the door posts and lintel with their rattles, uttered their characteristic cry of "Ho-ho-ho-ho-ho-ho," and thrust their heads in the door and withdrew them several times. Then they entered the room, shook their rattles over the sick person, went to the fireplace, dipped their hands in the ashes, and rubbed the ashes on the head and hair of the patient. This was thought to drive away the evil spirits causing the illness. As a reward for his services each masked performer was given a pail of "False-Face-pudding," a special preparation of parched cornmeal with trade sugar. Then the spirit impersonators departed to eat their puddings in private, for it was forbidden to unmask in public.

Probably all the tribes in what is now the southeastern United States had men's sodalities of restricted membership. The Creek, for instance, had schools with three grades for the training of medicine men; graduates of these schools shared a common secret knowledge of the healing art and, therefore, constituted a sodality. The peoples of the coastal plain from the Natchez to the Powhatan possessed priests who were in charge of temples and ossuaries. Such men necessarily received considerable training and joined each other in religious ceremonies.

Circum-Caribbean.—The common occurrence around the Caribbean of temples, priests, and idols suggests sodalities of priests. The scantiness of the record, however, makes it impossible to give the

425

frequency of such restricted sodalities or their precise geographical distribution. In a few localities all youths were initiated into a tribal sodality, which sometimes had a men's house which women were not allowed to enter.

The Mosquito and Sumo Indians of Central America divided their warriors into military ranks distinguished by feather insignia. These organizations staged a number of ceremonies from which women were barred. Assuming that membership in these military orders was on a basis of merit rather than heredity, we may label them sodalities.

The Guaymi of Central America had an initiation ceremony for adolescent boys, which seems to have included all boys and was secret. The leaders of the ceremony painted their bodies and wore masks, suggesting spirit-impersonation. These performers instructed the boys in the lore of the culture and gave each an official but secret name. The boys were taught to paint their faces, possibly to represent a spirit, and in some localities their teeth were chipped. They were not allowed to marry until after the ceremony. In addition, warriors belonged to a special "class" and were frequently given special burials.

The Bribri and Guetar, also of Central America, possessed organized priesthoods which sacrificed human captives at every new moon and at funerals. The victims were eaten.

The Calamari and neighboring tribes of Colombia had priests, temples, and idols. The great temple of Fincenú is said to have accommodated one thousand persons and housed twenty-four tall wooden idols covered with gold leaf and crowned with a tiara. Beside each idol a hammock suspended from a stake served as a receptacle for the offerings the religion demanded. Around the temple were the graves of important personages, each marked by a tree from which hung a gold bell, or covered by a mound of earth. Such an elaborate religious establishment could not have been operated without an organized priesthood. The Chibcha, the most famous Indian people of Colombia, possessed temples of comparable size.

The Achuaga of eastern Colombia and Venezuela had a men's clubhouse from which women were barred. Here the men lounged in their hammocks and chatted informally when they were not engaged in drunken festivities. For a drinking party they prepared

426

a large quantity of chicha, the local beer, in wooden troughs, then painted their bodies for the occasion and assembled in the club-house. The chief sat on a stool, as rulers generally did around the Caribbean, but the others had to squat. After servants had plied everyone with all the chicha he could hold, the men sang lustily to the accompaniment of musical instruments. The Achagua men also wore costumes and masks to represent supernatural beings at dance festivals, but because these resemble the ancestor cults of a neighboring tropical forest tribe to the south, the cult may be geared to kinship and therefore not a true sodality.

GREATEST ELABORATION OF SODALITIES

Probably all the peoples of Meso-America had sodalities of one kind or another, although this cannot be proved where the record is thinnest. Where the record is fullest, among the Aztecs, the number and importance of sodalities far exceeded that of any people in any other area.

At fifteen years of age all Aztec boys left their homes and went to live in one of two types of boarding schools. The first were the *Telpuchcalli*, or houses of youth, which were maintained by the demes, each deme educating its own youths. There were twenty houses of youth in Tenochtitlán because there were twenty demes in that city. Young men were given instruction in farming, in arts and crafts, in the bearing of arms, in the history and religion of their people, and in the duties of citizenship. In addition to formal instruction, the young men formed work parties to cultivate public lands and to build public buildings and irrigation works. They also served in the army, making up the bulk of the fighting force. The second type was the *Calmecac*, a school for priests, which was attended by a restricted number of youths, drawn principally from the upper classes. These schools were fewer in number, were located near the temples of important gods, and concentrated on the elaborate rituals which the pupils studied with the aid of pictographic writing in books. Both types of schools are described in more detail at the end of the chapter on Education, through quotation from a recent English translation of the original Nahuatl (Aztec) texts recorded by the famous Spanish priest Bernardino Sahagún.

427

Still other boarding schools trained a smaller group of young women to become priestesses. Their training and work was limited for the most part to weaving the priestly costumes and embroidering them with feathers. There were thus three kinds of sodalities dedicated to the education of the youth. There were also three additional sodalities restricted to men with outstanding military records who served as the lesser officers in the army. These military orders were called the Eagle, the Ocelot, and the Arrow.

In addition to the sodalities mentioned above, there was a host of religious cults of more restricted membership, each centering around the worship of a single deity. Vaillant (1941: 182–84) lists sixty-three Aztec gods, not to mention lesser spirits, and each of these gods had its special priests who joined one another in ceremonies propitiating their patron deity. Each of these sixty-odd groups of priests was a sodality dedicated to the service of its god, and young men were constantly being educated and initiated into the secret lore of each of these religious cults.

The organization of the priesthood converged with that of the government at the top. In Tenochtitlán a man called the "snake woman," one of the two top political officials, was in charge of the temples and the entire organization of the priesthood. Directly beneath him were two high priests who directed the worship respectively of the two highest gods, the war god and the rain god. Next in rank was a third priest who supervised the religious activities of conquered towns as well as acted as a deputy in Tenochtitlán for the higher-ranking priests. Below all of these officials were the sixty-odd priests in charge of the temple, worship, ritual, and sacrifice connected with each specific god. It was these priests who wore the dress of their patron divinities and impersonated them in the elaborate religious dramas which topped all others in native North America. It has been estimated that there were five thousand priests in Tenochtitlán alone. Therefore it seems likely that only the higher-ranking ones were full-time specialists, and that those who played the minor ritual roles were essentially religious-minded laymen who worked at utilitarian tasks or devoted part of their time to civic affairs or war.

The priesthood was the fountainhead from which the most

highly valued knowledge flowed. The priests were the ones who understood the complicated calendar system which was the core of the religion. There were 20 named days, 20 named "weeks" of 13 days each, and 18 named "months" of 20 days each; and each day, "week," and "month" was associated with a particular god or goddess. There were, in addition, 13 "hours" of daytime and 9 "hours" of nighttime, each with one of the same deities assigned to it. Each ritual for each god had to be performed on the proper "hour," day, "week," or "month" or it would bring harm instead of good.

It would have been impossible to carry on such an elaborate ceremonial cycle without a system of writing. Aztec writing was essentially pictographic, but a few phonetic syllables were beginning to emerge when the Spanish arrived and burned most of the native books. To these phonetic syllables, based on the pun, were added color, position, and abbreviations, all of which contained the germs of a true system of writing comparable to that of the hieroglyphs of the Egyptians, the cuneiform symbols of the Babylonians, or the early characters of the Chinese. There was no inkling of an alphabet which, even in the Old World, was invented only once. Much of Aztec writing was a series of mnemonic symbols, each associated with an oral tradition which was not only memorized but also probably chanted, the better to make it stick in the mind. All of such knowledge was lodged in the persons of the priests, who spent a considerable portion of their time imparting it to the less informed members of the cults as well as to new initiates.

The human sacrifices of war captives were carried on by these priestly sodalities. This so shocked the Spanish that they lost no time in destroying every manifestation of Aztec religion in sight. However, one case history of a sacrificial victim illustrates what must have been the common attitude toward this practice. It seems that a valiant Tlaxcalan chief, who was selected for sacrifice to the sun, fought so well with the inferior weapons given the victim on such occasions that he killed or wounded all his opponents. For this brave exhibition against overwhelming odds he was offered his freedom and a commission (chieftancy) in the army of Tenochtitlán. This he declined, however, because he preferred the greater honor associated with his major role as a sacrificial victim and the high-ranking position it assured him in the afterlife.

429

SUMMARY AND CONCLUSIONS

Our survey indicates that there were no sodalities of any kind on the Plateau, in the Great Basin, or in Northeast Mexico. In the Arctic, sodalities occurred only in Alaska south of Bering Strait where contact with the Northwest Coast was most pronounced. In the Sub-Arctic they were to be found only among the Cree and Ojibwa. The latter had considerable contact with the Iroquoians to the east as well as with Algonquians and Siouans to the south. Thus we see that the areas of poorest geographical environment, lowest population density, simplest division of labor, crudest material culture, lack of true political organization, and smallest differences in rank were the very ones which lacked sodalities entirely or had them only in limited numbers, in localities adjacent to other areas where they were well developed. The area with the greatest number of sodalities was Meso-America, which excelled all other areas in general cultural complexity. On the whole, therefore, there is a strong positive correlation between ramification of sodalities and general cultural complexity.

Tribal sodalities have a rather sporadic distribution. They seem to have occurred in southern Alaska, California, Baja California, Oasis, East, Circum-Caribbean, and Meso-America. All of these areas, except possibly Alaska, also had sodalities of more restricted membership. It was only on the Northwest Coast, Plains, and Prairies that restricted sodalities were the only type present.

Most sodalities were closely linked with religion. In fact, religious interests dominated sodalities everywhere except on the Plains, and even here some such organizations possessed religious features. Instruction in mythology and religion and personal contact with the supernatural were the rule in most sodality initiations, which were the nearest approach to formal education among most of the peoples possessing them.

Men's sodalities were much more frequent than those of women, although the latter were found in smaller numbers or with less conspicuous functions in most of the areas where men's sodalities prevailed. In most cases the women's sodalities appear to be modeled on the men's and to have been derived historically from those of the men. Sodalities of mixed male and female membership are most characteristic of the Iroquoians, although they also occur

430

among the Pueblos. Perhaps the dominance of matrilineal descent in both localities has something to do with the more equal opportunity accorded women in these cultures.

When we compare the sodality systems as wholes for the various culture areas, a number of linkages obtrude which are best explained in terms of contact between areas or by common origin. Thus Kroeber (1932: 408–15) makes out a good case for the common origin of a number of details in the initiation ceremonies of California, Baja California, and the Oasis, and Underhill (1948) extends the idea to other ceremonies.

The Midewiwin rites probably stem from the medicine sodalities of the Iroquois. This is shown directly by the origin legend of the Midewiwin among the Ojibwa, and indirectly from a comparison of ceremonial organization and behavior. Fenton (1953: 208–10) has made out a good case for the Iroquois deriving their Eagle Dance from the Calumet Dance of the Prairies, and some of its features from the Buzzard Cult of the Southeast, which in turn owed some of its inspiration to Meso-America. From these brief allusions to the diffusion factor, it is clear that while cultures must attain an economic surplus and a certain population density or community size before sodalities are likely to develop, such attainments do not explain the details of a particular sodality system in a particular locality. Such details are normally shared with neighboring tribes, as well as with tribes in other culture areas, and must be accounted for also by contact of peoples, diffusion, acculturation, and other historical processes.

REFERENCES

BEALS, 1943; BOAS, 1897; DENSMORE, 1929; DRIVER, 1936; DRUCK-ER, 1940, 1955; EGGAN, 1950; FENTON, 1936, 1941b; HOFFMAN, 1891; KROEBER, 1925, 1932; LANTIS, 1947; LAWSON, 1860; LOEB, 1932, 1933; LOWIE, 1916, 1935, 1948, 1954; MÜLLER, 1954; PARSONS, 1939; SPECK, 1945; STRACHEY, 1849; SWANTON, 1946; UNDERHILL, 1948; VAILLANT, 1941.

21: LIFE CYCLE

THE FOUR principal events in the life cycle of mammals are birth, the attainment of maturity, reproduction, and death. Man is no exception to this sequence, and everywhere in the world he devotes some special attention to these important events. Each is accompanied by anxiety, and, where this is great, a considerable elaboration of special behavior and belief tends to surround the occasion. However, the emphasis may vary tremendously from one primitive society to another. Puberty may be subjected to the greatest amount of ritual recognition in one culture, while death may be the dominant ceremonial occasion in another. On the whole, birth and marriage receive less attention than the other life crises, but are still regarded as important.

The supernatural is thought to be very close to man at the time of these four biological crises, in some cases for the better and in others for the worse. But whether the attitude of supernatural personalities is regarded as benevolent or malevolent, North American Indian peoples prescribe certain acts of behavior and forbid others, in order to attract the good or fend off the evil.

Apparently all American Indians were familiar with the essential facts of sexual reproduction and admitted that sexual intercourse is necessary to initiate conception and pregnancy. Anthropologists have not reported any cases from North America in which knowledge of the connection between the sex and conception was denied, as in native Australia and Melanesia. Many people in Christian nations today believe that God takes a hand in conception, that mere biology is not a sufficient explanation, and most Indians also believe the supernatural plays a role in such matters.

Newlyweds normally wanted children and, if none were born

432

after several years of marriage, this was often grounds for divorce. Where polygyny was approved, a younger sister of the barren wife might be taken as a second wife in the hope of producing off-spring. Where there was no younger sister or other relative available, the bride price was sometimes returned to the groom and the marriage dissolved. Sterility on the part of the husband does not seem to have been understood by many Indian peoples, because it is conspicuously absent in field reports and documentary data on Indians. Sons were valued more than daughters in areas where patrilineal descent prevailed or where men dominated the culture, but in matrilineal societies daughters were at a premium because they were the ones to carry on the family name and inherit the real estate.

When a woman realized she was pregnant, she performed certain positive acts thought to be beneficial to her health and that of the child, and avoided doing other things she believed would harm the child and herself. Dietary restrictions, especially the taboo on eating meat, were general at this time. The most common explanation of this is that the souls of the game animals would be offended if a pregnant woman had contact with their flesh and would broadcast the offense to all the game animals, with the result that none would permit themselves to be killed by the housemates of the unfortunate woman. To the meat taboo were often added taboos associated with water, such as the requirement that she must drink only a little water or drink through a special tube provided for the purpose. The pregnant woman was often secluded from the rest of the society in a screened-off part of the house or in a special hut nearby, especially toward the end of her period of gestation. Frequently she could scratch her body only with a stick provided for the purpose because her hands might give her a skin disease. Even her glance was sometimes thought to be harmful to others, so that she had to glance downward or cover her head when she went outdoors. As the time for birth drew near, such special behaviors increased in intensity and frequency until the blessed event itself took place.

Meso-America is the most deviant area with respect to the generalizations just offered. Here there was no formal seclusion, but only a gradual narrowing of participation in social and public life,

433

somewhat like that of the Victorian era in England or the United States. The expectant mother avoided "cold" foods, but was encouraged to indulge her cravings for other foods because of the belief that such cravings originated with the foetus. Pleasing the unborn child averted illness, miscarriage, or a difficult labor.

Voluntary abortion was practiced in all culture areas and probably by most tribes in every area. Devereux (1955) has assembled information on abortion for ninety North American Indian peoples, but the data are too meager to establish significant differences between culture areas. However, they do permit generalizations for the continent as a whole. The motivations for abortion, listed from most frequent to least frequent, are the following: illegitimacy of the pregnancy; desire to avoid the trouble and work of rearing children; fear of the pain, of injury to the mother's health, or of death at childbirth; poverty of the parents; desire to avoid bringing a child into the modern world with its discrimination against Indians and half-breeds; quarrels between parents and desertion of a pregnant woman by her husband or lover; fear of bringing into the world a child associated with coitus taboos, such as those during pregnancy or during the nursing period of a previous child; desire to avoid producing a child who will become a slave, a prisoner of war, or a person of any other undesirable status; desire to avoid producing offspring from an adulterous union.

The techniques of abortion are equally varied, but most of them fall into three principal categories: mechanical means, strenuous exercise, and drugs. These are reported in about equal frequency for North American Indians. The great variety of such techniques suggests that abortion was well known to North American Indians; nowhere was it considered a crime. Although illegitimate pregnancies and births are regarded by most anthropologists as being associated with less stigma among Indians than among modern western societies, the fact that the most frequently reported motivation for abortion was illegitimacy of the pregnancy suggests that there was greater disapproval than has been generally believed. The effect of abortion on population was probably not great because more than half the children died before they reached maturity; if no abortions had been performed, more children would have died at a later date from lack of food and other necessities.

434

BIRTH AND INFANCY

Birth took place in a special hut made for the purpose or in a screened-off portion of the house. The position the woman assumed in labor varied from tribe to tribe and area to area, but the most frequent ones for the continent as a whole seem to have been kneeling or squatting. Sitting, however, is more often mentioned for the Northwest Coast, California, and the Oasis. Standing or stooping is less often reported for the continent as a whole than the above postures, and lying flat on the back still less. The woman in labor, in all positions except lying, often supported herself by holding to one or two stakes in the ground, or to a cord attached to the roof of the dwelling. She was assisted by a midwife in most localities, if one were available or, if not, by a female relative. The husband less often helped at parturition because it was generally taboo for men to be present except for men shamans or other male native physicians supposed to be skilled in obstetrics.

Almost all Indians disposed of the placenta and the umbilical cord in some prescribed manner. The placenta might be buried in the earth floor of the house or otherwise disposed of where carnivores would not eat it; but the umbilical cord, after it had become disengaged from the infant's navel, was normally kept in some safe place in the house for a considerable time. Proper disposal of these objects insured the good health of the baby and sometimes of its mother.

Infanticide was practiced in every culture area, although it has been denied by informants from a number of individual societies and, therefore, was probably not universal. When the mother died at childbirth, there was no way of feeding the infant unless a wet nurse could be found. In the Arctic, Sub-Arctic, Great Basin, and Northeast Mexico, where population was sparsest and residential units smallest, a wet nurse was least likely to be available, and the frequency of infanticide from this cause was greatest. When no wet nurse could be found, the infant was most often buried with his mother. If the father of a newborn infant died suddenly, leaving the mother with several children to care for on her own, she might kill the new arrival in order to free herself to obtain a living for the other children more easily. In areas where the stigma attached to the illegitimate child was greatest, the unwed mother

435

might put her infant to death to spare him and herself from social censure. Deformed infants were frequently killed, especially in the more nomadic areas where they could not possibly measure up to the demands on children, not to mention those on adults. In the time of famine infants would more often be killed, because their chances of survival, with the mother's milk supply impaired by starvation, was slight.

Infanticide among the Eskimo in the Arctic has received more attention than that of any other region. In this area girl babies were killed more often than boys because the man was the hunter and more indispensable to survival than the woman. The mortality of adult males was about twice as high as that of adult females, because men were often killed in hunting or in fights with each other, so that some elimination of female infants was necessary to maintain a workable sex ratio later on in life.

In most North American Indian societies the parents had the power of life and death over their newborn infant and did not have to consult any higher authority to dispose of it. However, some societies placed a time limit on this power, as in the case of the Creeks where a mother possessed the option on her baby's life only for one month after its birth. She had to obtain the approval of her lineage or sib to put to death an older child.

Perhaps the harshness of living conditions for mother and child in some areas can best be conveyed to the reader with a quotation from Gonzalo de las Casas about the Chichimecs of Northeast Mexico in the sixteenth century.

They bear their children with great distress because, having no houses and roaming constantly, they often give birth while travelling. Even with the placenta hanging and dripping blood they walk on as if they were sheep or cows. They wash their infants or, if there is no water, cleanse them with herbs. They have nothing to give their children but their own milk, nor do they wrap them in blankets because they have none. They have no cradles, no houses for shelter, nothing more than a piece of cloth or a rock, and in such harsh conditions they live and rear their children. (Las Casas, 1944 [1574]:35–36.)

This inventory of birth customs would not be complete without mention of the couvade (from the French *couver*, "to hatch"). This term refers to the participation of the father in birth rites. In its extreme form the father lies in bed after the birth of his child, complains of labor pains, observes food taboos, and otherwise acts like a woman in confinement. The mother, on the other hand, gets up and assumes her normal household duties as soon as possible after giving birth, sometimes on the same day, and waits on the bedfast father. Thus the roles of the sexes are reversed. Nowhere on the mainland of North America did this extreme form of couvade prevail, but a number of California and Great Basin tribes practiced what might be called a half-couvade, with about equal restrictions on both parents after the birth of their child.

The fullest data on the half-couvade come from the Wappo Indians of California (Driver, 1936). Here the father was confined to his bed for four days, refrained from eating meat or fish, could not smoke, and could not talk loudly or rapidly. He got up on the fifth day, but only went a little way from the house. From the fifth to the tenth day he gradually resumed normal activities. If he tired himself too soon, it was thought that the child would become tired and weak, and if he smoked, the infant would have difficulty in breathing. After the fifth day he could gather acorns and other plant foods, but if he killed an animal before the tenth day, his baby was likely to die. On the tenth day he was permitted to hunt and kill deer, but could not kill a bear or catch fish for a still longer period. In recent times, when a man did not dare to leave his job for his confinement, he would place a stick or stone in his bed and admonish it to watch his baby while he was away. The mother of the infant observed about the same taboos as the father, except that she stayed indoors for the entire ten days.

Some restrictions on the father following the birth of a child were probably universal in aboriginal North America. California differs only in the greater emphasis placed on the role of the father as compared to most other areas. Some form of couvade has been reported for the Circum-Caribbean area and for South America east of the Andes as far south as Paraguay.

Around the Caribbean a stronger form of couvade has been recorded for a number of peoples including the Caribs of the West Indies. Here the mother fasted from all food except dried tapioca and drank only warm water for a few days. The restrictions on the father, however, were much more severe. Immediately after

437

the birth he complained of labor pains and went to a separate hut where he lay in a hammock. He stayed there for at least forty days after the birth of his first child, and for four or five days after the birth of each subsequent child. He went outdoors only at night and avoided meeting anyone for fear that he might be tempted to break his fast, causing the mother to become ill and the child to grow up a coward. For the first five days of the forty the father ate nothing at all; after that time he was allowed to drink corn beer, and after ten days to eat tapioca bread in increasing quantities. At the end of the forty-day period the father was brought outside and was stood on two large flat cakes of tapioca, where his body was scarified by two men chosen by the chief. A mixture of pepper seeds and tobacco juice was rubbed into the cuts and the blood which dripped from them was daubed on the face of the child to give it the courage shown by the father in undergoing this ordeal. The man was then fed the two tapioca cakes upon which he had stood and also a little fish which he could not swallow but had to spit out. He was not allowed to eat the meat of game animals for six months or a year, for fear that the child would become deformed.

The half-couvade in California and the Great Basin and the fuller couvade around the Caribbean probably represent independent historical developments. Because practically all tribes imposed restrictions of some sort on the father at the birth of a child, it is easy to see how an increase in the emphasis on the role of the father could produce parallelism in details, such as lying in bed, in the two areas.

Twins were probably as rare among Indians as among Europeans and were generally regarded or treated in some special manner. The emotional response to them ranged all the way from fear and anxiety to esteem and pleasure. Twins were generally thought to be caused by the supernatural and, where benevolent spirits were thought to be more numerous or powerful than malevolent ones, twins were welcomed; but where the reverse was true, they were feared. Incomplete information suggests that Indians were about equally divided on this score. Among the Pomo of California twins were feared, and it was thought that if sexual intercourse was done lying on the side, this would prevent the conception of twins. The Quinault Indians of the state of Washington thought that twins should always live together because separation would cause both to die. The Iroquois of New York State and other peoples in the East believed twins would grow up to possess supernatural power and would be able to foretell the future, and the southern California peoples and the adjacent River Yumans believed twins went to a special heaven for the highly esteemed. The belief that the death of one twin brings death to the other is most frequently reported on the Plateau and in the Great Basin, but it may also be common in other areas. The killing of one twin at birth has been reported for several culture areas but seems to have been most frequent in the Arctic where, when the twins were of both sexes, the girl was usually killed. If someone could be found to adopt one of the twins, however, both might be spared.

When a child was born, the pregnancy taboos surrounding the mother were not waived at once but, on the contrary, were intensified for a period of a few days to a few months. Dietary restrictions were broadened, seclusion was more severe, and the fear of the supernatural increased. At the end of this period the mother bathed, put on new clothing, and formally presented her child to her relatives or the public at a feast and ceremony. The child was usually given a name at this time. Names were often inherited from a deceased ancestor. Thus among the Eskimo not only was an infant given the name of a dead ancestor, but the soul of the ancestor was thought to reincarnate itself in the body of the child. Eskimo parents never slapped their children or otherwise abused them for fear of insulting the soul of the ancestor, which might decide to depart from the body of the baby and take its life away. Where descent was strictly patrilineal or matrilineal, personal names tended to be inherited in the same unilateral fashion, and in bilateral areas where male dominance over females was marked, as in the Sub-Arctic and on the North Pacific Coast from the Kwakiutl southward, patrilineal inheritance was the rule, at least for male names. In Meso-America, however, the personal name, as well as the fate of the individual, was determined by the date of birth. Such a system could prevail only in cultures with well-developed calendars and was therefore limited to this single area.

439

For other facts about personal names see the section on names in the chapter on Education.

Babies were kept in shallow, open containers of bark, basketry, and wood or were strapped to frames to make it easier for the mother to carry the infant and to anchor it out of reach of harm. These devices are called cradles by anthropologists, but none of them had rockers like the conventional European-derived cradle. In the Arctic the mother carried her baby inside her parka, supported by a hide sling under the baby's buttocks and over her shoulder. Inside the igloo the baby lay on the sleeping platform. Most Indians, however, bound the child to a flat board or framework which could be carried on the mother's back, with the infant facing backward, or could be suspended from a tree or leaned against the house. Such cradles were made of a single board in the Sub-Arctic, East, Prairies, Plains, Plateau, and on part of the Northwest Coast. In other areas a flat framework was made of small plant stems woven together like basketry, and the baby was strapped to this in the same manner. These areas were the ones where basketry dominated woodwork: California, Great Basin, Oasis, and Meso-America. On the Plains a thick, stiff piece of rawhide was also used as a cradle "board."

On the Northwest Coast as far south as the Columbia River, babies were kept in containers of two types: a doweled and sewn box made of boards, and a dugout wooden container. Bark containers were used for the same purpose in the Yukon Sub-Arctic and the Canadian Plateau, at least. And in northern California and southwestern Oregon a basketry container, in which the infant sat with his legs hanging out, was the characteristic cradle. Like the flat cradles of the paragraph above, these container cradles were carried on the backs of mothers, or suspended from above, leaned against some object, or laid down with the infant lying supine.

Babies were usually wrapped in some soft material before being strapped to or in the cradle. In the Sub-Arctic this took the form of a fur bag with moss in the bottom to absorb excretions. On the Plateau, Great Basin, California, Plains, Prairies, and East, the child was swaddled in a piece of buckskin; in the Oasis both buckskin and cloth were used for this purpose, while in Meso-America cloth was the dominant material.

440

In the more tropical regions of Meso-America and the Circum-Caribbean area, where it was too hot to wrap up the child, he was carried naked in a woven sling under his buttocks and over the mother's shoulder, and was kept in a hammock in the house. The hammock was widely used for this purpose also in highland Meso-America, although adults did not sleep in it in this region. Since the Spanish conquest, infants everywhere in Mexico and Central America have been carried in the elongated shawl called *rebozo*.

Mortality of infants was high everywhere in aboriginal North America compared to rates in modern civilized countries. It was especially high in the areas with the poorest natural resources and most severe climates: Arctic, Sub-Arctic, Great Basin, and Northeast Mexico. A study of a modern remnant group of Chichimecs in the last area, for the years 1946 to 1955, yielded the following figures: 30 per cent of the infants died in the first year; 50 per cent died in the first two years; and 67 per cent died in the first five years. These figures may have been even higher in pre-Columbian times, and were almost certainly higher in the sixteenth, seventeenth, and eighteenth centuries, when the Chichimecs were at war with the Spanish. They are probably not far from the average mortality for the continent as a whole in pre-Columbian times.

PUBERTY

For both girls and boys puberty is not an abrupt change, but one which extends over a period of years. However, there is one feature of feminine physiology which appears suddenly and makes it possible to say exactly when a girl has reached a stage of maturity, and that is first menstruation. All Indians make note of this event and give the pubescent girl some advice or instruction about the facts of life and the proper behavior of a female at this time. Because there is no generally accepted mark of maturity for the human male, ceremonies for boys cannot be properly called puberty rites. They have already been discussed in the chapter on Sodalities and Their Ceremonies.

First of all there are tremendous differences in the emphasis placed upon first menstruation from area to area and tribe to tribe. It probably received the least attention in Meso-America, especially when viewed in relation to the other activities and interests of these peoples. In this century the Indians of this area take a secretive attitude toward girls' puberty and usually do not explain this fact of life to girls in advance. When a mother learns of her daughter's first menstruation, she explains what she knows about it to the girl and tries to keep it a secret from the men of the house. There is no seclusion, dietary restrictions, or special avoidances, because these would only serve to call attention to the girl's condition. The Catholic priests and other early chroniclers have left so little information on this matter that positive statements are difficult to make about the aboriginal period in Meso-America. However, it seems likely that this event was more publicized in the sixteenth century and that some prescriptions and taboos were imposed upon the girl at this time, at least among the isolated mountain peoples. Nevertheless, the total emphasis must have been slight, or more information would have come down to us.

On the Plateau and in the Yukon Sub-Arctic, on the other hand, special behavior was required of a pubescent girl for a period of one year in most cases, two years in several instances, and four years among the Carrier of British Columbia. The fear of the harm that feminine physiology could bring to the girl, her family, and the whole community was intense, and every precaution was taken to see that the girl did not endanger the health and lives of others by breaking the rules.

The greatest publicity given to first menstruation was in northern California and among the Apaches of the Oasis, where the girl's puberty ceremony was the greatest ritual occasion in the entire culture. The ceremony was formerly held during the flow of menstrual fluid or just after it had ceased. It lasted for several days and included much feasting, singing, and dancing far into the night. Everyone in the local community was invited by the parents of the girl, and even outsiders were welcomed and sometimes urged to attend.

Still another example will illustrate the tremendous importance of female physiology to some Indians. In northwestern California, which is a part of the Northwest Coast culture area, elaborate annual rites called World Renewal Ceremonies are performed. The total published literature on these famous religious ceremonies is

442

about as bulky as this volume and constitutes one of the most thorough investigations of its kind in anthropological literature. Year after year Indians have performed these rites to renew the contaminated world. When the investigators finally got around to asking the Indians what it was that polluted the world and made the ceremony necessary, they said that menstrual fluid was the principal offender. Here we have an example in which the girls' puberty rite itself is of modest proportions and the subsequent menstruations of women are little talked about; yet this aspect of femine physiology is the center about which the greatest ceremonies of these societies revolve.

Along with the sharp differences just pointed out goes a substratum of beliefs and practices which occurred in every culture area and among a majority of tribes in all areas, except possibly Meso-America. The first is that the menstruant is in a state of close contact with the supernatural which may harm her or other persons if she does not behave properly. She is generally secluded. She especially avoids contact with hunters, fishermen, gamblers, shamans, and priests, all of whom are especially susceptible to harm at this time. She diets in order to avoid illness or bodily disfigurement, and especially abstains from meat so as not to spoil the hunting success of the men who killed the game. She must not touch her body with her hands, lest she catch a skin disease or lose her hair but must use a stick provided for the purpose. She is proctored by an older female relative and instructed in the proper behavior of a menstruating woman, in sex, and in her future duties as a wife and mother. It is also generally believed that the conduct of the girl at this time tends to predetermine her behavior throughout her future life; for example, if she works well at an assigned task, such as gathering firewood, she will grow up to be an industrious woman. At the end of the taboo period she is bathed and dressed in new clothing. These are the beliefs and practices that are the most widespread in native North America, and it is interesting to note that all of them occur in all other major areas of the primitive world as well. We seem to have here a very old and psychologically deep-seated set of notions surrounding feminine physiology.

Northwest Coast.—The Salish-speaking tribelets in the center of

443

this area possess the most elaborate public girls' puberty ceremony of the region. The girl is confined for a time in a wooden cubicle within the large plank house. Women who know the proper songs come daily to see the girl and to sing the songs to insure her a happy and successful future. They are paid for their services by being given an article of the girl's clothing or the products of her weaving during the period of seclusion. In the nineteenth century, pubescent girls were confined for months, or occasionally years, because the light skin which resulted from the lack of sunshine brought a higher bride price. The father's prestige was also increased by showing that he could afford to support an idle member of the family for so long a period.

There is an interesting case in this century of a father who confined his daughter longer than she or the women of her family thought necessary. The word was passed around to all the women who knew girls' puberty songs, and they came to visit the girl daily, each singing a song. When the matter of the gift for this service arose, each in turn asked the father for a sewing machine. This had by that time become a standard household item and a generous gift to receive for such a service. After the father had given away a dozen or more sewing machines and was approaching financial ruin, he was forced to release his daughter in order to avoid bankruptcy. Thus the women got their way in this matter and there were no more long puberty confinements in that family.

In the nineteenth-century practices of the Salish peoples, the girl went through a purification ceremony outdoors in a stream at the end of her seclusion. A group of men known as "washers" appeared in elaborate costumes impersonating spirits, sang the proper songs to the accompaniment of drums and sticks beaten on logs, and poured water over the girl as she stood in a stream. She was then physically and spiritually clean again. At a later date a potlatch feast was given to announce to a wider audience her coming of age and her eligibility for marriage. The tone and ostentation of the potlach was correlated with the wealth of her family and the amount of the bride price that would be paid for her hand.

Northern California.—In this region the pubescent girl was secluded in the usual way, observed dietary taboos, and carefully

444

controlled all her behavior, as in many other areas. The most distinctive belief here was that the girl must be kept awake as much as possible to prevent her from dreaming of ghosts of the dead. Such dreams were interpreted as actual visitations of the ghosts, who were maliciously inclined and likely to steal the soul of the girl, bringing her sickness or death. Therefore, on the first night following the beginning of her first menstruation, everyone in the community assembled near her place of seclusion and sang and danced all night to keep her awake. The pandemonium ceased only for a short time around midnight, when everyone except the girl feasted. Then they continued the dance until morning, when the girl ran toward the east carrying a rattle of deer hoofs in her hand. This singing and dancing was generally repeated for five successive nights, and the entire five-day performance was repeated on the next four subsequent menstruations of the girl, bringing the total ceremony up to twenty-five nights of singing and dancing for many tribelets. Some of the tribelets carried on the ceremonies for ten nights at a time instead of five, and one tribelet sang and danced throughout an entire month. Not only was everyone in the village invited, but friendly outsiders for miles around were sent invitations, and anyone who came on his own volition was welcome. The hosts were the girl's family, although everyone in the local community contributed food and, if the weather was bad, furnished housing for the visitors. In sharp contrast to the seriousness of the occasion for the girl was the spirit of merriment enjoyed by the guests, who sometimes indulged in sexual license on the last night. For some tribelets this was the best-attended ceremony and most joyous occasion of the year.

Oasis.—The Pueblo peoples paid the minimum of attention to puberty, but the Athapaskan-speaking Apaches had a girls' puberty rite that was a large public ceremony. It began as soon after first menstruation as the relatives of the girl could make the arrangements. They were hosts to all visitors, providing food and entertainment consisting of social dancing by both sexes, dancing by men wearing costumes similar to those of the Pueblo kachina dancers and impersonating mountain spirits, and also games and

445

races. The dancing took place at night by firelight, and the games and races were held in the daytime.

The more serious part of the ceremony took place inside a special tipi made for the girl. She danced continually, except for occasional rest periods, until midnight, to the singing of a shaman and the shaking of his deer hoof rattle. On the fourth night, the dancing of the girl continued until dawn. When morning came the shaman painted the girl's face red, then made a dry "painting" of the sun on his palm with pollen and other pigments, pressed this on the girl's head, and finally painted her arms and legs white. As all the guests filed past, the shaman marked them, in turn, with the same pigments. The girl then raced toward the east with children, who nowadays allow her to win, and the ceremony ends.

This ceremony was formerly given for each girl singly at her first menstruation, but more recently the relatives of several girls who have come of age within the last year give the ceremony jointly from the first to the fifth of July. The earlier games and races are now overshadowed by a round-up, with the men competing for honors in riding, bull-dogging, roping, and hog-tieing cattle. Thus the girls' puberty rite of the Apaches, which was the most important single ceremony in their culture, has been combined with one of our own important national ceremonies, the Fourth of July celebration.

A detailed analysis of girls' puberty rites (Driver, 1941) has shown an unexpected number of similarities between the Apache ceremony and that of Northern California and the Northwest Coast. Therefore it is likely that the public ceremonies in these three areas stem from a single origin, probably somewhere in the north, because the Apaches came from the north and arrived in the Oasis somewhere between five hundred and a thousand years ago.

A comparison of girls' puberty observances with those of other ritualized occasions, such as birth, death, vision-seeking, and war, shows that none of the details of individual behavior mentioned above are exclusively associated with first menstruation. All are shared with at least one other ritualized occasion and some, such as dietary restrictions, are shared by all. First menstruation, therefore, is only one of many critical occasions when rapport with the supernatural is close and special behavior is demanded of the individual to prevent harm to him or to his society.

The above examples of the reasons or rationalizations for observing the various taboos at first menstruation suggested that supernatural punishment for wrong-doing was more frequent than reward for right-doing. A fairly exhaustive tabulation of 283 rationalizations for the area west of the Rocky Mountains reveals that 81 per cent of them mention the harm that will befall the girl, other members of her society, or nature if she breaks the rules. Only 19 per cent mention the good things that will happen if the girl faithfully follows all the rules. This illustrates the predominantly negative character of the religious sanctions associated with girls' puberty rites.

Marriage is discussed in the chapter on Marriage and the Family. We need only add here that marriage ceremonies are predominantly secular, social, or civil in character rather than religious. Shamans and priests seldom play leading roles, as do our pastors and priests, and the sanction of the supernatural tends to be taken for granted rather than to be sought on this occasion.

DEATH

The causes of death among Indians were as varied as those for modern populations. Most deaths were attributable to disease or to the violence of the chase, wars, and feuds. A smaller number of deaths resulted from infanticide (discussed above under Birth), suicide, and parricide. The emotional disturbances responsible for suicide were caused by such experiences as disappointment in love, family troubles, illness and incapacitating senility, remorse after unintentionally causing the death of another, sorrow after the death of a loved one, fear of revenge after injuring another, fear of being taken captive by an enemy, and loss of rank in cultures which placed a premium on high rank. The techniques of suicide included hanging, drowning, stabbing, shooting, poisoning, and crawling under a deadfall and releasing the trigger. Neither the causes nor the techniques of suicide are well enough known to determine significant differences between areas, but suicide has been reported in some frequency in all culture areas.

Parricide and the killing of invalids is most frequently reported

447

in the Arctic and Sub-Arctic areas. A person too old or too ill to keep up with the hunting party was frequently abandoned to death by freezing and less often to the wolves. Sometimes the incapacitated person requested a son to kill him to put him out of his misery, because death at the hands of a non-relative might start a feud. Parricide or abandonment was also common in the Great Basin and Northeast Mexico, and probably occurred in lower frequency in many other culture areas as well.

In areas where houses were small, or temporary, or easily rebuilt, a person close to death might be allowed to die in his house. The house would then be abandoned, burned, or torn down and moved because of fear of the ghost of the deceased. In areas where houses were larger and more permanent, such as those occupied by extended families, or in the Arctic, where the extreme cold made it difficult to abandon a house, a dying person was sometimes removed from the house to a special hut in which to die. Another alternative, where fear of ghosts was obtrusive, was to exorcise the house after the death of an inmate to drive away the ghost. Still another practice was to remove the corpse through a specially made opening in the wall or roof rather than through the door, so that the ghost on returning would find the opening walled up and presumably would not know enough to use the door.

Most of the tribes in the United States killed a horse or a dog at the death of the owner as a sacrifice to the supernatural. On the Northwest Coast, and in the Southeast, Meso-America, and the Circum-Caribbean area human beings were normally sacrificed at the death of an important person. Such sacrificial victims might be slaves, war captives, and, in the three more southern areas, servants, a child of a civic-minded citizen, or the widow of the deceased.

Methods of disposing of the corpse show variation not only from tribe to tribe and area to area but also within single cultures. Chiefs or priests might be buried in special tombs or ossuaries above ground, the rank and file in graves below the surface, and shamans might be cremated. However, in most societies one practice was more common than the others.

In the Arctic the dead were most often left on the surface of the ground, because it was impractical to dig a grave in the frozen

448

soil, and there were no trees to provide poles for a raised scaffold or wood for a crematory fire. Sometimes the corpse was covered with stones, and with this protection might later be discovered by the archeologist, but in other instances it was left unprotected, to be devoured by hungry dogs or wolves. Surface burial was common also on the Northwest Coast, but here the dead were generally placed in wooden coffins, in canoes, or in more elaborate surface tombs of wood. Surface deposition in caves and rock shelters was practiced in the Arctic, on the Northwest Coast, Plateau, and Plains, and in the Great Basin and Oasis, at least; and on the Prairies and in the East a corpse was sometimes placed in a hollow log or tree.

Cremation was the dominant form of corpse disposal in three disconnected areas: Yukon Sub-Arctic, adjacent parts of the Northwest Coast, and Mackenzie Sub-Arctic; California and adjacent parts of the Plateau, Great Basin, and Oasis; Northeast Mexico and among a few peoples of Meso-America. As an alternative form of secondary or tertiary frequency, it has been reported for the Plateau, Great Basin, Plains, Prairies, and East. Because the necessary fuel was available in all areas except the Arctic, the limited distribution of cremation cannot be explained in any simple manner.

The placing of the dead on a scaffold or in a tree is dominant only in the Mackenzie Sub-Arctic, the northern Plains, the northern Prairies, and in the middle part of the Northwest Coast. In the last area a single tree trunk, carved like a totem pole, served as a mortuary column on top of which the wooden coffin was placed. Like other forms of totem poles, these belong to the historic period, after steel tools to carve them had been acquired from European trading ships. Scaffold or tree burial was also the rule in the winter in the Eastern Sub-Arctic, where the ground was frozen too deep to make the digging of a grave practical. However, corpses were buried in the ground in some localities by preference, and some of those placed on scaffolds and in trees in the winter were reburied in the earth in summer. Because Christian missionaries everywhere encouraged burial in the ground, it is difficult to decide how much inhumation in this area is native and how much is European.

Inhumation was the most widespread means of disposing of the dead, and, because it was dominant in the areas of heaviest population, it accounted for more individuals than any of the other three, and may possibly have disposed of more corpses than the other three combined. However, Christian influence increased the frequency of burial in the ground in the historic period, so that the data in A.D. 1492 would show less inhumation. Most Indians possessed nothing better for a digging tool than a sharpened stick, and almost half the tribes flexed the legs of the corpse and bound them against the body, so that a grave three feet long would suffice.

Funeral ceremonies for high-ranking persons were quite elaborate on the Northwest Coast, along the coastal plain of the Southeast, in Meso-America, and around the Caribbean. These are the areas where distinctions in rank and social class were most highly developed. In areas of simplest general culture level, such as the Arctic, Sub-Arctic, Great Basin, and Northeast Mexico, funerals were small family ceremonies with the minimum of ritual, although all persons residing in the community at the time of a death might have to practice certain taboos for a time. In the remaining culture areas they were of intermediate magnitude.

In a few areas large memorial ceremonies were held some months or years after death. The Hurons, and some of their neighbors in the northern parts of the Prairies and East, held an elaborate feast of the dead at intervals of twelve years. The corpses were retrieved from scaffolds and trees by their relatives and deposited in a huge community burial pit amidst wailing, singing, and speech-making.

In California an annual mourning ceremony was held for all those who had died during the previous year. This was a large public gathering lasting a week in the second half of the nineteenth century, and it was attended not only by everyone in the local tribelet sponsoring the event, but by outsiders as well. Among a number of tribelets it was the greatest single ceremony of the culture in terms of duration, numbers in attendance, and the sacred values associated with it. This dramatic ritual of a Yokuts tribelet has been recorded by a journalist named Stephen Powers who witnessed the spectacle in the 1870's.

While in Coarse Gold Gulch, it was my good fortune to witness the great dance for the dead (ko-tí-wa-chil), which was one of the most extraordinary human spectacles I ever beheld. It was not the regular annual dance, but a special one, held by request of Ko-ló-mus-nim, a subchief of the Chukchansi; but it was in all respects as strange, as awful, as imposing an exhibition of barbaric superstition and barbaric affection as is afforded by the formal anniversary. Not to my dying hour will the recollection of that frightful midnight pageant be effaced.

First, it will be well to explain that among the Yokuts the dance for the dead is protracted nearly a week. The first two or three nights, while they are waiting for the assembling of the tardy delegations, are occupied only in speech-making, story-telling, etc., until a late hour; but during the last three nights they dance throughout the night until morning, and on the third night, about daybreak, they burn the offerings consecrated to the dead. This happened to be the first of the last three nights, hence no burning occurred, but in every other respect it was complete, and all the exercises were conducted with more energy and with fuller choruses than they would have been after the Indians had become exhausted. . . .

. . . Sloknich, a little, old man, but straight as an arrow, with a sharp face and keen, little, basilisk eyes, stepped forth into the quadrangle and began to walk slowly to and fro around its three sides, making the opening proclamation. He spoke in extremely short, jerky sentences, with much repetition, substantially as follows:

"Make ready for the mourning. Let all make ready. Everybody make ready. Prepare your offerings. Your offerings to the dead. Have them all ready. Show them to the mourners. Let them see your sympathy. The mourning comes on. It hastens. Everybody make ready." . . .

For the last hour or so the mourners and their more intimate friends and sympathizers, mostly women, had been collecting in Kolomusnim's quarter, close behind the circle, and preparing their offerings. Occasionally a long, solitary wail came up, trembling on the cold night-wind. At the close of the third proclamation they began a death-dance, and the mourners crowded promiscuously in a great, open booth, and held aloft in their hands or on their heads, as they danced, the articles they intended to offer to the memory of the departed. It was a splendid exhibition of barbaric gew-gaws. Glittering necklaces of *Haliotis* and other rare marine shells; bits of American tapestry; baskets of the finest workmanship, on which they had toiled for months, perhaps for years, circled and furred with hundreds of little quail-plumes, bespangled, scalloped,

451

festooned, and embroidered with beadery until there was scarcely place for the handling; plumes, shawls, etc. Kolomusnim had a pretty plume of metallic-glistening ravens' feathers in his hand. But the most remarkable article was a great plume, nearly six feet long, shaped like a parasol slightly opened, mostly of ravens' feathers, but containing rare and brilliant plumage from many birds of the forest, topped with a smaller plume or kind of coronet, and lavishly bedecked through all its length with bulbs, shell-clusters, circlets of feathers, dangling festoons—a magnificent bauble, towering far above all, with its glittering spangles and nodding plume on plume contrasting so strangely with the tattered and howling savages over whom it gorgeously swayed and flaunted. Another woman had an image, rudely constructed of shawls and clothing, to represent the dead woman, sister to Kolomusnim.

The beholding of all these things, some of which had belonged to the departed, and the strong contagion of human sorrow, wrought the Indians into a frenzy. Wildly they leaped and wailed; some flung themselves upon the earth and beat their breasts. There were constant exhortations to grief. Sloknich, sitting on the ground, poured forth burning and piercing words: "We have all one heart. All our hearts bleed with yours. Our eyes weep tears like a living spring. O, think of the poor, dead woman in the grave." Kolomusnim, a savage of a majestic presence, bating his garb, though a hesitating orator, was so broken with grief that his few sobbing words moved the listeners, like a funeral knell. Beholding now and then a special friend in the circle, he would run and fall upon his knees before him, bow down his head to the earth, and give way to uncontrollable sorrow. Others of the mourners would do the same, presenting to the friend's gaze some object which had belonged to the lamented woman. The friend, if a man, would pour forth long condolences; if a woman, she would receive the mourner's head in her hands, tenderly stroke down her hair, and unite her tears and lamentations with hers. Many an eye, both of men and women, both of mourners and strangers, glistened in the flickering fire-light with copious and genuine tears. . . .

But now, at last, about one o'clock in the morning, upon some preconcerted signal, there was a sudden tumultuous rushing from all quarters of the quadrangle, amid which the interpreter and myself were almost borne down. For the first time during the night the women appeared conspicuously on the scene, thronged into the sacred circle, and quickly formed a ring close around the fire—a single circle of maidens, facing inward. The whole multitude of the populous camp crowded about them in confusion, jostling and struggling. A choir of male singers took their position hard by and commenced the death-song, though they were not audible except to the nearest listeners.

At the same instant the young women began their frightful dance, which consisted of two leaps on each foot alternately, causing the body to rock to and fro; and either hand was thrust out with the swaying, as if the offering it held were about to be consigned to the flames, while the breath was forced out with violence between the teeth, in regular cadence, with a harsh and grinding sound of *heh!* The blaze of the sacred fire flamed redly out between the bodies of the dancers, swaying in accord, while the disheveled locks of the leaping hags wildly snapping in the night wind, the blood-curdling rasp of their breath in concert, and the frightful ululations and writhings of the mourners, conspired to produce a terrible effect. At the sight of this weird, awful, and lurid spectacle, which was swung into motion so suddenly, I felt all the blood creep and tingle in my veins, and my eyes moisten with the tears of a nameless awe and terror. We were beholding now, at last, the great dance for the dead.

All the long remainder of that frenzied night, from one o'clock to two, to three, to four, to five, those women leaped in the maddening dance, through smoke, and choking dust, and darkness, and glaring light, and cold, and heat, amid the unceasing wail of the multitude, not knowing or heeding aught else on earth. Once in five or ten minutes, when the choir completed a chorus, there was a pause of a few seconds; but no one moved from her place for a moment. What wonder that only the strongest young maidens were chosen for the duty! What wonder that the men avoided this terrible ordeal!

About four o'clock, wearied, dinned, and benumbed with the cold of the mountains, I crept away to a friendly blanket and sought to sleep. But it was in vain, for still through the night-air were borne up to my ears the far-off crooning, the ululations, and that slow-pulsing, horrid *heh!* of the leaping witches, with all the distant voices, each more distinct than when heard nearer, of the mourning camp. The morning star drew itself far up into the blue reaches of heaven, blinking in the cold, dry California air, and still all the mournful riot of that Walpurgis-night went on.

Then slowly there was drawn over everything a soft curtain of oblivion; the distant voices blended into one undistinguishable murmur, then died away and were still; the mourning was ended; the dancers ceased because they were weary. (Powers, 1877:384–90.)

SUMMARY AND CONCLUSIONS

Taboos surrounding pregnancy and birth were numerous and general in native North America, which proves that these events were taken very seriously by Indians even though they were little publicized. Naming ceremonies for infants were common and, in the case of the Northwest Coast potlatches at least, were sometimes large affairs known to all, even though the attendance was restricted by formal invitation. Abortion and infanticide were general and were not regarded as crimes to be punished by legal authority. An understanding of the conditions of life under which women carried on their reproductive functions should make the reader more tolerant of these practices.

Girls' puberty rites at first menstruation exhibit a wide range of variation, extending all the way from secrecy in Meso-America to elaborate public ceremonies in northern California and among the Apaches of the Oasis which topped all other ritual occasions in those two areas. Public ceremonies for every girl who came of age were lacking in the most impoverished cultures, such as those of the Arctic, Sub-Arctic, Great Basin, and Northeast Mexico, and were also apparently lacking in the most complex cultures, those of Meso-America and around the Caribbean. In the Oasis they seem to have been introduced by the intrusive Apaches from the north. In the Plains, Prairies, and East combined, there were no public puberty rites for an individual girl, and only a single instance in the East of a "tribal" initiation ceremony for a group of girls. Therefore, public ceremonies for each girl at first menstruation achieved their greatest development among cultures at a "lower middle" level of general complexity. Such ceremonies occur only in the western part of the continent and appear to stem from a single origin.

Suicide and parricide probably occurred in all culture areas, although not necessarily in all individual societies within the areas. Death probably received more attention than any other life crisis for the continent as a whole, just as it does in many civilized nations. Funerals were most elaborate in areas where the general culture was relatively advanced, such as on the Northwest Coast, in the Southeast, in Meso-America, and around the Caribbean.

These were also the areas of greatest distinctions of rank and social class, and the amount of attention an individual received at death was highly correlated with his rank and eminence in the culture. Memorial celebrations, on the other hand, apparently reached their greatest development among cultures of intermediate general level, those in California and in the northern parts of the Prairies and East.

REFERENCES

Dawson, 1929; Devereux, 1955; Driver, 1936, 1941; Driver, Harold and Wilhelmine, MS; DuBois, MS; Las Casas, 1944 [1574]; Lawson, 1860; Libby, MS; MacLeod, 1925, 1926, 1933; Paul and Paul, 1952; Powers, 1877; Rouse, 1948; Voegelin, 1944; Wisse, 1933; Yarrow, 1880, 1881.

22: EDUCATION

THE TERM education, as used in this chapter,* refers to the entire process by which a person learns the way of life of the society into which he is born and reared. It is equivalent to *enculturation*, the term coined by Herskovits (1948). As we pointed out in the chapter on Sodalities and Their Ceremonies, the amount of formal instruction and actual schooling given Indian children or adolescents was indeed small as compared to education in the literate world. Areas without sodalities had no formal schooling at all, but relied exclusively on the uncontrolled learning of the child by observation and imitation, or on teaching by a parent or other older person. Even in areas where sodality initiations were performed at regular intervals, the schooling of the neophytes often lasted for only a few days. Most of the religious lore, deemed so essential for a successful life, was passed on to the next generation by individual tutoring.

Although the quantity of sodality elaboration is positively correlated with the amount of formal education given the young, this relationship is far from perfect. For example, the medicine men of the Navaho Indians were never organized into sodalities, yet it has been estimated that about one-third of the entire time of the Navaho adult male was occupied with religious ceremony of one kind or another. The verbal material in some of the chants performed by the "Singers" continues for many hours a day for several days. To memorize the verbal formulas and music for one chant of average length took months of close association between teacher and pupil. However, it must be remembered that the elab-

---

* This chapter, except for the last section on the Aztecs, is derived almost wholly from the excellent monograph of Pettitt (1946).

oration of Navaho ritual is to be explained in part by their contact with the Pueblo Indians for more than five hundred years. The Navaho have derived a great amount of ceremonial content from the Pueblos without acquiring the ceremonial organization of the latter. Few peoples without sodalities possess as much ritual as do the Navaho. Ceremonialism reached its greatest development in Meso-America, where it was carefully geared to the calendar system and an organized priesthood; yet the number of man hours consumed in it may not have been any greater per capita per annum than it was in the Oasis among the Navaho and Pueblos. On the whole, however, those peoples with the most elaborate development of sodalities gave the young the greatest amount of formal education or schooling.

In the chapter on Social and Religious Aspects of Subsistence it was mentioned that a boy learning to hunt was carefully taught by his father or other older relative. Every time he killed his first animal of a different species he was rewarded by praise and by being upgraded a rung on the ladder to manhood, but the principle of generosity was so important for him to learn that he was compelled to give away all the meat, at the same time receiving praise and recognition of achievement from the recipients of the food. The same rules applied in many areas to the first berries, roots, or seeds gathered by a girl. In both instances the emphasis was on reward rather than punishment, because children do not seem to have been punished for failure to take an animal or to gather plant foods. Praise for the young seems to have been less obtrusive in farming areas, but boys and girls labored in the fields and were carefully taught the techniques of agriculture.

DISCIPLINE

The emphasis on discipline in Europe and its derivative cultures seems to explain in part the frustration theory of Freudian psychologists. In its simplest form this theory holds that most learning is an adaptation of the child to frustrations imposed upon it by parents or other older persons who care for the child. This seems to be an extreme view, because children learn a great deal from unsupervised imitation of older children and adults. Although frustration is present here, it is of a different character from that consciously imposed on the child in the form of discipline by an adult. On the whole the North American Indians were very permissive with their children as compared to Europeans. Corporal punishment was far from lacking, but it was generally less frequent and less severe than in European cultures and their derivatives.

The close relationship of the young child to the supernatural served as a deterrent to corporal punishment. This concept is clearest among the Eskimo, who regard the infant's soul as being derived directly from a deceased ancestor. The infant's body provides a haven of refuge for the wandering ancestral soul and the infant, in turn, benefits from the knowledge and supernatural power possessed by the soul within. It is as unthinkable to slap or speak harshly to an infant as it is to an aged relative. Such mistreatment of a child may cause its soul to depart, bringing death; or, in other cases, may result in vengeance being taken on the parents by the child developing abnormally large ears, bowlegs, or a humpback. This concept is carried so far that adults explain their own limitations of personality or mental shortcomings in terms of rough treatment received in childhood. This is primitive psychoanalysis totally independent of that of Freud.

This notion that ill-treatment of a child may adversely affect its health and personality, and may even cause its death, has been found by Pettitt (1946: 9–11) to occur also in the Sub-Arctic, Northwest Coast, Oasis, Prairies, and East. This concept, in one form or another, has been regarded as universal in native North America. Although this seems to be an overgeneralization, the idea does account for much of the permissiveness that parents exhibit toward their young children.

Pettitt (1946: 9) also cites about a dozen instances of parents who avoid corporal punishment because they want their children to love them and to regard their home as a refuge from harm from the outside. After having physically restrained a disobedient child or finished with a moral lecture on the proper behavior, the parent may apologize for this mild discipline by saying that custom compels him to do his duty or that the child will be punished by the supernatural if he does not mend his ways. Where whipping is required by ritual, the parent or sponsor of the child may shield the child from the blows or submit to being whipped himself to prove that the treatment being administered to the child is meted out to others as well. Such apologetic behavior or shielding of the child from harm has been reported for the Arctic, Sub-Arctic, Plateau, Oasis, Plains, Prairies, and East, and no doubt occurred in other areas as well.

But the parent-child relationship was not universally affable: children were slapped, whipped, beaten, showered with hot coals or doused with cold water when their behavior failed to satisfy adults. Pettitt (1946:6–7) mentions such punishment for peoples in the Arctic, Northwest Coast, Plateau, Great Basin, California, and Oasis, and suggests that such instances tend to be more numerous as the level of cultural complexity increases. Thus among the Aztecs verbal rebuke was the principal disciplinary method up to the eighth year. From that time, a disobedient child was pricked in the hand with a maguey spine, exposed to the cold on a mountain at night, or compelled to lie bound and naked in a mud puddle. The postponement of such harsh measures to the eighth year is in keeping with the mild treatment of young children in native North America as a whole. Discipline was much stricter in the Aztec boarding schools, where youths of fifteen to twenty-two years of age were severely beaten and even killed for not obeying the rules.

Discipline is frequently administered by a relative more remote than a parent, such as an uncle or aunt. The mother's brother or the father's sister seems more often to serve as disciplinarian, teacher, and sponsor of the child or youth than does the father's brother or mother's sister. Pettitt (1946:22–24) explains the preference of the cross-uncle or aunt over the parallel uncle or aunt as due to a strong brother-sister tie, plus the fact that the mother's brother or father's sister never becomes a stepfather or stepmother to the child, but remains forever outside the nuclear family. In contrast, the custom of sororate, found among a majority of North American Indian societies would result in the mother's sister becoming the child's stepmother in the event of the mother's death. Similarly, the equally widespread levirate would shift the father's brother to the role of stepfather if the father died. The mother's brother, because of the universal brother-sister incest taboo, could never marry the mother, nor could the father's sister ever marry the father. Therefore the mother's brother and father's sister relationships are stable ones, and the nearest unalterable ones in the parental generation to the parents themselves.

At the same time, rules of residence and descent also seem to play a determining part. Most of the instances in which the mother's brother plays a prominent role in the disciplining of a child, as cited by Pettitt, are among societies which are either matrilocal or matrilineal. Because most of the socio-political and religious offices in matrilineal societies were held by males and descended to a man from his mother's brother, we can be sure that the mother's brother had a great deal more to do with the education and discipline of a youth than did the father. Areas where this pattern prevailed are the northern Northwest Coast, the northern Oasis, and the East. In patrilineal societies the father may have served as teacher and disciplinarian more often than did the mother's brother, but no one has collected enough instances to establish this point conclusively.

Grandparents also sometimes aid in the education and discipline of a child, both as grandparents and as foster parents in cases where the true parents have died. So far, no one has assembled enough data distinguishing paternal and maternal grandparents to show how closely their educational roles follow rules of residence and descent, but such correlations can be expected.

In the chapter on Sodalities and Their Ceremonies, we mentioned the frequent occurrence of spirit-impersonations by men masked or painted so as to disguise their identity. Even though such sodalities were usually secret, they normally performed in public upon occasion in full view of children. Most of the spirits represented were supposed to be dangerous, at least if angered, and parents often told a disobedient child that he would be beaten or killed and eaten by such a spirit if he did not behave properly. The initiation rights among peoples with secret sodalities and spirit-impersonations nearly always included some hazing features, such as striking the youth, exposing him to fire, depriving him of food, and frightening him with impersonations of evil spirits. The element of discipline and subordination to authority is prominent in all such initiations.

Whiting, Kluckhohn, and Anthony have recently shown a strong tendency for tribal initiations to be associated with cultures that have a strong mother-son tie. By a strong mother-son tie we mean a long nursing period, a long period when the son sleeps with his mother while the father sleeps in a separate place, and a long taboo on sexual intercourse between parents. Whiting's psychological interpretation of the world-wide correlation between male tribal initiations and a strong mother-son tie is that the isolation of the youth from his mother and the "hazing" he receives from the men during the initiation serves to break the close bond between mother and son, to reduce the hostility toward the father and by extension to other mature males, and thus to insure the identification of the young man with the mature males of the society.

The hazing features of initiations among North American Indians are nearly always administered by persons disguised as supernatural beings, and the neophytes seldom know the identity of the persons playing these roles. Thus part of the responsibility for the proper behavior of the child is shifted from parent, uncle, and aunt to the supernatural, much as in our culture some of it has been transferred from parent to schoolteacher.

In areas where sodalities were rare or absent, namely, the Arctic, Sub-Arctic, Plateau, and Great Basin, discipline was also referred to the supernatural. Individuals disguised themselves as spirits and went about warning or whipping disobedient children. Parents with problem children would arrange for someone outside their family to dress up like some evil spirit and play the disciplinary role. Such monsters represented owls, snakes, bears, ghosts, cannibal spirits, and other dangerous beings. Among the Sanpoil, a Plateau people, the following is reported:

When a child was guilty of serious misconduct it was told that "the old man from up the river" was coming down. The parents secretly notified the old man that locally acted as disciplinarian, who soon appeared disguised and wearing a large robe. . . . If the child cried, it was lashed more. When the old man finished . . . he said: "Now if you are not good the other man from up the river will come down and he is much stronger than I am. He'll whip you harder!" (Ray, 1932:131.)

461

In localities where there was no sodality organization, such disguised disciplinarians had no function in the culture other than to frighten problem children.

Without a doubt the referring of discipline to the supernatural helped keep hostility between parents and children, or between more remote older relatives and children, at a low level. But at the same time it sometimes disturbed children to the point that they continued to have nightmares about evil spirits for the remainder of their lives. The relatively permissive relationship between parents and children, which is encouraged so generally by child psychologists today, is frequently negated by the fear that the Indian child feels toward the supernatural.

PRAISE AND RIDICULE

Since corporal punishment was rare or mild in native North America as compared to Europe and Anglo-America in recent times, correction more often took the form of ridicule, which is reported for every culture area. In the juridical song contest of the Eskimo, mentioned in the chapter on Government and Social Control, two disputants ridiculed each other at length in song in public. This was a powerful deterrent to wrong-doing. Ridicule in song was also applied to persons who had done no wrong, but who had merely failed to accomplish what was expected of a mature person. For example, delay in getting married at the usual age was subject to ridicule, and even more serious was the failure to produce children after marriage. Both men and women were criticized for barrenness, but wife-lending may sometimes have spared a man or woman from this embarrassing predicament.

Ridicule was frequent in the Plains area. Among the Crow Indians a person was chided by his "joking relative," who was his father's brother's child or his father's male sib mate's child. These "joking relatives" were always in different sibs because descent was matrilineal. In the case of a marriage between a good-looking young man and an old maid, his female joking relative berated him in the following manner: "You had better marry a frog or mouse or some other animal than an old maid. What is an old maid good for?" The man did not reply but just sat laughing at the joke on himself. On the other hand a man might say to a woman who was his joking relative, "You are not good enough to attract any man; you have never put up a tent; you have never beaded any blankets; you never make moccasins for your husband; you have been kidnapped again and again." The last phrase means that she was a loose woman, because on certain occasions a man was permitted to kidnap any woman with whom he had had sexual relations before her marriage. Although the accusations leveled by joking relatives against each other were sometimes groundless, the threat of one's protagonist finding real holes in the armor of his personality was always present and served as a deterrent to deviant behavior. Other Plains tribes had similar practices.

Among the neighboring Blackfoot, a boy setting out on his first war party was given a derogatory name which stuck with him until he won honor in war by stealing a horse, killing an enemy, or tagging an enemy, "counting coup." Then he was given a new name symbolizing his brave deed. Women and girls, especially a young man's fiancée, took part in ridiculing a man among the Blackfoot, and the same thing is reported in association with cowardice in warfare among the Cree. For the Mandan and Hidatsa, girls who had won distinction in feminine pursuits might berate young men of their own age who had not yet won honors in war.

The difference between socially sanctioned and unsanctioned ridicule is illustrated by the Iroquois. If a mature man criticized a young man severely in ordinary conversation, the latter sometimes committed suicide; but if the occasion were during the War Dance, the same criticism would be taken lightly. On this occasion any spectator could step forward, make a gift to the dancers, and receive their permission to speak his mind for two or three minutes on any subject he chose, including the shortcomings of a particular individual.

It is noteworthy that personal criticism in public was seldom meted out by parents to their offspring, nor by members of the same sib to their younger sib mates. The family and sib presented a united front to the outside and sought to protect and defend their members rather than to ridicule them. We saw above that corporal punishment was often administered by someone outside the family and sib. Thus the two most obtrusive forms of punish-

463

ment were generally administered by persons outside the immediate kin group.

Reward in the form of praise for a deed well done is more obtrusive in the literature on Indians than is blame for failure. This
is true of all age levels but applies with greatest force to very
young children. Turning again to the Crow of the Plains, we find
that the father was always on hand to praise his son when the
latter was engaged in a shooting contest with the bow and arrow.
The father also gave his son many feasts at which friends made
laudatory speeches and predicted future success for the lad; and
when the boy returned from his first war party, it was the father's
sib mates who rallied round to dance and sing his praise. From
the Osage and Kansa of the Prairies we learn that when boys
fought informal duels, not only was the victor praised by the men,
but also the vanquished if he had fought bravely. Praise was also
the rule for the Shawnee in the same culture area:

> Children were taught that good conduct would earn a reward and
> evil conduct would bring sorrow. . . . A few words of praise from a
> parent or an elder was regarded as the highest prize that could be given
> for good conduct. A child would strive with all his might to win such
> praise while he would be indifferent to bodily punishment. One pun-
> ishment that was always a bitter one to an Indian child was to have
> some of his faults told to a visitor or a friend. (Alford, 1936: 19–21.)

Among the Natchez of the lower Mississippi boys practiced
shooting arrows at a bundle of grass thrown in the air. Every time
a youngster scored a hit he was praised by an old man in charge
of the group. The one who consistently shot best was named the
young warrior, and the next best the apprentice warrior. On ceremonial occasions when mature warriors had recounted their war
deeds and received applause, boys were encouraged to recount the
deeds they expected to perform in the future and were praised
just as much as those who had already achieved them.

Other parallel instances are reported from the Oasis. Among
the Hopi, parents and other onlookers bestowed loud applause on
the youngster who hit the target with bow and arrow. For the
Zuñi, we learn that a child was praised for every acceptable action, such as observing the right social etiquette and using the
proper terms of greeting when visiting.

On the Northwest Coast among the Nootka, boys frequently imitated famous orators before an audience of old men who encouraged the lad by predicting that he would do great things in the future.

The Eskimo celebrated the achievements of very young children with feasts to which neighbors were invited to hear the parents praise their offspring. Such a feast was given for a child when he was compelled to spend the night away from home because the return of his parents was delayed by a storm, or when he had worn out his first pair of boots.

When these examples are added to the praise children received for success in the hunt or in wild plant gathering, the total amount of praise received seems to top the total amount of ridicule.

FREE IMITATION AND DIRECTED LEARNING

All children in all cultures learn partly by voluntary imitation of older children or adults without the awareness of those imitated of their passive roles as teachers. At the same time all children in all cultures on other occasions receive specific instruction from elders in regard to the proper behavior. Indian children probably learned more by free imitation and less by conscious instruction than do children in the modern western world. Nevertheless many instances are reported of children being taught both essential tasks and games by parents or other elders. The distinction between work and play was less sharp among Indians than it is in our modern world. This was especially true of those peoples who did not farm, but lived entirely by hunting and gathering. Hunting was always a challenging adventure, and even the gathering of wild plant products necessitated travel over a considerable area with the chance of meeting neighbors and renewing old acquaintances. When an unusual quantity of wild food was obtained, it was always an occasion for festivities to which friends were invited.

For the most part, children played at activities which trained them for the work of adults; boys practiced shooting the bow and arrow, first at targets and later at small game, and girls played with dolls and at household tasks. The child's first weapon or doll was usually made by an elder and given to him. Later the child might

465

voluntarily make his own, with instruction from a parent. As the child matured, his dependence on elders for toys or help in making them was discouraged. In areas where a premium was placed on warfare, boys were taught the art of war in sham battles. The following excerpt is taken from a description of the games of the Mandans:

One of the most pleasing is the sham fight and sham scalp dance of the Mandan boys, which is a part of their regular exercise, and constitutes a material branch of their education. During the pleasant mornings of the summer, the little boys between the ages of seven and fifteen are called out, to the number of several hundred, and being divided into two companies, each of which is headed by some experienced warrior, who leads them on in the character of a teacher; they are led out into the prairies at sunrise, where this curious discipline is taught them. (Catlin, 1841:131–33.)

After shooting at each other with miniature bows and blunt arrows, the boys returned to the village where they put on a scalp dance with imitation scalps for an audience of girls. The girls, in turn, acted out their admiration for their young heroes.

Among the neighboring Sioux, a boy was given a small bow and blunt arrows as early as five years of age and instructed in their use. The father was most often the donor and teacher, but a grandfather or other older relative might substitute if the child were fatherless. One man recalled that his first bow was decorated to show the high rank of his father as a hunter and warrior. As the boy grew older and more skilled, the bow became larger, the arrows were pointed, and the stationary target was replaced by small game on the move. Finally he was given a man's weapons, or taught how to make them, and allowed to accompany the men on a buffalo hunt or raiding party.

Among the Eskimo, there is considerable evidence of the child's play being initiated and directed by parents. Little boys as young as three years of age were given toy bows and arrows, harpoons, bird darts, sleds, and ivory carvings of animals to play with. A father sometimes modeled snow animals for his son to shoot at. Little girls were given dolls, and later encouraged to make them and to make clothes for them out of skins. Puppies were even turned over to children who harnessed them to toy sleds; both the pups and the children were supposed to learn something of value from this experience. As a boy grew older, he would accompany his father on the hunt and would be allowed to go through the motions of killing the dead animal his father had taken. Similarly little girls were encouraged to help in skinning and butchering and in distributing meat. Successful participation by children in such useful tasks brought praise, and failure might bring ridicule.

In areas where weaving, pottery-making, and other such crafts were important, children received a great deal of instruction from adults. Often a single child was chosen to carry on a craft of a mature member of the family, since one such specialized individual per family was sufficient. In some instances a younger child denied formal instruction might learn the craft by voluntary imitation of an adult or an older child. Thus, directed learning and free imitation might exist side by side for the same task in the same family.

Throughout North America free imitation was combined with teaching. Every Indian society engaged in tasks requiring enough skill to demonstrate the advantage of actual instruction over unbridled mimicry. The survival of every society in the competitive Indian world depended in part on the skill with which it acquired its food, manufactured its tools, and defended itself against aggressors. Any people who dispensed with the tutoring of the young in such necessary skills could not have maintained its independent way of life for long. The fact that Indians often serve as hunting and fishing guides to those of European ancestry in the modern world is proof that they still possess marketable knowledge of wild life, a knowledge handed down to them by their Indian ancestors.

THE MARKERS OF MATURITY

All Indian languages possessed age-status terms to designate the various stages of the life cycle, and along with them went a series of other markers. In relation to education, the most important transition is from that of child or adolescent in need of further education to that of adult able to assume the responsibilities of the mature individual. The status markers of maturity were the

467

rewards for acquiring the abilities, skills, and knowledge of the adult. In the areas with sodalities the tribal initiations marked the acquisition of adult status on the part of the youths who were initiated. Tribal initiations were much less frequently conducted for girls, but all peoples recognized first menstruation as a marker of maturity, and a few of them held a public ceremony for each girl as she came of age (see Puberty in the chapter on Life Cycle).

In addition to the above major indicators of maturity there were a host of other achievements which helped raise the child to the status of an adult. On the Plains, Prairies, in the East, in Meso-America, and around the Caribbean, a successful war record was requisite to manhood. No young man could get married, speak in council, or dress like a man until he had gone to war and brought back evidence of having bested an enemy. Probably all the peoples in these areas distinguished warriors by special colors or patterns painted on the body, by the tattoo marks or designs on the body, by a special hair cut, and by special clothing and regalia. Some of the tribes in the remaining culture areas recognized similar signs of military distinction.

In the areas where game furnished the bulk of the diet (Map 3), success in the hunt was invariably prerequisite to marriage and full adult status. No woman would consider marrying a man who could not keep her supplied with food. This standard of success encouraged boys to bend every effort to acquire skill with the bow and arrow, and other weapons of the chase, and to learn all they could about the habits of game animals and the best means of outwitting them.

As we shall see in more detail below, a successful vision quest often assured success in hunting or warfare, permitted the youth to wear on his person the designs seen in the vision, and freed him from listening to moral lectures and other pearls of wisdom designed for the consumption of children. Participation in public religious ceremonies was often necessary to achieve full adult status. For example, among the Oglala Sioux a man could not claim the cardinal virtues of bravery, integrity, and generosity unless he had experienced the tortures of the Sun Dance and had scars on his body to prove it.

There were also dietary restrictions on children which were

468

lifted when they were successful in an adult pursuit. Thus among the Eskimo a youth was forbidden to eat young seal meat, eggs, entrails, heart, lungs, liver, narwhal, and small game until he had fully demonstrated himself to be an accomplished hunter. In other localities boys were given only cold food, served last, or not allowed to eat with elders when strangers were present.

These few examples will give some idea of the many ways in which the Indians distinguished the child from the adult. Although many of the rewards were deferred a number of years, they served as a constant incentive to further effort. With the mild amount of corporal punishment and a generally permissive early childhood, the bliss achieved by children was not sufficient to entice them to remain in the status of children indefinitely. Adults rewarded their achievements sufficiently to encourage them to become adults as soon as they were able. Their education included a series of carefully graded tasks to master before it could be considered complete.

PERSONAL NAMES

The use of nicknames of a trivial, ridiculous, or derogatory character is found in every culture area north of Mexico, although not every people in every area followed the practice. Such names were given to children of various ages and were not changed until the child had distinguished himself sufficiently to be given a new name appropriate to his deed of distinction. In some instances, however, a person was addressed by his nickname throughout life, or in jest, even though he had acquired new names by achievement and change of status. Examples of nicknames that a child would not want to keep are: turned up nose; flat head; long ears; turtle anus; intestines; hump on rump; big nose; without teeth; beaten into submission; ghost. Such names served as an incentive to the child to upgrade himself to the point of receiving a new name for some accomplishment.

The most common occasions on which new names were bestowed were at first menstruation for girls, initiation into a sodality for boys, success in hunting and war for boys, and the acquisition of supernatural power in the vision quest for both sexes but more often for boys. In some instances of hereditary names a youth

469

could not assume the name of his father until he had achieved a status comparable to that of his father, for example, in warfare. In other cases the entire community had to approve a new name for a young man before it would be applied to him. Some men acquired a dozen or more names in a lifetime by performing as many successive deeds of distinction. As men became older they turned to civil and religious affairs and were given new names for exceptional achievement in these activities. Examples of names describing achievement are: warrior walking; he who causes fear; two buffalo bulls; wisdom; brave chief; stampedes the grizzly bear; sacred hawk; big medicine; one who is loved.

There was a strong tendency in all culture areas north of Mexico to name a child after a distinguished person, with the hope of transferring the desirable personality of the elder to the younger, and sometimes even before the child had achieved anything of note. The donor was not of necessity an ancestor or collateral older relative of the child, although heredity was an important factor. The conflict between the status ascribed by heredity and that achieved by behavior was sometimes compromised by giving a child an hereditary nickname in the beginning, and later recognizing his accomplishments by bestowing on him a more serious hereditary name, often from the same ancestor. Persons of distinction normally acquired a series of names over a lifetime, so that it was possible to upgrade a young person by conferring such a series of names from a single important ancestor. In Meso-America, where the personal name was determined by the date of birth, this system was lacking. For other information on names, see pages 439–40 in the chapter on the Life Cycle.

VISION QUEST AND SPIRIT-HELPER

Dreams and hallucinations were interpreted as contact with the supernatural in all culture areas, although their importance in the life of the individual differed from area to area. Such personal experiences were of limited value in Meso-America, the Pueblo part of the Oasis, and in other localities where organized cults and priesthoods dominated the religious scene. Visionary experiences were most highly regarded in areas which lacked organized religions, such as the Plateau and Plains. Peoples in still other areas encouraged both individual contact with the supernatural in visions and group contact in organized ritual. All Indians agreed, however, that one's success in life was due not only to his own efforts, but in large part to the sanction of the supernatural.

In the process of acquiring the many markers of maturity, no experience was as important as the acquisition of a spirit-helper in a vision quest for at least half the culture areas of native North America. Without it a man would fail in all important undertakings, such as hunting, warfare, and curing the sick. Where visions were absolutely essential, individuals did not wait patiently to be touched by the divine hand, but sought out spirits on a vision quest. Such quests might be begun as early as five years of age, but more often the first quest was undertaken at about puberty. Both boys and girls went on vision quests on the Plateau, where the concept was perhaps most highly developed, but in other areas it was generally limited to boys.

A youth would travel to an isolated spot with a reputation as an abode of spirits, usually a mountain, or a lake, or an uninhabited wood. Here he remained for several days and nights, fasting from both food and water, naked in the cold, mutilating his body, and otherwise denying the desires of the flesh to the point that an hallucination was likely to occur. He prayed by asking a spirit to take pity on him in his condition of deprivation and want, the idea being that the more miserable his condition, the more likely was a spirit to come to his aid. Such "visions" usually took the form of both visual and auditory hallucinations. The neophyte would frequently see an animal spirit which would speak to him, teach him a song, or show him designs to paint on his body, clothing, or weapons for protection against the enemy. On returning home, the youth would eventually describe his experience to his family or camp mates, sing the songs he had acquired, and paint the designs on his possessions. If his demonstration was convincing, he might later acquire a following on a future hunting or warring expedition. If the knowledge he acquired in the vision was efficacious in curing the sick, he could set himself up as a medicine man. Such vision quests did not always end with an initial success but were sometimes continued at intervals throughout life in order to renew or supplement the first power acquired in youth.

471

The function of the vision in education was to instil confidence in a young person so that he would attempt things considered impossible before such a religious experience. With a spirit-helper at his beck and call, an insecure adolescent would become more self-sufficient and would take more initiative in such necessary activities as war and the chase. When the odds were against him, he would exert greater effort in the belief that his spirit-helper would get him out of his predicament.

Such supernatural experiences were of greatest importance for the religious leaders of the society who made careers out of their rapport with the divine. Those religious functionaries who are supposed to have had direct individual contact with the spirit world are generally called shamans. In some areas, such as the Plateau, where everyone of any consequence had a vision, there was no definite distinction between shaman and layman. The difference was one of degree; the shaman possessed more spirits or more powerful spirits than did the layman. In other areas, where visions were less universal, the shaman was more clearly distinguished from the layman. The shaman never stopped with a single initial vision obtained in youth, but renewed his contact with the supernatural by going into a trance or some other preoccupied state every time he functioned in his society. This was true regardless of whether he was trying to locate evasive game, find a lost child, make rain, cause a bad storm to cease, or cure the sick. He had visions again and again, and if he was intelligent enough to convince people of his power or to predict the weather in advance, he might rise to a position of leadership.

Religious leaders called priests depended less on visionary experiences as a means of acquiring competence and more on actual instruction by older priests. As mentioned in the chapter on Sodalities and Their Ceremonies, prospective priests were sometimes instructed in groups in schools, but north of Mexico individual tutoring was more common.

EDUCATION AMONG THE AZTECS

In the Aztec system of compulsory education, there were two types of schools, that is, organizations of students and teachers, the *telpuchcalli* or houses of youth and the *calmecac* or school for priests. Every Aztec youth entered one or the other; all sons of commoners and some of the sons of nobles entered the houses of youth at fifteen years of age, and other sons of nobles the schools for priests, sometimes at an earlier age. Youths remained in the houses of youth until twenty or twenty-two years of age, when they married. Those in the school for priests, for the most part, never married but stayed in the priesthood all their lives.

When a boy was born, he was taken by his parents either to one of the houses of youth or to the school for priests and enrolled as a future pupil in the school. At this time the parents prayed to the patron deity that their child, likened unto a precious jewel or brilliant quetzal feather, might grow up to be a brave warrior or a distinguished priest. When the boy attained the proper age, he was taken by his father to the school to which he had been dedicated in infancy.

In the houses of youth the duties of the boys were many. They swept the premises, built the fires, and joined with the others in singing and dancing at night. When they were still quite young, they were taken to the forests, where they cut logs and carried them back to their headquarters, first only one log, but when older, two at a time. They were also taken into battle at an early age to determine whether they were likely to be distinguished in war. If a youth was successful in such trials, discreet in speech, pure in heart, and had otherwise acquired a degree of maturity, he was promoted to the status of master of youths. If he enjoyed still further success, especially in warfare, he was advanced to the higher rank of a ruler of youths. In this capacity he was in charge of a group of younger youths and meted out justice in the form both of promotions and punishments to his underlings. Those who had taken four captives in battle were elevated to the still higher rank of constable and carried staves as symbols of office.

Work parties of young men from the houses of youth also made adobe bricks for walls, cultivated the fields belonging to the organization, and dug canals for the irrigation of the crops. Work always stopped just before sundown, when they returned to the school, bathed, painted, and adorned themselves for the evening festivities. Those of rank were distinguished from the others by special dress. A fire was built after sunset, when they sang and

473

danced until midnight. The higher-ranking and older men always slept with their paramours.

Drinking alcoholic beverages was a much more severe offense than unchastity. If a youth were found drunk and singing in a loud voice in public, or fallen into a stupor in a conspicuous place, he paid the extreme penalty. He was beaten to death with staves or strangled with a rope in a public place for all to see. However, if he were the son of a nobleman, he was strangled secretly so as not to stigmatize his family.

As the youths grew older they gradually acquired female mates, sometimes by twos and threes. When twenty to twenty-two years of age they were given permission to leave the boarding school, to get married to one woman, and to join the ranks of the mature citizens.

Rules in the school for priests were stricter. All the students slept in the school, arising before dawn to sweep the building. Some got up between midnight and dawn and went to the forest to gather firewood to replenish the perpetual (fifty-two-year) fires. Work parties performed the same tasks as those from the houses of youths, but they left the priests' house before dawn. About sunset they would cease their utilitarian tasks and cut maguey spines. After nightfall the young priests bathed themselves and gathered up their shell trumpets, incense ladles, sacks of incense, and pine torches in preparation for going forth to offer the maguey thorns to spirits residing in sacred spots. Each young man would walk from a half to two leagues to a forest, desert, or lake, where he placed his thorns.

The priests slept well apart without touching one another or being covered with the same blanket. They prepared their own food, and if one received a gift of food from his family he had to share it with the others. At midnight everyone was supposed to arise and pray. Those who overslept were punished by having blood drawn from their ears, breasts, thighs, or calves of the legs with maguey thorns or sharpened pieces of bone. Those who drank wine or had sexual relations with women were strangled, shot to death with arrows, or cast into fire alive. Small boys who committed minor sins had blood drawn from their ears or were switched with nettles.

474

At times of fasting some ate only once a day at noon, while others ate only at midnight. At such times they were forbidden to eat salt and chile or to drink water.

Emphasis was placed upon correct speech; those who spoke poorly or failed to address another in the proper manner were punished with bloodletting. All were taught the gods' songs and the calendar system from the book of dreams and the book of years.

Thus it is clear that the formal schooling of youths of the Aztecs and their neighbors in Meso-America went far beyond that of any other area. In fact, until recent times, few cultures anywhere in the world had as much formal education. The details of religion and ceremony were so complex that it took many years to master the knowledge necessary to be a head priest devoted to the worship of a single important god; and the time that it took to teach this knowledge to younger men was also great. This explains why the role of priest was a full-time and lifelong position and why it was necessary to have schools to maintain the system.

REFERENCES

Catlin, 1841; Heskovits, 1948; Lowie, 1935; Pettitt, 1946; Ray, 1932; Sahagún (Anderson and Dibble), 1950–58; Vaillant, 1941; Whiting, Kluckhohn, and Anthony, MS.

23: RELIGION, MAGIC,
AND MEDICINE

A STRIKING feature throughout the study of Indian cultures is the pervasiveness of the supernatural. In all areas, some direct or indirect reference to belief in the supernatural can always be detected in every activity. Often, its presence may be surprising in a particular context, such as food-getting activities, even though quite appropriate, given the circumstances of the Indians' existence. The search for food, being an everlasting problem to the Indians of many areas, shows a complex superimposition of technique associated with the supernatural. Animals were considered as much responsible for their capture or being killed as the actual manner and implements of taking them. They formed a kind of supernatural society to themselves and consequently the hunter had to please them all, in much the same manner that he would himself be pleased, with ritual, gifts, and praise, in order to gain their assent to be killed. Other food-getting activities, such as wild plant gathering and farming, were also attended by ritual and ceremony, although those rituals were not directed toward pleasing plants in the same way that hunting ceremonies were directed toward pleasing animals. A closer analogy between ceremonies for gaining the assent of an animal to be killed and farming ceremonies is the rain-making ritual, in which the spirit who caused rain required propitiation before his gift could be received. Some plants themselves were thought to be of a sacred nature, especially peyote, which is used even today in the religious ceremonies of the Native American Church. Such belief is hardly unexpected,

476

since the hallucinations brought about by the use of peyote rein-
force the religious beliefs of the user.

The life cycle is attended in every part by the appropriate religious ritual. The taboos and duties required of the mother during
and after her pregnancy are strict and demanding. They entail
seclusion from the other members of the household and dietary
restrictions as well as habits of movement, bowing the head, or
what may seem to us personal degradations. But the benefit of the
society is usually the object, and, in the case of bowing the head
in public, the specific purpose is to avoid displeasing the society
of animals and thereby endangering the food source. It appears
that the animals are no more prone to be eaten by a pregnant
woman than they are to be killed by a hunter who has met a
pregnant woman face to face. The dietary restrictions serve the
same function, to avoid endangering the food source, for the
animals are as careful in their choice of a successful hunter as
they are, after having been killed, cleaned, and cooked, in their
choice of who should eat them. Obviously, with the seriousness
of the results, possible starvation for the whole tribe, relaxation
of these restrictions would be difficult to achieve.

Direct references to the supernatural can be seen in the elaborate
architecture, the temples, pyramids, and astronomical observatories, of Meso-America, where the greater complexity of religious
belief and ritual is consistent with the greater complexity of the
culture as a whole. Among the Pueblo of the Oasis, where architecture was not elaborate but was permanent at least, the religious
structure called kiva was centrally located and usually circular—in
an area where other buildings were always a complex of cubicles.
True temples were also found in the Circum-Caribbean and Southeast areas, and the religious structures of California approached
the status of temples.

Rank and wealth were often displayed through possession of
corporeal and incorporeal property. Among the Kwakiutl of the
Northwest Coast, songs were marketable merchandise but, because
the songs themselves were religious, they measured the relation
of a man to the supernatural as well as his rank within the society.
The right to use ornamental religious devices was also marketable
and served the same purpose of ranking an individual in relation

477

both to the supernatural and the society. Medicine bundles from the Plains area were used in similar fashion, except that the increase in the demand, the value, and the turnover of medicine bundles as a result of the inflation brought about by the fur trade makes their value as property more evident.

Religion is as important in government and social control as in any other function of society. In those areas which lacked true political organization, the religious leader, or shaman, often enjoyed a position of great authority. In areas of borderline and mixed systems of government, the political leaders were also religious leaders, or at least were closely allied with them, and usually dependent upon them. If the shaman was not in a position of high governmental authority, it was simply because his time was more completely devoted to religious matters. Within the world view of the Indian, such interdependence was necessary because the sanction of the supernatural for all tribal activities, which the shaman was most likely to secure, was requisite for the success and well-being of the tribe. The shaman's position of power over individuals made him the most likely instrument for social control. The formula was simple: a recalcitrant person in need would not be helped, and the most valuable help came through the shaman from the supernatural.

Of course, any warring venture was absolutely dependent upon the aid of the supernatural. The spectacular rise and decline of the Ghost Dance religion of the 1890's, just after the warring spirit of the Indian had been whipped up to a high point in the swan song war against the invading Whites, is important in this respect. But this particular instance amounted to more, for here is an example of the need for supernatural sanction resulting in the establishment of a new religion rather than the extension of an existing one to cover the projected activity. This phenomenon invested all its potential in the power of the shaman, with the help of the dancers, to gain the approval of the supernatural in a cause with which by natural means the Indians were unable to cope. In a frenzy of panic at the recognition of impending failure and possible extinction, the hysteria induced by the weird ritual of the Ghost Dance encouraged a bravery and selflessness that transcended normal experience. But this last effort was ineffectual, the dead did not return, and more and more Indians sought refuge in the peyote religion.

Within most individual tribes, there were fraternal organizations ranging from completely religious in character to almost wholly social. But even those dedicated to the pleasure and brotherhood of their members indulged in some religious function, such as the establishment of rapport between the initiates and the supernatural. Another function of some sodalities was the group punishment of children, but since this was always accomplished by masked spirit impersonators, the supernatural entered into the problem of social behavior as well. In some areas, individuals were disguised to punish children singly. The nightmares that resulted from punishment by men in spirit disguise often lasted throughout an individual's lifetime. But because dreams were thought to be rapport with the supernatural, these resultant nightmares only strengthened the faith of the man in the truth of the disguises which he had learned since childhood were just that—disguises.

As can easily be seen from the examples above, the supernatural can no more be explained outside the ways and means of living than the customs of the Indian can be explained without reference to the supernatural. Such beliefs dictate in varying degrees every social action and are bound to have a deep effect upon those who hold them. But if the effect of existing beliefs upon a society seems great—the peyote religion served as a rallying point around which new societies were formed from the chaos left by defeat— the effect upon the individual personality will be as great—the formation of a new personality out of the pieces left by the disintegration of the old one. Some of these effects will be taken up in the next chapter.

Religion is regarded by anthropologists as the relation of man to supernatural personalities with anthropomorphic attributes. It includes *animism*, which is defined as the belief in spiritual beings or personalities. There is no generally accepted classification of spiritual personalities in books on primitive religion, but a division into gods, ghosts, and other spirits introduces a little order into the chaos of animism as a whole. *Gods* are important and powerful spirits, whose existence and power is recognized by every mature person in a culture. *Ghosts* are the souls of deceased ancestors,

479

which are propitiated principally by their own descendants, but which may also be recognized and supplicated collectively by the society as a whole. *Other spirits* is a residual category for all other spiritual personalities who have neither attained the rank of gods nor formerly lived as human beings on earth. Animism was universal in native North America.

Gods, ghosts, and other spirits are supposed to have intelligence, emotions, and free will comparable to those of man. They may intervene in the affairs of the world and of man in a manner consistent with a system of ethics or according to their whims of the moment. Because of their human-like emotions they may experience love, hate, joy, anger, jealousy, fear, courage, and may act according to their emotional state at the time. They may be benevolent, malevolent, or merely unconcerned, but they are generally susceptible to human pleading and bend an ear to prayers, sacrifices, and other forms of emotional appeal to their egos.

Such spiritual personalities are generally regarded as more intelligent and more powerful than man, although they may be assigned to different statuses and ranks in their own supernatural hierarchy. Their power is sometimes explained by the possession of a large quantity of the impersonal supernatural energy generally called by the Melanesian term *mana*. *Mana* may be compared to electricity or to atomic energy. When properly controlled by rubber gloves, lead shields, and switches, electricity and atomic energy can be extremely beneficial to the possessor, but they can quickly get out of hand and cause harm. So it is with *mana*. But because spiritual beings are generally superior to man, they usually exercise greater control over this impersonal supernatural energy than does man. Man may derive benefit from this infinite supply of power by asking a spirit who possesses it to help him. The concept of *mana* was also probably universal in native North America.

However, some men are able to maneuver impersonal supernatural power as well as to compel spiritual personalities to do their bidding. Their technique is called *magic*. If the proper spell is recited, if the proper manipulation of physical materials and objects is carried out, or if a symbolic pantomime is re-enacted, a certain result is destined to follow. A mere human being, therefore, is able to compel supernatural forces or personalities to fulfil his desires. The magician does not beg with tears in his eyes and a tremor in his voice for aid from a spirit, but goes methodically through the fixed routine which he believes is certain to bring about the desired result, unless someone else possesses a more powerful counter-magic. There need be no conflict between religion and magic, or for that matter between either of the two and modern science. Many persons employ all three in their daily lives. Thus a farmer may select the best hybrid corn seed available (science), plant it under a waxing moon (magic), and pray to God for rain when he goes to church on Sunday (religion). Indians normally employ mixed systems of religion, magic, and practical science which are difficult to analyze even with the aid of terms in native languages.

The term *sorcery* or *witchcraft* is applied to magic used for antisocial purposes. The harming or even the killing of a person by magical technique, when he is regarded by his society as a criminal, is not an antisocial act, because the people may agree that he should be killed. But when evil (black) magic is directed against an innocent person, only then does it become sorcery or witchcraft. It is then a form of unapproved aggression against a fellow member of a society. Magic, good and bad, was likewise universal in Indian America.

Because of its supposed compulsive character and inevitable sequence of cause and effect, magic has been compared to modern science. It resembles science in that specific formulas and techniques, verbal and non-verbal, are expected to produce specific predictable results. However, science possesses a rigid experimental technique which does not exist in the primitive world of magic. Let us take an example from the field of preventive medicine and contrast the Indian attitude with that of science.

In 1909 an anthropologist named Alanson Skinner went on a field trip to the Ojibwa Indians of Canada, where he observed a woman with a cross tattooed on each cheek. When asked the significance of the crosses, she said they were to prevent toothache. She believed there was a cause and effect relation between the presence of the crosses on her cheeks and the absence of toothaches. How does modern science test her hypothesis?

481

The common scientific procedure at the present time would be to select a population of naïve people from another locality who had not yet tattooed their cheeks, divide the population by some random device into two groups, an experimental group and a control group, tattoo crosses on the cheeks of the experimental group and then, over a period of years, observe the frequency of toothache in the two groups. If the Indian woman's hypothesis is correct, the frequencies of toothache in the non-tattooed group should be significantly greater than those in the tattooed group. If her hypothesis is incorrect, there should be no significant differences in the frequencies in the two groups. The scientific determination of significance is based on probability theory and requires the application of a statistical formula to the frequencies. It is obvious that no Indian culture ever worked out such a formula. The tendency of all naïve persons who believe in such magic is to remember only the positive cases, those persons whose cheeks are tattooed and who are free of toothaches, and those persons whose cheeks are not tattooed and who do have toothaches. The negative instances, those persons with tattooed cheeks who have toothaches and those with neither tattooed cheeks nor toothaches, are usually overlooked or forgotten. The test cases which Indians and other primitive peoples assemble to "prove" the efficacy of their magic never satisfy the criteria of modern science and are comparable to science only in a very superficial way.

If Indian shamans and priests have no adequate tests to demonstrate the efficacy of their arts, how do they build up reputations as religious or magical practitioners? The success of such operators may be explained in a number of ways: for instance, by the possession of foreknowledge of the outcome of some event which is doubtful to others. Thus the rain-maker may possess real skill in forecasting the weather by the direction of the winds, the appearance of the clouds, or his feeling for relative humidity and atmospheric pressure. Modern orthopedists have shown that changes in barometric pressure can be felt by persons with arthritis. The rain-maker may likewise feel such changes "in his bones" and, if the weather signs are unfavorable, postpone his rain-making rites to a time when he believes it more likely to rain.

The curing of disease with plant remedies is widespread among

482

Indians, and some of such curatives are known by modern pharmacology to be efficacious. The best-known examples of modern drugs of Indian origin came from South rather than North America. Thus the coca plant, which contributes ingredients to our cocaine and novocaine, was used by many Indian medicine men of South America to alleviate pain. Curare, used as arrow and dart poison by the tropical forest Indians of that continent, is now an important adjunct to modern anesthesia. And the bark of the quinoa tree, from which quinine was derived, was used in other medicines of South American Indians. In North America, after 25 of Cartier's men had died of scurvy, a band of friendly Iroquois cured the rest by giving them a decoction of pine bark and needles, thus proving that the pine products contained vitamin C.

Many of the cures effected by Indian medicine men belong to the category of psychotherapy. Psychosomatic or psychogenic disease is and was at least as common among Indians as in European societies and their derivatives. The Indian psychotherapist may be just as skilled in helping his patients as the best psychiatrist or analyst in the modern world. Any of the hundreds of kinds of medicine-men's cures may be equally as efficacious as modern psychotherapy for those who believe in them. The anthropologist has no criteria for ranking these many systems of psychotherapy, except utility.

The mention of psychotherapy leads to the relation of emotions to religion and magic. Everyone agrees that emotional responses are everywhere associated with religion and magic, but so little is known about human emotions that nothing concrete can be said about this relationship. A mere listing of words such as reverence, awe, and fear tells us little. Perhaps it is more meaningful to say that all human emotions, whatever they are, may be associated with one or another of the many behaviors and beliefs usually subsumed under religion and magic. The emotions would vary from culture to culture just as do the behaviors, verbal and nonverbal, which characterize each particular "system" of magic and religion. In extreme cases such emotions may be violent enough to cause death or, on the other side of the ledger, be able to cure a person of a psychosomatic ailment capable of causing death.

Physiologists and psychiatrists do not agree on the precise phys-

483

iological sequences which a human being experiences when he dies of emotional disturbance, but experiments with emotional stress on laboratory animals and observations of human patients undergoing severe stress from both physical injuries and emotional disturbance have thrown some light on the subject. At least two physiological stages may be distinguished: shock, and resistance to shock. Which comes first depends on the individual as well as on the nature of the stress. Stress which drives one individual to increased effort will cause another to fall into a faint, or to cease to live. The person who increases his physiological and physical activity under stress is resisting the stress, while the one who faints is succumbing to the stress and is in a state of shock.

Walter B. Cannon (1942) found that intense fear or anger is characterized by a powerful resistance to shock with the following effects on physiology: blood pressure is increased by the acceleration of the heart and the contraction of the small arteries; basal metabolism and body temperature rise; increased liberation of sugar into the blood from the liver occurs and increased liberation of adrenalin into the blood from the adrenal glands follows; increase in blood chlorides also takes place; and dilation of the small bronchial tubes to increase the amount of air to the lungs results, as well as increased rate and depth of breathing. These changes give the mammal, human or subhuman, increased energy which may be used in a fight with an opponent or in flight from an opponent. If the mammal wins the fight or escapes, these physiological changes return to normal, but if the stress continues or increases without the normal outlet into physical activity by which the mammal escapes the stress, shock and even death may follow.

The symptoms of shock are the opposite of those of resistance to shock. Blood pressure is lowered, not so much by deceleration of the heart as by loss of blood volume. Plasma escapes through the walls of the smaller arteries and veins, and other loss in body liquids is brought about by excessive sweating, vomiting, or diarrhea. This loss in body liquid is generally hastened by primitive medical prescriptions, which frequently forbid a patient to take food or water. At the approach of death from emotional disturbance the following symptoms should be found in a human being, according to Cannon: rapid but weak pulse; cool and moist skin from perspiration; high cell count of blood due to loss of plasma; high blood sugar; low blood pressure. Then, if the patient dies, the proof that he died of emotional disturbance rather than organic disease or injury would require a thorough autopsy of his remains. Needless to say, complete scientific proof of Indians dying of emotional disturbance has not yet been obtained, but many hard-headed scientists as well as anthropologists believe this is not only possible but that it has actually occurred over and over again. Deaths attributed to witchcraft may be of this kind, but organic disease may also be a factor in many such cases.

A recent study by Curt P. Richter (1957) modifies the sympathico-adrenal theory of Cannon and shows that death from emotional stress can be caused by overstimulation of the parasympathetic nervous system. Richter placed rats in glass cylinders filled with water, in which the rat was compelled to swim constantly in order to keep alive. He found that wild rats were much more "frightened" by this experience than were tame rats descended from other laboratory animals. Wild rats would cease swimming, sink to the bottom, and die in a matter of minutes, while tame rats would swim for as much as 60 hours. It was found that death was preceded by a slowing of the heart rate, slowing of respiration rate, and lowering of body temperature, in other words, exclusively by shock symptoms. That the difference in the length of swimming time between wild and tame rats was due to previous emotional conditioning, and not to genetics, was proven when it was found that wild rats could be conditioned to swim for long intervals if they were kept in the water for only very short intervals in the beginning. They could learn that the situation was not hopeless and that they would be rescued by their keepers. Then, when the swimming time was gradually extended, the wild rats would adjust to the longer intervals and eventually swim about as long as the tame rats. This proves conclusively that the sudden death of the unconditioned wild rats was due to emotional disturbance rather than to other factors. Let us return to human beings.

Having prostrated our Indian by the fear of witchcraft and the resulting shock, we need only bring in the priest or shaman with his counter-treatment to restore the patient to health. Under these conditions the Indian medicine-man may be more effective than all the statistically confirmed medical science in the books. This point has been recognized by some of our own physicians and surgeons who have worked among Indians.

A prominent abdominal surgeon, the late Dr. Thomas Noble of Indianapolis, began taking vacations in the Southwest in the 1940's. Here he contacted Navaho and Hopi Indians and made many friends among them. Being a surgeon, he was asked to treat the sick from time to time, and cases needing surgery were not lacking. Working in his trailer instead of in an operating room, with only his wife, who was a nurse, to help him, he performed appendectomies and other abdominal operations on Indians. But he never took a case without first obtaining the approval of a local medicine man, who engaged in his curative "chants" both before and after the operation. This surgeon believed that the patient's chances of recovery were greater if Indian curing rites were retained. Since that time, physicians employed by our Federal Government in Indian health programs have joined forces with the local medicine-men in the belief that treatment by the latter has psychotherapeutic value and can actually contribute to the saving of lives.

This introduction to Indian religion would not be complete without mention of the social aspects of religion, which include meetings of cults, group ceremonies produced by cults, and public attendance of rites centering around an individual, such as a menstruating girl or a sick person, where the cults were absent. In chapter xx we showed that religious organizations were lacking in most of the Arctic, Sub-Arctic, Plateau, Great Basin, and Northeast Mexico. But religious meetings for anyone who cared to attend occurred in all these areas. All these peoples conducted religious ceremonies of a public nature, whether for the benefit of a single individual or the entire group. All Indian religions, therefore, are reinforced by group participation.

THE GODS AND PRIESTS OF THE AZTECS

Aztec religion was dominated by an extensive pantheon, carefully ranked in authority and power, and equally numerous orders of priests, each dedicated to the propitiation of one of the gods. The priests were also ranked in a system parallel to that of the gods they served. The higher political officials of the Aztec

486

state were also technically priests, because all had been educated in the school for priests. Thus government and religion converged at the top of the hierarchy. Although religion, with its appeal to the emotions of supernatural personalities, was dominant, magic was also present. Medicine was a combination of religion, magic, and practical science. The many plant remedies (science) were regarded as ineffective without the proper incantations (magic) or prayers (religion). Physicians were sometimes priests, but more often appear to have been shamans and herb doctors not associated with the priesthoods.

Aztec gods numbered more than one hundred. Vaillant (1941: 182–84) lists the sixty-three principal ones, each of which had its own officially recognized cult of priests dedicated to its worship. He groups these gods into a number of classes to which we prefix the number in each class: 4 creative deities; 3 great gods; 15 fertility gods; 6 gods of rain and moisture; 3 fire gods; 4 *pulque* gods; 12 planetary and stellar gods; 6 gods of death and earth; 6 variants of great gods; 4 other gods.

The universe was divided horizontally and vertically into sections of religious significance. These were five horizontal divisions, the four cardinal directions plus the center; certain gods were assigned to each of these divisions. More significant, however, are the vertical divisions which reached a maximum of thirteen "heavens," with all of the gods being assigned to levels, according to rank, from top to bottom. This illustrates the generalization often made, that cultures possessing ranked social classes or other means of ranking their human members also tend to rank their gods in a parallel fashion. The creative deities were of highest rank, but were considered too remote from human affairs to be extensively worshipped. It was the second ranking group, the three great gods, who intervened most in the affairs of man and were the most worshipped: Huitzilopochtli, Humming-bird Wizard, War and Sun God, chief god of Tenochtitlán; Tezcatlipoca, Smoking Mirror, chief god of the pantheon, with solar attributes, and chief god of Texcoco; and Quetzalcoatl, Feathered Serpent, god of learning and of the priesthood, chief god of Cholula, frequently shown as Ehecatl, the Wind God.

The routine of worship included the reciting of prayers, the

487

performance of symbolic acts, and above all the giving of presents to the gods to persuade or induce them to operate for the benefit of man, or at least for the people living at the town or city of which the god was the patron. Of all the many things given to the gods as sacrifices, the most precious was the human heart. This was the food most desired by the gods and most nutritious to their beings. In order for man to win the many contests of the world, he must be aided by strong gods who, in turn, wax strongest on human hearts; and, because the hearts of brave enemies are the most difficult to obtain, they are the most strength-giving to the gods. This belief led to the vicious circle of more and more war and more and more human sacrifice, because the greater the success in war the greater must be the number of captives sacrificed to satisfy the divine appetite in order to maintain or augment the quantity of aid from the supernatural, without which victory would have been impossible. The brutality and sadism of some of the rituals of human sacrifice were so shocking to the participants that drugs, such as tobacco, alcohol, and hemp were frequently given to the priests as well as to the victims to steel their nerves for the terrible ordeal. In justice to the Aztecs, it should be mentioned that some of their sacrifices were staged with so much dignity and drama that the religious significance transcended the taking of human life. One such ceremony has been described by Vaillant.

In contrast to the callous brutality of the fire sacrifice, the ceremony in honor of the god Tezcatlipoca was strikingly dramatic, tinged with the pathos with which we view the taking of a life. The handsomest and bravest prisoner of war was selected a year before his execution. Priests taught him the manners of a ruler, and as he walked about, playing divine melodies upon his flute, he received the homage due Tezcatlipoca himself. A month before the day of sacrifice four lovely girls, dressed as goddesses, became his companions and attended to his every want. On the day of his death he took leave of his weeping consorts to lead a procession in his honor, marked by jubilation and feasting. Then he bade farewell to the glittering cortege and left for a small temple, accompanied by the eight priests who had attended him throughout the year. The priests preceded him up the steps of the temple, and he followed, breaking at each step a flute which he had played in the happy hours of his incarnation. At the top of the platform the priests turned him over the sacrificial block and wrenched out his heart. In deference to his former godhood his body was carried, not ignominiously flung, down the steps; but his head joined the other skulls spitted on the rack beside the temple. (Vaillant, 1941: 202–3.)

The Aztecs also believed that the ghosts of the dead lived on in afterworlds for an indefinite period. The ghosts of warriors who had died in battle, or in sacrifice to the gods, went to one of the multiple heavens, where they were accorded great honor amid much luxury. The ghosts of women who had died in childbirth were likewise accorded a place of honor in another special heaven, because they too had made the supreme sacrifice in an attempt to give birth to sons who might become great warriors. The ghosts of those who had died by drowning, by being struck by lightning, or by other means connected with precipitation and water, were likewise accorded a berth in one of the heavens, where there was perpetual summer and plenty to eat and drink. The souls of the rest of the dead went to an underworld, where the Lord of the Dead assigned them to one of the nine subdivisions according to their status and experiences on earth. The underworld, as compared to the heavens, were dreary and unattractive but they were not places of perpetual torture like the Christian hell, nor was there any stigma attached to being there. Offerings were made to the ghosts of the dead at regular intervals after death, but there was no cult of the dead nor enough formality involved to warrant labeling this practice ancestor worship.

In addition to gods and ghosts, there was an indefinite number of other spirits associated with fields, mountain-tops, springs, and other features of geography. There were also special spirits connected with individuals (personal spirit-helpers), families, demes, craft guilds, and the group of intinerant merchant-spies. However, the roles of the gods in Aztec religion dominated the parts played by lesser spirits and ghosts.

At the end of each sacred cycle of fifty-two years, all fires were allowed to go out or were extinguished. All the people destroyed their household furniture, fasted, and wept during the last five portentous days of the old cycle. Temple furnishings were also destroyed. At the exact moment when a certain star reached the meridian on the last night, the priests sacrificed a captive and kindled new fire with a wooden drill and hearth within the breast of

489

the sacrificial victim. Runners lit torches from the new fire and rekindled all the temple fires in the vicinity, whence the people obtained the new fire for the hearths of their homes. The next day everyone set to work renovating and refurnishing the houses and temples.

The organization of Aztec religion was briefly sketched above in chapter xx and need not be repeated here other than to say that it was merged with political organization at the top. Montezuma and other high officials were all graduates of the school for priests as well as that for laymen. It was this hierarchy of priests which was responsible for the almost perpetual round of religious ceremonies which, in both numbers of participants and numbers of observers, far exceeded those of any other area. In terms of its total configuration, the religion of the Aztecs, and some of their Meso-American neighbors as well, was far more elaborate than that of any other culture area in native North America.

Native North American medicine probably also reached its highest point among the Aztecs, who had built much of their knowledge on that of the Mayas and other Mexican peoples. Aztec medicine included, to be sure, many magical and religious elements. Healing was accompanied by charms, astrological symbols, dances, and incantations. Many medicinal plants were named after or associated with particular gods. Some remedies were used also as amulets, or chosen according to the principles of sympathetic magic. It represents, nonetheless, a significant advance in medicine, with medical and surgical specialization advanced to the point that they foreshadowed scientific experimentation. The emperor Montezuma, who devoted his magnificent pleasure gardens to flowers, blossoming fragrant trees, and aromatic or medicinal herbs, ordered his physicians to make experiments with the herbs and to employ only those thoroughly known and tested to cure illness in the imperial court. Furthermore, Aztec methods of animal and human sacrifice must have contributed to knowledge, at least by the priesthood, of internal anatomy.

At the time of the Spanish conquest the Aztecs distinguished several types of healers. The *ticitl* (diviners) chanted spells and administered charms. The *curanderos* relieved suffering manually or with medicines. The *tepati* were believed to cure disease by means

490

of knowledge and healing powers received from the gods. These three categories were, moreover, divided into specialists for various types of disease and injuries. In addition they distinguished *te-mixiuitiani* (midwives), *papiani* (pharmacists), and *panamacani* (dealers in drugs). Women as well as men were trained in the arts of medicine and divination. The medicinal values of herbs were common knowledge among the people, who concocted many home remedies from their own gardens.

Records of Aztec surgery are comparatively meager. We know, however, that the native doctors were skilful at trephining, castration, suturing facial wounds with hair, lancing boils and swellings, removing growths and white opacities from the eyes, and splicing long bones with slivers of bone or wood. Tumors which did not respond to herbal applications were lanced but not removed. Fractures were not only set but also were encased in plasters made of downy feathers, gum and resin with an outer coat of a rubber-like gum. Surgical instruments were made of sharpened wood or bone, thorns, obsidian, and probably of gold, silver, or copper. Thorn or bone needles were used for sewing up incisions. Wounds were washed with water, salt solution, urine, or herbal decoctions. Infected wounds or boils were sometimes cauterized with burning oil. Various wound dressings were used, including one of honey and salt.

Diseases were attributed by the Aztecs principally to punishment by the gods, but also to uncleanliness, all forms of personal intemperance, and atmospheric conditions of extreme heat, cold, humidity, wind, or dust. Prophylactic measures, in addition to cleanliness and sanitation, included fumigating with incense. Unpleasant fumes from burning mouse nests, hair, rubber-producing sap or odoriferous plants were thought to drive away disease or evil. Much of the incense, however, was pleasantly fragrant with oil of cedar, pine, copal, or aromatic herbs. The fragrance of flowers and herbs was used to dispel unpleasant odors and to treat fevers, melancholia, and fatigue. A prescription to relieve the weariness of government officials was made from sweet-smelling flowers and leaves. Other aromatic prescriptions included lotions for tired feet, for the fetid odor of invalids, and, after thorough bathing, to prevent armpit odor. Purificatory treatments included enemas, ear

491

syringing, brushing teeth and removing tartar, cold baths, steam baths, and baths in sulfur springs.

Pharmaceutical remedies were usually complex mixtures of plant extracts, to which mineral and animal ingredients were often added. Pearls, emeralds and other precious stones, and bezoars from lizards, birds, or mammals were used as medicines and as amulets. Mineral ingredients also included salt, nitre, alum, red ochre, and various other earths. Animal constituents included blood, bile, and brains; decoctions of snakes, scorpions and millipedes; human teeth or bones; ash from burnt horn, bone or excrement; and charcoal prepared from various animals. Most numerous, however, were the ingredients made from plants and trees. These included hundreds of medicinal substances, narcotics, analgesics, and stimulants, administered orally or by enema. Many of them were of practical therapeutic value, as for instance a species of *Ephedra*, used by the Aztecs in the treatment of common colds, and several species of *Datura*, containing hyoscyamine, atropine and scopalamine, which were included in various prescriptions to relieve pain.

A typical prescription is the following, for "treatment of the head." The shrubs *xiuhecapahtli, yztac ocoxochitl, teamoxtli*, and the precious stones *tetlahuitl, yztactlalli, eztetl, tematlatzin*, ground up together in cold water and applied to the head, were thought to stop heat in the head and, when ground up in hot water, to stop coldness therein. These hot or cold packs were applied three times a day, morning, noon, and evening, and the neck and throat were bound with the sinew of an eagle's foot and neck. One suffering from headache should eat onions in honey, should not sit in the sun, and should not work or enter the baths.

The early Spanish missionaries, although obligated to stamp out Mexican paganism with its horrendous human sacrifices, recognized the efficacy of Aztec medicine, and even considered it superior to their own for the treatment of native American diseases. They studied the prescriptions and methods of Aztec physicians and recorded them for European use. A course in Aztec medicine, taught by the best available Aztec doctors, was included along with philosophy, logic, the Aztec language, Spanish and Latin languages, arithmetic, and music, in the regular curriculum of the College of Santa Cruz, established by the Franciscans in 1536. At this college was produced by native Aztecs the first American medical book, now known as the Badianus Manuscript. This Aztec herbal, written in Aztec by the Aztec physician Martinus de la Cruz and translated into Latin in 1552 by his Spanish colleague Badianus, is a worthy companion to the great medieval herbals still in use in sixteenth century Europe. Except for the use of the Latin language and a few minor technicalities, it is a purely Mexican product, without European influence, written, illustrated, and translated by native Indians. Yet its formulas, with their odd mixture of efficacious medicines and magical animal substances and precious stones, are fascinatingly reminiscent of medieval and Renaissance prescriptions. On the basis of the Badianus Manuscript and sixteenth century books by Sahagún and other Spanish scholars we must conclude that Aztec herbal medicine, at least, was comparable to that of Europe at the time of the Spanish conquest of Mexico.

THE MAGIC AND MEDICINE MEN OF THE NAVAHO

Navaho religion, magic, and medicine are a mixture of the primitive shamanism of the Mackenzie Sub-Arctic with the priest-dominated religions of the Pueblo peoples. The acculturation of the Navaho to the Pueblo way of life began between five hundred and one thousand years ago when the former arrived in the Oasis. The Navaho religious leader has the attributes of both priest and shaman. The words of his chants are learned verbatim from an older medicine man, together with the associated tunes. Such a large body of fixed ritual is generally associated with organized priesthoods, but the Navaho medicine men are not organized into cults of any kind and in no sense are they officials of any governmental unit. Their individuality identifies them with the shaman. Although the chants were formerly employed to aid all human activities, including hunting and warfare, the gradual depletion of game after White contact and the abrupt cessation of warfare in 1868 did away with these uses of chants. At the present time the curative powers of chants dominate Navaho religion, magic, and medicine.

The Navaho classify personalities into two types: the Earth Sur-

493

face People, including living human beings and their ghosts after they die; the Holy People, the gods and lesser spirits who travel around on sunbeams, on the rainbow, and on flashes of lightning. Although the Holy People have great powers to help or harm human beings, they are not always superior in knowledge or in power to man, and they perform evil as well as good deeds. They are both supplicated and coerced, but it is coercion that dominates Navaho religion and magic.

Changing Woman is the dominant personality among the Holy People. She was the principal creator of man and helped teach him how to control and keep in harmony the forces of nature, such as the wind, storms, lightning, and animals. The meeting at which man was permitted to witness the ceremony of the Holy People harmonizing the forces of nature is re-enacted by man in the Blessing Way Chant. Second in importance to Changing Woman is her husband, the Sun. Sun symbolism penetrates every aspect of Navaho religion and magic. Third in rank are the Hero Twins, Monster Slayer and Child of the Water, who are propitiated in most ceremonies. Of lesser importance are First Man and First Woman. First Man was the creator of the universe. There are several groups of lesser spirits: Failed-To-Speak People, such as Water Sprinkler, Fringed Mouth, Hunchback, who are commonly impersonated in the great public "chants"; animals and personifications of natural forces, such as Coyote, Big Snake Man, Crooked Snake People, Thunder People, and Wind People; those who help the Holy People and serve as intermediaries between them and man, such as Big Fly and Corn Beetle. Of all these Holy People, it is only Changing Woman who is unchanging in her attitude toward man, who is always helpful to man. All the others play at times the roles of tricksters, witches, and other harmful beings and are feared. The ghosts of the dead are feared even more, so that the dominant feature of Navaho religion and magic is the warding off of evil.

The Holy People live in an underworld, as do also the ghosts of the dead. Life after death is neither pleasurable nor painful but is a bit on the dreary side. Fear of ghosts is intense; no matter how affectionate, helpful, and friendly a person has been while alive, his ghost is always potentially dangerous. Any slip in the complicated burial routine will offend the ghost and cause it to hover around

494

the grave, or the house where it lived while alive, in order to take revenge on the wrong-doer.

Witchcraft has been most thoroughly investigated among the Navaho, who, in their own language, divide it into several distinct categories: Witchery Way or witchcraft proper (*ʔant'i*); Sorcery (several types referred to by the *-nzin* stem); Wizardry (*ʔadagas*); and Frenzy Witchcraft (*ʔazile*). In addition they mention Disease Witchcraft and Eagle Pit Sorcery, both of which seem to be specialized forms of Sorcery.

The classic Witchery Way technique consists in the administration of "corpse poison," a concoction made from the flesh of corpses, preferably of dead children, that of twins being especially effective. It is ground into powder and may be given in food or cigarettes, blown into the victim's face, spread on his blanket, or dropped into his hogan through the smoke-hole. Witches are closely associated with the ghosts of the dead and with incest. Male witches are more numerous than female. Witchery is usually learned from an older relative, and the initiation into Witchery Way is said to include killing a brother or sister. Witches gain wealth by robbing graves or by fee-splitting; one witch makes a person ill and his partner witch cures the patient and collects a fee. Witches are thought to roam at night as were-animals (wolves, coyotes, bears, and owls), to meet in witches' sabbaths to plan and perform rites to kill or injure people, to have intercourse with dead women, to initiate new members, and to practice cannibalism.

Sorcery is considered a branch of witchery in the Navaho scheme. Sorcerers attend the witches' sabbath, but they are considered less violent than witches, and they use a different set of techniques. Sorcery is usually performed by contagious magic and incantation or spell. The sorcerer obtains a bit of the victim's hair, nails, excretions, or clothing, buries it in a grave or with something taken from a grave, and chants a spell over it. He may also make an "evil-wishing" sand painting, or, rarely, practice *envoûtement* by molding or carving an image of the victim and injuring it.

Wizardry is, to the Navaho, the practice of shooting "arrows" (foreign particles such as bits of stone, bone, quill, ashes, and charcoal) into the victim. English-speaking Navaho sometimes call it "bean-shooting," though actual beans are not used. Wizards are almost exclusively old men, but they do not become were-animals, nor do they attend the witches' sabbath.

Wizardry is normally cured by Sucking Way, which includes not only sucking but also singing and application of medicaments (dried and powdered blue lizard, "witchcraft plant," etc.) to the wound. The sucker is generally considered by the Navaho to be a wizard himself, or in league with wizards. Victims of Sorcery and Disease Witchcraft may be cured by recovery of the clothes, excrement or other buried materials, and by the smoke of the Game Way ceremony.

Victims of all types of witchcraft, but especially of its most serious form, Witchery Way, may be cured by catching the witch and obtaining his confession. If the witch refuses to confess, he is usually killed. If he confesses, the victim will gradually improve, and the witch will die within the year from the same symptoms which have afflicted the victim. Witchcraft of all sorts may also be counteracted by prayer ceremonials or by chants. Thus Prostitution Way chant (evil in itself) may be combined with Blessing Way to form a cure for Frenzy Witchcraft.

While the Navaho Indians have a definitely complex philosophy of disease, they also retain many of the primitive ideas shared with more primitive groups. Thus illness may be caused not only by sorcery or witchcraft, but by ghosts, by contact with the dead or things connected with the dead, by dreams of catastrophe or death, or by incompletely buried monsters. Their more complex theories of disease are bound up with the idea of taboo transgression and lack of harmony with the universe. Navaho life is full of restrictions, many of which are disregarded in ordinary circumstances and remembered only when illness or catastrophe strikes the offender. Ignorance is no excuse for transgression. Transgressions may, similarly, offend the spirits, who may retaliate by shooting invisible arrows or by inducing other forms of object, animal, or spirit intrusion. Diagnosis is made by medicine men who determine the cause of the illness by gazing at the heavenly bodies, "listening," or "trembling," or all three combined. The medicine man, guided by his innate supernatural power, sees a symbol of the ceremony which should be used for the cure.

Since all objects, beings, spirits, and events are thought to be in mystic relationship and sympathy, such diverse ceremonies as the Wind Chant, the Male Shooting Chant, the Big Star Chant, the Bead Chant, and the War Ceremony may be used to cure disease. All of these ceremonies are closely connected with Navaho myths of cosmogony and creation. In modern life many of them, especially the War Ceremony, have lost their former practical utility. Their principal function nowadays is therapeutic.

The Chants or Ways of the Navaho follow, to a large extent, the ceremonial procedures of the Pueblo Indians, whom the Navaho consider their superiors in the arts of the supernatural, and are extremely complex, elaborate, and colorful. The Navaho War Ceremony, however, suggests a relationship to Plains warfare and ritual. As conducted nowadays by the Navaho, these ceremonies have two principal aims: purification, to get rid of object, creature, or spirit intrusion; identification, to promote mystic harmony between the patient and other elements of the natural or supernatural world. Purification is attained through sweating, emetics, and bathing. Identification is achieved by means of chants, sand paintings, medicine bundles, and the like.

Ceremonies last from one to nine "nights." In the full nine-night ceremonies, the first night consists of an hour or two of singing and simple ritual. The early morning hours of the first four days are taken up with sweat-emetic rites to drive out evil and to purify not only the patient but all participants. The first four afternoons are devoted to the preparation of prayer sticks, which are prayed over and then placed at designated points as a compulsive invitation to the deities to attend the ceremony. At dawn on the fifth day the contents of the Singer's medicine bundle are laid out on an altar. The Singer prays over each object in turn and the patient touches each item as it is deposited on the altar.

On each of the next four days a sand painting is made inside the house. Some of these sand paintings are so elaborate as to require up to forty assistants working eight or ten hours. When the painting is finished, the patient sits on it, while the Singer applies sand from the various figures of the painting to specified parts of the patient's body and performs other ritualistic acts, all designed to identify the patient with the deities represented in the painting. The eighth day is called "The Day." Early in the morning the patient, with the aid of his relatives, shampoos his hair and bathes his body in suds made from the yucca (soapweed) root and dries himself with ceremonially ground cornmeal.

During each night the singing continues, becoming longer as the ceremony progresses. The Singer, who must know a vast number of songs, starts the required song and helps the chorus of laymen around him to sing it. On the ninth night, "The Night," the singing lasts until dawn, summarizing all the purification, invocation, attraction of power, and identification of the preceding rites. Throughout the vigil the patient concentrates on all the singing and ritual.

Participants, in addition to the patient, are supposed to be benefited in proportion to their proximity to the ritual. If the patient himself is not cured, failure is attributed to mistaken diagnosis and use of the wrong ceremony. Even minute errors in the proper chant may ruin its therapeutic efficacy. Occasionally, it is thought, a suitable chant may nonetheless injure the patient or the Singer by being "too strong" for his innate powers.

Many cures have been reported, sometimes in cases given up by the White physicians, not only by Navaho but by several unprejudiced White observers. Whether any of these can be rationally ascribed to the "chant lotions" and other remedies administered is uncertain. The Navaho, like most other Indian tribes, have an extensive pharmacopoeia, including a number of simples and compounds of real medicinal value. But Navaho ceremonialism functions most efficiently as a form of group psychotherapy, reinforcing the patient's faith in himself and in the moral support of his social group.

THE FORGIVING CREEKS

Perhaps the most distinctive feature of Creek religion and magic was the forgiving of every wrong short of murder at the greatest ceremony of the year, the Green Corn Dance. Offenders sometimes hid out in the woods until the time for this ceremony arrived, when they returned to their villages to be forgiven and reinstated as full citizens. The making of new fire, from which each housewife obtained fire for her hearth, is reminiscent of Meso-America. Like the Navaho, the Creek religious specialists possessed

498

attributes of both priests and shamans. They performed fixed rituals and uttered verbatim prayers at public ceremonies in the temples or council house, and also made direct contact with the supernatural in dreams and hallucinations. Young men were trained to be medicine men in schools, but these were much less formal than those of the Aztecs, although civil officials were chosen from the graduates. Creek medicine is a mixture of religion, magic, and herbalism, like that of so many other Indians, and its distinctive feature, if it has one, would be the emphasis on animals as the causers of disease.

The Creek Indians, formerly of Alabama and Georgia, believed in a supreme deity who lived in the sky and was associated with, but not identical to, the sun. His representative on earth was the spirit in the Busk fire or other sacred fires, who served as a sort of liaison officer between the supreme deity and man. There were a great number of lesser spirits difficult to classify. Among these were: (1) two other spirits closely connected with the Busk; (2) meteorological phenomena such as the wind; (3) pygmies or giants in human form who lived in the forest; (4) a host of other animal or animal-like spirits including water serpents, a horned snake, a monster lizard, eagles, hawks, owls, panthers, bears, deer, all of which were thought to have souls like human beings and to possess human attributes. In addition to this host of spiritual beings, the ghosts of the dead who had been slain by the enemy were thought to hover about the houses of their living relatives until their deaths had been avenged, when they departed to a spiritual world to join the other ghosts.

The earth was believed to be flat and square, and the sky a solid dome on which the supreme deity lived. Eclipses were supposed to be caused by an animal trying to swallow the sun or moon. The various mythological animals living in water were thought to control rain, starting or stopping it at will. Good ghosts went to dwell in the sky, while evil ones went west.

As in other Indian cultures, every important event was hedged by religion. Hunters, warriors, menstruants, parturients, mourners, and young men training to be medicine men secluded themselves, fasted, and observed a host of taboos supposed to protect them from harm or aid them in their undertaking. One White observer

499

was of the opinion that the fasting, and other taboos associated with a war expedition, were harder on the men than the actual traveling and fighting. There were many omens by which the success or failure of an undertaking was judged in advance, and numerous charms and fetishes to ward off evil.

The Green Corn Dance or Busk, held when the flour corn was in the roasting ear stage, in July or August, was the most important single ceremony among the Creeks. The Busk was the fourth and culminating ceremony in a series of similar rites which began about April. Up until the time of the Busk no one was permitted to eat any of the season's corn, on pain of being barred from attending the ceremony. The term "Busk" is a trader's corruption of the word *boskita*, meaning "to fast." This ceremony was a New Year rite to renew or regenerate the entire world and the plants, animals, and human beings who lived on it. It was believed to have been taught to the Creeks by the supreme deity and the leading roles were played by the highest-ranking medicine men, who made the new fire and brewed the Black Drink. While the selection of the date at the time of corn ripening establishes the fact that the ceremony centered around corn, animal spirits were also sometimes propitiated with an eye to better hunting, and a fresh start in moral matters was instituted by forgiving every offense short of murder. This last point was a remarkable concession for a people steeped in a tradition of blood feuds and "eye for an eye and tooth for a tooth" notions of justice. It meant that a measure of internal peace had been brought to irritable, vengeful personalities. While peace and tranquility were dominant during the Busk ceremony, the cause of war was not entirely omitted. The warriors occupied their graded bed platforms in the town square, were granted new names for distinguished war deeds of the past year, and advanced in position in the seating arrangement accordingly. They also put on a sham battle against enemy effigies.

The New Year's aspect included the manufacturing of new clothing, household articles, tools and weapons, and the destruction of the old articles. Furthermore, all house fires in the town were extinguished on the first day of the Busk and renewed afterwards on the fourth day from the sacred Busk fire made anew with the drill on the first day.

500

The ritual normally occupied four days but was sometimes repeated for a total of eight. While there was much variation in procedure from town to town, or from one historical source to another, the following is a generalized calendar of main events. On the first day, the town square was cleaned and arranged, and a new fire was started. On the second day, a feast on new corn was held. On the third day, there was fasting by all mature men, followed by drinking the emetic called the Black Drink, concocted from *Ilex vomitoria*. One the fourth day, a feast consisting of venison seasoned with salt was held. Ball games were played for amusement by young men; a wide variety of dances were given in the evening, largely for the same purpose. In later historic times the Busk served as a catch-all for almost every fragment of public ceremony left. Sexual continence was observed by everyone during the entire four days, the men sleeping in the town square.

Among a number of minor public ceremonies of a social or religious character, there was a celebration, whenever there had been a successful hunt, in which an entire town would take part in feasting and dancing. During epidemics everyone would fast and drink medicines publicly to counteract the disease. Council meetings were held periodically and were always preceded by the formal serving of the Black Drink, starting first with the chief and proceeding according to rank. Thus each individual's rank was demonstrated by the council seating arrangement and the order in which he was served. When the ball post was erected in the central area of a new town, a tree was felled without being allowed to touch the ground, and a scalp or skull was placed in the bottom of the post hole. There were at least thirty dances with animal names and mimicry which were danced at any time, mostly as entertainment. They were frequently given as informal additions to important ceremonies such as the Busk.

Medicine men derived some of their power from the supernatural and some from natural remedies such as herbs. While some of these were efficacious according to the standards of modern science, most probably were not. Their curing method consisted mostly of psychotherapy and was effective against the many fears and anxieties of native life, but against smallpox, measles, and other diseases of European origin, for which the Indian had no racial

501

immunity, it was unsuccessful and mortality was high. A neat distinction between natural and supernatural was seldom made by these Indians because, even when plant remedies were used, the medicine men had to collect and administer them along with verbal formulas in a manner satisfactory to the supernatural. The distinction between the shaman, who derives his power directly from the supernatural, and the priest, who learns rituals, songs, and verbal formulas from another priest, is not sharply drawn for this area. The same individuals often did both. For this reason the simpler term, medicine man, has been chosen.

There were several classes of medicine men among the Creeks: (1) a class of diviners called "knowers" who prophesied future events and diagnosed disease; twins were likely to belong to this class; (2) the graduates of the medicine men's school; (3) controllers of the weather (mostly rain) or of floods in streams, and dew makers; (4) witches or wizards, who were not always known because of the evil nature of their activities. The latter were supposed to be filled with lizards which forced them to commit murder, but they might be cured of this impulse by being made to throw up the lizards.

The medicine men's school was taught by an experienced "priest" of the highest degree, who tutored each student individually, sending him to an isolated spot to sweat, fast, and take medicines in order to attain direct contact with the supernatural. A student who succeeded in his first four-day attempt and obtained his "degree" was eligible to try again for the second "degree" a year or so later, with his second isolation period extended to eight days. Along with this vision-seeking went a considerable amount of instruction in songs, dances, verbal formulas and in concocting of medicines, all for a price, because the graduate medicine man always charged the laymen for his services. The third and final "degree" was obtained after a twelve-day vigil. The war leader and the head medicine man for town ceremonies was chosen from this group of third "degree" graduates, although proper sib affiliation also was a factor. This was the class of medicine men which was officially recognized and whose leaders might hold permanent town offices. Individuals wore insignia indicative of their achievements; a buzzard feather for one who could heal gunshot wounds;

a foxskin for one who could cure snake bite; an owl feather if he could trail the enemy in the dark.

Native classification of causes of disease is non-existent. Instead, we are given long lists of reptiles, birds, mammals, meteorological phenomena, mythological phenomena, and mythological characters as causers of specific ailments. For example, when mumps was caught from Whites in the eighteenth century, the Indians thought it was caused by cattle, because they were beginning to eat beef at that time. Their choice of cattle from among the dozens or hundreds of things they had derived from the Whites by that date reflects the persistence of the native notion that animals cause most disease. There is a suggestion in one account that the wrath of an animal spirit was inflamed by the breaking of some taboo in connection with the manner of hunting or disposing of its body parts. The cures were plant medicines which had to be concocted and administered in the correct way with the proper songs, dances, verbal formulas, and motions. Most of these medicines were taken internally. The gourd rattle was the instrument used to accompany the singing and dancing of the doctor, which was more often done to diagnose the disease than to cure it.

That foreign physical materials were thought to enter the body and cause disease is demonstrated by the bloodletting and sucking techniques to remove them. This is equivalent to lancing and poulticing an area of infection or poison and was certainly efficacious for such things as snake bite. The shaman sometimes sucked directly with his mouth, at other times through a bison horn, the large end of which was cupped over the wound. When nothing unusual was discharged from the infected area, the shaman would plant some small object in the discharge to convince the patient that he had extracted the cause of the ailment.

The sweat bath was prescribed by both laymen and doctors to cure disease. A dome-shaped hut, covered with hides or mats, was built especially for the purpose, and into this were rolled hot stones on which water was sprinkled to create water vapor. When the patient had had all of this he could endure, he plunged into the waters of the nearest stream. From the many accounts of this custom from many tribes of Indians, it seems quite possible that the heat was sufficient to induce an artificial fever, which would aid recovery from some ailments. The shock experienced by plunging into cold water after the sweat bath is parallel to hydrotherapy treatments so commonly used today for patients suffering from nervous tension. Therefore it was probably effective for ailments of a psychosomatic nature.

Bandages and splints were employed and the sick were transported on litters. A doctor who lost a patient was suspected of witchcraft and might himself be killed by the deceased patient's relatives.

THE VISION QUEST OF THE SANPOIL

The Sanpoil, who lived in eastern Washington State, in the Plateau culture area, had the minimum of social, political, and religious organization. Their emphasis was on the vision quest, the spirit-helpers obtained on the quest, and the multiple souls possessed by humans. Because every man went on a vision quest, and practically all claimed on return to have contacted the supernatural, there was no sharp distinction between shaman and layman. Shamans merely possessed a greater number of spirit-helpers or more powerful ones than the layman, and any layman might be upgraded to the position of shaman if he acquired more power or more spirits on another vision quest. Such quests were repeated throughout life and any unusual good fortune that befell a man was thought to have come from the supernatural. The concept of magic probably existed among the Sanpoil, but it was overshadowed by the plethora of spiritual personalities. Priests were totally absent because there were no religious organizations or standardized rituals. Natural diseases were more clearly distinguished from those of supernatural causation than is generally the case with Indians.

The Sanpoil distinguished six kinds of spiritual personalities. The first was the god Sweat Lodge who was the creator of animals and spirits, and perhaps human beings as well. He was a benevolent deity and answered the prayers of all who appealed to him by sweating in a sweat lodge and praying in song. The second kind was the soul which animated the living human body and resided in the viscera near the heart. Death would result if it left the body. When a person died, the soul left his body, going either

504

at once to the land of the dead or roaming about on earth after being transformed into a ghost. Ghosts belonged to the third class of spiritual beings. The fourth class consisted of spirits who had never resided in the bodies of human beings. They took on the forms of animals, plants, inanimate objects, and physical phenomena of nature. It was a spirit of this type which every youth sought on his quest for a spirit-helper, who became so identified with his human host that departure brought on sickness or death. When a person died, his spirit-helper did not cease to exist but underwent a transformation comparable to that from soul to ghost mentioned above. This transformed spirit, which belongs to a fifth class, may be called a spirit-ghost. Such spirit-ghosts could form an association with a relative of the deceased or with a shaman as an additional source of supernatural power, secondary to the primary spirit which everyone of any consequence acquired early in life. The sixth category included all dangerous supernatural personalities, embracing ogres, monsters, demons, and evil dwarfs. The Sanpoil make no attempt to quantify the numbers of spiritual beings in each of the six classes, but it is apparent that they total at least double the number of human beings on earth because most living persons possessed two.

A soul was possessed by human beings of all ages, including the unborn child. Because it never left the body without undergoing transformation, it was not assigned any visible form. Unconsciousness, as well as death, was attributed to soul loss, and no distinction in the Sanpoil language is made between unconsciousness and death. Here we have a fundamental difference between native ideology and that of modern medical science.

At death the soul had two alternatives: it could go at once to the land of the dead at the end of the Milky Way in the sky; or it could be transformed into a ghost and remain on earth. If it went to the land of the dead, it never returned to earth or communicated with men on earth. It gave up all individual activity and assumed a nirvana-like status which, strangely, was a desirable one. Everyone hoped his soul would attain the limbo of the land of the dead and not remain on earth as a ghost in a condition of perpetual torment. Ghosts varied from complete visibility to invisibility, but generally were shadowy or vague in outline. Some

505

were without heads or other body parts, but they were usually garbed in opaque clothing. They appeared both in the daytime and at night, but never to more than one person at a time. Ghosts remained on earth for different reasons: if a person before death had hidden an object of value in a place unknown to any human being, his ghost would stay on to watch the object; or if hair or nail parings of the deceased were left undestroyed, the ghost would hover around to watch them also. If a spirit-helper were buried with the corpse, or if the deceased had failed to confess some wrong-doing before death, the ghost was likewise compelled to remain on earth.

Spirits were most commonly animals, and every known animal functioned as a spirit-helper for somebody in the society. However, rocks, lakes, mountains, and even some inanimate objects possessed spirits, as did also whirlwinds and clouds. Such spirits were not arranged in a neat hierarchy of authority, although some were generally regarded as being more powerful than others. Although spirits were never equated with the souls and ghosts associated with human beings, they always assumed human form when appearing before men, only to change back again to their original forms when an interview was ended. Such spirits usually appeared to man only during vision quests, in dreams, at the winter dances, and in times of trouble. The loss of one's spirit-helper resulted in sickness and, if not found and returned to its host, in death. Shamans both recovered lost spirit-helpers and stole them on other occasions.

Every boy was compelled to seek a spirit-helper at an early age, and girls went on such quests if their parents encouraged them to do so. A young man past puberty who had failed to acquire a spirit-helper could look forward to only the most meager kind of life with the minimum of rewards. Not more than 10 per cent of youths failed to acquire spirit power in this manner. Perhaps 70 or 80 per cent of the girls did not obtain spirit-helpers but, as this was not mandatory for success in feminine pursuits, they led satisfactory lives without this experience. Most men boasted of more than one spirit-helper, and it was taken for granted that the most successful men possessed more than one such power. The

506

greatest Sanpoil shaman possessed six spirit-helpers and one spirit-ghost power.

A boy went on his first spirit-quest, a vigil of only one night, at about eight years of age. As he became older, the period was gradually extended to several nights. An old man, most often a grandfather, instructed the boy in the technique of acquiring a vision. The youngster would be told to go to the top of a certain mountain or to the shore of a particular lake where he was likely to find a spirit. The boy stayed out alone all night, sitting beside a fire on the mountain or diving repeatedly in the cold waters of the lake. To make sure that the boy went to the designated spot, the old man would give him a peculiarly shaped stick or piece of hide to leave at the spot, so that the latter could find the object the next day and confirm the fact that the boy had indeed been there. The youth was supposed to stay awake all night, but it is said that rule was often broken.

The vision involved seeing a spirit in the guise of a human being in a dream or hallucination. The spirit revealed its true identity to the child, told him the activities in which he would be especially successful as an adult, and listed the kinds of harm from which it would protect him. For instance, the lad might be told that he would be lucky in gambling, would be a great hunter, or would be able to bring rain in time of drought, and that he would be protected from injury in battle. Then the spirit taught the boy a song, which was supposed to be an original one different in detail, at least, from every other song and, when this was sung at a later date, it called forth the boy's supernatural power and assured his success in the undertakings listed by his spirit-helper. In addition to the loneliness and fear experienced by the boy, fasting from food and water on the longer quests increased his discomfort and helped induce the hallucinations or illusions regarded as visitations of spirits.

Shamanistic power was obtained in exactly the same manner as any other kind of power, and a young man could tell from the spirit's instructions and song whether he would become a successful shaman. Shamans normally possessed both more numerous spirit-helpers and more powerful ones than other men. Spirit-helpers were not sought in all-night vigils after the age of adolescence, but they were thought to contact men on their own volition up to almost any age.

The results of the first successful vision-quest in childhood or adolescence were not disclosed to anyone for many years. Then, when the visionary was twenty-five or thirty years of age, and had achieved full adult status, his spirit-helper would return. This caused him to get spirit sickness, a feeling of lonesomeness and despondency, which usually came on in the early winter. Only a shaman could cure such sickness. The shaman first located the spirit in the patient's body, then removed it, held it in his hands long enough to learn the song it had given the patient, and finally blew it back into the patient's body. Next the shaman sang the song, with the patient joining in before it was finished or repeating it a second time. After thus receiving back his spirit and his song, the patient recovered and was able to leave his bed, but he was not entirely well until he had sung the new song almost continuously for several days.

During the coldest part of the winter, when it was almost impossible to fish or hunt, the Sanpoil lived on stored foods for about two months. It was at this time that spirits most often recontacted their human hosts, and public dances were held to validate this renewal of spirit power. Such "winter dances" were sponsored most often by a shaman, but never by a group of shamans because they were not organized in any way. Sometimes, however, such a dance was sponsored by the individual who had received the power, or by one directed to do so by his spirit-helper. A "winter dance" lasted two or three nights and was attended by every adult who cared to witness the ceremony. Each person who had recently received supernatural power impersonated his spirit-helper in a dance. Many such dances occurred during this winter period and a single person might attend all within accessible distance of his home. These dances served as initiation ceremonies in which the shaman helped the young man to entice his spirit-helper to come to the dance house and ensconce itself in his body. This was the proof that the youth had acquired a personal spirit.

In the chapter on Sodalities and Their Ceremonies we pointed out again and again that the principal purpose of sodality initiations was to facilitate contact between the initiates and supernatural personalities. The Sanpoil "winter dances" had the same function, but the absence of any organization of shamans or other participants rules out the sodality there. Like the sodality ceremonies, the Sanpoil "winter dances" also gave the experienced shaman a chance to demonstrate his control over his supernatural powers, sometimes with the aid of illusory tricks.

Disease among the Sanpoil was divided into two major classes, natural and supernatural. Natural ailments included headaches, the common cold, injuries from inanimate objects such as sharp stones, and tuberculosis. Supernatural illnesses were divided into five subclasses: (1) injuries inflicted by animate beings other than men; (2) diffuse internal illnesses; (3) afflictions of the mind; (4) spirit illness; (5) magical "poisoning."

In the first supernatural subclass are included serious wounds resulting from attacks by bears, wolves, and snakes, which were interpreted as being caused by the spirits of the animals. The reason that these animal spirits wished to harm a man might be his failure to follow the dictates of his spirit-helper, or jealousy between his spirit-helper and the animal spirit.

The second subclass includes fevers and contagious diseases caused by intrusion into the body of foreign matter, and this, in turn, might be caused by the breaking of taboos or by sorcery initiated by an unfriendly shaman.

The third category, afflictions of the mind, were thought to be caused by a shaman projecting one of his spirit-helpers into the body of the victim. Such spirit intrusion brought on raving, delirium, and insanity, and could be cured by a more powerful shaman removing the foreign spirit.

The fourth type, spirit illness, was caused either by the sudden return of one's spirit-helper, or by its equally sudden departure. Loss of one's spirit came about by burying it with a corpse or by its being stolen by a shaman. The former case was hopeless, but the latter could be cured by the recovery of the stolen spirit by a more powerful shaman.

The fifth subclass, magical poisoning, was a form of contagious magic and was engaged in only by lay women, not men, and not women shamans. A lock of hair, some nail parings, or a piece of the victim's clothing was ground up in a witches' mixture of a certain root, red paint, the body of a bat, or a bit of bone from a corpse. As the mixture was being ground, the name of the victim and his desired fate was muttered, after which the stuff was placed in the victim's food or tossed on the dirtiest refuse heap in the vicinity. Soon the victim would wither away or break out in sores over his body. A cure was difficult, even for a shaman.

The first task of the shaman was to diagnose the ailment. After smoking a pipe of tobacco for a few moments, the shaman placed a hand on various parts of the patient's body, singing his doctoring songs at the same time. The audience then joined in the songs, beating time with sticks on the floor planks or on a log. When the intrusive object or spirit was located in the body of the patient, the shaman attempted to remove it by making a drawing-out motion with his hands or by "sucking" with deep inhalation an inch or two from the afflicted area of the body. The extracted spirit or object was immersed in a basket of water, where it was harmless. Shamans were paid only if they effected a definite cure. Some, however, used their power to cause illness in order to obtain the fee for curing it.

The Sanpoil used plant remedies to cure the ailments regarded as of natural causation. Verne Ray (1932: 217–22) lists forty-three species used for this purpose, but cautions that many such remedies have been forgotten and that the total would probably include half the total number of species available in the area. Knowledge of medicinal plants was not secret and was shared by both men and women. Plants were most often crushed, boiled in water, and applied both externally and internally according to the nature of the ailment. The sweat lodge was used for the curing of natural illnesses except for the common cold. Growths over the eye and warts anywhere on the body were removed by surgery, and boils were lanced.

THE POSSESSIONAL SHAMANISM OF THE ESKIMO

Possessional shamanism was the rule everywhere in the Arctic; although not lacking in other areas, this is the only area where it was universal. A soul or spirit from without was thought to enter the body of the shaman and take possession, causing the body to talk, sing, dance, and otherwise behave as if possessed. In most cases interpreted as spirit possession, the shaman seems to have been unconscious, because he does not remember how he behaved when possessed. In other instances, however, the shaman consciously puts on an act to impress his audience; and the same man might achieve possession at one seance and not at another. Perhaps the other most definitive aspect of Eskimo religion is soul flight. The shaman sends his soul to the spirit world to recover a stolen soul or to get a direct answer from the spirits concerning some question that has arisen on earth. Disease is most often attributed to breach of taboo and the theft of the patient's soul by offended spirits.

The Eskimo believed in many spirits or souls residing in persons, animals, inanimate objects, and places. Three kinds of human souls are generally distinguished: the immortal spirit which leaves the body at death and goes to live in a spiritual world; the breath and warmth of the body which ceases to exist at death; and the name-soul which lives for a time in a spirit world and is later reincarnated into the body of a baby descendant.

Disease was believed to be caused by soul loss, apparently of the first and third souls, because shamans were supposed to be able to recover them. Old or ill persons sometimes changed their names in the hope of acquiring a fresh name-soul to improve their health. Disease was less frequently thought to be caused by the intrusion into the body of an evil spirit. Soul loss or spirit intrusion usually resulted from the breaking of taboos, and isolation with dietary and other restrictions usually set the matter right. It was most often the shaman who diagnosed the difficulty and prescribed the cure.

Souls or spirits residing in animals, objects, and places were invariably called by terms translated as "man" or "person." This is substantial evidence for the unity of the soul concept. Rephrasing this idea, we might say that the soul was the personality of the animal, object, or place. The kinship between man and the animals has been amply illustrated in the section on religious aspects of hunting. Inanimate objects which possessed souls included parts of the bodies of animals (bones, teeth, claws), quartz crystals, iron, and carved images of humans or animals, including

511

masks. Places believed to possess souls were burial cairns, peculiar geographical features, and other less definable isolated places where shamans went to obtain spirit-helpers.

In addition to this indeterminate number of spirits or souls which flitted about continuously almost everywhere, there were several more powerful figures which were believed in by everyone and constituted a sort of pantheon. The most important of these was Sedna, a goddess who lived beneath the sea and controlled sea mammals. In a myth, Sedna had run away from her husband to live with another man. Her father, being of a moral nature, went after her in a boat to bring her back to her first husband. On the return trip a storm arose and her father, fearing the wrath of spirits toward his sinful daughter, decided to get rid of her. He threw her overboard but she clung to the gunwale with her hands. He picked up a hatchet and chopped off the first joints of her fingers and, when she still clung to the boat, finally the other joints. At last she lost her grip and was drowned. Her finger joints were transformed into sea mammals, and that is why the Eskimo always propitiate her when they are about to hunt sea mammals.

The moon was regarded as a male deity who lived in an incestuous relationship with his sister the sun. He controlled human reproduction: menstruation, fertility, pregnancy, childbirth; and punished taboo violators. He was supplicated to increase the ratio of boy babies to girls. To a lesser degree he controlled the reproduction of game animals, so that the breaking of human sexual taboos angered him and caused him to curtail the reproduction of the animals. His least important function was control of the tides.

The sun was much less important than the moon. She was not worshipped or propitiated in any way. A minority of localities celebrated the return of the sun in the spring by putting out all lamps and relighting them from new fire made with a drill; or made string figures (cat's cradles) only when the sun was absent in winter.

There was also a spirit of the air called Sila, who was vaguely regarded as half-personal and half-impersonal. This was a purely spiritual essence, apparently sexless and without any former earthly connections. It controlled the weather and, through the weather, the abundance or scarcity of game. When angered by a breach of taboo, it sent storms. This completes the pantheon.

Between the four deities and the multitude of souls of animals and ghosts of the dead was a class of spirits called Tornait. These were a legendary race of people who formerly lived in arctic regions, and some anthropologists believe they should be equated to the actual people of the Thule culture, which has been established by archeologists as having formerly existed almost everywhere in central and eastern Eskimo territory. These spirits served as shamans' helpers and escorted shamans' souls en route to Sedna beneath the sea or to the moon or Sila through the air. Some were like ghosts, that is, human in form; others were of grotesque and freakish appearance unlike any animal or human. On the whole they were malevolent, but they sometimes co-operated with persons whom they served as spirit-helpers.

Shamans were predominantly men, but included some women past the menopause in their ranks. They were religious intermediaries between man and the spiritual world. They had the power to send their souls to any of the spiritual personalities enumerated above and to lobby for aid to man.

Supernatural power in the form of some spirit sometimes first appeared, unsought by the shaman-to-be, in a dream or hallucination. At other times a person who wanted to become a shaman would go to a lonely spot where spirits were thought to dwell and seek contact with them there. This contact when it came was in the same form: dream or hallucination. These subjective experiences were interpreted as real by both the shaman and the public. The neophyte shaman saw or heard, and occasionally felt, a spirit which was most often in the form of either a human being or an animal, but sometimes rather grotesque. This might be a common ghost, a Tornait, or an animal spirit.

Shamans attempted to predict or control weather and the supply of game animals whose habits and hunting depended on weather. They also cured disease, brought fertility to barren women, and applied the head-lifting test to suspected taboo breakers. In order to impress the public with their powers they used ventriloquism and sleight of hand, and allowed themselves to be bound hand and foot by a rope from which they miraculously escaped. Like our modern stage magicians, the shamans performed these tricks in semi-darkness.

Possessional shamanism was universal. Every shaman went into a trance, at which time the spirit of some divinity was thought to enter his body and speak magical words, usually in a special brand of archaic language not understood by the people and doubtfully understood by shamans themselves.

A shaman might go into a trance and, instead of his body becoming possessed by an entering spirit, he might send his soul on a journey to contact his spirit-helper or some divinity such as Sedna. The psychological explanation is a simple one: that he dreamt that he went on these journeys. On regaining consciousness he would tell the people present what he had experienced on his soul flight and would often predict the future or prescribe behavior for the people which would be aimed at improving their plight.

The routine for making a barren woman fertile usually included her sleeping with the shaman. In cases of a husband who was sterile, this might have real efficacy. Shamans usually received fees, or demanded that some compensation be given to the spirit who had brought good health to a sick person. This payment to a spirit might amount to a female relative of the sick person sleeping with the shaman, or the patient herself doing the same after recovering. The material payment might be an article of clothing, a weapon, or an art object. When the shaman performed publicly during a time of famine, he received no specific pay other than personal advertising.

Spoken formulas, passed on from one shaman to another in the archaic language, were thought to bring definite results. Their effect was compulsive; the spirits or supernatural forces were forced to comply. They were therefore magical in character. Such magical formulas were sometimes bought and sold, or willed to another at the point of death. Other less secret verbiage could be heard and later uttered by anyone.

If there is any recurrent theme threading through all Eskimo religion, it is the consistent association of everything religious with the food quest. In a hostile environment where hundreds starved to death every winter, it is no wonder that the naïve person alleviated his anxieties over hunger by imagining that help could be obtained from the supernatural. Religion thus became an outlet for anxieties over problems beyond natural solution; the antics and verbalizations indulged in to influence the supernatural served to reduce highly charged emotions and ease tensions.

CONCLUSIONS

The number of spiritual personalities thought to exist probably exceeded that of living human beings everywhere in native North America for the simple reason that every people believed in ghosts, and there were as many ghosts as there were people who had died. There was a strong tendency to arrange gods in a ranked hierarchy in areas where people were ranked in similar manner, and to ignore such ranking where egalitarianism dominated human societies. Thus the peoples of Meso-America carefully ranked their gods, while those in the Sub-Arctic, Plateau, and Great Basin believed in large numbers of spirits of about equal rank. Other areas tended to be intermediate in this respect. Among the Pueblos, where many spiritual personalities were widely enough recognized to be designated as gods, there was little tendency toward ranking, just as there was near equality among human beings.

The number of public religious ceremonies, the number of participants, and the number of spectators, is correlated not only with the density of population but with general culture complexity and with a surplus of food and other necessities which made mass participation in the luxury of ceremonies possible. Here again Meso-America surpasses all other areas, while the Arctic, Sub-Arctic, and Great Basin fall at the other end of the scale. The Pueblos and Navaho of the Oasis may have devoted as much time per capita to religious activities as did the Meso-Americans, but their populations were much smaller and the total effect less spectacular.

Specialization in the priesthood parallels that in economic activities. Again Meso-America leads all other areas with its full-time priests, as well as in numbers of part-time participants in ritual. Around the Caribbean full-time priests were also present, but not as frequent as in Meso-America. The Pueblos, on the other hand, had no full-time priests; all priests worked at some primarily economic activity to earn their livings. If there were any full-time priests in the East, they were only to be found on the coastal plain of the Southeast, where the political ruler was linked with the sun, inherited his position, and had the power of life and death over all his subjects. In the Arctic, Sub-Arctic, Plateau, Great Basin, and probably Northeast Mexico there were no priests at all because there were no religious organizations, except in a few localities bordering on areas where organized religion prevailed. In these four or five culture areas shamans dominated religion, magic, and medicine. On the Northwest Coast, in California, in much of the Oasis, on the Plains, and Prairies, in most of the East, and in some of the Circum-Caribbean area, religious leaders shared the attributes of both priests and shamans. They belonged to cults, performed carefully memorized rituals, and sometimes appealed to generally recognized gods or powerful spirits; but at the same time they had visions and other direct contact with the supernatural from which they obtained what were regarded as original songs, cures, and the like. Shamans occurred even in Meso-America, and some of the priests there possessed attributes more characteristic of shamans elsewhere. The dichotomy of the priest as opposed to the shaman, therefore, fits about half of the culture areas of North America if only the major attributes of these religious functionaries are considered. It cannot be applied with much meaning to the other areas. The term medicine man has been applied where it is difficult to choose between priest and shaman.

Concerning medicine, we found that most ailments were thought to have been caused by the supernatural and could therefore be cured only with the aid of the supernatural. Where plant remedies were used, the Meso-Americans tended to mix a number of plants together into a single prescription for a single ailment. Peoples around the Caribbean, in the East, and in the Oasis concocted fewer plant mixtures, and those in remaining areas tended to prescribe a single plant for each ailment. Theories of disease show much variation, but intrusion of a foreign object may be the most frequent and a near universal. Intrusion of a disease-causing spirit is less often reported, although perhaps almost as common. Soul loss, or loss of spirit-helper, was formerly thought to be common only in the north, but more recent evidence has turned up some cases in every culture area, although the known continental frequency would be less than that of the other two major causes of illness.

Sorcery, by definition, is never condoned by Indian societies in which it is practiced, but the social scientist may regard it as a substitute for murder and other forms of physical aggression. A number of Indian societies, including the Canadian Ojibwa (Hallowell, 1955:277–90), have never heard of a case of murder. No one has ever been known to kill by physical means a member of his own group; but invariably such societies practice witchcraft. If a person feels he has been wronged by another, he attempts to injure or kill the offender by witchcraft. Although some persons become ill or may even die as a result of knowing they are being bewitched, many anthropologists believe that the mortality from witchcraft in these societies is less than that from murder in societies where murder takes place. Mortality from witchcraft was certainly less among the Ojibwa than death by murder among the Eskimo. The total amount of anxiety which sorcery creates in a society and the amount of disability such anxiety causes cannot be objectively measured; but neither can anxiety be measured in societies where murder is common. With mortality as the measure of disharmony, many anthropologists believe a society in which witchcraft occurs without physical murder is better off than one in which actual murder is committed. (less deaths.)

Social scientists possess no criteria for scaling Indian religions according to their total value for their believers. As examples of science, they all fail to measure up, but, as forms of psychotherapy, they all have been demonstrated to be efficacious. There is no unanimity of opinion in the anthropological profession on what to do about native religions in connection with modern programs of economic, medical, and educational aid to the Indians. Many persons would agree, however, that there is no point in trying to eliminate native religions until something else has been supplied to replace them. After the standard of living has been raised, modern medicine introduced, mortality reduced, and perhaps a program of insurance initiated, Indians will become less dependent psychologically on their own religions and will be willing to rely increasingly on these more tangible forms of security.

REFERENCES

CANNON, 1942; ELMORE, 1944; EMMART, 1940; FENTON, 1942; HALLOWELL, 1955; KLUCKHOHN, 1944; PARSONS, 1939; RAY, 1932; REICHARD, 1950; RICHTER, 1957; SAHAGÚN (Anderson and Dibble), 1950–58; SWANTON, 1928; VAILLANT, 1941; WEYER, 1932.

24: PERSONALITY AND CULTURE

THE WORD personality is used in psychology to refer to the total responses of a single individual, as opposed to other individuals, in a society. It includes emotional or physiological responses as well as overt behavior and language. Common synonyms for personality are character, disposition, and temperament. Social psychologists, as well as laboratory and clinical psychologists, treat the individual person as the unit of investigation. Generalizations about groups of persons are derived by statistical methods from the responses of individuals.

Anthropologists, on the other hand, extend the concept of personality, character, or temperament to social groups, often without making observations on a truly representative sample of all individuals in the group. Just as culture refers to the way of life shared by an entire society, personality may also refer to the composite personality of an entire society. Although all anthropologists recognize individual variation in personality within the small social groups they study, their chief interest is the normal or modal personality of the group as a whole.

The term modal personality is derived from the mode of the statistician, which is the interval on any scale of measurement where the largest number of persons (cases) are located. For instance, if we measure the stature of a group of college men to the nearest inch, we might find that more men are 5 feet 9 inches tall than are 5 feet 8, or 5 feet 10, etc. If that is true, then 5 feet 9 inches is the modal stature of the group. The mode is usually close to the average and may be identical to it, but is not always identical.

Just as hundreds of measurements and other observations may

519

be taken on the human body, so hundreds of measurements and observations of a psychological nature may be made on human responses. There may be as many modes for the personality of a single society as there are scales of measurement for traits of personality. Psychological statisticians have developed objective techniques for integrating the results of any number of separate measurements on the members of a society into a small number of clusters or factors, which describes the society as a whole. Although few anthropologists understand these techniques at the present time, they provide a conceptual framework needed by anthropology to give intelligent answers to the questions being raised about comparative personality. The concept of modal personality, as used by anthropologists, implies that it is a composite mode derived from a representative sample of all the kinds of responses made by all the members of the society.

At the present time many anthropologists believe that the thousands of societies in the world that we can now distinguish on the basis of race, language, and culture, could also be distinguished from one another in composite modal personality if our knowledge were more complete. Experience with the data of bioanthropology, language, and culture shows that if enough observations were obtained, the peoples of the world could be differentiated into very many units, each one distinguishable in some respect from every other one. On the basis of language alone, the American Indians of both continents have been divided into about two thousand entities, each with its own language. Add to this what we know of bioanthropology and culture differentiae, and the number would swell to many thousand. If we possessed enough observations on personality, it too should yield a large number of composite modal personality types, each one differing significantly from every other. Needless to say, we are very far from this goal at the present time.

Modal personality patterns are similar to the national character constructs of historians. Historians have not only distinguished the national character of nations, such as England, France, and Germany, but have also recognized differences within a single nation at different periods in its history. Thus the national character of the British would show differences at the time of Elizabeth I,

520

Cromwell, Victoria, and Elizabeth II. Historians have also recognized differences in personality in Europe according to social class. Nobles behave differently from commoners or slaves, and the rich show significant differences in behavior from the poor.

The above qualifications apply with equal force to Indian societies. Indian personality of a single tribe would be expected to change over the centuries since the first White contact, as well as to differ from tribe to tribe. In societies with social classes, the modal personality of each class should be distinguishable from that of every other class.

United States historians, up to a few decades ago, had tended to describe the personality of the Indian as that of a blood-thirsty savage struggling for survival in a howling wilderness. The Indian was viewed chiefly as an impediment to the spread of European civilization and Christianity, and was eliminated by some pioneers almost as ruthlessly as dangerous beasts, such as wolves, bears, and mountain lions. Little attention was given to personal relations within Indian society, except by a few romantic writers such as James Fenimore Cooper. The anthropologist today is concerned primarily with in-group personal relations, and only secondarily with out-group relations. The result is that the anthropologist gives a much more sympathetic picture of Indian personality than does the historian. The whole truth includes both views.

Two of the many determiners of personality, largely neglected by anthropologists today, are malnutrition and organic disease. A society in which malnutrition is widespread is not going to give forth bursts of energy or respond energetically to the anthropologist, colonial administrator, or business man. The scarcity of food in the Great Basin area of North America must have contributed to the dull unresponsive personalities that field workers have so often found there. Chronic diseases, such as malaria, yaws, and tuberculosis obviously limit the full participation of the sick in any kind of activity. An anthropologist recently studied personality in an Eskimo community without knowing that most of the population had tuberculosis. They had largely ceased to hunt, not because of some purely psychological defeatism, but principally because they did not have the physical strength to hunt.

The proof that psychosomatic disease is the cause of a person's

521

symptoms demands the elimination of organic disease by a series of careful and thorough laboratory tests. Only modern hospitals are equipped to diagnose accurately a wide range of organic diseases. For instance, when I was in Mexico on a field trip, a woman from the United States became seriously ill with jaundice, which a laboratory test identified as infectious hepatitis. Her Mexican servants and other unsophisticated local people, however, attributed her sickness to an argument she had had with her children's tutor. Her anger had made her ill, they thought. They said such cases were common among the Mexicans. The moral of this tale is that we cannot take an informant's word for the causation of disease. Informants in many primitive cultures believe all disease is caused by the supernatural; but the anthropologist should not interpret this to mean that practically all disease in the culture is of psychogenic origin. By extension, when a case is reported by informants of a person being killed by sorcery, the cause of death should not be labeled psychogenic by the anthropologist unless an autopsy revealing no organic disease has been performed by a well-equipped pathology laboratory.

There has also been considerable confusion between the actual behavior of persons and the ideal behavior that informants often prefer to talk about when speaking to an outsider. Much of the older ethnography seems to consist largely of an idealized picture derived from a small number of old informants who loved to glorify the past. Recent field reports tend to be much more candid and usually attempt to distinguish between ideal and manifest behavior.

Before narrowing down to descriptions of modal personality types in restricted areas, we can profit by quoting a recent general statement about North American Indian personality by George and Louise Spindler (1957).

Without attempting to document the many sources from which inferences and data were drawn, we can tentatively describe the psychological features most widely exhibited among the North American Indians as a whole in the following way: nondemonstrative emotionality and reserve accompanied by a high degree of control over interpersonal aggression within the in-group; a pattern of generosity that varies greatly in the extent to which it is a formalized social device without emotional depth; autonomy of the individual, a trait linked with socio-political structures low in dominance-submission hierarchies; ability to endure pain, hardship, hunger, and frustration without external evidence of discomfort; a positive valuation of bravery and courage that varies sharply with respect to emphasis on highly aggressive daring in military exploit; a generalized fear of the world as dangerous, and particularly a fear of witchcraft; a "practical joker" strain that is nearly everywhere highly channelized institutionally, as in the common brother-in-law joking prerogative, and that appears to be a safety valve for in-group aggressions held sharply in check; attention to the concrete realities of the present—what Rorschachists would call the "large D" approach to problem solving—practicality in contrast to abstract integration in terms of long-range goals; a dependence upon supernatural power outside one's self—power that determines one's fate, which is expressed to and can be acquired by the individual through dreams, and for which the individual is not held personally accountable, at least not in the sense that one's "will" is accountable for one's acts in Western cultures. (Spindler and Spindler, 1957:148-49.)

THE CONTROVERSIAL PUEBLOS

The modal personality of the Pueblo Indians of the Oasis was first described in detail by Ruth Benedict in her famous book, *Patterns of Culture* (1934). She concentrated on the Zuñi, among whom she had done field work. The present sketch will embrace both Hopi and Zuñi, between whom there were few differences with respect to personality and culture.

According to Benedict, the Pueblos were more wrapped up in religious ceremony than in any other aspect of their way of life, and they valued sobriety and inoffensiveness above all other virtues. Most prayers are magic formulas which must be recited verbatim to bring the desired result. They are not spontaneous outpourings of the troubled heart, but carefully memorized, emotionally mild requests asking for an orderly life, pleasant days, and protection from violence. Their religious dances likewise must be done exactly as prescribed by the gods themselves in order to carry enough appeal to the supernatural to be sure of bringing results to man. Practically all religious authority is vested in the four major and eight minor priesthoods, and all public religious ceremonies are conducted by one or the other of these groups. Almost all ceremonial activity is for the benefit of the entire Pueblo, and even

523

ceremonies to cure a sick person often have rain-making or fertility features built in.

Marriage was arranged with the minimum of courtship and tuning up of emotions. In the evening when all the girls went to the spring for water, a boy might ask the one he liked best for a drink. If she approved of him, she gave him the drink. He might also ask her to make him a throwing stick for the co-operative rabbit hunt and, if she did this, he would give her the rabbits he had killed. After no more contact than this, and no premarital sexual experience, the boy might go to the girl's house and, after the usual exchange of greetings, ask her father for her hand. The father did not make the decision, but called his daughter in to speak for herself. If she was willing, the mother made a bed in the next room and the young couple retired for the night. The next day the bride washed the groom's hair, and after four days she dressed in her best clothes and carried a large basket of finely ground corn meal to his mother as a present. There were no more formalities and nothing like a public wedding ceremony. Divorce was even simpler. If the marriage was childless or otherwise unsatisfactory to the bride, she would gather up her husband's personal possessions and place them on the doorsill. When the husband came home, he picked up the bundle, sometimes with tears, and returned to his own mother's house. The tears at separation were apparently the most emotional part of the whole procedure, and it was usually the man who cried.

As we have seen in the chapter on Marriage and the Family, the family unit is the matrilocal extended family embracing several generations. Authority is vested in the oldest woman in the female line or in all of the mature women collectively. A husband and wife combination, even if they have children, cannot make any decision of their own which runs contrary to the wishes of the larger extended family unit. The individual is again submerged in the group.

There were few differences in material wealth within Pueblo society, and those with more shared with those who had less. Everyone lived in the same kind of house, ate the same kind of food, and wore the same kind of clothing. Political and ceremonial leaders wore special costumes when appearing in official ceremonies, but not in daily life. The most prized possessions were ceremonial objects, but many might be borrowed by anyone who asked, and those too sacred to lend were used by the priest-owner to bring good fortune to all. Priestly positions were acquired by inheritance, by purchase from an older member of an organization, or by being chosen by older priests. In any case, the new priests had to memorize all the ritual, both verbal and non-verbal. Merit played a greater role than inheritance.

Pueblo men shunned authority and anyone ambitious to secure a high office was in danger of being persecuted for being a sorcerer. He might be hung by the thumbs until he confessed. If a man was involved in any conflict, even though he was in the right, it was held against him. If a man won foot races regularly he was barred from running because he spoiled the contest for the more mediocre. In these and other ways, the Pueblos discouraged individual distinction and placed a premium on mediocrity. The group interest always took precedence over individual interest.

In comparing the Pueblos with other North American Indian peoples, Benedict describes visions achieved during emotional states by other Indian tribes with the help of fasting, torture, drugs, and alcohol. The Pueblo people sought no visions and engaged in no emotional orgies of any kind.

There is little talk of sex among Pueblo peoples and no boasting about it, but a life of chastity is disapproved. No one in their folk tales is criticized more harshly than the proud girls who resist marriage in their youth. The gods come down to earth and sleep with such girls in order to educate their sexual responses to the point that they will want husbands. A moderate amount of extramarital sex experience is approved because sex is a part of the happy life.

The one experience mentioned by Benedict which is highly charged with emotions, is the initiation of boys into the secret cults. Boys from five to nine years of age are whipped and frightened by men disguised as evil spirits. Later, at about the age of fourteen, it is revealed to the boys that all the spirits appearing in the ceremonies are only men in disguise. Then the spirit impersonators whip the boys again, and the boys whip them in return. A long myth is then told the boys about how a certain boy in the past was killed for revealing this secret to women or younger chil-

perhaps initiations

dren. These traumatic experiences fill only a very small proportion of the space Benedict devotes to the Pueblos.

Benedict sums up the modal personality of the Pueblo people with the term Apollonian, which Nietzsche opposed to Dionysian. The Apollonian personality is modest, gentle, and co-operative, and does not indulge in disruptive psychological states. He is temperate, enjoys his sobriety to a moderate degree, and avoids the heights of ecstasy as well as the depths of despair.

Dorothy Eggan (1943) found the Hopi a much more disturbed group of adults than Benedict found at Zuñi.

In any prolonged contact with the Hopi Indians, an investigator who is interested in the psychic as well as in the more tangible phenomena of culture is struck with the mass maladjustment of these people, maladjustment being here defined as a state in which friction predominates in personal relations, and in which the worst is anxiously and habitually anticipated. The comment has been made by numerous persons who have worked with them that one Hopi is a delightful friend; two are often a problem; and more than that number are frequently a headache. Discord is apparent in inter-tribal relations as well, as most Hopi will testify; the younger ones particularly express annoyance over the needless arguments which accompany any group attempt to reach a decision in tribal matters. Gossip is rampant throughout the villages; witchcraft is an ever present threat, one's relatives as well as others being suspect; and in some cases individuals fear that they may be witches without being aware of it. Even sisterly love in this strongly matrilineal society seldom runs smoothly, although sisters present a united front to the rest of their world. (Dorothy Eggan, 1943:357.)

Dorothy Eggan reviews the generally accepted gentleness and permissiveness in the child-parent relationship, the threat of punishment from the spirits if the child does not behave properly, and the emotional shock that initiation brings to girls as well as boys. She concludes:

In summary, this preliminary study of Hopi psychology suggests that the first five or six years of childhood among them may have a different significance than Freudian theory allows. . . . It seems evident that the Hopi were not subject to the same set of early pressures which encompass western children, and even when the pressures were similar, they were much less intensely instigated. . . . Of greater weight in Hopi

526

personality development were the frustrating acculturation influences, the fears of various kinds which were ever present and inadequately sublimated, and the suppression of physical aggression. Probably the rather sudden shift from indulgence to control [at initiation] was also an important precipitating factor in personality formation. (Dorothy Eggan, 1943:373.)

Laura Thompson (1945), took essentially the same view of the Hopi that Benedict did of the Zuñi. Under a centered heading labelled "The Ideal Man," Thompson lists the attributes of the ideal Hopi personality.

Thus the *hopi* individual is: (1) strong (in the Hopi sense, i.e., he is psychically strong—self-controlled, intelligent, and wise—and he is physically strong); (2) poised (in the Hopi sense, i.e., he is balanced, free of anxiety, tranquil, "quiet of heart" and concentrated on "good" thoughts); (3) law-abiding (i.e., responsible, actively cooperative, kind and unselfish); (4) peaceful (i.e., non-aggressive, non-quarrelsome, modest); (5) protective (i.e., fertility-promoting and life-preserving, rather than injurious or destructive to life in any of its manifestations, including human beings, animals, and plants); (6) free of illness. (Thompson, 1945:733.)

Another challenge of Benedict's Apollonianism comes from Esther Goldfrank (1945a). Her interpretation holds that Pueblo personalities have their share of tension, suspicion, anxiety, hostility, fear, and ambition, but that outward manifestations of such emotions are suppressed by those in authority, and repressed by the fear on the part of the individual of being accused of witchcraft or of being bewitched.

Large-scale cooperation deriving primarily from the needs of irrigation is therefore vitally important to the life and well-being of the Pueblo community. It is no spontaneous expression of good-will or sociability. What may seem voluntary to some is the end of a long process of conditioning, often persuasive, but frequently harsh, that commences in infancy and continues throughout adulthood. (Goldfrank, 1945a: 519.)

To the need of irrigation we would like to add the need of defense against enemy raids, which was very real before the Spanish gained control.

Pueblo children loved extremely
when small; harsh treatment when initiated or adult
(personality factors?)

Goldfrank attacks the Freudian view that the treatment received in infancy and early childhood determines, to a great degree, the adult personality. All writers on Pueblo peoples agree that treatment of infants is unusually loving, gentle, and permissive. They are nursed when hungry, picked up whenever they fuss or cry, given a very gentle toilet training, and never slapped or spanked. However, when the child goes through his first initiation ceremony, he experiences harsh treatment which is a threat of worse things to come if he does not conform to the adult personality pattern.

But it is eminently clear that a study of the period of infancy alone would give few clues to the personality structure exhibited by the Pueblo adult. . . . But in the Pueblos where both severe discipline and substantial rewards derive from extersal agents who function most importantly in the "later" years, a study of the society as a whole and over time is absolutely necessary for any satisfactory understanding of the building of adult personality. (Goldfrank, 1945a: 537.)

The four descriptions of Pueblo personality, all published within a span of twelve years, clearly fall into two groups as John W. Bennett (1946) pointed out: the Benedict-Thompson Apollonian ideal; the Eggan-Goldfrank maladjusted actuality. How are these differences to be explained? To begin with, it is obvious that description of modal personality had not achieved much objectivity or singularity of purpose at the time the authors quoted above were writing. Benedict and Thompson were interested in portraying the ideal Pueblo personality, the perfect individual, while Eggan and Goldfrank were concerned with actual behavior and a psychological interpretation of it. Benedict especially selected the evidence about Pueblo life which agreed with her preconception of it, or perhaps her own ideal of an attractive personality pattern. She ignored evidence that pointed toward maladjustment. Her method of operation may be acceptable as impressionistic writing, but it failed as science because it did not present a representative sample of Pueblo behavior. Likewise she presented an extreme view of the Kwakiutl, as we shall see in more detail below, and her treatment of the Dobuans is also suspect. At the same time her book, *Patterns of Culture*, was most successful in conveying to the general reader the anthropological point of view, that each indi-

528

vidual culture may be centered about a small number of acquired drives or goals, but that taken collectively the many cultures of the world offer enormous variation from one to another. Just as the characters of a play are normally overwritten and overacted in the theater in order to be sure the audience will get the message, the differences between Benedict's three cultural characters were exaggerated in order to put them across to the general reader.

Thompson's treatment of the Hopi, cited above, was written in a technical journal for consumption by anthropologists but, as the title suggests, was more a philosophical and poetic treatment than a scientific investigation. Eggan and Goldfrank took a more candid look than Benedict and Thompson which revealed the less attractive side of Pueblo life. All four have made important contributions to our understanding of Pueblo personality. It is important to know the ideals toward which members of a society strive, and equally important to know how near they come to achieving their ideals. The low incidence of insanity (psychosis) and violence suggests that the behavior of the Pueblo people is not hopelessly far from their ethos, but that the maladjustments in personal relations nevertheless reveal a significant gap between the two.

THE EGOCENTRIC NORTHWEST COAST MEN

Benedict's (1934) account of the culture and personality of the Northwest Coast peoples will be considered first. Although the Northwest Coast peoples did not farm, they lived in permanent villages and accumulated more in the way of material possessions than did the Pueblos. Fish were so plentiful and easy to catch that the time spent in obtaining food was no greater than that of most farming peoples, and the inexhaustible supply of wood and other materials, plus the skill of the people in working these materials, provided a relatively rich and varied way of life. No other area of equal size without agriculture anywhere in the world enjoyed as much material prosperity as did the Northwest Coast.

Kwakiutl religion was loaded with intense emotional states, and those who did not have definite visionary experiences often had the chance to play the role of a person possessed by a powerful spirit in public performances. Initiates into the highest-ranking organization, the Cannibal Society, pretended that they had been

529

seized by a cannibal spirit and could not restrain themselves from eating human flesh (see pages 409–10). The potlatch (described on pages 225–27) was the occasion for giving away huge amounts of corporeal property to guests, who later returned them with "interest" to the donor. The man who gave away the most property was the winner of these contests. These give-aways were always associated with a transfer of status and title from one individual to another. Thus if a rich man died, his heir could not claim title to any of his inherited possessions until he had given a potlatch to validate or confirm his right to the inheritance.

Destruction of property was the most extreme form of wealth display. A man who was so rich that he could afford to destroy valuable possessions, instead of giving them away with the certainty that he would later receive return gifts of greater value, was indeed a great figure in the society. Canoes were chopped up or burned, and slaves killed, all to prove one's great wealth. The most valuable single object was a cold-hammered copper plate, which had no utility whatsoever, but was extremely valuable because of the scarcity of copper. Each "copper" had a name and a history as complicated as that of an original painting by a deceased and famous artist in Europe. It increased in value every time it changed hands at potlatches. To destroy a "copper" was the greatest act of all, unless it was the continued payment and repayment for the "copper" in sham exchanges after it had been destroyed and existed only in memory and tradition.

Among the Kwakiutl, marriage customs strongly reflect the dominant culture pattern and offer the greatest possible contrast with the Pueblos, where marriage was treated lightly. An important man desirous of acquiring a bride called his relatives and village mates together as he did in preparation for war and told them, "Now we shall make war upon the tribes. Help me bring my wife into the house." Then everyone collected his more valuable material possessions and they went in a group to the home of the bride's father. The more property the groom and his followers gave to the relatives of the bride, as a sort of bride price, the more they would receive in return from the bride's relatives at a potlatch of a later date. Sometimes the groom's party armed themselves and rushed upon the village of the bride, in which cases the bride's

530

party might counterattack. Although these were supposed to be sham attacks, sometimes tempers rose and people were actually killed, initiating endless bargaining over blood money. Return gifts from the bride's family were due after the birth of the first child, but they were often delayed until he was old enough to be initiated into the Cannibal Society. Then his father collected the large return from his mother's people and gave a huge potlatch to validate his son's membership in the secret society. An ambitious man might contract as many as four marriages in order to benefit economically by the exchange of property and to flaunt his wealth in public. The business aspects of marriage far outweighed the love of the principals which is not mentioned at all in most reports of marriages. The titles and prerogatives, so eagerly sought, were often passed on from a man to his daughter's child, but the son-in-law, who was the child's father, always gained status on these occasions.

Not mentioned by Benedict was the sharp division of labor between tasks performed by men and by women. Of the hundred jobs listed by Driver and Massey (1957:366) for the Kwakiutl, only five were shared by both sexes and these tasks were performed principally by women; 95 per cent of the occupations were associated exclusively with one sex. This is the sharpest division of labor known for all of aboriginal North America. In other areas more jobs were shared by both sexes. To this extreme sexual dimorphism of work must be added the extreme dominance of men over women. Nowhere is this reflected more clearly than in marriage customs, where the bride's preferences are not mentioned at all in most reports of marriages.

Although marriage was the principal means of acquiring enhanced rank in the culture, a man sometimes achieved it by murdering another man and appropriating his titles, crest, and privileges. A man could even raise his rank by claiming to kill a supernatural being, thus proving that he was more powerful than the spirit. By becoming a medicine man, one could receive all the trapping of noble rank directly from the spirits, and medicine men competed in contests to demonstrate their supernatural powers. They collected large fees for curing the sick and were the highest-ranking group in the culture.

Behavior on the Northwest Coast was dominated by the desire of every individual to show himself superior to his rivals. The speeches of chiefs at potlatches, which Benedict (1934: 190–93) quotes at length, were outbursts of self-glorification which she labels megalomania. The kings of Africa and Europe were modest in self-praise compared to Kwakiutl chiefs. Along with this bragging about one's self went ridicule of one's rivals; the greatest insult was to call a man a slave.

The Kwakiutl response to failure and frustration was sulking and acts of violence. Even when through no fault of his own a man's child died, he felt it necessary to redeem his loss in some concrete manner. After sulking on his bed for several days without speaking or eating, he arose and distributed property, went head-hunting, or committed suicide. There are no accurate figures on the frequency of suicide, but many cases are reported, often for reasons we would consider trivial. For instance, when a man's son stumbled in his initiation dance and failed to qualify as a secret society member, the man committed suicide because he was ruined financially. He had invested everything he owned in this ceremony to raise his son's status and knew that he could not raise enough material goods for a second try the next year.

Benedict sums up her description of the ideal Northwest Coast man by combining the term paranoid with the previously used megalomania and points out that our culture regards such behavior as abnormal. But what we regard as abnormal is the ideal personality pattern of the Kwakiutl and their neighbors on the Northwest Coast, as she sees it.

Helen Codere (1956) has challenged Benedict's position with respect to Kwakiutl culture in a paper aptly entitled, "The Amiable Side of Kwakiutl Life: The Potlatch and the Play Potlatch."

Field work among the Kwakiutl in 1951 produced evidence of a kind of potlatching, play potlatching or potlatching for fun, that has never been described but is of the greatest importance for an understanding of Kwakiutl life. The existence of playfulness in relation to potlatching requires reinterpretation of the character of both this institution and of the people participating in it. The 1951 field data include much new material on home life, child rearing, and humor that supports Boas' claim that the private life of the Kwakiutl possessed many amiable features, but it is the aim of this presentation to show that even in the public life of the ceremonials and potlatches there was mirth and friendliness. . . .

Even in those parts of Kwakiutl life in which a competitive, paranoid, atrocious character seems most unrelieved, there is evidence that such an extreme and unqualified characterization cannot be made. . . . The Kwakiutl are more real, more complex, more human than they have been represented to be. Even in their potlatches, their most extreme and flagrant institution, there are elements of humor and great complexity of thought and feeling: they are not single-minded; they are not lacking in insight; they do not put themselves and their most exigent interests beyond reflective thought and criticism. (Codere, 1956:334–50.)

It seems apparent from Codere's remarks that Benedict has again exaggerated almost to the point of caricature her portrait of Northwest Coast, and especially Kwakiutl, personality. Again Benedict has concentrated on an ideal personality, while Codere is more interested in manifest behavior over its entire range as well as at its central tendency. If we realize that Benedict selected her evidence to produce as sharp a contrast as possible with the Pueblo personality pattern, and that other evidence exists to modify her conclusions, we can still give her credit for first calling attention to the many differences in the ideal personalities of the Pueblos and Northwest Coasters.

What about the personality of the slaves, who are estimated to have made up 10 to 20 per cent of the population on the Northwest Coast? It is obvious that the concept of modal personality patterns is not adequate to describe personality patterns of class-structured societies, which are presumably multiple. Because about half the peoples of the world possess definite systems of rank or social classes, this is a serious limitation. This problem can be solved by introducing the concept of multiple modes, which in the present stage of personality studies in anthropology would demand multiple essays, one on each of the distinguishable social classes in each society. Where class distinctions are clear, as between freemen and slaves on the Northwest Coast, this would not be difficult to do; but where the presence or absence of class structure is debatable, the personality investigator would be compelled to help solve that problem, perhaps in part with his personality data.

THE MANLY-HEARTED PLAINS PEOPLE

Benedict (1932) gave a brief description of Plains modal personality, which did not elicit as much controversy as her characterizations of the Pueblos and Northwest Coast Indians. Later writers, such as Lewis (1941, 1942), Goldfrank (1943, 1945*b*), and Devereux (1951) enlarged her views and added more in the way of psychoanalysis.

Plains Indian mothers often nursed their children for years and treated them with considerable tenderness. Like most Indians, they swaddled their infants and bound them to cradle boards for the first year of life. Children were much more closely attached to the mother than to the father. Fathers were often away hunting or on the warpath, and mortality of fathers must have been about twice that of mothers. The mother then was not only the child's principal source of affection and security, but was his chief disciplinarian as well. The concept of the "manly-hearted woman" reflects the role many women played on the Plains. The result is that the child develops more hostility toward the mother than toward the father, thus transferring the Oedipus complex from the father to the mother. From the mother this hostility tends to be projected to the wife and even to other women. It is the father who helps his son gain rank by choosing one son as a favorite and honoring him in public. The relationship of a person to his father, then, tends to be more congenial than that toward his mother. It is also significant that spirit helpers are usually males, but they, like the father, are not all-powerful and cannot always help their protégé.

Devereux (1951:66) speaks of the "anti-sexual orientation" of Plains Indians. They sometimes boast of the length of time between their own birth and that of the next brother or sister, because it shows that their mother was more interested in nursing them than in renewing sexual relations with their father. Chastity in females is valued everywhere on the Plains although not expected of all of them, and ritual continence is also common. Along with this went a legitimized stealing of other men's wives for a few days by members of certain men's sodalities.

Conflicts arose from the notion that a woman should be chaste while a man should engage in sex adventures at every opportunity.

534

Thus a man would feel impelled to defend the honor of his wife and sisters at one moment, and to seek to dishonor another man's wife or sister at the next. A man who was both able to protect his wife and sisters from the sexual advances of other men and at the same time to achieve many conquests of other women enjoyed the most prestige. Thus relations with women became symbols of prestige. This ambivalence toward sex resulted in the infliction of rather severe penalties on wayward women by their husbands. They were sometimes beaten, ridiculed in public, mutilated in the nose to make them unattractive to other men, or forced in a revolting public spectacle to have sexual relations with all the men in camp. The dominance of men over women was probably stronger than in any other area north of Mexico except the Northwest Coast.

Rivalry and hostility between men was more institutionalized and given a healthier set of outlets by the culture. A man could raise his status by a successful vision quest, by public self-torture in the Sun Dance, by giving away horses and other property, by being a good hunter, and above all, by defeating the enemy in war. In the chapters on Violence, Feuds, Raids, and War (353–84) and on Rank and Social Classes (385–404) we have already seen the ways prestige was achieved on the Plains by men. The individual success of a man in male pursuits was generally of benefit to his entire band or tribe. Some men, however, had such a strong aversion to this ultra-masculine role that they would have been complete failures in the society if there had not been an escape for them. They donned the clothing of women, did women's work, and sometimes lived homosexually with another man. As *berdaches* they were accepted by their societies, and even allowed, like women, to carry scalps in the victory dance on the return of a successful war party.

All the Plains tribes observed the custom of recounting coup. On certain public occasions it was proper for a man to tell about his triumphs in war in a boastful manner. Some tribes even permitted a man to recount coup on women, to boast of his sexual exploits in public. Such examples of exhibitionism gave the partially rejected Plains male a chance to reinflate his ego.

The volatility of Plains emotions is well illustrated by the 1890

535

Ghost Dance religion, which swept the entire Plains area in a few years and continued for about a decade (Mooney, 1896). By 1890 the Plains Indians had all been defeated in wars with the Whites, most of them had been rounded up and confined to reservations, the buffalo were nearly exterminated, and many persons were starving. An Indian prophet from Nevada told them that he had experienced visions which indicated that all the Indians, dead as well as living, would be reunited upon a regenerated earth to live a life of happiness again, free from the Whites, misery, disease, and death. This package of prosperity was so attractive to the depressed, oppressed, repressed, and suppressed personality of the defeated Plains Indians, that they became converted to the new religion in droves. They actually thought a transformation of the world was about to take place and discussed the dates when it was supposed to happen.

Benedict characterizes Plains personality, as well as that of the Northwest Coasters, as Dionysian, given to extreme indulgence in violence, grief, trance, and other emotional states. While this is acceptable as far as it goes, Plains culture lacked the extreme egocentrism of the Northwest Coast which pointed in the direction of megalomania and paranoia. On the Plains there was nothing as extreme as the potlatch. Generosity was regarded as a virtue, but property given way was not returned with "interest" as on the Northwest Coast. There was little hereditary wealth on the Plains, and high honors were achieved principally by brave deeds in war, never by heredity. Plains culture, therefore, was much more democratic; a man of humble origin could rise to the top by his own achievements. Physical aggression against the enemy provided a socially approved outlet for rivalries and hostilities arising within the family, band, and tribe.

THE PSEUDO-APOLLONIANS OF THE SUB-ARCTIC

A significant series of studies in this area is that of A. Irving Hallowell (1955) which has been recently assembled in book form. Hallowell describes the Ojibwa of the Berens River, a small stream flowing into Lake Winnipeg from the east. This locality falls within the Eastern Sub-Arctic culture area.

536

The care of infants and children seems to have been as gentle and permissive as elsewhere in North America. The mother-child relationship is the warmest of any in the society. The infant is bound to the cradle board most of the time until he is able to walk, and is weaned gradually without marked emotional disturbance. Parents seldom inflict corporal punishment on their children, and Hallowell never witnessed boys and girls exchanging blows. The sexual activities of parents or other adults in the one-room dwellings are not concealed from children as they grow up. There is a little sex play among prepubescent children, but most of it is confined to those who are potential marriage mates: cross-cousins of the opposite sex. A relative in this relationship is the preferred person to marry, and the only relative one is allowed to marry. Even prepubescent youngsters in this relationship play practical jokes on one another and take liberties in speech that adults would discourage in children of any other relationship, for instance, brothers and sisters.

In former days all boys were sent out by their parents to obtain visions at the age of puberty or a little younger. If a boy had experienced sex before his vision quest, the supernatural would not bestow on him the blessings absolutely necessary to every man's successful life. To avoid this catastrophe parents probably watched their boys more carefully than their girls. After the vision quest of boys and the first menstruation of girls, which was kept as secret as possible, premarital sex activity took place. One gets the impression from Hallowell's writings that this was general, but not universal. However, it was allowed only when the parties involved were non-relatives or in the cross-cousin relationship and therefore potential mates. Ojibwa girls even planned excursions away from camp to make themselves available to boys they were interested in.

Genital sex activity was the only approved variety, as in our society. All other kinds of sex outlet were not only frowned upon but regarded as causes of illness. Marriage was polygynous until recent times, and was the only wholly approved form of sexual gratification. Neither impotence nor frigidity were understood by Ojibwa informants; they had never heard of a case of either. Younger men were expected to have intercourse nightly and, if a man failed to perform regularly, his wife might suspect him of

537

carrying on an adulterous affair with another woman. Sexual intercourse was resumed a month or so after the birth of a child; this is a very short period of postpartum continence. Extramarital sex experience was tolerated so long as the partners were unrelated or in the cross-cousin relationship, and was not a serious enough breach of the moral code to cause illness. However, faithfulness in marriage was the ideal, especially for women, and certain women were regarded as especially virtuous and good because they had never committed adultery.

Perhaps the most obtrusive characteristic of adult Ojibwa personality is the restraint exercised over almost all emotions in public; love, joy, hate, and fear are all repressed to an extreme degree. The one exception to this is laughter. There is a great deal of joking and laughing even during time of hunger, fatigue, and anxiety, and even their sacred myths contain Rabelaisian humor calculated to provoke a laugh. The greatest amount of joking is between cross-cousins of the opposite sex. Furthermore, face-to-face verbal quarreling or criticism of another is almost unheard of, although derogatory gossip behind a person's back is general. Along with this goes a hesitancy to command others, ready assent to requests from another, and much lending, sharing, and hospitality. Competition is discouraged and discretion is considered the better part of valor. Physical aggression and violence are totally unknown: no cases of murder have been reported; wars with other Indians or Whites have never existed; suicide is unknown; theft and brawls are extremely rare. To the casual observer, laughter, harmony, cooperation, modesty, patience, and self-control are the high points of Ojibwa modal personality. Here we seem to have as clear an example of the Apollonian ideal as can be found among the Pueblos or perhaps anywhere in the world.

But when we inquire into the reasons for this Apollonian behavior, we find that it is fear of illness and death. Serious illness can be caused by only two things: wrong-doing and sorcery. Wrong-doing includes all forms of deviant sexual behavior, cruelty to animals as well as to human beings, inconsiderate treatment of the dead, insult and ridicule of others, failure to share one's worldly goods, and a host of other acts running contrary to the cultural norm. Bad conduct is not punished by spirits or by any legal ma-

538

chinery, to which one may appeal his case, but directly according to a law of moral compensation. Punishment always takes the form of illness or death.

The other cause of illness and death is sorcery, inflicted on a person by a hostile human being, who may magically inject a poison object into his victim, or may steal his soul. In almost every case, the sorcerer is thought to be someone whom the victim has wronged in some way. Because physical aggression is wholly suppressed by the society, the wronged individual can get even only by making his enemy sick or by killing him with sorcery. Everyone believes himself to be in danger of being bewitched even by his own relatives, and everyone is at the same time a potential sorcerer. Physical murder is unknown but murder by witchcraft is thought to be common. Such a belief has social value as an inhibitor of aggressions against one's neighbor in a society which has no true government and little else in the way of social control.

Sickness caused by infraction of the moral code, without sorcery, can be cured by the patient through confessing his sins. He does not confess in private to the ear of a priest, psychoanalyst, or heavenly spirit, but must expound his sins at length for all to hear. It is only by making his bad conduct common public knowledge that he can become well again. Because everyone is ill at some time in his life, cases of wrong-doing are known to everybody and are easily obtained by the field worker.

Where witchcraft is thought to be the cause of illness, a medicine man can sometimes remove the intrusive poison object or recover the stolen soul of the patient. Because sorcerers work secretly and confess only if they themselves become ill, it is usually impossible to verify the source of the evil that is being inflicted on a person in this way. Persons accused of witchcraft may be innocent and those engaged in it may not be caught. Therefore anxiety over witchcraft never ceases to exist.

Fear of sickness and death, therefore, is the principal sanction which produces the pseudo-Apollonian behavior of the Berens River Ojibwa. Instead of achieving a truly Apollonian adjustment to life, their emotions remain ambivalent, shifting from the satisfactions derived from friendliness and sharing to the fear of retaliation if they do not please their associates. The threat of starvation in the past and the temptation to solve it by cannibalism is related to a neurosis or psychosis in which the afflicted person imagines himself to be transformed into a cannibalistic monster. This was the most severe emotional disturbance occurring among these people, but its frequency was apparently low. The repeated confession of bad conduct serves as a better barometer of their maladjustment, yet their ability to enjoy a full sex life, even up to old age, and their perpetual laughter suggests that their maladjustment on the whole is not extreme.

A comparison of the Berens River Ojibwa with the Kaska, who live over a thousand miles to the northwest in the Mackenzie drainage, suggests that modal personality in the Sub-Arctic was fairly uniform. Honigman (1949, 1954: 4–10) describes the Kaska's extreme distaste for overt hostility and acts of aggression, his suppression of all strong emotion, his relative independence and emotional isolation from his associates, and his employment of sorcery to harm an enemy. Sorcery, however, seems less developed than among the Ojibwa.

THE AGGRESSIVE BUT INSECURE IROQUOIANS

William Fenton (1948) compares Iroquois personality with that of the Berens River Ojibwa described by Hallowell. The Iroquois also stressed speaking kindly to others and avoiding argument and anger. Along with this went a strong individualism which permitted no one to give orders to another and contributed to the lack of real authority on the part of chiefs and a parallel absence of real cohesion in the League of the Iroquois. Membership in war parties was on a volunteer basis; warriors were never drafted. Parents were permissive of their children, never struck or whipped them, and lived in fear of child suicide, which actually happened occasionally. Child suicide suggests that there may have been too abrupt a change from indulgence to discipline. The Iroquois also resorted to sorcery to right wrongs inflicted on them by others, but it does not seem to have been as common as among the Ojibwa. Polite and impersonal forms of speech were used in public lest one's remarks be construed as personal criticism likely to arouse anger. Gossip and slander were ideally avoided and seem to have been less frequent than among the Ojibwa, although by no

540

means absent. Laughter, funny stories, and jesting songs provided escape from the severe emotional restraint in public. Hospitality, lending, and sharing were the rule in both private and public affairs. At the game of lacrosse the player who did not get angry was the ideal, although in practice these hotly contested matches often ended in brawls between the two sides. To nurse a grudge until an opportunity arose to even the score by ambush or sorcery was regarded as deplorable, although it sometimes occurred.

Like the Pueblos, and other Indians as well, the Iroquois withheld leadership from the man who was overanxious for prestige. Failing to keep an appointment was a breach of social form, and a group of local officials or the tribal council would always ignore a person's request if he did not show up to plead his case. After the petitioner had made his appeal he was asked to withdraw from the meeting while the officials discussed the issue, and they seldom came to a decision on the same day. Thus they avoided criticizing an individual to his face and arousing him to anger, and put off their decision until he had had time to become calm. The successful negotiator learned to divide up his request in the hope that if part were rejected the remainder might be accepted. A great deal of latitude was allowed in personal behavior so long as it did not affect the fate of the sib, tribe, or league; when it did, the councils denied the requests of the individual. Ideally chiefs were eventempered, mild-mannered men who neither engaged in nor paid attention to gossip. Their internal rule was by persuasion and reason, but their external rule of subject peoples was direct and backed by the threat of war.

Anthony Wallace (1958) contributes much to our knowledge of Iroquoian personality by his study of the dreams recorded by missionaries, mostly in the seventeenth century. We learn that dreams were regarded as wishes of the soul which must be satisfied lest the dreamer experience sickness or death. A person who was awakened after dreaming he was bathing got up and took a bath no matter how cold the weather. A man who dreamed he was a captive being tortured by the enemy insisted that his friends tie him up and burn his flesh the next day, in the belief that this would satisfy his soul's desire and prevent him from actually being captured by the enemy and tortured to death (see 375–77).

541

Sexual dreams created a problem. The Iroquois permitted premarital sex relations between unrelated young people in different sibs, who were therefore eligible as marriage mates, and divorce and remarriage were easy for adults. Like the Pueblos, it was the wife who most often divorced her husband, simply by tossing his personal possessions outside the longhouse door. But they were often rather shy in heterosexual contacts, and chastity in the young and marital fidelity in the mature were regarded as virtues. Nevertheless, when a certain man had a dream in which the culture hero ordered him to go to a certain village and cohabit with two married women for five days, his dream fulfilment was permitted by the village authorities for fear that the spirit would bring disaster upon them if disobeyed. Such sexual dreams were common.

Dreams of torture at the hands of the enemy were common among warriors. When one man who had had such a dream told it to others, a council was held. The chiefs agreed that steps should be taken to avoid the ill fortune that the dream foretold. They seized the dreamer and tortured him with fire, telling him that they pitied him and to take courage in his hour of agony. Finally the dreamer ran out of the ring of fires, seized a dog, and offered it as a sacrifice to a war spirit. The dog was killed, roasted in the flames, and eaten in a public feast just as they would eat a human captive. This routine was supposed to prevent the defeat, capture, and torture of warriors from the village where the dreamer lived. In one case it took the dreamer six months to recover from the burns his own tribesmen inflicted on him.

If a man dreamed he had killed a person, he felt impelled to commit murder. In one instance a Cayuga man dreamed he had killed a girl and eaten her flesh. He called the chiefs of the tribe to his cabin and asked them to guess his dream, as was the custom. When one chief finally guessed that he desired to eat human flesh, all of them became frightened to the point that they went out and selected a victim. When the dreamer was about to deal the death blow to the innocent girl, remorse seized him, he decided that his dream had been satisfied, and the girl's life was spared.

Boys at puberty went on vision quests to acquire a personal spirit-helper. They sought isolation in the woods, fasted, and denied themselves comforts so that spirits would take pity on them and come to their aid. After such experience, dreams about the spirit-helper recurred throughout life, and it was important to do whatever the spirit told a man to do. The sick, too, commonly had dreams which they had to fulfil in order to recover from their illnesses. Many religious ceremonies were initiated by dreaming, each type of dream being associated with a particular ceremony. It is easy to see that illnesses and states of anxiety caused by emotional disturbances could be cured by a dream and its re-enactment. The most successful members of Iroquoian society were those who had had many visions and dreams.

We see from these examples that dreams and their re-enactments served many purposes among the Iroquoians. They were the outlets for aggressions, for the desire for illicit sexual relations, and for the anxiety associated with capture and torture by the enemy or with illness. The most frequently recorded dreams seem to have come from three groups: pubescent youths; warriors; and the sick. Each of these groups was facing a crisis and was in need of the assurance a dream could bring.

William Fenton's study (1941) of suicide shows how the frustrated and rejected individual turned his aggressions on himself. Women committed suicide most often because of husbands deserting them in middle age; children because of too much restraint by elders; and men as an escape from torture by the enemy or death from blood revenge at the hands of the relatives of a murdered man. Taking a plant poison was the most common method of doing away with one's self, especially for women; men more often strangled, stabbed, or shot themselves with firearms. Public opinion tended to condemn suicides of men to escape physical suffering, but it condoned the suicides of women mistreated by lovers.

We see from this brief sketch of Iroquoian personality that although men were strong, brave, aggressive, and ultramasculine on the surface, they had their share of insecurity, anxiety, and fear on the inside. Few could maintain the hypermasculine role without some form of inner emotional repercussion. The Iroquoians seem closest in modal personality to the peoples of the Sub-Arctic and the Plains, yet the differences with both appear to be significant.

543

THE AMBIVALENT ESKIMO

One of the best descriptions of Eskimo personality is that of Robert F. Spencer (1959) in his excellent monograph on the North Alaskan Eskimo.

Children were wanted and were treated as indulgently as in other areas of native North America. Infants were nursed at their mother's breast whenever they cried from hunger. Shortly before one year of age a child was given a little broth and premasticated meat, but it might continue to nurse up to four or five years of age. Weaning was a gradual process; a mother might even nurse two children of different ages at the same time. There was no marked rejection of an older child by the mother in favor of a younger one, but sometimes it was sufficiently traumatic to the older child to cause temper tantrums. These were ignored by parents and seem not to have been severe.

Unlike infants of most North American peoples, who were swaddled and bound to cradle "boards," Eskimo infants were carried in hide slings inside their mothers' parkas. They were diapered with soft caribou skins containing moss. Although toilet training was started as early as two or three months by setting the infant over one of the wooden vessels used as a urinal by the family, there was no punishment for bed-wetting or other "accidents." On the whole toilet training was gentle.

Infants slept with their mothers or with both parents. Parents resumed intercourse soon after a birth, apparently in one or two months, and the child was not barred from the bed when the parents had sexual intercourse. Therefore, neither the father nor the infant was rejected in favor of the other by the mother. However, an older child would be shifted from the bed of his father and mother to that of an older female relative in the household when a new baby arrived. Infants were never left alone or completely rejected by members of the household. If the mother was busy at some household task, there was always another person to hold the child and otherwise take care of it.

Infants were not forced to walk or to talk. They walked at about a year or a little more and talked a little later. Parents encouraged a baby to walk and talk but allowed a slower child to take his time about both. Boy babies were subjected to a single

544

unpleasant experience; they were sometimes placed outdoors naked for a time when the north wind blew. This was thought to increase their ability to withstand the cold.

Boys and girls were separated much of the time in childhood. Girls stayed at home with their mothers, from whom they gradually learned household tasks. Boys accompanied their fathers on hunting expeditions as soon as they were old enough and began to learn the activities of men. Children were encouraged to speak softly and refrain from making any noise lest they drive away the game. Boys were allowed to eat only twice a day, at mealtime, but the rules were not so strict for girls. Although children were encouraged to become as proficient at necessary activities as they were able, boasting was frowned upon and modesty held up as the ideal. A good runner took care not to win races too often for fear of being regarded as too self-assertive. Industriousness, co-operation, generosity, and truthfulness were among the cardinal virtues.

The change from childhood to adulthood was not marked by formal initiations. For boys the piercing of the lower lip near the corners of the mouth for labrets ended the period of adolesence and marked the beginning of manhood. At first menstruation, girls were secluded from the rest of the family inside the house, were subject to restrictions on food and drink, could not prepare food for others, and the like, but the taboo period lasted for only five days. Their chins were tattooed soon afterward, and they were regarded as women ready for marriage.

Premarital sexual relations were the rule for both young men and young women, although the latter were warned not to become involved with several men lest they confuse the obligations between families which began with sexual ties and were aimed at marriage. Ideally parents preferred to arrange marriages for their children, and this was often associated with bride service, where the young man lived in his future bride's household and assisted her father in hunting for a year or more before the marriage.

Sexual intercourse was regarded as an end in itself and was always genital. One man was said to have had intercourse with dogs but was not stigmatized by this experience. Older people apparently accepted a myth relating how the Indians originated from a cross between an Eskimo man and a female dog. There was no

545

homosexuality and no transvestitism among these Eskimo. Sex play before intercourse was limited to kissing and biting; parts of female anatomy, such as the breasts and buttocks, were not important in sex play. In spite of the general permissiveness surrounding sex, rape sometimes occurred. If a woman objected, she could scream for her kin to come to her rescue. No instruction in sexual matters was given to young people at marriage. Every child witnessed the sex acts of his parents and of other adults in the one-room aboriginal dwellings, and most had had premarital sex relations.

Although most marriages seem to have been satisfactory to both parties, neither expressed his or her feelings for the other. In fact no one in Eskimo culture verbalized his feelings about anything. Feelings were repressed most of the time, but were occasionally expressed in outbursts of violence. If a man's wife was dissatisfied with her marriage but her relatives approved of her husband, the husband could punish her severely. He might tear her clothes to pieces. If she were a scold, he could rip her cheeks open from the corners of her mouth; and if she ran away too often, he might cut the Achilles tendons in her legs so she could not walk far.

Two wives in a polygynous union seem to have got along well with each other, and even two husbands in a polyandrous union with one wife generally had no difficulty. However, there was a definite taboo on the marriage of a man to two sisters or of a woman to two brothers. Both the sororate and the levirate were likewise forbidden; a widower could not marry his dead wife's sister, nor could a widow marry her dead husband's brother. One man, who had married his dead brother's wife without knowing it, committed suicide by hanging himself when he learned what he had done.

Old men, except possibly shamans, tended to lose prestige as their physical prowess waned. They turned to story-telling, singing and drumming, and to sedentary crafts such as making boats, sleds, and weapons. In the past, when life was more nomadic, the aged were abandoned when they could no longer maintain the pace necessary for the survival of the family as a whole. At present they are allowed to sit or live indoors after they have become incapable of outdoor tasks, and food and other necessities are given them until they die a natural death.

546

Old women, in contrast to men, sometimes became shamans after the menopause, or the wife of a shaman might take an active part in her husband's profession at this time. Those who were not shamans were often thought to possess evil supernatural powers with which they could harm another.

The grandmother, and to a lesser extent the grandfather, often became the baby sitters and guardians for their grandchildren. When rejected by a parent, a child frequently sought refuge in the arms of a grandparent. If we add to this the fact that children were usually given the names of deceased grandparents and were thought to have derived their souls from the same source, we see that the grandparent-grandchild relationship was second only to that of parent and child.

In a succinct but excellent paper entitled "Alaskan Eskimo Cultural Values," Margaret Lantis (1959), sheds much light on Eskimo personality. The Eskimo placed a premium on the self-reliance, self-confidence, quick thinking and skill of the successful hunter. This included skill in manufacturing weapons as well as skill and ingenuity in using them. Lack of skill meant starvation and death. Hunting achievements contributed most to a man's prestige and to his high ego ideal. After these traits had given a man a generous supply of the world's goods, he was expected to share them freely with others. There was even rivalry in public generosity; those with the most competed to see who could give away the most. Men even shared their wives with friends and guests.

Physical aggression toward other Eskimos was inhibited to the point of becoming completely repressed most of the time. Patience and a philosophy of fatalism were highly valued. So strong was the socialization of the individual that community survival was valued above individual survival. Infanticide, suicide, and the killing of invalids are to be explained in these terms. Eskimo religion placed greater value on human and animal souls than it did on the bodies. Thus it was proper to kill and eat a sea mammal if this was done in a manner which would not offend its soul. Such was the ideal pattern of Eskimo personal values and behavior.

When an Eskimo group was confined in cramped quarters by bad weather for a number of days, or when hunters came home

547

empty-handed and starvation became a threat, tensions rose and were relieved by aggression. The killing of animals was probably the most frequent outlet for hostility, but beating one's dogs in anger was common. Aggression often took the form of sorcery against another person, and less often of physical violence. Other outlets were the destruction of property and wife-stealing, not to mention the aggressions by a husband against his own wife, mentioned above. The most common social mechanism for dealing with such antisocial behavior was avoidance; the offender or the offended took to flight. But ultimately the culprit might be apprehended and forced to pay with his life for his deviations.

Frustrated individuals sometimes obtained relief from dreams or visions which were interpreted as soul flights and contact with spirits, and mythology constituted a kind of group fantasy or therapy. The personality of the shaman is largely to be explained in this manner.

If the ideal Eskimo personality described above was general throughout all of Eskimo territory, the amount of deviation from this ideal must have varied from one locality to another. For example, among the Musk Ox Eskimo of the central region, every adult man had killed at least one other man in a duel. This suggests a wide deviation from the ideal of co-operation, generosity, and friendliness. If more were known about personality and culture a number of cultures might be scaled according to the amount of adjustment or maladjustment of each to the ideals it professed. That some discrepancy between the ideal and the actual is general is suggested by the other sections in this chapter.

THE NEGATIVE MESO-AMERICAN COMMONERS

The concept of a single modal personality can scarcely be applied to Meso-America because of the class structure present there. Because the number of social classes cannot be determined with any degree of objectivity, it is impossible to determine the number of modes of personality. Nevertheless, some idea of the range of variation from top to bottom in these complex cultures has already been given on pages 348–50, 380–81, 393–96, 427–29, 486–90. Some excellent studies have been made of the personality of contemporary Indian minorities in Meso-America, but they portray only the character of the common man after four centuries of domination by an alien culture.

One of the best descriptions of this kind is that by Oscar Lewis of the contemporary people of Tepoztlán, an Aztec village two hours' drive south of Mexico City. The Tepoztecans exercise a great deal of emotional restraint and reserve, and rarely show any spontaneity in public. They prefer not to attract attention by word or deed and even in large public gatherings regarded as social occasions there is the minimum of noise. In the street most faces are sombre masks, smiles minimal, and laughter rare. Women and girls walk with downcast eyes lest they be accused of being too flirtatious, and adolescent girls maintain an emotionless facial expression because a smile or even a glance of interest may act as an invitation to some emotionally starved young male. Considerable restraint is practiced even at home and with relatives. Deviations from this strait and narrow path are tolerated only in the aged and in drunken men.

The lack of emotional expression is reflected in the limited development of arts and crafts. There are practically no traditional crafts such as basket-making, pottery-making, or weaving. Cultural missions sent by the Mexican federal government have introduced crocheting, embroidery, and other feminine crafts, but the designs used are all copied from patterns in stores or in style magazines; they are not created by the worker. There are no traditional dances for men and women together, and the men perform only a single simple Spanish dance. Modern social dancing is beginning to be indulged in by young people, but many parents will not permit their daughters to attend and dances tend to be dreary, monotonous affairs with little expression of pleasure. Unmarried youths sing Spanish songs to the accompaniment of the guitar, women and girls sing in the church choir, and men play badly in bands on important occasions. All music, however, is imported; there are no local composers and little individuality in performing Spanish music. The clothing of the Tepoztecans is more drab than that of many other Mexican towns of comparable economic level. Black, grey, and brown are much more common than red, yellow, or blue in the clothing of both sexes.

The shyness and restraint generally characteristic of the Tepoztlán personality applies also to the relations of the sexes. People do not express their affections warmly and generally avoid bodily contact. The principal exception to this rule is the mother-child relationship during the nursing period, when the mother shows genuine affection for her child. The double standard for adolescents is the rule. Boys are expected to have their sexual adventures but girls are severely punished if caught. The genitals are considered ugly and dirty; adolescent girls believe that sexual intercourse is necessarily painful, and even married women refer to the sex act as "the abuse by the man." Sex is a taboo subject in the home and sexual play among children as well as masturbation is punished. Between seven and ten years of age the sexes are separated both for work and for play; at adolescence the separation becomes intensified and continues until marriage. Girls are not told about menstruation, which so shocks them that they rarely tell even their mothers after it happens.

The negative emotions, such as anger, hate, fear, and envy, are more easily expressed than the positive emotions of love, kindness, sympathy, and joy. But because all emotions tend to be suppressed, the negative ones often take the form of suspicion and distrust or the harboring of a grudge. They may be expressed more definitely, however, in gossip, ridicule, stealing, destruction of another's property, and sorcery.

Successful persons tend to be targets of envy, criticism, and malicious gossip. Tourists, federal government agents, and other outsiders, whether Mexicans or from foreign nations, are ridiculed in private; no common citizen would dare to say such things in public, much less in face-to-face contact. Even the Catholic priest is not above criticism.

The repression of the negative emotions of envy, hate, anger, and the like sometimes gives rise to an illness called *muina*. The symptoms are loss of appetite, vomiting, loss of weight, and very often death. This sickness is primarily found among adults of both sexes, but sometimes occurs among children. It may be precipitated by misfortune, humiliation, or insult, according to native belief. However, unless it is proved by an adequately trained pathologist that the patient is free of organic disease, the psychosomatic causation is uncertain.

Aggression sometimes takes the form of beating one's wife, children, younger brothers or sisters, or domestic animals. But such cases seem to be the exception rather than the rule, and wife-beating is usually limited to times when the husband is drunk. People throw stones at the objects of their anger, husbands displeased with food may throw it on the ground, and wives sometimes toss around household objects when angered. Small children have temper tantrums and boys sometimes fight in the absence of adults. There is absolutely no sense of chivalry in fights between men. Face-to-face fights occur only when one or both men are drunk. At other times the aggressor attacks his enemy from behind, usually at night, and after a few shots or slashes with a machete, runs away to hide without any effort to determine how much damage he has done.

To offset fear, anxiety, and insecurity, the Tepoztecans rely on the moral virtues of hard work and thrift. A man who can provide his family with plenty of food, clothing, and shelter is a successful man. Those who accomplish less console themselves with the thought that they are hard-working and thrifty men, and measure their worth as much by the amount of their labor as by their economic gain. Men are reluctant to lend, borrow, or share with other men and prefer to remain independent, yet they share almost everything within the nuclear families they support, and may expect a little sharing with more distant relatives in time of need. Most men work alone in their fields or with the help of a son. This daily isolation probably contributes to the withdrawn character of the men. But family life does have its rewards. Even a poor provider remains the head of his household and maintains the respect of his children, who make few demands upon their parents. Few parents feel that they are poor providers for their children even though they fall below the average in objective terms.

With the negative emotions dominating the positive ones, one might infer that there was a great deal of competition within the society, but such is not the case. On the contrary, the people lack a competitive drive and do not try very hard to improve their lot or outdo their neighbors. They do not feel that they have much chance of bettering themselves and are resigned, if not content, to plod along from year to year. Most young men aspire to nothing more than the life of a farmer, like their fathers, and girls look forward to marrying and performing the household tasks.

Lewis' description of Tepoztlán was published in 1951 but was the result of field work done in the 1940's. Lewis has returned to Tepoztlán the last few years and has found many changes. Many young men have gone as laborers (*braceros*) to the United States and returned with a little capital, the first they have ever acquired in their lives. Many now operate small businesses of their own and never expect to farm. So great is the shift away from the farm that land, which had been getting progressively scarcer up to about fifteen years ago, now often goes unworked. After four centuries of little change in the rural areas, Mexico has finally got on the move, and Lewis' 1951 picture of Tepoztlán will soon be history. We can be certain that changes in personality are accompanying those in economics.

CONCLUSIONS

In this section a few of the theories of personality formation will be tested against the examples just described. The Freudian notion that the treatment of infants in the first few years of life is more important than any other period of comparable length in the life span will be discussed first. The survey above shows that infants were treated lovingly, affectionately, and permissively in all the Indian cultures described in this chapter. If infant care is uniformly gentle, it cannot explain the differences in adult personality revealed by the examples described above. Therefore, this Freudian generalization does not fit the facts.

Pettitt (1946:12) suggests that the binding of infants to cradling devices, which restrict arm as well as leg movements, may account in part for the general absence of overt expression of emotions. The "deadpan" face or "wooden Indian" restraint so common among North American Indians may be related to this physical restriction in infancy. An opposing view holds that swaddling or binding the limbs gives the infant a feeling of security comparable to that of the womb or the mother's arms, rather than frustrating him. Superficial comparison of personality in the Arctic and Tropic areas of North America, where infants are not swaddled or bound to cradling devices, suggests no marked differences in adult personality between these areas and the rest of the continent. Therefore, from areas where binding was the rule, this aspect of infant treatment seems to have little to do with adult personality.

North American Indians reveal no strong cases of the Oedipus complex anywhere, and it seems to be totally absent in many societies. There are several reasons for this absence. First, the gentle and affectionate treatment of infants would tend to keep hostilities at the minimum. Second, the transfer of discipline to the supernatural, as described in the chapter on Education, would tend to prevent the accumulation of much hostility toward either parent by children. Third, the extended family pattern, dominant in about half of our Indian societies, would tend to diffuse a child's emotional responses to a number of relatives rather than to concentrate them on one or two. Fourth, matrilocal residence and matrilineal descent, in areas where they occurred, tended to weaken the role of the father and to substitute the mother's brother for him. For these reasons the Oedipus complex was weak or absent in aboriginal North America.

The conclusion is that adult personality is a complex thing resulting from many causes which cannot be discussed piecemeal but must be related to each other. Experiences in adolescence and in later years, as well as those in childhood, determine the personality of the mature individual. The culture in which a person is reared can shape his personality to a large extent, but the limits of variation are set by the common heredity shared by all members of the Homo sapiens species. We are beginning to be aware of genetic differences in populations in different localities around the world, as in blood genes, and should not rule out entirely the possibility of differences in the genes controlling some aspects of personality. This will be an extremely difficult thing to measure, however, and is not likely to contribute much to explanations of personality formation in the foreseeable future. What is needed at present is an increased number of field studies in personality, to be followed as soon as possible with cross-cultural studies based on at least one hundred societies around the world. Cross-cultural studies made from adequate samples and sharpened by correlation methods can eventually give us many of the answers to the multitude of questions raised about personality formation.

REFERENCES

BENEDICT, 1932, 1934; BENNETT, 1946; CODERE, 1956; DEVEREUX, 1951; EGGAN, DOROTHY, 1943; FENTON, 1941*a*, 1948; GOLD-FRANK, 1943, 1945*a*, 1945*b;* HALLOWELL, 1955; HONIGMANN, 1949, 1954; LANTIS, 1959; LEWIS, 1941, 1942, 1951; MOONEY, 1896; SPINDLER AND SPINDLER, 1957; THOMPSON, 1945; WALLACE, 1952, 1958.

25: Language

Every time someone asks an anthropologist or a linguist if he knows the Indian language, he is actually voicing again the common assumption that there is, in fact, only one. The truth of the matter could hardly be more different. In A.D. 1492, there was a total of about 2,000 separate American Indian languages, each mutually unintelligible with respect to every other. This huge number has actually been listed and classified (Voegelin and Voegelin, 1944; McQuown, 1955), and although some of these language labels represent dialectic variants within languages rather than mutually unintelligible languages, there is every reason to believe that the number of languages not recorded at all would easily offset the dialects that have got into the list. The frequencies in round numbers for the three major subdivisions of the western hemisphere in A.D. 1492 were: Anglo-America, 200; Mexico and Central America, 350; South America and the West Indies, 1,450; or 2,000 separate languages, a total exceeding that for Europe and Asia at the same date but somewhat less than the 3,000 estimated for the entire eastern hemisphere. At present over half of the two thousand Indian languages are extinct.

Reports by traders, missionaries, soldiers, colonial officials, and others untrained in linguistics have sometimes described Indian languages as being made up of strange animal-like sounds combined into only a few hundred sloppily pronounced words bolstered by signs. There is no evidence that such rudimentary languages have existed anywhere in the world since the beginning of the Upper Old Stone Age, although they must be postulated as an early stage in the evolution of language. It is generally agreed that by the time man became physically Homo sapiens he was

555

probably using fully developed languages with thousands of words and precise systems of pronunciation and grammar. The first immigrants to the New World were indisputably Homo sapiens and must have possessed well-developed languages. Relatively few dictionaries for Indian languages have been compiled, but one published in 1890 on the Dakota (Sioux) language lists about 19,000 words. Some linguists believe this is about the minimum number of words in any language, and that most dictionaries of Indian languages are far from exhaustive. Languages of culturally more advanced peoples, such as the Meso-Americans, had much richer vocabularies.

PHONOLOGY

Because the Indian languages encountered by Europeans were totally unintelligible to them at first contact, the notion that they were composed of strange sounds of a very different character from those used in European languages was common. A handful of scholarly missionaries knew better, but they had little influence on the rank and file of the colonists, and the belief in the exotic character of Indian speech sounds persists to this day. When Indian speech is analyzed into the distinct elements of sound of which it is composed, called phonemes, even the strangest of these to our ears is paralleled in the languages of Europe and Asia. None is unique to the American Indian. Each phoneme in Indian languages, and for that matter in all languages, should be indicated by a single letter in an alphabet. Linguists employ principally the Roman alphabet, but bolster it with a few Greek letters, special signs, and numerous diacritical marks over, under, and on both sides of the letters. Thus a single, international alphabet of about one hundred symbols can record with sufficient accuracy the speech of all languages, including those of Indians.

A recent inventory of all the consonant phonemes in 176 representative Indian languages (Pierce, 1957) employs 61 different symbols. Thus there were only 61 essential consonant sounds in this large sample of Indian languages, and the addition of vowel sounds would not have increased the total number beyond about 80.

A common misconception about phonology is that the ability

to pronounce syllables, words, and phrases in an exotic language is determined by the form or shape of the speaker's vocal equipment. Some educated Europeans in Africa today believe that the thick lips of the Negro are necessary for the pronunciation of some of the sounds in African languages, and many persons in the Americas believe that some anatomical peculiarity of Indian speech organs must account for some of the strange noises emitted. It is interesting to note that Indian informants are often as naïve as linguistically unschooled Europeans in respect to the acquisition of the ability to pronounce their language. Some believe that an anthropologist or linguist who can pronounce their words correctly must have some Indian ancestry in his family tree. Every normal human being in the world, however, can learn to speak any language in the world like a native if exposed to the language in infancy or early childhood, or patiently taught the language at a later date by a trained and skilled linguist. No one inherits the specific content of any language. In short, babies are interchangeable from one language environment to another; each will learn correctly the language of the society in which he is reared. Every Indian child can learn English, or any other European written language, as effectively as children of European ancestry if given equal opportunity.

Still another misconception is the notion that Indians and other non-literates speak in a more slovenly manner than those whose languages have been taught them in schools with the aid of writing. On the whole, Indian languages are probably spoken more precisely and with less individual variation among speakers than the languages of Europe. Uniformity of speech is partly a function of the size of the language-bearing group and the closeness of contact among its members. In small, compact societies in which everyone is able to converse with every other person in the group, a high degree of uniformity of speech is the rule. In large language groups spread over large territories or made up of isolated pockets of people, each of whom may be exposed to a different language of a neighboring people, considerable variation in speech is likely to exist, and conditions are right for separate dialects to emerge. Such variation in speech is normal for language and should not be equated with the slovenly or substandard speech of a few sub-

557

normal persons. At the same time, some individual variation in speech is normal, as our recognition of voices of acquaintances over the telephone indicates. Such speech peculiarities of individuals, as long as they fall within the normal range, are called idiolects. Everyone has his own idiolect. In fact, if you can imitate the speech of another closely enough to be mistaken for him, you are considered clever and a potential entertainer. Each Indian speaker likewise spoke his own idiolect.

Even though most phonemes in Indian languages have parallels in European languages, the presence of a few kinds of sounds totally absent or rare in European languages makes it very difficult for a European to speak some Indian languages. In about a third of the American Indian languages, the stops *p*, *t*, or *k* are sometimes pronounced with the breath held at the glottis. This is so rare in European languages that few untrained Europeans are able to pronounce Indian words with such glottalized consonants. A skilled linguist can teach an apt pupil to pronounce these sounds in about an hour, but few adults ever learn to do it on their own. Another impediment to the amateur is phonemic tone. When the meaning of a word can be altered by changing only the pitch of one vowel, then the language is said to possess phonemic tone. The minimum number of tones is two, Mandarin Chinese has four, and a few languages of Southeast Asia possess about a dozen. Phonemic tone is less common in American Indian languages than it is in the languages of Southeast Asia or of Africa, but at the same time it is more common in Indian languages than in those of Europe. Unless the European has had training in tone languages or in music, he is likely to fail to learn the tones of an Indian language. Voiceless vowels, or whispered vowels, have phonemic value in a number of Indian languages and are likely to be observed only by trained linguists.

The isolated phonemes of an Indian language and a European language may match one another quite closely, yet they may be combined in different sequences and in different positions in words. In English the sounds *tl* occur in that sequence in the terminal or medial position, as in bottle or in bottling, but never in the initial position. For this reason the pronunciation of Indian words with *tl* in the initial position, as in anglicized *Tlingit*, is difficult for an English speaker. Another illustration is the *ts* combination, which occurs in the terminal position in the plural forms of all English nouns ending in *t*, and also quite frequently in the medial position, as in *catsup;* but it never occurs in the initial position in English. In Indian languages it frequently occurs in the initial position, where it is difficult for an English speaker to pronounce. When three or more consonants are combined into strange consonant clusters, the difficulty for an English speaker is increased. For instance, people who have no difficulty at all with the phrase "cat's pajamas" find it almost impossible to pronounce without the first two letters. The manner in which phonemes are combined and located in words, therefore, is as important to both speakers and hearers of a language as the nature of each in isolation. Because amateurs do not isolate phonemes of foreign languages, it is generally the combinations of phonemes which produce syllables and words that seem impossible to imitate. And finally, the combinations and permutations of phonemes taken two, three, four, or more at a time, as they appear in words, are so enormous that two languages could conceivably have identical sets of phonemes yet share not a single word or phrase in common.

GRAMMAR

The grammars of Indian languages show greater differences from European languages and more variation from one Indian language to another than do phonologies. So complex and variable are Indian grammatical structures that no comprehensive summary can be given in the space of one chapter, but a few illustrations can suggest how different these grammars are from those of the languages of Europe. For instance, inflections of verb forms outnumber those of nouns in most European languages and make the learning of verb forms in Spanish, French, and German more difficult than noun forms for a native English speaker. In some Indian languages, on the contrary, noun forms are complex, as in the following words for aunt in the tongue of the Chichimeca-Jonaz of Northeast Mexico.

	Singular	Dual	Plural
First person	natü	natüs	natün
Second person	utü	utüs	utün
Third person	erü	erüs	butün

These terms translate as follows:

	Singular	*Dual*	*Plural*
First person	my aunt	the aunt of us two	the aunt of us three or more
Second person	your aunt	the aunt of you two	the aunt of you three or more
Third person	his or her aunt	the aunt of those two	the aunt of those three or more

A glance at the native terms above is enough to reveal that pronouns are combined with nouns and that the stem for aunt changes with each person. With the change in number, however, the stem remains the same, except in the third person plural, while the ending changes. The dual is formed by suffixing *s* to the singular, as in English, and the plural is formed by adding *n* to the singular, as in German (and in some English words). So far the noun has been held constant and the pronoun varied; but the noun may also be varied by introducing dual and plural aunts. Each would yield nine more forms, making a total of twenty-seven. The terminal *n* in many Chichimeca-Jonaz words is unvoiced, but it may be detected by placing a small piece of paper in front of the speaker's nostrils and observing the deflection of the paper by the air exhaled through the nose. Such voiceless nasals occur in a number of other Indian languages and also in Welsh.

In the Chichimeca-Jonaz language it is impossible to express an unpossessed or unrelated noun concept. There is no way of saying "aunt" without saying whose aunt it is. Likewise, there is no way of saying "earth," "air," or "water" without indicating personal relation or possession. The Chichimeca-Jonaz word for earth has the same range of meaning as in English; it means anything from a handful of earth to the entire world. If one wishes to talk about the entire world without suggesting possession, the nearest he can come is "the world of those three or more," translated freely as "their world," or more freely as "world."

Those who believe in a close relationship between language and culture might infer from this language that property concepts were elaborately developed among these people. Such is not the case; in fact, the opposite is true. These people, at the time of first

Spanish contact, were nomads roaming daily in search of wild foods. They moved about constantly, carrying everything they owned on their backs or in their hands. Their material culture was among the simplest in all of North America, and the landscape was not owned by individuals or kinship groups but was open territory to all. Incorporeal property concepts seem to have been as poorly developed as those governing ownership of material possessions, yet the language demands a possession marker for every noun spoken. On the other hand a culture with an elaborate development of property rights could not exist without an adequate method of expressing possession in its language. Therefore, possession markers in language are necessary for the functioning of a property-minded culture, but are not sufficient to cause every culture that has them to develop complex property concepts.

The Yana language of California is peculiar because of the presence of distinct "male" and "female" forms for most words. These have nothing to do with sex gender, which is lacking in the language. Men use the "male" forms when speaking to men. "Female" forms are used for all other combinations of the sexes in conversation: by men speaking to women, women speaking to men, and women speaking to women. A few examples follow.

	Male	Female
deer	ba-na	ba'
grizzly bear	t'en'-na	t'et'
moon	wak!āra	wak!ar^a
person	yā-na	ya'
man	isi	is^i
woman	mari'mi	mare'm^i

The raised terminal vowels in the "female" forms are pronounced softly or whispered. Inspection of the examples above shows that the "female" forms are reductions of the "male" forms, either by eliminating the last syllable or by giving it less stress. Although Yana culture is not well described, there is no evidence to support the view that this linguistic feature is related to any trait or pattern of personality or culture.

Word length shows tremendous variation in Indian languages. Although linguists have not produced a satisfactory definition of a word that is applicable to all languages, it is possible to count empirically the number of phonemes in the words in published texts. For instance, a modest sample of Shawnee yielded an average of ten phonemes per word. This is significantly longer than the words in most English texts. It is perhaps better to label it a phrase, or call it by a compound term, word-phrase.

An unusually long word or phrase from the Southern Paiute language is this: *wii-to-kuchum-punku-rügani-yugwi-va-ntü-m(ü)*. In free translation it means "they who are going to sit and cut up with a knife a black cow (or bull) buffalo." In more literal translation in the order of the Indian elements it means "knife-black-buffalo-pet-cut-up-sit (plural)-future-participle-animate plural." In the language of the grammarian, this compound word or phrase is the plural of the future participle of a compound verb "to sit and cut up." The four grammatical elements at the end cannot stand alone, but must be joined to elements that precede them.

This single compound Paiute word, about which Sapir (1921, 30–32) has written two pages of analysis, should be enough to illustrate how grammatically complex some Indian languages can be. It takes years for a brilliant linguist to become fluent enough in such a language to understand every utterance by native speakers and to obtain a full description of the culture exclusively in the native language. Those who have known only a lightly inflected language, such as English, have great difficulty in mastering all the inflections in a more heavily inflected language; and where inflections are modest in number, a strange word order may create difficulties.

In English and other European languages most words fall into two classes, nouns and verbs. On the whole, verbs denote events of temporary or short duration, while nouns are used to label events or things that are long-lasting and stable; verbs denote processes of change, nouns the steady states. But English fails to distinguish consistently between the two classes on the continuum of experience. For example, *lightning, wave, flame, storm*, and *cycle* are nouns, although they represent both temporary events and processes of change. In contrast, *keep, adhere, continue*, and *dwell* are verbs, yet they describe long-lasting conditions or steady states. Therefore English arbitrarily tosses many of its words into one category or the other without adherence to any logical scheme.

562

The Hopi Indians do it better. They classify *lightning, wave, flame, storm,* and other things of short duration as verbs and consistently place experiences of longer duration and more steady character in a noun class. The Nootka, in contrast to both English and Hopi, do not make a basic distinction between nouns and verbs. They take a monistic view of the continuum of length of duration of experience.

Although the Hopi carefully distinguish nouns and verbs, their verbs have no tense, no past, present, or future. Instead, their verbs are distinguished according to aspects, validity forms, and clause-linkage forms. Aspect refers to the relative length of time an event lasts. Validity forms are of three kinds; the first denotes that the speaker is reporting a completed or an on-going action or event; the second indicates that the speaker expects that an action or event will take place; the third means that from his experience he knows the action or event is a regular or predictable occurrence. Clause-linkage forms relate the temporal characteristics of two or more verbs; they indicate which action is earlier, later, or going on simultaneously, with respect to another one or more verbs.

It should be clear from these illustrations of grammar that a linguist cannot describe Indian languages in terms of Latin grammar, as some have tried in the past. Each Indian language has its own grammar, which differs more or less from the grammars of other languages. Types of Indian grammar are not randomly distributed over the language map of native North America, but tend to cluster in adjacent areas, as will be suggested below in the section on language classification.

LANGUAGE AND CULTURE

The concept that has attracted most attention in discussions and writings on the relations of language and culture is the Sapir-Whorf hypothesis, named after the two men who pioneered its development in modern American linguistics. The following paragraph from the pen of Edward Sapir ably presented its essentials in 1929.

Language is a guide to "social reality." Though language is not ordinarily thought of as of essential interest to the students of social science, it powerfully conditions all our thinking about social problems and

563

processes. Human beings do not live in the objective world alone, nor alone in the world of social activity as ordinarily understood, but are very much at the mercy of the particular language which has become the medium of expression for their society. It is quite an illusion to imagine that one adjusts to reality essentially without the use of language and that language is merely an incidental means of solving specific problems of communication or reflection. The fact of the matter is that the "real world" is to a large extent unconsciously built up on the language habits of the group. No two languages are ever sufficiently similar to be considered as representing the same social reality. The worlds in which different societies live are distinct worlds, not merely the same world with different labels attached. (In Mandelbaum, 1949: 162.)

This statement tends to exaggerate the differences between the grammatical and semantic categories of various languages. Translation from one language to another may be difficult and cumbersome, but it is always possible for practical purposes if the translator is thoroughly qualified in both languages. The closer the languages are related historically, the easier the translation becomes. For two languages totally unrelated it is still possible, as the following example of Navaho and English will show. If we try to translate the English phrases "his horse" and "their horses" into Navaho we run into difficulty on two counts: Navaho lacks a distinction between "his," "her," "its," and "their"; and it lacks a distinction between singular and plural for nouns, in this case between "horse" and "horses." The nearest short equivalent in Navaho is *bìlí^{n}ʔ*, which is translated according to context as "his," "her," "its," or "their horse" or "horses." By rephrasing "his horse" to "one horse of one man," the following Navaho phrase suffices: *dìné-łà-bìlí^{n}ʔ-łàʔ*. This means literally "man-one-his-horse-one." Because horses were a symbol of prestige, it is certain that every Navaho knew how many horses he owned, as well as the number owned by his close relatives and friends. The failure of the language to include this information in its shortest grammatical forms does not mean that Navahos do not know who own the horses in their neighborhoods.

Another example is words for colors. Everyone who has had a physics course knows that color varies continuously from red to violet. The difference between the various colors along this continuum is a matter of the length of the light waves. There are almost as many ways of dividing up the color spectrum as there are languages which do it. The Navaho have only five principal terms for colors, which may be translated freely as "white," two kinds of "black," "red," and "blue or green." In color-matching tests the Navaho would be able to match fine gradations of blues and greens as accurately as we do, and we would be able to differentiate blacks and grays as carefully as they do. Perception is equally precise among members of both groups regardless of the arbitrary semantic categories of the languages, and no painter in either language group is handicapped by color semantics. However, recent experiments with English color semantics show that most people habitually communicate with the primary color categories of the language, even though all are capable of making finer distinctions. Although language may shape perceptions and thought, it does not limit its users to the conventional semantic categories when an occasion calling for finer distinctions arises.

Many other grammatical patterns in language are dead with respect to any real function in the thinking of the language users. A good example of this is sex gender for inanimate objects in German and French. Thus the word for sun in German, *Sonne*, is feminine, while that in French, *soleil*, is masculine. For moon the genders are reversed: *Mond* is masculine in German, and *lune* is feminine in French. Neither word has any gender in English. The gender of the sun and moon could not possibly have any effect on the attitude toward the sun and moon of the modern speakers and hearers of these languages. Gender categories for other inanimate objects are likewise non-functional today. Although the gender of the sun and moon may have had some influence on Indo-European thinking in the remote past, when religion and mythology regarded the sun and moon as gods, it is no longer functional. At any stage in the history of any language, it contains a considerable quantity of non-functional grammatical survivals.

One of the most carefully researched problems of language and culture is the relation of semantic categories in kinship terms to social structure. Above in chapter sixteen was mentioned the correlation between bifurcate merging classification of the mother-aunt categories and unilateral descent. Relatively large numbers of such correlations assembled by G. P. Murdock (1949, 139–83) and me (in Driver and Massey, 1957: 428–34) show that most of them fall in the medium and low range of magnitude. This means that there is only a tendency for semantic categories of kinship to match social structure; only about 60 or 70 per cent of the language-culture units (tribes) assembled for a single correlation support the Sapir-Whorf theory, with the remaining 30 or 40 per cent constituting the negative instances. This is a statistically significant difference but it is nowhere near as sweeping as Sapir and Whorf have suggested.

To sum up, the phonological and grammatical categories of structural linguistics have not yielded many significant correlations with culture so far and are not likely to do so in the future. Semantic categories, on the other hand, have exhibited many significant correlations of medium and low magnitude to date, and may be expected to produce more in the future. In the section on classification to follow, a comparison will be made between language family areas and culture areas to show the relation between these two over-all classifications of language and culture.

CLASSIFICATION

Languages are classified according to resemblances to one another, and resemblances are of at least four kinds: universal, convergent, diffusional, and genetic. Universals are those features of speech shared by all languages. With respect to phonology, for instance, all languages have stops, fricatives, and vowels, and these are produced by expulsion of the breath from the lungs, glottis, and oral cavity. Most of the meaning categories of the hundred basic words used by glottochronologists, given below, are universal or nearly so.

Convergent resemblances are those which arise independently in two or more languages. Many features of phonology are probably convergences and a few similar words seem to arise in this manner. For instance, the word for wood in the Wappo Indian language of California is *hol*, resembling the German *Holz*; and the Wappo word for valley, *tul*, is similar to the German *Tal*. A person fluent in both Wappo and German could surely find many more such convergences. There was no contact between Germans and California Indians before the nineteenth century, and not a shred of evidence to suggest common derivation of Wappo and German from common parent languages. The percentage of convergences among such short words (root morphemes) in historically unrelated languages is higher than one might suppose, about 4 per cent on the average (Greenberg, 1953: 270). This figure is admittedly achieved only when a generous interpretation of similarity is employed. A more critical appraisal of resemblances would lower the percentage.

Resemblances brought about by diffusion are those taken over by one language from another. The most obvious examples are so-called loan words such as tobacco, which spread around the world with the plant and its leaves as they were traded from tribe to tribe and nation to nation. Although there is more than one word for tobacco in Indian languages, the number of terms for this plant is much fewer than the number of languages, proving the diffusion of the words beyond all doubt.

A more subtle kind of influence of one language on another is the result of stimulus diffusion. In this case the clusters of sounds (morphemes or words) are not taken over by the alien language, but the categories of meaning are diffused nevertheless. For example, most Athapaskan numeral systems are based on tens, as in English, or on some complicated combination of threes, fours, and fives. Only a few Athapaskan systems are based throughout on fives. Wherever this deviant quinary system occurs it is adjacent to totally alien languages, such as Eskimo, in which counting is by fives. In this case the principle of counting by fives has been derived from the Eskimo, but the words contain only Athapaskan morphemes. The meanings of other words, such as kinship terms, may also diffuse from one language to another without the morphemes of the donor language. Stimulus diffusion of semantic categories is most likely to be implemented by considerable numbers of bilingual persons who speak both the donor and the recipient language. This would require prolonged contact, intermarriage, and other exchange of persons.

Genetic resemblances are those resulting from uninterrupted derivation from an earlier language. Thus Spanish is derived from Latin and may be described as a lineal descendant of Latin, as may also French; the relation of Spanish to French is a collateral one. Linguists often refer to the older language as the mother tongue and to the younger forms of speech as the daughter languages or, in relation to each other, the sister languages. Although the word "genetic" is a twentieth-century biological term, Darwin used comparative philology as an illustration of what he meant by common descent. Therefore the concept may be extended from biology to language without doing too much violence to the history of thought.

Genetic classifications of languages are the most meaningful to scholars in general, and especially to those outside the field of linguistics. The cultural anthropologist often uses genetic classification to reconstruct the past history of peoples and thus solve the many puzzles of cross-cultural research. For example, the Crow Indians are the only Plains tribe with matrilineal descent, a pattern which makes no functional sense in an otherwise male-dominated society where hunting and fighting skills carry the most prestige. This apparent anomaly is easily explained by genetic language classification, which places the Crow language nearest to that of the Hidatsa in the Siouan family. In the historic period the Hidatsa lived in North Dakota on the upper Missouri River where they obtained about half of their sustenance from the farm products raised exclusively by women on plots of land owned entirely by women. If we postulate that the Crow and the Hidatsa both farmed at some time from five hundred to a thousand years ago, when they spoke a single common language, the matrilineal descent of the Crow in the nineteenth century becomes a survival from an earlier period when women were more prominent in the society.

Although all languages are subject to change from elements received from neighboring languages, there is much evidence to suggest that language is more stable than the rest of culture, that its rate of change is slower in most instances. Such being the case, genetic language classification can reveal much information on past history and migrations of peoples that is not obtainable from any other kind of data. Where the results of modern studies in comparative linguistics are supported by documentary evidence dating back thousands of years, in the case for Indo-European languages about 2,700 years, genetic resemblances can usually be distinguished from similarities brought about by convergence or diffusion. But where practically no written sources appear until the post-Columbian era, as is the case for American Indian languages, it is much more difficult to distinguish these three kinds of resemblances. The picture is further complicated by the fact that convergences or diffusions can occur at any and all periods of time in the history or evolution of languages. A loan word may enter a language as a diffused element, only to be passed on by genetic descent to multiple daughter languages.

The surest way to prove that a group of languages has genetic unity, where documents cannot prove it directly, is to reconstruct the proto-language or mother tongue from which all members of the family are descended. This is a highly technical and time-consuming task, requiring the formulation of rules of both phonology and grammar, and has been achieved for only a few Indian language families, most completely for Algonquian.

A much easier but less exact way to proceed is to compare short lists of words. Table 4 gives a few Indian words from fifteen localities in California (Driver, 1937). Without worrying about how to pronounce these words exactly, a novice can see at a glance that the first six samples of speech are almost identical. They are regarded as one language by linguists, and Indian informants agree that they are all easily mutually intelligible. The next three samples show a progressive departure from the first six, with number nine being the most deviant. These middle three are classified as separate languages, although seven and eight are closer to each other than either is to nine. If we compare the middle three with the top six and the bottom six, it is apparent at once that the middle three are much closer to the top six, and in a twofold division would be classed with them. This package of nine, along with some others, was originally called the Shoshonean language family. It is now known to be a sub-family of the larger Uto-Aztecan family. Numbers ten to fifteen are all dialects of the Yokuts language, originally regarded as isolated but now accepted as a member of the California Penutian superfamily.

The first modern genetic classification of North American Indian languages was that of J. W. Powell (1891). Powell's scheme

TABLE 4

CALIFORNIA INDIAN WORDS

	Head/Hair	Eye	Ear	Tongue	Earth	Fire	Water	One	Two
1. Entimbich.....	wo	bus	nak	ego	tübop	kŏs	paya	sütmü'u	wahai
2. Woponuch.....	wo	bus	nak	ego	tübop	kŏso	paya	sütmü'u	wahai
3. Hodogida.....	wŏ	pus	nak	ego	tibop	kŏs	paya	sümü'ü	wahai
4. Tuhukwadj....	wo	pus	nakᵃ	ego	tibop	kŏs	paya	sümü	wahai
5. Big Pine......	wo	busi	nakᵃ	ego	tibip	koso	paya	sütmu'u	wahai
6. Independence...	wo	busi	nakᵃ	ego	tibipᵃ	koso	paya	sütmu'u	wahai
7. Koso..........	dzopipa	bui	nagi	ego	sŏgobi	kuna	paa	suutᵃ	waat
8. Kawaiisu......	tcopiwa	pui	nagabi	egu	tiipü	kunä	po'o	suyu	wahayu
9. Tubatulabal....	tcompmon	pundz	nang	lal	cuwal	kũt	pal	tcitc	wo
10. Yauelmani.....	ŏto	säsä	tük	talhat	paan	osït	ïlïk	yĕt	ponoi
11. Koyeti........	ŏto	säsä	tük	talhat	paan	osït	ïlïk	yĕt	ponoi
12. Nutumutu.....	otco	säsa	tuk	talhat	pa'an	osit	moyoxon	yĕt	ponoi
13. Paleuyami.....	ŏto	säsä	tuk	talhats	paan	osit	ïlïk	yĕt	ponoi.
14. Yaudanchi.....	ŏto	säsä	tük	talhat	paan	osït	ïdïk	yĕt	pongoi
15. Wukchumni....	ŏto	sasa	tük	talhats	pa'an	usit	ïdïk	yĕt	ponoi

was based principally on word lists, often of no more than a hundred items. The amazing thing about this classification is that none of the families Powell set up has been split apart by further research; all of them are regarded today as having genetic unity. However, most of them have been combined into genetic units of a larger order. At the present time the hierarchy of classes within classes approaches that of biology. Just as the biologist combines races or varieties of plants and animals into species, species into genera, genera into families, families into orders, orders into classes, and classes into phyla, so the linguists have used as many as seven or eight sizes of classes to construct their genetic classifications. There is no standard terminology for such classificatory units in linguistics or anthropology, but a workable set of labels, starting with the most specific would be: dialect, language, subfamily, family, superfamily, subphylum, phylum, and superphylum.

In a comparison of the validity of genetic language classification with that of biological taxonomy, language comes out second best. The principal difference is that, once biological forms have diverged enough to be classed as separate genera, they are no longer able to crossbreed. Dogs and cats, for instance, cannot crossbreed, and intermediate fossil forms may be safely regarded as common ancestors, not as hybrid forms. The fact that such intermediate forms are found only in the remote geological past and never in the recent period clinches the argument.

Not so for languages. Any two languages which come into contact may influence each other no matter how far apart they are in classification and history. Convergences may also arise at any time. Therefore, it is difficult to distinguish diffused elements and convergences from genetic resemblances without reconstructing the proto-languages for all the language families involved. Because this has not been done for most Indian language families, present genetic classifications are to be regarded as tentative or provisional. In the Americas, where writing was extremely rare and not alphabetic, it is impossible for the archeologist to discover "fossil" languages to prove which intermediate ones are ancestral types and which are hybrids.

About 1950 a new method of classifying languages and estimating how long ago the various daughter languages diverged from

571

ancestral tongues was devised by Morris Swadesh. It is now called glottochronology. Robert B. Lees (1953) compared the documented rates of change of thirteen streams of language, all Indo-European except Coptic and Chinese. He used a list of only about two hundred words, selected in advance for slow rate of change. Lees found that on the average these thirteen languages retained about eighty per cent and lost about twenty per cent of this basic vocabulary per thousand years. In other words, if one begins with a known mother language, such as Latin, he will find that after a thousand years the daughter tongues will retain about eighty per cent of these basic or conservative words and will have lost and replaced the remaining twenty per cent. Because there was relatively little difference in the rates of change of the thirteen languages investigated, Lees made the inference that all languages change at the same rate.

To derive a universal generalization for 5,000 languages from a sample of thirteen, with all but two from a single language family, breaks the rules of sampling and statistical inference. If one took only thirteen samples of physical type from the same localities in Europe and Asia and generalized for all mankind, he would characterize the human race as principally Caucasoid with a dash of Mongoloid. If he drew thirteen samples from Africa south of the Sahara or from native Australia, he would think everyone on earth was Negroid or Australoid. If a selected sample of thirteen cases is not likely to give a true picture of physical type over the face of the earth, there is no reason to suppose that it is adequate for linguistics. As a matter of fact, research since 1953 has revealed some rates of change which are significantly different from Lees's rates of that year. However, in spite of this shaky chronological basis, this method has greatly stimulated the reclassification of Indian languages. Most of the current studies in glottochronology operate with only the following one hundred basic words, which show an average rate of retention of about 86 per cent per thousand years:

I, thou, we, this, that, who, what, not, all, many, one, two, big, long, small, woman, man, person, fish, bird, dog, louse, tree, seed, leaf, root, bark, skin, flesh, blood, bone, grease, egg, horn, tail, feather, hair, head, ear, eye, nose, mouth, tooth, tongue, claw, foot, knee, hand, belly, neck, breasts, heart, liver, drink, eat, bite, see, hear, know, sleep, die, kill, swim, fly, walk, come, lie, sit, stand, give, say, sun, moon, star, water, rain, stone, sand, earth, cloud, smoke, fire, ash, burn, path, mountain, red, green, yellow, white, black, night, hot, cold, full, new, good, round, dry, name.

These words were chosen because experience in comparative linguistics has shown that most of them occur in every language on earth; and they are "culture free" in the sense that they are associated with simple as well as complex cultures, with literate and non-literate cultures, and need not change when important innovations revolutionize other vocabulary. For instance, everyone has a head regardless of the cut of his hair, his headgear, or his theory of the location of the center of intelligence in the body. Changes in these three "culture bound" items would not necessitate a change in the "culture free" term for head. Similarly the word "walk" is likely to be retained after horses, automobiles, airplanes, and space ships are introduced because people will still continue to walk. Although no word is entirely "culture free," much evidence shows that the words in the above list have a much slower rate of change than general vocabulary.

Once lists of words have been collected for a number of Indian languages, any two languages can be compared by determining the number of cognates shared. Words in two or more languages are said to be cognate when they can be proved to have been derived from a common mother tongue. They are often not identical but must share something in common to indicate divergence from a common ancestral language. Returning to the list of California Indian words (Table 4), it is apparent at once that all words in dialects ten to fifteen form clusters of cognates except the term *moyoxon* for "water," which may be an error. Similarly all words in dialects one to six fall into clusters of cognates. Languages seven, eight, and nine are not so obvious, but a little imagination suggests common origin for all the words for eye, ear, fire, water, and two. The word for tongue (*lal*) in language nine appears to be a loan word from dialects ten to fifteen, and the speakers of nine were indeed close neighbors of the speakers of dialects ten to fifteen. Without giving any more examples it should be clear that anyone can spot many cognates in word lists. To do an exhaustive and accurate job, however, requires linguistic training and experience.

Once cognates have been identified, any two languages in a sample may be compared by determining the percentage of cognates shared. Those sharing a high percentage of cognates are said to be linguistically close, while those sharing only a low percentage of cognates are linguistically distant. Experience shows that when twenty or thirty languages or dialects are compared in this manner, they often show a considerable range of linguistic distance. When each of say twenty languages is compared with the other nineteen, the number of relationships involved is

$$\frac{20 \times 19}{2} = 190$$

The general formula is

$$\frac{n(n-1)}{2}$$

where n is the number of languages.

In exhibiting such a large number of relationships it is convenient to arrange the figures in a square table identical in form to mileage tables on road maps. Just as one reads the mileage between any two towns or cities on the mileage table, so he may read the linguistic distance between any two dialects or languages on the linguistic table. Continuing our analogy, if the twenty largest cities in California were grouped on the same mileage table, they would fall into geographical clusters, one in the Los Angeles area and the other around San Francisco Bay. The mileage table would show two clusters of low mileages within each of these areas, and a cluster of high mileages between the areas.

Similarly, a linguistic table showing two clusters of languages with close internal relationships within each but distant external relationships between clusters suggests at once a classification into two families. Three or more clusters with close internal relationships and distant external relationships would suggest three or more linguistic classes, and so forth. The systematic determination of linguistic propinquity and distance between hundreds of North American Indian languages in the last ten years has greatly changed and sharpened our classifications. Groups of languages which no one had got around to comparing in the past have recently been shown to share at least some cognates.

574

The classification in Table 5 is based in part on phonology and grammar, as well as on the vocabularies of the glottochronologists. It shows only three sizes of language classes. In most cases the names of member languages correspond to those of "tribes" on the map at the end. The dotted lines on the tribal map separate dialects of the same language, the broken lines separate languages of the same language family, and the solid lines indicate boundaries between language families. The so-called tribal map is really a language map also. The same labels are used for both.

The nineteen largest classes have not been mapped because they are of little value in interpreting cultural data. It is the smaller, more compact classes of languages that are of value to the cultural anthropologist in reconstructing the history of Indian cultures. All of the language families mapped are generally accepted as genetic language units, although the proof is not yet complete. Some of the nineteen largest classes, in contrast, are based on fragmentary data and are still subject to debate. However, if the present trend of opinion continues, these largest classes are all likely to become generally accepted as genetic units in a short time. Some are already being combined to form still fewer major classes. For instance, recent research indicates a remote genetic connection between Gulf, Algonquian, and Coahuiltecan; and Yukian may be related to Hokan, Penutian, and Algonquian-Ritwan. The latest diagram by Morris Swadesh (1960: Fig. 1) shows many other remote relationships between the nineteen major classes listed, and even suggests that Wakashan be lumped with the Altai language family of Asia.

From about 1850 to 1950 linguists agreed that the principal process of linguistic change and the formation of new languages was one of diversification and rediversification from ancestral languages. Convergences and diffused elements were recognized but were assigned a minor role in linguistic change. It was assumed that every language fell definitely into one family and not into another. In the last ten years this view has been challenged more and more. Swadesh (1959a) uses the phrase "mesh principle" to describe the complicated relationships which glottochronology and other kinds of comparative research are bringing to light. This recent work shows that many languages and language families are linked to

575

TABLE 5

GENETIC CLASSIFICATION OF NORTH AMERICAN INDIAN LANGUAGES

I. Eskimo-Aleut
  A. Eskimo-Aleut (Map 37)
    1. Eskimo
    2. Aleut
II. Algonquian-Ritwan-Kutenai
  A. Algonquian-Ritwan
    1. Algonquian (Map 37)
    2. Ritwan
  B. Kutenai
III. Mosan
  A. Salishan (Map 37)
    1. Columbian
    2. Tillamookan
    3. Comoxan
    4. Bella Coolan
  B. Chimakuan
  C. Wakashan (Map 37)
IV. Na-Dene
  A. Haida
  B. Tlingit-Eyak-Athapas-
    kan
    1. Tlingit
    2. Eyak
    3. Athapaskan (Map 37)
V. Uto-Azteco-Tanoan
  A. Uto-Aztecan (Map 37)
    1. Basin Shoshonean
    2. Tubatulabal
    3. Luisenan
    4. Hopi
    5. Piman
    6. Taracahitan
    7. Coran
    8. Aztecan
  B. Tanoan
  C. Kiowa
VI. Penutian
  A. Chinook-Tsimshian
    1. Chinook
    2. Tsimshian
  B. Coos-Takelman
    1. Coosan (Alsea, Sius-
      law, Coos)
    2. Takelman (Takelma,
      Kalapuya)
  C. Klamath-Sahaptin (Map
    37)
    1. Klamath
    2. Molale
    3. Sahaptin
  D. California Penutian
    (Map 37)
    1. Yokuts
    2. Miwok-Costanoan
      a) Miwok
      b) Costanoan
    3. Maidu
    4. Wintun
VII. Yukian
VIII. Hokan-Coahuiltecan
  A. Hokan (Map 37)
    1. Achomawi
    2. Shasta
    3. Karok

    4. Chimariko
    5. Yana
    6. Pomo
    7. Washo
    8. Esselen
    9. Salinan
    10. Chumash
    11. Yuman
    12. Seri
    13. Tequistlatecan
  B. Coahuiltecan (Map 37)
    1. Coahuiltecan
    2. Comecrudan
    3. Karankawa
    4. Tonkawa
IX. Gulf
  A. Atakapan
  B. Tunican
  C. Chitimachan
  D. Natchezan
  E. Muskogean (Map 37)
  F. Timucuan
X. Siouan-Yuchi
  A. Siouan-Catawba
    1. Siouan (Map 37)
    2. Catawba
  B. Yuchi
XI. Iroquois-Caddoan
  A. Iroquoian (Map 37)
    1. Iroquoian proper
    2. Cherokee
  B. Caddoan (Map 37)
    1. Caddo
    2. Pawnee
XII. Keres
XIII. Zuñi
XIV. Tarascan
XV. Subtiaba
XVI. Zapotec-Otomian
  A. Zapotec
  B. Chinantec
  C. Mixtecan
    1. Mixtec
    2. Cuicatec
    3. Trique
    4. Amusgo
  D. Mazatecan
  E. Chorotegan
  F. Otomian-Pame (Map 37)
    1. Ocuiltecan
    2. Otomian
    3. Pame
XVII. Totonac-Mayan
  A. Totonacan
  B. Mizoquean
    1. Mixe
    2. Popoloca
    3. Zoque
  C. Huave
  D. Mayan (Map 37)
    1. Mayan proper
    2. Huastec
XVIII. Arawakan (Map 37)
XIX. Chibchan (Map 37)

many others by combinations of genetic and diffused resemblances which cannot be adequately described by family tree diagrams or by classes within classes, as in the classification given above in this book. These more complicated relationships between languages and language families must be expressed on language distance tables, mentioned above. Although such tables are two dimensional on paper, the variation of the distances in them may be multidimensional. The "mesh principle" does not demolish all order in linguistic classification. It merely requires a more sophisticated technique to express the more complicated kind of order that exists.

LANGUAGE AREAS AND CULTURE AREAS

A comparison of Maps 2 and 37 shows the geographical relations between culture areas and language family areas. Beginning in the north, the Eskimo-Aleut language family coincides exactly with the Arctic culture areas. Although the Arctic has been divided into two culture areas, the difference between the two is slight as compared to the difference of either from all other culture areas. Therefore, the correlation between language family and culture area is nearly perfect in this instance. This correlation may be explained by several factors: the relative uniformity of geographical environment throughout the Arctic; the relatively rapid migration of the Eskimo from west to east, probably within the last thousand years; and considerable isolation from neighbors. A single Eskimo language is spoken from the Yukon River in Alaska to eastern Greenland and Labrador. No other language in native North America was as widespread. The Polar Eskimo, who are estimated to have been isolated from other Eskimo as well as all other peoples for at least five hundred years, spoke a dialect which was easily intelligible to Eskimo guides from other localities when John Ross discovered them in 1818. This evidence has important bearing on the problem of causes of linguistic change; internal drift versus external contact with alien languages. In this case internal drift caused very little change, although the small population of only a few hundred and their complete isolation provided optimum conditions for drift. No other language areas and culture areas match as closely as do those in the Arctic, but a number else-

577

where exhibit a significant degree of correlation. For example, the Iroquoians and Muskogeans are both confined within the East culture area. If the East were divided into Northeast and Southeast, as it sometimes is, the correlations would be much higher. The Siouan languages are most numerous on the Prairies, with a little overflow in the East and a more recent expansion onto the northern Plains. The Caddoan group falls principally on the Prairies but also is found in the Southeast. Similarly the Klamath-Sahaptin group is confined to the Plateau area, which it shares with the Salish family, while the latter also appears on the adjacent Northwest Coast. The California Penutian language family is found entirely within the California culture area, although it shares this area with several other language families. The position of the Mayan family is similar; it is wholly confined to Meso-America but shares this area with other language families. Map 37 shows only part of the territories of the Arawakan and Chibchan families; both cover large areas in South America, and neither is confined to a single culture area, although Chibchan is more limited in this respect than Arawakan.

The distribution of the Athapaskan languages is a curious one because they are found in the Yukon and Mackenzie Sub-Arctic, on the North Pacific Coast, in the Oasis, Plains, and Northeast Mexico. About two thousand years ago there seems to have been only a single Athapaskan language or a close-knit mesh of dialects, each mutually intelligible to at least some of the others in the group. From this small area, presumably somewhere in the Yukon or Mackenzie Sub-Arctic, a series of southward migrations began. They did not cease until California was reached on the Pacific Coast and Mexico in the Southwest. As the various bands of Athapaskans moved southward, they adopted much of the cultures of the peoples they contacted, partly because of necessity in new geographical environments, and partly by preference. The end result of these migrations and acculturations, first observed in the nineteenth century, was three distinct types of culture so different from each other that without the linguistic evidence no one would have suspected a common origin for the bearers of these cultures.

The Athapaskans in the north remained wholly Sub-Arctic in

culture and personality as well. Those who reached California became so highly acculturated in their material goods that museum curators cannot distinguish the objects of the Athapaskan Hupa from the Ritwan-speaking Yurok or the Hokan-speaking Karok. Personality and ethos exhibit just as complete an acculturation; the Hupa are obsessed with the desire for wealth and social prestige as are all other North Pacific Coast peoples. The Navaho and Apache of the Southwest show varying degrees of acculturation to the Pueblo peoples and other earlier residents of that area. The Navaho have acquired horticulture, matrilineal descent, and much of their religious ritual from the Pueblos. In some respects they have even excelled the Pueblos in these acquired pursuits, for instance in their more elaborate sand paintings. The conclusion derived from Athapaskan history is that language is much more stable than culture; the languages changed much less than the cultures in these extensive migrations.

An even more startling example of the greater stability of language over culture is that of the Uto-Aztecans. These languages are thought to have been a single mother tongue about five thousand years ago. There is no agreement on the exact location of the homeland, but it may have been in southern California or the western Oasis. The presence of only three closely related languages in the Great Basin suggests relatively recent occupation of that area, probably during the Christian Era. The Comanche migrated from what is now Wyoming to Texas about A.D. 1700. The Aztecs arrived in the Valley of Mexico from the northwest only about two centuries before the Spanish conquest.

When the culture of the western Shoshoni in the Great Basin is compared with that of the Aztec in Meso-America, the range of complexity is as great as can be found anywhere on the continent. It seems likely that the Shoshoni experienced some deculturation in their postulated migration from southern California to the even more inhospitable deserts of Nevada and Utah. The Aztecs, on the other hand, seem to have experienced a rapid acculturation in the direction of the more complex cultures which preceded them in the Valley of Mexico. In spite of these extremes of deculturation and acculturation, the languages remained close enough to the an-

579

cestral form to be identified as members of the same language family, and a number of linguists hope to be able to reconstruct a proto-language for the entire group.

The geographical distributions of all the language families on Map 37 are explained by migrations. Loan words and other isolatable parts of language may spread by diffusion from one people to another, but whole languages spread only by migration of the speakers of the languages. However, not all the migrations will show on such a map because some languages have become extinct. There are instances from the historic period of the speakers of a language being reduced in numbers by war or disease and finally joining another society and acquiring its language. There must have been many cases of this kind in the thousands of years of Indian prehistory. Nevertheless, the evidence of migrations given by language classification is indeed impressive.

A comparison of Maps 2 and 37 also has bearing on the Sapir-Whorf hypothesis. If the relation of language and culture were as close as these linguists suggest, then language areas and culture areas should match each other more closely. The fact that they do not is evidence that culture can be altered drastically while language is undergoing only a moderate amount of change, and conversely that language can change more rapidly than culture, as among the California Penutians. It seems probable that grammatical or semantic categories of language have little to do with the execution of practical tasks, such as hunting, farming, weaving, or pottery making. At the present time the languages spoken by Indian members of the crews which fight forest fires seem to have nothing to do with the Indians' efficiency at this practical job. With respect to kinship, low to medium correlations have already been mentioned and are to be expected for such related topics as government and law. It is in the realm of religion, magic, mythology, and other fanciful or abstract areas of thought that semantic categories are most definitely linked with culture. This is inevitable because speech is the only manifestation obtainable of these imaginary aspects of culture, and the realization of this relationship is a tautology rather than a fresh generalization about language and culture. It is impossible to test experimentally the efficacy of various languages to communicate imaginary and fanciful ideas which have no objective existence outside of language and are not subject to verification by a system of common philosophy, such as that of modern science.

WRITING

The Aztecs, Mayas, and their neighbors in Meso-America possessed systems of writing. All of these appear to have had a common origin although no two of them are exactly alike. Aztec writing was in a pictographic or ideographic stage; objects such as bags of cochineal dye, bags of cacao beans, bales of raw cotton, cotton blankets, jars of cactus honey, and bundles of copal gum were drawn in conventionalized form and the quantity indicated by numeral signs. One was a dot or finger, and values up to nineteen were indicated by repetition of these symbols; twenty was a flag, four hundred a tree-like sign denoting hairs, and eight thousand a bag referring to the bags of cacao beans used to make change in trading transactions. For example, the number 8,421 would be indicated by one bag, one hair sign, one flag, and one dot. The number 8,848 would consist of one bag, two hair signs, two flags, and eight dots. These numeral symbols were drawn on top of the commodity symbols mentioned above, and the tax records for each subject town were kept in this manner.

The limitation of Aztec writing was its inability to express complex actions or abstract ideas. It functioned best in economics and government. The sacred books of the priests seem to have been mnemonic devices which helped the reader remember the chants and prayers associated with each symbol. However, at the time of the Spanish conquest a few symbols were regarded as representations of syllabic sounds and some were beginning to be combined in groups of two or more to indicate words by the pun principle. Each symbol stood for a syllable of a word. An analogy in English would be a drawing of a pear to represent the verb "to pare." The verb "permit" could likewise be indicated by a drawing of a pear and a baseball mitt. The number of syllables in most languages is far fewer than the number of words, and syllabaries have proven workable in the languages of the Far East, as well as those of the historic Cherokee and Cree Indians.

Mayan writing seems to have been more advanced than that of

581

the Aztecs. The number system employed a symbol for zero and twenty, a dot for units from one to four, and a bar for five. The Maya numbers were based on twenties, like those of the Aztecs, but position was indicative of value, as in our own Hindu-Arabic numeral system. We assign a multiple of ten for each position, proceeding from right to left. The Maya, in contrast, assigned a multiple of twenty for each position, proceeding from bottom to top. For example, the Maya represented twenty by a zero in the first position and a dot in the second position, meaning literally "one twenty." They wrote four hundred with zeros in the first two positions and a dot in the third, meaning "one twenty times twenty."

In addition to numbers, the Maya had twenty symbols for days, nineteen symbols for "months," nine other symbols for longer time periods, and symbols for astronomical bodies and signs of the zodiac. These and other glyphs that can be read total about 150. The remaining 250, out of a total of about 400, have not been deciphered to date. However, Norman McQuown (1960: 319) cites recent work by Y. K. Knorozov and other Russians which promises to solve this riddle of more than four centuries. Knorozov believes that most Mayan glyphs represent syllables and are therefore phonetic. Four hundred are far too many symbols for an alphabet and far too few for words but are an expectable number for syllables. If this is the case, the Mayan system of writing parallels that of the Babylonians and Hittites, although it differs in too many details to have been derived from that source. Because Mayan writing has been preserved on stone monuments and buildings for two thousand years, its decipherment will add a great deal to our knowledge of the history of the Maya and their neighbors.

REFERENCES

Driver, 1937; Hoijer, 1954; Hymes, 1959, 1960; Lamb, 1959; Lees, 1953; McQuown, 1960; Mandelbaum, 1949; Pierce, 1957; Powell, 1891; Sapir, 1921; Swadesh, 1959*a*, 1959*b*, 1960; Voegelin and Voegelin, 1944.

26: ACHIEVEMENTS
AND CONTRIBUTIONS

THIS chapter will be an evaluation of the achievements of Indian cultures as compared to those of the Old World before A.D. 1492, as well as an assessment of the contributions the Indians have made to the cultures of the modern world after European contact. The discovery of America by Christopher Columbus initiated the most dramatic and far-reaching cross-fertilization of cultures in the history of the world. Although European peoples also expanded into Asia, Africa, and Oceania after A.D. 1492, close contact and colonization of these areas came later than it did in the Americas, in most instances. The impact of these Old World peoples on European cultures was less sudden and precipitous than that of the Indians. To date anthropologists have concentrated principally on the effect of European cultures on those of the Indians and have given little attention to the ways in which Indian cultures have modified those of Europe and of the European colonists in the New World. The broad outlines of this two-way process, with reference to the final results in the twentieth century, will be sketched, following the topical order of the previous chapters of this book.

A glance at the common names for Indian domesticated plants (Table 1, pp. 43–44) reveals many species available in markets in the United States today. Some of these plant foods may be found in every nation of the Americas and probably in every nation or colony of the Old World as well. Many food plants first domesticated by American Indians are important in world diet today. *The Statistical Yearbook of the United Nations* (New York, 1958: 57–

583

67) gives the figures, in Table 6 below, on production of staple foods in 1957 for the entire world, except the U.S.S.R.

We see from this list of the seven most heavily produced world crops that the first four exceed all others by a wide margin. Of these four leading world crops, the total tonnage of the two originating in the Old World (rice and wheat) is almost exactly equal to the total tonnage of the two from the New World (potatoes and maize). Although other New World crops are less important than Old World barley, oats, and soybeans, the total world production of New World domesticates would add up to almost half of the total for the world today. Of the New World plants not listed by the United Nations source, manioc is probably the most important and is today a staple food in tropical Africa. The Ameri-

TABLE 6

WORLD (EXCEPT U.S.S.R.) PRODUCTION IN
METRIC TONS OF STAPLE CROPS IN 1957

Rice	206,600,000
Potatoes	194,600,000
Maize	164,000,000
Wheat	161,600,000
Barley	68,300,000
Oats	47,700,000
Soybeans	24,300,000

can sweet potato would not be far behind. Thus we see that Indian domesticated plants furnish almost half of the world's food supply today.

The history of the potato (Salaman, 1949) is a fascinating chapter in culture history. The potato was widely raised by Indians in the Andean Highlands of South America in pre-Columbian times and was first brought to Europe by the Spaniards in about 1570. Although it has been grown in Spain and other southern European countries continuously down to the present time, it has never been as important in the diet of southern Europe as it has in northwestern Europe. Its first recorded appearance in England was in 1596, over a century after Columbus discovered America, and by coincidence it was first mentioned by French writers in the same year. But it was in Ireland that it achieved its greatest importance in the diet. The earliest certain date for the presence of the potato in Ireland is 1606. Within the next fifty years it became the most important single source of food in that country. The climate and soils were ideal for the potato, and it was raised in increasing quantities until attacked by blight in 1845. The resulting potato famine initiated the emigration of large numbers of Irish to the United States. The term Irish potato was first used by an English herbalist in 1693, and the potato was first transferred from Ireland to the United States by a group of Irish Presbyterians in 1719 (Salaman, 1949: 188). Thus it reached the United States by way of Europe over two centuries after Columbus' discovery of America and has since become one of the staples of our diet. The potato also diffused northward from South America to Mexico, where it is called by the Peruvian term *papas,* but its rate of consumption in Mexico has never equalled that of the Andean region of South America, where it has maintained its prominent role in the diet in spite of the introduction of European foods after the Spanish conquest.

Maize was the main article of diet in aboriginal Mexico and has continued in first position down to the present time. According to the 1950 Mexican census the production of maize was over six times that of wheat, the second most important crop, and over twelve times that of beans. As much as two-thirds of the total crop land in Mexico was planted in maize in 1950, and there has probably been little change in this ratio in the last decade. The most significant innovation in the preparation of maize for food in Mexico is the mill operated by electric or gasoline power. This is spreading to many rural areas. In the United States we raise a tremendous amount of maize, but most of it is fed to cattle and hogs. It is only in the South that maize forms a significant part of human diet. Here cornbread, hominy, hominy grits, and succotash (corn and Lima beans) are all standard items on the menu. Maize has continued to be a staple crop in much of South America and, after A.D. 1492, achieved the rank of a staple in parts of Europe, Asia, and Africa.

Maize has obtained such a firm foothold in the dietary of Southeast Asia that some botanists believe it may be native to that area. If this is true there should be pre-Columbian mention of it in Chinese historical sources. However, the earliest reference to maize reported so far in China is 1555, but it was common enough

585

in that year to suggest that it was introduced two or three decades earlier (Ho, 1955). It was probably introduced into China by land from Southeast Asia as well as by ships landing on the Chinese coast. Therefore maize was introduced into Asia earlier than the potato into Europe, but there is no pre-Columbian evidence for it in documentary sources anywhere in the Old World.

If the American Indians had not domesticated any food plants, the world today would have less to eat and population would be smaller. Because each plant grows best in a limited range of soils and climates, Old World domesticated plants would not flourish as well in the regions most suited to New World domesticates. It took centuries to domesticate a plant to the point of high yield of nourishing food, and if the Indians had not achieved this for maize, potatoes, manioc, sweet potatoes, and some other food plants, it is doubtful if Europeans would ever have accomplished it for these species. They would almost certainly have devoted their attention to improving rice, wheat, and other plants familiar to them and would not have recognized the nutritional potential of the scrubby wild relatives of the American domesticates.

Turning to drugs and stimulants, tobacco is the best-known and most widely used non-edible American plant in the world today. Originating in South America, domesticated species spread out to about the limits of farming over both American continents by A.D. 1492, and were grown in Europe by about the middle of the sixteenth century. From there tobacco was taken by European colonists to Africa, Asia, and Oceania and, at the hands of the Russians, diffused across Siberia to Alaska. There it contacted native American tobaccos on the northern Northwest Coast. It traveled all the way around the world in about two centuries. New varieties became established in many parts of the Old World and many, such as Turkish, are imported back into the New World today.

Native American alcoholic beverages are still consumed in large quantities in Latin America today; for instance, the consumption of pulque in Mexico exceeds that of all other alcoholic drinks combined. With the aid of distillation, introduced from Europe after the Spanish conquest, native drinks have been converted into hard liquors, such as the tequila and mescal of Mexico. Native beverages and their distillates, however, form only a minor part of modern export trade to Anglo-America and the Old World. As export items they have been overshadowed by the products of the wine industry introduced from Europe soon after the Conquest. Probably nine-tenths of all the alcoholic drink consumed in the world today is of Old World origin.

Of the many native American drugs which have found their way into modern pharmacology, the best known are coca in cocaine and novocaine, curare in anesthetics, cinchona bark as the source of quinine, ephedra in ephedrine for clearing sinuses and nasal passages, datura in pain-relievers, and cascara in laxatives. So impressed were the Spanish with Aztec medicine that they included courses in that subject in the curriculum of the College of Santa Cruz, established by the Franciscans in 1536 (Emmart, 1940). During the Colonial period in both Anglo and Latin America, before modern medicine was known, Europeans leaned heavily on Indian medical treatment (e.g., Fenton, 1942). Since the development of scientific medicine, modern drugs of proven efficacy have progressively replaced Indian folk remedies, so that the latter flourish today only in the more backward regions where Indian cultures have been least disturbed.

Those Latin American nations with the largest Indian populations, namely Mexico, Guatemala, Ecuador, Peru, and Bolivia, still house many of their Indians in dwellings much like the pre-Columbian ones. The most conspicuous post-Columbian acquisition from the Spanish is the tile roof. Such primitive features as the earthen floor, the lack of a stove and chimney, the absence of windows, and the paucity of furnishings still persist. In the larger towns and cities, of course, European architecture dominates the scene, but huts of essentially Indian character often may be found in the poorer districts. As late as 1939 the Mexican census classified 45 per cent of its houses as native types, and the lack of sewage disposal characterized 86 per cent of all Mexican housing at that time. No features of aboriginal Indian housing seem to have diffused to the Old World after A.D. 1492, although many parallel housing traits of comparable simplicity may be found in that hemisphere.

In Mexico, along with the resurgence of Indian art in the

587

twentieth century, there has occurred a more limited trend toward a revival of Indian housing and architecture. For instance, in a very exclusive residential district on the south side of Mexico City in the Pedregal, tile roofs and iron balconies of Spanish origin are forbidden. The more recent public buildings in Mexico City, especially at the National Autonomous University of Mexico, also exhibit some features of native American architecture. No such trend occurs in the United States except for an inconsequential number of tourist accommodations in the West in the shape of tipis.

In the United States, where Indians number only about half a million, Indian housing has largely been replaced or at least modified. The Pueblo peoples still live in rectangular stone and adobe houses, some of which date from pre-Coronadan times, but doors, windows, and chimneys, as well as furniture from mail-order houses, have been added. The Navaho have abandoned most of their conical huts in favor of an eight-sided "log cabin" of post-Coronadan origin. For the United States as a whole, only a small fraction of 1 per cent of the present population resides in Indian-style housing.

In Canada, Alaska, and Greenland, aboriginal housing has been less completely replaced than in the United States. Native peoples loom larger, in proportion, and have been less overrun by Europeans. Nevertheless, modern housing will probably entirely replace aboriginal housing in these areas before this century has run its course.

One item of furniture commonly used in the tropical forest of South America and around the Caribbean Sea has been widely adopted by Old World cultures. This is the hammock. The hammock became the standard sleeping place on ships of European cultures, both in their navies and in their merchant marines. The hammock also serves as a bed for campers and as a lounging device around homes and summer resorts in the United States and in Europe as well. Before the discovery of America the hammock was unknown in the Old World.

The facts on Indian clothing parallel those on housing. In Latin American countries with large Indian populations, Indian materials and styles of clothing are conspicuous today. The woolen poncho with woven-in hole for the head is probably worn by the majority of men today in the Central Andes, where it was an aboriginal garment, and, in addition, has been acquired in the historic period by Indians almost as far north as the Mexico–United States border. The breechcloth, however, has been largely replaced by trousers of European origin. European shoes are probably less common today than sandals or bare feet for the Indians of Latin America as a whole, but in Mexico 54 per cent of the population (both men and women) wore shoes in 1950. Women's clothing today also exhibits aboriginal items in Latin America. For instance, the sleeveless blouse (*huipil*) and a poncho-like upper garment (*quesquemetl*) are still to be seen in Mexico. Women wear shoes less often than men, and wear sandals or go barefoot more often.

Of the materials most frequently worn by Latin American Indians in pre-Columbian times, namely cotton, wool, and maguey fiber, the first two are still the principal clothing materials. Mexico has undergone more change in this respect than has South America. The introduction of sheep into Mexico in the post-Columbian period has given that area an adequate source of wool, which was lacking in aboriginal times. To this may be added an increase in the amount of cotton, a more recent production of machine-made cotton cloth, and a breakdown of the class structure which limited the wearing of cotton cloth to the nobility. With the increase in the availability of both wool and cotton in Mexico, maguey fiber, formerly the most common clothing material, is now little worn. However, maguey fiber (*sisal*) has become an important export material for the making of cordage.

The commercial cottons of the world today are derived principally from the species and varieties cultivated by American Indians. For instance, all the cotton in the United States is of American Indian origin, as is the long-fiber cotton now raised in Egypt (Anderson, 1952:165) and in other parts of Africa as well. The total world production of cotton in 1957 was 7,600,000 metric tons, as compared to only 2,271,000 metric tons of wool (*Statistical Yearbook of the United Nations*, 1958). It is thus apparent that native American varieties of cotton supply much, if not most, of the world's clothing needs at the present time.

In Anglo-America, where Indians form a much smaller per-

589

centage of the population, a modified Indian dress is most conspicuous in Arizona and New Mexico. In other areas it may be worn on special occasions but is fast disappearing as daily garb. Nevertheless a few items have found their way into the costumes of people of European ancestry today. Most conspicuous of these is the parka, modeled on that of the Eskimo, but shorter and made of cotton, wool, or synthetic fibers instead of fur. From the Second World War to the present time, the parka has been a standard article of issue for troops in cold climates. It is also a standard garment in winter sports costumes. Another Indian item in our current dress is the moccasin, which is worn for house slippers; the moccasin toe is popular for outdoor shoes. The poncho, modified in both material and cut, is worn today as a raincoat. Ponchos of rubberized materials are spreading from the United States back into Latin American countries, where they are eagerly sought as raincoats by those who can afford them.

Indian clothing, with the exception of the parka, has not made much headway in the Old World. In the New World, in contrast, some of it has not only survived but has spread to new areas in the historic period and to people of European as well as of Indian ancestry.

Native crafts have survived in much the same way that housing and clothing have. They have been preserved best in those areas in the Americas where Indian population is largest. There has been relatively little diffusion of native crafts to new areas in the post-Columbian period. Although one may see many baskets, bags, and mats of Indian weaves with Indian design elements in the markets of Latin America, they are sometimes mass-produced by salaried workers instead of being made by craftsmen in their own homes. In Anglo-America twining and coiling, capable of producing watertight baskets, have been rapidly giving way to modern mass-produced metal containers. The plaiting of splint basketry in the eastern United States, originally characteristic only of the Southeast, has spread north to the Canadian border and a little beyond. Such baskets are made for sale to Whites as well as for home use, and this craft has become a minor source of income to Indian craftsmen. Birch-bark containers are still made in Canada, but they too are being rapidly replaced by mass-produced trade containers, mostly of metal. Spindle-whorls of pre-Columbian type, but sometimes with modifications, are still used for wool- and cotton-spinning from Arizona and New Mexico all the way to Chile, although less frequently than in pre-Columbian times. Colonists from Europe first brought the spinning wheel and flat-bed looms with foot treadles; later they invented or acquired more rapid mechanical spinning and weaving devices. Today most of the cotton cloth worn by those who regard themselves as Indians in Latin America is mechanically produced in relatively modern factories. It is sold as yard goods to Indian women who cut and sew it into garments. Today many Latin American women have acquired sewing machines, which greatly speed up this work. The pajama-like costumes of white cotton, so common in Mexico until the last few decades, were made in this manner. These still survive in the more backward areas but are rapidly being replaced elsewhere by factory-made shirts and pants modeled on those worn in the United States. Most of the women, however, still buy yard goods and make their own dresses. Hand methods of spinning and weaving, used aboriginally by the Indians, have not spread to the Old World since A.D. 1492, although similar methods are still employed in the more backward areas in the Old World. These appear to have been independently invented in the two hemispheres, although diffusion from Old to New World in pre-Columbian times is championed by some anthropologists.

Weaving reached a peak in pre-Columbian Peru, where some of the world's finest textiles were produced by hand methods. The fineness of the cotton or vicuña wool thread, the almost unbelievable variety of weaves, and the intricate designs of these weavers have never been surpassed and are only rarely equalled in the modern textile world. Today we excel Peruvian weavers only in speed of production. Because the finest weaving was done by virgin nuns called the "chosen women," and Inca religion was rapidly destroyed by the Spanish, the weaving done today in Peru does not come up to its pre-Columbian standards. For the same reason Peruvian weaving has not had much influence on weaving in the modern world. It remains an isolated peak of perfection to be admired by those privileged to study it, but unlikely to be equalled, much less excelled, by weavers of the future.

591

Handmade pottery is still produced in quantity in Latin America, but it too is being replaced by wheelmade or moldmade pottery, as well as by metal containers. Although wheel-like rotating devices may have been pre-Columbian in Mexico, and molding of pottery is unquestionably pre-Columbian, the appearance of European colonists with the true pottery wheel and other modern devices has stimulated the trend toward mass production in pottery.

A few hides are still dressed without tannic acid in the Indian manner, but are inconsequential compared to the amount of leather turned out by the tanning industry of today, which stemmed from Europe and Asia.

Indian metallurgical techniques have not survived to the present day, although many Indian craftsman have learned to work metal, especially silver, in the European manner. Indians both in our own Southwest and in Mexico, for instance, produce metal jewelry for the tourist trade, and some of their work may be purchased in cities in the United States as well as in those of Mexico. In spite of the fact that pre-Columbian metallurgists lacked knowledge of iron and of any kind of bellows, and produced principally non-utilitarian jewelry and ornamental objects, some of their techniques have not been improved upon to this day. For example, the "lost wax" method of casting was known in the pre-Spanish era from Mexico to Peru, and is used by dentists today to cast gold inlays to fill teeth. The same casting method was known in Europe and Asia in pre-Columbian times, and it is from this Old World source that dentistry derived the technique. Indian metallurgy on the whole is comparable to that of Egypt, Babylonia, and Pakistan in the third millenium B.C., before iron was known. It was inferior to the metallurgy of the Old World after about 1500 B.C.

In the United States a government-sponsored attempt was made by the Franklin D. Roosevelt administration to revive Indian arts and crafts in order to provide much needed income for the Indians. Congress passed the Indian Reorganization Act in 1934, and Roosevelt appointed John Collier to the position of Commissioner of Indian Affairs to direct the program. Although some Indians themselves disapproved of this program because it attempted to set the historical clock backward, most anthropologists and others aware of Indian problems supported this plan for the Indian to help himself. Stores were opened in cities to market Indian products, and more numerous and attractive stores and trading posts were also established in localities where Indians lived, to encourage tourists to do business with them. Whatever the ultimate effect of this program will be, its immediate effect was to place more Indian products in the shops and homes of the United States and to augment Indian income.

Other programs, aimed at getting Indians off the reservations and helping them to live and compete with Whites and thus become full citizens, are in operation in the United States at the present time. Government employees on reservations screen the Indians to select those most likely to adjust to the outside world. Their transportation is paid to cities and other places of employment, where they are helped in finding jobs. Many Indians have joined crews of migratory farm laborers, while others, especially those in the Oasis area, have formed fire-fighting crews, which are moved from one conflagration to another in the West during the summer season, thus contributing immeasurably to the preservation of our valuable forest resources.

Parallel programs to raise Indian income with the sale of products of their arts and crafts have been initiated in Latin America, especially in Mexico. Today in Mexico City there are a number of shops specializing in goods made by Mexican Indian artists and craftsmen.

As mentioned in the chapter on art, American Indian art has only recently been granted a place among the great art styles of the world. The art of Africa and Oceania, however, has had more influence on contemporary European art than has that of the American Indian. This is due in part to the fact that much of African and Oceanian art depicts the human figure, which is less common in American Indian art. From the time of the ancient Greeks the human figure has dominated European art, and the striking heads and complete figures carved in the hard tropical woods of Africa and Oceania have had enormous appeal to European artists from about a century ago to the present time. In comparison, American Indian art is more geometric and abstract or, when the human figure is attempted, a bit stiff and awkward.

593

Exceptions to this characterization are the superb pottery heads of pre-Incan Peru and the most naturalistic painting and sculpture of the Olmecs and Mayas of Mexico and adjacent Central America.

The greatest works of American Indian art ceased to be produced or were deliberately destroyed by the Spanish conquerors as soon as they gained political control of the New World. This art, from Mexico to Bolivia, had been closely associated with the nobility and the priesthood and, in conquering the Indian nobility and stamping out the heathen religions, the Spanish eradicated the art as well as the human sacrifice and other shocking aspects of Indian religions. The best examples of American Indian architecture were torn down and the stone used to build Christian churches. New cities of European style were built on the ruins of the Indian capitals, such as Cuzco and Mexico City, and at a speed unknown in Europe. No city of Europe up to the sixteenth century was built as rapidly as was the new Mexico City. After this almost complete obliteration of the best examples of American Indian art and architecture, the world was forced to wait until archeology discovered or rediscovered these distinctive art styles in order to become aware of their existence.

The more modest folk art, which manifested itself principally in the decoration of utilitarian objects such as tools, baskets, pots, and clothing, was much less disturbed by the European invasion and has continued, with modifications, down to the present time in areas where Indians survive in any numbers. Thus the Eskimo, who had little contact with Europeans until about a century ago, still engrave and carve in ivory and other hard materials. If the carvings in the round figured by Schaefer-Simmern (1958) are representative, Eskimo art has improved, or at least increased its appeal to Europeans since contact with them. A few art objects of the Eskimo have found their way into gift shops in cities in the United States and probably in those of other countries as well. Missionaries have taught Eskimo women weaving, braiding, embroidery, and beadwork, which they execute in a most colorful and attractive manner.

Porcupine quill embroidery on hide, aboriginally practiced in the Sub-Arctic, Plains, and Prairies, was the inspiration for the elaborate bead embroidery centering in the northern Plains and

Prairies (Hunt, 1951). The glass beads, needle, and thread were all furnished by European traders. With an inexhaustible supply of beads in a wider range of colors than was available to dye porcupine quills, beadwork became more frequent and elaborate than its predecessor, quillwork. It was applied principally to buckskin clothing: men's shirts, women's dresses, moccasins, mittens and gloves, belts and bands. Beadwork reached its florescence at the end of the nineteenth century, after most of the Indians were living on reservations, and survives in attenuated form to the present day.

On the Northwest Coast, art experienced a period of florescence in the first half of the nineteenth century due to the acquisition of steel tools, which were vastly superior to those of shell, bone, horn, and stone of the Indians of this area before European contact. Houses, totem poles, and canoes could be built and carved with steel tools in a fraction of the time required with native tool materials. This greater efficiency in production resulted in an increase in size and in the amount of carving on these large objects, where art was most conspicuously displayed. Smaller objects, such as boxes, rattles, household utensils, and clothing showed less change but also responded to the increase in wealth and leisure brought by the trade with European ships. Northwest Coast art has experienced a rapid decline in the twentieth century, although a few individuals manufacture small objects for the tourist trade. The climate in British Columbia and southeast Alaska does not attract artists of European ancestry as does that in the Southwest, and the market for art objects is too limited to support many native artists.

In Arizona and New Mexico, in contrast, artists of European ancestry have invaded the domain of the Indians in considerable numbers. Taos, for instance, has had an art colony for many years. The production of art works by Indians has also been greatly stimulated by purchases by tourists, who are more numerous in the Southwest than in any other area of comparable size in the United States. The tourist trade has kept alive the traditional arts such as weaving and pottery-making, and has lent support to the new arts of silversmithing (Adair, 1944) and painting (Tanner, 1957). Some of the Plains Indians have also taken up painting. This contemporary Indian painting is a new but hybrid form of art expression. It is a synthesis of Indian and European art styles, with perhaps a greater infusion of the latter, but distinctive and striking enough in its own right to command the attention of art connoisseurs and critics.

In the eastern United States, Indian art is almost a thing of the past, although its survives in modified form in areas where Indians still live in considerable numbers, for instance, among the Cherokees of the Carolinas, the Seminoles of Florida, and various tribes around the Great Lakes.

In Mexico and Guatemala, folk art survived the holocaust of the Spanish conquest, but not without modification. Textiles and pottery vessels were the most common mediums for its expression. The so-called native costumes distinctive of each local area in Mexico today are better termed colonial costumes. Post-Spanish items include trousers, woolen serapes or ponchos, woolen skirts, straw hats, sleeves on upper garments, and probably the long stole called *rebozo*. Decorations on such garments are normally of hybrid Indian-Spanish character, or show some modification from pre-Columbian designs.

Mexico, more than any other contemporary American nation, has developed a national art style which is an integration of Spanish and Indian elements. This is largely a twentieth-century development. For centuries the two art styles remained separated for the most part. European statues and paintings were conspicuous in churches, government buildings, and the homes of the Spanish families in the colonial period. Indian art was left to the Indians who formed the lower class. After Mexico won her independence from Spain in the revolution of 1810 to 1820, there was no significant change, but it was the revolution of the lower classes against the upper classes and the church, starting in 1910, that produced the kind of nationalism which could give rise to a new and integrated art style.

At the hands of such masters as Diego Rivera, José Clemente Orozco, David Alfaro Siqueiros, Rufino Tamayo, Miguel Covarrubias and Juan O'Gorman this art came to life and may be seen today in Mexico City in such public places as the *Palacio de Belles Artes*, the *Palacio Nacional*, and the National Autonomous University of Mexico. In the work of all these men, the Indian face and figure are portrayed beside those of the European. Many huge indoor mural paintings of this group depict important historical events in the history of Mexico, including the class struggle of the twentieth-century revolution. The buildings of the national university are adorned with mosaics full of eagles, serpents, jaguars, sun symbols, and other motifs derived from Indian art. These are combined with human figures in European as well as Indian dress, with horses, churches, buildings of classic architecture, and references to great Old World scholars such as Ptolemy and Copernicus. As if this variegated mixture were not enough, cries of the revolution, such as *Viva la Revolución* and *Tierra y Libertad*, are also displayed in these unusual tile mosaics. Mexico also has its school of more modern, abstract, and fanciful art; here also the human faces and figures are as often Indian as European.

In the United States today nearly all of our artists cling to the European tradition or to its modern derivatives and look to Paris for their inspiration. Indian art plays a much smaller role here than in Mexico.

American Indian music was enriched during the period after White contact as a result of increased contact of Indians with other Indians, as well as with Whites. The diffusion of the 1890 Ghost Dance music from the Great Basin to the Plains and the spread of Peyote music with that cult from the Oasis to the Plains have already been mentioned. The 1870 Ghost Dance diffusion in Nevada, California, and Oregon also carried its music along with other parts of the ceremony. Although less is known of earlier religious cults, we can be sure that music was an indispensable feature which spread along with each cult wherever it went.

The earliest known attempt in the United States to utilize Indian themes in music composed for White consumption was that of James Hewitt in 1794. He claims to have used Cherokee themes in a musical play called *Tammany*, about an Indian chief and a villain from Columbus's band (Covey, 1948:521). A century later, in his effort to develop national qualities in United States music, Edward MacDowell turned to the first published collection of Indian melodies, which appeared in 1882. The result was Mac-

597

Dowell's *Indian Suite*, written in 1891–92 and first performed in 1896. The next modern composition to use Indian musical motifs was Skilton's *Indian Dances*, published in 1915. These works of MacDowell and Skilton were among the 27 compositions of 12 composers which had the greatest number of performances in the United States from 1919 to 1926 (Hallowell, 1957:207).

The harmonized and otherwise altered tunes of composers such as Cadman (*Land of the Sky Blue Water*) and Lieurance (*By the Waters of Minnetonka*) are so far removed from the original Indian material from which they stemmed as to be unrecognizable to an Indian listener. The great differences in methods of voice production and in rhythms make it impossible to incorporate unaltered Indian music in our own compositions. The result is that such twentieth-century compositions based on Indian themes are much closer to European than to Indian music and are acceptable only as popular music. They do not constitute a new and vigorous style capable of producing great works of lasting fame.

Although it is enlightening to know that American Indian music has made some headway in the United States, it has been less popularly received than African Negro music and scarcely affects even 1 per cent of all the music heard in the United States today on radio, television, records, tapes, and in live performances. Of the composers mentioned by Hallowell (1957:207) all are minor figures, except possibly MacDowell, and their music has had little effect on the active musicians of the present time who are largely employed by universities, opera companies, symphony orchestras, and churches. Indian themes are less used in the United States today than they were in the first quarter of the twentieth century. In Latin America, on the other hand, the compositions of Carlos Chávez (especially his *Sinfonía India*) in Mexico and of Heitor Villa-Lobos in Brazil, based in part on Indian themes, are generally regarded as more significant contributions to twentieth-century musical style.

In the area of transportation, there has been considerable borrowing of Indian devices by Whites. When Europeans first penetrated the Arctic, they traveled almost exclusively by dog sled and hide boat, and continued to do so until the airplane took over most Arctic transportation. Completely decked boats, modeled on the kayak and maneuvered with a double-bladed paddle, are used in Europe and the United States today by sportsmen to run rapids in streams. In the Sub-Arctic, Whites were only too glad to use the moccasins, snowshoes, toboggans, and birch-bark canoes of the Indians of that area. On the Northwest Coast, on the other hand, the Indian dugout canoes were inferior to European vessels for large shipments across the open ocean, and competed with rowboats and other small craft in fjords and streams. Around the Caribbean the hand-paddled dugouts of the Indians were the envy of the Spanish on windless days when their sails went unfilled, but Spanish sailors never actually operated Indian canoes, although they may have hired them along with their crews from time to time. In the eastern United States the dugout canoe was used to some extent by colonial traders, but usually with Indians hired to do the paddling. In other areas of North America, where back packing by human beings was the principal method of transporting loads, there was little borrowing of Indian transportation devices by Whites. In downtown Mexico City today, Indian porters are still back packing loads with the aid of the forehead strap, which can also be observed in a great many other towns. However, Foster (1960:104) reports that the forehead strap is common in Galicia, Spain, today. Although its use in Spanish America has generally been attributed to Indian heritage, more research is necessary to determine possible Spanish origin in some localities.

The Whites, on the other hand, introduced beasts of burden: horses, mules, donkeys, and oxen. Of these animals, the donkey has been the most useful to the Indians of Latin America; he can live off the land, can withstand considerable heat, drought, and cold, and is not too expensive to purchase. The donkey is the most common beast of burden in those Latin American countries with large Indian populations today, except in the central Andes, where the llama is still used. Oxen are much used in the same areas for pulling the Spanish oxcart and plow, but are too expensive, to purchase and to feed, for the small farmer, who either hires his plowing done or cultivates his small plot by hand. Donkeys are too small for efficient plowing, but are sometimes so used. Mules are generally associated only with the larger farms, and horses are usually limited to the upper classes and are ridden more often than

599

driven. The same transportation animals were brought to the East Coast of the United States and Canada by English, French, and Dutch settlers, although donkeys and mules were fewer than in Latin America. In the Plains area, the horses derived from the Spanish greatly altered the pre-horse culture and gave rise to a new way of life which reached its climax in the first half of the nineteenth century.

In Anglo-America the railroad gradually replaced animals for the transportation of large shipments going long distances, and the automobile and the truck later took over local transportation from the animals. In Latin America, the same trend is occurring but it lags behind that of Anglo-America. As Ralph Beals has said, "If I were to rate the acculturative forces I have seen at work in various communities [in Mexico] I think I would suggest that one good road is worth about three schools and about fifty administrators." (Tax, 1952:232). At the present time Indian methods of transportation take care of only a small part of the total tonnage moved in the Americas, but are still the only methods known in the most backward areas.

Trade increased tremendously after European contact and has continued to expand to the present time. Indians are obtaining more mass-produced objects in trade every year and are using less and less of their own homemade products. Along with this trend goes a parallel trend in labor; Indians are working more and more for wages or to make articles they can sell for cash, and less and less to produce things for their own consumption. Regularly scheduled market days, common from Mexico to Peru in pre-Columbian times, have continued down to the present time in those areas where Indian population is heavy. These schedules have been adjusted to the Spanish calendar, with Sunday the most frequent market day.

Indian concepts of property and inheritance have partly been replaced by European systems, but those American nations with large Indian populations have generally permitted communities of Indians to own or use land in common as they did in pre-Columbian times. Sometimes farm plots are owned individually while grazing land is owned in common. Because unilateral descent has been giving way to bilateral descent, unilateral inheritance is also shifting toward bilateral in most such cases. As wage work by Indians increases, we may anticipate an increase in individually owned property and a decrease in the amount of property owned and inherited by kinship groups and communities. Individual ownership is usually accepted by Indians for chattels before it is accepted for land. The ownership of trapping territories by "families" in the Sub-Arctic is probably a post-European development, resulting from the increased demand for furs. Indian property concepts do not seem to have had any significant influence on the property systems of Whites, either during the colonial period or later.

Indian ideas and practices associated with marriage and kinship have been modified by White contact but not wholly altered to fit the White pattern. Bride "purchase" still prevails in areas where it was well developed in aboriginal times. Some polygyny also persists, although it is frowned upon, if not actually forbidden, by all American governments today. The extended family is losing its cohesion in favor of the nuclear family, along with the general trend toward individuality and bilateral structure. Kinship terminology has shifted from unilateral to bilateral systems in many areas, for instance in the Southeast (Eggan, 1937; Spoehr, 1947). The increasing amount of wage work, social security, medical care, and insurance will tend to weaken kinship groups, as the individual finds more security of another kind. Because kinship played a less prominent role in the aboriginal high cultures of Mexico and Peru, these areas of high culture have experienced less change in kinship than those of lower culture. Areas with rigid systems of unilateral descent, such as the northern Northwest Coast, Oasis, Prairies, and East have experienced a considerable lessening of the importance of kinship in the historic period. All of the major kinds of American Indian kinship groups, namely, families, clans, demes, lineages, sibs, moieties, and phratries, occurred in the Old World as well before A.D. 1492, but all the evidence points toward independent origin for the two hemispheres. There is no evidence of the diffusion of any of these institutions from one hemisphere to the other after A.D. 1492.

In Anglo-America almost all male immigrants brought wives with them or married women of their own nationality and culture after they arrived in the New World. Not so in Latin America. About 90 per cent of the Spanish immigrants were men who came over single, and married or cohabited with Indian women after arrival. Although most persons in Latin America today claim some dash of European ancestry, the percentage of European genes in entire populations is smaller than is generally known. In Mexico today more than 80 per cent of the genes in the entire population are probably Indian, with the remainder about equally divided between Negroes and Europeans. Only about 200,000 Europeans and 250,000 Negroes immigrated to Mexico up to A.D. 1810, and there has been little immigration since that time (Aguirre Beltrán and Pozas A., 1954:176). The Mexican census no longer attempts to differentiate Indians, Europeans, and Negroes. In the past, Indians were identified by language and culture. Those who spoke an Indian language, lived in a community with others speaking the language, shared in community property, participated in community ceremonies, retained some articles of clothing of Indian or colonial type, ground maize on the metate, etc., were regarded as Indians. As acculturation proceeds in Mexico such minority groups are growing smaller and smaller in proportion, although in absolute numbers they are becoming slightly larger.

The largest governmental unit in the New World before A.D. 1532 was the Inca Empire in the Andes of South America, with a population of several million and a territory 2,500 miles long. This compared in size with the pre-Christian empires of the Old World. It had a divine emperor at the top, a number of royal lineages related to that of the emperor, a lower class of nobility, and commoners at the bottom. It was as completely totalitarian and as highly centralized as any government in the history of the world, if the Spanish chroniclers have described it correctly. It reminds one of the social organization of the ants, bees, and termites, so completely regimented was everyone in the organization. Such a system of government is very unpopular in the Americas today and in most of the rest of the world as well, but whether we like it or not, it remains a major achievement of governmental organization. It was so over-dependent on orders from the top that when Pizarro captured the Inca there was little resistance left.

The city-state of the Aztecs of Tenochtitlán was both smaller and more democratic, but it too failed against the Spaniards after its leader, Montezuma, had been captured and slain by Cortez. Neither of these outstanding New World governments influenced colonial and modern governments in any significant way.

European colonial powers forced their systems of government on the Indians from the top, although they often retained some features of Indian local government at the bottom. From Mexico to Bolivia the Spanish conquerors eliminated the Indian nobility and put themselves in its place. They exploited the Indian lower classes in every conceivable manner and decimated the population in most areas. The combination of malnutrition, European disease, and overwork on Spanish building projects or in the mines took a heavy toll of the poor Indians. Spanish orders and demands were relayed to the common man through his own local leader. Thus the Spanish forced a European feudal system on the Indians in most of their colonies. The lower classes of Indians from Mexico to Bolivia acquiesced because they were accustomed to take orders from a ruling class and had no idea how to better themselves. Because the resources of land and water had been fully exploited by the Indians of central Mexico and Peru by A.D. 1492 and population was already heavy, there was no place left for rebellious Indians to go to escape the iron hand of the Spanish.

In Anglo-America it was very different. Indian governments in this area were much more democratic and allowed much more freedom to the individual. Men spent most of their time hunting and fighting and preferred to die fighting for their way of life than to yield to a conqueror. Furthermore, Anglo-American colonists stemmed from more democratic parts of Europe and in some instances (as with the Pilgrims) from near the bottom of European class structure, where few persons desired to regiment a group of others beneath them. Add to this the Christian religion, with its ethnocentric self-righteousness, and the heathen Indian became an impediment in the path of progress of Christianity and European culture. Although the French fraternized with the Indian to some extent in the colonial period, the English and most other European nationalities which settled in English-speaking

603

America were hostile toward Indians. They disregarded land claims and other rights of Indians in their westward expansion and deliberately drove the Indians from their path.

While there was probably some tribal organization on the Plains, Prairies, and in the East before White contact, its frequency seems to have increased sharply as a defense measure against the encroachment and threats of Whites. The confederacies which sprang up after European contact were also inspired by the necessity for mutual defense against the common enemy. Every Indian confederacy in Anglo-America, except that of the Iroquois, was a post-White development.

In spite of the sharp difference in attitude of Europeans toward Indians in Anglo, as opposed to Latin, America, the demographic results of European contact were not very different. Indian population in the territory that is now the United States dropped from an estimate of about a million in A.D. 1492 to about 200,000 in A.D. 1900. In central Mexico, Cook and Simpson (1948:46–48) estimate that population dropped from about 11 million in 1519 to about one and a half million in 1650. Although Cook seems to prefer the extreme figure in each direction, one cannot challenge his major conclusion. Therefore, the virtual enslavement of the Indian in Mexico was biologically about as destructive as the open hostilities against him in the United States. There was, however, a difference in the rate of population change. In Mexico, Indian population declined for about a century and a half and then increased for the next three centuries. In the United States the decline lasted for about three centuries and the increase began only about a half-century ago. In regard to genes Mexico is still at least 80 per cent Indian, while the United States might show 1 per cent Indian genes if there were any way to locate the hybrids with only a small percentage of Indian genes. The number of persons in the United States today on Indian tribal rolls is about half a million, but many are partially White.

During the colonial period, the Whites and Indians on the East Coast exchanged weapons and war tactics freely with each other. The Indian eagerly accepted the gun in exchange for furs, and the White pioneers learned to take cover behind rocks and trees and to engage in surprise attacks in the Indian manner. The fate of the close ranks of the British in Braddock's defeat was a bitter lesson to the British and the colonists, and George Washington, who witnessed the defeat, never later placed his own revolutionary army in such an untenable position. On the Plains in the nineteenth century, Whites learned from the Indians to ride on the side of a horse away from the direction of fire, so that the horse served as a shield.

In Mexico, the Spanish soon found that the reed arrows and darts of the Aztecs would split when they struck chain mail and go on to inflict serious wounds and even death. To remedy this weakness in their armor, they quickly took over the quilted cotton armor of the Aztecs, which was thick enough to stop any Aztec projectile. They even draped this Aztec armor on their horses to decrease their injury and mortality in battle. Once the Aztecs were conquered, the Spanish gladly employed Aztec warriors in their ranks in order to subdue other Indians.

In spite of considerable cross-fertilization of Indian and White cultures with respect to warfare from the sixteenth to the nineteenth century, the military organizations of American nations today have retained little or nothing of Indian fighting methods. The weapons and tactics of modern war have changed so rapidly in the last few decades that most elements of "primitive" war are obsolete.

With respect to rank and social classes in Anglo-America, early European contact often raised the rank of Indian leaders and encouraged greater centralization of authority in chiefs. This was especially true in the East and on the Prairies. In the extreme Southeast, however, the class structure of such peoples as the Natchez became rapidly obliterated. In the other area where social classes were most strongly developed, the Northwest Coast, the economic opportunities offered by European trade increased upward mobility. When we add to this the vacating of many titles by those who died of European diseases, we find many persons of "common" rank raising themselves into the titled nobility. Ultimately, however, most Indians in Anglo-America gravitated downward to a position second only to that of the Negro at the bottom. In spite of the sympathy that anthropologists and some minority

605

groups have shown the Indians in the United States, they are still treated as second-class citizens in most localities.

Indian sodalities have disappeared for the most part, or perform their ceremonies less often than in the past. In Latin America the Spanish succeeded in eliminating almost all organized native religious cults and in absorbing the Indians into the Roman Catholic faith. Almost all the natives in that area are nominally Catholics, and have been baptized into the church, although their knowledge of Christian theology is very spotty, and they are likely to equate the Catholic saints with their own pagan spirits. In Anglo-America, sodalities probably survive best among the Pueblos of the Oasis, although there too they are disappearing rapidly. The Midewiwin still continues in the Prairies area, and a minority of the Iroquois belong to a modified native religious group called the Longhouse People. None of these Indian sodalities have had any noticeable effect on parallel organizations of Whites, which remain wholly derived from Europe.

Indian beliefs and practices associated with the life cycle survive to a considerable extent in the areas where Indian population is most numerous. Because life cycle ceremonies were often small family affairs attracting little attention, they survived in areas where large public religious ceremonies were prohibited. Many infants today are brought into the world by non-literate Indian midwives, in much the same way that they were in pre-Columbian times. Boys' initiations at puberty have almost entirely disappeared, but girls at first menstruation are secluded and indoctrinated with the same old native taboos in many localities. Among the Apaches of the Oasis, where the girl's puberty rite was a public affair and the most important ceremonial occasion, it has assumed an even more prominent place in recent years. For the last thirty years or more it has been held from the first to the fourth of July, and combined with a rodeo (roundup) and the celebration of our national independence. Marriage and death ceremonies in Latin America have generally given way to those of the Catholic church, and in Anglo-America they tend also to follow White example for the most part. Burial in the ground is now much more common than other native ways of corpse disposal such as scaffold burial and cremation. Indian memorial ceremonies have also largely ceased to be given, although some Indians may decorate graves on our own Memorial Day.

Indian education has largely ceased to exist but still survives in areas where sodalities have survived, because the perpetuation of the cults demands the training of new ritualists to succeed the old. Education in native arts and crafts still exists in the areas of large Indian populations where these activities are carried on. The same may be said for farming and other utilitarian tasks. Indian educational methods have had no direct effect on those derived from Europe, but the trend in education in the United States today shows many parallels to Indian education. The permissive attitude toward children, the limited use of corporal punishment, and the greater emphasis on reward for a lesson well learned rather than censure for failure, are all accepted as obvious principles of enlightened education.

Indian religion and magic have survived to a considerable extent today in the hybridized religions now possessed by those regarded as Indians. The Roman Catholicism of Latin America, with its colorful ritual, had strong appeal to the Indians of that area. When combined with the permissive attitude of the Spanish Fathers toward native religions, which allowed the Indians to perform many of their aboriginal dances and rituals in and around the church edifice, the result was a complicated mixture of Catholic and pagan religion which is difficult for the anthropologist to separate today. For instance, the vision of the Virgin of Guadalupe appeared on the site of the temple of the Aztec maize goddess Tonantzin (Foster, 1960:166). Some details, such as the burning of incense, were shared by both religions; even the cross was a native American religious symbol in some localities.

The Protestant faiths which dominated Anglo-America, in contrast, were less generally accepted by Indians. This was because of the blandness of the ritual and the less compromising attitude of Protestant missionaries. Partly as a result of this failure to accept the Indians as full members of Protestant sects in Anglo-America, the Indians have formed new religions of their own. Although these religions do contain some Christian elements, their original inception and subsequent acquisition of followers has been independent of organized Christianity. As was pointed out in the section above on music, the Ghost Dance religions of 1870 and 1890 are examples of recent nativistic movements which ran their course in a few years and failed to survive. Two post-European religions which have survived to this day are the Indian Shakers and the Peyote Religion. The latter will serve as an example of a modern hybrid religion of Indians in the United States.

The Peyote Religion is known today as the Native American Church. Its history has already been sketched in the chapter on Narcotics and Stimulants. The doctrine includes the belief in supernatural power, in spirits, and in the incarnation of power in human beings. Spirits consist of the Christian Trinity (the Father, Son, and Holy Ghost), other Christian spirits, such as the devil and the angels, and still other spirits derived exclusively from Indian religions. The Christian spirits tend to be equated with comparable Indian spirits: God is the Great Spirit; Jesus is the culture hero, guardian spirit, or intercessor between God and man; the devil is an evil spirit bent on harming man; the angels are often the spirits of the four winds or cardinal directions, and are sometimes dressed like Indians. The pantheon is thus seen to be about an equal mixture of Indian and Christian spiritual beings.

The ethics of the Native American Church also closely parallel those of Christianity. Members should exhibit brotherly love by being helpful, friendly, honest, and truthful to one another, as in the golden rule (Matt. 7:12; Luke 6:31). Married couples should cherish and care for each other and their children, and should not commit adultery. Members should work steadily and reliably at their jobs to earn a good living, and above all, should avoid alcohol.

Peyote ritual, however, is heavily weighted in favor of Indian elements, such as the eagle-bone whistle, cedar incense, the fan of bird tail feathers, the bundle of sage sprigs, the gourd rattle, and the water drum. Ritual behavior, too, is principally Indian in character. Eating the peyote induces rapport with the supernatural and brings visions of spirits or departed loved ones, sometimes with aid in solving personal problems or with warning to abandon evil thoughts and deeds. Visions in Christianity occur in both the Old and the New Testament. To sum up, the Native American Church is a happy blend of about equal portions of Christian and Indian elements and patterns and provides a stabilizing force for the personalities of its followers today.

The total number of distinct (mutually unintelligible) Indian languages on both continents was about 2,000 in A.D. 1492. This total number breaks down by area approximately as follows: Anglo-America, 200 (Voegelin and Voegelin, 1944); Mexico and Central America, 350 (McQuown, 1955); South America and the West Indies, 1,450 (McQuown, 1955). In Anglo-America a little more than one-third of the 200 known Indian languages have become extinct, while in Mexico and Central America a little less than two-thirds of the 350 known native languages are no longer spoken. Therefore the rate of survival of Indian languages is significantly different in Anglo-America and in Latin America down to Panama. Anglo-America shows a higher percentage of survival.

From the 1950 census of Mexico we find figures on the number of Mexican citizens still speaking indigenous languages. From a total Mexican population of about 25,800,000, 3 per cent spoke only Indian languages, and another 7 per cent spoke both Indian languages and Spanish. These figures combined give a round 10 per cent of Mexican population using native languages in 1950. When we compare this figure with our estimate above, that about 80 per cent of the genes in the Mexican population today are of Indian origin, we see that Indian race has survived much better than Indian language.

All Indian languages spoken today have been influenced by the European languages contacted from A.D. 1492 to the present time. This influence has been restricted almost exclusively to vocabulary, especially to nouns. When new material objects were obtained from European traders, the European word was often incorporated in the native language, normally with modification of sound to fit the native phonology. In some instances, however, Indians "coined" new words and phrases in their own language and refused to accept the European term. Detailed analyses of European influence on a number of Indian languages would show different amounts of influence.

All European languages spoken in the Americas today have also been influenced by Indian languages. Thousands of geographical place names for lakes, rivers, mountains, towns, and states all over the Americas are derived from native languages. For instance, 23 of the states in the United States have Indian names (Wissler, 1937). Indian words incorporated into English include tobacco, hominy, succotash, toboggan, moccasin, wampum, wigwam, tipi, squaw, papoose, and thousands of others. A number of phrases, such as "go on the warpath," "bury the hatchet," "smoke the pipe of peace," and "run the gantlet," are meaningful only in the light of Indian culture. There are a number of special dictionaries containing etymologies of Indian words which have been incorporated into the various European languages. The most impressive is the huge three-volume *Diccionario General de Americanismos*, by Francisco J. Santa María, which gives tens of thousands of words which have been added to Spanish in Latin America. Most of such words are of Indian origin.

Literature produced in the Americas since A.D. 1492 also reflects the influence of the Indian. No doubt every reader knows of Henry Wadsworth Longfellow's *Hiawatha* and of James Fenimore Cooper's *Leather-Stocking Tales*. In the novels of Cooper, written from 1823 to 1851, his hero, Natty Bumppo, became the epitome of pioneer character, with a combination of the best personality traits of both Indians and Whites. He was reverent about religion, fearless of danger, and fair and just in his dealings with his fellow man. Chingachgook, the old Delaware warrior, is a more tragic figure, lonely, frustrated, drunken, yet proud. Every novel set in the pioneer period, which was as late as 1900 in some parts of the West, gives some space to Indians and their culture.

The Indian also figures prominently today in motion pictures and television melodramas of the West. Western pictures have never been more popular than at the present time, and the character of the White heroes of these tall tales is certainly influenced by that of the Indian. The strong, silent, fearless male talks softly with little outward emotion, but flies into action against evil "when the chips are down." Some of this personality type may be that of the generalized Anglo-American pioneer, and as true of Australia and South Africa as of America; but the American Indian was instrumental in producing the particular kind of western personality so admired at a popular level in the United States today.

610

On a more serious level, the psychoanalyst Carl Jung (1928) thought he could observe an Indian component in the character of some of his American patients. Although American patients exhibited significant differences from Europeans, it is questionable how much of this was derived from generalized frontier personality and how much was specifically Indian. Some certainly belongs to the latter category.

In the realm of science and mathematics the Indians made a few outstanding innovations. Perhaps the highest achievement of this kind was the mathematics, astronomy, and calendar system of the Maya. By 2,000 years ago the Maya had perfected a calendar accurate to the day for a period of 374,400 years (Morley, 1955: 183). This was equalled, but not excelled, by the calendar associated with Pope Gregory XIII a thousand years later in Europe. The Maya calendar was superior to those of such famous Old World civilizations as Egypt, Babylonia, Pakistan (Indus River), China, Greece, and Rome. The Maya priests in charge of the calendar were able to predict eclipses and the heliacal rising and setting of Venus.

The accurate recording of dates was made possible by a place numeral system with a symbol for zero. The Chinese of the first century B.C. also achieved a place numeral system, but without a symbol for zero. The zero was indicated by leaving an empty space (Goodrich, 1959: 48). A still earlier zero was invented by the Babylonians about 500 B.C. (Kroeber, 1948: 469–72). And finally a fourth invention of the zero occurred in India about A.D. 500. The Arabs adopted the Hindu place numeral system and passed it on to Europe as the Arabic system. Because the symbols for zero differ in all four localities, and the values of the places in the place numeral systems were different for all except the Chinese and Hindu (which were decimal), it seems highly probable that there were three or four independent inventions or discoveries of the concept. The Maya, therefore, take their place beside Babylonia, India, and China as one of the cradles of intellectual achievement. Because the Maya zero and calendar system were closely associated with their pagan religion, the Spanish burnt all the sacred books they found, and our knowledge of the system today is derived mostly from carvings on stone monuments which were difficult for the Spanish to destroy and equally impervious to the elements of nature.

We see, from this brief sketch of the achievements of the Indians and of their contributions to modern life, that much of their race, language, and culture is alive today in the Americas, and some has penetrated to other parts of the world as well. Although a quantitative comparison of these three aspects of man is difficult, it seems clear that race has survived to the greatest extent, and that language and culture have been subject to considerable acculturation. Although the acculturation of the Indian to European languages and cultures is the dominant direction of the trend, Europeans have also absorbed a large portion of Indian language and culture. The American Indian, therefore, takes his place among the major contributors to the current composite civilizations of the world today.

REFERENCES

AGUIRRE BELTRÁN AND POZAS A., 1954; ANDERSON, 1952; BARNETT, 1957; CHASE, 1955; COOK AND SIMPSON, 1948; COVEY, 1948; EGGAN, 1937; EMMART, 1940; FENTON, 1942; FOSTER, 1960; GOODRICH, 1959; HALLOWELL, 1957; HO, 1955; HUNT, 1951; JUNG, 1928; KROEBER, 1948; McQUOWN, 1955; MORLEY, 1955; ROSENBLAT, 1945; SALAMAN, 1949; SANTA MARÍA, 1942; SPOEHR, 1947; *Statistical Yearbook of the United Nations,* 1958; TAX, 1952; VOEGELIN AND VOEGELIN, 1944; WISSLER, 1937.

MAPS

MAP 1

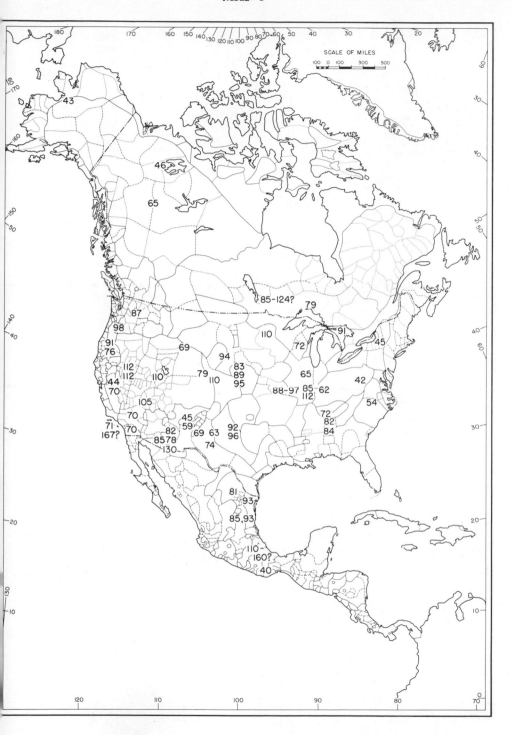

SCALE OF MILES
100 0   100   300   500

PRINCIPAL PALEO-INDIAN SITES WITH AGE IN CENTURIES AGO

MAP 2

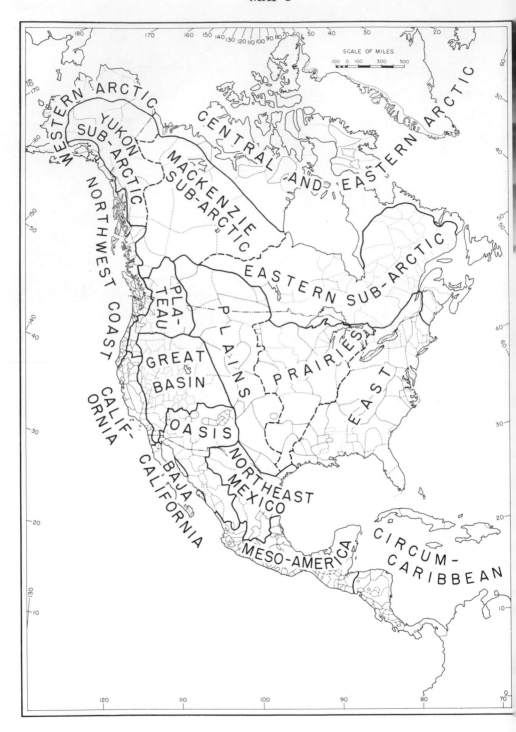

CULTURE AREAS. After Driver and Massey

MAP 3

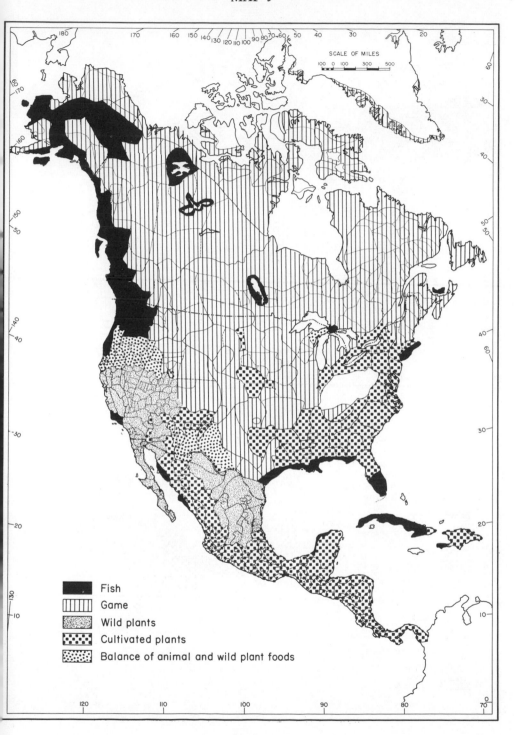

SCALE OF MILES
100 0 100   300   500

Fish
Game
Wild plants
Cultivated plants
Balance of animal and wild plant foods

DOMINANT TYPES OF SUBSISTENCE. Driver and Massey

MAP 4

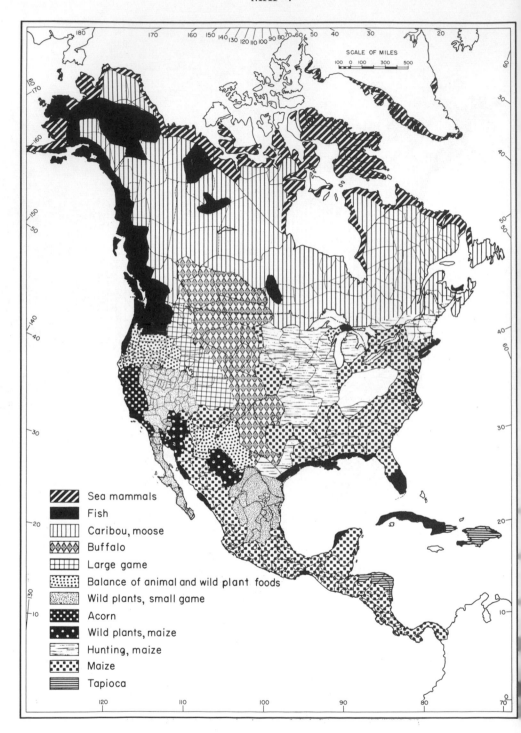

SCALE OF MILES

Sea mammals
Fish
Caribou, moose
Buffalo
Large game
Balance of animal and wild plant foods
Wild plants, small game
Acorn
Wild plants, maize
Hunting, maize
Maize
Tapioca

SUBSISTENCE AREAS. Driver and Massey

MAP 5

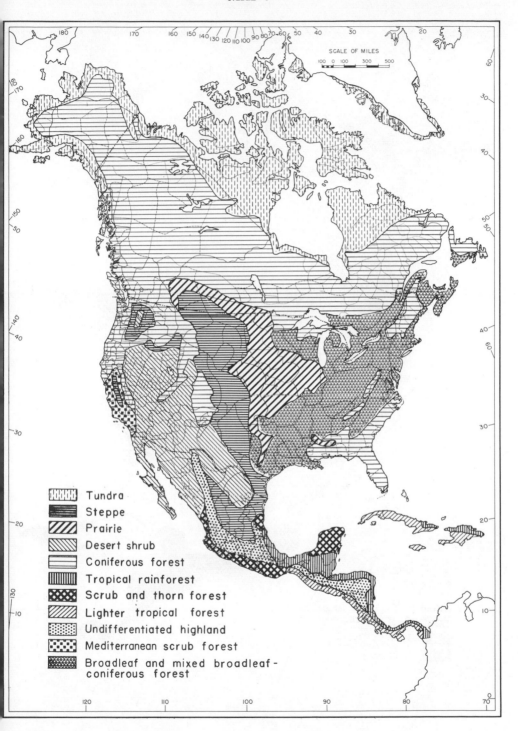

SCALE OF MILES
100 0 100   300   500

Legend:
- Tundra
- Steppe
- Prairie
- Desert shrub
- Coniferous forest
- Tropical rainforest
- Scrub and thorn forest
- Lighter tropical forest
- Undifferentiated highland
- Mediterranean scrub forest
- Broadleaf and mixed broadleaf-coniferous forest

NATURAL VEGETATION AREAS. Driver and Massey

MAP 6

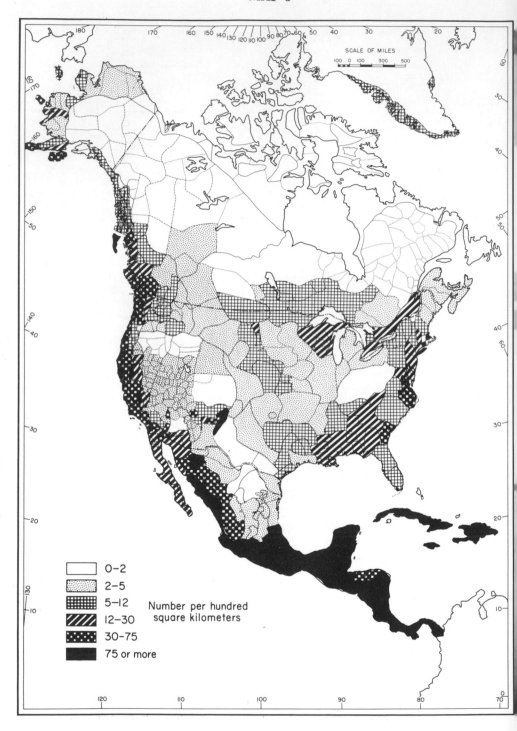

NATIVE POPULATION DENSITY. After Driver and Massey

MAP 7

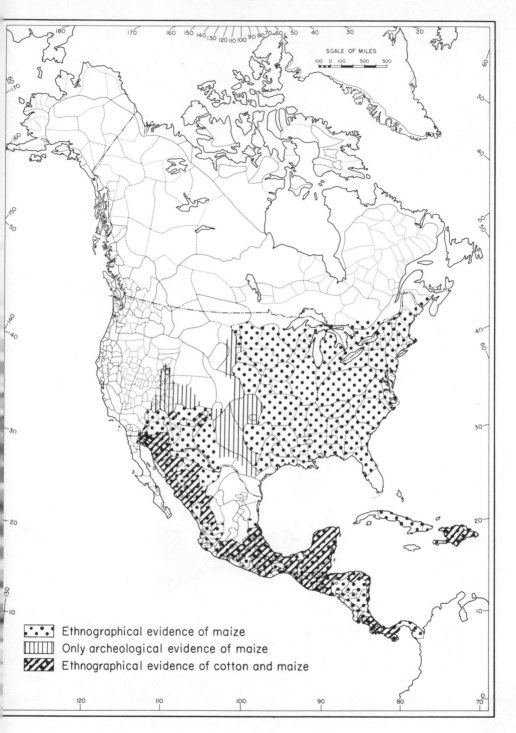

SCALE OF MILES
100 0 100   300   500

Ethnographical evidence of maize
Only archeological evidence of maize
Ethnographical evidence of cotton and maize

MAIZE AND COTTON. Driver and Massey

MAP 8

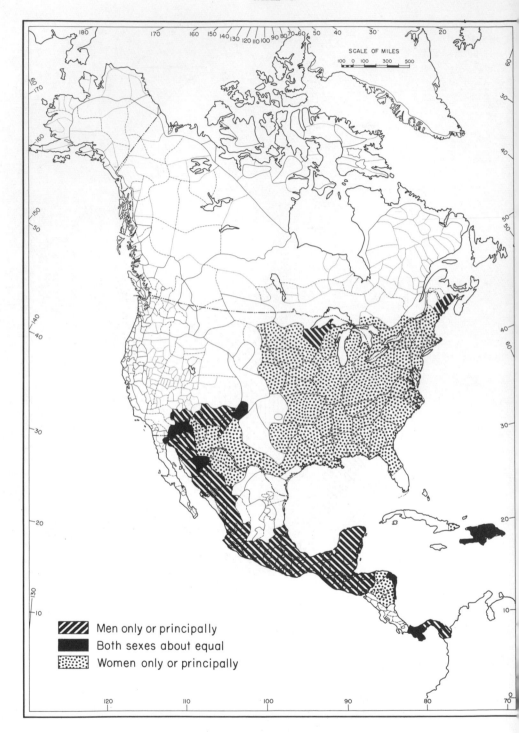

SCALE OF MILES
100 0 100   300   500

Men only or principally
Both sexes about equal
Women only or principally

HORTICULTURAL SEXUAL DIVISION OF LABOR. Driver and Massey

MAP 9

SCALE OF MILES
100 0 100 300 500

▨ Salt (Sodium Chloride)

Sᴀʟᴛ. Driver and Massey

MAP 10

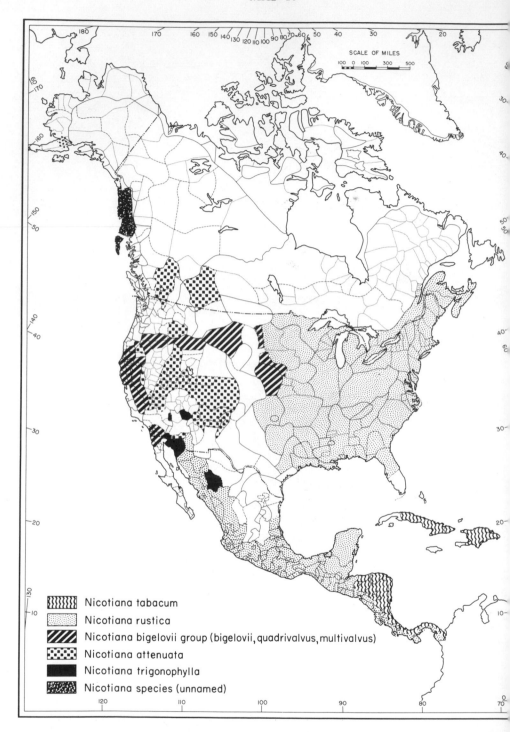

DOMINANT SPECIES OF TOBACCO. Driver and Massey

MAP 11

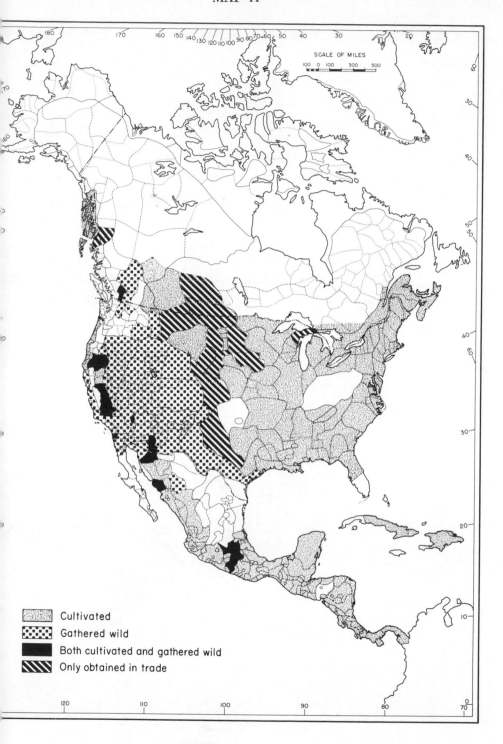

SCALE OF MILES

Cultivated
Gathered wild
Both cultivated and gathered wild
Only obtained in trade

PROBABLE ABORIGINAL SOURCES OF TOBACCO. Driver and Massey

MAP 12

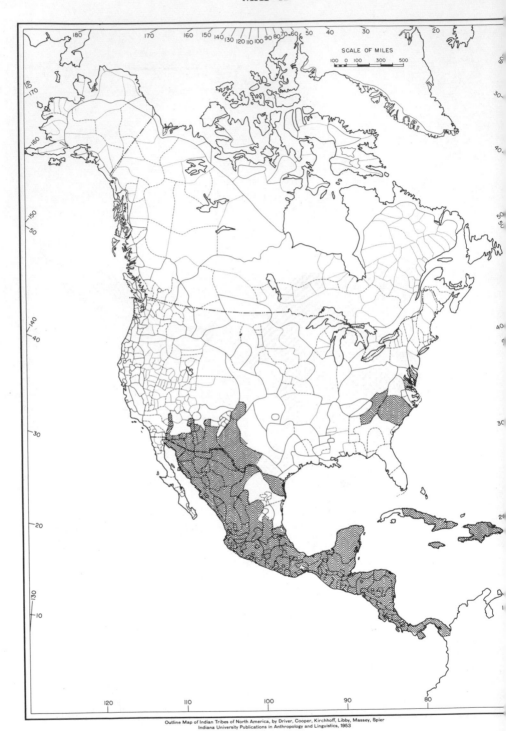

SCALE OF MILES

Outline Map of Indian Tribes of North America, by Driver, Cooper, Kirchhoff, Libby, Massey, Spier
Indiana University Publications in Anthropology and Linguistics, 1953

ALCOHOLIC BEVERAGES

MAP 13

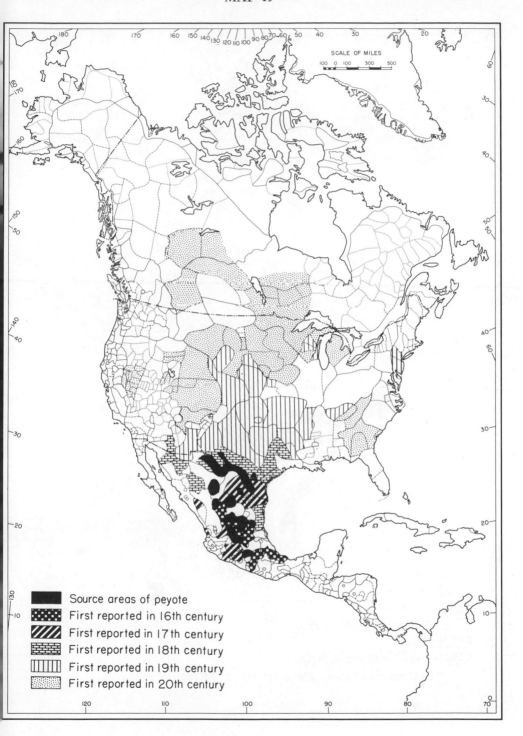

SCALE OF MILES
100 0 100   300   500

■ Source areas of peyote
▦ First reported in 16th century
▨ First reported in 17th century
▤ First reported in 18th century
▥ First reported in 19th century
░ First reported in 20th century

PEYOTE. After Driver and Massey

MAP 14

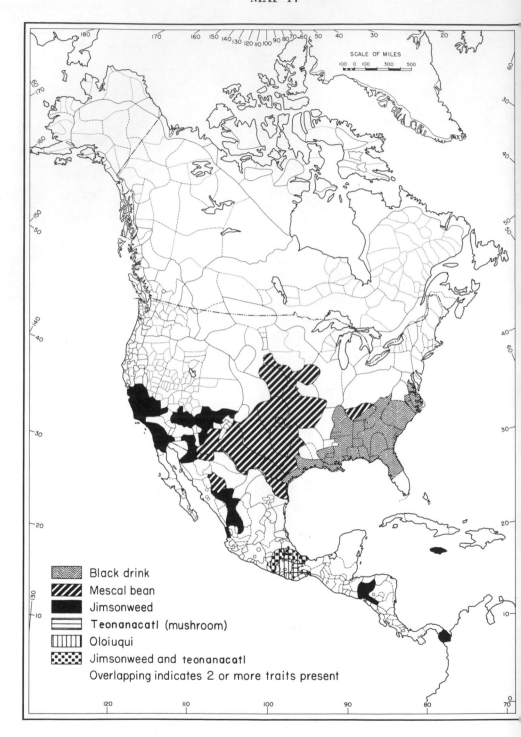

SCALE OF MILES
100 0 100 300 500

Black drink
Mescal bean
Jimsonweed
Teonanacatl (mushroom)
Oloiuqui
Jimsonweed and teonanacatl
Overlapping indicates 2 or more traits present

OTHER NARCOTICS. After Driver and Massey

MAP 15

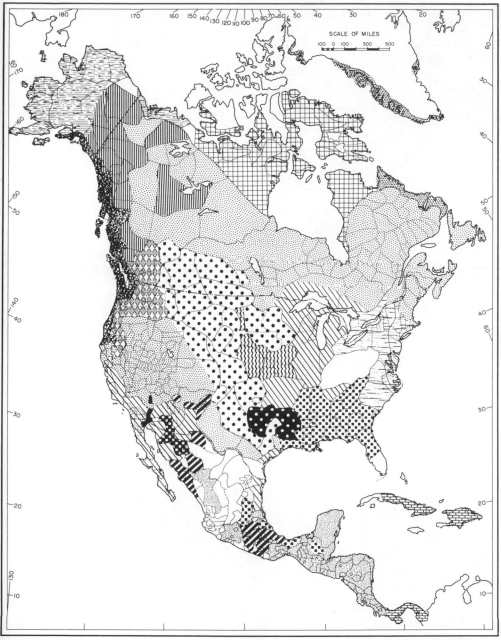

SCALE OF MILES
100 0 100   300   500

	Double lean-to		Pyramidal or hip-roof rectangloid house
	Rectangular plank house		Conical roof on cylinder, thatched
	Semi-subterranean Plateau house		Gothic dome, thatched house
	Prairie-Southeast earth lodge		Rectangular, gabled house, thatched
	Mohave type, 4-pitch-roof house		Domed bark, mat, thatch, hide house
	Crude conical tipi		Rectangular, barrel-roofed house
	Plains tipi		Rectangloid earth-covered Alaskan house
	Rectangular, flat roof house		Domed snow house
	Rectangular, domed roof house		Domoid stone–earth–whalebone house

DOMINANT HOUSE TYPES. Driver and Massey

MAP 16

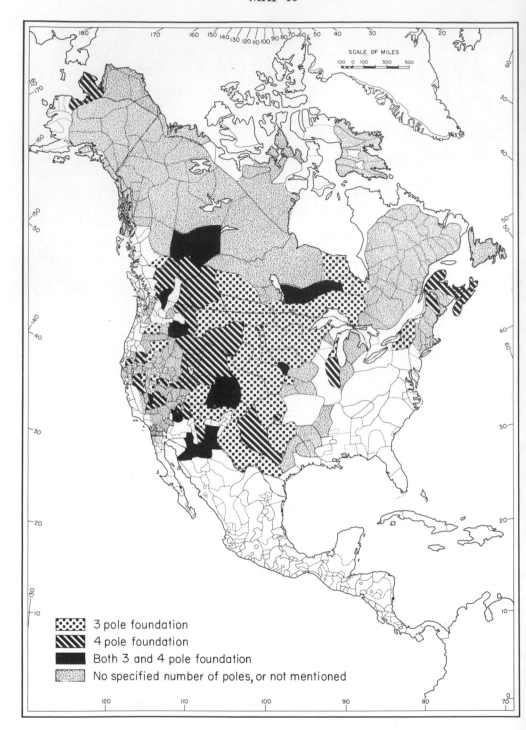

3 pole foundation
4 pole foundation
Both 3 and 4 pole foundation
No specified number of poles, or not mentioned

CONICAL AND SUB-CONICAL HOUSES. Driver and Massey

MAP 17

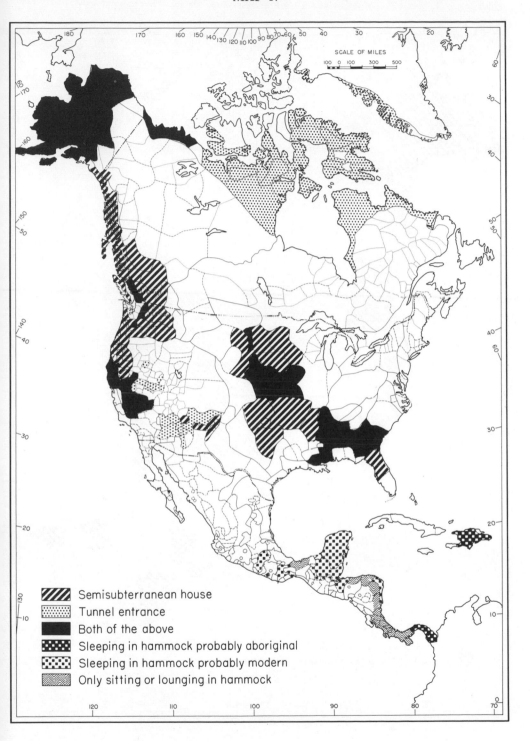

Semisubterranean house
Tunnel entrance
Both of the above
Sleeping in hammock probably aboriginal
Sleeping in hammock probably modern
Only sitting or lounging in hammock

SEMISUBTERRANEAN HOUSES, TUNNEL ENTRANCES, AND HAMMOCKS
Driver and Massey

MAP 18

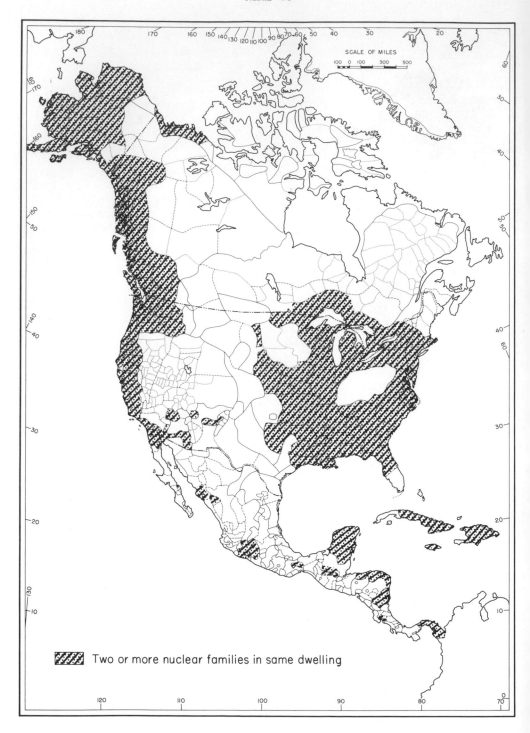

SCALE OF MILES
100 0 100   300   500

Two or more nuclear families in same dwelling

MULTIFAMILY HOUSES. Driver and Massey

MAP 19

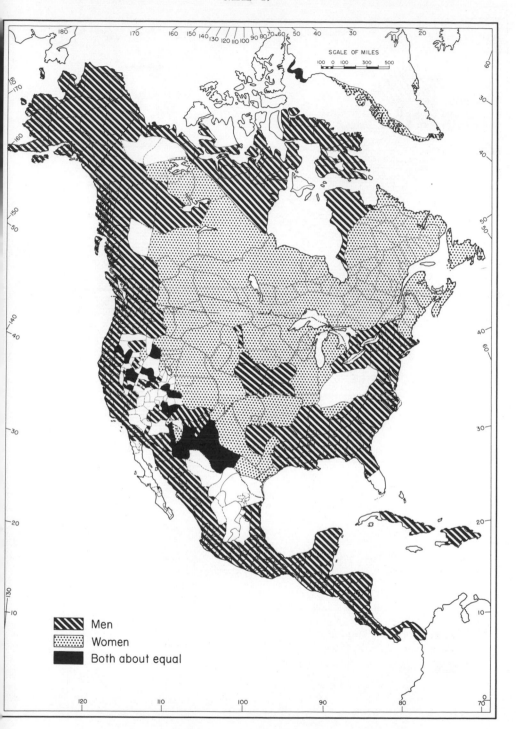

Men

Women

Both about equal

DOMINANT HOUSE-BUILDING DIVISION OF LABOR. Driver and Massey

MAP 20

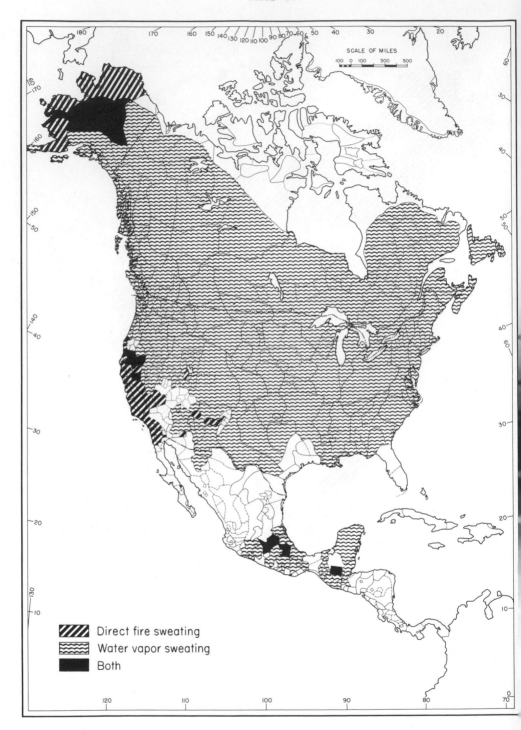

SCALE OF MILES
100 0 100 300 500

	Direct fire sweating
	Water vapor sweating
	Both

SWEATING. Driver and Massey

MAP 21

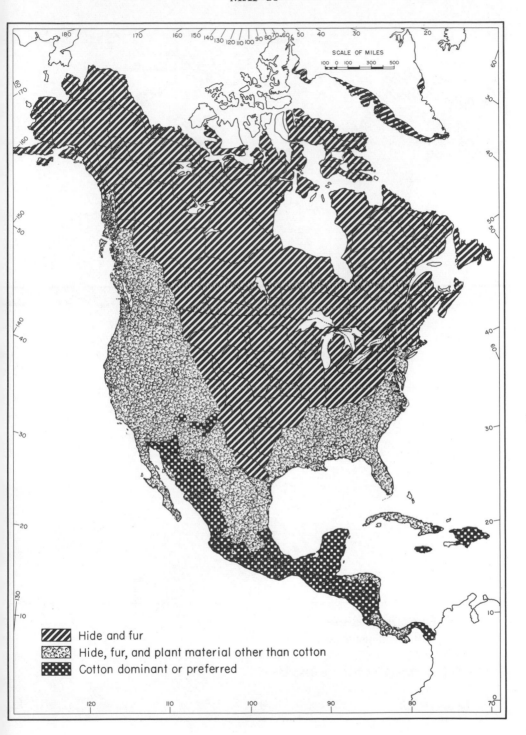

Hide and fur
Hide, fur, and plant material other than cotton
Cotton dominant or preferred

DOMINANT CLOTHING MATERIALS. Driver and Massey

MAP 22

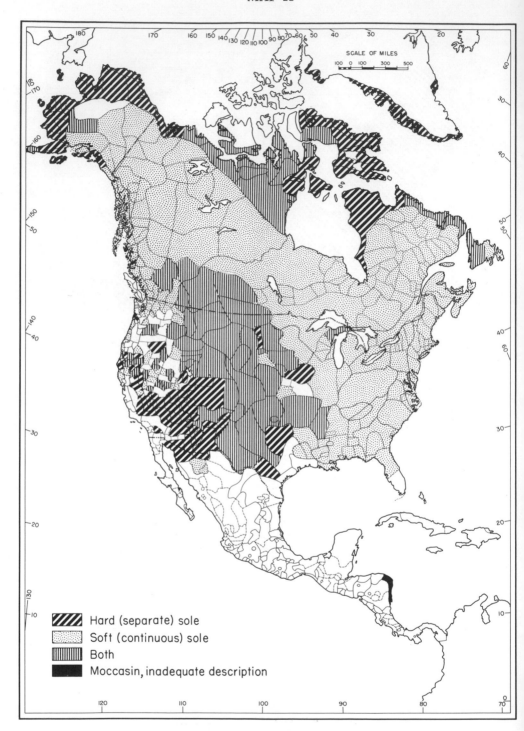

SCALE OF MILES
100 0 100   300   500

Hard (separate) sole
Soft (continuous) sole
Both
Moccasin, inadequate description

Moccasins. Driver and Massey

MAP 23

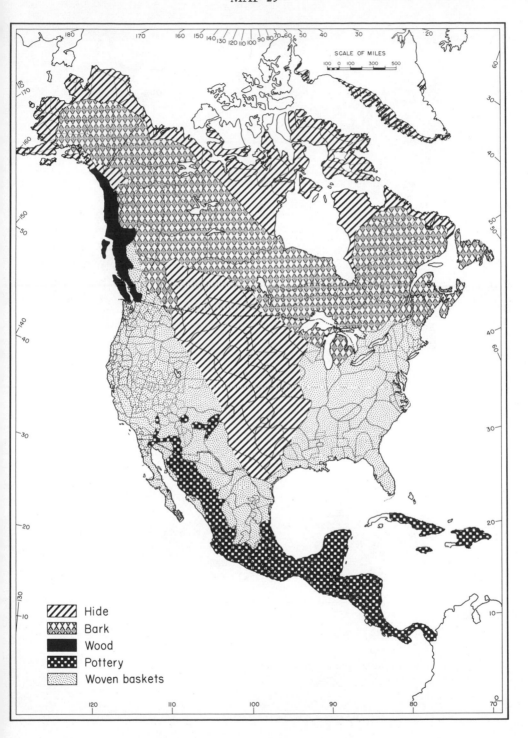

SCALE OF MILES
100 0 100 300 500

Hide
Bark
Wood
Pottery
Woven baskets

DOMINANT NON-COOKING CONTAINERS. Driver and Massey

MAP 24

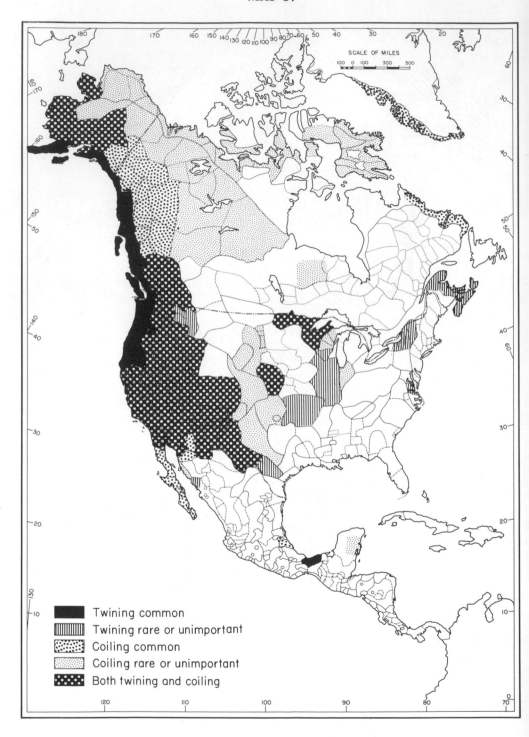

SCALE OF MILES

Twining common

Twining rare or unimportant

Coiling common

Coiling rare or unimportant

Both twining and coiling

TWINING OR COILING OF BASKETS, BAGS, OR MATS. Driver and Massey

MAP 25

SCALE OF MILES
100 0 100   300   500

Common

Rare or unimportant

PLAITING OF BASKETS, BAGS, OR MATS. Driver and Massey

MAP 26

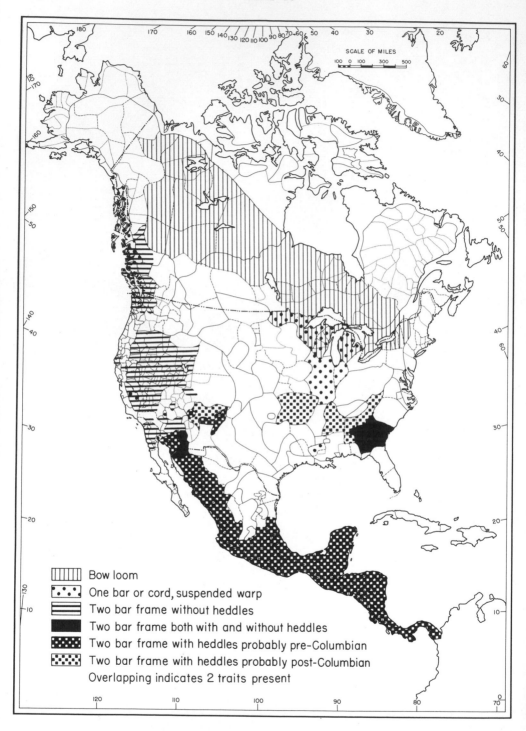

SCALE OF MILES
100 0 100 300 500

|||||| Bow loom
`.·.·.·.` One bar or cord, suspended warp
▤ Two bar frame without heddles
■ Two bar frame both with and without heddles
▦ Two bar frame with heddles probably pre-Columbian
▦ Two bar frame with heddles probably post-Columbian
Overlapping indicates 2 traits present

WEAVING DEVICES. Driver and Massey

MAP 27

SCALE OF MILES
100 0 100 300 500

▨ Ethnological data
▧ Only archeological data

POTTERY VESSELS. Driver and Massey

MAP 28

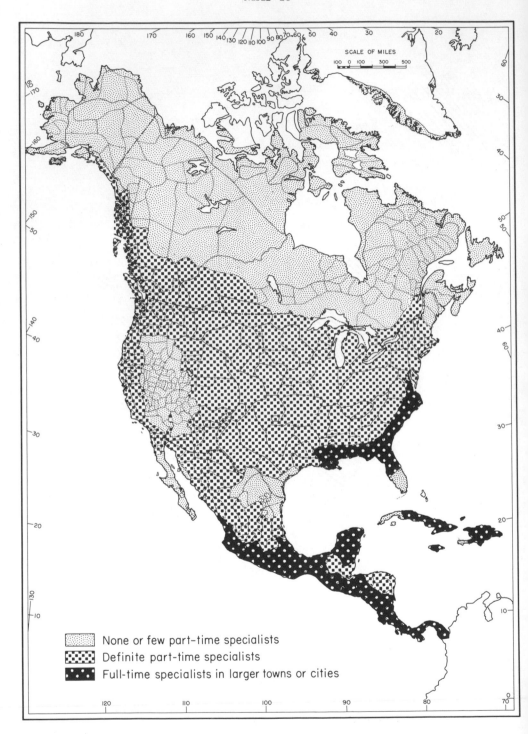

SCALE OF MILES
100 0 100   300   500

None or few part–time specialists
Definite part–time specialists
Full–time specialists in larger towns or cities

CRAFT SPECIALIZATION. After Driver and Massey

MAP 29

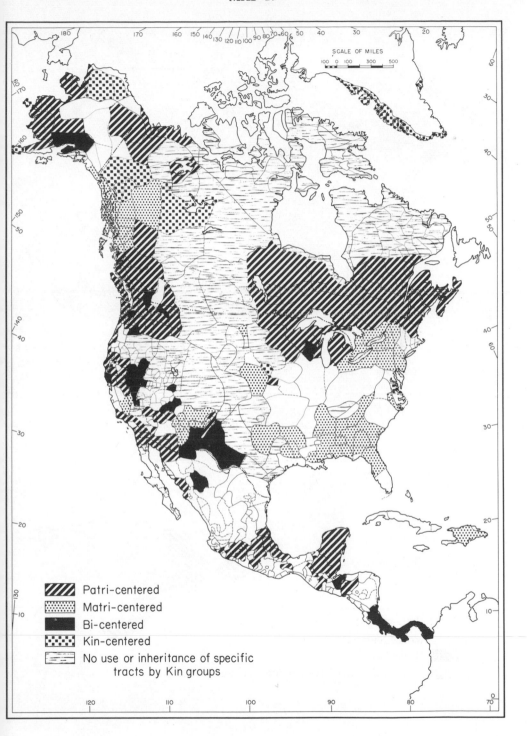

SCALE OF MILES
100 0 100 300 500

Patri-centered
Matri-centered
Bi-centered
Kin-centered
No use or inheritance of specific tracts by Kin groups

LAND TENURE. After Driver and Massey

MAP 30

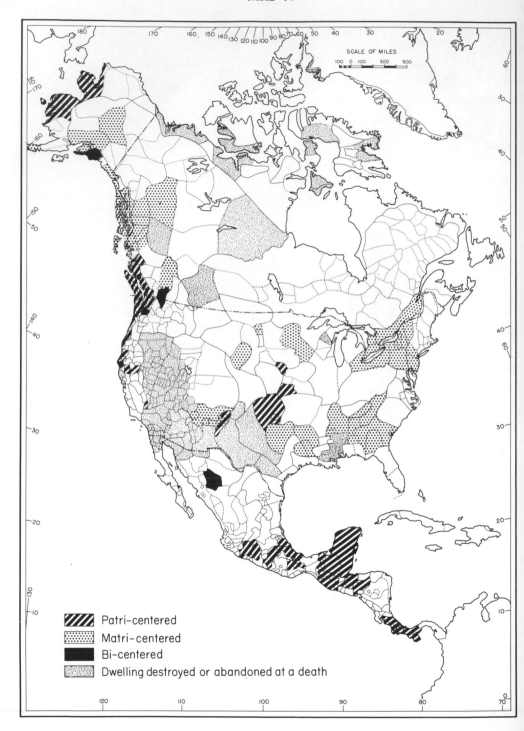

SCALE OF MILES
100 0 100 300 500

Patri-centered
Matri-centered
Bi-centered
Dwelling destroyed or abandoned at a death

OWNERSHIP AND INHERITANCE OF DWELLINGS. Driver and Massey

MAP 31

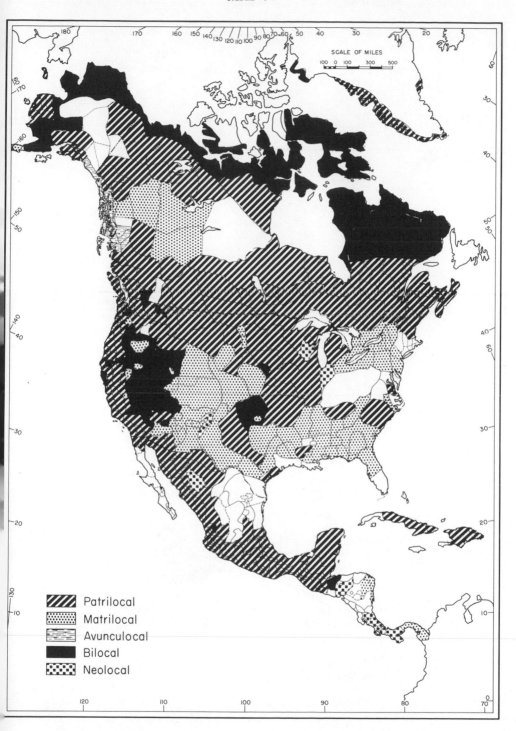

SCALE OF MILES
100 0 100 300 500

Patrilocal
Matrilocal
Avunculocal
Bilocal
Neolocal

Post-Nuptial Residence. After Driver and Massey

MAP 32

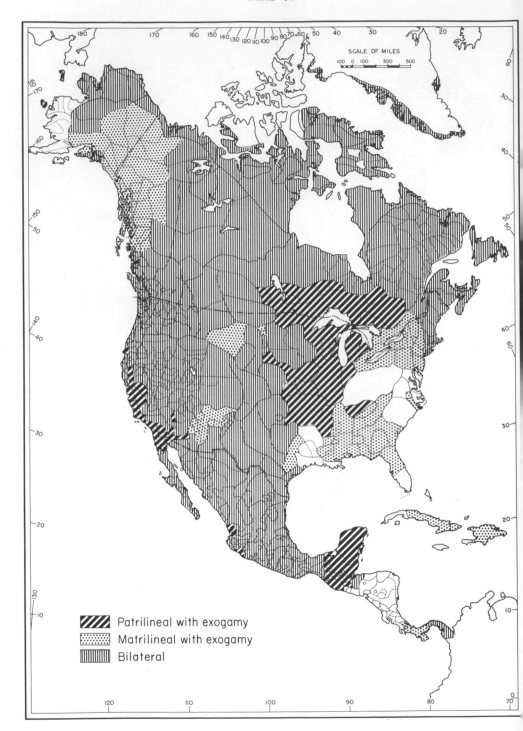

SCALE OF MILES
100 0 100   300   500

Patrilineal with exogamy
Matrilineal with exogamy
Bilateral

DESCENT. Driver and Massey

MAP 33

NUMBER OF MULTIPLE SIBS. Driver and Massey

MAP 34

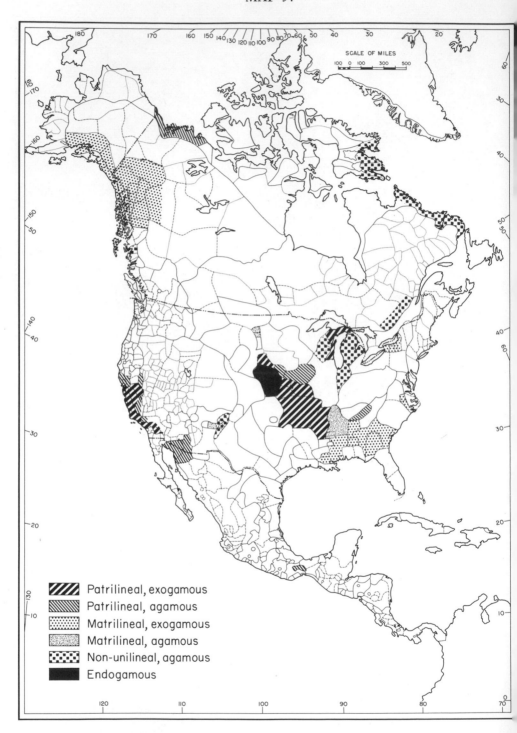

SCALE OF MILES
100 0 100   300   500

Patrilineal, exogamous
Patrilineal, agamous
Matrilineal, exogamous
Matrilineal, agamous
Non-unilineal, agamous
Endogamous

MOIETIES. Driver and Massey

MAP 35

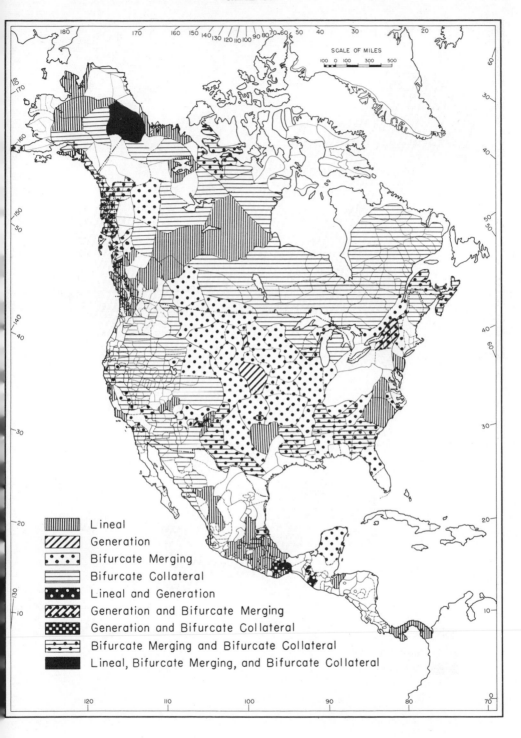

SCALE OF MILES
100 0 100   300   500

Lineal
Generation
Bifurcate Merging
Bifurcate Collateral
Lineal and Generation
Generation and Bifurcate Merging
Generation and Bifurcate Collateral
Bifurcate Merging and Bifurcate Collateral
Lineal, Bifurcate Merging, and Bifurcate Collateral

MOTHER-AUNT TERMS OF REFERENCE. After Driver and Massey

MAP 36

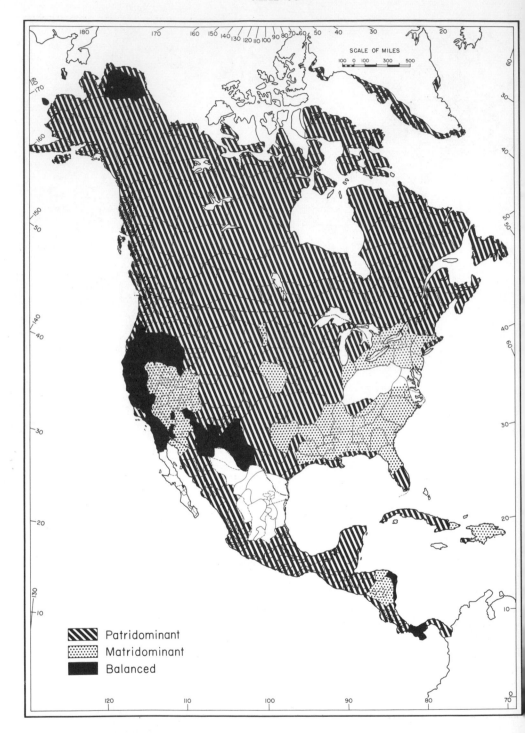

Patridominant

Matridominant

Balanced

SEXUAL DOMINANCE IN SUBSISTENCE PURSUITS. Driver and Massey

MAP 37

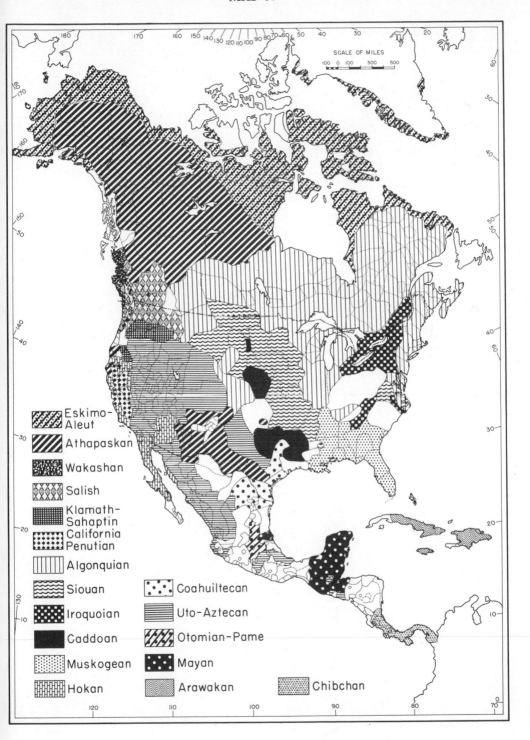

SCALE OF MILES
100 0 100   300   500

Eskimo-
Aleut

Athapaskan

Wakashan

Salish

Klamath-
Sahaptin

California
Penutian

Algonquian

Siouan   Coahuiltecan

Iroquoian   Uto-Aztecan

Caddoan   Otomian-Pame

Muskogean   Mayan

Hokan   Arawakan   Chibchan

LANGUAGE FAMILIES

BIBLIOGRAPHY

ABERLE, DAVID F., and STEWART, OMER C. 1957. *Navaho and Ute Peyotism.* Boulder: University of Colorado "Series in Anthropology," No. 6.

ACOSTA SAIGNES, MIGUEL. 1945. "Los Pocheta," *Acta Antropológica*, I, No. 1, 1–55. Mexico, D.F.

AGUILAR, C. H. 1946. "La Orfebrería en el México Precortesiano," *Acta Antropológica*, II, No. 2, 1–140. Mexico, D.F.

AGUIRRE BELTRÁN, GONZALO, and POZAS A., RICARDO. 1954. "Instituciones Indígenas en el México Actual," in *Metodos y Resultados de la Política Indigenista en México*, ed. ALFONSO CASO, pp. 171–87. Mexico, D.F.

ALEXANDER, H. B. 1939. "The Horse in American Indian Culture," in *So Live the Works of Men*, ed. DONALD BRAND and F. E. HARVEY, pp. 65–74. Albuquerque, N.M.

AMES, O. 1939. *Economic Annuals and Human Cultures.* Cambridge, Mass.: Botanical Museum, Harvard University.

AMSDEN, CHARLES. 1932. "The Loom and Its Prototypes," *American Anthropologist*, XXXIV, 216–35.

ANDERSON, EDGAR. 1952. *Plants, Man and Life.* Boston.

ARISS, ROBERT. 1939. "Distribution of Smoking Pipes in the Pueblo Area," *New Mexico Anthropologist*, III, 53–57.

ARMILLAS, P. 1949. "Notas sobre Sistemas de Cultivo en Meso-America," *Anales del Instituto Nacional de Antropología e Historia*, III, 85–113.

ARREOLA, J. M. 1920. "El Temezcal o Baño Mexicano de Vapor," *Ethnos*, I, No. 2, 28–33.

BANDELIER, ADOLPH F. 1877. "On the Art of War and Mode of Warfare of the Ancient Mexicans," Peabody Museum *Annual Report*, II, 95–161.

BARNETT, HOMER G. 1938. "The Nature of the Potlatch," *American Anthropologist*, XL, 349–58.

———. 1957. *Indian Shakers.* Carbondale, Ill.

BARTLETT, KATHERINE. 1933. *Pueblo Milling Stones of the Flagstaff Region and Their Relation to Others in the Southwest.* Flagstaff: Museum of Northern Arizona, *Bulletin 3*.

———. 1936. "The Utilization of Maize among the Ancient Pueblos," University of New Mexico *Bulletin 296*, pp. 29–34; "Anthropological Series," Vol. I, No. 5. Albuquerque, N.M.

BARTRAM, WILLIAM. 1853. "Observations on the Creek and Cherokee Indians," *Transactions of the American Ethnological Society*, Vol. III, Part I, pp. 1–81.

613

BEAGLEHOLE, ERNEST. 1937. *Notes on Hopi Economic Life.* New Haven: Yale University "Publications in Anthropology," No. 15.

BEALS, RALPH L. 1932a. *The Comparative Ethnology of Northern Mexico.* "Ibero-Americana," No. 2.

———. 1932b. "Unilateral Organization in Mexico," *American Anthropologist,* XXXIV, 467–75.

———. 1943. *The Aboriginal Culture of the Cáhita Indians.* "Ibero-Americana," No. 19.

BEALS, RALPH L.; CARRASCO, PEDRO; and McCORKLE, THOMAS. 1944. *Houses and House Use of the Sierra Tarascans.* Washington: Smithsonian Institution, *Institute of Social Anthropology,* No. 1.

BELL, WILLIS H., and CASTETTER, EDWARD F. 1937. *The Utilization of Mesquite and Screwbean by the Aborigines in the American Southwest.* Albuquerque: University of New Mexico *Bulletin,* "Biological Series," Vol. V, No. 2.

BENEDICT, RUTH. 1932. "Configurations of Culture in North America," *American Anthropologist,* XXXIV, 1–27.

———. 1934. *Patterns of Culture.* New York.

BENNETT, JOHN W. 1946. "The Interpretation of Pueblo Culture: A Question of Values," *Southwestern Journal of Anthropology,* II, 361–74.

BENNETT, WENDELL C., and BIRD, JUNIUS. 1949. *Andean Culture History.* New York: American Museum of Natural History, "Handbook Series," No. 15.

BENNETT, WENDELL C., and ZINGG, ROBERT M. 1935. *The Tarahumara: An Inland Tribe of Northern Mexico.* Chicago.

BIRKET-SMITH, KAJ. 1929. *The Caribou Eskimos:* II, *Analytical Part. Report of the Fifth Thule Expedition, 1921–24,* Vol. V, Part II. Copenhagen.

———. 1936. *The Eskimos.* New York.

———. 1945. *Ethnological Collection from the Northwest Passage. Report of the Fifth Thule Expedition, 1921–24,* VI, 218–88. Copenhagen.

———. 1953. *The Chugach Eskimo.* Nationalmusetts Skrifter Etnografish Raekke, VI. Copenhagen.

BIRKET-SMITH, KAJ, and LAGUNA, FREDERICA DE. 1938. *The Eyak Indians of the Copper River Delta.* Copenhagen.

BOAS, FRANZ. 1897. *The Social Organization and Secret Societies of the Kwakiutl Indians, Based on Personal Observations and Notes Made by George Hunt.* U.S. National Museum *Report* for 1895.

BONNERJEA, B. 1934. "Hunting Superstitions of the American Aborigines," *International Congress of Americanists,* XXXII, 167–84.

BRANT, CHARLES S. 1950. "Peyotism among the Kiowa-Apache and Neighboring Tribes," *Southwestern Journal of Anthropology,* VI, 212–22.

BROWN, W. L., and ANDERSON, EDGAR. 1947. "The Northern Flint Corns," *Annals of the Missouri Botanical Garden,* XXXIV, 1–28.

———. 1948. "The Southern Dent Corns," *Annals of the Missouri Botanical Garden,* XXXV, 255–68.

BRUMAN, H. J. MS. "Aboriginal Drink Areas in New Spain." Ph.D. dissertation, University of California, Berkeley.

BUSHNELL, DAVID I. 1908. "Ethnographic Material from North America in Swiss Collections," *American Anthropologist,* X, 1–15.

————. 1919. *Native Villages and Village Sites East of the Mississippi.* Washington: Bureau of American Ethnology, *Bulletin 69.*

————. 1922. *Villages of the Algonquian, Siouan, and Caddoan Tribes West of the Mississippi.* Washington: Bureau of American Ethnology, *Bulletin 77.*

CALDWELL, JOSEPH R. 1958. *Trend and Tradition in the Prehistory of the Eastern United States.* American Anthropological Association *Memoirs,* No. 88.

CANNON, WALTER B. 1942. "Voodoo Death," *American Anthropologist,* XLIV, 169–81.

CARR, L. 1897. "Dress and Ornaments of Certain American Indians," *Proceedings of the American Antiquarian Society,* N.S., XI, 381–454.

CARR, LLOYD G. 1947. "Native Drinks in the Southeast and Their Values, with Special Emphasis on Persimmon Beer," *Proceedings of the Delaware County Institute of Science,* X, 29–43.

CARTER, GEORGE F. 1945. *Plant Geography and Culture History in the American Southwest.* Viking Fund *Publications in Anthropology,* No. 5.

————. 1950. "Plant Evidence for Early Contacts with America," *Southwestern Journal of Anthropology,* VI, 161–82.

————. 1957. *Pleistocene Man at San Diego.* Baltimore, Md.

CARTER, GEORGE F., and ANDERSON, EDGAR. 1945. "A Preliminary Survey of Maize in the Southwestern United States," *Annals of the Missouri Botanical Garden,* XXXII, 297–322.

CASTETTER, EDWARD F. 1935. *Uncultivated Native Plants Used as Sources of Food.* Albuquerque: University of New Mexico *Bulletin,* "Biological Series," Vol. IV, No. 1.

————. 1943. "Early Tobacco Utilization and Cultivation in the American Southwest," *American Anthropologist,* XLV, 320–25.

CASTETTER, EDWARD F., and BELL, WILLIS. 1937a. *The Utilization of Mesquite and Screwbean by the Aborigines in the America Southwest.* Albuquerque: University of New Mexico *Bulletin,* "Biological Series," Vol. V, No. 2.

————. 1937b. *The Aboriginal Utilization of the Tall Cacti in the American Southwest.* Albuquerque: University of New Mexico *Bulletin,* "Biological Series," Vol. V, No. 1.

————. 1938. *The Early Utilization and Distribution of Agave in the American Southwest.* Albuquerque: University of New Mexico *Bulletin,* "Biological Series," Vol. V, No. 4.

————. 1942. *Pima and Papago Indian Agriculture.* Albuquerque: University of New Mexico, "Inter-American Studies," No. 1.

————. 1951. *Yuman Indian Agriculture.* Albuquerque, N.M.

CASTETTER, EDWARD F., and OPLER, MORRIS E. 1936. *The Ethnobiology of the Chiricahua and Mescalero Apache.* Albuquerque: University of New Mexico *Bulletin,* "Biological Series," Vol. IV, No. 5.

CATLIN, GEORGE. 1841. *Letters and Notes on the Manners, Customs, and Conditions of the North American Indians.* New York.

CHAMPLAIN, SAMUEL DE. 1619. *Voyages,* BIGGAR ed., III, 1–230.

CHARD, CHESTER S. 1950. "Pre-Columbian Trade between North and South America," *Kroeber Anthropological Society Papers,* No. 1, 1–27.

CHASE, GILBERT. 1955. *America's Music from the Pilgrims to the Present.* New York.

CLAVIGERO, FRANCISCO J. 1945. *Historia Antigua de México,* Vol. II. Mexico, D.F.

CODERE, HELEN. 1951. *Fighting with Property. Monographs of the American Ethnological Society,* No. 18.

———. 1956. "The Amiable Side of Kwakiutl Life: The Potlatch and the Play Potlatch," *American Anthropologist,* LVIII, 334–51.

———. 1957. "Kwakiutl Society: Rank without Class," *American Anthropologist,* LIX, 473–86.

COLTON, H. S. 1941. "Prehistoric Trade in the Southwest," *Scientific Monthly,* LII 308–19.

CONN, RICHARD. MS. "A Classification of Aboriginal North American Clothing." M.A. thesis, University of Washington.

COOK, SHERBURNE F. 1946. "Human Sacrifice and Warfare as Factors in the Demography of Pre-Colonial Mexico," *Human Biology,* XVIII, 81–102.

———. 1954. "The Epidemic of 1830–1833 in California and Oregon," University of California *Publications in American Archaeology and Ethnology,* XLIII, 303–26.

———. 1955. "The Aboriginal Population of the San Joaquin Valley, California," University of California *Anthropological Records,* XVI, 31–78.

COOK, SHERBURNE F., and SIMPSON, LESLEY B. 1948. *The Population of Central Mexico in the Sixteenth Century.* "Ibero-Americana," No. 31.

COOPER, JOHN M. 1938. *Snares, Deadfalls, and Other Traps of the Northern Algonquians and Northern Athapaskans,* Catholic University of America "Anthropological Series," No. 5.

———. 1939. "Is the Algonquian Family Hunting Ground System Pre-Columbian?" *American Anthropologist,* XLI, 66–90.

COVARRUBIAS, MIGUEL. 1954. *The Eagle, the Jaguar, and the Serpent: Indian Art of the Americas.* New York.

COVEY, CYCLONE. 1948. "Of Music, and of America Singing," *Seeds of Liberty,* by MAX SAVELLE, 490–552. New York.

CRANE, H. R., and GRIFFIN, JAMES B. 1958. "University of Michigan Radiocarbon Dates II," *Science,* CXXVII, 1098–1105.

CRESSON, F. M., JR. 1938. "Maya and Mexican Sweat Houses," *American Anthropologist,* XL, 88–104.

CROOK, WILSON W., and HARRIS, R. K. 1958. "A Pleistocene Campsite near Lewisville, Texas," *American Antiquity,* XXIII, 233–46.

CUSHING, FRANK H. 1894. "Primitive Copper Working," *American Anthropologist,* VII, 93–117.

DAHLGREN DE JORDAN, BARBRO. 1954. *La Mixteca, su Cultura e Historia Prehispánicas.* Mexico, Colección Cultura Mexicana.

DAIFUKU, HIROSHI. 1952. "The Pit House in the Old World and in Native North America," *American Antiquity,* XVIII, 1–6.

DAVIDSON, D. S. 1935. "Knotless Netting in America and Oceania," *American Anthropologist,* XXXVII, 117–34.

DAWSON, WARREN. 1929. *The Custom of Couvade. Publications of the University of Manchester,* No. 194, "Ethnological Series," No. 4,

DEMBO, A., and IMBELLONI, J. 1938. *Deformaciones Intencionales*. Buenos Aires.

DENHARDT, ROBERT M. 1948. *The Horse of the Americas*. Norman, Okla.

DENSMORE, FRANCES. 1926. *The American Indians and Their Music*. New York.

———. 1929. *Chippewa Customs*. Washington: Bureau of American Ethnology, *Bulletin 86*.

DEVEREUX, GEORGE. 1951. *Reality and Dreams: Psychotherapy of a Plains Indian*. New York.

———. 1955. *A Study of Abortion in Primitive Societies*. New York.

DIENES, ANDRE DE. 1947. "Costumes of the Southwest Indians," *Natural History*, LVI, 360–67.

DINGWALL, E. J. 1931. *Artificial Cranial Deformation*. London.

DORSEY, J. OWEN. 1897. "Siouan Sociology." *Annual Report of the Bureau of American Ethnology*, No. 15, 213–44.

DOUGLAS, FREDERICK H. 1932. *New England Houses, Forts and Villages: Colonial Period*. Denver Art Museum "Indian Leaflet Series," No. 39.

DOUGLAS, FREDERICK H., and D'HARNONCOURT, RENÉ. 1941. *Indian Art of the United States*. New York.

DRIVER, HAROLD E. 1936. "Wappo Ethnography." University of California *Publications in American Archaeology and Ethnology*, XXXVI, 179–220.

———. 1941. "Girls' Puberty Rites in Western North America." University of California *Anthropological Records*, VI, 21–90.

———. 1953*a*. "The Acorn in North American Indian Diet," *Proceedings of the Indiana Academy of Science*, LXII, 56–62.

———. 1953*b*. "The Spatial and Temporal Distribution of the Musical Rasp in the New World," *Anthropos*, XLVIII, 578–92.

DRIVER, HAROLD E., and MASSEY, WM. C. 1957. *Comparative Studies of North American Indians*. "Transactions of the American Philosophical Society," XLVII, 165–456.

DRIVER, HAROLD E., and RIESENBERG, SAUL H. 1950. *Hoof Rattles and Girls' Puberty Rites in North and South America*. Indiana University *Publications in Anthropology and Linguistics*, Memoir 4.

DRIVER, HAROLD E. and WILHELMINE. MS. "Ethnography and Acculturation of the Chichimeca-Jonaz of Central Mexico."

DRUCKER, PHILIP. 1939. "Rank, Wealth, and Kinship in Northwest Coast Society," *American Anthropologist*, XLI, 55–65.

———. 1940. "Kwakiutl Dancing Societies," University of California *Anthropological Records*, II, 201–30.

———. 1955. *Indians of the Northwest Coast*. New York.

EDMONSON, MUNRO S. 1958. *Status Terminology and the Social Structure of the North American Indians*. American Ethnological Society, Seattle.

EGGAN, DOROTHY. 1943. "The General Problem of Hopi Adjustment," *American Anthropologist*, XLV, 357–73.

EGGAN, FRED. 1937. "Historical Changes in the Choctaw Kinship System," *American Anthropologist*, XXXIX, 34–52.

———. 1950. *Social Organization of the Western Pueblos*. Chicago.

EGGAN, FRED. 1955. "Social Anthropology: Methods and Results," in FRED EGGAN (ed.), *Social Anthropology of the North American Tribes*, 485–551. Chicago.

EINZIG, PAUL. 1948. *Primitive Money in Its Ethnological, Historical, and Economic Aspects.* London.

ELLIS, FLORENCE HAWLEY. 1951. "Patterns of Aggression and the War Cult in Southwestern Pueblos," *Southwestern Journal of Anthropology*, VII, 177–201.

ELMORE, FRANCIS H. 1944. *Ethnobotany of the Navaho.* "Monographs of the School of American Research," No. 8. Santa Fe, N.M.

EMMART, EMILY W. 1940. *The Badianus Manuscript.* Baltimore.

EWERS, JOHN C. 1939. *Plains Indian Painting.* New York.

———. 1955*a*. "The Bear Cult among the Assiniboin and Their Neighbors of the Northern Plains," *Southwestern Journal of Anthropology*, XI, 1–14.

———. 1955*b*. *The Horse in Blackfoot Indian Culture.* Bureau of American Ethnology, *Bulletin 159.*

FAIRBANKS, C. H. 1946. "The Macon Earth Lodge," *American Antiquity*, XII, 94–108.

FARABEE, W. C. 1921. "Dress among the Plains Indian Women," University of Pennsylvania Museum *Journal*, XII, 239–51.

FARMER, MALCOLM F. 1957. "A Suggested Typology for Defensive Systems of the Southwest," *Journal of Anthropology*, XIII, 249–67.

FENTON, WM. N. 1936. "An Outline of Seneca Ceremonies at Coldspring Longhouse," Yale University *Publications in Anthropology*, No. 9, 1–23.

———. 1941*a*. *Iroquois Suicide: A Study in the Stability of a Culture Pattern.* Bureau of American Ethnology, *Bulletin 128*, 79–137.

———. 1941*b*. "Masked Medicine Societies of the Iroquois," *Smithsonian Report for 1940*, 397–430.

———. 1942. "Contacts between Iroquois Herbalism and Colonial Medicine," *Smithsonian Report for 1941*, 503–26.

———. 1948. "The Present Status of Anthropology in Northeastern America," *American Anthropologist*, L, 494–513.

———. 1953. *The Iroquois Eagle Dance, an Offshoot of the Calumet Dance.* Bureau of American Ethnology, *Bulletin 156.*

FEWKES, VLADIMIR J. 1944. "Catawba Pottery Making," *Proceedings of the American Philosophical Society*, LXXXVIII, 69–124.

FISHER, R. G. 1939. "An Outline of Pueblo Government," in *So Live the Works of Men*, eds. D. D. BRAND and F. E. HARVEY, 147–57, Albuquerque, N.M.

FLANNERY, REGINA. 1939. *An Analysis of Coastal Algonquian Culture.* Catholic University of America "Anthropological Series," No. 7.

———. 1946. "The Culture of the Northeastern Indian Hunters: A Descriptive Survey," in *Man in Northeastern North America*, FREDERICK JOHNSON (ed.), *Papers of the Robert S. Peabody Foundation for Archaeology*, III, 263–71.

FOSTER, GEORGE M. 1948. "Some Implications of Modern Mexican Mold-made Pottery," *Southwestern Journal of Anthropology*, IV, 356–70.

———. 1949. "Sierra Popoluca Kinship Terminology and Its Wider Relationships," *Southwestern Journal of Anthropology*, V, 330–44.

———. 1955. *Contemporary Pottery Techniques in Southern and Central Mexico.* Tulane University Middle American Research Institute, No. 22.

———. 1959. "The Coyotepec *Molde* and Some Associated Problems," *Southwestern Journal of Anthropology,* XV, 53–63.

———. 1960. *Culture and Conquest: America's Spanish Heritage.* Viking Fund Publications in Anthropology, No. 27.

GAYTON, ANN H. 1930. "Yokuts-Mono Chiefs and Shamans," University of California *Publications in American Archaeology and Ethnology,* XXIV, 361–420.

———. 1945. "Yokuts and Western Mono Social Organization," *American Anthropologist,* XLVII, 409–26.

———. MS. "The Narcotic Plant Datura in Aboriginal American Culture." Ph.D. dissertation, University of California, Berkeley.

GIFFEN, NAOMI M. 1930. *The Roles of Men and Women in Eskimo Culture.* University of Chicago Publications in Anthropology, "Ethnological Series."

GIFFORD, EDWARD W. 1916. "Miwok Moieties," University of California *Publications in American Archaeology and Ethnology,* XII, 139–94.

———. 1926. "Miwok Lineages and the Political Unit in Aboriginal California," *American Anthropologist,* XXVIII, 389–401.

———. 1928. "Pottery-making in the Southwest," University of California *Publications in American Archaeology and Ethnology,* XXIII, 353–73.

———. 1932. "The Southeastern Yavapai." University of California *Publications in American Archaeology and Ethnology,* XXIX, 177–252.

———. 1936. "Northeastern and Western Yavapai," University of California *Publications in American Archaeology and Ethnology,* XXXIV, 247–354.

———. 1944. "Miwok Lineages," *American Anthropologist,* XLVI, 376–81.

GODDARD, PLINY E. 1945. *Indians of the Northwest Coast.* New York.

GOGGIN, JOHN M. 1949. "Plaited Basketry in the New World," *Southwestern Journal of Anthropology,* V, 165–68.

GOLDFRANK, ESTHER S. 1943. "Historic Change and Social Character, a Study of the Teton Dakota," *American Anthropologist,* XLV, 67–83.

———. 1945a. "Socialization, Personality, and the Structure of Pueblo Society," *American Anthropologist,* XLVII, 516–39.

———. 1945b. *Changing Configurations in the Social Organization of a Blackfoot Tribe during the Reserve Period.* American Ethnological Society Monographs, No. 8.

GOLDMAN, IRVING. 1941. "Alkatcho Carrier: Historical Background of Crest Prerogatives," *American Anthropologist,* XLIII, 396–418.

GOLDSCHMIDT, WALTER R. 1948. "Social Organization in Native California and the Origin of Clans," *American Anthropologist,* L, 444–56.

GOLDSCHMIDT, WALTER R., and HASS, THEODORE H. 1946. *Possessory Rights of the Natives of Southeastern Alaska. Report of the Commissioner of Indian Affairs,* Washington.

GOODRICH, L. CARRINGTON. 1959. *A Short History of the Chinese People.* 3d ed. New York.

GOODWIN, GRENVILLE. 1942. *The Social Organization of the Western Apache.* Chicago.

619

GRIFFIN, JAMES B. 1935. "Aboriginal Methods of Pottery Manufacture in the Eastern United States," *Pennsylvania Archaeologist*, V, 19–24.
———. (ed.). 1952. *Archaeology of Eastern United States.* Chicago.
GRIFFIN, JAMES B., and KRIEGER, ALEX D. 1947. "Notes on Some Ceramic Techniques and Intrusions in Central Mexico," *American Antiquity*, XII, 156–68.
GUERRA, F., and OLIVERA, H. 1954. *Las Plantas Fantásticas de México.* Mexico, D.F.
GUNTHER, ERNA. 1928. "A Further Analysis of the First Salmon Ceremony," University of Washington *Publications in Anthropology*, II, 129–73.
———. 1945. "Ethnobotany of Western Washington," University of Washington *Publications in Anthropology*, X, 1–61.
HAAG, W. G. 1948. *An Osteometric Analysis of Some Aboriginal Dogs.* University of Kentucky *Reports in Anthropology*, Vol. VII, No. 3.
HADLOCK, WENDEL S. 1947. "Warfare among the Northeastern Woodland Indians," *American Anthropologist*, XLV, 204–21.
HAINES, FRANCIS. 1938a. "Where Did the Plains Indians Get Their Horses?" *American Anthropologist*, XL, 112–17.
———. 1938b. "The Northward Spread of Horses among the Plains Indians," *American Anthropologist*, XL, 429–37.
HALLOWELL, A. IRVING. 1926. "Bear Ceremonialism in the Northern Hemisphere," *American Anthropologist*, XXVIII, 1–175.
———. 1937. "Cross-cousin Marriage in the Lake Winnipeg Area," *Publications of the Philadelphia Anthropological Society*, I, 95–110.
———. 1949. "The Size of Algonkin Hunting Territories," *American Anthropologist*, LI, 35–45.
———. 1955. *Culture and Experience.* Philadelphia.
———. 1957. "The Impact of the American Indian on American Culture," *American Anthropologist*, LIX, 201–17.
HARRIS, BARBARA D. MS a. "Social Organization of the Western Eskimo and Aleut." M.A. thesis, Indiana University.
———. MS b. "Economy of the Western Eskimo."
HATT, GUDMUND. 1916. "Moccasins and Their Relation to Arctic Footwear," American Anthropological Association *Memoirs*, No. 3, 149–250.
HAURY, EMIL W. 1947. "A Large Pre-Columbian Copper Bell from the Southwest," *American Antiquity*, XIII, 80–82.
HAWLEY, E. E., and GARDEN, G. 1941. *The Art and Science of Nutrition.* St. Louis.
HEISER, CHARLES B., JR. 1951. "The Sunflower among the North American Indians," *Proceedings of the American Philosophical Society*, XC, 432–48.
HEIZER, ROBERT F. 1940. "The Botanical Identification of Northwest Coast Tobacco," *American Anthropologist*, XLII, 704–6.
———. 1953. *Aboriginal Fish Poisons.* Bureau of American Ethnology, *Bulletin 151*, pp. 225–84.
HERSKOVITS, MELVILLE J. 1948. *Man and His Works.* New York.
———. 1952. *Economic Anthropology.* New York.
HERZOG, GEORGE. 1928a. "Musical Styles in North America," *Proceedings of the Twenty-third International Congress of Americanists*, 455–58.

620

——. 1928*b*. "The Yuman Musical Style," *Journal of American Folklore,* XLI, 183–231.

——. 1934. "Speech-Melody and Primitive Music," *Musical Quarterly,* XX, 452–66.

——. 1935*a*. "Plains Ghost Dance and Great Basin Music," *American Anthropologist,* XXXVII, 403–19.

——. 1935*b*. "Special Song Types in North American Indian Music," *Zeitschrift für Vergleichende Musikwissenschaft,* III 23–33.

——. 1936. *Materials and Resources in Folk and Primitive Music in the U.S.A.* American Council of Learned Societies, *Bulletin 25.*

——. 1938. "A Comparison of Pueblo and Pima Musical Styles," *Journal of American Folklore,* XLIX, 283–417.

——. 1949. "Salish Music," in SMITH, MARIAN E. (ed.), *Indians of the Urban Northwest,* 93–110. New York.

HICKERSON, NANCY P. MS. "The Institution of Slavery in Societies of Northwestern North America." M.A. thesis, Indiana University.

HILL, W. W. 1938. *The Agriculture and Hunting Methods of the Navaho Indians.* Yale University *Publications in Anthropology,* XVIII, 1–194.

HIND, H. Y. 1863. *Explorations in the Labrador Peninsula.* 2 vols. London.

HO, PING-TI. 1955. "The Introduction of American Food Plants into China," *American Anthropologist,* LVII, 191–201.

HOEBEL, E. ADAMSON. 1939. "Comanche and Hekandika Shoshoni Relationship Systems," *American Anthropologist,* XLI, 440–57.

——. 1940. *The Political Organization and Law-ways of the Comanche Indians.* American Anthropological Association *Memoirs,* No. 54.

——. 1941. "Law-ways of the Primitive Eskimos," *Journal of Criminal Law and Criminology,* XXXI, 663–83.

——. 1958. *Man in the Primitive World.* New York.

HOFFMAN, WALTER J. 1891. "The Midewiwin or Grand Medicine Society of the Ojibwa," Bureau of American Ethnology *Annual Report for 1885–1886,* 143–300.

——. 1897. "The Graphic Art of the Eskimos," *Report of the United States National Museum for 1895,* 739–968.

HOIJER, HARRY (ed.). 1954. *Language in Culture.* American Anthropological Association *Memoirs,* No. 79.

——. 1956*a*. "The Chronology of the Athapaskan Languages," *International Journal of American Linguistics,* XXII, 219–32.

——. 1956*b*. "Athapaskan Kinship Systems," *American Anthropologist,* LVIII, 309–33.

HONIGMAN, JOHN J. 1946. *Ethnography and Acculturation of Fort Nelson Slave.* Yale University *Publications in Anthropology,* No. 33.

——. 1949. *Culture and Ethos of Kaska Society.* Yale University *Publications in Anthropology,* No. 40.

——. 1954. *Culture and Personality.* New York

HOWARD, JAMES H. 1957. "The Mescal Bean Cult of the Central and Southern Plains," *American Anthropologist,* LIX, 75–87.

HUNT, GEORGE T. 1940. *The Wars of the Iroquois.* Madison, Wis.

HUNT, WALTER BERNARD. 1951. *American Indian Beadwork.* Milwaukee, Wis.

HUNTER, H. V. 1940. *The Ethnography of Salt in Aboriginal North America.* Philadelphia.

HYMES, DELL H. 1957. "A Note on Athapaskan Glottochronology," *International Journal of American Linguistics*, XXIII, 291–97.

———. 1959. "Genetic Classification: Retrospect and Prospect," *Anthropological Linguistics*, I, 50–66.

———. 1960. "Lexicostatistics So Far," *Current Anthropology*, I, 3–44.

INVERARITY, ROBERT BRUCE. 1950. *Art of the Northwest Coast Indians.* Berkeley and Los Angeles.

IZIKOWITZ, KARL G. 1935. *Musical and other Sound Instruments of the South American Indians.* Göteborg.

JABLOW, JOSEPH. 1951. *The Cheyenne in Plains Indian Trade Relations, 1795–1840. Monographs of the American Ethnological Society*, No. 19.

JACOBSON, OSCAR B. 1952. *North American Indian Costumes.* Nice, France.

JAEGER, E. C. 1940. *Desert Wild Flowers.* Stanford.

JENNESS, DIAMOND. 1932. *Indians of Canada. Bulletin of the Canada Department of Mines*, No. 65, National Museum of Canada, Ottawa.

JENNINGS, JESSE D. 1957. *Danger Cave. Memoirs of the Society for American Archaeology*, No. 4.

JOHNSON, IRMGARD WEITLANER. 1953. "El Quechquemitl y el Huipil," in *Huastecos, Totonacos y sus Vecinos*, IGNACIO BERNAL and EUSEBIO DÁVALOS HURTADO (eds.). Mexico, D.F.

JOHNSON, JEAN B. 1939*a.* "Some Notes on the Mazatec," *Revista Mexicana de Estudios Antropológicos*, III, 142–56.

———. 1939*b.* "The Elements of Mazatec Witchcraft," *Ethnological Studies*, IX, 128–50.

JONES, VOLNEY H. 1944. "Was Tobacco Smoked in the Pueblo Region in Pre-Spanish Times?" *American Antiquity*, IX, 451–56.

———. 1949. "Magic from the Davis Site: Its Nature and Interpretation," in *The George C. Davis Site, Cherokee County, Texas*, by H. NEWELL and ALEX KRIEGER, *Memoirs of the Society of American Archaeology*, Vol. XIV, No. 4.

JUDD, NEIL M. 1948. "Pyramids of the New World," *National Geographic Magazine*, XCIII, 105–28.

JUEL, E. 1945. "Notes on Seal-hunting Ceremonialism in the Arctic," *Ethnos*, X, 143–64.

JUNG, CARL G. 1928. *Contributions to Analytical Psychology.* London.

KELEMEN, PÁL. 1956. *Medieval American Art.* New York.

KELLEY, ISABEL. 1943. "West Mexico and the Hohokam," in *El Norte de México y El Sur de los Estados Unidos*, 206–22. Mexico, D.F.

KELLY, WM. H. 1942. "Cocopa Gentes," *American Anthropologist*, XLIV, 675–91.

KENT, KATE P. 1957. *The Cultivation and Weaving of Cotton in the Prehistoric Southwestern United States.* "Transactions of the American Philosophical Society," XLVII, 457–732.

KING, ARDEN R. MS. "Aboriginal Skin Dressing in Western North America." Ph.D. dissertation, University of California, Berkeley.

KINIETZ, VERNON. 1940. "Notes on the Roached Headdress of Animal Hair among the North American Indians," *Papers of the Michigan Academy of Science, Arts, and Letters,* XXVI, 463–67.

KLUCKHOHN, CLYDE. 1944. *Navaho Witchcraft.* Harvard University *Papers of the Peabody Museum of American Archaeology and Ethnology,* XXII, 1–149.

KNOWLES, NATHANIEL. 1940. "The Torture of Captives by the Indians of North America," *Proceedings of the American Philosophical Society,* LXXXII, 151–225.

KRICKEBERG, W. 1939. "The Indian Sweatbath," *Ciba Symposia,* I, 19–35.

KRIEGER, ALEX D. and GRIFFIN, JAMES B. 1947. "Notes on Some Ceramic Techniques and Intrusions in Central Mexico," *American Antiquity,* XII, 156–68.

KRIEGER, H. W. 1929. "American Indian Costumes in the United States National Museum," *Annual Report of the Smithsonian Institution for 1928,* 623–61.

KROEBER, ALFRED L. 1925. *Handbook of the Indians of California.* Bureau of American Ethnology, *Bulletin 78.*

——. 1928. "Native Culture of the Southwest," University of California *Publications in American Archaeology and Ethnology,* XXIII, 375–98.

——. 1932. "The Patwin and Their Neighbors," University of California *Publications in American Archaeology and Ethnology,* XXIX, 253–364.

——. (ed.) 1935. *Walapai Ethnography. Memoirs of the American Anthropological Association,* No. 42.

——. 1937. "Athabascan Kin Term Systems," *American Anthropologist,* XXXIX, 602–9.

——. 1939. *Cultural and Natural Areas of Native North America.* University of California *Publications in American Archaeology and Ethnology,* XXXVIII.

——. 1940. "Stimulus Diffusion," *American Anthropologist,* XLII, 1–20.

——. 1941. "Salt, Dogs, and Tobacco," University of California *Anthropological Records,* VI, 1–20.

——. 1948. *Anthropology.* New York.

——. 1955. "Nature of the Land-holding Group," *Ethnohistory,* II, 303–14.

LABARRE, WESTON. 1938a. "Native American Beers," *American Anthropologist,* XL, 224–34.

——. 1938b. *The Peyote Cult.* Yale University *Publications in Anthropology,* XIX, 1–188.

——. 1960. "Twenty Years of Peyote Studies," *Current Anthropology,* I, 45–60.

LAGUNA, FREDERICA DE. 1932–33. "A Comparison of Eskimo and Paleolithic Art," *American Journal of Archaeology,* XXXVI, 477–508; XXXVII, 77–107.

——. 1940. "Eskimo Lamps and Pots," *Journal of the Royal Anthropological Institute of Great Britain and Ireland,* LXX, 53–76.

LAMB, SYDNEY. 1959. "Some Proposals for Linguistic Taxonomy," *Anthropological Linguistics,* I, 33–49.

LANTIS, MARGARET. 1938. "The Alaskan Whale Cult and Its Affinities," *American Anthropologist*, XL, 438–64.

———. 1947. *Alaskan Eskimo Ceremonialism.* "Monographs of the American Ethnological Society," No. 11.

———. 1959. "Alaskan Eskimo Cultural Values," *Polar Notes*, No. 1, pp. 35–48. Dartmouth College, Hanover, N.H.

LAS CASAS, GONZALO DE. 1944 [1574]. *La Guerra de los Chichimecas.* Mexico, D.F.

LASSWELL, HAROLD D. 1935. "Collective Autism as a Consequence of Cultural Contact; Notes on Religious Training and the Peyote Cult at Taos," *Zeitschrift für Social Forschung*, IV, 232–47.

LAWSON, JOHN. 1860. *History of Carolina.* Raleigh, N.C.

LEACOCK, ELEANOR. N.D. *The Montagnais Hunting Territory and the Fur Trade.* American Anthropological Association *Memoirs*, No. 78.

———. 1955. "Matrilocality in a Simple Hunting Economy," *Southwestern Journal of Anthropology*, XI, 31–47.

LEES, ROBERT B. 1953. "The Basis of Glottochronology," *Language*, XXIX, 113–27.

LEONARD, IRVING A. 1942. "Peyote and the Mexican Inquisition," *American Anthropologist*, XLIV, 324–26.

LEWIS, OSCAR. 1941. "Manly-Hearted Women among the North Piegan," *American Anthropologist*, XLIII, 173–87.

———. 1942. *The Effect of White Contact upon Blackfoot Culture.* "Monographs of the American Ethnological Society," No. 6.

———. 1951. *Life in a Mexican Village: Tepoztlán Restudied.* Urbana, Ill.

LIBBY, DOROTHY RAINIER. MS. *Girls' Puberty Observances among Northern Athapaskans.* PhD. dissertation, University of California, Berkeley.

LIBBY, WILLARD F. 1955. *Radiocarbon Dating.* 2d ed. Chicago.

LID, N. 1948. "On the Dual Division of North American Tribes," *Proceedings of the International Congress of Americanists*, Paris, 1947, 277–82.

LINTON, RALPH. 1924a. *Use of Tobacco among North American Indians.* Field Museum of Natural History "Anthropological Leaflets," No. 15.

———. 1924b. "The Origin of the Plains Earth Lodge," *American Anthropologist*, XXVI, 247–57.

———. 1942. "Land Tenure in Aboriginal America," in *Changing Indian*, OLIVER LA FARGE (ed.), pp. 42–54, Norman, Okla.

———. 1944. "North American Cooking Pots," *American Antiquity*, IX, 369–80.

LIPS, JULIUS E. 1947. *Naskapi Law (Lake St. John and Lake Mistassini Bands): Law and Order in a Hunting Society.* "Transactions of the American Philosophical Society," XXXVII, 379–492.

LLEWELLYN, K. N., and HOEBEL, E. ADAMSON. 1941. *The Cheyenne Way.* Norman, Okla.

LOEB, E. M. 1932. "The Western Kuksu Cult." University of California *Publications in American Archaeology and Ethnology*, XXXIII, 1–138.

———. 1933. "The Eastern Kuksu Cult." University of California *Publications in American Archaeology and Ethnology*, XXXIII, 139–232.

LORM, A. J. DE. 1945. *Kunstzin der Eskimós.* The Hague, Holland.

LOTHROP, SAMUEL K. 1952. "Metals from the Cenote of Sacrifice, Chichén Itzá, Yucatan," Harvard University *Memoirs of the Peabody Museum of American Archaeology and Ethnology*, X, No. 2.

LOWIE, ROBERT H. 1916. "Plains Indian Age-Societies," *Anthropological Papers of the American Museum of Natural History*, XI, 877–992.

——. 1920. *Primitive Society*. New York.

——. 1935. *The Crow Indians*. New York.

——. 1940. *An Introduction to Cultural Anthropology*. Rev. ed. New York.

——. 1948. *Social Organization*. New York.

——. 1951. "Some Aspects of Political Organization among the American Aborigines," *Journal of the Royal Anthropological Institute of Great Britain and Ireland*, Vol. LXXVIII, Parts 1–2, 11–24.

——. 1954. *Indians of the Plains*. New York.

McALLESTER, DAVID P. 1954. *Enemy Way Music*. Papers of the Peabody Museum of American Archaeology and Ethnology, Vol. XLI, No. 3.

McCUE, GEORGE A. 1952. "The History of the Use of the Tomato: An Annotated Bibliography," *Annals of the Missouri Botanical Garden*, XXXIX, 289–348.

McGUIRE, J. D. 1897. *Pipes and Smoking Customs of the American Aborigines. Report of the United States National Museum for 1897*, pp. 351–645.

McILLWRAITH, T. F. 1948. *The Bella Coola Indians*. 2 vols. Toronto.

MacLEOD, W. C. 1925. "Certain Mortuary Aspects of Northwest Coast Culture," *American Anthropologist*, XXVII, 122–48.

——. 1926. "Priests, Temples and the Practice of Mummification in S.E. North America," *Proceedings of the International Congress of Americanists*, XXII, 207–30.

——. 1933. "Mortuary and Sacrifical Anthropophagy on the Northwest Coast," *Journal de la Société des Américanistes*, XXV, 335–66.

MacNEISH, RICHARD S. 1955. "Ancient Maize and Mexico," *Archaeology*, VIII, 108–15.

——. 1960. "Agricultural Origins in Middle America and Their Diffusion into North America," *Katunob*, I, No. 2, no pagination.

McQUOWN, NORMAN. 1955. "Indigenous Languages of Native America," *American Anthropologist*, LVII, 501–70 .

——. 1960. "American Indian and General Linguistics," *American Anthropologist*, LXII, 318–26.

MANDELBAUM, DAVID. 1949. *Selected Writings of Edward Sapir*. Berkeley and Los Angeles.

MARQUINA, IGNACIO. 1951. *Architectura Prehispánica*. Mexico, D.F.

MARTIN, PAUL S.; QUIMBY, GEORGE I.; and COLLIER, DONALD. 1947. *Indians before Columbus*. Chicago.

MARTÍNEZ, MAXIMINO. 1936. *Plantas Utiles de México*. Mexico, D.F.

MARTÍNEZ DEL RÍO, P. 1954. "La Comarca Lagunera a Fines del Siglo 16 y Principios del 17 Según las Fuentes Escritas," *Publicaciones del Instituto de Historia*, XXX, 63–98.

MASON, J. ALDEN. 1924. *Use of Tobacco in Mexico and South America*. Field Museum of Natural History "Anthropological Leaflets," No. 16.

625

MASON, J. ALDEN. 1948. "The Tepehuan and other Aborigines of the Mexican Sierra Madre Occidental," *América Indígena*, VIII, No. 4, 289–300.

MASON, OTIS T. 1891. "Aboriginal Skin-dressing," *Report of the United States National Museum for 1889*, pp. 553–89.

———. 1896. "Primitive Travel and Transportation," *Report of the United States National Museum for 1893–94*, pp. 237–593.

———. 1901. "Aboriginal American Harpoons," *Report of the United States National Museum for 1899–1900*, pp. 191–304.

———. 1904. "Aboriginal American Basketry," *Report of the United States National Museum for 1901–2*, pp. 171–548.

MEIGHAN, C. W.; PENDERGAST, D. M.; SWARTZ, B. K.; and WISSLER, M. D. 1958. "Ecological Interpretation in Archaeology," *American Antiquity*, XXIV, 1–23; 131–150.

MENDIETA Y NÚÑEZ, L. L. (ed.). 1949. *Los Zapotecos*. Universidad Nacional Autónoma de México, Mexico, D.F.

MENDIZÁBAL, MIGUEL DE. 1930. "Influencia de la Sal en la Distribución Geográfica de los Grupos Indígenas de México," *Twenty-third International Congress of Americanists*, 1928, pp. 93–100. New York.

———. 1942. "La Evolución de los Culturas Indígenas de México y la División de Trabajo," *Cuadernos Americanos*, I, No. 1, 121–31.

MERA, HARRY P. 1937. *The "Rain Bird": A Study in Pueblo Design*. Laboratory of Anthropology *Memoirs*, No. 2.

———. 1939. *Style Trends of Pueblo Pottery*. Laboratory of Anthropology *Memoirs*, No. 3.

MERRIAM, ALAN P. and BARBARA W. N.D. *Flathead Indian Music*.

MILLER, CARL F. 1950. "Early Cultural Horizons in the Southeastern United States," *American Antiquity*, XV, 273–88.

MILLER, WALTER B. 1955. "Two Concepts of Authority," *American Anthropologist*, LVII, 271–89.

MOONEY, JAMES. 1896. *The Ghost-Dance Religion*. Bureau of American Ethnology, *Annual Report*, XIV, No. 2.

MORGAN, LEWIS H. 1871. *Systems of Consanguinity and Affinity*. Smithsonian Institution *Contributions to Knowledge*, XVII.

———. 1877. *Ancient Society*. Chicago.

———. 1881. *Houses and House-Life of the American Aborigines*. Contributions to North American Ethnology, IV, 1–281.

MORLEY, SYLVANUS G. 1955. "The Maya of Yucatan," in *National Geographic on Indians of the Americas*, 183–216.

MORRIS, EARL H., and BURGH, ROBERT F. 1941. *Anasazi Basketry*. Carnegie Institution of Washington, *Publication 533*.

MÜLLER, WERNER. 1954. *Die Blaue Hütte: zum Sinnbild der Perle bei Nordamerikanischen Indianern*. Studien zur Kulturkunde, No. 12. Wiesbaden, Germany.

MURDOCK, GEORGE P. 1934. *Our Primitive Contemporaries*. New York.

———. 1949. *Social Structure*. New York.

———. 1957. "World Ethnographic Sample," *American Anthropologist*, LIX, 664–87.

NADEAU, GABRIEL. 1944. "Indian Scalping Techniques in Different Tribes," *Ciba Symposia*, V, No. 10, 1677–84.

NELSON, E. W. 1899. *The Eskimo about Bering Strait.* Bureau of American Ethnology, *Annual Report*, XVIII, 3–518.

NETTL, BRUNO. 1954. "North American Indian Musical Styles," *Journal of American Folklore*, LXVII, 45–56, 297–307, 351–68.

NEUMANN, GEORG K. 1940. "Evidence for the Antiquity of Scalping from Central Illinois," *American Antiquity*, V, 287–89.

NEWCOMB, W. W. JR. 1950. "A Re-examination of the Causes of Plains Warfare," *American Anthropologist*, LII, 317–30.

OLSON, RONALD L. 1927. "Adze, Canoe, and House Types of the Northwest Coast," University of Washington *Publications in Anthropology*, II, 1–38.

———. 1933. "Clan and Moiety in Native America," University of California *Publications in American Archaeology and Ethnology*, XXXIII, 351–422.

O'NEALE, LILA M. 1945. *Textiles of Highland Guatemala.* Carnegie Institution of Washington, *Publication 567.*

OPLER, MORRIS E. 1941. *An Apache Life Way.* Chicago.

ORCHARD, W. C. 1929. *Beads and Beadwork of the American Indians.* Heye Foundation *Contributions from Museum of the American Indian*, XI, 3–140.

OSGOOD, CORNELIUS. 1936. *Contributions to the Ethnography of the Kutchin.* Yale University *Publications in Anthropology*, XIV, 1–189.

———. 1937. *The Ethnography of the Tanaina.* Yale University *Publications in Anthropology*, XVI, 1–229.

PARSONS, ELSIE C. 1939. *Pueblo Indian Religion.* 2 vols. Chicago.

PASSIN, HERBERT. 1944. "Some Relationships in Northwest Mexican Kinship Systems," *El México Antiguo*, VI, 205–18.

PAUL, BENJAMIN D. and LOIS. 1952. "Life Cycle," in *Heritage of Conquest*, SOL TAX, ed., Chicago.

PETTITT, GEORGE A. 1946. *Primitive Education in North America.* University of California *Publications in American Archaeology and Ethnology*, XLIII, 1–182.

PIERCE, JOE E. 1957. "A Statistical Study of Consonants in New World Languages," *International Journal of American Linguistics*, XIII, 36–45, 94–108.

POLLOCK, H. E. D. 1936. *Round Structures of Aboriginal Middle America.* Carnegie Institution of Washington, *Publication 471.*

PORTER, MURIEL N. 1948. "Pipas Precortesianas," *Acta Antropológica*, III, No. 2.

POWELL, J. W. 1891. *Indian Linguistic Families North of Mexico.* Bureau of American Ethnology *Annual Report*, VII, 1–142.

POWERS, STEPHEN. 1877. *Tribes of California. Contributions to North American Ethnology*, III. Washington, D.C.

QUIMBY, GEORGE I. 1948. "Culture Contact on the Northwest Coast, 1785–1795," *American Anthropologist*, L, 247–55.

RAY, VERNE F. 1932. *The Sanpoil and Nespelem.* University of Washington *Publications in Anthropology*, V, 1–237.

———. 1939. *Cultural Relations in the Plateau of Northwestern America.* Publications of the Frederick Webb Hodge Anniversary Publication Fund, No. 3. Los Angeles, Southwest Museum.

REICHARD, GLADYS A. 1950. *Navaho Religion.* 2 vols. New York.

627

RICHTER, CURT P. 1957. "On the Phenomenon of Sudden Death in Animals and Man," *Psychosomatic Medicine*, XIX, 191–98.

RICKARD, T. A. 1934. "The Use of Native Copper by the Indigenes of North America," *Journal of the Royal Anthropological Institute of Great Britain and Ireland*, LXIV, 265–87.

RIVET, PAUL, and ARSANDAUX, H. 1946. *La Metallurgie en Amérique Precolombienne. Travaux et mémoires de l'Institut d'Ethnologie*, XXXIX. Musée de l'Homme, Paris.

ROBERTS, HELEN H. 1936. "Musical Areas in Aboriginal North America," Yale University *Publications in Anthropology*, XII, 1–41.

ROE, FRANK G. 1939. "From Dogs to Horses among the Western Indian Tribes," *Proceedings and Transactions of the Royal Society of Canada*, Third Series, Vol. XXXIII, Section 2, pp. 209–75.

———. 1952. *The North American Buffalo*. Toronto.

———. 1955. *The Indian and the Horse*. Norman, Okla.

ROEDIGER, VIRGINIA M. 1941. *Ceremonial Costumes of the Pueblo Indians*. Berkeley and Los Angeles.

ROJAS, G. F. 1942. "Estudio Histórico-etnográfico del Alcoholismo entre los Indios de México," *Revista Mexicana de Sociología*, IV, No. 2, 111–25.

ROSENBLAT, A. 1945. *La Población Indígena de América desde 1492 hasta la Actualidad.* "Cuadernos de la Series Stirps Quaestionis." Institución Cultural Española, Buenos Aires.

ROSTLUND, ERHARD. 1952. *Freshwater Fish and Fishing in Native North America.* University of California *Publications in Geography*, No. 9.

ROUSE, IRVING. 1948. "The Carib," *Handbook of South American Indians*, JULIAN H. STEWARD (ed.), Bureau of American Ethnology, *Bulletin 143*, Vol. IV, pp. 547–65.

ROYS, RALPH L. 1943. *The Indian Background of Colonial Yucatan*. Carnegie Institution of Washington, *Publication 584*.

———. 1957. *The Political Geography of the Yucatan Maya*. Carnegie Institution of Washington, *Publication 613*.

RUPPERT, KARL; THOMPSON, J. ERIC S.; and PROSKOURIAKOFF, TATIANA. 1955. *Bonampak, Chiapas, Mexico*. Carnegie Institution of Washington, *Publication 602*.

SAFFORD, W. E. 1917. "Narcotic Plants and Stimulants of the Ancient Americans," *Annual Report of the Smithsonian Institution for 1916*, 387–424.

SAHAGÚN, FRAY BERNARDINO DE. 1950–58. *Florentine Codex: General History of the Things of New Spain*. Translated from Aztec to English by ARTHUR J. O. ANDERSON and CHARLES E. DIBBLE. Sante Fe and Salt Lake City.

SALAMAN, REDCLIFFE N. 1949. *The History and Social Influence of the Potato*. Cambridge, England.

SALAS, ALBERTO M. 1947. "Armas de la Conquista: Venenos y Gases," *Cuadernos Americanos*, Año 6, Vol. XXXII, pp. 135–52.

SANFORD, TRENT ELWOOD. 1947. *The Story of Architecture in Mexico*. New York.

SANTA MARÍA, FRANCISCO J. 1942. *Diccionario General de Americanismos*. 3 vols. Mexico, D.F.

SAPIR, EDWARD. 1921. *Language*. New York.

SAPPER, CARL. 1924. "Die Zahl und Volksdichte der Indianischen Bevölkerung in Amerika vor der Conquista und in der Gegenwart," *International Congress of Americanists*, Session 21, The Hague, pp. 95–104.

SATTERTHWAITE, LINTON, JR. 1952. *Piedras Negras Archaeology: Architecture: Part V, Sweathouses.* University Museum, University of Pennsylvania.

SAUER, CARL O. 1935. *Aboriginal Population of Northwestern Mexico.* "Ibero-Americana," No. 10.

———. 1939. *Man in Nature.* New York.

———. 1950. "Cultivated Plants of South and Central America," in *Handbook of South American Indians*, Bureau of American Ethnology, *Bulletin 143*, Vol. VI, 487–543.

———. 1952. *Agricultural Origins and Dispersals.* New York.

SAUER, JONATHAN D. 1950. "The Grain Amaranths: A Survey of Their History and Classification," *Annals of the Missouri Botanical Garden*, XXXVII, 561–632.

SAVILLE, MARSHALL H. 1920. *The Goldsmith's Art in Ancient Mexico.* Museum of the American Indian, Heye Foundation, "Indian Notes and Monographs."

SCHAEFER-SIMMERN, HENRY. 1958. *Eskimo-Plastik aus Kanada.* Kassel, Germany.

SCHERY, R. W. 1952. *Plants for Man.* New York.

SCHULTES, R. E. 1940. "Teonanacatl, the Narcotic Mushroom of the Aztecs," *American Anthropologist*, XLII, 429–43.

SECOY, FRANK R. 1953. *Changing Military Patterns on the Great Plains.* American Ethnological Society *Monograph*, No. 21.

SELLARDS, E. H. 1952. *Early Man in America.* Austin, Texas.

SETCHELL, W. A. 1921. "Aboriginal Tobaccos," *American Anthropologist*, XXIII, 397–414.

SHIMKIN, DEMETRI B. 1941. "The Uto-Aztecan Systems of Kinship Terminology," *American Anthropologist*, XLIII, 223–45.

SINCLAIR, A. T. 1909. "Tattooing of the North American Indians," *American Anthropologist*, XI, 362–400.

SLOTKIN, J. S. 1952. *Menomini Peyotism.* "Transactions of the American Philosophical Society," Vol. XLII, Part 4.

———. 1955. "Peyotism, 1521–1891," *American Anthropologist*, LVII, 202–30.

———. 1956. *The Peyote Religion: A Study in Indian-White Relations.* Glencoe, Ill.

SLOTKIN, J. S., and SCHMIDT, KARL. 1949. "Studies of Wampum," *American Anthropologist*, LI, 223–36.

SMITH, A. L. 1940. "The Corbeled Arch in the New World," in *The Mayas and Their Neighbors.* New York.

SMITH, MARIAN W. 1938. "The War Complex of the Plains Indians," *American Philosophical Society Proceedings*, LXXVIII, 425–64.

———. 1951. "American Indian Warfare," *New York Academy of Sciences Transactions*, Ser. 2, Vol. XIII, pp. 348–65.

SNYDERMAN, GEORGE S. 1948. *Behind the Tree of Peace: A Sociological Analysis of Iroquois Warfare.* Pennsylvania Archaeologist, Vol. XVIII, Nos. 3–4.

629

SOLIER, W. DU. 1950. *Indumentaria Antigua Mexicana.* Mexico, D.F.

SOUSTELLE, JACQUES. 1956. *La Vida Cotidiana de los Aztecas en Vísperas de la Conquista.* Mexico, D.F.

SPECK, FRANK G. 1911. "Huron Moose Hair Embroidery," *American Anthropologist,* XIII, 1–14.

———. 1915. *Family Hunting Territories and Social Life of Various Algonkian Bands of the Ottawa Valley.* Canadian Department of Mines, Geological Survey, *Memoir 70,* "Anthropology Series," No. 8.

———. 1917. *The Social Structure of the Northern Algonkian.* American Sociological Society *Proceedings,* N.S. XII, 82–100.

———. 1918. "Kinship Terms and the Family Band among the Northeastern Algonkian," *American Anthropologist,* XX, 143–61.

———. 1919. "The Functions of Wampum among the Eastern Algonkian," American Anthropological Association *Memoirs,* VI, 3–71.

———. 1920a. "Decorative Art and Basketry of the Cherokee." Public Museum of the City of Milwaukee, *Bulletin 2,* pp. 53–86.

———. 1920b. "Correction to Kinship Terms among the Northeastern Algonkian," *American Anthropologist,* XXII, 85.

———. 1928. *Chapters on the Ethnology of the Powhatan Tribes of Virginia.* Museum of the American Indian, Heye Foundation *Indian Notes and Monographs,* I, 225–455.

———. 1931. "Birch-bark in the Ancestry of Pottery Forms," *Anthropos,* XXVI, 407–11.

———. 1935. *Naskapi.* Norman, Okla.

———. 1937. "Analysis of Eskimo and Indian Skin-dressing Methods in Labrador," *Ethnos,* II, 345–53.

———. 1938. "The Question of Matrilineal Descent in the Southeastern Siouan Area," *American Anthropologist,* XL, 1–12.

———. 1945. *The Iroquois, a Study in Cultural Evolution.* Cranbrook Institute of Science, *Bulletin 23.*

SPECK, FRANK G., and EISELEY, LOREN C. 1939. "The Significance of Hunting Territory Systems of the Algonkian in Social Theory," *American Anthropologist,* XLI, 269–80.

SPENCER, ROBERT F. 1959. *The North Alaskan Eskimo.* Bureau of American Ethnology, *Bulletin 171.*

SPIER, LESLIE. 1925. "The Distribution of Kinship Systems in North America," University of Washington *Publications in Anthropology,* I, 69–88.

———. 1928. "Havasupai Ethnography," American Museum of Natural History *Anthropological Papers,* XXIX, 83–392.

SPINDLER, GEORGE D. and LOUISE S. 1957. "American Indian Personality Types and Their Sociocultural Roots," *Annals of the American Academy of Political and Social Science,* CCCXI, 147–57.

SPOEHR, ALEXANDER. 1947. *Changing Kinship Systems.* Field Museum of Natural History, "Anthropological Series," XXXIII, 153–235.

Statistical Yearbook. 1958. United Nations, New York.

STEVENSON, MATILDE COXE. 1904. *The Zuñi Indians: Their Mythology, Esoteric Societies, and Ceremonies.* Bureau of American Ethnology *Annual Report,* XXIII.

STEWARD, JULIAN H. 1938. *Basin-Plateau Aboriginal Sociopolitical Groups.* Bureau of American Ethnology, *Bulletin 120.*

———. (ed.). 1948. *Handbook of South American Indians.* Bureau of American Ethnology, *Bulletin 143,* Vol. IV.

———. 1949. "The Native Population of South America." in *Handbook of South American Indians,* JULIAN H. STEWARD (ed.), Bureau of American Ethnology, *Bulletin 143,* Vol. V, 655–68.

STEWART, KENNETH M. 1947. "Mohave Warfare," *Southwestern Journal of Anthropology,* III, 257–78.

STEWART, OMER C. 1944. "Washo-Northern Paiute Peyotism," University of California *Publications in American Archaeology and Ethnology,* XL, 63–142.

STRACHEY, WM. 1849. *The Historie of Travaile into Virginia Britannia.* London.

STRONG, WM. D. 1929. "Cross-cousin Marriage and the Culture of the Northeastern Algonkian," *American Anthropologist,* XXXI, 277–88.

SUTTLES, WAYNE. 1958. "Private Knowledge, Morality, and Social Classes among the Coast Salish," *American Anthropologist,* LX, 497–507.

SWADESH, MORRIS. 1959a. "The Mesh Principle in Comparative Linguistics," *Anthropological Linguistics,* I, 7–14.

———. 1959b. *Mapas de Clasificación Lingüística de México y las Américas.* Cuadernos del Instituto de Historia, "Serie Antropológica," No. 8. Universidad Nacional Autónoma de México.

———. 1960. *La Lingüística como Instrumento de la Prehistoria.* Instituto Nacional de Antropología e Historia.

SWANTON, JOHN R. 1909. *Contributions to the Ethnology of the Haida.* American Museum of Natural History *Memoirs,* VIII, 1–300.

———. 1911. *Indian Tribes of the Lower Mississippi Valley and Adjacent Coast of the Gulf of Mexico.* Bureau of American Ethnology, *Bulletin 43.*

———. 1928a. "Religious Beliefs and Medical Practices of the Creek Indians," Bureau of American Ethnology *Annual Report,* XLII, 473–672.

———. 1946. *The Indians of the Southeastern United States.* Bureau of American Ethnology, *Bulletin 137.*

TANNER, CLARA LEE. 1957. *Southwest Indian Painting.* Tucson.

TAX, SOL (ed.). 1952. *Heritage of Conquest.* Chicago.

———. 1953. *Penny Capitalism: A Guatemalan Indian Economy.* Smithsonian Institution, *Institute of Social Anthropology,* No. 16.

THOMPSON, J. ERIC S. 1940. *Mexico before Cortez.* New York.

———. 1954. *The Rise and Fall of Maya Civilization.* Norman, Okla.

THOMPSON, LAURA. 1945. "Logico-Aesthetic Integration in Hopi Culture," *American Anthropologist,* XLVII, 540–53.

———. 1950. *Culture in Crisis: A Study of the Hopi Indians.* New York.

THWAITES, REUBEN G. 1897–1901. *Jesuit Relations and Allied Documents.* 73 vols. Cleveland.

TOOR, FRANCES. 1947. *A Treasury of Mexican Folkways.* New York.

UNDERHILL, RUTH. 1939. *Social Organization of the Papago Indians.* Columbia University *Contributions to Anthropology,* No. 30.

631

UNDERHILL, RUTH. 1948. *Ceremonial Patterns in the Greater Southwest.* "Monographs of the American Ethnological Society," No. 13.
——. N.D. *Workaday Life of the Pueblos.* Washington, D.C.
VAILLANT, GEORGE. 1941. *Aztecs of Mexico.* New York.
VOEGELIN, CARL F. and ERMINIE W. 1944. *Map of North American Indian Languages.* American Ethnological Society, *Publication 20.*
VOEGELIN, ERMINIE WHEELER. 1944. *Mortuary Customs of the Shawnee and Other Eastern Tribes.* Indiana Historical Society, "Prehistory Research Series," II, 227–444.
WALLACE, ANTHONY F. 1952. *The Modal Personality of the Tuscarora Indians: As Revealed by the Rorschach Test.* Bureau of American Ethnology, *Bulletin 150.*
——. 1958. "Dreams and the Wishes of the Soul: A Type of Psychoanalytic Theory among the Seventeenth-Century Iroquois," *American Anthropologist,* LX, 234–48.
WATERMAN, T. T. 1924. "North American Indian Dwellings," *Geographical Review,* XIV, 1–25.
WAUGH, F. W. 1919. "Canadian Aboriginal Canoes," *Canadian Field Naturalist,* XXXIII, 23–33.
WEATHERWAX, PAUL. 1954. *Indian Corn in Old America.* New York.
WELLHAUSEN, E. J.; ROBERTS, L. M.; HERNÁNDEZ, E.; and MANGELSDORF, P. C. 1952. *Races of Maize in Mexico.* Cambridge: Bussey Institution of Harvard University.
WELTFISH, GENE. 1930. "Prehistoric North American Basketry Techniques and Modern Distributions," *American Anthropologist,* XXXII, 454–95.
WEST, G. A. 1934. *Tobacco, Pipes, and Smoking Customs of the American Indians.* 2 vols. Public Museum of the City of Milwaukee, *Bulletin 17.*
WEYER, EDWARD M. 1932. *The Eskimos.* New Haven, Conn.
WHITAKER, THOMAS W. 1948. "Lagenaria: A Pre-Columbian Cultivated Plant in the Americas," *Southwestern Journal of Anthropology,* IV, 49–68.
WHITAKER, THOMAS W.; CUTLER, HUGH C.; and MacNEISH, RICHARD S. 1957. "Cucurbit Materials from Three Caves near Ocampo, Tamaulipas," *American Antiquity,* XXII, 352–58.
WHITING, JOHN W. M.; KLUCKHOHN, RICHARD; and ANTHONY, ALBERT. MS. "The Functions of Male Initiation Ceremonies at Puberty."
WILSON, GILBERT L. 1917. *Agriculture of the Hidatsa Indians: An Indian Interpretation.* University of Minnesota "Studies in the Social Sciences," No. 9.
——. 1924. "The Horse and the Dog in Hidatsa Culture," *Anthropological Papers of the American Museum of Natural History,* XV, 125–311.
——. 1934. "The Hidatsa Earth Lodge," *Anthropological Papers of the American Museum of Natural History,* XXXIII, 341–420.
WINTENBERG, W. J. 1942. "The Geographical Distribution of Aboriginal Pottery in Canada," *American Antiquity,* VIII, 129–41.
WISSE, JAKOB. 1933. *Selbstmord und Todesfurcht bei den Naturvölkern.* Zutphen, Holland.
WISSLER, CLARK. 1908. "Types of Dwellings and Their Distribution in Central North America," *Sixteenth International Congress of Americanists,* 477–87.
——. 1914. "The Influence of the Horse in the Development of Plains Culture," *American Anthropologist,* XVI, 1–25.

——. 1916. "Costumes of the Plains Indians," *Anthropological Papers of the American Museum of Natural History*, XVII, 39–91.

——. 1926. *Indian Costumes in the United States*. American Museum of Natural History "Guide Leaflet Series," No. 63, pp. 1–32.

——. 1937. "Contribution of the American Indian," in *Our Racial and National Minorities*, eds. FRANCIS J. BROWN and JOSEPH S. ROUCEK. New York.

——. 1938. *The American Indian*. New York.

——. 1941. *North American Indians of the Plains*. New York.

WITTHOFT, JOHN. 1949. *Green Corn Ceremonialism in the Eastern Woodlands*. Museum of Anthropology, University of Michigan, *Occasional Papers*, No. 13.

WORMINGTON, H. M. 1957. *Ancient Man in North America*. 4th ed., rev. Denver Museum of Natural History "Popular Series," No. 4.

YANOVSKY, E. 1936. *Food Plants of North American Indians*. United States Department of Agriculture *Miscellaneous Publications*, No. 237.

YANOVSKY, E., and KINGSBURY, R. M. 1938. "Analysis of Some Indian Food Plants," *Journal of the Association of Official Agricultural Chemists*, XXI, 648–65.

YARROW, H. C. 1880. *Introduction to the Study of Mortuary Customs among the North American Indians*. Washington.

——. 1881. *A Further Contribution to the Study of Mortuary Customs of the North American Indians*. Bureau of American Ethnology *Annual Report*, I, 89–203.

Index

637

Comanche, 16, 125, 287, 307, 315, 340, 579

Combination suit (of clothes), 135

Communal ownership, 248, 252, 332

Communities, 85, 181, 224, 244, 248, 265, 268, 271, 279, 299, 300, 303, 305, 431, 601, 602; Arctic, 79, 327, 356, 450; California, 256, 304, 306; Circum-Caribbean, 184, 238, 307; East, 304, 321; Great Basin, 450; Meso-America, 99, 130, 185, 238, 259, 304, 307; Northeast Mexico, 450; Northwest Coast, 184, 304, 442; Oasis, 258, 289; Plateau, 252; Prairies, 254, 304, 420; Sub-Arctic, 332, 420, 450. *See also* Bands, Local group, *and* Villages

Compensation, blood money, indemnity, weregild, 226, 335, 358, 361, 362, 364, 365, 371, 374, 531

Composition in art, 188, 193, 208

Compulsory military service, 378, 380

Confederacies, confederations, leagues, 344, 345, 347, 348, 352, 353, 354, 366, 371, 374, 401, 540, 541, 604

Conical roof on cylinder, thatched house, 112, 114, 123, Fig. 19 (p. 122), Map 15

Conical and sub-conical houses, 106, 110, 112, 113, 118, 120, 123, 124–25, 127, 128, 588, Map 16. *See also* Tipis

Coniferous forest, 13, 14, Map 5

Containers, kettles, vessels, 157–59, 161, 163, 172, 182, 189, 190, 203, 205, 222, 223, 232, 234, 240, 369, 440, 590, 596, May 23; boiling vessels, 66–67, Map 23. *See also* Bark, Basketry, Hide, Pottery, *and* Wood

Continental drift, theory of, 8

Conventionalization in art, 190, 191, 197, 199, 200, 201, 203, 204, 205, 206

Convergences in language, 566, 569, 571, 575

Cook, Captain James, 149

Cook, Sherburne F., 35, 36, 604

Cooking. *See* Boiling, Broiling and roasting, *and* Food preparation and preservation

Cooper, James Fenimore, 521, 610

Copan, Honduras, Fig. 20 (p. 131)

Copper, 50, 146, 175, 176, 177, 178, 182, 190, 204, 223, 227, 229, 230, 231, 235, 237, 238, 240, 491. *See also* Tools and utensils

Copper Eskimos, 229

Copper plate as symbol of prestige and wealth, 176, 190, 227, 530

Coppermine River, 175, 230

Coptic language, 572

Corn. *See* Maize

Corporal punishment of children. *See* Education: discipline

Corporeal property: 244, 263, 264, 387, 394, 402, 477, 530

Corpse. *See* Burial

Corral or inclosure for hunting, 59, 234, 253

Correlations, 89, 314, 315, 316, 565, 566, 577, 578, 581

Cortez, Hernando, 18, 349, 382, 603

Costumes. *See* Regalia

Cotton, 589, 590, 591, Table 1 (pp. 43–44), Map 7; bast mistaken for cotton, 147, 168; origin and history, 45–46, 147–48; spinning, 164. *Culture areas:* Circum-Caribbean, 147; Meso-America, 75, 145, 147, 150, 151, 231, 240, 380, 395, 581, 605; Oasis, 142–43, 144, 147, 195, 197, 231

Councils, 234, 371, 468; Meso-America, 259, 307, 348, 349, 395; Northeast, 92, 288, 340, 401, 541, 542; Oasis, 95, 337, 338, 366, 367, 397, 398, 417; Plains, 340, 341, 342; Plateau, 335; Prairies, 92, 301, 340, 343; Southeast, 92, 105, 126, 201, 289, 340, 345, 346, 347, 400, 499, 501

Counting or recounting coup, 373, 402, 463, 464, 535

Courtship. *See* Love

Cousin marriage. *See* Marriage

Couvade, 436–38

Covarrubias, Miguel, 187, 199, 596

Cow-parsnip, 65, Table 2 (p. 65)

Cradle board, 142, 537, 544

Cradles, 138, 190, 440, 534, 552

Crafts and craftsmen, 157–85, 204, 229, 238, 260, 395, 396, 398, 427, 467, 489, 546, 549, 590–93, 607, Map 28. *See also* Bags, Basketry, Clothing, Division of labor, House-building, Mats and matting, Metallurgy, Pottery, Skin-dressing, Specialization of labor, Weaving, *and* Wood

Crane, H. R., 10

Cree, 101, 273, 274, 276, 357, 370, 407, 430, 463, 581

Creek (tribe): art, 200–201; crafts, 166, 168; family, 289; government, 345–47;

641

333; Oasis, 258, 414; Prairies, 254; Sub-Arctic, 251, 262

Matrilineal sib. *See* Matrisib

Matrilocal extended family, 247, 282, 296, 297; Fig. 34 (p. 283), Figs. 38–39 (pp. 297–98); Circum-Caribbean, 291; East, 254, 288, 289; Oasis, 290, 292, 337, 524; Plains, 308; Plateau, 287; Prairies, 288

Matrilocal residence, 247, 268, 270, 274, 278, 280, 305, 322, 323, 460, 553, Map 31; California, 256; East, 276, 289, 398–99; Northwest Coast, 390; Oasis, 279; Plains, 308; Prairies, 307

Matrisib (maternal or matrilineal sib), 247, 248, 254, 255, 258, 303, 345, 399

Mats and matting, 6, 115, 123, 128, 129, 147, 159, 160, 161, 162, 163, 261, 503, 590, Maps 24, 25

Maximilian of Wied, 418

Mayan language family, 578, Table 5 (p. 576), Map 37

Mayas, Mayan: architecture, 131, 132; art, 205, 206, 207, 208, 209, 594; culture area, 18, 19; family, 290, 291; government, 348; kinship, 296, 299, 305, 307; marriage, 274; narcotics and stimulants, 97, 104; origins, 11; rank, 394; religion, 490; science, 611; subsistence, 52–53, 72, 86; trade, 239–40; writing, 581

Mazatecs, 104

Meat, 60, 64, 65, 67, 68, 71, 73, 80, 81, 99, 232, 233, 238, 327, 433, 437, 438, 443. *See also* Hunting, Nutritional value of diet

Media of exchange, 230, 238, 239, 241, 242. *See also* Money

Medicine bundles, 92, 158, 219, 234, 263, 264, 341, 402, 419, 421, 478, 497

Medicine and curing practices: of Aztecs, 490–93, 587; confession as cure, 539; of Creeks, 501–4; education of physicians, 221, 263–64, 410, 412–13, 424–25, 499; enemas, 492; fee charged, 336, 390, 414, 531; Jimson weed, 103–4, 587; music, 218, 221, 263–64, 490, 493; of Navaho, 221, 496–98; obstetricians, 435; of Ojibwa, 420–22, 538–39; peyote, 99; property aspect of cures, 244–45, 263–64; plant remedies in general, 87, 482, 483, 490, 491, 492, 493, 499, 501, 502, 503, 510, 516, 587; recovery of lost soul, 509–10, 511; of

Sanpoil, 509–10; scurvy cured, 483; sodalities for curing, 415, 416, 420–22, 424–25; surgery, 491; sweating, 129; tobacco, 92; visions revealed cures. 471, 508. *See also* Disease

Medicine men, 30, 81, 104, 190, 219, 263, 264, 336, 337, 379, 412, 425, 456, 471, 483, 485, 486, 493, 496, 499, 500, 501, 502, 516, 531, 539. *See also* Priests, Ritualists, *and* Shamans

Mediterranean scrub forest, Map 5

Megalomania, 532, 536

Melanesia, 432, 480

Memorial ceremonies. *See* Mourning

Menomini, 28

Men's house or clubhouse, 128, 129, 406, 409, 428, 472, 473

Menstruation, 80, 81, 226, 267, 413, 441, 443, 444, 446, 454, 468, 469, 512, 537, 550, 606; taboos, 441–47, 499, 545. *See also* Puberty

Mescal bean, 104–5; Map 14

Mescalero, 96, 100, 306

Mesh principle in linguistic relationships, 575–77, 578

Meso-America culture area: art, 200, 202, 203, 204–10; clothing, 144–46, 147, 148, 149, 150, 153, 156, Fig. 26 (p. 145); crafts, 159, 161, 162, 163, 165, 167, 168, 170, 172, 173, 175, 177, 179, 180, 181, 184–85; definition, 11, 18–19; education, 457, 468, 470; family, 290; government, 329, 339, 347, 348–50, 351; housing and architecture, 121–23, 124, 128, 130, 131, 132, Fig. 18 (p. 121), Fig. 20 (p. 131); kinship, 321; language, 556, 578, 579; life cycle, 433, 439, 440, 441, 442, 443, 448, 449, 450, 454; marriage, 266, 280; music, 214, 220, 222–23; narcotics and stimulants, 91, 92, 94, 95, 97, 104; personality, 548–52; property, 259–60, 261, 264; rank, 393–96, 397, 398, 402, 403, 404; religion, 477, 486–93, 498, 515, 516; sodalities, 410, 427–29, 430, 431; subsistence, 23, 32, 33, 34, 35, 36, 38, 50–51, 54, 60, 62, 65, 66, 70, 71, 72, 73, 74, 78, 80, 83, 84, 85, 86; trade, 231, 237, 238–40; transportation, 228, 229; war, 353, 359, 379–82, 383, 384; writing, 581–82

Mesquite, 30, 96

Metallurgy, metalwork, metal, 157, 175–78, 185, 204, 287, 592; trade objects of metal, 230, 232, 234, 238, 241, 590–91,

PRINTED IN U.S.A.